Ite missa est–Ritual Interactions around Mass in Chinese Society (1583–1720)

Studies in the History of Christianity in East Asia

Editors-in-Chief

M. Antoni J. Ucerler, sj
Wu Xiaoxin 吳小新
Ricci Institute for Chinese-Western Cultural History–Boston College

Editorial Board

Donald L. Baker (*University of British Columbia, Canada*)
Anthony Clark (*Whitworth University, USA*)
Kiri Paramore (*Leiden University, The Netherlands*)
Stephen J. Roddy (*University of San Francisco, USA*)

VOLUME 7

The titles published in this series are listed at *brill.com/hcea*

Ite missa est–Ritual Interactions around Mass in Chinese Society (1583–1720)

By

Yang Hongfan

BRILL

LEIDEN | BOSTON

Cover illustration: "The Last Supper," by Chinese Catholic artist Luke Chen Yuandu 陈缘督 (1902–1967). Courtesy to St. Michael Seminary, Beijing Archdiocese.

Library of Congress Cataloging-in-Publication Data

Names: Yang, Hongfan (Thérèse), author.
Title: Ite missa est : ritual interactions around mass in Chinese society (1583-1720) / by Yang Hongfan.
Description: Leiden : Brill, [2022] | Series: Studies in the history of Christianity in East Asia, 2542-3681 ; volume 7 | Includes bibliographical references and index.
Identifiers: LCCN 2021048775 (print) | LCCN 2021048776 (ebook) | ISBN 9789004499577 (hardback) | ISBN 9789004501027 (ebook)
Subjects: LCSH: Mass–History. | Catholic Church–China–Liturgy. | Catholic Church–China–History. | Christianity and culture–China–History.
Classification: LCC BX2230.5 .Y36 2022 (print) | LCC BX2230.5 (ebook) | DDC 264/.020360951–dc23/eng/20211029 LC record available at https://lccn.loc.gov/2021048775 LC ebook record available at https://lccn.loc.gov/2021048776

Typeface for the Latin, Greek, and Cyrillic scripts: "Brill." See and download: brill.com/brill-typeface.

ISSN 2542-3681
ISBN 978-90-04-49957-7 (hardback)
ISBN 978-90-04-50102-7 (e-book)

Copyright 2022 by Yang Hongfan. Published by Koninklijke Brill NV, Leiden, The Netherlands.
Koninklijke Brill NV incorporates the imprints Brill, Brill Nijhoff, Brill Hotei, Brill Schöningh, Brill Fink, Brill mentis, Vandenhoeck & Ruprecht, Böhlau Verlag and V&R Unipress.
Koninklijke Brill NV reserves the right to protect this publication against unauthorized use. Requests for re-use and/or translations must be addressed to Koninklijke Brill NV via brill.com or copyright.com.

This book is printed on acid-free paper and produced in a sustainable manner.

Contents

Acknowledgments IX
List of Figures and Tables XI
Abbreviations XII

Introduction to Ritual Interactions around Mass 1
1 Prologue 1
2 Paradigm of Ritual Interaction 3
3 *Ite Missa Est* 5
4 Structure and Sources 9

1 Object of Worship: Grand Ritual of Sacrifice to the Lord of Heaven 11
1 The Lord of Heaven as Object of Worship 11
   1.1 *Is Mass a Usurpation of the Worship of Heaven?* 11
   1.2 *Is Heaven Identical to the Lord of Heaven?* 17
   1.3 *Twofold Depiction of the Ultimately Honorable and the Ultimately Intimate* 22
2 Jesus as Object of Worship in Mass 36
   2.1 *Title as the Lord of Heaven Jesus* 36
   2.2 *Relationship between Reception of Suffering and Mass* 41
   2.3 *Litany of Jesus' Holy Body* 58
3 Conclusion 77

2 Intention of Worship: Mass for Salvation of the Souls of the Deceased 79
1 Salvation of the Souls of the Deceased at Catholic Funeral 79
   1.1 *Sharing Concern of the Souls of the Deceased* 79
   1.2 *Catholic Funeral with Mass at the Core* 81
   1.3 *Best Practices to Express Filial Piety* 85
2 Relationship between Mass and Sacrifice to Ancestors 88
   2.1 *Disadvantages of Forbidding Sacrifice to Ancestors* 88
   2.2 *Original Intention of Sacrifice to Ancestors* 91
   2.3 *Distinction between Mass and Sacrifice to Ancestors* 96
   2.4 *Sacrifice to Parents and Sacrifice to the Lord of Heaven* 99
   2.5 *Practical Intention of Vegetarian Fasting as Comparison* 102
3 Salvation of Souls of the Deceased in the Communion of Merits 106
   3.1 *Most Efficacious Practices for the Deceased* 107
   3.2 *Two Types of Narration of Apparition of A Deceased Soul* 113

	3.3	*Statutes of Confraternities Regarding the Deceased* 117
	3.4	*Care of the Souls of Deceased Strangers* 121
4	Conclusion 123

3 Performer of Worship: Indigenous Clergy along with Indigenous Liturgy 125

1 Catholic Priest's Multiple Identities in China 125
   1.1 *Exclusive Celebrant of Mass* 125
   1.2 *Western Confucianist* 134
   1.3 *Religious Professional* 137
   1.4 *Conspirator* 140
2 Anticlericalism against Catholic Priest 143
   2.1 *Anticlericalism in Chinese Society* 143
   2.2 *Sexuality* 144
   2.3 *Violence* 146
   2.4 *Sorcery* 153
3 Indigenous Clergy and Indigenous Liturgy 160
   3.1 *Establishment of Indigenous Clergy* 160
   3.2 *Ritual Manuals for Mass* 167
   3.3 *Sacrificial Hat* 174
   3.4 *Wu Li and "The Musical Sound of Mass"* 186
4 Conclusion 204

4 Place of Worship: Ritual Space and Ritual Time of Mass 206

1 Ritual Space of Mass 206
   1.1 *Hall of the Lord of Heaven* 206
   1.2 *The Altar and Objects around It* 216
   1.3 *Beamless Palace* 224
2 Ritual Time of Mass 229
   2.1 *Day of Worship* 229
   2.2 *List of Worship* 234
   2.3 *To Observe the Day of Worship* 240
3 Christendom in Chinese Society 247
   3.1 *Ritual of the Assembly* 247
   3.2 *Female Catholics' Participation* 253
   3.3 *Foundation of Christendom* 258
4 Conclusion 269

5 On-Going Interactions 270
    1   Glocalization of Catholic Rituals in Chinese Society 270
    2   Applications of the Metaphor of Weaving 274
    3   Tension between Inheritance and Adaptation 277
    4   The Intermediary 283

Bibliography 287

Index 314

Acknowledgments

Four hundred years ago, Jesuit missionaries wrote manuscripts in Chinese, then Chinese Catholics commented, polished the language, and helped with the publication. Texts resulted from their collaboration become major sources in this book, whose own publication is also a fruit of beautiful collaboration. This time, a young Chinese scholar traveled to Europe, wrote a manuscript in English, and made it to publication, with tremendous support of Western Jesuits.

I am most indebted to Prof. Dr. Nicolas Standaert, SJ, who kindly invited me twice to KU Leuven and has guided me through a whole process in which a preliminary outline turned to many drafts, then to a manuscript, and finally to a book. My amazing proofreader Mr. Brendan Gottschall, SJ, has contributed to improving this book in many ways. Prof. Dr. Thierry Meynard, SJ, and Prof. Dr. Benoît Vermander, SJ, generously provided me with useful primary and secondary sources.

I adapted the early manuscript into my doctoral dissertation at Peking University. Entering through the Gate of Philosophy (*zhexue men* 哲學門) has transformed me from a student to a scholar. I am deeply indebted to Prof. Dr. Sun Shangyang 孫尚揚 for seeing the potential in me and for his earnest instruction. Prof. Dr. Xu Fenglin 徐鳳林 and Prof. Dr. Xu Longfei 徐龍飛 offered invaluable suggestions during my writing process.

The first pages were begun and the final manuscript was finished at the Department of Sinology, KU Leuven. Prof. Dr. Carine Defoort has offered me on-going support since my very first day in Europe. Dr. Ad Dudink kindly provided me with articles and answered my questions. Dr. Noël Golvers patiently taught me to transcribe and to translate Latin letters. Ms. Silvia Toro, Ms. Valentina Lin Yang Yang, and Ms. Moira De Graef have commented on parts of the manuscript. Librarians in KU Leuven have done a great service even in quarantine, such as Ms. Benedicte Vaerman in the East-Asian Library. I am also grateful to Fr. Anthony Yuan Wei 袁偉, to Dr. Carine Dujardin of KADOC, to Fr. Jeroom Heyndrickx, CICM, and Fr. Matthew Gong Zhixi 龔志喜 of the Ferdinand Verbiest Foundation.

Within the team of Brill Publisher, Ms. Patricia Radder and Mr. Stephen Ford have patiently walked me through the publication process. I would like to thank Dr. Wu Xiaoxin and Dr. M. Antoni J. Üçerler, SJ, of Ricci Institute for Chinese-Western Cultural History, and two anonymous reviewers as well. China Scholarship Council has supported my research in KU Leuven from 2015 to 2017. Finally, I deeply appreciate the love and prayers from my parents, my aunt, and my cousin sisters.

This book is made to publication because of all the people who have supported me in one way or another, named or not in the limited acknowledgments. As the missionaries and Chinese Catholics humbly addressed themselves, I am but a young pupil (*houxue* 後學), who, despite of all her shortcomings, tries to contribute to the field.

Thérèse Yang Hongfan 楊虹帆
19 March, 2021

Figures and Tables

Figures

1. To institute the grand ritual of Holy Body 46
2. The Last Supper: the institution 50
3. The Picture of the Lord of Heaven Jesus initiating the sacrificial ritual 51
4. The Picture of the Lord of Heaven Jesus hanging on the cross 59
5. The Picture of the Lord of Heaven Jesus on the cross 60
6. Beginning invocation and petitions in Latin 63
7. Beginning invocation and petitions in Greek 64
8. Beginning invocation in Chinese 65
9. Petitions in Chinese 66
10. Sacrificial hat 177

Tables

1. Titles in eight categories 67
2. Act of priest and allegorical explanation 193
3. Comparison of allegorical explanation 201
4. Altar and objects around it 217
5. Names of days of worship 231
6. Transliteration of seven sacraments 248

Abbreviations

ARSI Jap. Sin.	Archivum Romanum Societatis Iesu, Japonica-Sinica Collection, Rome.
CCT ARSI	*Yesuhui Luoma dang'anguan Mingqing tianzhujiao wenxian* 耶穌會羅馬檔案館明清天主教文獻. 12 vols, edited by Nicolas Standaert 鐘鳴旦 and Ad Dudink 杜鼎克. Taipei: Taipei Ricci Institute 臺北利氏學社, 2002.
CCT BAV (1)	*Fandigang tushuguancang Mingqing zhongxi wenhuajiaoliushi wenxian congkan diyiji* (1) 梵蒂岡圖書館藏明清中西文化交流史文獻叢刊（第一輯）. 44 vols, edited by Zhang Xiping 張西平, Federico Masini, Ren Dayuan 任大援, and Ambrogio M. Piazzoni. Zhengzhou: Elephant Press 大象出版社, 2014.
CCT BnF	*Faguo guojia tushuguan Mingqing tianzhujiao wenxian* 法國國家圖書館明清天主教文獻. 26 vols, edited by Nicolas Standaert 鐘鳴旦, Ad Dudink 杜鼎克, and Nathalie Monnet 蒙曦. Taipei: Taipei Ricci Institute 臺北利氏學社, 2009.
CCT-database	The Chinese Christian Texts Database.
CCT ZKW	*Xujiahui cangshulou Mingqing tianzhujiao wenxian* 徐家匯藏書樓明清天主教文獻. 5 vols, edited by Nicolas Standaert 鐘鳴旦, Adrian Dudink 杜鼎克, Huang Yi-long 黃一農, and Chu Ping-Yi 祝平一. Taipei: Faculty of Theology, Fu Jen Catholic University 輔仁大學神學院, 1996.
DCFY	*Dongchuan fuyin* 東傳福音, 25 vols, edited by Zhou Xiefan 周燮藩 and Wang Meixiu 王美秀. Hefei: *Huangshan shushe* 黃山書社, 2005.
Eruson	Beijing Eruson shuweihua jishu yanjiu zhongxin Zhongguo jiben gujiku 北京愛如生數位化技術研究中心中國基本古籍庫.
SCCT ZKW	*Xujiahui cangshulou Mingqing tianzhujiao wenxian xubian* 徐家匯藏書樓明清天主教文獻續編. 34 vols, edited by Nicolas Standaert 鐘鳴旦, Ad Dudink 杜鼎克, and Wang Renfang 王仁芳. Taipei: Taipei Ricci Institute 臺北利氏學社, 2013.
TZJDCWXSB	*Tianzhujiao dongchuan wenxian sanbian* 天主教東傳文獻三編, 6 vols, edited by Wu Xiangxiang 吳相湘. Taipei: Taiwan xuesheng shuju 臺灣學生書局, 1984.

Introduction to Ritual Interactions around Mass

1   **Prologue**

On 16 July 1632, an Educational Official named Chen visited the missionary Giulio Aleni (Ai Rulüe 艾儒略, SJ, 1582–1649) in the south of China.

> The Educational Official asked again: "The Lord of Heaven must be worshiped. This I know well. Humble as I am, I still have some doubts. The Son of Heaven sacrifices to Heaven and Earth; feudal lords sacrifice to mountains and rivers; senior officials sacrifice to the five gods; common people sacrifice to their ancestors. Now every family in your Teaching reverences the Lord of Heaven. Is this not a usurpation? Moreover, the homes of common people, small and shabby, also must reverence the Lord of Heaven's image. Is that not a grave blasphemy?" Master Aleni said: "Sacrifice and reverence are different. In China only the Son of Heaven can perform the ritual to Heaven and Earth; this is to value his esteem. In the Holy Teaching only a priest can perform the ritual of Mass; this is to value his responsibility. What is called the reverence is because the Lord of Heaven creates heaven to cover us, creates earth to hold us, creates angels to guard us, and creates all things to nourish us. All these great graces, who does not receive them daily? Who does not want to repay them? Nevertheless, even to reverence day and night can only express one ten-thousandth of gratitude. How can this be called a 'sacrifice'? How can this be called a 'usurpation' or a 'blasphemy'?"[1]

This conversation is recorded in *Li Jiubiao's Diary of Oral Admonitions* (*Kouduo richao* 口鐸日抄, 1630–1640), a record of daily conversations in the Christian community of Fujian 福建. The Educational Official Chen (Chen Guangwen

---

1 "廣文復問口：'天主當敬，予稔知之。但竊有疑者，天子祭天地，諸侯祭山川，大夫祭五祀，士庶人祭其先，今貴教家家供奉天主，不亦僭乎？況士庶之家，蝸居蓬戶，亦必供奉主像，毋乃太褻耶？' 先生曰：'祭祀與奉事不同。夫郊社之禮，在中邦，非天子不舉，重其事也；彌撒之禮，在聖教，非鐸德不行，重其職也。若所云奉事者，為天主生天覆我，生地載我，生神守我，生萬物以安養我。種種大恩，何人不日受？何人不思圖報？然則朝夕瞻依奉事，亦聊盡感酬萬一耳，豈曰祭之云乎，豈曰僭而褻之云乎？'" Li Jiubiao 李九標, *Kouduo richao* 口鐸日抄, juan 3, fol. 21b2–fol. 22a3, in CCT ARSI, vol. 7, 220–221. See also Erik Zürcher, *Kou duo ri chao: Li Jiubiao's Diary of Oral Admonitions: A Late Ming Christian Journal* (Sankt Augustin: Institut Monumenta Serica, 2007), vol. 1, III. 28 (Xianyou, Saturday, 16 July 1632), 357–358.

陳廣文) is the catechumen Chen Zhongdan 陳衷丹 from Xianyou 仙遊.[2] He raised two questions concerning Catholic rituals to Aleni. Firstly, there is a clear hierarchy in the Confucian sacrificial rituals, where the object of sacrifice varies according to the social status. In the Teaching of the Lord of Heaven (*tianzhujiao* 天主教, Catholicism), however, everyone can reverence the Lord of Heaven. Is this a usurpation of the worship of Heaven by the emperor who is called the Son of Heaven? Secondly, the Lord of Heaven's image can be reverenced even in the shabby homes of common people. Is this a blasphemy to the Lord of Heaven? These two questions were representative in Chinese society where Confucianism was dominant. Moreover, they refer to three perspectives of worship, e.g., the object, the performer, and the place.

Aleni distinguished two verbs used by Chen Zhongdan: "to sacrifice" (*ji* 祭) used for the Confucian sacrificial rituals; "to reverence" (*gongfeng* 供奉) for the Teaching of the Lord of Heaven. Then he responded to the first question by explaining the difference between sacrifice and reverence, and to the second question by defending the validity of reverence. In fact, Chen Zhongdan emphasized the reverence of the Lord of Heaven in the familial sphere, such as every family (*jiajia* 家家) and the homes of common people (*shishu zhi jia* 士庶之家), with no direct reference to Mass. It is Aleni who reoriented the emphasis to Mass and drew a comparison between the celebrant of the ritual to Heaven and Earth (*jiaoshe zhi li* 郊社之禮) and that of the ritual of Mass (*misa zhi li* 彌撒之禮). Since these two rituals have different celebrants and emphases, the ritual of Mass does not usurp the ritual to Heaven and Earth. Next, Aleni pointed out that Chinese Catholics adored the Lord of Heaven not by sacrifice but by reverence, and that their worship intended to repay all the great graces bestowed by the Lord of Heaven. His response to the second question connected to the first one, because in the Catholic Church a priest is the exclusive celebrant of Mass. Furthermore, Chinese Catholics reverenced the Lord of Heaven in order to express their gratitude to him. By mentioning Mass and the comparison with celebrants of the two rituals, Aleni's skillful response introduced greater complexity and nuance. Regrettably, the conversation ended with Aleni's rhetorical questions, not with Chen Zhongdan's reaction to his response. Nevertheless, their conversation serves as an excellent introduction of this book's theme: ritual interaction around Mass in late Ming and early Qing.

---

2 In 1632, Chen Zhongdan was only a tribute student, yet he obtained the title of the Educational Official afterward. In the eighth volume of *Kouduo richao* (August 1639), Chen Zhongdan was already a Chinese Catholic. Zürcher, *Kou duo ri chao*, vol. 1, III. 28, 357.

2   Paradigm of Ritual Interaction

For a long time, research on the communication between China and Europe in late Ming and early Qing has been focused on doctrines and various kinds of sciences introduced into Chinese society by Western missionaries. Rituals in Chinese society in general and Catholic rituals in particular have not received enough attention. Even the research on the Chinese Rites Controversy mainly focuses on debates among various religious orders and missionaries with various nationalities, while the specific procedures, meanings, and practices of Catholic rituals have been rarely studied.

In recent decades a paradigm shift has taken place from missiological viewpoint to sinological one and from Eurocentric approach to Sinocentric one.[3] Since then, Christianity has been considered a vaster cultural phenomenon, including abundant and diverse cultural elements produced by the Christian faith and practices. For example, Jacque Gernet's work *China and Christianity: Action and Reaction* (*Chine et christianisme: Action et réaction*) underlines the reaction of the Chinese to Christianity in the Sinocentric paradigm.[4] While Gernet focuses on the anti-Catholic texts, which indicated that Christianity and Chinese culture essentially contradicted each other, Gianni Criveller argues that these texts should be examined along side those written by missionaries and Chinese Catholics.[5] The paradigm of interaction encourages scholars to shift away from both Eurocentric and Sinocentric approaches.[6] Although Christianity and Chinese culture began dialogue in misunderstandings during late Ming and early Qing, these misunderstandings do not prove that interaction must inevitably end in confusion. In addition to action and reaction, contrast and confrontation, the paradigm of interaction examines how missionaries and Chinese people established relationships with each other. In the

---

3 Nicolas Standaert, *The Interweaving of Rituals: Funerals in the Cultural Exchange between China and Europe* (Seattle: University of Washington Press, 2008), 4. This book focuses on the interaction between the Catholic rites of death and funerals to the relevant traditional Chinese rites. It is an outstanding model of applying the new paradigm of interaction, providing creative findings about the interaction between the Chinese ritual tradition and the Catholic one.

4 The title of this work changed several times, such as *China and the Christian Impact: A Conflict of Cultures* in English, *Christus kam bis nach China. Eine erste Begegnung und ihr Scheitern* in German, and *La première confrontation* in the second edition in French. For the respective emphasis of each version, see Nicolas Standaert, "New Trends in the Historiography of Christianity in China," *Catholic Historical Review* vol. 83, no. 4 (1997): 580.

5 Gianni Criveller, *Preaching Christ in Late Ming China* (Taipei: Taipei Ricci Institute, 1997), 406–408.

6 Standaert, *The Interweaving of Rituals*, 5.

study of interaction, the focus is not comprehension or incomprehension, not the transmitter or the receiver, but a permanent tension in between.[7] Taking place in various situations, the interaction could be diverse and dynamic. A text, a ritual, or a social network produced by the communication between the transmitter and the receiver could be considered the fruit of interaction. In this sense, a shift of methodology takes place, from the search for the other to the search for the space of interaction, from differences between the two sides to what lies "in-between."[8]

There has been a basic shift in the general study of ritual as well. Ritual is not merely the communication of meanings and values any more but becomes a group of specific activities which construct particular meanings and values.[9] In the past, the study of Catholic rituals was strongly theological; the medieval Europe was in fact considered essentially Christian. Yet, in the second half of the twentieth century, a historiographical shift urged scholars to reconsider the medieval religious life.[10] The research subject changed from the clerical elite to ordinary people; the researcher from theologians, church historians, and members of religious orders to a broader group of scholars, such as sociologists of religion, historical anthropologists, and art historians.[11] New research in the historiographical shift reveals that although the Catholic Church was dominant in medieval Europe, ordinary people's actual practices did not totally follow the church doctrines; in fact magic and various superstitions were popular.[12] Moreover, the shift in the study of medieval Christianity is rather the result of new questions than of new discoveries. Scholars tend to study how religious teachings and institutions shaped ordinary lives and how the latter in turn shaped the former.[13] For example, Van Engen suggests interpreting medieval culture in Europe by a basic question about the extent of Christianization in medieval society, i.e., to explore how much the Christian teachings and practices shaped

---

7   Nicolas Standaert, *L'«autre» dans la mission: leçon à partir de la Chine* (Bruxelles: Lessius, 2003), 119. This book gives the methodological thinking on the communication between China and Europe in the seventeenth century. It discusses the Christian communities, the inculturation of thoughts, and the cultural interactions. Chapter Five "The Communities of Effective Rituals" provides practical instructions on the study of ritual interaction.
8   Standaert, *The Interweaving of Rituals*, 214–215.
9   Catherine Bell, *Ritual: Perspectives and Dimensions* (New York: Oxford University Press, 1997), 82.
10 John Van Engen, "The Christian Middle Ages as an Historiographical Problem," *American Historical Review* 91, no. 3 (1986): 520.
11 Van Engen, "The Christian Middle Ages," 522, 549.
12 Van Engen, "The Christian Middle Ages," 536.
13 Van Engen, "The Christian Middle Ages," 536.

the cultural milieu of people in various social classes at medieval times.[14] Consequently, Christianization becomes the research subject in the discipline of history and an essential part of medieval culture. The historiographical shift of medieval religious life can be an inspiration to the study of Catholic rituals in late Ming and early Qing.

Contrary to its dominant role in medieval Europe, the Catholic Church was weak in late Ming and early Qing China. Erik Zürcher suggests that Chinese culture especially Confucianism has formed a cultural imperative in Chinese society. Confronted with the cultural imperative, religions of foreign origin, such as Buddhism, Muslim, Judaism, and Christianity, must adapt themselves to Confucianism in order to take root in Chinese society. Following a consistent pattern of adaptation, all the aforementioned religions tried to build connection with Confucianism, to prove their existence in early Chinese history, and to adapt to Chinese mores and rituals.[15] In light of the historiographical shift of medieval religious life, the study of Catholic rituals in late Ming and early Qing can raise new questions concerning the cultural imperative. For example, to examine to what extent Catholic rituals shaped ordinary lives (both Catholic and non-Catholic) and how the latter in turn shaped the former. In other words, to explore the diverse and dynamic interaction of both Christianization in Chinese society and Sinicization of Catholic rituals.

3   Ite Missa Est

The usage of the word *missa* has a long and complex history. In summary, this word usually means "to send, to dismiss" (*dimissio*) in Latin. The early Catholic Church used it to dismiss the catechumen before the second part of Mass. In the fourth century, Ambrose (339–397) used *missa* to describe the whole ritual, including the Eucharist.[16] Solid written material shows that the Catholic Church began to use the formula *Ite missa est* (Go, [the Church] has been sent) in the fourth century. The deacon would face the congregation and using this formula proclaimed in a high voice that the Mass is ended; the congregation would respond *Deo gratias* (Thanks be to God). Yet, Joseph Jungmann suggests that the history of using this formula might be as long as that of the

---

14   Van Engen, "The Christian Middle Ages," 537.
15   Erik Zürcher, "Jesuit Accommodation and the Chinese Cultural Imperative," in *The Chinese Rites Controversy: Its History and Meaning*, ed. D.E. Mungello (Monumenta Serica Monograph Series XXXIII, Nettetal: Steyler Verlag, 1994), 34–41.
16   Éric Palazzo, *Liturgie et société au Moyen Âge* (Paris: Aubier, 2000), 31.

Latin Mass.[17] In Rome, at first the formula was used in every Mass. In the early eleventh century, a new closing formula *Benedicamus Domino* (Let us bless the Lord) which probably originated in Gaul appeared. This new formula was usually used in the daily Mass and *Ite missa est* was used on feast days. Since the twelfth century, another formula *Requiescant in pace* (May they rest in peace) was used specifically in Requiem Masses, because *Ite missa est* was seen as the expression of joy.[18]

In *The Meaning of the Sacrifice of Mass* (*Misa jiyi* 彌撒祭義, 1629), the first book dedicated to Mass in late Ming and early Qing, Aleni transliterated *Ite missa est* as "*yi-de misa e-si-de* 依得彌撒厄斯得,"[19] shortened as "*yi-de misa* 依得彌撒." He also explained the meaning in Latin: "Fourth, [the priest] says to the people '*yi-de misa*' etc., the translation of 'the Mass is ended, people may leave now.'"[20] *Rules of Confraternity of Charity* (*Renhui yue* 仁會約, 1634) teaches what Catholics shall do after Mass: "When [the priest] ends speaking, [the congregants] are dismissed and faithfully obey [what the priest speaks about]."[21] Here Philippe Wang Zheng 王徵 (1571–1644) not only expressed the literal meaning of *Ite missa est* but also revealed the deeper meaning that the congregants are sent forth to bring the fruits of Mass to the whole world. Following the deeper meaning of *Ite missa est*, European missionaries introduced Catholic rituals into China; Chinese Catholics, together with missionaries, propagated these rituals in Chinese society.

The time frame for this book begins with the introduction of Catholicism to the mainland China by the Jesuits in 1583 and ends with the official prohibition of the practice of Catholicism by the Kangxi emperor in 1720. In 1583, Michele Ruggieri (Luo Mingjian 羅明堅, SJ, 1543–1607) and Matteo Ricci (Li Madou 利瑪竇, SJ, 1552–1610) gained the permission to settle in Zhaoqing 肇慶 from the local official Wang Pan 王泮.[22] Earlier on their first arrival, the two missionaries met a young man whose surname was Chen 陳 and gave him an altar for

---

17 Joseph Jungmann, *The Mass of the Roman Rite: Its Origins and Development* (*Missarum Sollemnia*), trans. F. Brunner (London: Burns & Oates, 1961, 4th ed.), 434.

18 Jungmann, *The Mass*, 435–436.

19 "四、又向眾人念：依德彌撒，厄斯得。" Giulio Aleni 艾儒略, *Misa jiyi* 彌撒祭義, *juan* 2, fol. 3a5, in CCT BnF, vol. 16, 557.

20 "第四、又向眾人念'依得彌撒' 云云，譯言 '彌撒已畢，眾人可去矣。'" Aleni, *Misa jiyi, juan* 2, fol. 36 b1–2, 624.

21 "講畢各散，依信奉行。" Wang Zheng 王徵, *Renhui yue* 仁會約, fol. 41a1, in CCT BnF, vol. 6, 609.

22 For an introduction of Wang Pan, see Lin Jinshui 林金水, *Li Madou yu Zhongguo* 利瑪竇與中國 (Beijing: Zhongguo shehuikexue chubanshe 中國社會科學出版社, 1996), 14, note 5.

INTRODUCTION

the celebration of Mass. Chen put the altar in a small room at home, where a wooden tablet written "the Lord of Heaven" (*tianzhu* 天主) was in the middle of the altar, also seven or eight oil lamps and burning incense were on it. Chen knelt down before the altar and prayed to the Lord of Heaven daily. When Ruggieri and Ricci came back to Zhaoqing to settle, they celebrated Mass daily at the altar in this room.[23] This altar was probably the first one in mainland China where Mass was celebrated regularly and directly connected to Chinese people. In this regard, the year 1583 is an initial mark for the propagation of Mass in China. Moreover, given Ricci's evangelical mission in China, the years 1583 to 1610 can be considered the foundation of the mission in China.[24]

On the other end, from December 1720 to March 1721, the apostolic visitor Carlo Ambrogio Mezzabarba (Jia Le 嘉樂, 1685–1741) presented to the Kangxi emperor Rome's rejection of traditional Chinese rituals, such as sacrifice to ancestors and sacrifice to Confucius. Consequently, the Kangxi emperor decided to prohibit the Teaching of the Lord of Heaven: "From now on, it is unnecessary for the Western people to propagate their teaching in China. It is proper to prohibit it lest many troubles should happen."[25] The emperor's prohibition became a remarkable event in the Chinese Rites Controversy and caused heavy damage to ritual interactions of the Catholic Church in China. In this regard, this book chooses the years 1583 to 1720 as the time frame and occasionally mentions situations before 1583 or after 1720.

Many studies have been devoted to the cultural communication between China and Europe in late Ming and early Qing, but few focus on Catholic rituals in Chinese society, especially the sacraments. Yet, a major portion of the missionary activities in China was explicitly introducing and explaining the sacraments, especially the Eucharist. In this early stage of the mission in China, of all the Catholic rituals Jesuit missionaries discussed the Eucharist the most.[26] Called the Sacrament of sacraments (*sacramentum sacramentorum*),

---

23 Matteo Ricci 利瑪竇, *Yesuhui yu tianzhujiao jinru Zhongguo shi* 耶穌會與天主教進入中國史, trans. Wen Zheng 文錚, ed. Eugenio Menegon 梅歐金 (Beijing: The Commercial Press 商務印書館, 2014), 97.
24 François Bontinck, *La Lutte autour de la liturgie chinoise aux XVIIe et XVIIIe siècles* (Louvain: Nauwelaerts, 1962), 6.
25 "以後不必西洋人在中國行教，禁止可也，免得多事。" Chen Yuan 陳垣, ed., *Kangxi yu Luoma shijie guanxi wenji* 康熙與羅馬使節關係文集 (Taipei: Wenhai chubanshe 文海出版社, 1974), 96.
26 Song Gang, *Giulio Aleni, Kouduo richao, and Christian-Confucian Dialogism in Late Ming Fujian* (Abingdon, Oxon/New York: Routledge, 2018), 305. The fifth chapter of this book focuses on the propagation in Chinese society, especially the liturgical life in the Christian communities in Fujian. Section 5.3.3 discusses specially on the Mass.

the Eucharist is an essential Catholic ritual.[27] The Mass is the supreme religious practice in the Catholic Church, because it is where the Eucharist takes place. Mass contains two main parts: the Liturgy of the Word and the Liturgy of the Eucharist; the first part could be seen as a preparation for the second. Because of their inseparable relationship, the Eucharist is also called Mass.[28]

Nevertheless, it seemed that Chinese Catholics in late Ming and early Qing preferred confession to the Eucharist.[29] Moreover, some Chinese Catholics considered baptism and confession as the two most important sacraments. For example, Matthew Zhang Geng 張賡 (1570–1646/1647) wrote *Explanation of Baptism and Confession Two Important Rules Set by the Lord of Heaven Himself* (*Tianzhu qinli lingxi gaojie er yaogui zhi li* 天主親立領洗告解二要規之理, 1630–1640). The Eucharist, the other sacrament set by the Lord of Heaven, was not included in the title. For another example, Thomas Li Jiugong 李九功 (?–1681) valued the effect of sacraments, especially of baptism and confession, because he thought that these Catholic rituals contain a dimension which the Confucian tradition lacks.[30] Yet, the Chinese converts showed full admiration for the holy liturgy and were fond of the festive celebration.[31] Their fervent celebration of Christmas and Holy Week kept recurring in the missionaries' reports.[32] In this regard, questions as follows await further research. How did

---

27   "I. The Eucharist—Source and Summit of Ecclesial Life," *Catechism of the Catholic Church*, 1324–1327, last accessed September 29, 2021,
     https://www.vatican.va/archive/ENG0015/__P3X.HTM.

28   For various ways to call this sacrament, such as Eucharist, Holy Communion, Holy Mass, see "II. What is This Sacrament Called?" *Catechism of the Catholic Church*, 1328–1332, last accessed September 29, 2021,
     https://www.vatican.va/archive/ENG0015/__P3Y.HTM.

29   Liam Matthew Brockey, "Illuminating the Shades of Sin: The Society of Jesus and Confession in Seventeenth-Century China," in *Forgive Us Our Sins: Confession in Late Ming and Early Qing China*, ed. Nicolas Standaert and Ad Dudink (Monumenta Serica Monograph Series LV, Sankt Augustin: Institut Monumenta Serica, 2006), 138–140. Brockey examines the propagation of confession by the Jesuits in the seventeenth century China. Missionaries tried to make confession an effective way for Chinese Catholics' moral reformation. Efforts were made not only between the missionaries and the Chinese Catholics but also in the whole social network of Chinese society.

30   You Bin 游斌, "Hetian, heren yu heji: Wanming tianzhujiao rushi Li Jiugong de bijiaojingxue shijian 和天、和人與和己：晚明天主教儒士李九功的比較經學實踐," in *Bijiao jingxue* 比較經學 vol. 1 (Beijing: Zongjiao wenhua chubanshe 宗教文化出版社, 2013), 23.

31   Xaver Bürkler, *Die Sonn-und Festtagsfeier in der katholischen Chinamission: Eine geschichtlich pastorale Untersuchung* (Roma: Herder, 1942), 14. The book discussed the celebration of Sunday and other feast days in different periods in the Catholic Church in China, unfolding the dynamic development full of tension.

32   Bürkler, *Die Sonn-und Festtagsfeier*, 16.

missionaries introduce and propagate Mass in Chinese society? How did Chinese Catholics and anti-Catholics understand Mass? What were the cultural adaptations of Mass in the local Christian community?

Catherine Bell categorizes rituals in six types which are not completely separated from each other: rites of passage; calendrical and commemorative rites; rites of exchange and communion; rites of feasting, fasting, and festivals; rites of affliction; political rituals.[33] For the study of Catholic rituals, the theological typology distinguishes the sacraments (baptism, confirmation, Eucharist, confession, marriage, ordination to priesthood, extreme unction) from the non-sacramental rites (fasting, recitative prayers, exorcism, blessings, funerals).[34] As the focus of this book, Mass is located in the intersection of four aforementioned types: sacraments; calendrical and commemorative rites; rites of exchange and communion; rites of feasting, fasting, and festivals. The exploration of ritual interactions around Mass is not restricted within the Christian communities, but extends to various cultural expressions of Chinese society, such as traditional religion, architecture, art, literature, government, and theology; it also extends from China to Europe, especially to Rome.

4   Structure and Sources

The conversation between Aleni and Chen Zhongdan in the prologue contains four elements of worship: the Lord of Heaven relates to the object of worship; to express gratitude to the intention of worship; the celebrant of the ritual to the performer of worship; families and homes to the place of worship. Each chapter in this book explores one element of worship, unfolding ritual interactions around Mass. The conclusion reflects on the three major questions below, which are treated through the whole book. How was the Mass introduced and propagated in late Ming and early Qing? At what levels, between whom, and regarding what questions did ritual interactions around Mass take place in Chinese society? In comparison with the ritual in Europe, what was the inheritance and adaptation of the Mass in China?

The primary sources in the current book can be roughly categorized as prescriptive and descriptive, with some overlap in certain texts. The prescriptive sources include catechisms, ritual manuals, statutes of confraternities, and official documents, which reflect the procedure, meaning, and regulations of Mass

---

33 Bell, *Ritual: Perspectives and Dimensions*, 94.
34 Standaert, *The Interweaving of Rituals*, 5.

as conceived in Chinese society. The descriptive sources include letters, poems, journals, and account books, which reflect the actual practice, thoughts, and interpretation of Mass. The majority of primary sources are chosen from the years 1583 to 1720, mainly in the seventeenth century. A few texts are currently undatable as to the publishing date. The geographic areas from which the primary sources originate include various cities, towns, and villages in various provinces. The focus is mainly on Beijing 北京, and south-western provinces such as Fujian, Jiangsu 江蘇, and Zhejiang 浙江, where most Christian communities were located. The primary sources are mainly in Chinese and unless otherwise noted translations are my own and tend to be more literal. The original text of translations and other scholar's translation are given as a reference in the footnote.

Only a few works among the primary sources are solely dedicated to Mass, such as *The Meaning of the Sacrifice of Mass* (*Misa jiyi* 彌撒祭義, 1629) and *The Classics of the Mass* (*Misa jingdian* 彌撒經典, 1670). Studies on the Mass in late Ming and early Qing usually focus on the few aforementioned works, however, this book analyzes several texts which have not been studied from the ritual perspective before, such as the Litany of Jesus' Holy Body (*Yesu shengti daowen* 耶穌聖體禱文), "The Musical Sound of Mass" (*Misa yueyin* 彌撒樂音), and *The Regulation of the Cap of Mass* (*Misa guan yi* 彌撒冠儀). In addition to the works dedicated to Mass, this book selects a large number of scattered material. In fact, the majority of the references related to Mass can be found in various texts, in the form of chapters, sections, paragraphs, and even sentences. These pieces of material are like tiles varied in size, shape, and color. With the Mass in late Ming and early Qing as its theme, this book puts these tiles together to form a mosaic which depicts ritual interactions of the Catholic Church in Chinese society.[35] The materials relating to this topic are quite extensive so it lies beyond the scope of this book to exhaustively catalog everything pertaining to the Mass in late Ming and early Qing. This book usually supports its arguments by several examples selected from different texts. Occasionally, the examples do not connect with each other directly but are combined together to support one argument. This situation resembles the gaps among tiles in a mosaic. When staring at a specific detail in one mosaic, one only sees the individual tiles instead of an image that carries the meaning. It takes certain distance to look at a mosaic as a whole, with all the tiles presenting a clear and colorful image together.

---

35 The mosaic imagery is borrowed from Jungmann, who described *Missarum Sollemnia* in this way. Jungmann, foreword to *The Mass*, 7.

CHAPTER 1

Object of Worship: Grand Ritual of Sacrifice to the Lord of Heaven

This chapter examines how the object of worship in Mass was introduced and understood in late Ming and early Qing. In the first part, introducing the Lord of Heaven as the object of worship in Mass, the Catholic Church in China had to answer two crucial questions: "Is Mass a usurpation of the worship of Heaven?" and "Is Heaven identical to the Lord of Heaven?" During the introduction and understanding of the Lord of Heaven, the Christian communities revealed the twofold depiction of the ultimately honorable and the ultimately intimate. The second part discusses Jesus as the object of worship in Mass from three perspectives: the title as the Lord of Heaven Jesus; the relationship between the reception of suffering and Mass; and the Litany of Jesus' Holy Body.

1   The Lord of Heaven as Object of Worship

1.1   *Is Mass a Usurpation of the Worship of Heaven?*

In late Ming and early Qing, Chinese Catholics attended Mass to worship the Lord of Heaven. As Francesco Brancati (Pan Guoguang 潘國光, SJ, 1607–1671) proclaimed: "Mass is the grand ritual of sacrifice to the Lord of Heaven (*ji tianzhu zhi dali* 祭天主之大禮)."[1] The object of worship in Mass is the Christian God, which was addressed by Brancati as "the Lord of Heaven" (*tianzhu* 天主) in Chinese. Since the beginning of the mission in China, missionaries were facing the question of the terms, which was as inevitable as the question of the rites.[2] It was problematic for them to choose a Chinese word for the Christian God to differ him from all the other gods.

---

[1] "彌撒者，祭天主之大禮，" Francesco Brancati 潘國光, *Tianshen huike* 天神會課, fol. 62a7, in CCT BnF, vol. 20, 127. See also "為祭獻天主的大礼，" Nicolas-Joseph Raux 羅廣祥, *Shengshi wenda* 聖事問答, fol. 6b3–4, in CCT BnF, vol. 20, 458.

[2] Bontinck, *La Lutte*, 59. This is a classic work on questions pertaining to Catholic rituals in Ming and Qing. With a large number of historical sources, Bontinck presents in detail rituals in different periods in the Catholic Church in the seventeenth and eighteenth centuries, the efforts made by missionaries in China to initiate Chinese Catholic rituals, and Rome's reac-

Ricci's strategy is to borrow suitable terms from the religious vocabulary in Chinese to express Catholic notions, which Diego de Pantoja (Pang Diwo 龐迪我, SJ, 1571–1618), Alfonso Vagnone (Wang Fengsu 王豐肅/Gao Yizhi 高一志, SJ, 1568–1640), and Nicolas Trigault (Jin Nige 金尼閣, SJ, 1577–1629) followed.[3] The first missionaries in late Ming chose two terms: the High Lord (*shangdi* 上帝), the Lord of Heaven (*tianzhu* 天主). The first term was borrowed from the Confucian Classics in order to approach Confucianism; the second had been used in Buddhism and Taoism. To borrow terms used in the existent religion resembles the Jesuits' strategy in Japan decades ago. For example, Francis Xavier (Sha Wulüe 沙勿略, SJ, 1506–1552) used the Buddhist term "Dainichi" to translate God. Yet, it was easy for the Japanese to mistake the Jesuits for Buddhist preachers. Therefore, the Jesuits decided to employ a Japanese transliteration from Latin or Portuguese terms.[4] In 1613 (Wanli 41), the missionary in Japan João Rodrigues (Lu Ruohan 陸若漢, SJ, 1561–1633) entered mainland China and stayed for two years.[5] Some of his Jesuit brothers in China declared that the Chinese in ancient times already knew God in order to approach the literati. Based on his solid experience in Japan, Rodrigues thought that this approach was wrong and opposed using terms already used in the Chinese tradition. Particularly for the term "the Lord of Heaven," he pointed out in a letter written in 1616: "in addition to being the name of a famous pagoda [deity] among them, it does not mean God but something else very different."[6]

Coincidentally, the well-known Buddhist monk Yunqi Zhuhong 雲棲祩宏 (1535–1615) echoed Rodrigues' opinion on the Lord of Heaven in the anti-Catholic text *On Heaven* (*Tian shuo* 天說, 1615).

> According to the classics, what they call the Lord of Heaven is the King of Heaven Tāvatiṃsa, the lord of the thirty-three heavens in the four great continents. In the four great continents, to count from one to one thousand is called a small chiliocosms, and there are one thousand Lords of Heaven; to count from one small chiliocosms to one thousand is called a medium chiliocosm, and there are one million Lords of Heaven; to count

---

tion and action. Furthermore, the appendix provides abundant original texts of discussions on rituals written by missionaries in different periods and Rome's responses. The Catholic rituals in discussion were mainly Mass and Holy Orders.

3   Bontinck, *La Lutte*, 60.
4   Michael Cooper, SJ, *Rodrigues the Interpreter: An Early Jesuit in Japan and China* (New York and Tokyo: Weatherhill, 1974), 285.
5   João Rodrigues entered mainland China in June 1613, but his two-year itinerary was vague. Cooper, *Rodrigues the Interpreter*, 279.
6   Cooper, *Rodrigues the Interpreter*, 282.

from one medium chiliocosm to one thousand is called a great chiliocosm, and there are one trillion Lords of Heaven. It is the King of Heaven Mahābrahmā that governs a great trichiliocosm. The one whom they call the Lord of Heaven the most high and honorable to the King of Heaven Mahābrahmā is as a thousand and eight hundred princes to the Son of Heaven in Zhou dynasty. The one whom they know is but one among one trillion Lords of Heaven.[7]

Since "the Lord of Heaven" (*tianzhu* 天主) has a Buddhist origin,[8] Zhuhong firstly used the Buddhist classics to prove that missionaries misunderstood the heaven and mistook one Lord of Heaven as the most high and honorable god. Secondly, he pointed out that the sacrificial ritual to the High Lord complied with the bureaucratic hierarchy, and that the heaven in the ancient Chinese classics embodied the imperial system (*wangzhi* 王制).[9]

For missionaries such as Rodrigues, it is wrong and dangerous to borrow terms from the existent religions. Yet, for missionaries such as Ricci, it is common for different religions to use the same terms. In addition, the Chinese were far less receptive to the transliteration from European languages than the Japanese.[10] Nevertheless, Ricci's successor Niccolò Longobardo (Long Huamin 龍華民, SJ, 1565–1655), after reading the Four Books (*sishu* 四書), noticed that the idea of the High Lord is opposite to the divine nature.[11] Therefore, he agreed with Rodrigues and preferred the strategy similar to that in Japan. From the end of 1627 to the beginning of 1628, eleven Jesuits and four Catholic literati held a conference in Jiading 嘉定, Zhejiang to discuss the question of terms.

---

[7] "按經以證，彼所稱天主者，切利天王，一四天下三十三天之主也。此一四天下，從一數之而至於千，名小千世界，則有千天主矣。又從一小千數之而複至於千，名中千世界，則有百萬天主矣。又從一中千數之而複至於千，名大千世界，則有萬億天主矣。統此三千大千世界者，大梵天王是也。彼所稱最尊無上之天主，梵天視之，畧似周天子視千八百諸侯也。彼所知者，萬億天主中之一耳。" Shi Zhuhong 釋袾宏, *Tian shuo 1* 天說一, fol. 1 a9–b7, in *Shengchao poxie ji* 聖朝破邪集, vol. 7, ed. Xu Changzhi 徐昌治, Lan Jifu 藍吉富, ed., *Dazangjing bubian* 大藏经补编, vol. 28 (Taipei: Huayu chubanshe 華宇出版社, 1986), 322–323.

[8] "諸天之帝主也。最勝王經八日 '有王法心論，名天主教法。'" Ding Fubao 丁福保, ed., *Foxue dacidian* 佛學大辭典 (Beijing: Wenwu chubanshe 文物出版社, 1984), 234.

[9] Zhuhong, *Tian shuo 3*, fol. 3b4–8, 324.

[10] Cooper, *Rodrigues the Interpreter*, 286–287.

[11] "… ayant lû selon la coûtume de nostre Compagnie les quatre Livers de Confucius, je remarquay que l'idée que divers Commentateurs donnoient du *Xangti*, estoit opposée à la nature divine." Nicolò Longobardi, *Traité sur quelques points de la religion des Chinois* (Paris: Louis Guerin, 1701), 1.

Yet, the disagreement among the missionaries intensified during and after the Jiading conference. The Visitor André Palmeiro (SJ, 1569–1635) ceased the discussions and ordered that *tianzhu* be used while *tian* and *shangdi* be rejected.[12] The usage of terms in Chinese was not only a concern to the Jesuits in China but also to Rome. In 1645, Innocent X (1574–1655, papacy: 1644–1655) condemned the usage of "Heaven" and "the High Lord."[13] In order to differ the Christian God from all the other gods, Rome forbade terms chosen from the Confucian Classics yet kept the usage of "the Lord of Heaven." Nevertheless, Innocent X's condemnation did not stop the usage of "Heaven" and "the High Lord" in the Catholic Church in China. Along with the Jesuits, some Chinese Catholics supported Ricci's strategy.

In *Examination on Similarity & Dissimilarity between the Study of Heaven and Confucianism* (*Tian ru tongyi kao* 天儒同異考, 1702–1715), Ignatius Zhang Xingyao 張星曜 (1633–ca. 1715) articulated that "In our China, all know that the Lord of Heaven the High Lord exists."[14] Zhang Xingyao identified the Lord of Heaven with the High Lord worshiped in ancient China. In this context, it is easy for the Chinese to consider the heaven or the High Lord the object of worship in Mass. Recalling the conversation cited at the beginning of this book, Chen Zhongdan asked Aleni two questions, focusing on the object of worship. In the first question, Chen Zhongdan identified the Lord of Heaven with the heaven worshiped in China and wondered if it is a usurpation of the traditional Chinese ritual that every Christian could worship the Lord of Heaven. In the second one, he acknowledged the high status of the Lord of Heaven and wondered if it is a blasphemy to the Lord of Heaven that every Christian could hang his picture in their house. These two questions aroused from a typical Chinese mind which was accustomed to the traditional bureaucratic hierarchy.

The bureaucratic hierarchy derives from ancient China, where the king had a sacred character, being the highest priest as well as the highest ruler. Thus, the king and his officials were priests of the official cult.[15] With the development of bureaucracy in late Imperial China, the role as the Son of Heaven (*tianzi* 天子) legitimized the emperor as the highest ruler in the state. The emperor was the legitimate agent of heaven, empowered to rule the world as long as the heaven was satisfactory with him. As the exclusive celebrant of the ritual to Heaven

---

12   Bontinck, *La Lutte*, 60–61. Liam Matthew M. Brockey, *Journey to the East: The Jesuit Mission to China, 1579–1724* (Cambridge: Harvard University Press, 2008), 87–88.
13   Bontinck, *La Lutte*, 61.
14   "我中國皆知有天主上帝也。" Zhang Xingyao 張星曜, *Tianru tongyi kao* 天儒同異考, in CCT BnF, vol. 8, 433.
15   Henri Maspero, *La Chine antique* (Paris: Presses Universitaires de France, 1965), 157.

and Earth (*jiaoshe zhi li* 郊社之禮), the emperor could be understood as the highest priest. Accordingly, the officials celebrated other state rituals as priests, which became one of the main responsibilities of the literati-officials.[16] With the emperor at the top and various classes of officials as subjects, the traditional bureaucratic hierarchy was elaborately constructed.

In addition to the political dimension, the bureaucratic hierarchy operated its power in the religious dimension, supported by Confucianism. With the worship of Heaven and sacrifice to ancestors as its core, Confucianism can be defined as a religious system including a series of worships.[17] According to C.K. Yang, with no independent theology, clergy, or institution, Confucianism is a diffused religion which functions as a part of the secular social institution.[18] Under Confucian ideology, the state educated the people to distinguish orthodoxy from heterodoxy and prevented any religious groups from challenging the state's authority.[19] In this sense, Confucianism was an official state religion and the religion of the literati.[20]

As regards the bureaucratic hierarchy, some literati considered the worship of the Lord of Heaven a usurpation. In 1616 (Wanli 44.5), Shen Que 沈㴶 (1556–1624), an official in the Ministry of Rites in Nanjing 南京, wrote *Memorial to Impeach Barbarians from Far Away* (*Can yuanyi shu* 參遠夷疏, 1616).

> When the Three Dynasties were prosperous, the person who governed the feudal lords was called the King of Heaven, and who ruled the whole world was called the Son of Heaven. The current dynasty examines the ancient rules and establishes systems. Every time the announcement of the imperial order says "to carry out [the order of] Heaven." Yet, the barbarians cunningly call [their god] "the Lord of Heaven," as if he rules over the Son of Heaven.[21]

---

16 Clerical responsibilities differ according to the official level, see Sun Shangyang 孫尚揚, *Zongjiao shehuixue* 宗教社會學 (Beijing: Peking University Press, 2001), 201.
17 Sun, *Zongjiao shehuixue*, 196.
18 C.K. Yang, *Religion in Chinese society: a study of contemporary social functions of religion and some of their historical factors* (Berkeley: University of California press, 1961), 295.
19 Jochim suggested that the definition of civil religion by Dunbar Moodie is suited for the discussion of traditional Chinese state religion. Confucianism was an integral part of the state instead of an independent faith. Confucian scriptures were the basis for civil faith and civil ritual. In these two spheres, Confucian literati-officials guided the interpretation of scriptures. Christian Jochim, *Chinese Religions: A Cultural Perspective* (Englewood Cliffs N.J.: Prentice Hall, 1986), 144.
20 Vincent Goossaert, *Dans les temples de la Chine. Histoire des cultes Vie des communautés* (Paris: Albin Michel, 2000), 14.
21 "三代之隆也，臨諸侯曰'天王'，君天下曰'天子'。本朝稽古定制，每詔誥之

The Three Dynasties refer to the Xia dynasty (ca. 2070 BC–ca. 1600 BC), the Shang dynasty (ca. 1600 BC–ca. 1046 BC), and the Zhou dynasty (ca. 1046 BC–256 BC). Shen Que underlined how the Ming dynasty inherited the ancient rules and how the Son of Heaven represents the heaven's order. Around 1634 (Chongzhen 7), Huang Zhen 黃貞 accused the Teaching of the Lord of Heaven of using the terms similar to those which refer to the imperial reign: "What suspiciously resemble the imperial system the most are the High Lord (*shangdi* 上帝), the heaven's order (*tianming* 天命), and the heaven (*tian* 天) these five characters."[22] Huang Wendao 黃問道 thought that the worship of the Lord of Heaven "threatens the heaven, profanes the heaven, usurps the heaven, and blasphemes the heaven."[23]

Nevertheless, the Shunzhi emperor and the Kangxi emperor did not consider the worship of the Lord of Heaven a usurpation to the worship of Heaven. In 1652 (Shunzhi 9), the reconstruction of the church at Xuanwu men 宣武門 had been completed. The Shunzhi emperor bestowed the tablet (*paibian* 牌匾) with the inscription "To Adore the Way of Heaven" (*qinchong tiandao* 欽崇天道).[24] On 12 July 1675 (Kangxi 14.5.20), the Kangxi emperor visited the Jesuit church and residence at Xuanwu men with imperial family members, officials, and courtiers. The twenty-one-year-old emperor wrote two characters "*jingtian* 敬天" (To Revere Heaven) to Ferdinand Verbiest (Nan Huairen 南懷仁, SJ, 1623–1688). The following day, the Kangxi emperor wrote the same characters in larger size, approved them with the imperial seal, and bestowed them to the Jesuits. The tablet with the inscription "To Revere Heaven" written by the emperor was hang at the best place in the church.[25]

This section collects various responses to the question "Is Mass a usurpation of the worship of Heaven?" The Shunzhi emperor and the Kangxi emperor considered the worship of the Lord of Heaven an ordinary religious practice; the anti-Catholics, such as Shen Que, Huang Zhen, and Huang Wendao, crit-

---

下，皆曰'奉天'。而彼夷詭稱'天主'，若將駕軼其上者然。" Shen Que 沈㴆, *Can yuanyi shu* 參遠夷疏, fol. 6b7–fol. 7a1, in *Poxie ji*, vol. 1, 221.

22 "其最受朱紫疑似者，莫若上帝，天命與天之五字。" Huang Zhen 黃貞, *Zunru jijing* 尊儒亟鏡, fol. 13b10–fol. 14a1, in *Poxie ji*, vol. 3, 260.

23 "邀天褻天僭天瀆天，" Huang Wendao 黃問道, *Pixie jie* 闢邪解, fol. 20b6–7, in *Poxie ji*, vol. 5, 304.

24 Sun Shangyang 孫尚揚 and Nicolas Standaert, *1840 nian qian de Zhongguo jidujiao* 一八四零年前的中國基督教 (Beijing: Xueyuan chubanshe 學苑出版社, 2004), 327.

25 Claudia von Collani, "Jing Tian—The Kangxi Emperor's Gift to Ferdinand Verbiest in the Rites Controversy," in *Ferdinand Verbiest (1623–1688): Jesuit Missionary, Scientist, Engineer and Diplomat*, ed. John W. Witek (Monumenta Serica Monograph Series XXX, Nettetal: Steyler Verlag, 1994), 453–455.

icized Mass as the usurpation to the traditional Chinese ritual; the Chinese Catholics such as Chen Zhongdan tried to understand the relationship between the object of worship in Mass and that in traditional Chinese rituals. Next section discusses another question derived from Chen Zhongdan's conversation with Aleni.

1.2 Is Heaven Identical to the Lord of Heaven?

Since the Chinese in late Ming and early Qing tended to consider heaven the object of worship in Mass, the Catholic Church in China had to answer if heaven was identical to the Lord of Heaven. To answer Chen Zhongdan's two questions, Aleni distinguished Mass from the traditional Chinese sacrificial ritual. Nevertheless, he did not distinguish the heaven worshiped by the emperor as Son of Heaven from the Lord of Heaven worshiped by Chinese Catholics. Aleni and some other Jesuits tacitly agreed that the Son of Heaven and Chinese Catholics worship the same Lord of Heaven or the same heaven. The missionaries reinforced this tacit agreement with the aforementioned tablet with the inscription "To Revere Heaven."

It seems that the Kangxi emperor identified heaven with the Lord of Heaven. In one imperial edict (*yu* 諭), he said: "'To Revere Heaven' written by me means to worship 'the Lord of Heaven.'"[26] The Kangxi emperor also wrote "To Revere Heaven" and had it hang in his room, which belonged to a trend to worship a personalized Heaven propagated by some Confucianists in late Ming and early Qing.[27] Through out history heaven in Chinese had developed rich meanings.[28] Nevertheless, Philippe Couplet (Bo Yingli 柏應理, SJ, 1623–1693) explained to European readers that the *"tian* 天*"* (heaven) written by the emperor is the Chinese way to speak of *"tianzhu* 天主*"* (the Lord of Heaven).[29] The Jesuits, some Franciscans, some Augustinians, and the Chinese Dominican Luo Wenzhao 羅文炤 (Gregorio López, OP, 1617–1691) hang the tablet bestowed by the emperor in many halls of the Lord of Heaven across China as the sign of imperial protec-

---

26 "朕書 '敬天，' 即敬 '天主' 也。" "Yushu jingtian erzi bian'e 御書敬天二字匾額," Huang Bolu 黃伯祿, ed., *Zhengjiao fengbao* 正教奉褒 (Shanghai: Cimu tang 慈母堂, 1894), vol. 1, fol. 69b10–fol. 70a1.
27 Liu Yunhua 劉耘華, *Yitian liyi: Qingdai qianzhongqi Jiangnan wenren yingdui tianzhujiao wenhua yanjiu* 依天立義：清代前中期江南文人應對天主教文化研究 (Shanghai: Shanghai guji chubanshe 上海古籍出版社, 2014), 139–140.
28 See Liu, *Yitian liyi*, 266–271.
29 Philippe Couplet, *Histoire d'une dame chrétienne de la Chine où par occasion les usages de ces peuples, l'établissement de la religion, les manieres des missionaires, & les exercices de pieté des nouveaux chrétiens sont expliquez* (Paris: Estienne Michallet, 1688), 119.

tion.³⁰ Candida Xu 許甘第大 (1607–1680) paid for two beautiful replicas of the tablet "To Revere Heaven" in the church in Shanghai 上海 and that in Songjiang 松江.³¹ On 14 February 1676 (Kangxi 15.1.1), a replica of the tablet was inaugurated in the church in Changshu 常熟, Jiangsu. The account book of François de Rougemont (Lu Riman 魯日滿, SJ, 1624–1676) recorded the construction and installment of the replica.³² The tablet's wide circulation showed the pendulum of using Chinese terms among missionaries in China. On the one hand, Innocent X condemned the usage of "*tian* 天" (heaven) in 1645; on the other, the missionaries wanted to publicize the Kangxi emperor's favor, regardless of the pope's condemnation.³³

Missionaries from different religious orders differed in the attitude toward the tablet. Some Franciscans thought that the inscription "To Revere Heaven" reveals a pagan view of God and prohibited the tablet hanging in the church. Michael Fernandez-Oliver (Nan Huaide 南懷德, OFM, 1665–1726), however, took a more accommodating attitude toward the Chinese terms than most Franciscans, accepting the tacit agreement that the Lord of Heaven identifies heaven.³⁴ Fernandez-Oliver had the tablet hang in the new building of the East Hall (*dongtang* 東堂) in Ji'nan 濟南, Shandong 山東. One non-Christian literatus Zhu contributed to the construction of the East Hall, by having a gilded inscription made to hang over the altar. At first the literatus Zhu planned to write "To Revere Heaven" on the tablet, however, Fernandez-Oliver insisted on writing "To Revere the Lord of Heaven" (*jing tianzhu* 敬天主). To add the character "*zhu* 主" (the Lord) distinguished the Christian God from the heaven in the Chinese notion.³⁵ Fernandez-Oliver made a compromising decision because to claim that the Chinese did not know the Christian God might prevent them from approaching Catholicism.

In order to prove that the Chinese know the Christian God, Louis Le Comte (Li Ming 李明, SJ, 1655–1728) made a bold argument identifying the heaven worshiped in ancient China with the Lord of Heaven: "So that this people has kept for nearly two thousand years the knowledge of the true God and has honored

---

30 Buddhists, Taoists, Muslims, and Jews in China hang the same tablet in their religious buildings. Collani, "Jing Tian," 456–457.
31 Couplet, *Histoire d'une dame*, 119–120.
32 Noël Golvers, *François de Rougemont, S.J., Missionary in Ch'ang-Shu (Chiang-Nan): A Study of the Account Book (1674–1676) and the Elogium* (Leuven: Leuven University Press, 1999), 380.
33 Brockey, *Journey to the East*, 137.
34 D.E. Mungello, *The Spirit and the Flesh in Shandong, 1650–1785* (Lanham, New York, Boulder, and Oxford: Rowman and Littlefield, 2001), 84.
35 Mungello, *Spirit and the Flesh*, 88.

Him in a way that can serve as example and as instruction even to the Christians."[36] The idea that the Chinese has known the Christian God for almost two thousand years was astonishing to the European mind. In 1700, the theologians of the University of Paris condemned the Jesuits' books, especially those by Le Comte and by Charles Le Gobien (Guo Bi'en 郭弼恩, SJ, 1653–1708).[37] Missionaries in China confronted more tension, when a European vicar apostolic made rash decisions in this unfamiliar land.

On 26 March 1693 (Kangxi 32.2.20), the Vicar Apostolic of Fujian Charles Maigrot (Yan Dang 顏璫, MEP, 1652–1730) issued *Mandatum seu Edictum* (Mandated edict). There are seven articles in his edict pertaining to the Chinese rites, which were valid at least to all the missionaries in Fujian.[38] The first article forbade the usage of "Heaven" and "the High Lord." The second forbade hanging the aforementioned tablet in the church, because Maigrot thought that the general understanding of the tablet is to revere the material heaven.[39] Innocent XII (1615–1700, papacy: 1691–1700) appointed Maigrot as the bishop of Conon in 1696. On 13 March 1700 (Kangxi 39.1.24), the bishop of Beijing Bemardino della Chiesa (Yi Daren 伊大仁, OFM, 1644–1721) officially ordained Maigrot as the bishop of Conon. The ordination Mass was celebrated in a church owned by the Jesuits in Jiaxing 嘉興, Zhejiang. Ironically, Maigrot was ordained under the tablet with the inscription "To Revere Heaven" which he had forbidden yet he did not protest.[40]

On 1 April 1700 (Kangxi 39.2.12), Mgr. Maigrot returned to Fuzhou 福州, Fujian and found that Giampaolo Gozani (Lu Baolu 魯保祿/Luo Baolu 駱保祿, SJ, 1659–1732) and João de Saa (Yang Ruowang 楊若望/Yang Ruohan 楊若翰, SJ, 1672–1731) did not obey his mandate, so he suspended the two Jesuits from administering the sacraments. As a result, from 12 to 18 April 1700 what Dehergne called "the regrettable incidents" took place in Fuzhou.[41]

---

36 "De sorte que ce peuple a conservé près de deux mille ans la connaissance du véritable Dieu et l'a honoré d'une manière qui peut servir d'exemple et d'instruction même aux chrétiens." Louis Lecomte, *Un jésuite à Pékin: Nouveaux mémoires sur l'état présent de la Chine, 1687–1692*, texte établi, annoté et présenté par Frédérique Touboul-Bouyeure (Paris: Phébus, 1990), 362.

37 Claudia von Collani, "Charles Maigrot's Role in the Chinese Rites Controversy," in *The Chinese Rites Controversy*, 158.

38 For the seven articles, see Collani, "Charles Maigrot's Role," 152–154.

39 Collani, "Jing Tian," 458–459.

40 See Collani, "Jing Tian," 463. See also Collani, "Charles Maigrot's Role," 159–160.

41 Joseph Dehergne, *La Chine centrale vers 1700. II. Les vicariats apostoliques de la côte. Étude de géographie missionnaire* (Rome: Archivum Historicum Societatis Iesu, 1961): 337. *Study of Missionary Geography* (Éetude de géographie missionnaire) is a series of articles with a large research region. It examines missions in villages, towns, and cities in China. Although

It was Easter season but the local Chinese Catholics could not confess or attend Mass because Mgr. Maigrot suspended Gozani and de Saa. From 17 to 18 April 1700 (Kangxi 39.2.28–29), a group of local Chinese Catholics assembled in front of Mgr. Maigrot's residence to beg him to stop suspending the two Jesuits. Mgr. Maigrot tried to chase them out but got involved into a conflict. Wu Min 吳旻 and Han Qi 韓琦 find three descriptions of this conflict: the first one was probably written by a missionary from the Dominican order or from the Society of Foreign Missions of Paris; the second was probably written by a Jesuit, with a testimony by local Chinese Catholics; the third was a letter written by the local Chinese Catholics in Fuzhou.[42] This section conveys the voice of the local Chinese Catholics in the third description.

On 17 April (Kangxi 39.2.28), local Chinese Catholics knelt down and begged in front of the bishop residence, but Mgr. Maigrot insisted that Gozani must remove the tablet first. On 18 April (Kangxi 39.2.29), because Mgr. Maigrot ignored the local Chinese Catholics, they held one crucifix in front of his residence and cried aloud, then Mgr. Maigrot went out to chase them away. Seeing that Mgr. Maigrot did not pay respect to the crucifix, the local Chinese Catholics thought that "the bishop disrespects the Lord of Heaven, so we disrespect the bishop." They forced Mgr. Maigrot to kneel down before the crucifix, however, Mgr. Maigrot lied that they beat him and forbade them from attending Mass. On the same day, the local Chinese Catholics in Fuzhou wrote one letter to describe the conflict in detail and sent copies to several bishops and vicars apostolic in China.

In the letter, the local Chinese Catholics praised the Jesuits and took responsibility for the conflict. Yet, they strongly criticized Mgr. Maigrot: "The bishop has not bestowed any grace but hands out heavy punishment on people. ...

---

the research period is mainly around 1700, it often mentions different periods from the end of the fifteenth century to the beginning of the twentieth century. With abundant historical sources, Dehergne presents precious information from various regions, such as the initiation of mission, church construction, the population receiving baptism, confession, and the Eucharist.

42 1, *Lettre écrite de la province de Fukien dans la Chine sur la fin de l'année 1700 où l'on rapporte le cruel traitement que les chrétiens des Jésuites ont fait à Mr. Maigrot, Evéque de Conon & Vicaire Apostolique, au R.P. Croquet de l'ordre de S. Dominique; & où l'on voit un échantillon du respect qu'ont les Jésuites pour les Evéques & pour S. Siège*, anonymous, undated; 2, *Relation abregée des insultes faites à M. l'Evéque de Conon par quelques chrétiens de Fotcheou*, anonymous, undated; 3, the letter to Carlo Giovanni Turcotti (Du Jialu 都加祿, SJ, 1643–1706) written by the local Chinese Catholics, with 25 signatures, on 18 April 1700 (Kangxi 39.2.29).

Why does he not destroy the tablet by himself but passes the order to others to do so?" To remove the replica of the imperial gift was considered a huge disrespect for the Kangxi emperor. In this regard, the local Chinese Catholics thought that Mgr. Maigrot wanted Gozani and them to take the blame for him. They analyzed their situation: "If we obey the bishop and remove the tablet, our bodies shall die according to the strict imperial law; if we do not remove the tablet, our souls die permanently. It is such a dilemma which matters a lot."[43] In order to maintain the pure Catholic ritual in his mind, Mgr. Maigrot put local Chinese Catholics in Fuzhou into a dilemma. On 22 May 1700 (Kangxi 39.4.4), he compromised and allowed the two Jesuits to administer sacraments.[44] Nevertheless, on 20 November 1704, Clement XI (1649–1721, papacy: 1700–1721) confirmed most of Mgr. Maigrot's edict in the decree *Cum Deus Optimus* (With the Best God),[45] putting some missionaries and Chinese Catholics into a dilemma again.

On 2 August 1706 (Kangxi 45.6.24), the Kangxi emperor met Mgr. Maigrot at his mountain resort in Chengde 承德, Hebei 河北. Their conversation was rather embarrassing: Mgr. Maigrot did not understand the emperor and needed an interpreter; he did not remember anything from the ancient Chinese Classics the Four Books; of an inscription with four characters the emperor asked him to read, he only knew two characters. Then, the Kangxi emperor pointed out that the meaning of "*ji* 祭" (sacrifice) varies according to different contexts and that Mgr. Maigrot forbade traditional Chinese rites out of his ignorance. The emperor declared that if local Catholics in Fujian follow Mgr. Maigrot's order to abandon the rites of "*jingtian* 敬天" (revering Heaven), they are not his Chinese subjects anymore.[46] What the Kangxi emperor told Mgr. Maigrot is what every missionary in China need to know: the meaning of one character varies in different contexts, therefore one shall not interpret the character totally literally. The Kangxi emperor got angry that the King of Teaching (*jiao-*

---

43 "若遵主教，摘去其匾，皇法甚嚴，肉身該死；若不去匾，靈魂永死。其事兩難，關係甚大。" Wu Min 吳旻 and Han Qi 韓琦, "Liyi zhi zheng yu Zhongguo tianzhujiaotu—yi Fujian jiaotu he Yan Dang de chongtu weili 禮儀之爭與中國天主教徒——以福建教徒和顏璫的衝突為例," *Lishi yanjiu* 歷史研究 6 (2004): 91.

44 Collani, "Charles Maigrot's Role," 160.

45 Wu and Han, "Liyi zhi zheng," 84. Collani, "Charles Maigrot's Role," 158.

46 For a contemporary record in Western language, see Kilian Stumpf, SJ, *The Acta Pekinensia or Historical Records of the Maillard de Tournon Legation*, volume I, December 1705–August 1706, ed. Paul Rule and Claudia von Collani (Rome: Institutum Historicum Societatis Iesu, 2015), 578–580.

hua wang 教化王, the pope) confirmed Mgr. Maigrot's edict, so he ordered to expel the missionaries who did not obey Ricci's rule (*Li Madou de guiju* 利瑪竇的規矩).[47]

In late Ming and early Qing, to introduce the object of worship in Mass was extremely problematic. Missionaries confronted questions not only from the Chinese but also from Rome and European theologians. In the sixteenth and seventeenth centuries, to translate the Christian God into indigenous languages was a common problem in the Jesuit overseas missions. For example, Jesuit missionaries in South America translated various instructional texts in indigenous languages but they could not find a proper word to translate God.[48] In India, Roberto de Nobili (SJ, 1577–1656) thought that the translation of essential expressions and the transliteration of the sacraments were incorrect or inappropriate.[49] The mission to Japan faced the same problem, and when the experienced missionary in Japan Rodrigues visited China, he thought it is too difficult to find a Chinese translation to express the precise meaning of a European theological term.[50] Nevertheless, instead of finding the most precise translation of the Christian God, it might be more practical to build a proper context in indigenous languages to propagate the extant translation. Specific depiction and interpretation can assist to identify the Christian God. In fact, the Christian communities in China developed remarkable interpretations of God. Some Chinese Catholics, as well as missionaries, explained the Lord of Heaven's twofold depiction.

1.3 Twofold Depiction of the Ultimately Honorable and the Ultimately Intimate

In late Ming and early Qing some Chinese Catholics, such as Philippe Wang Zheng and Thomas Han Lin 韓霖 (1596?–1649), understood the Lord of Heaven as an omnipotent creator and a strict judge. Erik Zürcher suggests that they reinterpreted salvation by minimizing the doctrines of the original sin and the Incarnation; that their belief in the Lord of Heaven is closer to the Confucian doctrine based on the innate goodness of human nature.[51] In this sense, what these Chinese Catholics believed was in fact a "Confucian monotheism,"

---

47   Chen, *Kangxi*, 13.
48   Robert H. Jackson, *Demographic Change and Ethnic Survival among the Sedentary Populations on the Jesuit Mission Frontiers of Spanish South America, 1609–1803* (Leiden: Brill, 2015), 35.
49   Henri Bernard, SJ, *Le père Matthieu Ricci et la société chinoise de son temps (1552–1610)* (Tientsin: Hautes études, 1937), première partie, 99.
50   Cooper, *Rodrigues the Interpreter*, 284.
51   Zürcher, "Jesuit Accommodation," 47.

where redemption only plays a marginal role.[52] The suggestion of Confucian monotheism indicates that Chinese Catholics conceived an original theological notion: a combination of Confucianism and Catholicism.

Nevertheless, the depiction of an omnipotent creator and a strict judge only appeared in certain works and did not necessarily contradict the depiction of a loving Father and a redeemer. In fact, the Chinese Catholics' understanding of the Lord of Heaven was not restricted to Confucian monotheism. When discussing the heaven understood by Chinese Catholics in late Ming and early Qing, Nicolas Standaert mentions the theory of Rudolf Otto (1869–1937). In *The Idea of the Holy* (*Das Heilige*, 1917), Rudolf Otto suggests that the human being's encounter with the holy can be addressed both as the terrifying mystery (*mysterium tremendum*) and the fascinating mystery (*mysterium fascinosum*). It is remarkable that Chinese Catholics in the seventeenth century had a similar twofold depiction of the Lord of Heaven.[53] This section reveals the twofold depiction in the texts pertaining to Mass.

Some Chinese Catholics supported the tacit agreement to identify the Lord of Heaven with the heaven in the Chinese tradition. The Catholic literatus Michael Yang Tingyun 楊廷筠 (1562–1627) agreed that the original Confucianism has revealed the belief in a personalized God.[54] He showed his understanding of the Lord of Heaven in the explanation of Mass. In *Compilation of Doubts [on Behalf of Literatus]* (*Daiyi pian* 代疑篇, 1621), Yang Tingyun made up one literatus (*daru* 大儒) who raises questions about the Teaching of the Lord of Heaven. The literatus said: "Only the Son of Heaven could perform the ritual of the worship of Heaven. Now [Catholics] perform the ritual of Mass daily, this is either usurpation or blasphemy."[55] Chen Zhongdan raised the same question as mentioned in section 1 of the Introduction. Both Chen Zhongdan and the litertus in the *Compilation of Doubts* identified the Lord of Heaven with the heaven in the Chinese tradition and questioned the ritual of Mass where every Catholic can worship the Lord of Heaven.

Similar to Aleni's response in section 1 of the Introduction, Yang Tingyun distinguished the Chinese traditional sacrificial ritual from Mass but his answer was more thorough. Yang Tingyun pointed out that "some rituals are the same

---

52 Zürcher, "Jesuit Accommodation," 50.
53 Nicolas Standaert, *The Fascinating God: A Challenge to Modern Chinese Theology Presented by a text on the name of God written by a 17th century Chinese student of theology* (Rome: Pontificia Università Gregoriana, 1995), 131.
54 Zürcher, "Jesuit Accommodation," 43.
55 "禮惟天子祭天，今日日行彌撒禮，非僭即瀆，" Yang Tingyun 楊廷筠, *Daiyi pian* 代疑篇, *juan shang*, fol. 32a4–5, in CCT BAV (1), vol. 23, 101.

in name but different in nature."⁵⁶ The worship of Heaven and Mass are different in nature because the former is performed by the Son of Heaven, which "values the status [of the Son of Heaven]" (*zhong mingfen* 重名分);⁵⁷ the latter is instituted by Jesus who "offered [sacrifice to] the Lord of Heaven the Father" (*feng tianzhufu* 奉天主父) daily when he was on earth. The Western Confucianists (*xiru* 西儒) "offer sacrifice to Jesus" (*fengji Yesu* 奉祭耶穌) daily in order to express gratitude to the Lord of Heaven's grace and to follow Jesus' order.⁵⁸

Yang Tingyun's answer revealed a clear theological understanding of the Trinity. The sacrifice of Mass reflects three levels of relationship: the relationship between Jesus and the Lord of Heaven; the one between human beings and the Lord of Heaven; the one between human beings and Jesus. At the first level, Jesus the Son offered sacrifice to the Lord of Heaven the Father; at the second, human beings offer sacrifice to express gratitude to the Father; at the third, human beings offer sacrifice to follow the Son's order. The first level shows the relationship within the Trinity, and the last two show the relationship between human beings and the Trinity. The two phrases "offered [sacrifice to] the Lord of Heaven the Father" and "offer sacrifice to Jesus" (*fengji Yesu* 奉祭耶穌) reveal the extraordinary theological point of Mass—the object of worship identifies with the performer of worship. After the distinction, Yang Tingyun recommended a text called *Explanation of Mass* (*Misa jie* 彌撒解), which explains why perform Mass daily and why it is neither usurpation or blasphemy.⁵⁹ According to Li Tiangang, the *Explanation of Mass* has not been discovered yet and it might be an unpublished manuscript.⁶⁰ Yang Tingyun's distinction implies that the worship of Heaven and Mass differ in both the object of worship and the performer of worship.

56 "禮有名同實異者，" Yang, *Daiyi pian, juan shang*, fol. 32a6, 101.
57 The Japanese scholar Nakae Tōju (1608–1648) made a similar explanation that all human beings could have a direct relationship with Heaven, regardless of their status. Nicolas Standaert, *Yang Tingyun, Confucian and Christian in Late Ming China: His Life and Thought* (Leiden: Brill, 1988), 160.
58 "此為大祀之首，典禮最重，諸侯王通不得僭之，重名分也。若西教之彌撒禮，非此之謂。…… 耶穌在世，亦日日虔奉罷德肋，親定此禮，為萬民表率。故西士亦謹守其傳，日日奉祭耶穌，一是感天主之恩，一是遵耶穌之命。" Yang, *Daiyi pian, juan shang*, fol. 32a9–b8, 101–102.
59 "有《彌撒解》一編，…… 解則此禮當行，自無一日可少，非僭非瀆也。" Yang, *Daiyi pian, juan shang*, fol. 32b9–33a2, 102–103.
60 Li Tiangang 李天綱, comp. and annot., *Mingmo tianzhujiao sanzhushi wenjianzhu—Xu Guangqi, Li Zhizao, Yang Tingyun lunjiao wenji* 明末天主教三柱石文箋注——徐光啟、李之藻、楊廷筠論教文集 (Hongkong: Logos and Pneuma Press 道風書社, 2007), 247, note 136.

Nevertheless, Yang Tingyun still identified the Lord of Heaven with the heaven following Ricci's strategy. He expressed the regret that the Chinese had lost the correct understanding of the Lord of Heaven.

> Today people only see the Lord of Heaven as the ultimately honorable and the highest, who is far away and not intimate with themselves. They do not know that as regards the status in this world, the Lord of Heaven sees human beings as his children, regardless of the noble and the humble, regardless of the wise and the fool, all from one Great Father. This is the reason why he is called the Great Father and Mother, who is honorable and intimate; no one could be far away from him.[61]

Yang Tingyun did not trace the depiction of the Lord of Heaven to the heaven worshiped since ancient China but brought up that the Lord of Heaven is honorable and intimate (*zun erqie qin* 尊而且親), a fresh notion that reveals the twofold depiction. Instead of an omnipotent creator and a strict judge, the Catholic literatus depicted one Great Father (*dafu* 大父) and called him the Great Father and Mother (*dafumu* 大父母).

More than a decade earlier, Ricci had already connected filial piety (*xiaodao* 孝道) with the worship of the Lord of Heaven. The usage of "the Great Father and Mother" in the Catholic Church in China firstly appeared in *The True Meaning of the Lord of Heaven* (*Tianzhu shiyi* 天主實義, 1603).[62] The missionaries continued this usage, such as Aleni in *The Meaning of the Sacrifice of Mass* and *Four Character Classic of the Lord of Heaven's Holy Teaching* (*Tianzhu shengjiao sizi jingwen* 天主聖教四字經文, 1642).[63] So did some Chinese Catholics in their works. In *Records of the Holy Water* (*Shengshui jiyan* 聖水紀言, ca. 1613–1616), Yang Tingyun expounded that the Creator is our human beings' Great

---

61 "今人止視天主至尊至高，與己邈不相親。不知在人世，則論名分，天主視人無非其子，無貴賤、無賢愚，皆一大父所出，故謂之大父母，尊而且親，無人可得遠之。" Yang, *Daiyi pian, juan shang*, fol. 33a3–6, 103.

62 "夫父母授我以身體髮膚，我固當孝；君長賜我以田里樹畜，使仰事俯育，我又當尊；矧此天主之為大父母也，大君也，為眾祖之所出，眾君之所命，生養萬物，奚可錯認而忘之？" Matteo Ricci 利瑪竇, *Tianzhu shiyi* 天主實義, *shang juan*, fol. 22b5–8, in DCFY, vol. 2, 42.

63 Aleni, *Misa jiyi, juan* 2, fol. 37a6, 625. Giulio Aleni 艾儒略, *Tianzhu shengjiao sizi jingwen* 天主聖教四字經文, fol. 2a4, in CCT ARSI, vol. 2, 311. For more references of *dafumu*, see Joseph de Mailla 馮秉正, *Shengti ren'aijing guitiao* 聖體仁愛經規條, fol. 1a3, in CCT BnF, vol. 20, 295. See also Brancati, *Tianshen huike*, fol. 15b1, 34; fol. 17a3, 37. See also Ferdinand Verbiest 南懷仁, *Jiaoyao xulun* 教要序論, fol. 14a9, in CCT BnF, vol. 24, 45.

Father and Mother (*wuren dafumu* 吾人大父母).[64] In the preface of *Records of the Holy Water*, Leo Li Zhizao 李之藻 (1565–1630) connected the father and mother of one family with the Great Father and Mother of the whole world: "I have father and mother, how can I not love them or respectfully serve them? Human beings have the Great Father and Mother, how can we not love him or respectfully serve him?"[65] In *Expounding How to Fear Heaven and to Love Human Beings* (*Weitian airen jilun* 畏天愛人極論, 1628), Wang Zheng similarly claimed: "Human beings know serving their parents, yet they do not know that the Lord of Heaven is the Great Father and Mother."[66] In *The Book of the Warning Bell* (*Duoshu* 鐸書, ca. 1640), Han Lin articulated: "We must know that the heaven is the Great Father and Mother."[67] This Catholic literatus implicitly identified the Lord of Heaven with the heaven in his moral guidebook for the local community.

In the late sixteenth century, an early translation of the *Pater Noster* (the Our Father) in Chinese used the similar term "the Great Father" (*dafu* 大父) eight times.[68] *General Collection of Prayer Recitation in the Holy Teaching of the Lord of Heaven* (*Tianzhu shengjiao nianjing zongdu* 天主聖教念經總牘, 1628) used the term from time to time. For example, [Prayer] Recited before Receiving the Holy Body (*ling shengti yiqian nian* 領聖體已前念) called the Lord Jesus "my Great Father" (*wo zhi dafu* 我之大父).[69] Later on, Aleni described Mass as the ritual where Catholics gather in a church "to adore one Great Father together."[70] Li Jiugong claimed that to celebrate Mass for the salvation of ancestors' souls "purely conforms with the Lord of Heaven the Great Father's

---

64 Sun Xueshi 孫學詩, *Shengshui jiyan* 聖水紀言, *juan* 2, fol. b3–4, in CCT ARSI, vol. 8, 16.

65 "我有父母可不愛不敬事乎哉？則人ᘰ有大父母又可不愛不敬事乎哉？" Li Zhizao 李之藻, "Ke *Shengshui jiyan* xu 刻《聖水紀言》序," fol. 1b5–fol. 2a1, in *Shengshui jiyan* 聖水紀言, 4–5.

66 "夫人知事其父母，而不知天主之為大父母。" Wang Zheng 王徵, *Weitian airen jilun* 畏天愛人極論, fol. 16b1–2, BnF Chinois 6868.

67 "吾人要知天為大父母。" Han Lin 韓霖, *Duoshu* 鐸書, in *Duoshu jiaozhu* 鐸書校注, annot. Sun Shangyang 孫尚揚, Xiao Qinghe 肖清和, et al. (Beijing: Huaxia chubanshe 華夏出版社, 2007), 60. See also "必信天上有大主宰，為吾人大父母。" Han, *Duoshu*, 167.

68 Michele Ruggieri 羅明堅, *Tianzhu shilu* 天主實錄, in CCT ARSI, vol. 1, 84–85. This version of the *Pater Noster*, together with the *Ave Maria* on the same loose folio, might be written in 1583 or 1584 by Michele Ruggieri and Matteo Ricci, see *Baigao xian Ma-li-ya* 拜告仙媽利呀, the CCT-database, accessed March 19, 2021,
http://heron-net.be/pa_cct/index.php/Detail/objects/6856.

69 *Tianzhu shengjiao nianjing zongdu* 天主聖教念經總牘, *juan* 2, fol. 85a7, in CCT BAV (1), vol. 16, 439.

70 "共仰一大父，" Aleni, *Misa jiyi, juan* 1, fol. 16 b9, 516.

order, thus being called a great expression of filial piety."[71] Zhang Xingyao used both the Great Father and the Great Father and Mother in *Examination on Similarity & Dissimilarity between the Study of Heaven and Confucianism*.[72] In addition, Vagnone proclaimed that the Lord of Heaven is "our human beings' Great Father and Great Mother" (*wuren zhi dafu damu* 吾人之大父大母).[73]

The Great Father and Mother is a typical Chinese expression which contrasts with the traditional Western concept of God only as the Father. The word "*fumu* 父母" (father and mother) contains two dimensions. In the first dimension, the human being's love and respectful service to heaven is identified with a child's to his or her parents; in the second, the heaven's love and nurture to the human being is identified with the parents' to the child.[74] In this sense, the heaven or the Lord of Heaven is the parent of every human being. The Great Father and Mother is an indigenous term to depict the Lord of Heaven. The relationship between the Lord of Heaven and the human being is stressed by the human being's status (*mingfen* 名分) as the Great Father and Mother's child.

Yang Tingyun connected the human being's status with filial piety, the essential virtue in the Chinese tradition. To offer Mass to the Lord of Heaven is like "the child serving the parents (*zi shi fumu* 子事父母) ... how can someone do not fulfill this responsibility daily and accuse it as usurpation and blasphemy?"[75] Since the Great Father and Mother is the object of worship in Mass, the human being's status as a child justifies the daily celebration of Mass. In the *Regulation of Reciting the Beads* (*Song nianzhu guicheng* 誦念珠規程, ca. 1619), João da Rocha (Luo Ruwang 羅儒望, SJ, 1565–1623) underlined the human being's status as a child by praying: "Also, like carrying one heavy and large Cross by the body, grant me the ability to often take up the Cross of holy filial piety."[76] The Cross of holy filial piety (*shengxiao zhi shizi* 聖孝之十字) is an

---

71 "純合天主大父之旨，而稱孝之大者矣。" Li Jiugong 李九功, *Zhengli chuyi* 證禮蒭議, in CCT ARSI, vol. 9, 81.
72 "宇宙之大父也，" Zhang, *Tianru tongyi kao*, 476. "天主為生人之大父母，" Zhang, *Tianru tongyi kao*, 503–504. "天主之為人大父母，" Zhang, *Tianru tongyi kao*, 551.
73 Vagnone, *Jiaoyao jielüe, shang juan*, fol. 14b1, 152.
74 Standaert, *Yang Tingyun*, 116–118. For more texts using "the Great Father and Mother," see Standaert, *Yang Tingyun*, 116, note 32. It is noteworthy that the "father and mother" could be applied to a single person, see Standaert, *Yang Tingyun*, 117.
75 "子事父母 …… 豈有父母之前，可一日不盡其分，以僭與瀆罪之耶？" Yang, *Daiyi pian, juan shang*, fol. 33a6–8, 103.
76 "亦如身負重大的十字架一般，又賜我能勤荷聖孝之十字。" João da Rocha 羅儒望, *Song nianzhu guicheng* 誦念珠規程, fol. 20b3–4, in CCT ARSI, vol. 1, 554.

original expression interwoven by the Catholic spiritual teaching and the Chinese traditional virtue. Missionaries encouraged Chinese Catholics to fulfill the holy filial piety toward the Lord of Heaven.

In 1627 (Tianqi 7), the literatus-official Ye Xianggao 葉向高 (1559–1627) invited Aleni and the literatus-official Cao Xuequan 曹學佺 (1574–1646) to his residence Cotton Rose Garden (*Furong yuan* 芙蓉園) at Fuzhou, where they had many discussions over Confucianism and Catholicism.[77] Ye Xianggao suspected the Lord of Heaven's Incarnation: "Isn't it blasphemy that the one who is honored as the lord of all things in heaven and on earth descended and became human?"[78] Similar to Yang Tingyun, Aleni explained that the Lord of Heaven is not only the ultimately honorable (*zhizun* 至尊) but also the ultimately intimate (*zhiqin* 至親).

> If [the Lord of Heaven] did not descend to the world, people would say that he is high above, far away and unrelated to us. Although the Lord of Heaven is the ultimately honorable, he gently loves all people and his love is the ultimately intimate. In fact he is intimate with us but we do not know.[79]

Then, Aleni further explained that human beings should treat the Great Father and Mother of all people (*wanmin dafumu* 萬民大父母) the way the filial son serves his parents day and night. Only by doing so can a person be called the filial son of the Lord of Heaven (*tianzhu zhi xiaozi* 天主之孝子).[80]

In 1641 (Chongzhen 14), the Chinese Catholic Zuo Guangxian 左光先 (1580–1659) talked with Aleni in Shaowu 邵武.[81] He pointed out that Confucianism and Catholicism worship the High Lord in different ways.

---

[77] These discussions among Ye Xianggao, Aleni, and Cao Xuequan probably took place between 17 and 29 June, 1627. Lin Jinshui 林金水, "Ai Rulüe yu Ye Xianggao Sanshan lunxue jiqi shidi kao 艾儒略與葉向高三山論學及其時地考," *Zongjiaoxue yanjiu* 宗教學研究 1 (2015): 196.

[78] "且尊為天地萬有之主，複降為人，豈不甚褻？" Li Sixuan 李嗣玄, *Xihai Ai xiansheng yulu* 西海艾先生語錄, *shang*, in CCT ARSI, vol. 12, 284.

[79] "不降世，則人將謂高高在上，遠而不相涉也。天主至尊，而其孺愛萬民，情又至親也。實與我親，而我輩不知。" Li, *Yulu, shang*, 284–285.

[80] Li, *Yulu, shang*, 289–290. See also "善人，天主之孝子也。" Li, *Yulu, xia*, 305.

[81] Huang Yi-long suggests that Zuo Guangxian probably received Baptism in 1625 (Tianqi 5). Huang Yi-long 黃一農, *Liangtoushe: Mingmo Qingchu diyidai tianzhujiaotu* 兩頭蛇：明末清初第一代天主教徒 (Shanghai: Shanghai guji chubanshe 上海古籍出版社, 2006), 217.

When our Confucians worship the High Lord, we know that he is honorable but we do not know that he is intimate. Not until I learned about Catholicism did I know that the High Lord is truly our human beings' Great Father and Mother (*wuren dafumu* 吾人大父母), that he is both the ultimately honorable and the ultimately intimate.[82]

Zuo Guangxian embodied his understanding by leading people to build a church and naming it the Hall of the Honorable and Intimate (*Zunqin tang* 尊親堂).[83] As a Catholic-literatus, Zuo Guangxian thought that Catholicism completes the partial understanding of the High Lord in Confucianism.[84] Similar to Yang Tingyun, he identified the High Lord with the Lord of Heaven and understood him as the Great Father and Mother who is both honorable and intimate. Still in 1641 (Chongzhen 14.6), Zuo Guangxian issued an official proclamation as the local official in Jianning 建甯 county, declaring that the Teaching of the Lord of Heaven worships "the common Lord of the whole world, the Great Father of human beings, who is the ultimately honorable and ultimately intimate."[85] At the end of the proclamation, Zuo Guangxian praised how the missionaries, such as Aleni, made every effort to convert the Chinese to "the great Lord who is the ultimately honorable and ultimately intimate" (*zhizun zhiqin zhi dazhu* 至尊至親之大主).[86]

Generally, the Great Father and Mother, as well as the Great Father, referred to the first Person of the Trinity. Yet, in the Litany of Jesus' Holy Name (*Yesu shenghao daowen* 耶穌聖號禱文, ca. 1640), João Monteiro (Meng Ruwang 孟儒

---

[82] "且吾儒之事上帝也，知尊而不知親。聞公教，乃知上帝之真為吾人大父母也，斯尊親至矣。" Li Sixuan 李嗣玄, *Xihai Ai xiansheng xinglüe* 西海艾先生行略, in CCT ARSI, vol. 12, 252–253.

[83] Li, *Xinglüe*, 253. Li Sixuan pointed out on purpose that Zuo Guangxian is the little brother of Zuo Guangdou 左光鬥 (1575–1626), a literatus who belonged to the Donglin party 東林黨. Li Sixuan and Zuo Guangxian were friends. Both were active in the Christian community network in Fujian. See Xiao Qinghe 肖清和, *Tianhui yu wudang: Mingmo Qingchu tianzhujiaotu qunti yanjiu* 天會與吾黨：明末清初天主教徒群體研究 (Beijing: Zhonghua shuju 中華書局, 2015), 157. Pan Feng-chuan suggests that Zuo Guangxian built the Hall of the Honorable and Intimate to cultivate local people, but it was not a church. Pan Feng-chuan 潘鳳娟, *Xilai Kongzi Ai Rulüe: Gengxin bianhua de zongjiao huiyu* 西來孔子艾儒略——更新變化的宗教會遇 (Taipei: Shengjing ziyuan zhongxin 聖經資源中心, 2002), 64.

[84] See also Lin Jinshui 林金水, "Shilun Ai Rulüe chuanbo jidujiao de celue yu fangfa 試論艾儒略傳播基督教的策略與方法," *Shijie zongjiao yanjiu* 世界宗教研究 1 (1995): 37.

[85] "其所昭事者，乃普世之共主，羣生之大父，至尊至親，" Zuo Guangxian 左光先, "Jianning xian Zuomingfu gaoshi 建甯縣左明府告示," in *Zhengjiao fengzhuan* 正教奉傳, Huang Bolu 黃伯祿, ed. (Shanghai: Cimu tang 慈母堂, 1877), fol. 3a4–5.

[86] Zuo, "Jianning xian Zuomingfu," fol. 3b–4a.

望, SJ, 1602–1648) referred it to the second Person: "Jesus who is people's Great Father and Mother."[87] Similarly, Matthew Zhang Geng referred "your Great Father" (*er dafu* 爾大父) to the second Person: "Since you believe that the Lord of Heaven is your Great Father and that the Lord of Heaven was born into this world, you shall also believe the rules of the Teaching established by your Great Father after he was born into this world."[88] The Great Father and Mother is an original term coined by the Catholic Church in China, which can be considered "the heritage of the tradition of the Church in China."[89] Although an excellent example of inculturation, the Great Father and Mother is rarely used in the Catholic Church in China today.[90]

Yang Tingyun's biography *Supernatural Events of Mr. Yang Qiyuan* (*Yang Qiyuan xiansheng chaoxing shiji* 楊淇園先生超性事蹟, ca. 1628) recorded that the Jesuits taught Yang Tingyun about transubstantiation.[91]

> One day, Master Jin Sibiao and the member of the Society from Macao Zhong Nianjiang discussed the doctrines with Mr. [Yang], and therefore they expounded the meaning of the grand sacrifice in the Western ritual. Since the meaning—between the appearance of the bread the Lord of Heaven truly descends—is so profound, they worried that Mr. [Yang] would not believe.[92]

Master Jin referred to Nicolas Trigault (Jin Nige 金尼閣) whose courtesy name is Sibiao 四表. Zhong referred to Zhong Mingren 鐘鳴仁 (Sebastien Fernandes, SJ,

---

87 "耶穌諸人之大父母者，矜憐我等。" João Monteiro 孟儒望, *Yesu shenghao daowen* 耶穌聖號禱文, fol. 5a5, Anon., *Tongku jingji* 痛苦經蹟, in TZJDCWXSB, vol. 3, 1073.
88 "爾既信天主為爾大父矣，爾既信天主亦曾降生矣，則亦應信爾大父降生時所定教規矣。" Zhang Geng 張賡, *Tianxue jiehuo* 天學解惑, fol. 8b5–7, in CCT BnF, vol. 7, 44.
89 "中國的教會傳統之遺產," Sun Shangyang 孫尚揚, "Fengbi de jidutu yu danfang shouyi de ruye duihua—yi Huang Baoluo de yanjiu weili 封閉的基督徒與單方受益的儒耶對話——以黃保羅的研究為例," *Zhexue yanjiu* 哲學研究 5 (2009): 55.
90 Inculturation emphasizes that the Catholic Church should be open to non-Christian cultures during evangelization and embrace their diversity, thus achieving a mutual enrichment. It was the Jesuits who introduced this term to missiological discussions. The Belgian Jesuit Joseph Masson firstly promoted "a Catholicism inculturated in a polymorphous way" (un catholicisme inculturé d'une façon polymorphe). J. Masson, "L'Église ouverte sur le monde," *Nouvelle Revue Théologique* 84 (1962): 1038–1039.
91 Standaert, *Yang Tingyun*, 55.
92 "一日，金四表先生及粵中會士鐘念江與公論道，因揆明西禮大祭之義，以麵像之間，天主實式臨之，其義深遠，而猶慮公之未諶也。" Ding Zhilin 丁志麟, *Yang Qiyuan xiansheng chaoxing shiji* 楊淇園先生超性事蹟, fol. 3a2–4, in CCT ZKW, vol. 1, 221.

1562–1621) whose courtesy name is Nianjiang 念江. The two Jesuits explained the meaning of Mass to the catechumen Yang Tingyun, focusing on the real presence (*praesentia realis*). The *Supernatural Events of Mr. Yang Qiyuan* used "*shi shilin zhi* 實式臨之" (to truly descend) to describe the real presence of the Lord of Heaven in Mass. During the Ming dynasty, "to truly descend" was a formal and literary expression which was usually used to describe the presence of a royal ancestor's soul,[93] sometimes the High Lord's presence and the emperor's power.[94] Ding Zhilin 丁志麟, a Chinese Catholic from Jinjiang 晉江, wrote *Supernatural Events of Mr. Yang Qiyuan* based on Aleni's narration. He probably borrowed the formal and literary expression from the existent Chinese texts.

Early in *Brief Explanation of Catechism* (*Jiaoyao jielüe* 教要解畧, 1615), Vagnone had already explained transubstantiation, which takes place in Mass.

> After [the priest] reciting the prayer (*jing* 經). The appearance and taste of the bread remain, but the substance (*ti* 體) of the bread has changed into the body (*ti* 體) of Jesus. His body is the living body, with the soul and the holy blood ... therefore the Lord of Heaven's nature (*tianzhuxing* 天主性) is inside. It is the same with the wine.[95]

Vagnone's explanation conforms with the decree issued in October 1551 during the Council of Trent (13 December 1545–4 December 1563), declaring: "In the sacrament of the most holy Eucharist, are contained truly, really, and substantially, the body and blood together with the soul and divinity of our Lord Jesus Christ, and consequently the whole Christ."[96]

---

93   "成湯之靈，顯顯在廟，實式臨之，" Shi Hao 史浩, *Shangshu jiangyi* 尚書講義, vol. 8, Eruson, 64. "九廟神靈，實式臨之，" Li Sancai 李三才, *Jichen guojia zhiluan daguanshu* 極陳國家治亂大關疏, in *Wanli shuchao* 萬曆疏鈔, juan 1, comp. Wu Liang 吳亮, Eruson, 89.

94   "天皇上帝，實式臨之，" Qu Jiusi 瞿九思, comp., *Wanli wugong lu* 萬曆武功錄, vol. 13, Eruson, 136. "以陛下之斧鉞，實式臨之，" Qu, *Wanli wugong lu*, vol. 3, 554.

95   "念經後，麵色、餅味存，而其體變易為耶穌之體。其體既為活體，併有魂靈，併有聖血。…… 故有天主性在其中焉。惟酒亦然。" Alfonso Vagnone 王豐肅, *Jiaoyao jielüe* 教要解畧, *shang juan*, fol. 53a7-b2, in CCT ARSI, vol. 1, 229–230. See also "但念過成聖體之經言，獨有吾主耶穌聖體，而無麵體。只存麵之形、味、香、色，而已。" Francesco Brancati 潘國光, *Shengjiao sigui* 聖教四規, in CCT ARSI, vol. 5, 290–291.

96   "Decree concerning the most holy sacrament of the Eucharist," in *The Canons and Decrees of the Sacred and Oecumenical Council of Trent*, ed. and trans. J. Waterworth (London: Dolman, 1848), 82.

Brancati also mentioned the Lord of Heaven's body, soul, and nature in *Four Rules of the Holy Teaching* (*Shengjiao sigui* 聖教四規, ca. 1662): "Therefore to receive the holy body (*shengti* 聖體) is to receive Jesus' holy body (*shengshen* 聖身), holy soul, and the Lord of Heaven's nature and substance (*tianzhu xingti* 天主性體)."[97] Based on Christian theology, Brancati distinguished the terminology of transubstantiation from the traditional usage of "*shen* 身" and "*ti* 體" in Chinese philosophy.

An inspiring comparison posed in the twenty-first century is worth mentioning. Roger Darrobers borrows a Christian theological notion to explain the idea of "principle" (*li* 理) in Neo-Confucianism: "The unique, immaterial, and irreducible principle incorporates and innervates the multiple and material energies, according to a mode comparable to the transubstantiation."[98] The way the principle works in the "energies" (*qi* 氣) is compared to the way the Lord of Heaven works in the bread, drawing a parallel with the missionaries' approach. Instead of connecting with Chinese philosophical notions, missionaries in late Ming and early Qing preferred to explain transubstantiation in the Tridentine way.

The real presence is a grand mystery which the corporeal eyes (*rouyan* 肉眼) are unable to see and it requires the eyes of the soul (*lingmu* 靈目) to believe.[99] The eyes of the soul derives from *oculis fidei* (the eyes of faith), a phrase used by Augustine (354–430) in *The City of God* (*De civitate Dei*, 426).[100] Christian theologians in later generations used the phrase to express that certain mysteries in Catholicism can only be accepted by faith.

Similarly, Aleni translated *oculis fidei* as "*shenmu* 神目" (the spiritual eyes). On 24 June 1637 (Chongzhen 10.5.3), he told the Chinese Catholics in Haikou 海口: "Our Lord truly descends (*shi jianglin* 實降臨) in the ritual of the holy body but he borrows the form of the bread to hide. Those who have the spir-

---

97 "故領聖體即領吾主耶穌聖身、聖䰟，并天主性體，" Brancati, *Shengjiao sigui*, 290.

98 "Le Principe, unique, immatériel et irréductible, s'incorpore et innerve les énergies multiples et matérielles, selon un mode comparable à la transsubstantiation," Roger Darrobers, *Zhu Xi et la synthèse confucéenne* (Paris: Éditions Points, 2016), 79. My gratitude to Prof. Thierry Meynard for providing this valuable information to me.

99 "天主歷顯大聖蹟，而開人靈目以信之，但非肉眼可得而見也。" Brancati, *Shengjiao sigui*, 290. See also "天主時顯大聖跡，以証其理，開人靈目以信之，但非肉眼可見也。" Brancati, *Tianshen huike*, fol. 67b1–2, 138. See also "惟吾以靈目信麵酒外像，實幕覆主體焉。" Manuel Dias 陽瑪諾, *Qingshi jinshu* 輕世金書, *juan* 4 (S.L.: S.N., 1848), fol. 11a3–4.

100 "Oculis fidei libentissime spectant, gaudere cum gaudentibus," Augustinus, *De civitate Dei*, tomus II, libri XIV (Lipsiae [Leipzig]: sumtibus et typis Caroli Tauchnitii, 1825), 13.

itual eyes (*shenmu* 神目) believe it without doubt; those who only have physical eyes inevitably see it with contempt."[101] Aleni called Mass the ritual of the holy body (*shengti zhi li* 聖體之禮) to underline that the real presence is true.

It is reasonable that Trigault and Zhong Mingren worried that Yang Tingyun might not believe the real presence. Yet, Yang Tingyun accepted it smoothly, saying: "Our Lord loves the world infinitely. The event and grace of his nativity and redemption of the world did not take place groundlessly. How can anyone doubt?"[102] After discussing transubstantiation with the two Jesuits, he learned about the life of Christ, which connects the sacrifice of Mass and the sacrifice of Jesus on the Cross.

The nativity of Christ and the Crucifixion particularly highlighted the Lord of Heaven being the ultimately intimate. On 22 March 1631 (Chongzhen 4.3.20), Rudomina Andrzej (Lu Ande 盧安德, SJ, 1595–1631) explained in the homily the story of the prodigal son told by Jesus in the Gospel of Luke (Lk 15:11–32). Andrzej asked the Chinese Catholics in Fuzhou: "You know about the dignity of the Lord of Heaven. Do you also know about the mercy of the Lord of Heaven?"[103] The dignity of the Lord of Heaven (*tianzhu zhi zunyan* 天主之尊嚴) referred to the ultimately honorable, and the mercy of the Lord of Heaven (*tianzhu zhi cibei* 天主之慈悲) the ultimately intimate.

On 3 May 1633 (Chongzhen 6.3.26), Bento de Matos (Lin Bendu 林本篤, SJ, 1600–1651) exemplified the Lord of Heaven's twofold depiction during a talk with the Chinese Catholics in the church in Fuzhou: "The Lord of Heaven is honorable (*zun* 尊). Why does He descend into the humble one's body? Thus, we can see that the Lord of Heaven is the most benevolent and the most merciful (*zhiren zhici* 至仁至慈) Lord."[104]

On 21 March 1636 (Chongzhen 9.3.15, Good Friday), Aleni celebrated Mass with the Chinese Catholics in Yongchun 詠春. Good Friday was called the wor-

---

101 "卽聖體之禮，吾主實降臨其中，不過借麵形以蔽之耳。有神目者，尊信無疑；其肉眼者，不免褻慢視之。" Li, *Kouduo richao*, juan 7, fol. 27b6–8, 510. Zürcher, *Kou duo ri chao*, vol. 1, VII. 33 (Haikou, Wednesday, 24 June 1637), 562.
102 "吾主愛世之心無已，其降生贖世之事之恩，非出無稽，更何復有致疑者乎？" Ding, *Yang Qiyuan*, fol. 3a5–6, 221.
103 "二十日，瞻禮甫畢。盧先生語余輩曰：'子等知天主之尊嚴，亦知天主之慈悲乎？今日《萬日畧經》，載吾主設譬有云 ……'" Li, *Kouduo richao*, juan 1, fol. 23a9–b1, 81–82. See also Zürcher, *Kou duo ri chao*, vol. 1, I. 39 (Fuzhou, Saturday, 22 March 1631), 244.
104 "天主尊矣，何為降此卑賤者之身？可見天主者，原至仁至慈之上主。" Li, *Kouduo richao*, juan 4, fol. 15 a6–7, 283. Zürcher, *Kou duo ri chao*, vol. 1, IV. 15 (Fuzhou, Monday, 2 May 1633), 406.

ship of reception of suffering (*shounan zhanli* 受難瞻禮) and Aleni vividly described it as the day of dolor (*tongku ri* 痛苦日).[105] During the homily, Aleni asked a series of questions pertaining to the reception of suffering and the Chinese Catholics answered them.

> Question: "Who is the one that receives suffering today?"
> Answer: "The most honorable, the most potent."
> Question: "What suffering does he receive?"
> Answer: "The most humiliating, the most bitter."
> Question: "Why does the most honorable receive the most humiliating suffering, and why does the most potent receive the most bitter one?"
> Answer: "[For he is] the most good, the most merciful. [He does so] to redeem our sins, to save us."[106]

By the series of questions and answers, Aleni guided the Chinese Catholics to understand the Lord of Heaven's twofold depiction. The local Chinese Catholics understood that the reception of suffering does not indicate the Lord of Heaven's incompetence but his mercy toward human beings.

On 25 December 1697 (Kangxi 36.11.13, Christmas Day), the Chinese Catholic Zhao Lun 趙侖 in Jiading recorded how the indigenous priest Wu Li 吳歷 (Simon-Xavier a Cunha, SJ, 1632–1718) talked about the Lord of Heaven's twofold depiction.

> On the day of the holy nativity of Jesus, Master went to the church and preached. His profound discourse ran so smoothly that I could not record everything. Yet, it is necessary to memorize these two sentences, saying: "It is how pleased the Lord of Heaven is to receive suffering that shows how honorable the Lord of Heaven is."[107]

---

105 "十五日，為受難瞻禮。遐邇畢集，先生曰：'今日痛苦日，'" Li, *Kouduo richao, juan* 6, fol. 19b8, 424.

106 "問：'今日受難者為誰？'曰：'至尊也，至能也。'問：'受是何難？'曰：'至辱也，至苦也。'夫至尊何而受至辱，至能為何而受至苦？'曰：'至善耳，至慈耳。為贖我罪，為救我耳。'" Li, *Kouduo richao, juan* 6, fol. 20a7–b1, 425–426. See also Zürcher, *Kou duo ri chao*, vol. 1, VI. 34 (Yongchun, [Good] Friday, 21 March 1636), 507.

107 "耶穌聖誕日，先生登堂講道，名論亹亹，不能勝紀，中有二語當切記，曰：'天主之甘受苦，正見天主之尊也。'" Zhao Lun 趙侖, *Xu Kouduo richao* 續口鐸日抄, in *Wu Yushan ji jianzhu* 吳漁山集箋注, *juan* 8, annot. Zhang Wenqin 章文欽 (Beijing: Zhonghua shuju 中華書局, 2007), 628.

In *One Hundred Questions and Answers of the Lord of Heaven's Holy Teaching* (*Tianzhu shengjiao baiwenda* 天主聖教百問答, 1675), Couplet connected the reception of suffering with the Lord of Heaven's love for human beings.

> Question: "Our Lord received suffering and instituted the grand ritual of the holy body. What does this mean?"
> Answer: "[Our Lord] wants to express that he loves human beings infinitely. By this ritual he nourishes their souls and provides what they lack, thus making human beings always remember the enormous grace of the reception of suffering."[108]

Called the grand ritual of the holy body (*shengti dali* 聖體大禮), Mass fully expresses the twofold depiction of the ultimately honorable and the ultimately intimate. The reception of suffering and transubstantiation were important in the Jesuit catechism and preaching. After his discussion with the two Jesuits, Yang Tingyun began to understand the Lord of Heaven's twofold depiction and asked for baptism.[109]

Toward the twofold depiction of the ultimately honorable and the ultimately intimate, human beings reciprocally produce fear and love, two sentiments which Han Lin discussed in *The Book of the Warning Bell*.

> Respect is produced by the two sentiments fear and love. Yet, the two sentiments do not tolerate each other. If fear triumphs, love will certainly declines. Fear is from the heart of common people; love from the virtue of the superior man. Respect should be produced mainly by love.[110]

Human beings' respect toward the Lord of Heaven is produced by fear and love, which coexist yet when one increases the other decreases. Han Lin acknowledged that human beings fear the Lord of Heaven, meanwhile he underlined that they should respect the Lord of Heaven mainly out of love. In the *Expounding How to Fear Heaven and to Love Human Beings*, Wang Zheng described another type of relationship between the two sentiments: "Whoever truly loves the Lord of human beings must have fear, then fear generates respect, and

---

108 "問：'吾主受難，立聖體大禮，有何意思？' 答：'欲顯愛人無量，以此養育人靈，補存其弱，使人常念受難之洪恩。'" Philippe Couplet 柏應理, *Tianzhu shengjiao baiwenda* 天主聖教百問答, fol. 10b, in CCT BnF, vol. 24, 240.
109 "因矢志為主功臣，求領聖洗。" Ding, *Yang Qiyuan*, fol. 3a5–7, 221.
110 "尊敬者，畏愛二情之所發也。然二情不并容，畏情勝，愛情必衰。畏者，小人之心也；愛者，君子之德也。尊敬者，尤當以愛情為主。" Han, *Duoshu*, 67.

respect generates love."[111] Sun Shangyang thinks that Wang Zheng's description is a unique part of the Catholic understanding of the holy love.[112] In *Meditations* (*Shensi lu* 慎思錄, 1682) Li Jiugong considered fear and love two basic virtues of human beings toward the Lord of Heaven: "Human beings worship the Lord only by fear and love the two virtues, which are two wings for improvement, two stairs for ascension to Heaven."[113] Li Jiugong tried to "transform and transcend the Confucian tradition" by combining the Confucian teaching to fear the heaven and to love human beings (*weitian airen* 畏天愛人) with the Catholic teaching to fear and to love the Lord.[114]

In order to justify the ritual of Mass in Chinese society, missionaries and Chinese Catholics had to distinguish it from the worship of Heaven in Chinese tradition. Nevertheless, some of them reached a tacit agreement to identify the object of worship in Mass with the heaven worshiped since ancient China. Furthermore, in the introduction and propagation of Mass, the Christian communities depicted the Lord of Heaven as the ultimately honorable and the ultimately intimate. In the depiction of the object of worship in Mass, the second Person of the Trinity was noteworthy in the Chinese Christian texts in late Ming and early Qing.

2   Jesus as Object of Worship in Mass

2.1   *Title as the Lord of Heaven Jesus*

Despite the debate over the Chinese terms, the Christian communities in China commonly called the object of worship in Mass the Lord of Heaven Jesus (*tianzhu Yesu* 天主耶穌). In *Brief Explanation of Catechism*, Vagnone described the institution of the Eucharist as below.

> On the day before the reception of suffering, the Lord of Heaven Jesus assembled the holy disciples. He desired to abolish the ancient sacrificial ritual and to replace it with the new sacrificial ritual which is true and earnest. Therefore, he gave the bread to the holy disciples, saying: "You

---

111   "真爱人主者，必由畏起敬，由敬起爱。" Wang, *Weitian airen*, fol. 46a8–9.
112   Sun Shangyang 孫尚揚, *Mingmo tianzhujiao yu ruxue de hudong: yizhong sixiangshi de shijiao* 明末天主教與儒學的互動：一種思想史的視角 (Beijing: Zongjiao wenhua chubanshe 宗教文化出版社, 2013), 193.
113   "人生事主，惟有畏愛二德，為進脩之兩翼，升天之兩梯也。" Li Jiugong 李九功, *Shensi lu* 慎思錄, *ji* 1, fol. 6b7–8, in CCT ARSI, vol. 9, 158.
114   "轉化和超越儒學傳統," You, "Hetian," 22–23.

shall eat it for this is my body." Then he poured the wine into the chalice and gave it to them, saying: "You shall drink it for this is my blood."[115]

The words left by Jesus during the Last Supper referred to the Words of institution (*verba institutionis*), which became the consecration prayer recited in Mass.[116] In *Four Rules of the Holy Teaching*, Brancati explained the consecration prayer's effect as the change of substance (*ti* 體).

> It is better for people in the Teaching to believe the holy words left by the Lord of Heaven Jesus. Before consecrating the holy body, there is indeed the substance of the bread in the Host. Yet, after reciting the prayer of consecrating the holy body, there is only our Lord Jesus' holy body and no substance of the bread. What remains is only the shape, taste, smell, and appearance of the bread.[117]

The theological term for the consecration prayer's effect is transubstantiation (*transubstantiatio*), translated today as *"tibian* 體變" (the change of substance) and *"zhibian* 質變" (the change of nature).[118] The Lord of Heaven Jesus was an extraordinary title for the object of worship in Mass. The Chinese Christian texts pertaining to Mass emphasized the second Person, which was often called Jesus (*Yesu* 耶穌) instead of Christ (*Ji-li-si-du* 基利斯督) or Jesus Christ.

In addition to the Lord of Heaven Jesus, the second Person was emphasized by being attached to the holy body (*shengti* 聖體). Instead of the literal translation of *Corpus Christi* (*Ji-li-si-du shengti* 基利斯督聖體), the Host was called *"Yesu shengti* 耶穌聖體" (*Corpus Iesu*). In the aforementioned explanation in *Four Rules of the Holy Teaching*, Brancati called the Host our Lord Jesus' holy body (*wuzhu Yesu shengti* 吾主耶穌聖體). In *Statutes of the Confraternity of the Angels* (*Tianshen huike* 天神會課, ca. 1673), Brancati again emphasized that

---

115 "天主耶穌，未受難前一日，聚聖宗徒，欲令革去古祭禮，而易眞切之新祭禮。因以麵餅授聖徒曰：'爾等食此，吾體也。' 又以爵注葡萄酒授之曰：'爾等飲此，吾血也。'" Vagnone, *Jiaoyao jielüe, shang juan*, fol. 53a2–4, 229.
116 See Matthew 26:26–29; Mark 14:22–25; Luke 22:14–20; First Corinthians 11:23–26.
117 "教中人宜信天主耶穌所遺之聖言而已。未成聖體以前，阿斯底亞之內，果有麵體，但念過成聖體之經言，獨有吾主耶穌聖體，而無麵體。只存麵之形、味、香、色，而已。" Brancati, *Shengjiao sigui*, 290–291.
118 Fu Jen Theological Publications Association 輔仁神學著作編譯會, *Jiduzongjiao waiyu Hanyu shenxue ciyu huibian* 基督宗教外語漢語神學詞語彙編 (Shanghai: Guangqi Press 天主教上海教區光啟社, 2007), 1046.

"our Lord Jesus' holy body is indeed really present."[119] After transubstantiation, the real presence of the Lord of Heaven descends at Mass, which the physical eyes cannot see but only the eyes of the soul (*lingmu* 靈目) can. Brancati reiterated that "people in the Teaching shall believe the words left by Jesus,"[120] and he explained the meaning of the Host. In the question of the bread of soul (*linghun zhi liang* 靈魂之糧), "Question: 'What is the bread of soul?' Answer: 'the holy grace of the Lord of Heaven, our Lord Jesus' holy body (*wuzhu Yesu shengti* 吾主耶穌聖體), and various spiritual merits in the Holy Teaching.'"[121] To the question how come our Lord Jesus' holy body becomes the bread of soul, the answer is that those who receive the holy body gain the Lord of Heaven's holy grace.[122]

Furthermore, in *Prayer of the Confraternity of the Holy Body's Benevolence to Give Thanks to the Lord of Heaven* (*Shengti ren'aihui xianxie tianzhu zhuwen* 聖體仁愛會獻謝天主祝文), the beginning reads: "Thanks to the grace and blessing of our Lord Jesus Christ's holy body," and the end reads: "to respectfully repay the enormous grace of mercy and love of our Lord Jesus' holy body."[123] This prayer calls the Host wholly as "our Lord Jesus Christ's holy body" (*wuzhu Yesu Qi-li-si-du shengti* 吾主耶穌契利斯督聖體), which is often shortened as "Jesus' holy body" (*Yesu shengti* 耶穌聖體). To the question when Jesus' holy body (*Yesu shengti* 耶穌聖體) is present at Mass, the answer articulates: "In Mass, before holding up the holy body, after reciting the prayer of consecrating the holy body, our Lord Jesus is really present."[124] The Host can also be called "our Lord's holy body" (*wuzhu shengti* 吾主聖體).[125] Later on, *Questions & Answers of the Holy Sacrament* (*Shengshi wenda* 聖事問答, before 1789)

---

119 "吾主耶穌聖體，果然實在。" Brancati, *Tianshen huike*, fol. 67b1, 138. See also "我們是罪人，如何敢領吾主耶穌聖體？" Brancati, *Tianshen huike*, fol. 69a2, 141.
120 "天主時顯大聖跡，以証其理，開人靈目以信之，但非肉眼可見也。教中人應信耶穌所遺之言而已。" Brancati, *Tianshen huike*, fol. 67b1-3, 138.
121 "問：'靈魂之糧是何？' 答：'天主聖寵，并吾主耶穌聖體，及聖教各樣神功。'" Brancati, *Tianshen huike*, fol. 17b2-3, 38.
122 "問：'吾主耶穌聖體，怎麼為靈魂之糧？' 答：'領聖體者，得天主聖寵，能力行天上之路，堅守十誡，易退魔之誘惑，故聖體為靈魂之糧。'" Brancati, *Tianshen huike*, fol. 17b8-fol. 18a1, 38–39.
123 "託賴吾主耶穌契利斯督聖體寵祐，…… 以仰報吾主耶穌聖體仁愛弘恩，亞孟。" Brancati, "Shengti ren'aihui xianxie tianzhu zhuwen," *Tianshen huike*, fol. 7b6–fol. 8a4, 270–271.
124 "問：'成過聖體以後，與未成聖體以前，不見稍異，未知耶穌聖體，何時而在？' 答：'彌撒中，舉揚聖體前，念過成聖體之經，吾主耶穌即已實在。'" Brancati, *Tianshen huike*, fol. 67b4-7, 138.
125 "吾主聖體之心，當超越尋常，" de Mailla, *Shengti ren'aijing*, fol. 5b8, 304. See also "吾主聖體即時在焉，" Couplet, *Baiwenda*, fol. 10b, 240.

directly pointed out the second Person: "Do not think that the holy body we receive is only the empty image of Jesus. It is truly the second Person of the Lord of Heaven (*tianzhu di'er wei* 天主第二位), the only holy Son of the holy Father."[126]

Occasionally, missionaries emphasized the Trinity as a whole when discussing the Host. On 23 June 1634 (Chongzhen 7.5.28), Aleni told the Chinese Catholics in Haikou: "When I receive the holy body, the three Persons of the Lord of Heaven all descend into my body."[127] *Rules of Prayer to the Holy Body's Benevolence* (*Shengti ren'aijing guitiao* 聖體仁愛經規條, 1719) occasionally called the Host the body of the ultimately honorable Lord of Heaven (*zhizun tianzhu zhi ti* 至尊天主之體).[128]

The holy body generally referred to the Host or Jesus' body, however, in *Life of the Holy Mother* (*Shengmu xingshi* 聖母行實, 1631), Vagnone called Mary's body "the holy Mother's holy body" (*shengmu shengti* 聖母聖體).[129] In addition, Mary was exceptionally placed together with the Host. In the end of *Catechism of the Lord of Heaven* (*Tianzhu jiaoyao* 天主教要, ca. 1650–1700) are two short prayers: "Praise to the Holy Body: Blessed in the world is our Lord Jesus, whose body is the ultimately holy. Praise to the Holy Mother: And blessed is the holy Mother, whose conception is immaculate."[130] Praise to the Holy Body (*Shengtizan* 聖體讚) and Praise to the Holy Mother (*Shengmuzan* 聖母讚) are in fact a coherent prayer.[131] In *Rules of Prayer to the Holy Body's Benevolence*, the members shall add the prayer "Praise to the Holy Body and the Holy Mother" (*Shengti shengmu hezan* 聖體聖母合讚) in their vespers.[132]

The Lord of Heaven Jesus, a unique expression coined in the Catholic Church in China, seemed to identify Jesus with the heaven and the High Lord, thus inciting the anti-Catholic sentiments. In the Preface of *Anthology of Destroy-*

---

126 "別想我們領的聖體不過是耶穌的虛像。真是天主第二位，聖父惟一聖子。" Raux, *Shengshi wenda*, fol. 1a5–6, 447.
127 "我領聖體，則天主三位，俱降臨我身也。" Li, *Kouduo richao*, juan 5, fol. 25a4–5, 369. Zürcher, *Kou duo ri chao*, vol. 1, v. 33 (Haikou, Friday, 21 June 1634), 466. The date in Zürcher's translation is misprinted.
128 de Mailla, *Shengti ren'aijing*, fol. 2a6, 297.
129 Alfonso Vagnone 高一志, *Shengmu xingshi* 聖母行實, juan 2, fol. 34a6, in TZJDCWXSB, vol. 3, 1395.
130 "聖體讚：伏願吾主耶穌，至聖之體，普見稱頌。聖母讚：又願聖母，無原罪之始胎，併見稱頌。" Anon., *Tianzhu jiaoyao* 天主教要, fol. 32b5–fol. 33a4, in CCT ARSI, vol. 1, 372–373. See Dudink, "Manual for Attending Mass," 285, note 265.
131 For a French translation of the prayer, see Brunner, *L'euchologe*, 111.
132 "一、在籍之人，每日 ⋯⋯ 晚課加誦聖體聖母合讚一遍，" de Mailla, *Shengti ren'aijing*, fol. 10a4–5, 313.

ing the Pernicious (*Poxie ji xu* 破邪集序, 1638), the high-ranking official Jiang Dejing 蔣德璟 (1593–1646) explained why he used to communicate with missionaries.

> I read their books and found out that they steal our Confucians' purpose to serve the heaven and call it "the Lord of Heaven," that is, "the High Lord" worshiped in our China. Yet, I did not know that they take Jesus at the time of the Ai emperor in the Han dynasty as the Lord of Heaven.[133]

Jiang Dejing disapproved how missionaries related the heaven in the Confucian Classics to a foreigner who lived at the time of the reign of the Ai emperor (27 BC–1 BC).

The Buddhist Huang Zhen's opposition was fiercer: "Yet our Chinese combine the barbarian's Lord of Heaven Jesus with the Emperor Heaven in our Confucian Classics. How is this different from combining the noise of the strange bird and the strange rat with the voice of the phoenix?"[134] The noise of the strange bird and the strange rat means empty talk in the Buddhist texts.[135] Huang Zhen used this Buddhist analogy to deride the Lord of Heaven Jesus.

While Huang Zhen paid attention to Jesus the second Person, Xu Dashou 許大受 focused on the notion of the Trinity.

> They made up the talk of one nature three Persons, with no similarity and no difference. Those who have not read the Buddhist books might find the talk profound, but they do not know that it is stolen from the idea of law, retribution, and transformation of the three bodies, then they [the missionaries] have rudely given it a vulgar explanation. In which sense is it profound?[136]

---

[133] "比讀其書，第知其竊吾儒事天之旨，以為'天主'，即吾中國所奉'上帝'，不知其以漢哀帝時耶穌為天主也。" Jiang Dejing 蔣德璟, "*Poxie ji* xu 破邪集序," fol. 1a5–8, in *Poxie ji*, vol. 3, 254.

[134] "而我華人以夷之天主耶穌，為合吾儒之經書帝天者，何異以鳥空鼠即為合鳳凰之音也與？" Huang, *Zunru jijing*, fol. 15b6–8, 261.

[135] "鳥鼠者蝙蝠之異名，……如鼠唧唧聲，鳥空空聲，謂無意味之語也。止觀八曰'鼠唧鳥空。'" Ding, *Foxue*, 973.

[136] "彼又遁之以一性三位、非同非異之說；未讀佛書者，以爲精微，殊不知此特竊法、報、化三身之意，而橫成惡解，有何精微之有？" Xu Dashou 許大受, "Sanpi liexing," 三闢裂性, *Shengchao zuopi* 聖朝佐闢, in *Shengchao zuopi jiaozhu* 聖朝佐闢校注, annot. Thierry Meynard and Yang Hongfan 楊虹帆 (Gaoxiong: Foguang wenhua shiye youxian gongsi 佛光文化事業有限公司, 2018), 100.

Since the three Persons (*sanwei* 三位) in Catholicism resembled the three bodies (*sanshen* 三身) in Buddhism, Xu Dashou accused missionaries of stealing and distorting the Buddhist notion.[137]

Although the object of worship in Mass is the Lord of Heaven, it is Jesus the second Person that was often emphasized in the Chinese Christian texts pertaining to Mass. From the theological perspective, to describe Jesus as the object of worship in Mass is closely related to Christology, especially to the Crucifixion.

2.2 *Relationship between Reception of Suffering and Mass*

In late Ming and early Qing, to describe Jesus as the object of worship in Mass found its theological basis in Christology, where the Crucifixion is an essential event. In the seventeenth century, the Christological controversy broke out in the Catholic Church in China. Since their arrival in China, the mendicants were suspicious of the Jesuit preaching strategy. In 1635 (Chongzhen 8), Juan Bautista de Morales (Li Yufan 黎玉範, OP, 1597–1664) and Antonio de Santa Maria Caballero (Li Andang 利安當, OFM, 1602–1669) wrote the reports (*Informaciones*) to their superiors in the Philippines to accuse the Jesuit strategy. Their most serious charge was that the Jesuits hid the crucifix in the public eye and did not mention the Crucifixion.[138] Nevertheless, Gianni Criveller's study of the Christology in late Ming reaches the conclusion that the Jesuits did not conceal the reception of suffering and that the crucified Christ was at the core of the spiritual formation of catechumens and Catholics.[139] Based on this conclusion, this section suggests that the teaching of the reception of suffering emphasized Jesus as the object of worship in Mass.

In the early stage of the Mission in China, Ricci presented Jesus as a teacher and a miracle performer.[140] As the Catholic Church in China grew, the Jesuits began to explain the Crucifixion in the depiction of Jesus, which was often called the reception of suffering (*shounan* 受難) in late Ming and early Qing. In *Brief Explanation of Catechism*, Vagnone explained the three meanings of the institution of Mass.

---

137 Several Buddhist notions related to the three bodies resemble the Trinity. Ding, *Foxue*, 151–152.
138 Criveller, *Preaching Christ*, 81.
139 Criveller, *Preaching Christ*, 437.
140 Gianni Criveller, "Christ Introduced to Late Ming China by Giulio Aleni S.J. (1582–1649)," in *The Chinese face of Jesus Christ*, vol. 2, ed. Roman Malek (Netteltal: Steyler Verlag, 2003), 442.

> The Lord of Heaven Jesus instituted this ritual with three meanings: first, he desires to nourish and preserve the human spirit by the ritual; second, he desires that human beings prepare the sacrificial ritual to the Lord of Heaven by it; third, he desires that human beings consider it the symbol (*haoji* 號記) of the holy grace.[141]

The human spirit (*renshen* 人神) in the first meaning referred to the human soul, whose existence relies on the Lord's protection and grace. The preparation in the second meaning referred to the ordination of the Catholic priest, who is the exclusive celebrant of Mass. The symbol in the third meaning reminds people to memorize the Lord of Heaven Jesus' grace.

> Yet, among the ten thousand graces, only the reception of bitterness and suffering (*shou kunan* 受苦難) is the great one. Therefore the worship must particularly be the symbol of this grace, which makes the pious followers of the Teaching see Jesus in the appearance of bread and wine when they see the worship.[142]

Vagnone explained transubstantiation in plain language and underlined the reception of suffering as an essential event to memorize in the celebration of Mass.

Four Rules of the Holy Teaching exhorts Chinese Catholics to be solemn at Mass: "When attending Mass, … one shall meditate on our Lord Jesus' reception of suffering (*wuzhu Yesu shounan* 吾主耶穌受難)."[143] Similar exhortations appeared in the *Statutes of the Confraternity of the Angels*: "One should think about the event of our Lord Jesus' reception of suffering,"[144] and "to meditate on the enormous grace of our Lord Jesus' reception of suffering."[145] Furthermore, the Jesuits wrote the depiction of the Crucifixion to assist Chinese Catholics to meditate during Mass. Around 1610, de Pantoja wrote *Reception of Suffering of the Lord of Heaven Jesus from the Beginning to the End* (*Tianzhu Yesu shounan*

---

141 "天主耶穌，定立此禮，具有三義。第一、欲以補存人神；第二、欲人以此俻祭天主之禮；第三、欲人以為聖恩之號記。" Vagnone, *Jiaoyao jieliie, shang juan*, fol. 53b6–fol. 54a1, 230–231.
142 "但其萬恩之中，獨當時受苦難一事為大。所以祭祀者，尤切為此恩之號記，令誠心奉教者，見祭時，則見耶穌於餅酒色中，" Vagnone, *Jiaoyao jieliie, shang juan*, fol. 54b1–3, 232.
143 "與彌撒之時，宜用心端肅，……即當默想吾主耶穌受難，不拘幾端，若不知行默想之功，口中謹念，不拘何聖經可也。" Brancati, *Shengjiao sigui*, 273–274.
144 "該想吾主耶穌受難之事，" Brancati, *Tianshen huike*, fol. 62b4, 128.
145 "默想吾主耶穌受難洪恩。" Brancati, *Tianshen huike*, fol. 69b2, 142.

shimo 天主耶穌受難始末, ca. 1610). Based on the Gospels (mainly John 13–19), de Pantoja provided detailed depiction from the Last Supper to the entombment of Jesus.[146] This text is the first complete account of the Crucifixion and the doctrine of redemption.[147]

Around 1619, *Regulation of Reciting the Beads* was published as the first manual of the Rosary in Chinese.[148] In the fifteen traditional mysteries of the Rosary, the five Sorrowful Mysteries focus on the reception of suffering: the Agony of Jesus in the Garden; the Scourging at the Pillar; Jesus is Crowned with Thorns; Jesus Carried the Cross; the Crucifixion of our Lord. In the petition of the fourth suffering (*tongku si* 痛苦四, the fourth Sorrowful Mystery), the person who prays shall "beg [the Lord of Heaven] to grant me the power to carry the Cross of the holy filial piety as to carry a heavy and huge Cross."[149] It is remarkable that the love of human beings for the Lord of Heaven was called the holy filial piety (*shengxiao* 聖孝), interweaving the essential Catholic teaching with the essential Chinese one.

Moreover, the *Regulation of Reciting the Beads* provided one illustration for each mystery. The fifteen woodcut illustrations were derived from the copperplate engravings in *Illustrations of the Gospel Stories from the order of the Gospels, recited in the Sacrifice of Mass the whole year* (*Evangelicae historiae imagines ex ordine evangeliorum, quae toto anno in missae sacrificio recitantur*) by Jerónimo Nadal (SJ, 1507–1580). Firstly published in 1593, *Evangelicae historiae imagines* collected 153 engravings of gospel scenes in accordance with the Roman Missal's liturgical order.[150] The Jesuits introduced *Evangelicae historiae imagines* to various missions in the world, including China. As a result, the Chinese were not only able to learn the reception of suffering by words but also by illustrations, which revealed to them the connection between the iconography of Christ's sacrifice and his sacramental presence in the sacrifice of Mass.[151]

---

146 Diego de Pantoja 龐迪我, *Tianzhu Yesu shounan shimo* 天主耶穌受難始末, *Pangzi yiquan* 龐子遺詮, *juan* 2, fol. 1b–fol. 8b, in CCT ARSI, vol. 2, 61–76.

147 Criveller, *Preaching Christ*, 425.

148 The text has been attributed to João da Rocha yet Fu Ji points out that the author is in fact Gaspar Ferreira (Fei Qigui 費奇規, SJ, 1571–1649). Fu Ji, *Prêcher, réciter et illustrer le Rosaire en Chine au XVIIe siècle: Étude du Song nianzhu guicheng* (*Règles pour la récitation du Rosaire*), (Mémoire de recherche, École du Louvre, 2016), 42.

149 "求亦如身負重大的十字架一般，又賜我能勤荷聖孝之十字。" da Rocha, *Nianzhu guicheng*, fol. 20b3-4, 554.

150 Fu, *Prêcher, réciter et illustrer*, 58–59.

151 Mark A Lewis, SJ, "Annotations and Meditations on the Gospels by Jerome Nadal," *Renaissance Quarterly* vol. 59, no. 3 (2006): 878.

Similarly, *Rules of Prayer to the Holy Body's Benevolence* connected the reception of suffering with the sacrifice in Mass: "Now our Lord Jesus forsakes the ultimately honorable blood in his body and let it flow to the ground in order to save me and to redeem me."[152] The character "*jin* 今" (now) implied that the sacrifice on the Cross is once and for all (*semel*).[153] Thus, the reception of suffering was connected with Mass, to some extent even identified with Mass.[154] Later on, João Fróis (Fu Ruowang 伏若望, SJ, 1591–1638) translated the Litany of the Passion into the Litany of Jesus' Reception of Suffering (*Yesu shounan daowen* 耶穌受難禱文, ca. 1628–1638).[155]

In 1637 (Chongzhen 10), Aleni published *Explanation of the Incarnation and Life of the Lord of Heaven* (*Tianzhu jiangsheng chuxiang jingjie* 天主降生出像經解, 1637). It was the first time that the Chinese could learn about the life of Christ thoroughly from pictures.[156] The book's European source is *Annotations and Meditations on the Gospels which Read in the Holy Sacrifice of Mass the Whole Year* (*Annotationes et meditationes in Evangelia qvae in sacrosancto Missae sacrificio toto anno legvntur*, 1595) by Nadal.[157] The word "*chuxiang* 出像" referred to a type of illustrated book that was common in late Ming and early Qing.[158] The life of Christ in Nadal's work is fully illustrated while in Aleni's work it is partially illustrated.[159] Among the 53 unnumbered pictures in Aleni's work,[160] three were closely related to Mass: picture 20, "Five Breads and Two

---

152 "今吾主耶穌，捨身內至尊至貴之血，流注至地，救我贖我，" de Mailla, *Shengti ren'aijing*, fol. 3b4–5, 300.
153 Hebrew 7:27, 9:12, 10:10.
154 "The sacrifice of Christ and the sacrifice of the Eucharist are one single sacrifice," "The Sacrament of the Eucharist," 1367, accessed January 28, 2021,
     https://www.vatican.va/archive/ccc_css/archive/catechism/p2s2c1a3.htm.
155 The litany was included in the anonymous Jesuit prayer book *The Prayers of Sufferings* (*Tongku jingji* 痛苦經蹟, ca. 1640s). Paul Brunner, *L'euchologe de la mission de Chine: Editio princeps 1628 et développements jusqu'à nos jours* (*Contribution à l'histoire des livres de prières*) (Münster: Aschendorffsche, 1964), 90.
156 Criveller, *Preaching Christ*, 238.
157 *Annotations and Meditations on the Gospels* is an enlarged edition of *Evangelicae historiae imagines*. Gianni Criveller, "Christ Introduced," 448.
158 The word "*chuxiang* 出像" in *Le Grand Ricci* does not contain this meaning, however, the following word "*chuxiang* 出相" contains the meaning that a book whose pages are occupied by pictures on high and an explanative text below. *Le Grand Dictionnaire Ricci de la langue chinoise* II (Paris: Desclée de Brouwer, 2001), 114.
159 Sun Yuming suggests that the word "*chuxiang* 出像" means partially illustrated whereas "*quanxiang* 全像" means fully illustrated. Both partially and fully illustrated books were common in late Ming. Sun Yuming, "Cultural Translatability and the Presentation of Christ as Portrayed in Visual Images from Ricci to Aleni," in *The Chinese face of Jesus Christ* vol. 2, 477–478.
160 Picture 25 was a repetition of picture 21, and picture 26 of picture 22. Yet, Alexander Bai-

Fishes Feeding Five Thousand People" (*Wubing eryu xiang wuqianren* 五餅二魚餉五千人); picture 41, "To Institute the Grand Ritual of Holy Body" (*Li shengti dali* 立聖體大禮); picture 47, "Many Miracles Occurred When Jesus Was Crucified" (*Yesu beiding lingji diexian* 耶穌被釘靈蹟叠現).[161]

As shown in figure 1, picture 41 contains four scenes marked by the characters *jia* 甲, *yi* 乙, *bing* 丙, and *ding* 丁. Under the picture are four descriptions in accordance with the four scenes. Picture 41 depicts the Last Supper on a large square table in a room, with Jesus sitting in the middle and the twelve disciples on two sides. In the round picture hang high on the middle of the wall is the scene *jia* 甲, which is a miniature of the room. Yet, what on the table is the lamb instead of the tableware. The description *jia* 甲 tells: "Jesus first ate the lamb according to the ancient ritual to express that the old ritual had ended and the whole work of world salvation had completed."[162]

The scene *yi* 乙 is on the large square table, where there are plates, knives, two bottles, one small cup, several pieces of bread, and one large cup in front of Jesus. The large cup and two bottles resemble the sacrificial objects used in Mass. The description *yi* 乙 depicts how Jesus performed the consecration of bread and wine.

> Jesus washed the disciples' feet, then he went back to the seat and by his omnipotence consecrated the bread and wine into the holy body and holy blood, which remain in the world forever to comfort the disciples and those who serve the Teaching in later generations.[163]

The scene *bing* 丙 has two marks on the twelve disciples sitting on the two sides. The description *bing* 丙 tells: "the disciples piously received the holy body with clean heart, in order to nourish their spirit and to increase various virtues and blessings."[164] The scene *ding* 丁 is beside Judas sitting at the end of one side

---

ley suggests that the anonymous Chinese artists produced more than 57 pictures. Gauvin Alexander Bailey, "The Image of Jesus in Chinese Art during the Time of the Jesuit Missions (16th–18th Centuries)," in *The Chinese face of Jesus Christ* vol. 2, 408–409.

161 Picture 20, Giulio Aleni 艾儒略, *Tianzhu jiangsheng chuxiang jingjie* 天主降生出像經解, in CCT ARSI, vol. 3, 548. Picture 41, Aleni, *Chuxiang jingjie*, 569. Picture 47, Aleni, *Chuxiang jingjie*, 575.
162 "甲、耶穌先依古禮食綿羊羔以示舊禮已終而救世全功已竣矣；" Aleni, *Chuxiang jingjie*, 569.
163 "乙、耶穌濯宗徒足，復就座，將麵餅及酒以其全能化成聖體聖血，永留在世，以慰宗徒及後世諸奉教者；" Aleni, *Chuxiang jingjie*, 569.
164 "丙、宗徒心潔而虔領聖體，以護養其神魂，增諸德慶；" Aleni, *Chuxiang jingjie*, 569.

FIGURE 1   To institute the grand ritual of Holy Body
COURTESY OF © ARCHIVUM ROMANUM SOCIETATIS IESU

near the reader. The description *ding* 丁 tells: "Judas impudently took the grace as well. Since his idea of corruption was not eliminated, Satan entered his heart and finally ruined him."[165]

Each description starts with the actor or actors in each corresponding scene, thus guiding the reader to watch the four scenes in order. In the first two scenes, Jesus is the actor who fulfilled the ancient Jewish ritual and instituted the new ritual for all human beings. In the third scene, the disciples are the actors who piously received the holy body as the congregants of the very first Mass. A contrary attitude is shown by the actor in the fourth scene Judas, who conceived the idea of betrayal after receiving the holy body.

In the end of the four descriptions, Aleni suggested the reader to read the first three sections of Chapter 7 in *Brief Account of the Lord of Heaven's Incarnation, Sayings, and Acts* (*Tianzhu jiangsheng yanxing jilüe* 天主降生言行紀畧, 1635). Aleni probably adapted this book from an abbreviated version of *Life of Christ* (*Vita Christi*, 1474) by Ludolf of Saxony (ca. 1300–1378). In the sixteenth and seventeenth centuries, *Life of Christ* was very popular in Europe and its use of active imagination influenced Ignacio de Loyola (SJ, 1491–1556) in the writing of the *Spiritual Exercises*.[166] It is not surprising that Aleni adapted the first biography of Jesus in Chinese from this popular book.[167]

The first section in Chapter 7 of *Brief Account of the Lord of Heaven's Incarnation, Sayings, and Acts* is "To Perform the Ancient Ritual on the Night before the Reception of Suffering" (*shounan qianxi xing guli* 受難前夕行古禮); the second is "To Wash Feet and to Give Instruction" (*zhuozu chuixun* 濯足垂訓); the third "To Institute the Grand Ritual of Holy Body" (*li shengti dali* 立聖體大禮). Since *Explanation of the Incarnation and Life of the Lord of Heaven* and *Brief Account of the Lord of Heaven's Incarnation, Sayings, and Acts* complement each other,[168] Aleni suggested the reader to read sections in the latter in order to understand the scenes in the former. Being exceptional in late Ming and early Qing, the structure of four scenes in one picture with chronicle marks and descriptions was adapted from *Annotationes et meditationes in Evangelia*.[169]

---

165 "丁、茹荅斯亦冒受其恩，貪污之心不除，魔遂入其心而終敗。（見《行紀》七卷三）" Aleni, *Chuxiang jingjie*, 569.
166 Nicolas Standaert, "The Bible in Early Seventeenth-century China," in *Bible in Modern China: The Literary and Intellectual Impact*, ed. Irene Eber, Sze-kar Wan, and Knut Walf (Sankt Augustin: Institut Monumenta Serica, 1999), 40–41.
167 Criveller, "Giulio Aleni," 446.
168 Standaert, "The Bible," 40.
169 The Passion narratives is the longest and most complex in Nadal's work. Lewis, "Annotations and Meditations," 878.

One distinctive feature in *Annotationes et meditationes in Evangelia* is the combination of letters in the picture and the description below, which well embodies the tradition to meditate in the composition of place (*compositio loci*).[170] Under each picture are several descriptions referring to the Gospel, each with a letter marked in the picture. The reader can follow the letters and meditate oneself in one place in the picture by chronicle order. Thus, the picture becomes the composition of place, which enables the reader to be present in the Gospel scene.[171] *Explanation of the Incarnation and Life of the Lord of Heaven* introduced the tradition to meditate in the composition of place into Chinese society. The characters *jia* 甲, *yi* 乙, *bing* 丙, *ding* 丁 marked in the picture and at the beginning of the corresponding descriptions are Sinicized from the letters A, B, C, D.

In addition to the characters, Aleni made other adaptations to approach the reader in Chinese society. Qu Yi points out two adaptations in picture 41: firstly, the addition of a dog under the large square table, a theme which can be traced from the Chinese picture tradition; secondly, the curtain and the tablecloth were decorated with the Chinese patterns that resemble the decoration in the upper-class literati's room, which probably implied to the Chinese reader that Jesus has a rather high social status.[172] As visual representation of the Gospel, picture 41 not only depicts the Last Supper but also serves for liturgical and meditative prayers.[173] The four scenes enable the reader to be present at the institution of the grand ritual, thus deepening their understanding of Mass. Moreover, their presence in the scene helps them to experience the presence of the Lord of Heaven Jesus vividly. Focusing on depicting life of Christ, especially the reception of suffering, Aleni used the name "Jesus" in his works more frequently than Ricci.[174] The works focused on the Lord of Heaven Jesus assisted Chinese Catholics to develop a personal experience with Jesus and a spiritual life centered on him.[175]

The Jesuits carried on the publication of pictures to introduce and propagate the Mass. On 8 September 1640 (Chongzhen 13.7.23), Johann Adam Schall

---

170 Lewis, "Annotations and Meditations," 878.
171 Nicolas Standaert, "The Composition of Place: Creating Space for an Encounter," *The Way* 46, no. 1 (2007): 14.
172 Qu Yi 曲藝, "Mingmo jidujiao chatu zhong de rujia yuansu: yi *Tianzhu jiangsheng chuxiang jingjie* weili 明末基督教插圖中的儒家元素：以《天主降生出像經解》為例," *Shijie zongjiao yanjiu* 世界宗教研究 2 (2015): 145–146.
173 Standaert, "The Composition of Place," 12–13.
174 Sun Yuming, "Cultural Translatability and the Presentation of Christ as Portrayed in Visual Images from Ricci to Aleni," in *The Chinese face of Jesus Christ* vol. 2, 485.
175 Criveller, "Giulio Aleni," 460.

von Bell (Tang Ruowang 湯若望, SJ, 1592–1666) submitted *Pictures in a Booklet Presented to His Majesty* (*Jincheng shuxiang* 進呈書像, 1640) to the Chongzhen emperor.[176] This book is an illustrated *Life of Christ* with 48 pictures, four of which are closely related to Mass: picture 21, "The Picture of the Holy Deed of the Lord of Heaven Jesus Feeding the Crowd" (*Tianzhu Yesu xiangzhong shengji xiang* 天主耶穌餉衆聖蹟像, the Multiplication of Loaves and Fishes); picture 30, "The Picture of the Lord of Heaven Jesus Practicing the Ancient Ritual on the Night Before the Reception of Suffering" (*Tianzhu Yesu shounan qianxi xing guli xiang* 天主耶穌受難前夕行古禮像, the Last Supper: the Eating of A Lamb); picture 32, "The Picture of the Lord of Heaven Jesus Initiating the Sacrificial Ritual" (*Tianzhu Yesu chuangding jili xiang* 天主耶穌創定祭禮像, the Last Supper: the Institution); picture 43, "The Picture of the Lord of Heaven Jesus Hanging on the Cross" (*Tianzhu Yesu xuanjia shuli xiang* 天主耶穌懸架豎立像, Christ on the Cross).[177] When titling the pictures, Aleni underlined the expression the Lord of Heaven Jesus.

Picture 32 (figure 3) directly describes the institution of Mass, and its European prototype is "The Last Supper: the Institution" (figure 2) engraved by Hendrick Goltzius (1558–1617) in 1598.[178] The reproduction of the European prototype adapted to the Chinese style. The figure, the background, and the scene in picture 32 were familiar to the Chinese and certain details resembled the Buddhist illustrations.[179]

The text corresponding to picture 32 does not describe the picture but explains the bread and wine, which are called the two sacrificial offerings (*jipin* 祭品). The bread must be made of pure flour, the wine pure grape. Jesus' reception of suffering is compared to the pureness of the two sacrificial offerings, accordingly, Mass is called the most honorable and immeasurable sacrifice (*zhizun wuliang zhi ji* 至尊無量之祭). In the end of the explanation, the comparison to the bread of wine extends to all the Catholics.

---

176 Nicolas Standaert, *An Illustrated Life of Christ Presented to the Chinese Emperor. The History of the Jincheng shuxiang (1640)* (Monumenta serica monograph series LIX, Sankt Augustin: Institut Monumenta Serica, 2007), 11.
177 For the picture with European prototype and the text with an English translation, picture 21, see Standaert, *An Illustrated Life*, 193–196. Picture 30, Standaert, *An Illustrated Life*, 237–240. Picture 32, Standaert, *An Illustrated Life*, 245–248. Picture 43, Standaert, *An Illustrated Life*, 293–298.
178 Figure 2, Standaert, *An Illustrated Life*, 247. Figure 3, Standaert, *An Illustrated Life*, 246.
179 Xiao Qinghe 肖清和, "Quanshi yu qibian: Yesu xingxiang zai Mingqing shehuili de chuanbo jiqi fanying 詮釋與歧變：耶穌形象在明清社會裡的傳播及其反應," *Guangdong shehui kexue* 廣東社會科學 4 (2011): 142.

FIGURE 2   The Last Supper: the institution
COURTESY OF THE ROYAL LIBRARY OF BELGIUM (KBR)

OBJECT OF WORSHIP 51

FIGURE 3   The Picture of the Lord of Heaven Jesus initiating the sacrificial ritual
COURTESY OF BIBLIOTECA NAZIONALE CENTRALE "VITTORIO EMANUELE II"

> The bread is made from much flour, and the wine from many grapes. They can be compared to those who worship the Teaching of the Lord of Heaven. Many hearts shall assemble into one heart, and many bodies in one body, in order to be presented to the Lord of Heaven.[180]

As Jesus is the offering on the altar, Catholics themselves assemble to be one offering. The essence of Mass is to worship the Lord as an assembly.

The Jesuits connected the reception of suffering with Mass and described the connection both by words and pictures. Furthermore, they discussed the reception of suffering with Chinese Catholics in daily life. On 3 May 1630 (Chongzhen 3.3.21), Aleni talked about the primary merit (*shougong* 首功) to repay the Lord of Heaven with Stephanus Li Jiubiao 李九標 (1597?–1647?) in Fuzhou. Aleni explained: "None [of the merits] is greater than carrying one's own Cross for the Lord of Heaven. In the past when speaking to the apostles, Jesus only said: 'You shall carry your own Cross daily to follow me.'"[181] It was the day of Finding of the Holy Cross (*xundao shizi shengjia ri* 尋到十字聖架日, the feast of the Finding of the Holy Cross). According to the Catholic liturgical calendar, Aleni connected the Cross carried by Jesus with the one that every Catholic should carry in daily life. He cited Jesus' words in the Gospels to underline the merit gained by carrying of the Cross.[182]

> As for the Cross, there is the visible one and the invisible one. When you entered the Way you have already found the Cross. It is better that you carry it, for if you do not want to and drag it along, it would become heavier. The Cross refers to various virtues, such as self-restraint, patience, and renunciation of desire ... Furthermore, there are two kinds of carriers: those who carry the Cross reluctantly, and those who carry it joyfully; to carry the Cross joyfully gains greater merit.[183]

---

180 "麪多麥合成，酒多葡萄合成，比之奉教之人，合眾心成一心，合眾體為一體，以上獻天主也。" Johann Adam Schall von Bell 湯若望, *Jincheng shuxiang* 進呈書像, fol. 34, in *An Illustrated Life*, 248.

181 "未有大于為天主而負己之十字架者。昔耶穌之語宗徒，亦惟曰：'爾其日日負己之十字架以從我。'" Li, *Kouduo richao*, *juan* 1, fol. 10b2–5, 56. Zürcher, *Kou duo ri chao*, vol. 1, I. 17 (Fuzhou, Friday, 3 May 1630), 218.

182 "Et qui non accipit crucem suam et sequitur me non est me dignus," Matthew 10:38. "Si quis vult post me sequi deneget se ipsum et tollat crucem suam et sequatur me," Mark 8:34. "Si quis vult post me venire abneget se ipsum et tollat crucem suam cotidie et sequatur me," Luke 9:23.

183 "夫十字架，有有形者，有無形者。子自入道以來，業已尋得十字架矣。子宜負焉，如不願負而拖之，則更重矣。蓋指克己忍耐絕欲諸德也。……卽負

The visible Cross and the invisible Cross echo to the feast. To become a Catholic signifies the finding of the invisible Cross, and it is every Catholic's responsibility to carry the Cross.

On 3 May 1631 (Chongzhen 4.4.3), then the feast of the Finding of the Holy Cross, in Fuzhou, Chen Rutiao 陳汝調 asked Andrzej about the practice of collecting relics of the Holy Cross.

> Chen Rutiao asked Master Lu: "I have heard that the Holy Cross has been split and taken by various countries in the Great West and that the pieces of the Cross have been treasured as the most precious. Is that true?"
>
> Master said: "Yes, that is true. In the beginning the Cross was but an instrument of torture. Once our Lord had received the suffering to redeem us, it was honored, venerated, loved, and admired by everyone. Certain kings even added it on the top of the crown. Therefore, various countries in the Great West split the Holy Cross which had been found and treasured the pieces as the most precious."[184]

Andrzej confirmed the relic collection of the Holy Cross, then, on his own initiative, he explained that the Cross was originally an instrument of torture but Jesus' suffering made the Cross an object worthy of veneration. Through the homilies and talks on the reception of suffering, the Jesuits tried to instill into Chinese Catholics the devotional approach toward Jesus.[185]

In return, Chinese Catholics showed their understanding of the reception of suffering by various practices. In 1639 (Chongzhen 12), Rodrigo de Figueiredo (Fei Lede 費樂德, SJ, 1608–1642) founded the Confraternity of the Holy Cross in Kaifeng 開封, Henan 河南. The members commemorated the reception of suffering by a series practices, such as kneeling down to pray the Litany of Jesus' Reception of Suffering, kissing the foot of the Cross, giving short talk on the reception of suffering, and carrying the Cross by turns during Mass.[186] In the

---

十字架，亦有兩等：有強負者，有欣負者，而欣負之功更大矣。" Li, *Kouduo richao*, juan 1, fol. 10b5–9, 56. Zürcher, *Kou duo ri chao*, vol. 1, I. 17 (Fuzhou, Friday, 3 May 1630), 218. Zürcher ignored the translation for the sentence of the virtues.

184 "初三日，尋到十字聖架日也。陳汝調問盧先生曰：'聞十字聖架，大西諸國，各取而分之，珍為至寶，未知然否？'先生曰：'然，夫十字架者，初直刑具耳。一經吾主受難，救贖我眾，遂無不尊之崇，愛之慕之，且有加之冕旒之上者。以故大西諸國，將尋到之聖架，各各分之，珍為至寶。'" Li, *Kouduo richao*, juan 2, fol. 2a1–6, 101. Zürcher, *Kou duo ri chao*, vol. 2, II. 2 (Fuzhou, Saturday, 3 May 1631), 254–255.

185 Criveller, "Giulio Aleni," 458.

186 Brockey, *Journey to the East*, 375–377.

aforementioned conflict with Mgr. Maigrot, local Catholics in Fuzhou showed how much they honored the crucifix in their letter written on 18 April 1700.

> We sinners did not know what else to do but to hold the Lord of Heaven's bitter image (*tianzhu kuxiang* 天主苦像) and to cry together, hoping to move Monsignor's heart … Suddenly Mgr. Maigrot opened the door … expelled us. He saw Jesus' bitter image (*Yesu kuxiang* 耶穌苦像) but was too arrogant to kneel down … We sinners became angry: seeing that Monsignor dared to treat the Lord of Heaven disrespectfully, we can treat him disrespectfully. Together we pulled him down on his knees.[187]

Since late Ming and early Qing, the crucifix, whether a sculpture or a picture, has been called the bitter image (*kuxiang* 苦像). The character "*ku* 苦" (bitter) embodies Jesus' reception of suffering. Out of deep respect for the bitter image, local Chinese Catholics at first thought that the bitter image may make Mgr. Maigrot be merciful to them; when they saw that Mgr. Maigrot did not honor the bitter image, they forced him to.

In addition, Chinese Catholics wrote down their understanding of the reception of suffering. In *Basic Knowledge of the Study of Heaven* (*Tianxue mengyin* 天學蒙引, ca. 1655), Jacobus Zhou Zhi 周志 described the institution of Mass in poetic form.

> Jesus took the bread to consecrate: "The disciples share and distribute it
>   to energize your souls.
> This is my true real body, eat it and you will enjoy the everlasting life."
> Again [Jesus] took the wine to consecrate: "The disciples share and
>   drink it from myself.
> This is my true body and blood, which will be poured on the Cross
>   tomorrow."
> Jesus was about to receive suffering and to return to the Father, so [he]
>   left the ritual to nourish human spirit.[188]

---

[187] "眾罪人情極無奈，只得抱請天主苦像，合眾哀號，感動主教之心……顏主教忽開房門……驅逐眾人，親見耶穌苦像，傲慢竟不下跪……眾罪人心中不平：主教敢不敬天主，吾輩亦不敬主教，齊扯其跪。" Wu and Han, "Liyi zhi zheng," 89.

[188] "耶穌取餅來祝聖，分與群徒健爾靈，此即吾之真實體，食來便得享常生。又取葡萄酒祝聖，分飲群徒自我身，此即吾之真體血，明朝架上所來傾。耶穌受難將歸父，故留此禮養人神。" Zhou Zhi 周志, *Tianxue mengyin* 天學蒙引, fol. 9a–b, in CCT BnF, vol. 7, 349–350.

The form is very poetic: each sentence has seven characters; the character *"ling* 靈*"* rhymes with *"qing* 傾*,"* and *"shen* 身*"* with *"shen* 神*."* This poetic description conforms with the institution of Mass in the Synoptic Gospels (Matthew 26:26–29; Mark 14:22–25; and Luke 22:14–20). Particularly, the actions and words of Jesus closely resemble the verses in the Gospel of Matthew.[189] The verb *"qu* 取*"* in Chinese echoes the verb *accipere* in Latin, and *"fen* 分*"* echoes *frangere dedereque*. The Chinese Christian communities added to the verb *"zhusheng* 祝聖*"* the meaning "to consecrate" (*consecrare*).

After the consecration, Jesus declared to the disciples that the bread is *corpus meum* and the wine *sanguis meus*. To highlight the real presence, the description not only uses *"wu* 吾*"* (my) but also *"zhen* 眞*"* (true). The Buddhist sutras had already used the expression "true real body" (*zhen shiti* 眞實體), for example the *Flower Adornment Sutra* (Avataṃsaka Sūtra) reads: "capable to see the Buddha's true real body."[190] Yet, the expression "true body and blood" (*zhen tixue* 眞體血), rarely seen in the traditional Chinese texts, was a specific term used in the Teaching of the Lord of Heaven.

Zhou Zhi almost rewrote the verse *novi testamenti qui pro multis effunditur in remissionem peccatorum* (Matthew 26:28) in Chinese. He omitted *novi testamenti* and *remissionem peccatorum*, yet specified that the blood would be poured "on the Cross" (*jiashang* 架上), and declared the effects of Mass: "to energize your souls" (*jian erling* 健爾靈) and "to enjoy the everlasting life" (*xiang changsheng* 享常生). Chinese Catholics learned the notion of the everlasting life from missionaries. Early in *Brief Explanation of Catechism*, Vagnone explained: "Everlasting life means that the body is beautiful and the soul is ultimately joyful, permanently without intermission."[191] Zhou Zhi explicitly mentioned the reception of suffering and implied the resurrection and ascension of Jesus by the phrase "return to the Father" (*guifu* 歸父). In the last sentence he explained that Jesus instituted Mass to nourish human spirit (*yang renshen* 養人神). With an emphasis on Jesus, Zhou Zhi did not merely repeat the Synoptic Gospels but connected the Cross, the reception of suffering, and Mass together.

---

189 "Cenantibus autem eis accepit Iesus panem et benedixit ac fregit deditque discipulis suis et ait accipite et comedite hoc est corpus meum et accipiens calicem gratias egit et dedit illis dicens bibite ex hoc omnes hic est enim sanguis meus novi testamenti qui pro multis effunditur in remissionem peccatorum dico autem vobis non bibam amodo de hoc genimine vitis usque in diem illum cum illud bibam vobiscum novum in regno Patris mei." Matthew 26:26–29.

190 "能見如來真實體，" Śikṣānanda 實叉難陀, trans., *Dafang guang fo huayan jing* 大方廣佛華嚴經, *juan* 5, Eruson, 54.

191 "常生者，四體美好，靈冕至樂，永無間斷之期也。" Vagnone, *Jiaoyao jieliie*, *shang juan*, fol. 42b1–2, 208.

The Jesuits did not hide the explanation of the reception of suffering within the Christian communities. The Chongzhen emperor read *Pictures in a Booklet Presented to His Majesty* and asked Schall to explain the illustrations. As Schall recorded, when they reached the reception of suffering, the Chongzhen emperor put the book down and knelt down, so Schall knelt down beside him and explained the reception of suffering. Schall had talked about the same teaching to many literati who either did not pay any attention or mocked it. The Chongzhen emperor was unlike them: "On the contrary the monarch so powerful genuflected with so much humility" (*hic vero tantus Monarcha cum tanta humilitate se in genua proiecit*).[192] The description may exaggerate the emperor's reaction yet at least exemplified that the Chongzhen emperor respected the reception of suffering. Schall compared different reactions to the reception of suffering outside the Christian communities. The Chongzhen emperor paid respect; some literati showed indifference; some showed mockery.

In addition, some Chinese showed disgust and contempt to the reception of suffering. For anti-Catholics in late Ming and early Qing, Jesus's reception of suffering was too incomprehensible and unacceptable.[193] Some officials were not anti-Catholic yet considered the bitter image sorcery. In July 1600 (Wanli 28.5) in Linqing 臨清, Shandong, the powerful eunuch Ma Tang 馬堂 inspected the gifts which Ricci prepared for the Wanli emperor and saw a picture of the reception of suffering. In September 1600 (Wanli 28.8) in Tianjin 天津, Ma Tang spread the rumor that Ricci wanted to use this pernicious picture to practice sorcery against the emperor.[194]

Similarly, the Nanjing official document made a list of books and pictures found in the missionary's residence in 1617 (Wanli 45.5). One item on the list reads "three ivory statues of [Jesus] being crucified to death."[195] Since the late sixteenth century, the craftsmen in Fujian, especially in Zhangzhou 漳州, produced and exported ivories with Catholic themes to Macao, the Philippines, India, the Americas, and Europe. The craftsmen imitated the European models and blended certain Chinese style in the ivories. The ivory statue of the Cru-

---

192 Joannes Adamus Schall, sj, *Relation historique, texte latin avec traduction française de Paul Bornet* (Tientsin: Hautes études, 1942), 287.
193 Xiao, "Quanshi," 144.
194 Lin, *Li Madou yu Zhongguo*, 80, 254.
195 "釘死牙像叁個，" Nanjing libu zhuke qinglisi 南京礼部主客清吏司, *Qingcha yiwu you yi'an* 清查夷物又一案, in *Nangong shudu*, juan 3, fol. 44a3. The title in the text was misprinted. The character "*wen* 文" should be "*you* 又."

cifixion was but a popular production to them,[196] however, to the officials in Nanjing, it "belongs to pernicious sorcery" and should be destroyed.[197]

The anti-Catholic Chinese heard about the reception of suffering and emphasized that the Cross was an instrument of torture. Xu Dashou thought that missionaries made up the reception of suffering: "[They] falsely proclaim: for human beings Jesus was willingly to be sentenced and be crucified to death on the cross-shaped instrument of torture (*shizi jia* 十字枷)."[198] He accused missionaries of commanding Chinese Catholics "to worship one cross-shaped instrument of torture in every family."[199] On 8 August 1634 (Chongzhen 7.8.15), the Buddhist monk Shi Purun 釋普潤 accused Chinese Catholics of "burning the holy statues and only worshiping the cross-shaped instrument of torture (*shizi xingjia* 十字刑枷)."[200] Around 1634, Huang Zhen suspiciously described missionaries: "Today the pernicious barbarians shower the holy water, smear the holy oil, and use the cross-shaped instrument of torture (*shizi xingjia* 十字刑枷) to shackle their own body and mind."[201]

In 1664 (Kangxi 3), Yang Guangxian 楊光先 (1597–1669) criticized three pictures in *Pictures in a Booklet Presented to His Majesty*,[202] including "The Picture of the Lord of Heaven Jesus Returning to the Capital" (*Tianzhu Yesu fandu xiang* 天主耶穌返都像), chosen from picture 28, "Christ's Entry into Jerusalem;" "The Picture of Jesus Being Crucified" (*Yesu fangding xingjia xiang* 耶穌方釘刑架像), from picture 42, "The Crucifixion;" "The Picture of the Lord of Heaven Jesus on the Cross" (*Tianzhu Yesu lijia xiang* 天主耶穌立架像), from picture 43, "The Picture of the Lord of Heaven Jesus Hanging on the Cross."[203]

---

196 Bailey, "The Image of Jesus," 397–400.
197 "釘像的係邪術魘魅," Nanjing libu, *Qingcha yiwu you yi'an*, fol. 44b2.
198 "詭言：耶穌爲人甘罪，釘死於十字枷上。" Xu, "Yipi kuangshi 一闢誑世," *Shengchao zuopi*, 85. See also "謂天主曾爲眾生釘死於十字枷上。" Xu, "Qipi qiefo hefo zhongzhong zuiguo 七闢竊佛呵佛種種罪過," *Shengchao zuopi*, 134.
199 "戶供一十字枷," Xu, "Liupi feisi 六闢廢祀," *Shengchao zuopi*, 121.
200 "火神聖之像，但供十字刑枷," Shi Purun 釋普潤, *Zhuzuo ji yuanqi* 誅左集緣起, fol. 21b4–5, in *Poxie ji* vol. 8, 352.
201 "如今日妖夷淋聖水，擦聖油，運十字刑枷以自桎梏其身心，" Huang, *Zunru jijing*, fol. 19a6–7, 263.
202 Yang Guangxian 楊光先, *Lin Tang Ruowang jincheng tuxiang shuo* 臨湯若望進呈圖像說, *Budeyi* 不得已, fol. 32 b, fol. 33b, fol. 34b, in SCCT ZKW, vol. 5, 566, 568, 570. See also Yang Guangxian 楊光先, *Xiejiao santu shuoping* 邪教三圖說評, *Budeyi fu erzhong* 不得已附二種, annot. Chen Zhanshan 陳占山 (Hefei: Huangshan shushe 黃山書社, 2000), 31–33. See also Albert Chan, SJ, *Chinese Books and Documents in the Jesuit Archives in Rome: A Descriptive Catalogue: Japonica-Sinica I–IV* (Armonk&London: M.E. Sharpe, 2002), 143.
203 Picture 28, see Standaert, *An Illustrated Life*, 223–229. Picture 42, Standaert, *An Illustrated Life*, 287–291. Picture 43, Standaert, *An Illustrated Life*, 293–298.

Yang Guangxian miswrote the name "*Yesu* 耶穌" (Jesus) as "*Yesu* 耶蘇," which might be a move to show his derision. In *On Copies of Pictures Presented by Adam Schall* (*Lin Tang Ruowang jincheng tuxiang shuo* 臨湯若望進呈圖像說), Yang Guangxian used the three pictures to prove that "Jesus was the thief leader of those who conspired against the orthodox law" (*Yesu nai moufan zhengfa zhi zeishou* 耶蘇乃謀反正法之賊首) and that he was crucified because of his crime.[204] Yang Guangxian considered the Crucifixion a pure political event and emphasized Jesus' secular image as a criminal.[205] He made three rough copies from Schall's book in order to defame Jesus' image.[206] For example, Schall adapted the possible European prototype "Christ on the Cross" into picture 43 (figure 4), then Yang Guangxian simplified picture 43 into "The Picture of the Lord of Heaven Jesus on the Cross" (figure 5).[207]

This section unfolds the close relationship between the reception of suffering and Mass. Jesus as the object of worship in Mass was emphasized in the explanation of the reception of suffering, by pictures as well as by words. Both within and outside the Christian communities, the Chinese learnt about the Lord of Heaven Jesus and shaped their own understanding.

2.3   Litany of Jesus' Holy Body

After settled in Fujian, Aleni changed his missionary method by writing fifteen books or booklets about spirituality, catechism, and liturgy, the majority of which focused on Christ's mysteries. This change can be seen as a Christological shift which reflects not only Aleni's pastoral consideration but also his inclination toward a Christocentric spirituality shaped during his Jesuit formation.[208] In this Christological shift, of the seven sacraments Aleni discussed the Eucharist the most.[209] The Litany of Jesus' Holy Body (*Yesu shengti daowen* 耶穌聖體禱文) is a remarkable example that describes Jesus as the object of worship in Mass, however, only a few basic information is given on this prayer.

---

204   Yang, *Lin Tang Ruowang*, fol. 32 a8, 565. See also Yang, *Xiejiao santu*, 30.
205   Xiao, "Quanshi," 142.
206   Criveller, *Preaching Christ*, 244.
207   Figure 4, Standaert, *An Illustrated Life*, 294. This picture was probably adapted from J. Nadal, *Adnotationes et meditations in Evangelica*, Antwerpen, 1607, no. 130. Standaert, *An Illustrated Life*, 295. Figure 5, Yang, *Lin Tang Ruowang*, fol. 34b, 570.
208   Criveller, "Giulio Aleni," 443.
209   Lin, "Shilun," 41.

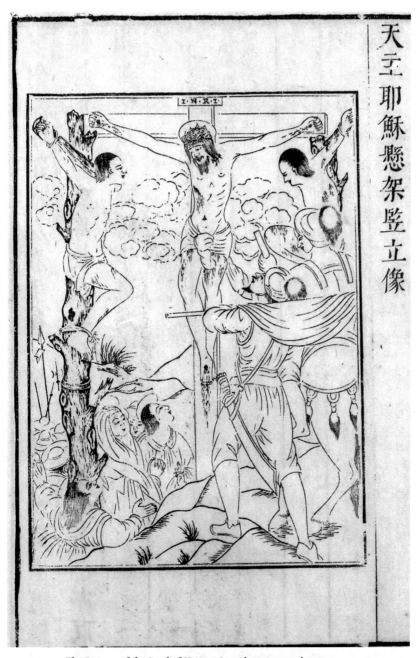

FIGURE 4   The Picture of the Lord of Heaven Jesus hanging on the cross
COURTESY OF BIBLIOTECA NAZIONALE CENTRALE "VITTORIO
EMANUELE II"

FIGURE 5   The Picture of the Lord of Heaven Jesus on the cross
COURTESY OF © ARCHIVUM ROMANUM SOCIETATIS IESU

OBJECT OF WORSHIP 61

Henri Bernard mentions that Aleni published the prayer around 1627;[210] Paul Brunner suggests that it was published between 1638 and 1649;[211] Gianni Criveller suggests that the prayer was first published as an appendix to the first edition of *Treatise on the Holy Body* (*Shengti yaoli* 聖體要理, ca. 1638) then it was published separately.[212] The Litany of Jesus' Holy Body was often re-edited in later collections of prayers.[213]

This section examines the edition which is an appendix of *Treatise on the Holy Body* in the CCT BnF series. The prayer has six and a half pages (13 folios).[214] Bernard translates the Chinese title into French as *Litanies de la Sainte Eucharistie* (Litany of the Holy Eucharist); Brunner translates it as *Litanies du Saint Sacrement* (Litany of the Holy Sacrament); and Criveller translates it as the Litany of the Holy Eucharist. This section translates it literally as the Litany of Jesus' Holy Body, whose variant title is the Litany of the Holy Body (*Shengti daowen* 聖體禱文). The CCT-database indicates that Aleni adapted the prayer from *Fasciculus sacrarum litaniarum ex sanctis scripturis et patribus* (*Fascicle of Sacred Litanies from the Holy Scriptures and the Fathers*), a prayer book in Latin and Greek by Georg Mayr (SJ, 1564–1623).[215] The title in Latin

---

210 In *Les Adaptations I*, it is put in the group of "1628, 天啓 7 (XI. 25)–崇禎 1 (XII. 7)" as work no. 159. Henri Bernard, *Les Adaptations chinoises d'ouvrages européens: Bibliographie chronologique depuis la venue des Portugais à Canton jusqu'à la mission française de Pékin 1514–1688* (Monumenta serica vol. 10, 1945), 341.

211 Brunner, *L'euchologe*, 97.

212 Criveller, *Preaching Christ*, 189. Criveller translates the title "*Shengti yaoli* 聖體要理" as *Treatise on the Eucharist*. For the publish date of this book, see Ad Dudink, "The Holy Mass in Seventeenth-and Eighteenth-Century China: Introduction to and Annotated Translation of 與彌撒功程 (1721), Manual for Attending Mass," in *A Life Long Dedication to the China Mission: Essays Presented in Honor of Father Jeroom Heyndrickx, CICM, on the Occasion of His 75th Birthday and the 25th Anniversary of the F. Verbiest Institute, K.U.Leuven*, ed. Noël Golvers and Sara Lievens (Leuven Chinese studies XVII, Leuven: Ferdinand Verbiest Institute, K.U.Leuven, 2007), 310, note 327. Based on the text *Yu Misa Gongcheng* 與彌撒功程, this article analyzes how missionaries explained the procedure to attend Mass in the seventeenth and eighteenth centuries. It summarizes the interpretation in the text of what the congregants see or hear during Mass, such as the priest's actions, gestures, and voices.

213 Bernard, *Les Adaptations chinoises*, 341. It is not frequently recited in the Catholic Church in China today.

214 Giulio Aleni 艾儒略, *Yesu shengti daowen* 耶穌聖體禱文, fol. 1a–fol. 7a, *Shengti yaoli* 聖體要理, in CCT BnF, vol. 18, 289–301.

215 Georg Mayr, *Fasciculus sacrarum litaniarum ex sanctis scripturis et patribus* (Augustae Vindelicorum, 1614), 291–302. *Shengti daowen* 聖體禱文, the CCT-database, accessed March 19, 2021, http://heron-net.be/pa_cct/index.php/Detail/objects/7393.

is *Litaniae de Venerabili Sacramento* (the Litany of the Venerable Sacrament, shortened as *Litaniae de V. Sacramento*).[216]

A classic form of the litany begins with *Kyrie eleison* (Lord, have mercy), continues with the invocations to the three Persons, then goes through the beads with the invocations to Christ or to a particular saint.[217] Accordingly, *Litaniae de V. Sacramento* is structured in three parts: the beginning invocation, the specific petition, and the closure. In fact, the litanies in *Fasciculus sacrarum litaniarum* share the same structure and even the same beginning invocation. The first half of the beginning invocation is *Kyrie eleison*; the second is the invocations to the Father, the Son, the Holy Spirit, and the Trinity. Each invocation in the second half is followed by the response *Miserere nobis* (Have mercy on us). The responsorial form is a remarkable characteristic in the Catholic litanies. When reciting the litany in an assembly, one person acts as the leader who begins each verse and the rest responds as a whole. The following part is the specific petition, where petitions are listed one by one, while a same response written vertically on the right side of the page, with a large bracket as indication (figure 6); the Greek version takes the same structure (figure 7). There are two groups of specific petitions in *Litaniae de V. Sacramento*. The response to the first group is *Miserere nobis* and that to the second group is *Libera nos Domine* (Save us, Lord). The closure includes a long communal prayer recited by the leader alone, followed by the *Pater Noster* and other prayers. Adapted from *Litaniae de V. Sacramento*, the Litany of Jesus' Holy Body highlights the responsorial form much more. Two characters "*qi* 啓" (versicle) and "*ying* 應" (response) appear since the beginning invocation (figure 8) and continue in the specific petitions (figure 9). The leader recites the verse indicated by "*qi* 啓" and the rest recites that indicated by "*ying* 應."[218] Consequently, the Chinese version takes up more space than the Latin version and the Greek one.

The response is given to each petition, although a number of petitions share the same one. "*Qi* 啓" and "*ying* 應" are clear indications guiding Chinese Catholics to recite the litany. Aleni translated the response to the first group of specific petitions as "*jinlian wodeng* 矜憐我等" (*Miserere nobis*) and that to the second as "*zhu jiu wodeng* 主救我等" (*Libera nos Domine*). In the first group, the verse after "*ying* 應" is always "*jinlian wodeng* 矜憐我等" (*Miserere nobis*) while the verse after "*qi* 啓" varies in each petition. There are forty petitions in the

---

216 Mayr, *Fasciculus sacrarum litaniarum*, 291.
217 Brunner, *L'euchologe*, 93.
218 Figure 6, Mayr, *Fasciculus sacrarum litaniarum*, 291. Figure 7, Mayr, *Fasciculus sacrarum litaniarum*, 292. Figure 8, Aleni, *Shengti daowen*, fol. 1a, 289. Figure 9, Aleni, *Shengti daowen*, fol. 1b, 290.

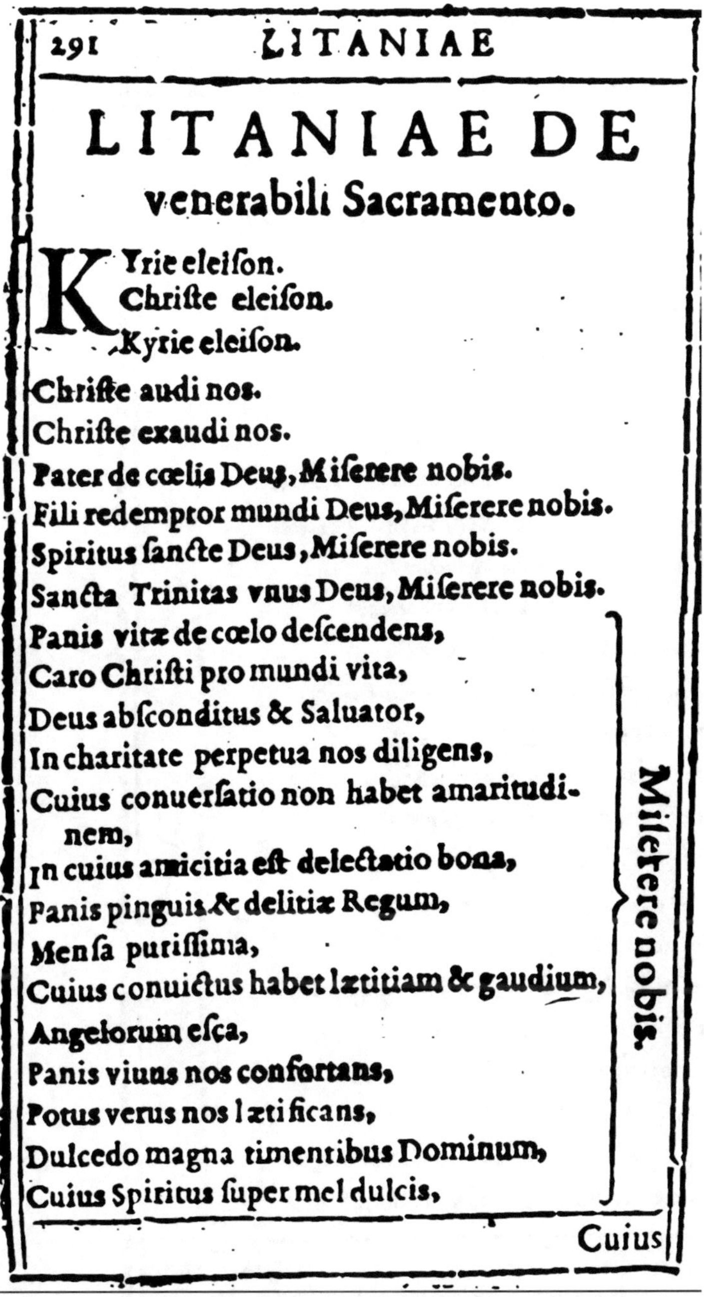

OBJECT OF WORSHIP 63

291   LITANIAE

LITANIAE DE
venerabili Sacramento.

Kyrie eleison.
Christe eleison.
Kyrie eleison.
Christe audi nos.
Christe exaudi nos.
Pater de cœlis Deus, Miserere nobis.
Fili redemptor mundi Deus, Miserere nobis.
Spiritus sancte Deus, Miserere nobis.
Sancta Trinitas vnus Deus, Miserere nobis.
Panis vitæ de cœlo descendens,
Caro Christi pro mundi vita,
Deus absconditus & Saluator,
In charitate perpetua nos diligens,
Cuius conuersatio non habet amaritudinem,
In cuius amicitia est delectatio bona,
Panis pinguis & delitiæ Regum,
Mensa purissima,
Cuius conuictus habet lætitiam & gaudium,
Angelorum esca,
Panis viuus nos confortans,
Potus verus nos lætificans,
Dulcedo magna timentibus Dominum,
Cuius Spiritus super mel dulcis,

} Miserere nobis.

Cuius

FIGURE 6   Beginning invocation and petitions in Latin
                COURTESY OF BIBLIOTECA NAZIONALE CENTRALE "VITTORIO
                EMANUELE II"

de V. Sacramento. 292

ΛΙΤΑΝΕΙΑΙ
περὶ σεβασμίας εὐχαριστίας.

Κύριε ἐλέησον.
Χριστὲ ἐλέησον.
Κύριε ἐλέησον.
Χριστὲ ἄκουσον ἡμῶν.
Χριστὲ εἰσάκουσον ἡμῶν.
Πάτερ ὁ ἐκ τῶν οὐρανῶν θεὸς, ἐλέησον ἡμᾶς.
Υἱὲ λυτρωτὰ τοῦ κόσμου θεὸς, ἐλέησον ἡμᾶς.
Πνεῦμα ἅγιον θεὸς, ἐλέησον ἡμᾶς.
Ἁγία τριὰς, εἷς θεὸς, ἐλέησον ἡμᾶς.
Ἄρτε τῆς ζωῆς ὁ ἐκ τοῦ οὐρανοῦ καταβὰς,
Σὰρξ τοῦ χριστοῦ ὑπὲρ τοῦ τοῦ κόσμου ζωῆς,
Θεὸς ὁ ἀποκεκρυμμένος καὶ σωτήρ,
Ἀγάπησιν αἰώνιον ἀγαπῶν ἡμᾶς,
Οὗ συναναστροφὴ οὐκ ἔχει πικρίαν,
Ἐν οὗ φιλίᾳ τέρψις ἐστὶν ἀγαθὴ,
Ἄρτῳ πίων, καὶ τρυφὴ τῶν βασιλέων,
Τράπεζα καθαρωτάτη,
Οὗ συμβιώσις ἔχει ἀφροσύνην καὶ χαράν,
Ἡ τῶν ἀγγέλων τροφὴ,
Ἄρτε ζῶν ἡμᾶς ἐπισχύων,
Πόσις ἀληθινὴ ἡμᾶς εὐφραίνουσα,
Ἡ ἐλπὶς μεγάλη τῆς φοβουμένοις τὸν κύριον,
Οὗ πνεῦμα γλυκύτερον ὑπὲρ μέλι,

} ἐλέησον ἡμᾶς.

Οὗ κλη.

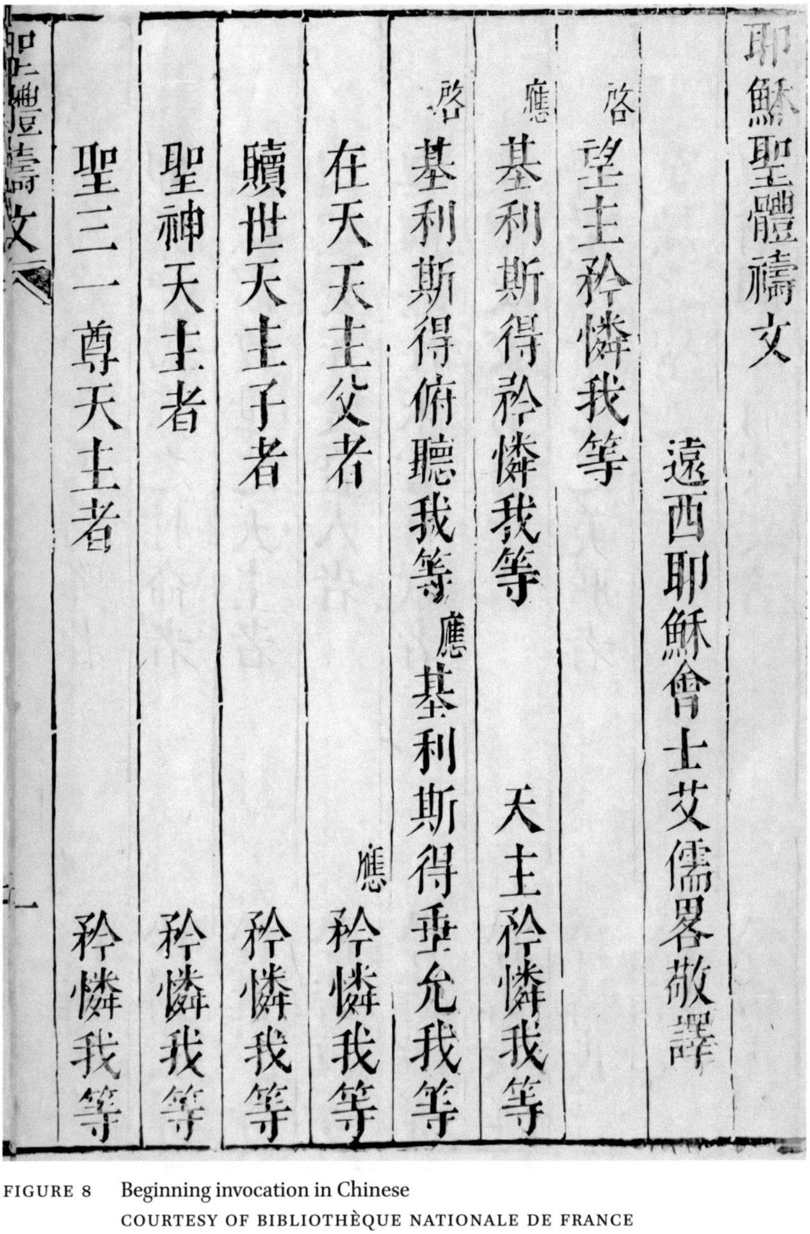
耶穌聖體禱文
遠西耶穌會士艾儒畧敬譯
啓 望主矜憐我等
應 基利斯得矜憐我等 天主矜憐我等
啓 基利斯得俯聽我等 應 基利斯得垂允我等
在天天主父者 應 矜憐我等
贖世天主子者 矜憐我等
聖神天主者 矜憐我等
聖三一尊天主者 矜憐我等
聖體禱文 一

FIGURE 8 Beginning invocation in Chinese
COURTESY OF BIBLIOTHÈQUE NATIONALE DE FRANCE

性命之糧自天而降者。應矜憐我等
耶穌聖體人之性命者。矜憐我等
隱藏以救世之天主者。矜憐我等
以聖愛永愛吾人者。矜憐我等
與爾遊徃未嘗有厭者。矜憐我等
與爾交友有善樂者。矜憐我等
膏粱及帝王之美膳者。矜憐我等
至潔之聖筵。矜憐我等
與爾同席有安樂者。矜憐我等

FIGURE 9　Petitions in Chinese
COURTESY OF BIBLIOTHÈQUE NATIONALE DE FRANCE

OBJECT OF WORSHIP 67

first group, each time addressing Jesus' holy body in a different title. This section puts the forty titles in eight categories: food & drink, the feast, medicine, sacrifice, the Lord, friend, graces, and merit for the deceased. Table 1 presents the eight categories, the Latin titles used by Mayr, and the Chinese ones used by Aleni.[219]

TABLE 1   Titles in eight categories

Category	Latin by Mayr	Chinese by Aleni
1st food & drink	*Panis vitae de caelo descendens*	性命之糧自天而降者
	Panis pinguis & deliciae Regum	膏粱及帝王之美膳者
	Angelorum esca	天神之糧
	Frumentun electorum	簡越者之神糧
	Panis vivus nos confortans	活糧健裨吾輩者
	Manna absconditu	隱藏之瑪納
	Panis supersubstantialis	厚養人之糧者
	Potus verus nos laetificans	眞飲樂我輩者
	Vinum germinans virgines	生育童貞之酒
	Resectio animarum sanctarum	諸聖蒐之飽飫
2nd the feast	*Mensa purissima*	至潔之聖筵
	Dulcissimum conuiuium cui assistunt Angeli ministrantes	至甘之筵，天神所使役者
3rd medicine	*Caeleste antidotum quo a peccatis praeservamur*	預防諸罪之天藥者
	Pharmacu immortalitatis	常生不死之丹
4th sacrifice	*Agnus absque macula*	無玷之棉羔者
	Hostia sancta & calix benedictionis	聖祭之聖品，及降福之爵者
	Offerens & oblatio	自為獻品，而且為獻者
5th the Lord	*Deus absconditus & Salvator*	隱藏以救世之天主者
	In charitate perpetua nos diligens	以聖愛永愛吾人者
	Verbu caro factum	費畧降生之本體
	Cibus & conviva	以本體為珎餚以筵賓者

219 For the Latin titles, Mayr, *Fasciculus sacrarum litaniarum*, 291–295. For the Chinese titles, Aleni, *Shengti daowen*, fol. 1b1–fol. 3b4, 290–294.

TABLE 1   Titles in eight categories (cont.)

Category	Latin by Mayr	Chinese by Aleni
6th friend	*Cuius conversatio non habet amaritudinem*	與爾遊徃，未嘗有厭者
	In cuius amicitia est delectatio bona	與爾交友，有善樂者
	Cuius convictus habet laetitiam & gaudium	與爾同席有安樂者
	Habitans in nobis	與世遊王者
	Cuius haereditas super mel & favum	爾之遺物，勝于甘美
	Cuius Spiritus super mel dulcis	爾之神氣甘于蜜
	Spiritalis dulcedo in proprio fonte degustata	神飴嘗於本原者
7th graces	*Caro Christi pro mundi vita*	耶穌聖體，人之性命者
	Dulcedo magna timentibus Dominum	敬畏主者之大慰
	Memoria mirabilium Dei	天主奇異諸事之標蹟
	Memoriale praecipuum divini amoris	天主仁愛之首榜者
	Donum transcendens omnem plenitudinem	恩賜之第一恩賜者
	Vera propiciatio pro peccatis nostris	吾眾罪之恩赦者
	Divinae affluentia largitatis	天主恩惠之流溢
	Vinculu charitatis	仁愛之連合
	In quo omnis spes vitae & virtutis	吾生吾德，諸望所從出者
	In quo omnis gratia viae & veritatis	眞道正學之恩所繇來者
8th merit for the deceased	*Viaticum in Domino morientium*	以德終者升天之資
	Pignus futurae gloriae	身後眞福之質當

The category "food & drink" contains ten titles, most of which are based on the biblical verses. The title "the hidden Manna" (*yincang zhi mana* 隱藏之瑪納, *Manna absconditu*) is followed by a note explaining that "Manna is a miraculous food descended from heaven in ancient times," based on Exodus 16:4.[220] On 24 June 1634 (Chongzhen 7.5.29), Aleni told the Chinese Catholics in Haikou how the Lord of Heaven descended manna from heaven to feed the Israelites in the wilderness. He pointed out that this food in the Old Testament was considered the prefiguration of the holy body (*shengti zhi yuxiang* 聖體之豫象) by the Catholic theologians.[221] Aleni translated *praefiguratio* as

220   "瑪納者，古時自天降來奇糧。" Aleni, *Shengti daowen*, fol. 2b9, 291.
221   "有天上降來之糧，名瑪納者，食之人人皆可得飽，⋯⋯ 後賢推論此事，正

"*yuxiang* 豫象" and talked about the exegesis by prefiguration which was new to the Chinese.[222]

The title "the food of angels" (*tianshen zhi liang* 天神之糧, *Angelorum esca*) is based on Sapientiae 16:20, a verse referring to manna in Exodus 16. The explanation of the Host was one of the few occasions where Chinese Catholics in late Ming and early Qing caught a glimpse of the Old Testament.[223] In *Treatise on the Holy Body*, Aleni wrote the section "The Prefiguration of the Holy Body in the Ancient Scriptures" (*gujing shengti yuxiang* 古經聖體預像). The word "*gujing* 古經" refers to the Old Testament and "*yuxiang* 預像" is the variant of "*yuxiang* 豫象". In this section, Aleni discussed Exodus 16:1–4 and John 6:32–51, explaining that manna is the figuration of the holy body predicted by the Lord of Heaven (*tianzhu yuzhi shengti zhi xiang* 天主預指聖體之像).[224]

The title "the food that generously nourishes human beings" (*houyang ren zhi liang zhe* 厚養人之糧者, *Panis supersubstantialis*) is based on Matthew 6:11 (*panem nostrum supersubstantialem da nobis hodie*), which is part of the prayer *Pater Noster* taught by Jesus himself. The synoptic verse is Luke 11:3 (*panem nostrum cotidianum da nobis cotidie*). The Lord of Heaven's Prayer (*tianzhujing* 天主經), the Chinese translation of the *Pater Noster*, used the verse in the Gospel of Luke and translated *panem nostrum cotidianum* (our daily bread) as "*wo riyong liang* 我日用糧" (our daily food).[225] As the liturgical prayer in the Roman Missal, the *Pater Noster* used the same biblical verse.[226] In the Chinese Roman Missal *The Meaning of the Sacrifice of Mass*, the prayer is briefly mentioned in the fifth section of the second part: "To recite the Lord's Prayer 'In Heaven our [Father] …' in a loud voice."[227] In late Ming and early Qing, priests recited the *Pater Noster* in Latin while those who attended Mass recited the same prayer in Chinese.[228]

Yet, the title in *Litaniae de V. Sacramento* used the verse from the Gospel of Matthew. Accordingly, Aleni translated *Panis supersubstantialis* (life-sustaining

---

為聖體之豫象。" Li, *Kouduo richao, juan* 5, fol. 25b6–8, 370. Zürcher, *Kou duo ri chao*, vol. 1, v. 34 (Haikou, Saturday, 24 June 1634), 467.

222 Zürcher, *Kou duo ri chao*, vol. 1, v. 34, 468.
223 Zürcher, *Kou duo ri chao*, vol. 1, v. 34, 467.
224 Aleni, *Shengti yaoli, shang juan*, fol. 9a9, 251.
225 There were two frequent variants used in texts in late Ming and early Qing: "*Zhujing* 主經" (the Lord's Prayer) and "*Zaitian* 在天" (In Heaven, *Pater Noster*). For the whole content, see Matteo Ricci 利瑪竇, *Shengjing yuelu* 聖經約錄, in CCT ARSI, vol. 1, 89–90.
226 "Ordinarium Missae," Sodi, Manlio, and Achille Maria Triacca, eds, *Missale Romanum: editio princeps (1570)* (Città del Vaticano: Libreria editrice Vaticana, 2012), 348, no. 1531.
227 "高聲頌主經在天我等云云，" Aleni, *Misa jiyi, juan* 2, fol. 26b6, 625.
228 Dudink, "Manual for Attending Mass," 279, note 242.

bread) into "*houyang ren zhi liang zhe* 厚養人之糧者" in the Litany of Jesus' Holy Body. It is the human soul that the holy body nourishes. Again on 24 June 1634 (Chongzhen 7.5.29), Aleni told the Chinese Catholics in Haikou: "The great grace of the holy body nourishes (*yang* 養) every human being's soul."[229] Earlier on 2 May 1633 (Chongzhen 6.3.25), de Matos also told the Chinese Catholics in Fuzhou: "To nourish (*yang* 養) the flesh with the crops, and to nourish our soul with Jesus' holy body."[230]

The title "the food of life descending from heaven" (*xingming zhi liang zi tian er jiang zhe* 性命之糧自天而降者, *Panis vitae de caelo descendens*) is based on John 6:50 (*Hic est panis de coelo descendens*). The character "*jiang* 降" indicates the relationship between the Host consecrated in Mass and manna in the Old Testament. The title "the living food that benefits us" (*huoliang jianbi wubei zhe* 活糧健裨吾輩者, *Panis vivus nos confortans*) is based on John 6:51 (*Ego sum panis vivus, qui de cælo descendi*). The title "the true drink that makes us joyful" (*zhenyin yue wobei zhe* 眞飲樂我輩者, *Potus verus nos laetificans*) is based on John 6:55 (*Caro enim mea verus est cibus, et sanguis meus verus est potus*). In *Golden Book with Contempt of the World* (*Qingshi jinshu* 輕世金書, ca. 1680), Manuel Dias (Yang Manuo 陽瑪諾, SJ, 1574–1659) translated the same biblical verse into "My body, true food; [my] blood, true drink."[231]

The second category "the feast" underlines the reception of the Host as a communion shared by Catholics as an assembly. In the early church, Mass was called the Lord's table (*mensa Domini*), whereas the title "the holy feast" (*shengyan* 聖筵, *mensa*) particularly refers to the Host.

The third category "the medicine" contains two titles which were familiar to the Chinese in late Ming and early Qing. The first title "the heavenly medicine" (*tianyao* 天藥, *Caeleste antidotum*) has certain Taoist connotation,[232] and the second "the elixir that provides everlasting life and immortality" (*changsheng busi zhi dan* 常生不死之丹, *Pharmacu immortalitatis*) has an even stronger Taoist connotation. The character "*dan* 丹" (elixir) implies the Taoist practice of external elixir (*waidan* 外丹). For a long time, the Taoist believed that everlasting life and immortality (*changsheng busi* 長生不死) can be achieved by taking

---

229 "聖體大恩，人人靈蔦皆得所養也。" Li, *Kouduo richao*, *juan* 5, fol. 26a3, 371. Zürcher, *Kou duo ri chao*, vol. 1, v. 34, 467.
230 "五穀以養肉軀，耶穌聖體以養吾之靈魂。" Li, *Kouduo richao*, *juan* 4, fol. 14b1–2, 282. Zürcher, *Kou duo ri chao*, vol. 1, IV. 15 (Fuzhou, Monday, 2 May 1633), 405.
231 "予体，味眞；血，飲眞，" Dias, *Qingshi jinshu*, *juan* 4, fol. 1a6–7.
232 "乃修齋建醮，相率進香，天桃天藥，相率表賀。" Hai Rui 海瑞, *Hai Zhongjie gong wenji* 海忠介公文集, in *Ming jingshi wenbian* 明經世文編, *juan* 390, Eruson, 2859. "先天藥，後天藥，此是陰陽真妙物。" Li Xiyue 李西月, *Zhang Sanfeng xiansheng quanji* 張三丰先生全集, *juan* 4, Eruson, 85.

elixir.[233] In the end of Han dynasty (202 BC–220), a Taoist book had already recorded a prescription of elixir to achieve everlasting life and immortality.[234] As a variant of *"changsheng* 長生*"* (everlasting life), the word *"changsheng* 常生*"* was much less used in Chinese, however, the Catholic Church in China has been using *"changsheng* 常生*"* since late Ming. Vagnone translated *vitam aeternam* in the Apostles' Creed as *"changsheng* 常生*."*[235] Monteiro called Jesus the tree of everlasting life (*changsheng zhi shu* 常生之樹) in the Litany of Jesus' Holy Name.[236] One possible reason is that the Teaching of the Lord of Heaven wants to differ from the traditional Chinese religions who aim at *"changsheng* 長生*."*

The title "the elixir that provides everlasting life and immortality" resembles *Prescription of Elixir that Revives Human Beings* (*Huoren danfang* 活人丹方, ca. 1630) written by Wang Zheng. *Prescription of Elixir that Revives Human Beings* was published and circulated in the form of a sheet. Huang Yi-long presents the whole text and gives a brief introduction.[237] In the epilogue, Han Lin's brother Vital Han Yun 韓雲 (?–1639) suggested that those who desire everlasting life and immortality (*changsheng busi* 常生不死) consult Wang Zheng.[238] The prescription lists several virtues in analogy with human organs, such as the true heart that worships Heaven (*jingtian zhenxin* 敬天真心), the warm gut that loves human (*airen rechang* 愛人熱腸), and the liver of fidelity (*zhonggan* 忠肝).[239] The elixir in *Prescription of Elixir that Revives Human Beings* is in fact the human being, whereas the elixir in the Litany of Jesus' Holy Body is Jesus.

Still on 24 June 1634 (Chongzhen 7.5.29), Aleni told the Chinese Catholics in Haikou an analogy of receiving the Host.

---

233 "古有煉丹術士鎔冶金石鍛煉藥物，或翼得常生不死之丹，或貪求黃白致富之術。" Qilu Zhuren 杞廬主人, comp., "Huaxue 1 化學一," *Shiwu tongkao* 時務通考, *juan* 24, Eruson, 2547.

234 [Attributed to] Gu Gangzi 孤剛子, *Huangdi jiuding shendan jingjue* 黃帝九鼎神丹經訣, *juan* 1, Eruson, 3–4.

235 Vagnone, *Jiaoyao jielüe, shang juan*, fol. 42a7–fol. 43a6, 207–209.

236 "耶穌常生之樹者，矜憐我等。" Monteiro, *Shenghao daowen*, fol. 4b5, 1072.

237 Huang, *Liangtoushe*, 150–151.

238 "若欲常生不夙，惟用一味拔弟斯摩水，試問之葵心先生。" Huang, *Liangtoushe*, 151. For an introduction of the Han brothers, see Fang, Fang Hao 方豪, *Zhongguo tianzhujiaoshi renwu zhuan shang* 中國天主教史人物傳上 (Beijing: Zhonghua shuju 中華書局, 1988), 254–255.

239 Huang, *Liangtoushe*, 151.

A saint in the past once said: "For good people the reception of holy body is medicine (*yao* 藥), yet for evil people it is poison (*du* 毒); for good people it is the fortitude of everlasting life (*changsheng* 常生), yet for evil people it is the punishment of permanent death."[240]

Although Aleni did not tell the saint's name, the analogy resembles St. Paul's warning in the first letter to the Corinthians: "For anyone who eats and drinks without discerning the body, eats and drinks judgment on himself." (*qui enim manducat et bibit indigne iudicium sibi manducat et bibit non diiudicans corpus*, 1 Corinthians 11:29).

The three titles in the fourth category "sacrifice" are purely Catholic. The first title "a lamb without blemish" (*wudian zhi gaoyang zhe* 無玷之棉羔者, *Agnus absque macula*) is based on Exodus 12:5 (*erit autem agnus absque macula masculus anniculus*). Similarly to manna, the lamb in this biblical verse is the Host's prefiguration in the Old Testament. The second title "the holy object of the holy sacrifice and the chalice of fortitude descendance" (*shengji zhi shengpin ji jiangfu zhi jue zhe* 聖祭之聖品，及降福之爵者, *Hostia sancta & calix benedictionis*) refers to the bread and wine consecrated in Mass. Yet, instead of the common translation "*shengti* 聖體" (the holy body), Aleni translated *Hostia sancta* as "*shengpin* 聖品" (the holy object), and he added "*shengji zhi* 聖祭之" (of the holy sacrifice) to specify that the holy object is consecrated in Mass. Since late Ming and early Qing, "*jiangfu* 降福" (fortitude descendance/to descend fortitude) is the translation of both *benedictio* (benediction) and *benedicere* (to bless). Borrowed from the traditional Chinese ritual term, the character "*jue* 爵" refers to an ancient wine vessel with three legs and a loop handle, used as a ritual object since the Shang dynasty (ca. 1600 BC–ca. 1046 BC). The third title "the one who is the offering himself and the celebrant" (*zi wei xianpin erqie wei xian zhe* 自為獻品，而且為獻者, *Offerens & oblatio*) shows one characteristic of Mass, i.e., Jesus presents himself as the offering and at the same time he celebrate Mass as the high priest. Contrary to the Latin verse, Aleni put "*xianpin* 獻品" (*oblatio*) in front of "*xian* 獻" (*offerens*), and he added the character "*zi* 自" (oneself) to underline the real presence.

The fifth category "the Lord" shows the Lord of Heaven as the ultimately honorable. The word "*yincang* 隱藏" (to hide, *absconditus*) in the title "the Lord of Heaven who hides in order to save the world" (*yincang yi jiushi zhi tianzhu zhe* 隱藏以救世之天主者, *Deus absconditus & Salvator*) echoes the word "*yincang*

---

240 "前聖有云：'人之領聖體也，善者為藥，不善者為毒；善者為常生之福，不善者為永歿之罰。'" Li, *Kouduo richao*, juan 5, fol. 26a6–8, 371. Zürcher, *Kou duo ri chao*, vol. 1, V. 35, 468.

隱藏" (hidden, absconditu) in the title "the hidden Manna" (yincang zhi mana 隱藏之瑪納, Manna absconditu) in the first category. Instead of manna, the one who hides in the fifth category is the Lord of Heaven. Aleni did not translate *salvator* into a noun as "*jiushi zhe* 救世者" (the savior of the world) but attached it to the Lord of Heaven.

In the title "the one who perpetually loves us human beings with the holy love" (*yi sheng'ai yong ai wuren zhe* 以聖愛永愛吾人者, *In charitate perpetua nos diligens*), Aleni added two characters in the translation. Adding the character "*sheng* 聖" (holy), he changed perpetual love (*charitate perpetua*) into the holy love (*sheng'ai* 聖愛) and "perpetual" into "perpetually" (*yong* 永). Earlier in *Humble Attempt at Discussing Matters Pertaining to the Soul* (*Lingyan lishao* 靈言蠡勺, 1624), Francesco Sambiasi (Bi Fangji 畢方濟, SJ, 1582–1649) and Paulus Xu Guangqi 徐光啟 (1562–1633) already used the holy love (*sheng'ai* 聖愛).[241] Later on, in *Methodical Exposition of the Essence of the Faith* (*Jiaoyao xulun* 教要序論, 1670), Verbiest used the same word.[242] Similarly, Chinese Catholics talked about the holy love in their works, such as Cosmas Zhu Zongyuan 朱宗元 (ca. 1615–1660), Wang Zheng, and Han Lin.[243] The second added character is "*ren* 人" (human beings), referring to the relationship between the Lord of Heaven and all human beings. The two added characters indicate the Lord of Heaven's twofold depiction as the ultimately honorable and the ultimately intimate. On the one hand, the Lord of Heaven is a holy and distant God; on the other, he deigns to love human beings.

The title "the substance of the Son who was born" (*feilüe jiangsheng zhi benti* 費畧降生之本體, *Verbu caro factum*) underlines the second Person of the Trinity. The Latin title is based on John 1:14 (*Et Verbum caro factum est*) and Aleni paraphrased the biblical verse in Chinese. He changed the Word (*Verbum*) into "*feilüe* 費畧," the transliteration of *Filius* (the Son). He translated the event of Incarnation (*caro factum*) simply as "*jiangsheng* 降生" (to be born) and added the word "*benti* 本體" (substance) to emphasize that the second Person became a human being himself. One possible reason why Aleni did not give a faithful translation is that the Incarnation was too difficult for the Chinese to comprehend. Today, the biblical verse "*et Verbum caro factum est*" is translated as

---

241 "居於聖愛者則與天主偕，而天主亦與之偕焉。" Francesco Sambiasi 畢方濟 and Xu Guangqi 徐光啟, *Lingyan lishao* 靈言蠡勺, *juan xia*, fol. 6a4–5, in DCFY, vol. 2, 521. "Traité du l' âme humaine," Bernard, *Les Adaptations chinoises*, 337.

242 "天主聖愛原是實實全發之愛。" Verbiest, *Jiaoyao xulun*, fol. 27a7–8, 71. "Exposition méthodique de l' essential de la foi," Bernard, *Les Adaptations chinoises*, 372.

243 Sun Shangyang 孫尚揚, "Lüelun Mingmo shidafu tianzhujiaotu dui qixinyang de bentuhua quanshi 略論明末士大夫天主教徒對其信仰的本土化詮釋," *Beijing xingzheng xueyuan xuebao* 北京行政學院學報 4 (2006): 79.

"the Holy Word became flesh" (*shengyan chengle xuerou* 聖言成了血肉) in the Catholic Church.

The title "the one who treats guests at the feast with the substance as precious food" (*yi benti wei zhenyao yi yanbin zhe* 以本體為珎餚以筵賓者, *Cibus & conviva*) is also paraphrased in Chinese. The word *conviva* describes Jesus as the companion at the feast, which can fit in the sixth category, however, Aleni hid this noun in the translation and added the word "*benti* 本體" again. The Chinese Christian texts borrowed "*benti* 本體" (substance) from Confucianism and attached the Catholic theological connotation.

The sixth category "friend" describes the Lord of Heaven as the ultimately intimate. The neutral word *cuius* (whose) appears in five titles in the category, and Aleni paraphrased it into "*er* 爾" (you), an intimate word used between friends. The five titles describe the intimate relationship between Jesus' holy body and human beings: 1, who interacts with you has no boredom (*yu er youwang weichang you yan zhe* 與爾遊往，未嘗有厭者, *Cuius conversatio non habet amaritudinem*); 2, who makes friends with you has good joy (*yu er jiaoyou you shanle zhe* 與爾交友，有善樂者, *In cuius amicitia est delectatio bona*); 3, who sits close to you has comfort and joy (*yu er tongxi you anle zhe* 與爾同席有安樂者, *Cuius convictus habet laetitiam & gaudium*); 4, your legacy is better than sweetness (*er zhi yiwu sheng yu ganmei* 爾之遺物，勝于甘美, *Cuius haereditas super mel & favum*); 5, your divine Spirit is sweeter than honey (*er zhi shenqi gan yu mi* 爾之神氣甘于蜜, *Cuius Spiritus super mel dulcis*). The title "the itinerant king in the world" (*yu shi youwang zhe* 與世遊王者, *Habitans in nobis*) echoes the title "the substance of the Son who was born" in the fifth category. The Latin title is based on the same biblical verse (John 1:14) yet Aleni paraphrased it differently to underline Jesus as the king.

The seventh category "graces" lists the graces bestowed by Jesus' holy body in ten titles. In the title "Jesus' holy body, life of human beings" (*Yesu shengti ren zhi xingming zhe* 耶穌聖體人之性命者, *Caro Christi pro mundi vita*), Aleni changed "Christ's flesh" (*Caro Christi*) into "Jesus' holy body" (*Yesu shengti* 耶穌聖體), underlining the object in the Litany of Jesus' Holy Body. He changed "for the world" (*pro mundi*) into "of human beings" (*ren zhi* 人之), which indicates the relationship between Jesus and human beings. The title "the first on the board of benevolence of the Lord of Heaven" (*tianzhu ren'ai zhi shoubang zhe* 天主仁愛之首榜者, *Memoriale praecipuum divini amoris*) has certain Confucian connotation. Aleni borrowed the word "*ren'ai* 仁愛" (benevolence) from Confucianism and applied it to the Lord of Heaven's divine love (*divini amoris*). The title "the bond of benevolence" (*ren'ai zhi lianhe* 仁愛之連合, *Vinculu charitatis*) continues applying "*ren'ai* 仁愛" to the Christian charity (*charitatis*).

To the title "the origin of the grace of true way and of orthodox knowledge" (*zhendao zhengxue zhi en suo youlai zhe* 眞道正學之恩所繇來者, *In quo omnis gratia viae & veritatis*), Aleni applied the Confucian notion by adding the character "*zhen* 眞" (true) to "*dao* 道" (way, *viae*) and "*zheng* 正" (orthodox) to "*xue* 學" (knowledge, *veritatis*). The phrase "*zhendao zhengxue* 眞道正學" (true way and orthodox knowledge) indicates that Catholicism conforms with Confucianism. During the apostolate through books in late Ming and early Qing, the Catholic Church used words such as "*zhenjiao* 眞教" and "*zhengjiao* 正教" in order to differ from the so-called "*xiejiao* 邪教" (the pernicious teaching) which was persecuted by the state.[244]

The eighth category "merit for the deceased" contains petitions for the special grace for the souls of the deceased. The title "the provision for ascending to Heaven of those who die with virtue" (*yi de zhong zhe shengtian zhi zi* 以德終者升天之資, *Viaticum in Domino morientium*) means the grace for the deceased good Catholics. Jesus' holy body is the provision (*zi* 資) for human being's soul to enter heaven.[245] On 20 March 1636 (Chongzhen 9.3.14), the day of worship of Jesus Initiating [the Ritual of] the Holy Body (*Yesu ding shengti zhanli* 耶穌定聖體瞻禮, Holy Thursday), Aleni made the analogy of provision to the Chinese Catholics in Yongchun.

> Those who travel a long distance bring the provision in advance. Now we all plan to ascend to Heaven. Since the journey is difficult, Jesus has mercy and gives us the food … We not only dare not to receive [the holy body] but also dare not to not receive [it], thus not being ungrateful to the food of the holy body given by our Lord.[246]

Using multiple negation, Aleni urged the Chinese Catholics to properly receive the food of the holy body (*shengti zhi liang* 聖體之糧).

The title "the pledge of true fortitude after death" (*shenhou zhenfu zhi zhidang* 身後眞福之質當, *Pignus futurae gloriae*) describes the grace for all the

---

[244] Zhang Xianqing 張先清, "'Bailian,' 'wuwei' yu 'tianzhu': Qingqianqi de tianzhujiao yu minjian zongjiao guanxi '白蓮'、'無為' 與 '天主'：清前朝的天主教與民間宗教關係," *Aomen ligong xuebao* 澳門理工學報 1 (2017): 82.

[245] Today, the expression "*shengtian* 升天" usually refers to the ascension of Jesus and the assumption of Mary.

[246] "行遠途者宿齎糧，今吾儕咸擬升天矣，耶穌憫此途之難也，而畀之糧。……非惟不敢領，且不敢不領，以毋負吾主畀此聖體之糧也。" Li, *Kouduo richao*, *juan* 6, fol. 19a7–b2, 423–424. See also Zürcher, *Kou duo ri chao*, vol. 1, VI. 32 (Yongchun, Thursday, 20 March 1636), 506. Zürcher translates the character "*su* 宿" as "for the night," yet this section suggests that "*su* 宿" in this context means in advance.

souls of the deceased. A literal translation of *futurae gloriae* would be "*weilai guangrong zhi* 未來光榮之" (of future glory), however, Aleni used a translation more appealing to the Chinese. In late Ming and early Qing, the Chinese cared about what happened after death (*shenhou* 身後) rather than in the future (*futurae*). Confucianism, Buddhism, Taoism, and popular religions offered various possibilities for the afterlife. The souls of the deceased may transmigrate, become a ghost, or become a god, while the idea that the souls of the deceased may vanish was faint in people's mind. Many people pursued a better life after death and Catholicism offered a new possibility. To enter heaven is the true fortitude (*zhenfu* 真福) whereas other possibilities are false. In *Treatise on the Holy Body*, Aleni made the analogy: "To obtain the reception of the holy body is like to obtain the ticket that ensures the ascending to Heaven after death (*shenhou shengtian zhi fuquan* 身後升天之符券)."[247]

In *Examination on Similarity & Dissimilarity between the Study of Heaven and Confucianism*, Zhang Xingyao used similar expressions.

> [The Lord of Heaven] commanded the apostles to eat the holy body and to drink the holy blood so that they will never die. His method has been passed on, because the Lord of Heaven wants human beings to stay away from sins and to approach good in order to seek the true fortitude of everlasting life (*changsheng zhenfu* 長生真福).[248]

Later in the same book, Zhang Xingyao went further at a theological level: "The Lord of Heaven becomes the offering himself to release the Lord of Heaven Father's anger, and he becomes the offering himself to be received by human beings and to give human beings the ticket for ascending to Heaven (*shengtian zhi quan* 升天之券)."[249] Zhang Xingyao's explanation echoes the title "the elixir that provides everlasting life and immortality" in the third category and "the one who is the offering himself and the celebrant" in the fourth. Later on, Dias continued the similar usage in *Golden Book with Contempt of the World*:

> The holy body which satiates the soul is the pledge of the Heavenly kingdom ... The holy body is the spiritual medicine, which ceases evil and

---

247 "獲領聖體猶獲一身後升天之符券也。" Aleni, *Shengti yaoli, shang juan*, fol. 5b2–3, 244.
248 "以聖體聖血命宗徒飲食可得不死，其法流傳至今，蓋天主欲人遠罪遷善以求長生真福，" Zhang, *Tianru tongyi kao*, 510.
249 "天主以身為祭品以解天主父之怒，又以身為祭品以使人領受，予人以升天之券。" Zhang, *Tianru tongyi kao*, 542.

perfects good, ... when human beings receive the holy body, the Lord becomes the honored guest, the good friend, and the excellent companion.[250]

The forty titles in the petitions of the first group exemplify Aleni's effort to construct an understanding of Jesus as the holy body in Chinese. In order to make the depiction more familiar to the Chinese, Aleni did not hesitate to borrow words from Confucianism, Buddhism, and Taoism. It is necessary to notice that a Chinese Christian text was usually a collaboration between missionaries and Chinese Catholics. Beautifully written, the Litany of Jesus' Holy Body was probably polished by a Chinese Catholic. To propagate Catholic spiritual texts pertaining to Mass, such as the Litany of Jesus' Holy Body, Aleni actively assimilated contemporary Chinese texts and adapted to the Chinese culture.

3   Conclusion

Interacting with the Chinese, missionaries introduced the object of worship in Mass in Chinese society. The Christian communities developed various fresh depictions on the Lord of Heaven, by interweaving the tradition in the Catholic Church with that in Chinese society. For example, they depicted the Lord of Heaven as the Great Father and Mother, human beings as the filial son; thus to celebrate Mass was to express filial piety to the loving parent of all human beings. Some missionaries and Chinese Catholics boldly identified the Lord of Heaven with the heaven in Chinese tradition; some propagated the reception of suffering. All these efforts indicate an inculturation of the Catholic ritual in Chinese society.

Nevertheless, missionaries and Chinese Catholics were confronted with tremendous tension between the two traditions. The debate over the object of worship in Mass incited suspicions and even attacks toward them. Moreover, the missionaries who opposed the tacit agreement to identify the Lord of Heaven with the heaven in the Chinese tradition began heated arguments in Europe as well as in China. As regards terms, the Christian communities in China were unable to reach a unanimous solution that was satisfactory to both Chinese society and Rome. Consequently, the heated arguments of the object of worship in Mass became a crucial issue at stake in the Chinese Rites Con-

---

250   "聖體飫靈，天國劕也。…… 聖體，神藥也，止惡集善，…… 人領聖體，主為上賓、益友、良伴，" Dias, *Qingshi jinshu*, juan 4, fol. 5a2–7.

troversy. Another crucial issue in the Chinese Rites Controversy was sacrifice to ancestors, which is discussed in the next chapter. Chapter two focuses on a major intention offered by Chinese Catholics at Mass: the salvation of the souls of the deceased.

CHAPTER 2

Intention of Worship: Mass for Salvation of the Souls of the Deceased

In the celebration of Mass, human beings not only express gratitude to the Lord of Heaven but also beg him for various intentions. This chapter argues that the salvation of the souls of the deceased as one major intention greatly assisted to propagate Mass in Chinese society. The first section examines the salvation of the souls of the deceased in Catholic funerals, with Mass at the core. The second section reflects on the relationship between Mass and sacrifice to ancestors, where the intention of worship is the decisive element. The third section analyzes the communion of merits, the key notion to propagate Mass as the most efficacious ritual to achieve the salvation of the souls of the deceased.

1 Salvation of the Souls of the Deceased at Catholic Funeral

1.1 *Sharing Concern of the Souls of the Deceased*

To take care of a deceased soul has a long tradition in Chinese society and this spiritual need is served mainly by the institutional religion, such as Buddhism.[1] Both China and India share a huge concern for the deceased. Since its entrance in China, Buddhism introduced and propagated a series of rituals to take care of the souls of the deceased.[2] The Teaching of the Lord of Heaven, another institutional religion in Chinese society, shares the concern for the souls of the deceased.

In the early church, the Christians had already celebrated Mass for the deceased. As the apocryphal *Acts of St. John* (*Acta Johannis*) recorded, some Christians in Asia Minor celebrated Mass for the deceased at the grave on the third day after the burial in 170 AD.[3] In *The Meaning of the Sacrifice of Mass*, Aleni described three general intentions of Mass: to pray, to express gratitude,

---

1 Yang, *Religion in Chinese society*, 301.
2 Stephen F. Teiser, *The Ghost Festival in Medieval China* (Princeton, N.J.: Princeton University Press, 1996), 31.
3 Jungmann, *The Mass*, 217.

and to sacrifice.[4] In addition, Catholics may carry specific desires (*vota*) at Mass which they ask God to fulfill and to save the souls of the deceased was a common desire since the early church.[5] The common tradition of caring for the souls of the deceased helped to propagate Catholic rituals in Chinese society.

The propagation of the care of the soul and its practices in the Catholic Church attracted the Chinese from different social classes. Since Confucianism holds a cautious and conservative attitude toward the afterlife, the literati in Ming and Qing went out from Confucianism (*churu* 出儒) and entered Buddhism (*rufo* 入佛) or even entered Christianity (*ruye* 入耶).[6] In the third and fourth chapters of *Ten Paradoxes* (*Jiren shipian* 畸人十篇, 1608), Ricci explained the Catholic theory of the soul to Xu Guangqi. At the age of 63, this Catholic literatus co-translated with Sambiasi *Humble Attempt at Discussing Matters Pertaining to the Soul* to introduce Aristotle's theory of soul.[7] A seventy-year-old patient in Shanxi 山西 converted because he was attracted by the Catholic teaching on the salvation of the soul. Some Buddhist monks told him that he would become a horse in the next life, and he became extremely worried. Then he heard about the Teaching of the Lord of Heaven, which did not propagate reincarnation. The man told Le Comte the reason why he longed for baptism: "Whatever it takes, I still prefer to be a Christian rather than to become a beast."[8]

In the Catholic Church care of the soul starts when one is alive: "Among the principles of the Holy Teaching, the first is to take care of human's soul."[9] The efficacious practice to take care of the soul is to attend Mass in the church. In *Rules of Prayer to the Holy Body's Benevolence*, Joseph de Mailla (Feng Bingzheng 馮秉正, SJ, 1669–1748) drew an analogy between daily life and the spiritual life:

---

4   "蓋祭或為祈禱，彌撒亦祈禱；或為謝恩，彌撒亦謝恩；或為奉獻，彌撒亦奉獻。" Aleni, *Misa jiyi, juan* 1, fol. 3b1–2, 489.
5   Jungmann, *The Mass*, 217. As one major creation in the Catholic liturgy in the ninth century, the Votive Mass serves for the fulfillment of diverse desires, such as a good harvest, a child, and the salvation of the souls of the deceased. Palazzo, *Liturgie et société*, 104. Since the primary sources in Chinese do not directly mention the Votive Mass, this chapter does not use this term.
6   Li Tiangang 李天綱, "Sanjiao tongti: shidafu de zongjiao taidu 三教通體：士大夫的宗教態度," *Xueshu yuekan* 學術月刊 5 (2015): 120.
7   Sun, *Mingmo tianzhujiao*, 142–143.
8   "Et quoi qu'il m'en coûte, j'aime encore mieux être chrétien que de devenir bête." Lecomte, *Un jésuite à Pékin*, 374.
9   "聖教之理，第一先該管顧人之靈冕。" Brancati, *Tianshen huike*, fol. 51a6, 105.

"The secular work has its market, and the holy work has its hall. Going to the market can nourish the body and going to the church can nourish the soul."[10]

Caring for a deceased soul is a continuation of care for a living human's soul. In the Chinese ritual tradition, care for the souls of the dead mainly focused on the salvation of ancestors' souls. Therefore, the salvation of ancestors' souls became a crucial issue for the Christian communities to interweave the Catholic ritual tradition and the Chinese one. For example, de Mailla combined salvation of ancestors' souls with filial piety: "One should know that to express filial piety to parents is the first responsibility of the Holy Teaching. To only nourish their body and not to save their soul is not true filial piety."[11] In Chinese society the salvation of an ancestor's soul began at the funeral, an occasion where Buddhist monks (*heshang* 和尚) and nuns (*nigu* 尼姑) played a key role in the rituals.[12] To compete with the popular Buddhist funeral rituals, missionaries propagated the Catholic ones with Mass at the core.

1.2 Catholic Funeral with Mass at the Core

In the seventeenth century, missionaries began to propagate Catholic funeral rituals in Chinese society. At first, they performed funeral rituals in a way similar to Europe, with Mass as the central ritual and a priest as the main celebrant.[13] For example, on 11 May 1610 Ricci passed away, and two days later his coffin was moved to the church where a Mass was said, then the coffin was moved back to the residence. On 3 May 1611, the new Jesuit superior in China Longobardo arrived in Beijing. On 1 November All Saint's Day, Longobardo led the Chinese Catholics, including Xu Guangqi, in celebrating Mass for Ricci at the Zhalan er 栅栏儿 cemetery, then they held the entombment ceremony.[14] Several decades later, the Christian communities had to cope with a more complex situation in Chinese society. Due to the lack of priests and other difficulties, local Christian communities and various lay confraternities gradu-

---

10 "俗業有市，聖業有堂。到市可以養身，到堂可以養靈。" de Mailla, *Shengti ren'aijing*, fol. 8b1, 310.
11 "當知孝敬父母，乃聖教愛人之首務。徒養其身，不救其靈魂，非眞孝也。" de Mailla, *Shengti ren'aijing*, fol. 34b5–6, 362.
12 Vincent Goossaert, *Dans les temples de la Chine. Histoire des cultes Vie des communautés* (Paris: Albin Michel, 2000), 15. Buddhist monks' main community function was to assist the souls of the deceased to the underworld, which probably made them relatively better in popular stories than Taoist priests. Philip A. Kuhn, *Soulstealers: The Chinese Sorcery Scare of 1768* (Cambridge, MA: Harvard University Press, 1990), 113.
13 Mass took a long process to become the essential part of Catholic funeral rituals in Europe. Standaert, *The Interweaving of Rituals*, 225.
14 Lin, *Li Madou yu Zhongguo*, 135–136, 142–143.

ally played an essential role in maintaining all sorts of activities, including the funeral rituals. Moreover, the frequency of the celebration of Mass decreased because of the lack of priests. Consequently, the lay-oriented communities grafted Catholic funeral rituals onto the existing family rituals.[15]

This section suggests that although the celebration of Mass became less common at Catholic funerals, it remained a most crucial practice to ensure the salvation of an ancestor's soul. In the late seventeenth century, "Ritual Sequence for Attending Funerals and Organizing the Procession" (*Linsang chubin yishi* 臨喪出殯儀式, 1685), a funeral ritual guideline for the Christian communities, was written by the catechist Antonio Li Andang 李安當 and revised by Leontius Li Anrui 李安瑞.[16] Among four different versions of the guideline,[17] this section examines the later version of "Ritual Sequence for Attending Funerals and Organizing the Procession" and the earlier version of "Ritual Sequence for Funerals and Burials" (*Sangzang yishi* 喪葬儀式).

In "Ritual Sequence for Attending Funerals and Organizing the Procession," statute 1 is a warning about the proper performance of Catholic rituals, which excludes all non-Catholic religious professionals in Catholic funerals. Statute 2 is the actual first step in Catholic funerals.

> When a person in the Teaching leaves the world, it is better that the family members immediately inform a Spiritual Father and ask him to celebrate Mass for the souls of the deceased. They should not inform him late, in case the soul is harmed.[18]

The first step underlines the intention to save the souls of the deceased in Catholic funerals, where Mass is the first suggested ritual. Since late Ming and early Qing, Chinese Catholics called a Catholic priest "Spiritual Father" (*shenfu*

---

15 Standaert, *The Interweaving of Rituals*, 228.
16 Albert Chan marked Francesco Saverio Filippucci (Fang-ji-ge 方濟各, SJ, 1632–1692) as the author but he pointed out that Francesco asked the catechist Mr. Li (Li *xianggong* 李相公) to write the guideline. Chan, *Chinese books and documents*, 204–205.
17 The four versions are: 1, earlier version of "Ritual Sequence for Attending Funerals and organizing the Procession" (*Linsang chubin yishi* 臨喪出殯儀式); 2, later version of "Ritual Sequence for Attending Funerals and organizing the Procession;" 3, earlier version of "Ritual Sequence for Funerals and Burials" (*Sangzang yishi* 喪葬儀式); 4, later version of "Ritual Sequence for Funerals and Burials." For their textual history, see Standaert, *The Interweaving of Rituals*, 140–142.
18 "二、教中人若棄世，其家人即宜先報神父，請神父做彌撒，為先亡之靈魂。不該遲報，免靈魂之害。" Li Andang 李安當, *Linsang chubin yishi* 臨喪出殯儀式, in CCT ARSI, vol. 5, 450. For an English translation, see Standaert, *The Interweaving of Rituals*, 142.

神父), a title implying the close relationship between them and priests.[19] Following the first step, the family members bring the salvation of the souls of the deceased from the familial sphere into the ecclesiastical sphere. The salvation of the souls of the deceased is not purely a familial issue, nor purely a local community issue, but an ecclesiastical one.

The statute 2 in the earlier version of "Ritual Sequence for Funerals and Burials" emphasizes Mass as the immediate practice to save the souls of the deceased from purgatory.

> When a follower of the Teaching abandons the world, it is better that the family members first inform a Spiritual Father and soon ask him to celebrate Mass to pray for the souls of the deceased, which may exempt the soul from the bitterness of purgatory.[20]

In the Buddhist and Taoist rituals, the care for the souls of the deceased already has a remarkable salvific dimension. The family members ask Buddhist monks, Taoist priests, or both at the same time, to save the souls of the deceased from the suffering of the underworld. Missionaries introduced a new type of the underworld in Chinese society and propagated Catholic rituals to save the souls of the deceased from purgatory.[21] The Christian community at Mopan Mountain (Mopan shan 磨盤山, Hubei 湖北) has been observing statute 2 for centuries. When a Catholic dies, the family members immediately go to the church to dedicate a Mass (*xian misa* 獻彌撒) for the souls of the deceased.[22]

Although Catholic funerals excluded all non-Catholic religious professionals, the Christian communities consented to the ritual of the seven sevens (*qiqi* 七七), which was a popular funeral ritual in China. The family members usually invited the Buddhist monks or the Taoist priests at home to perform the

---

19   Later on, the anti-Catholics who did not want to apply "father" to Catholic priests changed the character "*fu* 父" into its variant "*fu* 甫." Today, some people mistake "*shenfu* 神甫" for a respectful title of Catholic priests, which is in fact a derision.
20   "二、奉教者棄世，其家人即宜先報神父，速請做彌撒，為亡者之靈魂祈求，庶免煉罪之苦。" Li Andang 李安當, *Sangzang yishi* 喪葬儀式, in CCT ARSI, vol. 5, 472.
21   The notion of purgatory (*purgatorium*) was constructed around the twelfth century. In the Middle Age purgatory was seen as the place where the souls of the deceased purify their sin. The belief in purgatory is "the process of spatialisation of the thought," an important phenomenon in the history of ideas and mentalities. Jacques Le Goff, *La naissance du Purgatoire* (Paris: Gallimard, 1981), 11–13.
22   Kang Zhijie 康志傑, *Shangzhu de putaoyuan: E xibei Mopan shan tianzhujiao shequ yanjiu, 1634-2005* 上主的葡萄園：鄂西北磨盤山天主教社區研究，1634-2005 (Xinbei: Fu Jen Catholic University Press 輔仁大學出版社, 2006), 306.

ritual.²³ In the seventeenth century, the ritual of the seven sevens was allowed in Catholic funerals with strings attached, as statute 17 reads: "The ritual of the seven sevens is allowed to be in use, as long as all superstitious and pernicious things are removed."²⁴ This concession was made probably for non-Catholic members of the family and lineage, since the Catholic family may clearly abandon this ritual. For example, the Catholic villages at Mopan Mountain have long abandoned the ritual of the seven sevens. In that area, the performance of this ritual distinguishes non-Catholics from Catholics.²⁵

Statute 18 prescribes that attending Mass takes priority over performing the seven sevens: "If the time to perform the seven sevens coincides with the date of Mass, [Catholics] must first go to church to hear Mass and then they can go to the deceased's family to perform the ritual of the seven sevens."²⁶ To attend Mass on Sunday or feast days is a strict rule and no exception is made, not even for a funeral. As the explanation of the third commandment in the Ten Commandments reads: "Whenever it is Sunday and a feast day, it is better to attend Mass."²⁷ Statute 24 reiterates the priority to attend Mass: "The date to carry the coffin to the grave can be fixed by the filial son himself. Nevertheless, it should not impede the date of Sundays and feast days, when [Catholics] go to church to hear Mass."²⁸ The specification of the filial son (*xiaozi* 孝子) implies that this statute is for the funeral of the parent. The statutes in "Ritual Sequence for Attending Funerals and Organizing the Procession" establish a direct connection between the celebration of Mass and the salvation of the souls of the deceased.

---

23 The seven sevens is the period of forty-nine days after the person's death. Every seventh day certain ritual is held until the forty ninth day. In Buddhism the seven sevens assists to achieve the salvation of the souls of the deceased. Ding, *Fuxue*, 48. It is problematic that these rituals are called "masses" in *A Dictionary of Chinese Buddhist Terms*, and to perform them is called "masses are said." William Edward Soothill and Lewis Hodous, ed., *A Dictionary of Chinese Buddhist Terms: with Sanskrit and English Equivalents and a Sanskrit-Pali Index* (Taipei: Ch'eng Wen Publishing Company reprinted, 1975), 10.

24 "十七、七旬之禮，除侵雜邪事可用。" Li, *Linsang chubin*, 456. For an English translation, see Standaert, *The Interweaving of Rituals*, 144.

25 Kang, *Shangzhu*, 310.

26 "十八、若做七的時候，偶遇着瞻禮之日期，先要到堂聽彌撒完，隨後能徃伊家，做七旬之禮。" Li, *Linsang chubin*, 457. For an English translation, see Standaert, *The Interweaving of Rituals*, 144. See also "十八、做七之日偶遇瞻禮之期，先要到聖堂聽彌撒，然後徃喪家做七。" Li, *Sangzang yishi*, 475.

27 Brancati, *Tianshen huike*, fol. 49a3–5, 101. It is also the first rule in *Four Rules of the Holy Teaching*. "凡主日暨諸禮之日宜與彌撒，" Brancati, *Tianshen huike*, fol. 61a3, 125.

28 "廿四、出殯日期，聽孝子自訂。但不要碍瞻禮到堂聽彌撒之日期。" Li, *Linsang chubin*, 460–461. For an English translation, see Standaert, *The Interweaving of Rituals*, 146.

1.3 Best Practices to Express Filial Piety

To further propagate Catholic funeral rituals, the Christian communities proclaimed several best practices to express filial piety, especially Mass. Yet, unlike the traditional Chinese funeral rituals, the Catholic ones bring the salvation of the souls of the deceased into the ecclesiastical sphere. In the traditional Chinese funeral rituals, the transformation of the deceased is from a corpse into an ancestor, i.e., a biologically dead person is transformed into a member of the social continuity, where the family holds the primary place.[29] In Catholic funeral rituals, a transformation of the deceased also takes place from a corpse into a saint in heaven.[30]

Every Catholic is a member of the communion of saints, which contains three states: the living in the world; the dead in purgatory; and the saint in heaven.[31] In Catholic funeral rituals, transformation into an ancestor solidifies the familial bond between the living family members and the dead ones; transformation into a saint in heaven solidifies the local Christian community and strengthens the communion of saints. As Christian Herdtricht (En Lige 恩理格, SJ, 1625–1684) recorded, at a funeral held by non-Catholics there is the comedy at night, whereas at a Catholic funeral Chinese Catholics sit around the coffin and have devout discussions at night. What the congregants do in the funeral is "not only relatives for relatives, but, in entirely communal and universal love, Christians for a Christian."[32] Again, Herdtricht underlined the Catholic funeral not just as a familial issue or a local one but an ecclesiastical one.

In addition to the timing of asking for the celebration of Mass and the date to attend Mass, "Ritual Sequence for Attending Funerals and Organizing the Procession" seems to suggest that the celebration of Mass for the deceased only takes place in the church and the mourner's attendance is not required.[33] Yet, in the introduction to *A Rustic Opinion about Rites* (*Zhengli chuyi* 證禮蒭議, ca. 1670s), Li Jiugong offered another angle to examine the Mass at Catholic funerals for parents.

   See also "二十三、出殯之期聽孝子自定。但勿碍守瞻礼之日為妥。宜於前二日預請教中會長及諸友。" Li, *Sangzang yishi*, 477.
29 Standaert, *The Interweaving of Rituals*, 157.
30 Standaert, *The Interweaving of Rituals*, 155.
31 "蓋聖教之體雖一，而教會之處有三。" Aleni, *Misa jiyi*, juan 2, fol. 28b7–8, 608. These three states of human beings relate closely to the three spaces of the Catholic Church, including the world, purgatory, and heaven. Purgatory, a comparatively new notion, is in-between (*entre-deux*), see Le Goff, *La naissance du Purgatoire*, 16.
32 "Nec solum propinquos ut propinquos, sed amore omnino communi ac universali Xtiani erga Xtianum," "Letterae Annae, Collegium Pekinense, Anno 1677," ARSI Jap. Sin. 116, fol. 217.
33 Standaert, *The Interweaving of Rituals*, 150.

Within the hundred days of the new funeral, while the sad memory is still sharp, one shall often beg the priest to offer sacrifice to the Lord of Heaven, and to communicate merits with the companions of the Teaching [for the deceased]. Either in the church or at home is decided by the host of the funeral.[34]

A Rustic Opinion about Rites prescribes the proper entombment: "In addition to the relatives' accompany to the entombment, the priest and the friends of the Teaching are particularly desired to go to the mountain and to offer sacrifice in order to communicate merits for the deceased."[35] To offer sacrifice (*fengji* 奉祭) is a variant of the celebration of Mass. *A Rustic Opinion about Rites* clearly demonstrates that Mass can be celebrated at the home and the grave as well.

The transformation from a corpse into an ancestor takes place at Mass as well. In the traditional Chinese funeral rituals, this transformation is the passage where a recently deceased and threatening ghost transforms into a stable and venerated ancestor.[36] In Catholic funeral rituals, Mass ensures the salvation of the souls of the deceased and soothes the grief memory of the living. In 1716 (Kangxi 55.9), Carlo di Orazio da Castorano (Kang Hezi 康和子, OFM, 1673–1755) proclaimed that five practices in Catholic funerals are the best way to express filial piety.

> As for the funeral for people in the Teaching, there are the best [practices to express] filial piety. First, to fast; second, to give alms; third, to communicate merits; fourth, to commemorate the deceased in Requiem Masses; fifth, to beg a Spiritual Father to celebrate Masses.[37]

---

34 "當其初喪，百日之內，正切哀思，應多為之求鐸德，奉祭天主，暨諸同教通功。此或於堂於家皆從喪主所便。" Li Jiugong 李九功, *Zhengli chuyi yin* 證禮蒭議引, in CCT ARSI, vol. 9, 103–104.

35 "如本日親人送塋外，尤欲鐸德并同教友上山，為之奉祭通功。" Li, *Zhengli chuyi*, 69. See also Li, "Zhengli chuyi yin," 104–105. The usage of "a rustic opinion" in the title reveals that Li Jiugong hoped leaders in the Catholic Church consider his suggestions. He combined Chinese classics with Catholic doctrines, attempting accommodation in funeral rituals, sacrifice to ancestors, and sacrifice to Confucius. Chan, *Chinese books and documents*, 57.

36 Teiser, *The Ghost Festival*, 13.

37 Despite his negative response to Chinese Catholics on the rites, da Castorano made a sound remark on Catholic funerals in the early eighteenth century. "論教中人喪事，有最好的孝敬。一守斎，二施捨，三通功，四做安所追思，五求神父做彌撒。" Petrus Wang 王伯多祿 et al., *Jingdu zonghuizhang Wang Bo-duo-lu deng shiba ren zhi waisheng getang huizhang shu, gao Kangxi wushiwu nian jiuyue zhuren yu Shandong Linqing daizhujiao Kang shenfu tan liyi wenti* 京都總會長王伯多祿等十八人致外省

Out of the five practices two directly refer to Mass. Early Chinese Catholics had already performed several of the five practices. The Jesuit annual letter in 1619 records the funeral of Yang Tingyun's father Yang Zhaofang 楊兆坊 (ca. 1535–1619). Yang Zhaofang had received baptism three years ago, and before dying he received all the last rites. He told Yang Tingyun to do various charitable works at his funeral for his salvation and to save the entombment expense for giving alms to the poor. In addition to these instructions, Yang Tingyun held a solemn Requiem Mass for his father in a church which belonged to the Jesuits.[38] Likewise, Yang Tingyun's funeral contained two parts which contributed to the salvation of his soul: the first was the charitable work, the second a Requiem Mass.[39]

In late Ming and early Qing, the Christian community entered into the familial sphere by providing Catholic funeral rituals. The entrance brought the family community into the wider Christian community and reaffirmed the family's relation with the wider social circle.[40] Furthermore, the celebration of Mass exerts a different function than other Catholic funeral rituals. When a Catholic dies, instead of inviting a priest into the family, the Catholic Church urged the family members immediately to go to a priest and ask for Mass, whose celebration brings the family into the ecclesiastical sphere. With Mass at the core, Catholic funeral rituals promote the transformation of the deceased from a corpse into an ancestor and into a saint in heaven. These two transformations are not instantaneous upon completion of the immediate funeral rituals. The salvation of a deceased soul requires further ongoing rituals.

各堂會長書，告康熙五十五年九月諸人與山東臨清堂代主教康神父談禮儀問題, in CCT ARSI, vol. 10, 500. In addition to *Requiem*, mass for the deceased can also be called *Missa pro Defunctis* and *Missa defunctorum* in Latin.

[38] Manuel Dias, Wencelaus Pantaleon Kirwitzer, and Nicolas Trigault, *Histoire de ce qui s'est passé à la Chine et du Iapon, tirée des lettres escritesés années 1619. 1620. & 1621, adressées au R.P. Mutio Vitelleschi, general de la Compagnie de Iesus: Traduicte de l'Italien en François par le P. Pierre Morin de la même Compagnie* (Paris: Sébastien Cramoisy, 1625), 43–44. This annual letter is translated from Italian to French. In fact, its content is the same with a Jesuit annual letter in 1618 written in Portugal. Dong Shaoxin 董少新 and Liu Geng 劉耿, trans., annot., "1618 nian Yesuhui Zhongguo nianxin yizhu bing xu shang 1618 年耶穌會中國年信譯注並序（上）," *Guoji hanxue* 國際漢學 4 (2017): 135.

[39] Standaert, *Yang Tingyun*, 94–95.

[40] Yang, *Religion in Chinese society*, 34–38.

2 Relationship between Mass and Sacrifice to Ancestors

Among various traditional Chinese rituals, sacrificing to ancestors is the most common for continuing to advance the salvation of the souls of the deceased. Therefore, dealing with sacrifice to ancestors became one crucial issue to the Christian communities in late Ming and early Qing. Since the early stage of the mission in China, missionaries and Chinese Catholics had made a number of analyses of sacrifice to ancestors. Later in the Chinese Rites Controversy, the polemic on traditional Chinese sacrificial rituals became even more heated. These analyses usually discuss sacrifice to ancestors and sacrifice to Confucius together. Since the latter, a tremendous issue by itself, is beyond the field of this section, the focus remains on the former.

In this section, I argue that the salvation of an ancestor's soul served as an essential intention to build a connection between Mass and sacrifice to ancestors. This section translates the term "*jizu* 祭祖" as sacrifice to ancestors, thus showing its literary resemblance in Chinese with Mass. It is noteworthy that missionaries and Chinese Catholics did not deny Mass as a sacrifice, that they did not totally divide it and the traditional Chinese sacrifices, regardless of their attitude toward the latter.[41] In the seventeenth century, missionaries and Chinese Catholics tended to compare and contrast sacrifice to ancestors with the Mass. In their analyses, the intention of worship was the decisive element that justified sacrifice to ancestors, distinguished it from Mass, and connected it with Mass.

2.1 *Disadvantages of Forbidding Sacrifice to Ancestors*

It was difficult for the Christian communities to decide which traditional Chinese rituals can be allowed and which have to be abandoned.[42] For Chinese Catholics and the missionaries who knew about Chinese society, the disadvantages of forbidding sacrifice to ancestors were very clear. Yet, the newly arrived mendicant orders wanted to replace this traditional ritual with Catholic ones. In the history of church, it happened that Mass replaced the ancient sacrifice to the deceased, such as *refrigerium* (the funerary banquet) in the Latin tradi-

---

41 According to Wang Ding'an, certain missionaries and Chinese Catholics denied Mass as a sacrifice and totally divided Mass and traditional Chinese sacrifices. Wang Ding'an 王定安, "Misa shifou jisi: Mingqing zhi ji bei yizhi huati zhi chongxin zhankai 彌撒是否祭祀：明清之際被抑制話題之重新展開," *Zhexue yu wenhua* 哲學與文化 46 (Taipei: Zhexue yu wenhua yuekanshe 哲學與文化月刊社, 2019): 107, 115.

42 Zürcher, "Jesuit Accommodation," 58.

tion.⁴³ The ancient Roman ritual as a meal with food and drink can be easily related to Mass, since the Catholic ritual is a symbolic meal. The most ancient celebration of the Eucharist was called the breaking of the bread, which indicated a meal and took the form of a meal.⁴⁴

Nevertheless, it was unrealistic to replace sacrifice to ancestors with Mass in late Imperial China. Since the sixteenth century, kinship (*zongzu* 宗族) gradually became powerful in Chinese society and lineage rituals were popularized. Under the reign of the Jiajing emperor (1522–1566), sacrifice to ancestors had obtained a legitimate status.⁴⁵ Therefore, what the Christian communities faced was not only a popular ritual at the local level but also an orthodox ritual at state level. Li Jiugong even considered sacrifice to ancestors "the most important ritual in China since ancient times."⁴⁶

While the Jesuits decided to allow Chinese Catholics to attend sacrifice to ancestors, the mendicant orders criticized the Jesuit strategy. Early in 1635, the Franciscan missionary Caballero debated with Aleni over sacrifice to ancestors in Fujian, attacking the Confucian rituals in public.⁴⁷ In the same year, the Dominicans and the Franciscans forbade Chinese Catholics in Fujian from participating in sacrifice to ancestors. Such a move alienated a number of Catholic men, especially some literati who carried on ritual duties at grand local ceremonies.⁴⁸ In Shandong, since local people accused Chinese Catholics of lacking filial piety to ancestors, Fernandez-Oliver allowed the participation of sacrifice to ancestors.⁴⁹

After hearing missionaries' contradictory decisions and local people's criticism, Chinese Catholics made a series of analyses on the crucial issue. One frequent argument was that to forbid sacrifice to ancestors hinders the Catholic Church in China. In the *Study on Sacrifice to Ancestors* (*Jizu kao* 祭祖考, 1680–1685), Paulus Yan Mo 嚴謨 (ca. 1640–?) cited the *Book of the Rites* (*Liji* 禮記)

---

43   *Refrigerium* is the memorial meal eaten at the graveside of the deceased, probably without reference to a fixed day. Jungmann, *The Mass*, 218.
44   Josef A. Jungmann, SJ, *La liturgie des premiers siècles jusqu'à l'époque de Grégoire le Grand* (Paris: Cerf, 1962), 54–55.
45   David Faure 科大衛, *Mingqing shehui yu liyi* 明清社會與禮儀, trans. Zeng Xianguan 曾憲冠 (Beijing: Beijing Normal University Press 北京師範大學出版社, 2016), 320–321.
46   "從古迄今，為中邦最重之礼也。" Li, *Zhengli chuyi*, 73.
47   Li Tiangang 李天綱, *Zhongguo liyi zhi zheng: lishi, wenxian he yiyi* 中國禮儀之爭：歷史、文獻和意義 (Shanghai: Shanghai guji chubanshe 上海古籍出版社, 1998), 308.
48   Eugenio Menegon, *Ancestors, Virgins, and Friars: Christianity as a Local Religion in Late Imperial China* (Harvard-Yenching Institute Monograph Series 69, Cambridge Massachusetts and London: Harvard University Press, 2009), 83.
49   Mungello, *Spirit and the Flesh*, 84.

to show that it is the filial son's responsibility to worship the ancestor.⁵⁰ Furthermore, Yan Mo weighed the advantages and disadvantages of performing sacrifice to ancestors.

> If we perform it, the faith of the Holy Teaching is not hindered. If we do not, people who have not yet known the Holy Teaching's profound and delicate ritual only see the appearance. They will definitely slander us and say that we do not acknowledge our ancestors, which is unethical and inhuman. What has been disputed is not an obstacle, whereas what is being hindered is the spread of the Holy Teaching.⁵¹

Yan Mo argued that sacrifice to ancestors should be allowed for the benefit of the Catholic Church in China. In the *Imitation of Sacrificial Rituals* (*Jili paozhi* 祭禮泡製, 1698), Mathias Xia Dachang 夏大常, a catechist at Ganzhou 贛州,⁵² made the same argument: "If the sacrificial ritual is forbidden, the Chinese mind will certainly suspect that people of the Holy Teaching have come to disturb the law of the [Confucian] Teaching."⁵³ The sacrificial ritual refers to sacrifice to ancestors, and the law of the Teaching refers to the Confucian ethics.

The author of *Refutation of the Buddhist's Absurdities* (*Pi shishi zhuwang* 闢釋氏諸妄, ca. 1615–1680) claimed: "It is rumored among the secular people that the orthodox Teaching of the Lord of Heaven does not honor ancestors."⁵⁴

---

50 "《禮記·祭統篇》曰：'孝子之事親也，有三道焉。生則養，沒則喪，々畢則祭。養則觀其順也，喪則觀其哀也，祭則觀其敬而時也。盡此三道者，孝子之行也。'" Yan, *Jizu kao*, fol. 1a–b, 8. For the citation from the *Book of the Rites*, see "*Jitong* 祭統," fol. 2b8–fol. 3a1, Zheng Xuan 鄭玄, annot., Kong Yingda 孔穎達, comm., *Liji* 禮記, vol. 49, Ruan Yuan 阮元, ed., *Shisanjing zhushu* 十三經注疏 (Taipei: Yiwen yinshuguan 藝文印書館, 1981), vol. 5, 830–831.

51 "行之無碍於聖教信德之事。不行之，人未解更有聖教深微之禮，但見其外面，必相誣以不認祖先，大不道，非人類矣。是所爭者無碍之事，而所阻者聖教之行。" Yan Mo 嚴謨, *Jizu kao* 祭祖考, fol. 11b, in CCT ARSI, vol. 11, 28. In this text, Yan Mo rarely talked about the Catholic teaching yet shed much ink on the Confucian teaching. Only at the end of the text, he betrayed his deep concern about the evangelization in China.

52 Standaert, *Chinese voices*, 51.

53 "若禁祭禮，中國人心，必疑聖教中人，來亂教法矣。" Xia Mathias 夏瑪第亞, *Jili paozhi* 祭禮泡製, fol. 1b1–4, in CCT ARSI, vol. 10, 82. Mathias (Ma-di-ya 瑪第亞) is Xia Dachang's baptismal name. Li, *Zhongguo liyi*, 228.

54 "世俗訛傳天主正教，不奉祖先。" Xu Guangqi 徐光啟, *Pi shishi zhuwang* 闢釋氏諸妄, fol. 16b6, in CCT ZKW, vol. 1, 68. This text is attributed to Xu Guangqi, yet the earliest version is from 1670's. It is probably composed by the Jesuits and the Chinese Catholics. Ad Dudink, "The Image of Xu Guangqi as Author of Christian Texts: A Bibliographical

Then, the author explained that the first three commandments of the Ten Commandments teach how to love the Lord while the last seven teach how to love human beings, underlining: "And the first of the [last] seven commandments says to show filial piety to parents. Right after the commandments to love the Lord of Heaven, this is the most important."[55] Since to show filial piety to parents is an important commandment, Chinese Catholics must honor ancestors, however, they should replace the falsehood and emptiness (*jiawei xuwu* 假偽虛物) valued in Buddhism with offering Mass to the Lord of Heaven, doing charitable work, and praying. Not admitting that some missionaries forbade sacrificing to ancestors, the author reasoned from Catholic doctrines and emphasized that Chinese Catholics should honor ancestors through Catholic practices. Still based on Catholic doctrines, missionaries and Chinese Catholics focused on interpreting the original intention of sacrifice to ancestors.

2.2 *Original Intention of Sacrifice to Ancestors*

Since sacrifice to ancestors has a long tradition that can be traced back to ancient China, the early missionaries and Chinese Catholics tried to find out if the ritual's original intention could justify the Chinese Catholics' participation. The intention of the ritual was a decisive element to decide if this traditional ritual could be allowed in the Christian communities. Ricci argued that in ancient time people built ancestral temples as memorials to the deceased family members, however, as time went by people began to pray for blessing and protection.[56] To express great affection for ancestors is permitted but seeking to gain benefit for the living family members by praying to the deceased is not. According to Catholic doctrines, to pray to the deceased is wrong because only the Lord of Heaven can bestow blessing and protection on human beings. In this sense, with the original intention of worship, Chinese Catholics can participate in sacrifice to ancestors.

In fact, Ricci's argument does not totally reconcile with the development of sacrifice to ancestors. Since the Shang dynasty (ca. 1600 BC–ca. 1046 BC), on behalf of common people, the royal family prayed through the souls of the

---

Appraisal." in *Statecraft and Intellectual Renewal in Late Ming China: The Cross-Cultural Synthesis of Xu Guangqi (1562–1633)*, ed. Catherine Jami, Peter Engelfriet, and Gregory Blue (Leiden: Brill, 2001), 115–124.

55   "而七誡之首，曰孝敬父母。誠以愛天主之下，莫如此為重也。" Xu Guangqi, *Pi wang*, fol. 16b8–9, 68.

56   "上古之時，人甚愚直，不識天主，或見世人畧有威權，或自戀愛己親，及其死，而立之貌像，建之祠宇廟禰，以為思慕之跡。暨其久也，人或進香獻紙，以祈福佑，" Matteo Ricci, *Tianzhu shiyi, xia juan*, fol. 54a5–8, 86.

deceased royal ancestors to the High Lord. In the early Zhou dynasty (1046 BC–256 BC), people already believed that ancestors' souls can bestow fortune and misfortune. Throughout history various thinkers had explained sacrifice to ancestors in different perspectives.[57] Some missionaries and Chinese Catholics carried on and developed Ricci's strategy. In the seventeenth century, a tendency to correct the intention of the traditional sacrificial rituals emerged in the Christian communities. Aleni articulated to Chinese Catholics that the deceased are unable to ensure the living's fortune.

> A living person, whose eyes can see, ears can hear, mouth can talk, hands can hold, and feet can walk, is unable to bless the descendants with wealth or nobility. How can the person after death, whose eyes cannot see, ears cannot hear, mouth cannot talk, hands cannot hold, and feet cannot walk, be able to bless the descendants with wealth or nobility? Isn't it a delusion?[58]

Therefore, Chinese Catholics can commemorate ancestors but should not ask for blessing. Accordingly, some Chinese Catholics adjusted the intention of sacrifice to ancestors. Yan Mo confirmed that "to sacrifice to ancestors is only to commemorate them, without the intention to beg for any good fortune."[59] Xia Dachang cited the chapter *Tangong pian* 檀弓篇 of *Book of the Rites* to explain that "the heart of the Chinese who offers sacrifice clearly knows that the deceased has no authority or power ... The sacrifice has no intention to beg for good fortune."[60] Li Jiugong pointed out that since all fortune and blessing come from the Lord of Heaven, ancestors are unable to bestow any fortune, moreover, "what [sacrifice to ancestors] values is to repay not to pray."[61]

Furthermore, Chinese Catholics claimed that there is no actual presence of ancestors during the sacrificial ritual, therefore it is not an actual sacrifice. One sentence from the *Analects* (*Lunyu* 論語) is common in their analyses of sac-

---

57 Sun, *Mingmo tianzhujiao*, 10–11.
58 "人之生也，目能視，耳能聽，口能言，手足能持行，而不能庇其子孫，或富且貴。岂既死之後，目不能視，耳不能聽，口不能言，手足不能持行，而能庇子孫以富貴，岂不惑哉？" Li, *Kouduo richao, juan* 1, fol. 8b7–fol. 10a5, 52–55. Zürcher, *Kou duo ri chao*, vol. 1, I. 15 (Fuzhou, Sunday, 28 April 1630), 214.
59 "祭祖宗，止為思念妣者之意，並無求福也。" Yan, *Jizu kao*, fol. 10a, 25.
60 "《檀弓篇》第五十葉云：'惟祭祀之禮，主人自盡焉耳，岂知神之所饗，亦以主人有齊敬之心也。'……可知中國奉祭之心，明知死者，並無權柄力量也。……祭祀非為求福矣。" Xia, *Jili paozhi*, fol. 2a3–6, 83.
61 "主報不主祈也，" Li, *Zhengli chuyi*, 79. See also Li, "Zhengli chuyi yin," 109.

rifice to ancestors. Yan Mo cited the sentence twice in the *Study on Sacrifice to Ancestors*. The first time is the original sentence followed by his own commentary: "The *Analects* says: 'To sacrifice as if they were present (*ji ru zai* 祭如在).' Since it is 'as if they were present,' they are clearly not present."[62] The second time is the original sentence followed by the commentary by Zhu Xi 朱熹 (1130–1200).

> The *Analects* says: "To sacrifice as if they were present." Zhu Xi's commentary says: "The disciples recorded Confucius' sincerity of the sacrifice. Confucius performed sacrifice to ancestors with a heart of pure filial piety. Although the deceased were far away, he commemorated them according to the times. As if their voice and visage were still tangible, he worshiped them with a heart of ultimately filial piety."[63]

The sentence "to sacrifice as if they were present" also appeared in Catholic ritual practices. On 10 April 1718, Fernandez-Oliver held the funeral of Girolamo Franchi (Fang Quanji 方全紀, SJ, 1667–1718) at the West Hall in Ji'nan. The funeral's floor plan drawn by Matteo Ripa (Ma Guoxian 馬國賢, SJ, 1682–1746) shows that the inscription of "as if they were present" (*ru zai* 如在) was hung right above the altar.[64] The missionaries omitted the character "*ji* 祭" (to sacrifice) to avoid the implication of sacrifice to ancestors. In addition, the floor plan shows that various offerings were placed on both sides in the church.

---

62 "《論語》'祭如在。'夫以為如在，則不在可知矣。" Yan, *Jizu kao*, fol. 9a, 23. For the citation, see *"Bayi* 八佾," fol. 7a8, He Yan 何晏, annot., Xing Bing 邢昺, comm., *Lunyu* 論語, vol. 3, *Shisanjing zhushu*, vol. 8, 28. See also "是以《論語》記孔子祭先曰'祭如在'。如之云者，明非真有在也。" Li, *Zhengli chuyi*, 74. For the original text and the Latin translation which had been sent to Rome, and an English translation, see Nicolas Standaert, *Chinese voices in the Rites Controversy: Travelling Books, Community Networks, Intercultural Arguments* (Bibliotheca Instituti Historici SI 75, 2012), 53–56. This book focuses on the voices of Chinese Catholics which came from different Christian communities, expressing their understanding of Mass and traditional Chinese rituals. The Chinese Catholics wrote in Chinese, then the missionaries made partial translations and brought them together with the original texts to Rome, as references for its decision on rituals in the Catholic Church in China. For a similar citation, see "所問祭先不過如事生，既無求福免禍之意，聖教原未嘗禁，" Simao Rodrigues 李西滿, *Bianji canping* 辯祭參評, in CCT ARSI, vol. 10, 399.
63 "《論語》曰：'祭如在。'朱注曰：'此門人記孔子祭祀之誠意。孔子祭先祖，孝心純篤，雖死者已遠，因時追思，若聲容可接，得竭盡孝心以祀之。'" Yan, *Jizu kao*, fol. 3a, 11.
64 For the floor plan of Franchi's funeral in the West Church in Ji'nan (7–10 April, 1718), see Mungello, *Spirit and the Flesh*, 97.

Bernardino della Chiesa suspected that the offerings to Franchi indicated a worship to false gods, however, Fernandez-Oliver clarified that the offerings placed at the funeral were not sacrifices to Franchi's soul and that the only sacrifice was offered to God in Mass.[65] Fernandez-Oliver underlined the contrast between the sacrifice offered to God who is present at Mass and the offerings to the deceased, who is not present at funeral.

In addition to the *Book of the Rites* and the *Analects*, some Chinese Catholics considered the Neo-Confucian book *Family Rituals* (*Jiali* 家禮) an authority in Catholic funeral rituals.[66] Yan Mo cited the *Family Rituals* as a major authority along with the *Book of the Rites* and the *Analects*. He gave high praise to the Neo-Confucians in the Song dynasty, especially to Zhu Xi: "No one observes the ancient rituals more strictly than the Song Confucians. [Zhu Xi] wrote the book *Family Rituals*, prescribing most diverse and prosperous rituals for sacrifice and funeral, even more serious than people in ancient times."[67] Yan Mo also cited other Neo-Confucians, such as Zhang Zai 張載 (1020–1077) and Cheng Yi 程頤 (1033–1107).[68]

It is noteworthy that a Chinese Catholic in the seventeenth century gave so much credit to the Song Confucians. The citations and praise indicate a shift in the Jesuit strategy. At first, Ricci criticized Neo-Confucianism as a distortion of the ancient times. Although Neo-Confucianism was already established as the official orthodoxy in late Ming, the creative and open cultural climate allowed critiques, whereas in early Qing, the authority of Neo-Confucianism was strengthened and the cultural climate became more conservative. Consequently, the Jesuits and their Chinese supporters began to harmonize Neo-Confucianism with Catholicism.[69] In his apologetic work, Zhang Xiangcan 張象燦 established the pattern "People denigrate the Teaching of the Lord of Heaven for … however, the *Family Rituals* says …" He first listed the Catholic doctrines which incited criticism then cited the *Family Rituals* to justify them. For example, "Secular people denigrate the Teaching of the Lord of Heaven

---

65 Mungello, *Spirit and the Flesh*, 97–99.
66 Standaert, *The Interweaving of Rituals*, 94.
67 "且最遵古禮者莫如宋朝諸儒。著為《家禮》一書，祭葬之禮極其繁重，比古人有更認真者。" Yan, *Jizu kao*, fol. 9b, 24.
68 Yan, *Jizu kao*, fol. 5a, 15.
69 David Mungello, *Curious Land: Jesuit Accommodation and the Origins of Sinology* (Stuttgart: F. Steiner, 1985), 62. On the one hand, it is worthy of notice that the Jesuit accommodation was "powerfully shaped by internal Chinese developments," that Ricci's strategy had been evolving in the seventeenth century, Mungello, *Curious Land*, 18. On the other hand, it is remarkable that besides all these shifts, "Ricci's basic strategy for a Chinese-Christian synthesis" had been maintained, Mungello, *Curious Land*, 347.

for not feeding hungry ghosts, nor breaking the hell to save the souls of the deceased, nor … however, the *Family Rituals* says: 'Do not perform Buddhist rites.'"[70]

Yang Tingyun exemplified by practice how much Chinese Catholics acknowledged the authority of the *Family Rituals*. Relatives and friends persuaded him to perform Buddhist rituals for his deceased parents. Showing them the *Family Rituals*, Yang Tingyun declared that people should obey rules in this book instead of Buddhist rituals. No one could argue with that and Yang Tingyun held Catholic funerals for his parents.[71] In late Ming and early Qing, the Confucian intellectuals began a movement to rejuvenate orthodox Confucian rituals, consequently, Chinese Catholics claimed that Catholic rituals comply with the *Family Rituals* while Buddhist and Taoist rituals are incompatible.[72] In *A Mirror for Self-Cultivation* (*Lixiu yijian* 勵修一鑑, 1645), Li Jiugong cited Yang Tingyun as a model of how Chinese Catholics should honor parents (*shiqin* 事親).[73]

Chinese people expressed their care for ancestors' souls by various traditional practices, such as the Ghost Festival, burning the paper money, and inviting a Buddhist monk or Taoist priest to the funeral. Yan Mo cited Zhu Xi as the support for not performing the Buddhist rituals on the Ghost Festival: "Master Zhu in the Song dynasty said: 'On the fifteenth day of the seventh month, people employ Buddhist monks to arrange the sacrifice with vegetarian food. I do not.'"[74] Yan Mo further argued that since Chinese people performed sacrificial rituals long before the entrance of Buddhism, "had sacrificial rituals of the

---

70 "一、世人詆天主教不施食、破獄、道場、出殯、洒掃，而《家禮》云：'不作佛事。'" Zhang, *Jiali hejiao*, 288.
71 Ding, *Yang Qiyuan*, fol. 4b5–fol. 5a1, 224–225.
72 Zhang Xianqing 張先清, "Liyi de duihua: Zhang Xiangcan jiqi *Jiali hejiao lu* 禮儀的對話：張象燦及其《家禮合教錄》," in *Xiao lishi: Mingqing zhiji de Zhongxi wenhua xiangyu* 小歷史：明清之際的中西文化相遇 (Beijing: The Commercial Press 商務印書館, 2015), 59–60.
73 Li Jiugong 李九功, *Lixiu yijian* 勵修一鑑, *shang juan*, fol. 26a1–fol. 27a8, in CCT BnF, vol. 7, 145–147. For this compilation of miracle stories in Christian literature, see Erik Zürcher, "The Lord of Heaven and the Demons—Strange Stories from a Late Ming Christian Manuscript," in *Religion und Philosophie in Ostasien: Festschrift für Hans Steininger zum 65. Geburtstag*, ed. Gert Naundorf, Karl-Heinz Pohl, Hans-Hermann Schmidt (Würzburg: Köningshausen & Neumann, 1985), 360.
74 "宋朱子曰：'七月十五，用浮屠設素饌祭。某不用。'" Yan, *Jizu kao*, fol. 7b, 20. See also "且朱子曰：'七月十五，用浮屠設素饌祭。不用。'" Zhang Xiangcan 張象燦, *Jiali hejiao lu* 家禮合教錄, in CCT ARSI, vol. 11, 290. The original sentence is "但七月十五素饌用浮屠，某不用耳。" Zhu Xi 朱熹, *Zhuzi yulei* 朱子語類 vol. 6, *juan* 90, ed., Li jingde 黎靖德 (Beijing: Zhonghua shuju 中華書局, 2004), 2321.

ancient people related to the Buddhist theory? There is no need to consider it."[75] In addition to the original intention, the Christian communities had to distinguish sacrifice to ancestors from Mass.

2.3 Distinction between Mass and Sacrifice to Ancestors

To celebrate Mass is often simply called "*fengji* 奉祭" or "*xianji* 獻祭" (to offer sacrifice) in Chinese.[76] Since the character "*ji* 祭" (sacrifice) is a common usage, certain names of traditional Chinese rituals resemble Mass, including sacrifice to ancestors. To the Christian communities, such resemblance seemed to be a transgression of the Lord of Heaven. To justify sacrifice to ancestors, the Christian communities had to explain the ritual's name. Verbiest distinguished the Catholic rituals to care for ancestors from the secular ones: the former express the true heart and true sentiment (*shixin shiqing* 實心實情) of filial piety for the deceased parents, whereas the latter is mostly empty ritual (*xuli* 虛禮) performed in the secular world.[77] The word "secular" (*shisu* 世俗) implies the distinction between the holy Catholic rituals and the secular non-Catholic rituals, including traditional Chinese rituals. In this regard, sacrifice to ancestors is an empty ritual.

Two Chinese Catholics in Ningde 寧德, Fujian used a similar word. On 16 December 1637 (Chongzhen 10.11.1), Huang Dacheng 黃大成 and Guo Bangyong 郭邦雍 (ca. 1582–1649) apologized the Teaching of the Lord of Heaven before the local official. They directly addressed sacrifice to ancestors as empty words (*xuwen* 虛文).[78] As a main leader in local Christian communities, Guo Bangyong agreed with the Jesuits that the contemporary sacrifice to ancestors violated Confucius' original teachings.[79] Similarly, in *Imitation of Sacrificial Rituals*, Xia Dachang used the empty useless name (*kongshu wuyong zhi ming* 空疎無用之名), however, he argued that despite its seeming resemblance to Mass, sacrifice to ancestors does not ask for any fortunes or worship any false gods, therefore it does not transgress the Lord of Heaven.

---

75 "古人之祭禮亦何關於佛說？不必慮也。" Yan, *Jizu kao*, fol. 8b, 22.
76 Mass has the character of sacrifice, see A. Michel, *Dictionnaire de théologie catholique*, tome dixième, première partie (Paris: 1928), 1058.
77 "則表其致愛致慤，孝敬感恩之實心實情，與夫世俗多行虛禮者，大不同也。" Ferdinand Verbiest 南懷仁, *Tianzhujiao sangli wenda* 天主教喪禮問答, fol. 1b4–5, in CCT ARSI, vol. 5, 496.
78 "有生員黃大成、郭邦雍忿忿不平，直赴本道為夷人護法，極口稱人間追遠祭祀為虛文，惟天主為真實，" Shi Bangyao 施邦曜, "*Fujian xunhaidao gaoshi* 福建巡海道告示," fol. 33b8–10, in *Poxie ji* vol. 2, 251.
79 Menegon, *Ancestors, Virgins, and Friars*, 86.

In the analyses of sacrifice to ancestors, one frequent argument is the distinction between the true sacrifice to the true God and the true sacrifice to the false god. In the *Dialogue on Sacrifice* (*Bianji* 辯祭, ca. 1650–1660), Francisco Varo (Wan Jiguo 萬濟國, OP, 1627–1687) who entered China in 1649 rejected sacrifice to ancestors and sacrifice to Confucius. Based on the works of Thomas Aquinas (OP, 1224/6–1274), Varo considered traditional Chinese rituals superstition.[80] In *Summa Theologiae* (1265–1274), Aquinas distinguished two species of superstition. The first species is about the mode, when the divine worship is given to whom it ought to be given, namely to the true God, but in an undue mode; the second is about the object, when the divine worship is given to whom it ought not to be given. Furthermore, in the second species of superstition, when divine worship is given to a creature, it is idolatry.[81] Varo claimed that the true ritual can only be offered to the Lord of Heaven and that to offer sacrifice to any creatures is blasphemy.[82]

In *Commentary on Dialogue on Sacrifice* (*Bianji canping* 辯祭參評, 1680–1685) to refute Varo, Simao Rodrigues (Li Ximan 李西滿, SJ, 1645–1704) made a further distinction between Mass and sacrifice to ancestors.[83] First of all, Mass is the true ritual to worship the true Lord (*jing zhenzhu zhi zhenli* 敬真主之真禮). If sacrifice to ancestors considers the ancestors gods, it worships the false lord by the true ritual (*yi zhenli jing weizhu* 以真禮敬偽主), however, sacrifice to ancestors in fact only expresses filial piety to the deceased family members.

As Rodrigues emphasized, to the Lord of Heaven alone shall people perform the internal sacrifice (spiritually) and external sacrifice (materially). Because the internal sacrifice and external sacrifice are unified in Mass, it is forbidden to perform the sacrifice of Mass (*misa zhi ji* 彌撒之祭) to anyone other than the Lord of Heaven. To pray to any creatures with the intention to gain good fortune

---

80 Menegon, *Ancestors, Virgins, and Friars*, 112.
81 Thomas Aquinas, *Summa Theologiae*, II-II, Question 92, Article 2 (Steubenville, Ohio: St. Paul Center), accessed January 28, 2021,
    https://aquinas.cc/la/en/~ST.II-II.Q92.A2.Obj1.
    Later on, Aquinas confirmed that idolatry belongs to superstition. Aquinas, *Summa Theologiae*, II-II, Question 94, Article 1, accessed January 28, 2021,
    https://aquinas.cc/la/en/~ST.II-II.Q94.A1.
82 Wang Ding'an analyzes Varo's *Dialogue on Sacrifice* with the distinction of the superstition made by Aquinas. Wang Ding'an 王定安, "Zhongguo liyi zhi zheng zhong de rujia zongjiaoxing wenti 中國禮儀之爭中的儒家宗教性問題," *Xueshu yuekan* 學術月刊 7 (Shanghai: Shanghai shi shehui kexue lianhehui 上海市社會科學聯合會, 2016): 176. The article focuses on the discussion of Confucian sacrificial rituals in the Chinese Rites Controversy. Since missionaries' discussions often pertained to Mass, the analysis in the article relates to theological thoughts of Catholic rituals.
83 Chan, *Chinese books and documents*, 50–51.

and to exempt misfortune is as if to apply to them the Mass which is the true ritual to the true Lord.[84] Nevertheless, the character "*ji* 祭" (sacrifice) has various meanings in China and the traditional rituals' intention is not necessarily to gain good fortune.[85] Rodrigues confirmed: "The Chinese ritual is neither the true ritual to the false lord nor the false ritual to the true Lord."[86] Although not as grand as the Mass, the Chinese sacrificial rituals are not empty words (*xuwen* 虛文),[87] the same word used by Huang Dacheng and Guo Bangyong.

Holding a positive attitude toward Chinese sacrificial rituals, Rodrigues pointed out the clear distinction between Mass and sacrifice to ancestors but did not criticize the latter.[88] Sacrifice to ancestors "is but instituted by human beings … clearly belongs to human beings. It does not beg for protection of non-human beings."[89] Rodrigues seems to imply that Mass as the true ritual is instituted by the Lord of Heaven Jesus.[90] Based on Catholic doctrines, Rodrigues denied that sacrifice to ancestors is heterodoxy (*yiduan* 異端) and clarified its intention: "[Chinese sacrificial rituals,] such as sacrifice to ancestors and sacrifice to sages, do not worship them as the false lords and do not mingled with heterodoxy. Moreover, the intention is to express gratitude not to pray."[91] According to Wang Ding'an, Rodrigues totally distinguished the Confucian sacrifices from Mass because he wanted to understand the former in the Confucian Classics system.[92]

---

84   Rodrigues, *Bianji canping*, 371–372.
85   Rodrigues, *Bianji canping*, 381.
86   "中國之礼非真礼向於偽主也亦非偽礼向於真主也，" Rodrigues, *Bianji canping*, 382.
87   "吾向言中國祀典不是彌撒，而亦不是虛文。" Rodrigues, *Bianji canping*, 394.
88   "祭先祭聖，果如彌撒之祭主乎？ …… 則其祭祀之礼而非類我祭天主之礼也愈明矣。" Rodrigues, *Bianji canping*, 386–387. This argument was confirmed again, see Rodrigues, *Bianji canping*, 391.
89   "不過人立之也 …… 明屬人類，非求庇於人類之外者等矣。" Rodrigues, *Bianji canping*, 382. See also "蓋其祭只屬人類之情，" Rodrigues, *Bianji canping*, 391.
90   It is Jesus that instituted the Eucharist, thus making Mass the essential ritual in the Catholic Church. "聖教之有彌撒也，命之自天主，傳之至聖人，至為貴鉅。" Aleni, *Misa jiyi, xu*, fol. 5a6–8, 479. "吾主親定，" Aleni, *Misa jiyi, juan* 1, fol. 2b3, 488. "天主降世之後躬定新教祭獻大禮，" Li Mei 李梅, *Haishuidi* 海水滴, *xiapian*, in CCT BnF, vol. 7, 501. "聖教之有聖軀之禮也，亦吾主耶穌之所親定，" Li Mei 李梅, *Juehuo ji* 爝火集, in CCT BnF, vol. 7, 550.
91   "如祀先祀聖非同偽主并無異端可雜，亦但主報而不主祈。" Rodrigues, *Bianji canping*, 391. Li Jiugong declared that the intention is not for fortunes (*qifu* 祈福), see Li Jiugong 李九功, *Lisu mingbian* 禮俗明辯, in CCT ARSI, vol. 9, 38. A clear distinction must be made between the expression of gratitude "*bao* 報" and selfish prayer "*qi* 祈," see Zürcher, "Jesuit Accommodation," 61.
92   Wang, "Zongjiaoxing wenti," 179.

In *Clear Discussion on Ritual and Custom* (*Lisu mingbian* 禮俗明辯, 1670s), Li Jiugong proclaimed loud and clear that it is proper to perform sacrifice to ancestors.[93] Since the two intentions—to worship the Lord and to love ancestors—do not contradict each other, Chinese Catholics can participate in sacrifice to ancestors.[94] Furthermore, the salvation of ancestors' souls is an important intention at Mass: "Ask the priest to offer sacrifice to the Lord of Heaven for the ancestors' souls, either to reduce their punishment for sin in purgatory or to increase their fortitude and joy in heaven."[95] Therefore, the celebration of Mass became a meeting point of the two crucial intentions in the Christian communities.

2.4 Sacrifice to Parents and Sacrifice to the Lord of Heaven

In addition to distinguish Mass from sacrifice to ancestors, some missionaries and Chinese Catholics connected the two sacrifices in various ways. Rodrigues deepened the relationship between Mass and sacrifice to ancestors.

> Today, some Chinese people gradually come to clearly know that Mass is the true ritual (*zhenli* 真禮). As a result, they will also clearly know that sacrifice to ancestors and sacrifice to sages are not the most important and the ultimately noble ritual. Why would there be any obstacles?[96]

The more Chinese people understand Mass, the more they understand Chinese sacrificial rituals. Thus, Chinese people will notice the difference between these two rituals and acknowledge that Mass is the most important and the ultimately noble ritual (*jizhong zhizun zhi li* 極重至尊之礼).

Xia Dachang conceived a potentially dynamic interaction between the two sacrifices. Although he distinguished the name "*ji* 祭" of traditional Chinese sacrificial rituals from that of Mass, he draw an analogy between the two sacrifices: "To offer sacrifice to the Lord of Heaven is to worship him as the Great

---

93 "今當先明孔子祖宗二祭之當行，" Li, *Lisu mingbian*, 31.
94 "庶于敬主爱親，兩者俱可無背矣。" Li, *Zhengli chuyi*, 80. See also Li, "Zhengli chuyi yin," 111.
95 "為之求鐸德祭獻天主，或以消其煉所罪譴，或以增其天堂福樂，" Li, *Zhengli chuyi*, 80.
96 "則今中國亦漸有人明知彌撒為真礼，則亦自然明知祭聖祀先非極重至尊之礼，何相碍之有耶？" Rodrigues, *Bianji canping*, 413. See also "天地之上有至尊者之位 …… 行至尊之礼以敬之 …… 宜設至尊之礼以敬之 …… 以至尊之礼敬至尊之主，" Rodrigues, *Bianji canping*, 410.

Father and Mother of all the creatures, while to offer sacrifice to ancestors is to worship minor fathers and mothers of only one family."[97] By addressing the Lord of Heaven as the Great Father and Mother, the ecclesiastical sphere is combined with the familial sphere.

In *Imitation of Sacrificial Rituals*, Xia Dachang cited various parts of the *Book of the Rites*, such as *Quli pian* 曲禮篇, *Tangong pian* 檀弓篇, *Wangzhi pian* 王制篇, *Liqi pian* 禮器篇, *Jiaotesheng* 郊特牲, *Jiyi* 祭義, *Jitong* 祭統, *Fangji* 坊記, and *Pinyi* 聘義. His explanations are mostly based on the annotations made by Chen Hao 陳澔 (1261–1341).[98] Xia Dachang applied the Catholic doctrines of the supernatural and natural law:

> The supernatural shall repay the Lord of Heaven, and the natural shall also repay parents. To repay, to be grateful, and not to forget by whom we are created, how can such practices prove the sin of offending the Lord of Heaven? Take the sacrifice to honor parents as the introduction of the supernatural sacrifice to worship the Lord of Heaven. It is more clear when applying the analogy of the natural.[99]

Xia Dachang connected the natural (*benxing* 本性) and the supernatural (*chaoxing* 超性) to underline that the intention to repay parents conforms with repaying the Great Father and Mother. Since people repay parents according to the natural, then they shall repay the Lord of Heaven according to the supernatural. In this sense, sacrifice to ancestors serves as an introduction to the sacrifice to the Lord of Heaven. The term "supernatural" (*supernaturalis*) has a strong Catholic philosophical connotation. The supernatural is what exceeds the natural of every creature, yet it does not oppose the natural but perfects it.[100] Xia Dachang developed a classical Thomistic understanding: grace does not destroy nature but perfects it (*gratia non tollat naturam, sed perfi-*

---

97 "奉祭天主者，奉其為天地萬物之大父母。奉祭祖先者，不過奉其為一家一身之小父母而已耳。" Xia, *Jili paozhi*, fol. 6a6–7, 91.
98 Chan, *Chinese books and documents*, 42.
99 "超性固當反本報始于天主，本性亦當反本報始于父母矣。反本報始，不忘所生，豈得證為得罪天主之罪耶？惟取奉祭父母之祭，引入超性奉祭天主之祭，直以本性喻之，尤明矣。" Xia, *Jili paozhi*, fol. 7a1–2, 93. "唯社，丘乘共粢盛，所以報本反始也。" "*Jiaotesheng* 郊特牲," fol. 20b8, *Liji*, vol. 25, *Shisanjing zhushu*, 489.
100 A. Michel, *Dictionnaire de théologie catholique*, tome quatorzième, deuxième partie (Paris: 1941), 2851. Buglio adapted parts of *Summa Theologiae* into the book *Summary of the Supernatural* (*Chaoxing xueyao* 超性學要, 1654–1677).

ciat).¹⁰¹ Combining the traditional Chinese thought with Catholic philosophy, Xia Dachang expounded his method.

> They say that a person shall not forget the one who gives birth to the flesh. We should take this idea and lead it to the other, saying that a person shall especially not forget the one who gives birth to the spirit. They say that a person shall pay homage, express one's emotion, and spare no effort to serve in order to repay parents' grace. We should take this idea and lead it to the other, saying that a person shall especially pay homage, express one's emotion, and spare no effort to serve in order to repay the Lord of Heaven's grace. It is no use to destroy their original nature. We might as well approach their original nature and lead it into the supernatural, then it is useful.¹⁰²

The word "they" refers to ordinary Chinese people, and "we" refers to people in the Christian communities. Xia Dachang took the most advantage of filial piety to connect Mass and sacrifice to ancestors.

When dealing with the resemblance between the Catholic ritual and the Chinese one, Xia Dachang's method is quite feasible. Sometimes, the resemblance is not in the name but in the act. In *Questions & Answers of Sacrificial Rituals* (*Jisi wenda* 祭祀問答, ca. 1680) Ignatius Hong 洪依納爵 discussed the offering of wine to ancestors three times and the raising of the chalice at Mass.¹⁰³

> Someone says that to respectfully offer wine to ancestors three times resembles to raise the chalice at Mass. This saying is more wrong. Because in China the offering of wine is not performed exclusively at sacrifice to

---

101   Aquinas, *Summa Theologiae*, I, Question 1, Article 8, Reply to Objection 2, accessed January 28, 2021,
        https://aquinas.cc/la/en/~ST.I.Q1.A8.Rep2.
102   "他曰肉身之所由生者不可忘，我當從而引之曰：靈性之所由生者，尤不可忘也。他曰致其敬，發其情，竭力從事，以報父母之恩者，我當從而引之曰：尤當致其敬，發其情，竭力從事，以報天主之恩也。徒然破他本性，無用也。不如就他本性，引入超性，乃為有用矣。" Xia, *Jili paozhi*, fol. 7a8–b2, 93–94. "君子反古復始，不忘其所由生也。是以致其敬，發其情，竭力從事，以報其親，不敢弗盡也。" *Jiyi* 祭義, fol. 1a4–5, *Liji*, vol. 48, *Shisanjing zhushu*, 819.
103   The author is probably Hong Ji 洪濟, see Standaert, *Chinese voices*, 51. As the title shows, the text is a series of questions and answers concerning traditional Chinese sacrificial rituals. The missionary is the one to pose questions and the Chinese Catholic is the one to answer.

ancestors. Whenever it is the celebration of birthdays and marriages, the young generation kneel before the honorable elderly and offer them three chalices of wine. The young generation wait until the elderly drink up then kowtow and stand up. This is but an expression of filial love and respect for parents. Do people respect their parents by performing the ritual to worship the High Lord?[104]

Ignatius Hong clearly distinguished the act of offering wine in family events from that of raising the chalice at Mass. Yet, in light of Xia Dachang's method, the act of offering wine can be used as an introduction for Chinese people to understand the act of raising the chalice. Using the resemblance rather than denying it could have made the celebration of Mass more acceptable in Chinese society. Xia Dachang held a very positive attitude toward sacrifice to ancestors: instead of abandoning or merely tolerating the traditional ritual, the Christian communities should encourage it because it is of its great use to assist the Chinese mind to accept Mass. His method of using the resemblance between the two sacrifices is exceptional and inspiring. It is "as a Chinese and as a Christian" that Xia Dachang discussed the crucial issue of sacrifice to ancestors.[105]

2.5   *Practical Intention of Vegetarian Fasting as Comparison*

This section discusses the Christian communities' attitude toward the vegetarian fasting, as a comparison to their attitude toward sacrifice to ancestors. Although fasting is not a remarkable symbol of Catholicism, it is a regular religious practice in Christian communities. For example, both priests and the faithful are required to fast before Mass. In *The Meaning of the Sacrifice of Mass*, Aleni mentioned that if Mass is celebrated in the morning of ordinary days, priests must observe fasting beforehand: "The priest must perform the ritual before breakfast. If he eats anything accidentally, he must not perform the ritual of Mass."[106] In *Instructions of the Priest* (*Siduo dianyao* 司鐸典要, 1676), Lodovico Buglio (Li Leisi 利類思, SJ, 1606–1682) described in detail how priests must observe the fasting to empty his heart (*kongxin zhai* 空心齋).

---

104   "如云恭呈三獻以為類夫彌撒中之舉揚聖爵，此說更非。中邦盖不特祭祖行之，凡于壽誕婚姻，子弟則尊長前，跪獻酒醴三爵，候其飲畢再拜而起。此不過子孫行其孝敬尊親之意，豈亦以事上帝之禮奉其尊親也哉？" Ignatius Hong 洪依納爵, *Jisi wenda* 祭祀問答, in CCT ARSI, vol. 11, 242. For a study of raising chalice, see Dudink, "Manual for Attending Mass," 219, 224, 231–240, 268–269.
105   Chan, *Chinese books and documents*, 42.
106   "鐸德行是禮，必須朝食以前。若偶進飲食，必不得行彌撒之禮，" Aleni, *Misa jiyi*, *juan* 1, fol. 3b8–9, 490.

> To empty the heart means that before the sacrifice, from the hour of midnight to the moment of receiving the holy body, it is better for the priest to empty his heart, that is, not to eat anything or drink anything. Otherwise, he commits a mortal sin, even if he is ill.[107]

Buglio explained the two intentions of this severe rule: "One intention for the Holy Church to establish this abstinence is to adore the holy body; the other is to beg the holy grace for us through love."[108] Those who attend Mass and receive communion must observe the fasting to empty the heart as well, although the rule is less severe.

> From the hour of midnight to the reception of the holy body, it is better to empty the heart, that is, not to eat anything or drink anything. Otherwise, one commits a mortal sin. For those who are ill, it is alright to receive the holy body after eating and drinking.[109]

In *Victory over Fasting* (*Zhaike* 齋克, 1634), Giacomo Rho (Luo Yagu 羅雅谷, SJ, 1592–1638) expounded the Catholic rules of fasting, which require abstinence from meat but not from fish, shrimp, and other aquatic animals.[110] There are two categories of food for human beings, i.e., vegetables (*su* 素) and meat (*hun* 葷). In the category of meat, there is primary meat (*dahun* 大葷), such as birds and beasts; and secondary meat (*xiaohun* 小葷), such as fishes and turtles.[111] Then, Rho pointed out that some practices of abstaining from primary meat are true and some are false.

As for the false practices, some people do not eat blood and meat by nature, which is "fasting by nature" (*xingzhai* 性齋); some cannot eat meat because they are poor, which is "fasting by poverty" (*qiongzhai* 窮齋); some observe

---

107 "空心者，鐸德祭前，自子時正，至領聖體時，宜空心，不吃一粒食，飲一滴水，否則得重罪，雖抱病亦然。" Lodovico Buglio 利類思, *Siduo dianyao* 司鐸典要, *juan shang*, fol. 9 b4–5, in CCT BnF, vol. 19, 32.
108 "聖教會設此戒，一為欽崇聖體；一為我等以愛德求聖寵。" Buglio, *Siduo dianyao, juan shang*, fol. 9b10–fol. 10a1, 32–33.
109 "宜空心，自子時至領聖體，纖食不進，滴水不下，否則得重罪。病危者，飲食後領聖體亦可。" Buglio, *Siduo dianyao, juan shang*, fol. 45a1–3, 103. See also "領聖體，自子正至領時，宜空心，一些食，一滴水，不宜進。" Buglio, *Siduo dianyao, juan xia*, fol. 60b7–8, 274.
110 "飛走肉食，均在所戒。惟水族不與焉。" Giacomo Rho 羅雅谷, *Zhaike* 齋克, *juan* 3, fol. 1a9, in CCT BnF, vol. 19, 577. See also "凡飛走肉食，皆戒。水族不與焉。" Buglio, *Siduo dianyao, juan xia*, fol. 54a8–9, 261.
111 "然葷之中，又鳥獸類，名大葷；魚鱉類，名小葷。" Rho, *Zhaike, juan* 3, fol. 11b9–fol. 12a2, 598–599.

fasting in order to beg for richness and longevity, which is "fasting by avarice" (*tanxin zhi zhai* 貪心之齋); some are deluded by the theory of reincarnation to abstain from killing, and this is "fasting by delusion (*miumi zhi zhai* 謬迷之齋), which produces no merit but commits sin;" some do not eat meat because they find the death of animal miserable.[112] Among these false intentions for fasting, Rho most harshly criticized fasting by delusion referring to the Buddhist theory of reincarnation.

In the Buddhist counterattack against Catholicism, Xu Dashou defended the theory of reincarnation and mocked the abstinence of the Christian communities.

> The barbarians speak of two fasting days during which it is simply allowed to eat aquatic animals, in order to control themselves and to correct their thoughts. Is that true or false? … Moreover, they make fasting purely symbolic and distinguish aquatic animals from meat, considering them vegetables. Isn't it as ridiculous as the custom of Huihui who do not eat pork and only eat meat killed by themselves?[113]

Particularly promoted by Buddhism and some popular religions, fasting has been popular in Chinese society for a long time. Since vegetables are usually the only food allowed to eat, it is rather odd that the Catholic Church allows the consumption of aquatic animals. Yet, local fishermen were happy that Chinese Catholics bought fishes on days to fast.[114]

Some Chinese wanted to maintain fasting by only eating vegetables after converting to the Catholic Church. Whether or not to baptize those who insisted on a vegetarian fast became a major argument among missionaries. In the early 1630's, the Franciscans and the Dominicans, who had entered China more recently, criticized the Jesuits, claiming that they do not give Chinese Catholics a full introduction to the Catholic fasting, and that their loose requirement has

---

112 "戒大葷之意，有真有偽。如人之本性 …… 雖勉強必不能食，此謂之曰性齋，非真有意于齋也；又有家貧，財不能備肉食 …… 此之謂窮齋，亦非有意于齋也；或有從世福起見 …… 此乃貪心之齋，齋而無功者也；又有一種惑于輪廻謬說 …… 此乃謬迷之齋，不但無功，而且有罪者也；或有謂物雖可食，但其濱死痛苦 …… 以小慈而滅大禮，亦非哀矜之實；凡此皆齋之偽者也。" Rho, *Zhaike*, juan 3, fol. 12a3–fol. 12b8, 599–600.

113 "夷言克已正念二齋日，單食水族，是耶非耶？…… 而以齋爲號、又別水族異於牲牷、宜充素食者，與回回之單不食肫、自殺自食之可咲，有何異哉？" Xu, "Qipi," 138–139.

114 "買魚喜有守齋戶。" Wu Li 吳歷, "Yufu yin 漁夫吟," *Sanyu ji* 三餘集, in Zhang, *Wu Yushan ji*, 331.

led some Catholics to disobey basic rules, for instance, not observing the fast before Sunday Mass. One particular criticism was that some Jesuits baptized those who observed fasting by only eating vegetables.

Although their attitude was comparatively more open than other religious orders, the Jesuits did not achieve unanimity on this issue. For some Jesuits, as long as those who observe fasting by only eating vegetables changed the intention of fasting, they are allowed to receive baptism. In 1647, Aleni allowed local people in Wuyi Mountain (*Wuyi shan* 武夷山) who were accustomed to fasting to receive baptism and to keep only eating vegetables. He especially warned that to observe fasting is no longer to worship idols but to adore the Lord of Heaven. According to Aleni's report, many local people converted and became pious Catholics.[115] During the Canton Conference (18 December 1667– 26 January 1668), the rule of fasting by only eating vegetables was still loose. Chinese Catholics can keep only eating vegetables, but they should understand that their fasting is for the Lord of Heaven, not for any gods or buddhas.[116]

Some Jesuits did suggest forbidding those who observe fasting by only eating vegetables from receiving baptism. Whoever desires baptism must first eat meat to break their old abstinence. Adrien Grelon (Nie Zhongqian 聶仲遷, SJ, 1618–1696) analyzed the suggestion from two perspectives. Firstly, from the perspective of Catholic theology, one act has two sides: material act which is the act itself; formal act which is the intention. To consider the specific content of eating only vegetables from the side of material act, the act itself is not a popular practice in the Catholic Church and it is difficult to dispel the Buddhist connotation. To consider the personal intention from the side of formal act, without breaking the abstinence, it is difficult to prove that the intention of fasting is purely for the Lord of Heaven. Secondly, from the perspective of Chinese society, if Chinese Catholics observe fasting by only eating vegetables, Catholicism might be misunderstood as a popular religion. What is even more dangerous is that the state might consider the Teaching pernicious. In fact, when some followers of Manicheism who observed fasting by only eating vegetables were caught, they claimed themselves to be Catholics.[117]

---

115 Thierry Meynard 梅謙立, "Fojiao zhaijie nengfou rongru tianzhujiao—yi 1668 nian Guangzhou huiyi yu Nie Zhongqian de baogao weili 佛教齋戒能否融入天主教——以 1668 年廣州會議與聶仲遷的報告為例," *Foguang xuebao* 佛光學報 *xinsi juan*, 2 (2018): 480.
116 Meynard, "Fojiao zhaijie," 487.
117 Meynard, "Fojiao zhaijie," 492–496.

Most of the Franciscans and the Dominicans strictly followed the Catholic tradition. They forbad Chinese Catholics from attending traditional Chinese religious practices, from sacrifice to ancestors and fasting by only eating vegetables. Yet, other missionaries, mostly the Jesuits, tried to combine the Catholic tradition and the Chinese one, in hope of rooting the Catholic Church in Chinese society and attracting more Chinese converts. In the discussion of whether to keep certain traditional Chinese practices in the Christian communities, it was necessary to identify the intention of practice and to consider the status of the practices in Chinese society. For example, most of the Jesuits allowed Chinese Catholics to participate in sacrificing to ancestors, a practice promoted by Confucianism; yet only some of them allowed fasting by only eating vegetables, a practice promoted by Buddhism.

In order to propagate Catholic rituals in Chinese society, the Jesuits applied a new method to interpret the intention of sacrifice to ancestors. From Ricci's time to Verbiest's, the original intention of sacrifice to ancestors was well justified with the support of the Confucian texts, as well as Catholic doctrines. Moreover, the converted literati examined sacrifice to ancestors from the new perspective of Catholic doctrines, meanwhile they cited the ancient Chinese classics and the Neo-Confucians as main authority. Nevertheless, sacrifice to ancestors was still forbidden because of its suspicious intention and became a crucial issue in the Chinese Rites Controversy.

3 Salvation of Souls of the Deceased in the Communion of Merits

The celebration of Mass is for the living as for the deceased (*pro vivis quam pro defunctis*).[118] According to *The Meaning of the Sacrifice of Mass*, the Lord of Heaven bestows graces on three categories of human beings at Mass, i.e., human beings of the past, of the present, and of the future, referring to the dead in purgatory, the living in the world, and the saint in heaven.[119] Both from the temporal and spatial dimensions, the communion of saints connects the living and the dead "in the unity of one same mystic body whose head is Jesus Christ and in the solidarity of one same life," thus being called the spiritual solidarity.[120] Since for Chinese people the family is composed of the living and the dead, there seems to be a solidarity of the living and the dead in Chinese

---

118 Jungmann, *The Mass*, 224, note 85.
119 "又指已過現在未來之人，盡此三等，無不披吾主之恩澤。" Aleni, *Misa jiyi, juan* 2, fol. 29a5–6, 609.
120 R.-S. Bour, *Dictionnaire de théologie catholique*, tome troixième (Paris: 1908), 429.

society, as well as in the Catholic Church.[121] This section further explores the salvation of all the souls of the deceased in the ecclesiastical sphere.

3.1   Most Efficacious Practices for the Deceased

In the late sixteenth century, missionaries introduced a new notion of the communion of saints (*communio sanctorum*) into Chinese society. Since late Ming and early Qing, the translation of the term literally means the communion of merits of saints (*zhusheng xiangtonggong* 諸聖相通功). The word "*xiangtong* 相通" means to be in communication, to communicate with, interchangeable, and corresponding; marked with Catholic theological connotation, the word "*xiangtonggong* 相通功" means the communication of merits.[122] In the Chinese Christian texts in late Ming and early Qing, "the communion of merits of saints" is often shortened as "the communion of merits" (*xiangtonggong* 相通功 or *tonggong* 通功). Its variant is "the communion of merits through the Holy Spirit" (*shengshen xiangtonggong* 聖神相通功, *communio Sancti Spiritus*).

The Apostles' Creed puts the church and the communion of saints together: "holy and Catholic *ecclesia*, the communion of merits of saints" (*you sheng er gong e-ge-le-xi-ya zhusheng xiangtonggong* 有聖而公厄格勒西亞，諸聖相通功, *sanctam Ecclesiam catholicam, sanctorum communionem*).[123] The variant is "holy and Catholic *ecclesia* [and] the communion of merits through the Holy Spirit" (*you sheng er gong e-ge-le-xi-ya shengshen xiangtonggong* 有聖而公厄格勒西亞聖神相通功).[124] In the section "The Apostles' Creed" (*shi'er ya-bo-si-duo-luo xing-bo-lu* 十二亞玻斯多羅性薄錄, *Symbolum Apostolorum*) of the *Brief Explanation of Catechism*, Vagnone explained the communion of merits through the Holy Spirit by the analogy of one body.[125] People in the Holy Teaching are like hundreds parts of one body which are connected together, therefore "the goodness they do and the merits they gain are communicated with each other."[126]

---

121   For the notion of spontaneous solidarity, see Teiser, *The Ghost Festival*, 13–14.
122   See *Le Grand Ricci* II, 1003. See also Dudink, "Manual for Attending Mass," 275–276, note 232. Dudink's translation of this term is "the communication of merits among saints." Zürcher's translation is "to pass on the merit" and he equals the practice with suffrages, Zürcher, *Kou duo ri chao*, vol. 1, I. 26 (Haikou, Sunday, 3 November 1630), 228.
123   Ricci, *Shengjing yuelu*, 99. See also Brancati, *Tianshen huike*, fol. 37b6–fol. 38a2, 78–79.
124   Vagnone, *Jiaoyao jielüe, shang juan*, fol. 38b7–fol. 40a1, 200–203. The character "*you* 有" acts as a prefix without specific meaning before the adjectives.
125   According to Dudink, Vagnone's explanation reflects the two meanings of *communio sanctorum*: 1, the communion of saints (*sancti*); 2, the communion of sacred goods (*sancta*) or merits. Dudink, "Manual for Attending Mass," 276, note 232.
126   "其所行善，其所得功，彼此相通，""聖神相通功，" Vagnone, *Jiaoyao jielüe, shang*

In a similar section, de Pantoja reiterated the analogy of the church (*e-ge-le-xi-ya* 厄格勒西亞, *ecclesia*) as one living body. In the answer to "what is called the communion of merits through the Holy Spirit," he explained that merits and work made by various parts of the body are shared thoroughly by the whole body.[127] In the answer to "the communion of merits, why does it solely speak of the Holy Spirit," de Pantoja underlined the notion of grace (*e-la-ji-ya* 額辣濟亞, *gratia*): "Since ordinary human beings have eliminated all the sins and their hearts are covered by the Lord of Heaven's grace, they are all favored and loved by the Lord of Heaven. Therefore, it is called the Holy Spirit."[128] Accordingly, people who are excommunicated are addressed as people who break off from the common merits (*tonggong* 同功) of the Holy Teaching.[129] Around 1619, da Rocha gave a similar explanation.

> Master: "How do you explain the communion of merits through the Holy Spirit?"
> Student: "We communicate with each other the virtuous deeds and the merits of praying made by all the people in the church. It is like the human body, when one part is peaceful, all the parts are peaceful."[130]

The communion of merits of saints (*zhusheng xiangtonggong* 諸聖相通功) is an innovative term.[131] The modern translation is the communion of saints (*shengren de xiangtong* 聖人的相通), whereas the translation in late Ming and early Qing added the character "*gong* 功," which acts like a complement or an interpretation rather than a translation. In the various meanings of "*gong*

---

juan, fol. 40a1–b2, 203–204. See also "聖神實相通功," Giacomo Rho 羅雅谷, *Aijin xingquan* 哀矜行詮, *juan* 3, fol. 44a6, in CCT ARSI, vol. 5, 245.

127 "厄格勒西亞，總猶活身也。其中諸聖神者，猶百體也，一身百體，功業雖殊，而其功業之利益，則無不通達於全身。" de Pantoja, "Quan yousheng er gong e-ge-le-xi-ya shengshen xiangtonggong 詮有聖而公厄格勒西亞聖神相通功," *Pangzi yiquan*, *juan* 3, fol. 18b6–8, 162.

128 "凡人既已除一切罪而心被天主額辣濟亞，則皆天主所寵愛者，故謂聖神，" de Pantoja, "Xiangtonggong," *Pangzi yiquan*, *juan* 3, fol. 19b1–3, 164.

129 "絕出于聖教之同功者," Lodovico Buglio 利類思, *Shengshi lidian* 聖事禮典, fol. 67a9, in CCT ARSI, vol. 11, 491.

130 "師：'神聖相通功，怎麼解說？'學：'凡陀格勒西亞中人，所為的德行，所行禱的功，我們皆互相有分通用的。如人身一肢安，眾肢皆安。'" João da Rocha 羅儒望, *Tianzhu shengjiao qimeng* 天主聖教啟蒙, fol. 23b5–8, in CCT ARSI, vol. 1, 422. The word "*shensheng* 神聖" should be "*shengshen* 聖神."

131 As Standaert points out, "It is noteworthy that the Chinese translation of these European concepts is built on the key notion of 'merit' (*gong* 功)." Standaert, *The Interweaving of Rituals*, 157.

功,"¹³² the meaning of merit (*gongde* 功德) is especially crucial in Chinese religious life.¹³³ Since the word "*gongde* 功德" (merit) is a very important Buddhist notion,¹³⁴ one may say that Buddhism had laid the foundation for Chinese people to accept the notion of the communion of merits. The majority people in Chinese society do not have an exclusive religious affiliation. They make offerings to Buddhist monks in order to ensure the salvation of ancestors' souls, because Buddhism teaches that the donations can produce merits for their ancestors.¹³⁵ At the funeral of Xu Dashou's mother, he invited Buddhist monks to his home to pray for his mother's and other ancestors' souls. The Buddhist monks exhorted Xu Dashou that if he wanted great merits (*magna merita*) he had to attack Catholicism.¹³⁶

The Buddhist monks' exhortation is probably a counterattack, because missionaries forbade inviting Buddhist monks and Taoist priests to funerals and they denied the efficacy of the traditional Chinese practices. When seeing someone raising a banner (*fan* 幡) to establish merit (*jiangong* 建功) for the deceased, Aleni laughed at the idea that "someone during his lifetime has gained no merit yet relies on his offspring to establish it on his behalf."¹³⁷ According to Catholic doctrine, only the communion of saints provides a means of the communication between the living and the deceased. The liv-

---

132   Among the ten meanings of "*gong* 功" given by *Le Grand Ricci*, the first one is merit. The meaning of effort and that of effect can also be applied to the term. *Le Grand Ricci* III, 991. For the table of merit and fault (*gongguo ge* 功過格) to record the daily deeds, see *Le Grand Ricci* III, 992.
133   Same as "*gong* 功," the first meaning of "*gongde* 功德" is merit; the second is the liturgical service in Taoism for the souls of the deceased; the third is the merit in Buddhism, as the translation of the Sanskrit word *puṇya*. *Le Grand Ricci* III, 993.
134   "功者福利之功能，此功能為善行之德，故曰功德。又德者得也，修功有所得，故曰功德。" Ding, *Foxue*, 464.
135   Teiser, "Introduction," *The Ghost Festival*, 3.
136   "*In ea Idolo ut continuo ibi demortuo matris animam, aliorumque parentum Diis suis commendarent. Illi eundem hortantur si magna merita colligere vellet, ut Legem Dei, quam Jacobus aliique consanguinei sequebantur persequeretur.*" Thomas-Ignatius Dunyn-Szpot, ms. *Hist. Sin. 1610–1625*, ARSI, Jap. Sin. 107, 222. For a Chinese translation and discussion, see "Daolun 導論," *Shengchao zuopi*, 42. Since the information is provided by the Jesuits, it is unclear whether the word "merit" here contains a more Buddhist connotation or a Catholic one.
137   "比歸途，見有揚幡于道者，先生問曰：'之何為乎？' 允鑒曰：'為亡者建功耳。' 先生笑曰：'生前無功，而待後人建之'," Li, *Kouduo richao, juan* 1, fol. 13b6–9, 62. Zürcher, *Kou duo ri chao*, vol. 1, I. 26 (Haikou, Sunday, 3 November 1630), 228. According to Zürcher, the raised banner is a Buddhist practice to save souls of the deceased. As Zürcher points out, it is difficult for non-Catholics to distinguish Catholic practice of saving souls of the deceased and the Buddhist one.

ing can only gain and share merits with the deceased by attending Catholic rituals while the deceased is unable to offer the living any blessing or protection.

Refutation of the Buddhist's Absurdities criticizes various Buddhist rituals which take care of the souls of the deceased. For "the absurdity of breaking the hell" (*poyu zhi wang* 破獄之妄), if the hell exists, it should be unbreakable. Even if it could be broken, it is unfair to free only one soul for someone's sake. Moreover, there is a huge difference between the rich and the poor to prepare offerings and to invite Buddhist monks, "therefore, who has money survives the hell, and who has no money dies."[138] For "the absurdity of almsgiving [to souls of the deceased]" (*shishi zhi wang* 施食之妄), how can the souls captured in the hell go out? Which place shall they go to, if there is almsgiving both in the east and in the west? "If the souls of the deceased go to every almsgiving, then they would stay in the living world all year round, wandering and eating ... Why bother to establish the hell?"[139] For "the absurdity of the lonely soul without a lord in the blood lake" (*wuzhu guhun xuehu zhi wang* 無主孤魂血湖之妄), the author claimed: "Whether for human or for ghost, the High Lord is their Lord."[140]

For "the absurdity of burning paper" (*shaozhi zhi wang* 燒紙之妄), first, the ghosts have no need of money; second, the burnt paper does not turn into true money; third, before the invention of paper or even money, how poor must the ghosts have been; fourth, since the descendants burn paper for their ancestors generation after generation, "their hearts are hard enough to suppose that their ancestors stay in the hell forever. Is this really filial piety?"[141] For "the absurdity of reincarnation" (*lunhui zhi wang* 輪回之妄), first, if to commit bad karma is that easy, "it takes less than one hundred years for human beings to die out;" second, if the deceased family member is rebirthed as human again, "one's father might become one's son, mother might become wife," which violates the five cardinal relationships (*wulun* 五倫), and if the deceased family member is rebirthed as animal, one might kill the animal and commits parricide; third, since the Catholic notion of soul is different from the Buddhist one, "who believes in the High Lord naturally does not believe reincarnation."[142] The

---

138 "是地獄亦有錢得生，無錢得死也。" Xu Guangqi, *Pi wang*, fol. 2a3–4, 39.
139 "如凡施食之地皆赴，則魂終年在世，饗用優遊，⋯⋯ 地獄之設，不滋多事乎？" Xu Guangqi, *Pi wang*, fol. 2b8–fol. 3a2, 40–41.
140 "無論人與鬼，皆上帝為主。" Xu Guangqi, *Pi wang*, fol. 3b4–5, 42.
141 "忍擬祖父永處於地獄，孝乎不孝乎？" Xu Guangqi, *Pi wang*, fol. 7b8–9, 50.
142 "不百年而人類盡矣 ⋯⋯ 父或為子，母或為妻 ⋯⋯ 信上主，自不信輪廻矣。" Xu Guangqi, *Pi wang*, fol. 10a8–12a3, 55–59.

Christian communities propagated a new and exclusive alternative to save the souls of the deceased in Chinese society.

The Christian communities combined the traditional Chinese notion of merit with the Catholic doctrine of communion to coin the Chinese phrase "*xiangtonggong* 相通功" (the communion of merits), which has been frequently used in the texts pertaining to Catholic rituals. For example, Li Jiugong described how to commemorate a newly deceased Catholic: "The friends [in the Teaching] shall gather and demand the priest to offer sacrifice to the Lord of Heaven for the deceased. In addition, each shall fast and give alms in order to communicate merits to the deceased."[143] Furthermore, the communion of merits closely relates to the Host. In fact, to receive the Host is called the Eucharistic communion. In the *Dictionary of Catholic Theology (Dictionnaire de théologie catholique)*, the Eucharistic communion is discussed right after the communion of saints.[144] In the summary of the institution of Mass in the *Treatise on the Holy Body*, Aleni listed six main meanings of Mass. The third meaning is to show the Lord's ultimate love (*zhiai* 至愛) for human beings. Aleni pointed out the relationship between love and communion: "The essence of love is communion. The truer the love is, the closer the communion shall be."[145] There are three levels of communion: all the universe created by the Lord provides for human beings, this is the communion of creatures (*tong qiwu* 通其物); the birth and the Crucifixion of Jesus save human beings, this is the communion of his merits (*tong qigongde* 通其功德); Jesus instituted the grand ritual to feed people with his own body, which is "the ultimate communion" (*xiangtong zhi ji* 相通之極).[146] The ultimate communion is to receive the Host at Mass, which earlier in *The Meaning of the Sacrifice of Mass*, Aleni described as "to communicate spiritually with the Lord of Heaven, as if we are one body."[147]

The Chinese translation of the Host and that of Jesus' body are identical; this is a firm profession of transubstantiation. Using the plain terminology, the missionaries infused a profound theological teaching into Chinese Catholics' mind. In *The Meaning of the Sacrifice of Mass*, Jesus' body sacrificed on the cross and the bread consecrated at Mass are both called the holy body (*shengti* 聖

---

143 "合眾友，為之請鐸德，祭獻天主，并各行齋施等，以通其功。" Li, *Zhengli chuyi*, 64. See also Li, "Zhengli chuyi yin," 98.
144 H. Moureau, *Dictionnaire de théologie catholique*, tome troixième (Paris: 1908), 480.
145 "其三、以顯其至愛。蓋愛之情在于相通。其愛也彌挚，其相通也彌切。" Aleni, *Shengti yaoli, shang juan*, fol. 4b6–7, 242.
146 Aleni, *Shengti yaoli, shang juan*, fol. 4b6–fol. 5a3, 242–243.
147 "與天主神合，猶如一體，" Aleni, *Misa jiyi, juan* 1, fol. 5a2, 493.

體);[148] Jesus' blood shed on the cross and the wine consecrated at Mass are both the holy blood (*shengxue* 聖血).[149] Verbiest used the identification in the *Answers to Questions about the Holy Body* (*Shengti dayi* 聖體答疑, ca. 1675). Jesus sacrificed his holy body on the cross, then he designated his holy body as the grand ritual of the new Teaching (*xinjiao dali* 新教大禮), which produces unlimited merits (*wuqiong zhi gong* 無窮之功) to atone for the sins committed by people daily.[150] The atonement of sins is one crucial function of Mass. In *Treatise on the Holy Body* (*Shengti yaoli*), Aleni listed sixteen articles to summarize the unlimited graces bestowed on human beings by the holy body. The very first article is "to exempt the sins committed by human beings and to bestow the holy grace."[151] The celebration of Mass is the proper remedy to gain the atonement of sins for the living and the dead.[152] Therefore, Mass is a crucial practice to save the souls in purgatory whose sins are purified through suffering.

It is necessary to note that Mass is not the only practice for the salvation of the souls of the deceased. The Catholic Church approves other efficacious practices, such as prayer, almsgiving, and fasting. Yet, among all the good works done by the living for the deceased, the celebration of Mass holds the pride of place.[153] This long tradition can be traced back to the early Church Fathers, especially Augustine, who acknowledged the efficacy of the suffrages for the deceased.[154] Augustine provided Mass, prayer, and almsgiving as a trilogy of aids for the dead, among which Mass is the first and is called the sacrifice offered at the altar.[155] Gregory the Great (ca. 540–604, papacy: 590–604) affirmed the trilogy of aids for the dead and underlined Mass as the sacred offering of the salvific Host.[156] Aquinas further solidified the trilogy of aids for the dead as "the principal means of aiding the dead" (*praecipua mortuorum sub-*

---

148 The word "*shengti* 聖體" also means the body of Jesus before and after his resurrection, see Aleni, *Misa jiyi, juan* 1, fol. 18b5, 520; fol. 24b5, 532; fol. 26b6, 536.
149 Aleni, *Misa jiyi, juan* 2, fol. 18b3, 588.
150 "吾主耶穌降世，既以無玷之聖體，豎十字架上，奉獻于天主，為萬民重罪之寶價。又以其聖體超貴于萬物，定為新教大禮，令司教者于行彌撒時獻之，卽借其無窮之功，以補贖眾人日日所犯諸罪。" Ferdinand Verbiest 南懷仁, *Shengti dayi* 聖體答疑, fol. 8b4–7, in CCT BnF, vol. 18, 398.
151 "赦免人罪，加以聖寵，一也。" Aleni, *Shengti yaoli, shang juan*, fol. 8a7–9, 249.
152 The Protestant tradition denies the celebration of Mass for the living and the dead, for the absolution of sin, and for penitence. Jungmann, *The Mass*, 132.
153 Michel, *Dictionnaire de théologie catholique*, tome dixième, première partie, 1303.
154 Le Goff, *La naissance du Purgatoire*, 94.
155 Le Goff, *La naissance du Purgatoire*, 113.
156 Le Goff, *La naissance du Purgatoire*, 126–128.

sidia).[157] The suffrage of the Mass contains both sacrifice and prayer. As regards the sacrifice, the Mass profits equally all the souls of the deceased; as regards the prayers, a special Mass for the dead is most profitable for the deceased soul.[158] It is remarkable that in *Description of Mercy on Souls in Purgatory* (*Aijin lianling shuo* 哀矜煉靈說, 1696?), Pedro de la Piñuela (Shi Duolu 石鐸琭, OFM, 1650–1704) cited the trilogy of aids for the dead: "Saint Augustine has said, 'to perform Mass, to give alms, and to fast for the souls in purgatory, the merit is extraordinary and incomparable.'"[159] In addition to theological developments, there was a popular literary genre which reinforced the merit produced by the celebration of Mass: the narration of an apparition of a deceased soul.

3.2 Two Types of Narration of Apparition of A Deceased Soul

In the thirteenth century, a type of narration became popular in the Catholic Church, that is, the apparition to the living of a deceased soul who suffers in purgatory. The deceased soul usually appears to the living to demand suffrages, and sometimes they warn the living to convert from evil in order to avoid the suffering of purgatory.[160] Aquinas denied any communication between the living and the dead, because the souls departed are in a state of separation from the living (*segregatae sunt a conversatione viventium*), however, he explained that an apparition of a deceased soul may happen "by the special dispensation of God; in order that the souls of the dead may interfere in affairs of the living—and this is to be accounted as miraculous" (*per specialem Dei dispensationem, ut animae mortuorum rebus viventium intersint, et est inter divina miracula computandum*).[161]

On 4 March 1631 in Fuzhou, Li Jiubiao asked how the souls of the deceased appear in this world and Andrzej answered that there are two opinions. The

---

157 Aquinas, *Summa Theologiae*, Sup., Question 71, Article 9, accessed January 28, 2021,
     https://aquinas.cc/la/en/~ST.IIISup.Q71.A9.C.
158 Aquinas, *Summa Theologiae*, Sup., Question 71, Article 9, Reply to Objection 5, accessed January 28, 2021,
     https://aquinas.cc/la/en/~ST.IIISup.Q71.A9.Rep5.
159 "聖奧吾斯定有言：'為煉靈行彌撒及施舍、大齋等，其功非尋常可比。'" Pedro de la Piñuela 石鐸琭, *Aijin lianling shuo* 哀矜煉靈說, fol. 1a7–8, in CCT BnF, vol. 24, 257. The publish date is uncertain, see *Aijin lianling shuo* 哀矜煉靈說, the CCT-database, accessed March 19, 2021,
     http://heron-net.be/pa_cct/index.php/Detail/objects/95.
160 Le Goff, *La naissance du Purgatoire*, 241. This type of narration has its prototype since the eleventh century, Le Goff, *La naissance du Purgatoire*, 243.
161 Aquinas, *Summa Theologiae*, I, Question 89, Article 8, Reply to Objection 2, accessed January 28, 2021,
     https://aquinas.cc/la/en/~ST.I.Q89.A8.Rep2.

first opinion is that the devil makes the illusion in the rituals which aim at merits, such as the Taoist offering ritual "*jiao* 醮;" the second is that the Lord of Heaven sometimes allows a deceased soul to temporarily appear.[162] The first opinion opposed traditional Chinese rituals to gain merits; the second follows Aquinas' explanation. On 14 September 1639 in Fuzhou, Li Jiubiao again asked Aleni about the apparition of ghosts. Instead of explaining ghosts, Aleni repeated Andrzej's answer that the Lord of Heaven sometimes allows a deceased soul to appear. Then, he narrated that decades ago in Naples, the Lord of Heaven allowed a deceased soul to rectify the wrongdoing in this world and to ask for the communion of merits (*tonggong* 通功).[163] The story in Naples is an example of the narration of the apparition of a deceased soul, which had been circulated in Europe since medieval times.[164]

In the *Dialogue on Miracles* (*Dialogus miraculorum*, 1219–1223), Caesarius of Heisterbach (OCist, ca. 1180–ca. 1240) recorded an apparition to his friend of a deceased soul in purgatory. The soul of the deceased explains why the offering of Mass is so particularly efficacious for the salvation of the soul: it is Christ that prays in Mass; his body and blood are almsgiving.[165] In this sense, the other two practices in the trilogy of aids for the dead are combined in Mass. Missionaries introduced into China narrations of apparitions of the deceased souls who suffer in purgatory. Various Chinese Christian texts in late Ming and early Qing recorded this type of narration. The four apparitions below further confirm that Mass is the most efficacious practice to save souls from purgatory.

In *Ritual Rules of the Holy Body* (*Shengti guiyi* 聖體規儀, 1658), Brancati recorded eight miracles performed by the eucharistic Host, which is usually called "the holy body" (*shengti* 聖體) in Chinese. The second miracle is about the salvation of a soul in purgatory through the grace of the holy body. A certain Dominican pastor was once praying in the church when suddenly a deceased friend appeared to him. The deceased friend said that he had been in purgatory for fifteen years and begged the pastor to save his soul. Then, the pastor celebrated one Mass for his friend. While raising the Host, he cried and begged the

---

162 "一則魔鬼計較甚多，諸如建功設醮之類，其有幻現諸相者，皆魔鬼所變弄，以誘世人者也；一則地獄中靈魂，天主亦有時暫容其出現，以示靈魂不滅意耳。" Li, *Kouduo richao*, juan 1, fol. 18b3–6, 72. Zürcher, *Kou duo ri chao*, vol. 1, I. 31 (Fuzhou, Tuesday, 4 March 1631), 236.

163 Li, *Kouduo richao*, juan 8, fol. 18b3–6, 72. Zürcher, *Kou duo ri chao*, vol. 1, VIII. 23 (Fuzhou, Friday, 14 September 1639), 604. Li Jiugong included the story in *A Mirror for Self-Cultivation*. Li, *Lixiu yijian, shang juan*, fol. 42b3–fol. 43a4, 178–179.

164 Erik Zürcher suggests that Aleni heard the story in Naples from the Neapolitan Jesuit Francesco Sambiasi. Zürcher, *Kou duo ri chao*, vol. 1, VIII. 23, 605.

165 Le Goff, *La naissance du Purgatoire*, 413.

Lord to save his deceased friend from suffering. At night his friend appeared again and thanked the pastor, saying: "Because of the grace of the holy body, I obtained atonement from suffering in purgatory."[166]

In *Explanation on Works of Mercy* (*Aijin xingquan* 哀矜行詮, 1633), Rho recorded two similar miracle stories that took place in the West. In the first story, a deceased soul appeared to one female relative and urged her to go to the church and to ask the priest to celebrate the Mass three times. The female relative did so and the deceased soul ascended in heaven.[167] In the next story, Aquinas saw his deceased sister in church asking for Mass to save her soul. Aquinas obliged and three days later his sister appeared again, saying: "The Lord of Heaven accepted the merit produced by your offering for me and has commuted my suffering."[168] Rho underlined the notion of merit rather than that of grace and explained that the Catholic Church designates annually the days to perform the merit of praying to the Lord (*xing qizhu zhi gong* 行祈主之功) by celebrating Mass for the souls in purgatory.[169]

In the fourth story, a boy very close to Schall was ill but his parents did not care about him enough. When the boy died, Schall offered for him sacrifices of Mass to God (*pro eo missae sacrificia Deo*). A few days later, after celebrating Mass for the boy, Schall heard a voice calling him "Father" two times when he was barely asleep. Schall woke up and saw the boy standing near his bed with three companions and the boy illuminated his bed with light. Then, Schall heard the boy saying in distinctive voice: "My father and my mother have abandoned me, but the Lord has accepted me" (*Pater meus et mater mea dereliquerunt me, Dominus autem assumpsit me*). Schall emphasized that "the vision is perhaps a hallucination, but not the hearing" (*si visus forte est hallucinatus, non tamen auditus*). As Schall recalled, Michel Trigault (Jin Mige 金彌格, SJ, 1602–1666) saw in a dream that Vagnone only stayed three days in purgatory. Yet, Schall thought that the apparition he experienced is happier and more probable (*laetiora et probabiliora*).[170]

In the apparitions of a deceased soul recorded in the Chinese Christian texts, the suffering soul usually appears to a living family member or a friend and demands Mass for salvation from purgatory. Occasionally, the deceased soul

---

166 "為聖體之恩，我得免煉獄之苦。" Francesco Brancati 潘國光, *Shengti guiyi* 聖體規儀, fol. 19a7–fol. 20a2, in CCT BnF, vol. 18, 347–349.
167 Rho, *Aijin xingquan, juan* 3, fol. 46a5–fol. 47a3, 249–251. Li Jiugong included the story in *A Mirror for Self-Cultivation*. Li, *Lixiu yijian, shang juan*, fol. 41b3–fol. 42b2, 176–178.
168 "天主享爾為我所獻之功，已減我苦，" Rho, *Aijin xingquan, juan* 3, fol. 47a7–8, 251.
169 "聖教中因每歲定日，以本禮為煉處行祈主之功。" Rho, *Aijin xingquan, juan* 3, fol. 47a7–8, 251.
170 Schall, *Relation historique*, 357–359.

demands other practices, for instance prayer, for salvation. In accordance with the genre of narration in Europe, the soul in purgatory appears firstly to the immediate family, siblings, parents, or descendants; secondly to the spouse; thirdly to friends and acquaintances, especially to monastics.[171] Missionaries also introduced another type of narration into China, i.e., the visit of the living to purgatory. The miracle story below is an indigenous example which circulated among Chinese Catholics in late Ming and early Qing.

According to *Clear Evidence of Judgement of the Lord of Heaven* (*Tianzhu shenpan mingzheng* 天主審判明證, 1640), at the midnight of 30 August 1640 (Chongzhen 13.7.14), Yan Kuibin 顏魁賓, an elderly Catholic in Quanzhou, experienced the visit to purgatory,[172] and his son Yan Weisheng 顏維聖 recorded this visit.[173] While in purgatory, a deceased Catholic in Quanzhou Zhang Ergu 張爾谷 asked Yan Kuibin to tell Zhang's family that he demands local Catholics to pray for his salvation from purgatory. After the visit, Yan Kuibin awoke and desired the great grace of the holy body (*shengti da'en* 聖體大恩). In this narration, the deceased soul in purgatory demanded from his family prayer, the second practice in the trilogy of aids for the dead. As for the visitor Yan Kuibin, receiving the Host is the most urgent demand after such a miraculous yet terrifying visit. The mysterious experience of visiting purgatory can incite the living's sense of awesomeness or even the sense of fear toward religion, thus enhancing Chinese Catholics' religious commitment.[174]

In the communion of saints, Mass produces merits both for the living and the dead; and through this ritual, the living share their merits with the dead. With Mass being the most efficacious, the religious practices in the Catholic Church strengthen the relationship between the living and the dead. Solidarity between the living and the dead is reinforced in the family, the local Christian

---

171 The deceased soul usually appears to the living again to confirm the efficacy or the inefficacy of the asked suffrage. Le Goff, *La naissance du Purgatoire*, 393–394.

172 Yan Weisheng 顏維聖, *Tianzhu shenpan mingzheng* 天主審判明證, *Jingjiao yiban* 景教一斑, *juan* 1, in CCT BnF, vol. 23, 207–212. For a translation of the story in English, see Nicolas Standaert, "Chinese Catholic Visits to the Underworld," in *Conflict and Accommodation in Early Modern East Asia*, ed. Leonard Blussé and Harriet T. Zurndorfer (Leiden: Brill, 1993), 61–63.

173 Yan Weisheng was an active Catholic in the Christian community in Fujian, a co-compiler of the third and seventh volumes in *Kouduo richao*. His narrative probably combined the Catholic notion of purgatory with the Chinese notion of hell in popular religion. Pan, *Xilai Kongzi*, 91–92.

174 Sun Shangyang 孫尚揚, "Cong *Kouduo richao* kan Mingmo Fujian tianzhujiaotu de zongjiao weishen 從《口鐸日抄》看明末福建天主教徒的宗教委身," *Hangzhou shifan daxue xuebao: shehui kexue ban* 杭州師範大學學報：社會科學版 vol. 35, 6 (2013): 23.

community, and the whole Catholic Church. Based on the newly-developed theory of purgatory,[175] this solidarity was new and strange in late Imperial China because it broke off the familial sphere. The care of a deceased soul of the family is extended to the care of all the souls in purgatory. Through the communion of saints, merits gained by the living at Mass can be shared with the souls in purgatory.[176] Later on, as the theory of purgatory developed, the living can ask the souls in purgatory to pray for them. In Donger gou 洞兒溝 (the Cave Gully) Catholic village, Shanxi, local Catholics circulated one miracle story about how the souls in purgatory protected the villagers during the Boxer Uprising.[177]

3.3 Statutes of Confraternities Regarding the Deceased

To attend Mass for the salvation of a deceased soul is a frequent demand in statutes of confraternities in late Ming and early Qing. Most of the statutes pertaining to Mass point to the benefit for the souls of the deceased. This section puts these statutes into three categories: for the deceased Catholics who are not members; for the deceased members; generally, for all the souls in purgatory.

In the first category for the deceased Catholics, the priest should be informed as soon as someone dies in order to pray for the newly deceased at Mass. In *Ordinances of the Holy Teaching* (*Shengjiao guicheng* 聖教規程, ca. 1670) for Chinese Catholics in general, Pacheco Feliciano (Cheng Jili 成際理, SJ, 1622–1687) wrote that the deceased's information should be written down and delivered to the priest, such as baptismal name, secular name, and death date.[178] In *Summary of Confraternity Statutes* (*Huigui zongyao* 會規總要, ca. 1650–1700), when it is a Catholic's death anniversary, the members should inform the priest to pray for the soul of the deceased at Mass.[179] In *Rules of Prayer to the Holy Body's Benevolence*, de Mailla wrote that every Monday (*zhanli er* 瞻禮二), Friday (*zhanli liu* 瞻禮六), and Wednesday (*zhanli si* 瞻禮四), the Confraternity of

---

175 Le Goff, *La naissance du Purgatoire*, 315.
176 See "Division du fruit de la messe," Michel, *Dictionnaire de théologie catholique*, tome dixième, première partie, 1310.
177 Henrietta Harrison, *The Missionary's Curse and Other Tales from a Chinese Catholic Village* (Berkeley: University of California Press, 2013), 92.
178 "若終後當寫其聖名、姓字、某日亡故，遣人報知本堂以便彌撒中祈求也。" Pacheco Feliciano 成際理, *Shengjiao guicheng* 聖教規程, Hubert Germain Verhaeren, "Ordonnances de la Sainte Église," *Monumenta serica* 4 (1939–1940): 472. For the attribution to Feliciano, see Verhaeren, Préface, "Ordonnances," 452. Brunner states that the text was promulgated in January 1668, see Brunner, *L'euchologe*, 85.
179 "一、凡遇教中先亡，即通神父。彌撒中祈主為彼靈魂。" Anon., *Huigui zongyao* 會規總要, in CCT ARSI, vol. 12, 476.

the Holy Body's Benevolence celebrates Mass with the specific intention that one Catholic's soul in purgatory will ascend into heaven.[180]

For the deceased members in the second category, in *Statutes of Confraternity of the Holy Mother* (*Shengmuhui gui* 聖母會規, 1660), Humbert Augery (Hong Duzhen 洪度貞, SJ, 1618–1673) wrote that the prefect in the Confraternity of the Holy Mother should ask the priest to dedicate two Masses for a newly deceased brother.[181] In *Statutes of Confraternity of the Third Order of St. Francis* (*Sheng Fangjige disanhui gui* 聖方濟各第三會規, ca. 1582–1840), de la Piñuela wrote that on 2 November, the day to commemorate all the deceased in the Teaching (*zhuisi jiaozhong xianwang zhi ri* 追思教中先亡之日),[182] the members should ask the priest to say one Requiem Mass (*ansuo* 安所, *Missa pro Defunctis*) for all the deceased ones.[183] Members who are wealthy enough can offer some money for the whole confraternity to celebrate Requiem Masses for the deceased ones.[184]

With the Host as its patron, the Confraternity of the Holy Body's Benevolence has more statutes pertaining to Mass than other confraternities. Its two texts *Rules of Prayer to the Holy Body's Benevolence* and *Statutes of Confraternity of the Holy Body* (*Shengtihui gui* 聖體會規, ca. 1582–1719) overlap and complement each other. The members monthly receive the holy body for the deceased members, in order to offer up an indulgence (*dashe* 大赦, *indulgentia*) to the souls in purgatory.[185] Indulgences are the remission of sins, theologically based on the dogma of the communion of saints: "The merits of the head and the members of the church as a whole form an only and same treasure."[186] On 2 November and the seven following days, and every Monday the members cele-

---

180 "又本堂另有恩赦彌撒，可專救教中一煉靈升天。" de Mailla, *Shengti ren'aijing*, fol. 30a5–7, 353.
181 "一、兄弟中有棄世者，會長求鐸德奉彌撒二次，代其補贖煉罪之功。⋯⋯ 以祈大主祐其靈魂安所。" Humbert Augery 洪度貞, *Shengmuhui gui* 聖母會規, fol. 5a1–2, in CCT ARSI, vol. 12, 455.
182 In the middle of the eleventh century, Cluny established the Commemoration of the Deceased in 2 November, and this "Feast of the Dead" had been celebrated soon through the Catholic Church. Since then, the dead have their own day in the Catholic liturgical calendar. Le Goff, *La naissance du Purgatoire*, 171–173.
183 "十四、⋯⋯ 遇追思已亡瞻礼日，求鐸德為本会先亡者做一安所，" Pedro de la Piñuela 石鐸琭, *Sheng Fangjige disanhui gui* 聖方濟各第三會規, in CCT BnF, vol. 20, 177.
184 "有力者，獻些錢与全会之人做安所，或分与貧人，求鐸德做彌撒，求天主保祐全会，加力量恒德。" de la Piñuela, *Sheng Fanjige*, 179.
185 "每月一會之友同為本會亡者領聖體，通大赦于煉靈。" Anon., *Shengtihui gui* 聖體會規, fol. 9b1–2, in CCT BnF, vol. 20, 274.
186 E.T. Magnin, *Dictionnaire de théologie catholique*, tome septième, deuxième partie (Paris: 1923), 1594. The Church doctors in the thirteenth century, especially St. Bonaventure (OFM,

brate Mass for the deceased members to save one soul from purgatory.[187] Every Monday, Wednesday, and Friday, the local church celebrates Mass with the specific intention that one member's soul in purgatory will ascend into heaven.[188]

As one branch of the Confraternity of the Holy Body's Benevolence, the Confraternity of St. Joseph (*sheng Ruosehui* 聖若瑟會) focuses on loving the deceased, so the members follow more statutes in this regard. On the first Sunday of each month, the members must attend Requiem Mass.[189] On any day within 2 November and the seven following days, and every Sunday and Friday, if the members ask the priest to celebrate Mass for the deceased members of the local church, each Mass will save one soul from purgatory to heaven.[190] A similar statute of attending Mass on any day within 2 November and the seven following days, and every Wednesday applies to the Confraternity of St. Francis Xavier (*sheng Fangjigehui* 聖方濟各會), another branch of the Confraternity of the Holy Body's Benevolence.[191] Moreover, *Rules to Communicate Merit with the Deceased in the Confraternity of the Holy Body's Benevolence* (*Wei shengti ren'aihui zhong wangzhe tonggong gui* 為聖體仁愛會中亡者通功規) has six rules pertaining to the deceased members in six ranks.

1, for the Prefect (*zonghuizhang* 總會長), the whole confraternity shall hear three Masses;[192]
2, for vice-Prefect (*fuhuizhang* 副會長), the whole confraternity shall hear two Masses;

---

ca. 1217–1274) affirmed for the first time that indulgences are applicable to the souls in purgatory, see Magnin, *Dictionnaire de théologie catholique*, 1611.

187 "本堂祭臺逢追思亡者瞻禮日，連後七日並每瞻禮二，為本會亡者做一彌撒，救一煉靈。" Anon., *Shengtihui gui*, fol. 2a4, 259. See also de Mailla, *Shengti ren'aijing*, fol. 43a7–b1, 379–380.

188 de Mailla, *Shengti ren'aijing*, fol. 30a5–6, 353. "The local church" in the original text is written as "*bentang* 本堂." Verhaeren translates it as "les curés," see Verhaeren, "Ordonnances," 652. This section suggests that "*bentang* 本堂" in this context signifies the place rather than the person.

189 "每月第一主日做安所，在若瑟會者必到。" Anon., *Shengtihui gui*, fol. 2a4–5, 259.

190 "一、奉聖若瑟主保者，追思教中先亡之日，或追思八日內之一日，或每主日瞻禮六，為籍中亡者，於本堂內求神父行彌撒，每一次可救一煉靈升天。" de Mailla, *Shengti ren'aijing*, fol. 43b7–8, 380.

191 "一、奉聖方濟各沙勿略主保者，追思教中先亡之日，或追思八日內之一日，或每主日瞻禮四，為籍中亡者，於本堂內求神父行彌撒，每一次可救一煉靈升天。" de Mailla, *Shengti ren'aijing*, fol. 43b5–7, 380.

192 Verhaeren translates "*ting misa* 聽彌撒" as "écouter la messe," Verhaeren, "Ordonnances," 475. The phrase "hear Mass" (*ting misa* 聽彌撒) in this section means to attend Mass and does not deny the receiving of the Host.

3, for secretary (*zongbi* 綜筆), doorkeeper (*zongtang* 綜堂), and treasurer (*zong* 綜□),[193] the whole confraternity shall hear one Mass;

4, for the prefect of each subordinate confraternity (*huizhang* 會長), the whole confraternity shall hear one Mass; all members of the same subordinate confraternity shall hear three Masses;

5, for sacristan of each subordinate confraternity (*ge huizhu* 各會祝), the whole confraternity shall pray the Our Father (*Zaitian* 在天, *Pater Noster*) and the Hail Mary (*Yawu* 亞物, *Ave Maria*) seven times for three days; all members of the same subordinate confraternity shall hear two Masses;

6, for the member, the whole confraternity shall pray the Our Father and the Hail Mary seven times for two days; all members of the same subordinate confraternity shall hear one Mass.[194]

The third category considers all the souls in purgatory, including non-Catholic strangers. Since to save the souls in purgatory is a particularly Franciscan tradition, the Third Order of St. Francis bestows enormous generosity in this regard. Its members shall pray unceasingly: "From now on until our death, we will recite prayers, hear Mass, receive the holy body, and do charitable work to gain indulgences. Once gained, indulgences will be shared with the souls in purgatory through our Lord."[195] In another statute, de la Piñuela repeats offering indulgences for the souls in purgatory.

> To see Mass or to recite other prayers, to receive the holy body or to do other charitable work, all indulgences, once gained, should be shared with the souls who are about to leave purgatory, who suffer the most, and who are with no support.[196]

The statute implies that to see Mass (*kan misa* 看彌撒, *videre missam*) contains the recitation of prayers.[197] Instead of family members, relatives, and friends,

---

[193] The word should be "*zongku* 綜庫" according to the pattern on the previous page, yet the character "*ku* 庫" is missing. Anon., *Shengtihui gui*, fol. 6b5, 268.

[194] Anon., *Shengtihui gui*, fol. 7a7–b4, 269–270. For the translation of six ranks, see Verhaeren's translation of officials, "règles des divers officiers: prefect, vice-prefects, secrétaire, trésorier, sacristain, chefs de section et leurs assitants," Verhaeren, "Ordonnances," 647.

[195] "自今至死時，凡我念經，聽彌撒，領圣体並所行善功，有可得大赦者，若得之，俱賴吾主分与煉罪灵魂。" de la Piñuela, *Sheng Fanjige*, 199.

[196] "又為看彌撒或念別樣的經，領圣体或行別樣的善功，凡有大赦，都分与將出的煉灵、最苦的煉灵、無托的煉灵。" de la Piñuela, *Sheng Fanjige*, 200.

[197] Ad Dudink translates "*kan misa* 看彌撒" as "to see the Mass." Dudink, "Manual for Attending Mass," 229.

indulgences should be shared with those who are most in need. Moreover, part of the money offered to the Third Order of St. Francis shall be given to the prisoners and the poor to celebrate Masses in general and especially Requiem Masses.[198] Similarly, in *Statutes of the Confraternity of the Annunciation to the Holy Mother* (*Shengmu lingbaohui gui* 聖母領報會規, 1694), José Soares (Su Lin 蘇霖, SJ, 1656–1736) wrote that the members shall offer money according to their capacity to ask the priest to celebrate a Requiem Mass.[199] In addition, on the first Sunday of every month, the members of the Confraternity of the Holy Body's Benevolence receive the Host for the benefit of the souls in purgatory, as well as for their own souls.[200]

The salvation of the souls of the deceased was an important motivation for Chinese Catholics to attend Mass. When the Christian community was unable to celebrate Mass due to the lack of priests, Chinese Catholics performed other practices as replacements, such as prayer, almsgiving, and fasting. As Jacques Le Goff points out, through these practices Catholics can obtain two satisfactions at the same time: their solidarity with their deceased parents and relatives and the hope to be the beneficiary of these suffrages after their own death.[201] The communion of saints comprised of all members of the Catholic Church, i.e., in the world, in purgatory, and in heaven. As members of the communion of saints, Chinese Catholics not only care about ancestors' souls but also the souls of deceased strangers.

3.4   *Care of the Souls of Deceased Strangers*

The category of the souls of deceased strangers includes the souls of Catholics in other family and the soul which no lineage is attached to, i.e., the souls of the deceased without the care from the family, be it Catholic or non-Catholic. In Chinese culture, the soul which no lineage is attached to is considered an unattended soul. Since unattended souls either wander around or haunt in one place, it is believed that they carry certain potential danger to the living. Consequently, the living perform rituals to take care of unattended souls, thus soothing the fear of the potential danger. In Imperial China, such rituals were mainly conducted by Buddhist monks and two related Buddhist festivals became popular since then. The first one is called the Festival of Water and Land (*shuilu*

---

198   "該分与監牢及貧人，作瞻礼，作安所，" de la Piñuela, *Sheng Fanjige*, 209.
199   "各隨力捐貲，求鐸德于堂中，做彌撒以祈安所。" José Soares 蘇霖, *Shengmu lingbaohui gui* 聖母領報會規, *gui* 5, a1–2, in CCT BnF, vol. 20, 237.
200   "每月第一主日，為沾善終大赦之恩，或為煉靈，領聖體，" Anon., *Shengtihui gui*, fol. 9a4–5, 273.
201   Le Goff, *La naissance du Purgatoire*, 183.

hui 水陸會).²⁰² This festival had been developed in the Song dynasty, then the monk Zhuhong revitalized and revised the liturgies in the Ming dynasty.²⁰³ The second is the Ghost Festival, which was introduced from India and developed in the Tang dynasty. Although the festival is mainly for the communication between the souls of the deceased and family members, people try to appease hungry ghosts on this day as well.

In addition to Buddhism, rituals to take care of unattended souls made their way into the state sphere in late Imperial China. The altar for *li* (*litan* 厲壇) was established as an unprecedented regime in the Ming dynasty. The unattended soul that harbors a strong feeling of injustice and hatred is called "*li* 厲." During the end of Yuan and the beginning of Ming, the number of *li* souls surged because of the war. In February 1369 (Hongwu 3.2), the regime of the altar for *li* was established, and the annual sacrifice for *li* was obliged to officials from the national level to various local levels.²⁰⁴ For the first time, the state made the ritual to take care of unattended souls orthodoxy.

Although the rituals to take care of unattended souls had already been familiar to Chinese people, the Christian communities criticized these rituals and proclaimed that the Catholic rituals' intention is different. According to Catholic doctrine, a deceased soul does not carry any potential danger to the living. Instead of fear, Catholics shall take care of unattended souls out of mercy and love. They performed Catholic rituals for the benefit of strangers' souls and Catholics' souls in other families. Nevertheless, the Christian communities still took social relationships into consideration. First of all, it is ancestors' souls that gained the most care; then among the deceased souls outside the family, the soul of the member of the same confraternity received care more frequently than a total stranger's.

In the communion of saints, Chinese Catholics extended the care for ancestors' souls which is confined in the familial sphere to the care of all deceased souls. The aforementioned statutes pertaining to All Souls Day on 2 November provide the best example. In addition to the confraternity's collective care, there was also individual care of the deceased souls outside family. A remarkable example is Candida Xu who offered the Mass for all the souls of the

---

202   The Festival of Water and Land is attributed to a dream of the Wudi 武帝 emperor (464–549) in the Liang dynasty. It begins with placing food in the water for water sprites and on land for ghosts, see *Chinese Buddhist Terms*, 160. Ding, *Foxue*, 345.
203   Teiser, *The Ghost Festival*, 108.
204   For an introduction of the altar for *li*, see Atsutoshi Hamashima 濱島敦俊, *Mingqing Jiangnan nongcun shehui yu minjian xinyang* 明清江南農村社會與民間信仰, trans. Zhu Haibin 朱海濱 (Xiamen: Xiamen University Press 廈門大學出版社, 2008), 109–110.

deceased in the Christian communities of Shanghai and Songjiang.[205] One day, either in a dream or a vision, her deceased husband and child appeared to her, ensuring that they were on the passage of salvation by the Lord's mercy.[206] Another remarkable example of the communion of saints is the memorial prayer card, whose translation in Chinese literally means the card of the communion of merits (*tonggong dan* 通功單).[207] In addition to the basic information of the deceased, such as baptismal name, death date, and age, the card contains the intention to ask other Catholics to pray for the salvation of the souls of the deceased. The Chinese translation underlines the intention to communicate merits gained by the living to the deceased. The card of the communion of merits is generally distributed by the deceased's family members. By distributing the cards to Catholics outside the family, the family members acknowledge that the salvation of ancestors' souls is not only a familial issue but that merits for ancestors can be gained and shared by Catholics outside the family. Today, to distribute the card of the communion of merits is still a common practice in the Catholic Church in China. As a combination of the traditional Chinese notion of merit and the Catholic doctrine of the communion of saints, the notion and practice of the communion of merits took root in the Christian communities and has been passed down since late Ming and early Qing.

4   Conclusion

As a common concern shared between Chinese society and the Catholic Church, the salvation of the souls of the deceased became one major intention at Mass. The Christian communities propagated Catholic rituals as the only efficacious practices to save the souls of the deceased, with Mass being the most efficacious. Through the communion of merits, Chinese Catholics not only brought the care for ancestors' souls from the familial sphere into the ecclesiastical sphere but also extended the care to all the souls in purgatory. To attend Mass for the salvation of all the souls of the deceased shed new light on the spectrum of religious life in Chinese society. Meanwhile, the Christian communities evaluated the traditional Chinese practices of caring for the souls of the deceased by examining the intention as the decisive element. After a series of heated debates and insightful analyses, Chinese Catholics had to even-

---

205   Couplet, *Histoire d'une dame*, 128.
206   Couplet, *Histoire d'une dame*, 129–130.
207   For three cards of the communion of merits printed in 1740 (Qianlong 5), see Anon., *Tonggong dan* 通功單, CCT BnF, vol. 18, 631–635.

tually abandon many traditional practices, including sacrifice to ancestors. All the efforts made by the missionaries and the Chinese Catholics were moving toward an indigenous liturgy. The next chapter takes a closer look at indigenous clergy and indigenous liturgy in the Catholic Church in China.

CHAPTER 3

Performer of Worship: Indigenous Clergy along with Indigenous Liturgy

Catholic clergy is closely related to Catholic liturgy, especially to Mass. In late Ming and early Qing, the establishment of indigenous clergy went along with that of indigenous liturgy. The first section examines the Catholic priest's identity in the Christian communities and how this identity was reshaped in Chinese society. During anti-Catholic movements, missionaries noticed more acutely the urgency to create indigenous clergy and indigenous liturgy. The second section explores these movements from an anticlerical angle. The third section focuses on the close relationship between indigenous clergy and indigenous liturgy in the Christian communities. In the diverse religious life in Chinese society, the installation of Catholic clergy in late Ming and early Qing is a distinct process.

1 Catholic Priest's Multiple Identities in China

1.1 *Exclusive Celebrant of Mass*

In the early Catechism books in Chinese, missionaries highlighted Catholic priest's identity by introducing the hierarchy of the Church. In *Brief Record of Holy Prayers* (*Shengjing yuelu* 聖經約錄, ca. 1610), Ricci transliterated basic terms from Portuguese into Chinese.[1] He called the sixth sacrament "*a-er-deng* 阿兒等" (*ordo*), which means "*pinji* 品级" (orders). Then, Ricci introduced specific requirements for ordination to priesthood.

> A man in the Holy Teaching, who wants to serve specifically for the sacrifice to the Lord of Heaven, shall master well the Holy Teaching's ritual classics, must pass the exam and receive the seventh order from the bishop, then he shall achieve the honorable order of the priest, be in charge of Mass the grand sacrifice, and never marry.[2]

---

1 Ad Dudink, "Sacramental Initiation in Matteo Ricci's Mission," in *Scienza, Ragione, Fede: Il genio di Padre Matteo Ricci*, Macerata: Edizioni universita di Macerata, ed. Claudio Giuliodori (2012), 192–193. This article analyzes the translation of the sacraments in the early stage in the Catholic Church in China, especially the Eucharist.

2 "六、阿兒等。譯言品级也。聖教中人，自願專事天主祭祀等情，精習聖教礼文，

In the introduction, the celebrant of Mass, the grand sacrifice (*misa daji* 弥撒大祭), is a priest's essential identity. The variant for the term "*sa-ze-er-duo-de* 撒責耳鐸德" (*sacerdote*, priest) is "*sa-ze-er-duo-de* 撒責爾鐸德," both shortened as "*duode* 鐸德." The mention of "*bi-si-bo* 俾斯玻" (*bispo*, bishop) implies the hierarchy of the Catholic Church.[3]

In *Instructions of the Priest*, Buglio explained: "The Lord of Heaven designated priests to specifically serve for the sacrifice to the true Lord."[4] He referred priests to the ancient Jewish priest and the Catholic one, then distinguished the latter from the former. Only a Catholic priest "has the power (*quan* 權) to consecrate Jesus' holy body."[5] The exclusive power to consecrate the bread and wine at Mass guarantees a priest's authority in the Christian communities. In *The Meaning of the Sacrifice of Mass*, Aleni prescribed three ranks of the celebrant of Mass. The first rank is the pope, "who governs the Holy Teaching in the world on behalf of the Lord of Heaven" (*dai tianzhu guanshe putian shengjiao zhi shi zhe* 代天主管攝普天聖教之事者). Aleni subtly depicted that rulers of various countries are not the pope's subjects yet they respect him as the common master (*gonggongshi* 公共師) and the common Father (*gonggongfu* 公共父). The pope is not hereditary but is "appointed by the Lord of Heaven" (*tianzhu suoyu* 天主所與).[6] The other two ranks are the bishop and the priest, who are sent by the pope to various countries to evangelize. Aleni highlighted their role as the celebrant of Mass: "Although they are specifically in charge of the propagation of the Teaching, their role as the celebrant of the sacrifice is most important."[7]

In the *Sketch of Landscape in Capital Beijing* (*Dijing jingwu lüe* 帝京景物略, 1635), Liu Tong 劉侗 (ca. 1593–ca. 1637) and Yu Yizheng 于奕正 (1597–1636) misunderstood the three ranks of the celebrant of Mass.

> In their Teaching, Jesus is called Christ; the leader of their Law is called bishop; the preacher of their Law is called priest (for example Matteo

---

須從俾斯玻考取，歷授七等品級，乃至撒責耳鐸德之尊品，則承彌撒之大祭，而終身不娶矣。" Ricci, *Shengjing yuelu*, fol. 13b5–fol. 14a1, 114–115. See also Vagnone, *Jiaoyao jieliie*, *shang juan*, fol. 49a1–7, 221. See also Anon., *Tianzhu jiaoyao*, fol. 18b2–6, 344.

3 For Portuguese words *sacerdote* and *bispo*, see Dudink, "Sacramental Initiation," 192.
4 "天主設定撒責爾鐸德專於奉事祭祀眞主，" Buglio, *Siduo dianyao, juan shang*, fol. 2a7–8, 17.
5 "有成耶穌聖體之權，" Buglio, *Siduo dianyao, juan shang*, fol. 3a6–7, 19. See also "而承彌撒大祭之權，" Anon., *Tianzhu jiaoyao*, fol. 18b5–6, 344.
6 Aleni, *Misa jiyi, juan* 1, fol. 10a2–5, 503.
7 "其職雖專行教，尤重主祭，" Aleni, *Misa jiyi, juan* 1, fol. 10a7–a8, 503.

Ricci). The person who follows their Teaching is called Christian (for example Qiu Lianghou 丘良厚).[8]

Instead of the Vicar of Christ, this description attributes "*Qi-li-si-du* 契利斯督" (*Christo*, Christ) to the first rank. The Chinese term for the second rank is correct yet "*bi-si-bo* 俾斯玻" (*bispo*, bishop) is considered the leader of their Law (*fawang* 法王), a Buddhist term for Buddha or a Buddhist leader.[9] As for the third rank, the Chinese term "*sa-ze-er-duo-de* 撒責而鐸德" (*sacerdote*, priest) mistakes the character "*er* 而" for "*er* 爾" and a priest is considered a preacher of their Law (*chuanfa zhe* 傳法者), a Buddhist term in accordance with "*fawang* 法王*.*" Although "Law" (*fa* 法) in this description has a strong Buddhist connotation, it echoes Western words frequently used by missionaries in the seventeenth century. In Western languages, the Teaching of the Lord of Heaven was called *nobis legis*;[10] *legem Dei, la loi de Dieu*;[11] *S. Legis nostrae, notre sainte loi*;[12] *divinae Legis*;[13] and *la loi chrétienne*.[14] Following the third rank is a note in smaller size, which mentions Ricci as an example of priests.[15] Following the description of "*qi-li-si-dang* 契利斯當" (*Christam*, Christian) is a note in smaller size, which mentions the Chinese Jesuit Qiu Lianghou 丘良厚 (SJ, 1584–1640) as an example.[16] The three ranks are described in one sentence, the Christian in another, implying a distinction between clergy and the faithful. Although inaccurately, the two authors Liu Tong and Yu Yizheng knew the hierarchy of

---

8 "其教，耶穌曰契利斯督，法王曰俾斯玻，傳法者曰撒責而鐸德，如利瑪竇等。奉教者曰契利斯當。如丘良厚等。" Liu Tong 劉侗 and Yu Yizheng 于奕正, *Dijing jingwu lüe* 帝京景物略, *juan* 4 (Beijing: Beijing guji chubanshe 北京古籍出版社, 1983), 153.
9 Ding, *Foxue*, 690.
10 Schall, *Relation historique*, 281.
11 Schall, *Relation historique*, 283. Manuel Dias, Wenceslaus Pantaleon Kirwitzer, and Nicolas Trigault, *Histoire de ce qui s'est passé*, 32. For the usage of "the Law of God" (*Legem Dei*) in the seventeenth century, see Nicolas Standaert, "The Jesuits Did NOT Manufacture 'Confucianism'," *East Asian Science, Technology and Medicine* 16 (1999): 118–120.
12 "Letterae Annae, Collegium Pekinense, Anno 1677," ARSI Jap. Sin. 116, fol. 216–fol. 217. Manuel Dias, Wenceslaus Pantaleon Kirwitzer, and Nicolas Trigault, *Histoire de ce qui s'est passé*, 28, 33. Lecomte, *Un jésuite à Pékin*, 404, 471.
13 "Letterae Annae, Collegium Pekinense, Anno 1677," ARSI Jap. Sin. 116, fol. 217. Schall also used *Legis divinae*. Schall, *Relation historique*, 11.
14 Lecomte, *Un jésuite à Pékin*, 103, 251, 469, 470, 476, 484.
15 For Portuguese words *Christo* and *Christam*, see Dudink, "Sacramental Initiation," 190–191.
16 Qiu Lianghou, courtesy name Yongxiu 永修, Baptism name Paschal, born in Macao, joined the Society of Jesus in 1610, assisted da Rocha, Sambiasi, and Longobardo. Fang, *Zhongguo tianzhujiaoshi shang*, 167–168.

the Catholic Church. The historian Tan Qian 談遷 (1594–1658) gave almost the same description in *Record of Trip in Beijing* (*Beiyou lu* 北游錄, 1654).[17]

Some Chinese rejected the pope's high status because it resembles the emperor's.

> They say that there are two rulers in [their] countries, one is called the emperor who rules the world; the other the emperor who teaches. Who rules the world controls politics of one country; who teaches has power over all the countries … It is like two Suns in one sky and two lords in one country.[18]

Nevertheless, missionaries introduced the hierarchy of the Catholic Church by emphasizing Catholic priest's identity as the exclusive celebrant of Mass. As Aleni highlighted, people who are not in the three ranks, regardless how great or sage, are not allowed to celebrate Mass.[19] The identity as the exclusive celebrant of Mass traces back to Jesus: "Jesus is the first priest throughout history, who is constantly present and never leaves."[20] Given this premise, a Catholic priest inherits Jesus' intermediary role, "between the Lord of Heaven and human beings, as the intermediary."[21] When consecrating the bread and wine at Mass, a priest represents Jesus' words and gestures in the Last Supper, thus being the central mediator of Catholics' relationship with God.[22] In this sense, Aleni coined the Chinese term "the intermediary" (*jujian zhe* 居間者) and this identity brings great power to priests. In the chapter "Two Powers of the Priest" (*Duode liangquan* 鐸德兩權), in *Instructions of the Priest*, Buglio underlined a priest's power to celebrate Mass.

---

17 "其教耶穌曰契利斯督。法王曰俾斯玻。傳法者曰撒責而鐸德如利瑪竇等。奉教者曰契利斯當。" Tan Qian 談遷, *Beiyou lu* 北游錄, in *Qingdai shiliao biji congkan* 清代史料筆記叢刊, rev. Wang Beiping 汪北平 (Beijing: Zhonghua shuju 中華書局, 1997), 46. For an English translation, see Albert Chan, SJ, "Johann Adam Schall in the Pei-Yu Lu of T'an Ch'ien and in the Eyes of His Contemporaries," in *Western Learning and Christianity in China: The Contribution and Impact of Johann Adam Schall von Bell, S.J. (1592–1666)* vol. 1, ed. Roman Malek, SVD (Monumenta Serica monograph series XXXV, Nettetal: Steyler Verlag, 1998), 276.

18 "彼云國中君主有二，一稱治世皇帝，一稱教化皇帝。治世者攝一國之政，教化者統萬國之權。…… 是一天而二日，一國而二主也。" Zhang Guangtian 張廣湉, *Pixie zhaiyao lüeyi* 闢邪摘要畧議, in *Poxie ji*, vol. 5, fol. 28b1–6, 308.

19 Aleni, *Misa jiyi*, juan 1, fol. 4a9–b1, 491.

20 "吾主耶穌為古今第一撒責耳鐸德，常在不遷。" Aleni, *Misa jiyi*, juan 1, fol. 15a3–4, 513.

21 "所謂介天主與人之中，而為之居間者也。" Aleni, *Misa jiyi*, juan 1, fol. 12a5–6, 507.

22 Claude Macherel, "Le corps du pain et la maison du père," in *L'Uomo* vol. 3, n.s.–n. 1 (1990): 129. Since the twelfth century in Europe, as the dispensers of the life-bringing sacraments,

The priest has two powers, the power of the spiritual order is the first; the power to supervise the subordinate is the second. The power of the spiritual order is to sacrifice to the Lord of Heaven, to consecrate the bread and wine into the holy body and holy blood.[23]

In the explanation of the seven sacraments, Brancati posed one question: what power and responsibility (*quanneng* 權能) does a priest have? The Chinese word "*quanneng* 權能" is a combination of power (*quanli* 權力) and responsibility (*zhineng* 職能). The answer discusses two responsibilities (*erneng* 二能): to judge people's sin and to give penance on behalf of the Lord of Heaven; to perform the grand ritual which is called Mass.[24] The first responsibility refers to the sacrament of confession, and the second, the sacrament of the Eucharist.

Aleni made further explanation of a priest's power (*quan* 權): "How solemn it is, the ritual of Mass! The celebrant of this ritual holds very important power. The acolyte of this ritual holds utmost honor, because a priest is near the Lord of Heaven and the acolyte near a priest."[25] In *Golden Book with Contempt of the World*, Dias has the Lord himself acknowledge a priest's capability to celebrate Mass:

> How enormous is the capability of a priest, what a majestic responsibility! The angels cannot compete. Only he is able to celebrate the sacrifice and to consecrate the bread and wine, thus making the holy body hidden under the appearance [of the bread and wine]. A priest is the Lord's miraculous vessel, which obeys the Lord's order to show the miracle. The Lord is the primary craftsman.[26]

In *Answers to Questions about the Holy Body*, Verbiest explained the priest's power and responsibility in the form of question and answer.

---

     priests were seen as the intermediaries whom the people depended on. Van Engen, "The Christian Middle Ages," 547.

23 "鐸德權有二，神品權一，管屬下權二。神品權，卽祭祀天主，祝聖麵酒，成為聖體聖血。" Buglio, *Siduo dianyao, juan shang*, fol. 4b10–fol. 5a2, 22–23.

24 "問：鐸德有何權能？答：有二能，一代天主審人罪過而分處之；二行大祭之禮，所謂彌撒是也。" Brancati, *Tianshen huike*, fol. 76a4–6, 155. The confirmation is reserved to the bishop, see Brancati, *Tianshen huike*, fol. 73b8–9, 150.

25 "嚴哉，彌撒之禮也。主此禮者，其權甚重。輔此禮者，其幸莫大。蓋鐸德近天主，而輔彌撒者近鐸德，" Aleni, *Misa jiyi, juan 1*, fol. 26a4–5, 535.

26 "巨矣司祭之能，厥職巍哉！天神莫逮，獨彼克祭，克聖麵酒，俾聖體隱含像內。司祭，乃主奇器，遵命著奇，主乃首工，" Dias, *Qingshi jinshu, juan 4*, fol. 6b4–6.

> Someone asks: "All creation changes with work, only gradually and sequentially. Yet, the holy body is consecrated immediately once [the priest] recites the prayer. What can compare with such a power?"
>
> The answer: "It is all because of the power of the Lord of Heaven. Don't you see that once the sunlight shines, it sprays to billions of miles away? And don't you see that once the cannon is fired, the powder explodes, the thunder arises, and they shake and change right away faster than the priest's recitation of the prayer?"[27]

The question acknowledges that priest's power of reciting the prayer of consecration is extraordinary. The answer explains that because of the Lord of Heaven's power, some natural phenomena are even faster than transubstantiation realized by reciting the prayer of consecration. It is remarkable that Verbiest used knowledge of astronomy and cannon to explain the Eucharist. In 1669 (Kangxi 8), Verbiest became the vice-Director of the Imperial Astronomical Bureau (*Qintian jian* 欽天監), and in 1674 (Kangxi 13), he began to construct cannons under the Kangxi emperor's order.[28] *Answers to Questions about the Holy Body* was finished around 1675. Whether intentionally or not, Verbiest infused the knowledge he used daily at the Qing court into the explanation of Catholic doctrines. Verbiest was fully occupied with work but still wrote one text on Mass, showing how much he valued this ritual.

In his account book written in Changshu, Rougemont took eight notes on his celebration of Mass.

> My mind was absent several times during the Mass and in other occasions; (on 5 December 1674)
> My mind was often absent during the Mass. (on 7 December 1674)
> I plan to practice a thorough meditation before the Mass. (on 27 February 1675)
> Your attention was not focused during the Mass. (undated)
> My mind was absent several times during the Mass. (on 24 July 1675)

27　"或曰：'萬物變化之功，由先後漸次而成。此經言一誦，即成聖體。如此能力，有何可比？'曰：'此全係天主之能力。何不見日光一出，即射億萬里之遠；又何不見砲火一燃，藥迸雷起，即刻震動變化，較司教者之經言更速？'" Verbiest, *Shengti dayi*, fol. 4b3–7, 390.

28　For Verbiest's work at the Astronomical Bureau, see Nicole Halsberghe and Keizô Hashimoto, "Astronomy," in *Handbook of Christianity in China. Volume One: 635–1800*, ed. Nicolas Standaert, (Leiden: Brill, 2001), 718. For his construction of cannon, see Giovanni Stary, "Cannon," in *Handbook of Christianity*, 772.

> I made the mistake of hesitation during the Mass. God, pardon me. (on 27 July 1675)
>
> You hesitated as yesterday. You recited the prayer of the Mass at an inappropriate time. (on 28 July 1675)
>
> You barely had recollection after receiving the Host. (undated)[29]

These notes present Rougemont's reflection as the celebrant of Mass. He was concerned about his spiritual state during, before, and after Mass, showing how much he valued the power and responsibility to celebrate Mass.

Although a priest is the exclusive celebrant of Mass, it was forbidden for him to celebrate Mass alone. In addition to the celebrant (*zhufeng misa zhe* 主奉彌撒者), this grand ritual required the presence of other people, i.e., the acolyte (*fu misa zhe* 輔彌撒者) and the congregant (*yu misa zhe* 與彌撒者).[30] The celebration of Mass required co-celebrants (*cooperatores*) in order to safeguard the social, plural character of this sacrificial ritual.[31] Nevertheless, there was a strict requirement: "The acolyte is indispensable, proper to be a man not a woman. When in times of crisis, it is preferred to have no acolyte rather than to have a woman as the acolyte."[32] On 8 September 1696 (Kangxi 35.8.13, feast of the Nativity of Virgin Mary), the Chinese priest Wu Li told Zhao Lun, a leader of the Confraternity of St. Francis Xavier, that being an acolyte is not an arrogant act but contains profound meaning. After distinguishing between a priest and a confraternity leader, Wu Li explained that since the acolyte is closer to the altar than the congregant, he receives more graces from the Lord of Heaven. Then Wu Li encouraged Zhao Lun to take the responsibility (*zhi* 職) of the acolyte. Wu Li lent *A Manual for Acolytes* (*Fu misa jing* 輔彌撒經) to Zhao Lun and asked him to memorize the content. The next Sunday, Zhao Lun returned the manual and served as an acolyte in Mass.[33] *A Manual for Acolytes* might be a manual book on Mass, which circulated in late Ming and early Qing.

As the intermediary between the Lord of Heaven and human beings, the celebrant of Mass extends his power from ritual to daily religious life. Chinese Catholics asked a priest to pray for them because he is the most closest per-

---

29 Golvers, *François de Rougemont*, 137–141.
30 Aleni, *Misa jiyi, juan* 1, fol. 16b6, 516.
31 Jungmann, *The Mass*, 226.
32 "輔祭者必不可無，宜男子，不宜女人，若值緊要時，寧無輔祭，萬不宜用女人輔。" Buglio, *Siduo dianyao, juan shang*, fol. 13a10–b1, 39–40.
33 Zhao, *Xu Kouduo*, 590–591. Later in the text it became *A Manual for Mass* (*Misa jing* 彌撒經), where the character "*fu* 輔" might be missing.

son to the Lord of Heaven, therefore his prayer contains the most power.[34] In the Christian communities, "*sa-ze-er-duo-de* 撒責爾鐸德" (priest) was an encompassing term for the celebrant of Mass while other terms stressed different aspects of his identity. As master of the Teaching (*zhangjiao zhi shi* 掌教之士), a priest saves human souls into heaven: "Common people all call the master of the Teaching 'Spiritual Father.' Spiritual Father refers to someone who is capable saving human souls and making them ascend into heaven. When common people have any demands or sufferings, they tell him."[35] Since eleventh or twelfth century, the celebration of Mass was one crucial means to save human souls.[36] Consequently, since late Ming and early Qing, Chinese Catholics call priests "Spiritual Father" (*shenfu* 神父). The relationship between a Spiritual Father and Chinese Catholics can be very close. For example, one child of a prince (*beile* 貝勒) showed great affection toward Schall. Once Schall and the prince were sitting together, the child saw them but directly ran to Schall, paying no attention to his own father. People around them considered the child's affection toward Schall destined love (*fatali amore*), yet Schall attributed it to a spiritual cause (*spiritualem causam*).[37] In the official document of the Nanjing persecution, Chinese Catholics called a priest "Master" (*xiansheng* 先生) and "Sir" (*laoye* 老爺) during daily conversation, which were respectful but without religious connotation.[38] Similarly, the early edition of *Li Jiubiao's Diary of Oral Admonitions* addressed priests as "*xiansheng* 先生." Xiao Qinghe suggests that Li Jiubiao was lingering between Confucianism and Catholicism; his communication with Aleni can be seen as the traditional Confucian apprenticeship.[39] The edition in the early Qing replaced it with "*siduo* 司鐸" (the priest), thus decreasing the Confucian connotation.[40]

The celebration of Mass closely connected priests and Chinese Catholics. In the active Christian communities in Fujian, community leaders were in charge of preaching, indoctrination, and even baptism, however, only a priest had the power to celebrate Mass.[41] In late Ming and early Qing, missionaries ceded an

---

34 Aleni, *Misa jiyi, juan* 2, fol. 12a4–6, 575.
35 "掌教之士，庶民俱稱為神父。々々者，謂能救援人之靈魂，使升天堂也。有所求，有所苦，則告之。" Wang, *Renhui yue*, fol. 40b5–7, 608.
36 Le Goff, *La naissance du Purgatoire*, 11–13.
37 Schall, *Relation historique*, 347.
38 Wu Ercheng 吳爾成, *Huishen Zhong Mingli dengfan yi'an* 會審鐘明禮等犯一案, fol. 8a8, in *Poxie ji*, vol. 2, 238. See also Wu, *Huishen Zhong Mingli*, fol. 8b6, 238.
39 Xiao, *Tianhui yu wudang*, 192–193.
40 Xiao, *Tianhui yu wudang*, 143.
41 This is also the case for confession where only a priest has the authority to absolve sins. Erik Zürcher, "Buddhist Chanhui and Christian Confession in Seventeenth-Century

important part of their power to perform rituals.[42] The Jesuits deputized Chinese catechists the right to baptize, to exhort, and to teach catechism so they themselves had more time to hear confession and to celebrate Mass. Chinese catechists played a central role in supporting the Jesuits' pastoral activities. When a local Christian community could not attend Mass due to the lack of priests, the catechist would lead the members to pray as an assembly. Since most of the Christian communities could not attend Mass frequently, they took praying as the essential religious practice over Mass. Yet, to pray as an assembly was "a sorry substitute" for the sacraments and the priest's pastoral care.[43] The function of Chinese catechists was effective but could not replace completely the function of a priest. In the mid seventeenth century, some zealous Chinese Catholics were not satisfied with the substitute of praying as an assembly. They desired more administration of the sacraments and more interaction with priests.[44] The lack of priests resulted in a dearth of certain sacraments, such as the Eucharist, confession, and extreme unction. Consequently, some Chinese Catholics expressed a greater desire for Mass and confession.[45] Yet, some Chinese Catholics who lived far from missionaries became cold and indifferent to gathering in church, as Buenaventura Ibáñez (Wen Dula 文都辣, OFM, 1650–1690) noticed.[46] Also, up to 1699 the Christian community in Shanxi had greatly shrunken due to the lack of priests.[47]

The irreplaceable power to celebrate Mass established the priest's authority among Chinese Catholics and a close relationship between them. This is not the case for the relationship between religious professionals and people in traditional Chinese religions, such as Buddhism, Taoism, and popular religions. Generally, ordinary people do not affiliate with a specific religious community. They invited the religious professionals in different temples or different religions to perform the rituals according to their specific intentions. The religious professional does not have the authority to interfere people's personal life.[48]

China," in *Forgive Us Our Sins: Confession in Late Ming and Early Qing China*, 105. Menegon emphasizes that rituals such as confession and Mass solidified the priest's authority in the Christian communities. Occasionally, a priest had to protect his authority as the religious professional against some local community leaders. Menegon, "Deliver Us from Evil," 71.

42 Brockey, *Journey to the East*, 357.
43 Brockey, *Journey to the East*, 139.
44 Brockey, *Journey to the East*, 338.
45 Brockey, *Journey to the East*, 138–141.
46 Bürkler, *Die Sonn-und Festtagsfeier*, 20.
47 Joseph Dehergne, *Les Missions du Nord de la Chine vers 1700. Étude de géographie missionnaire* (Rome: Archivum Historicum Societatis Iesu, 1955), 276.
48 See Yang, *Religion in Chinese Society*, 327–329.

On the contrary, a Catholic priest explained the Mass to Chinese Catholics, exhorted them to attend Mass, and even intervened in their personal life, all of which incited anti-Catholic movements.

1.2 *Western Confucianist*

As the exclusive celebrant of Mass, the priest has great power in the Christian community. Yet in late Ming and early Qing, the Catholic priest's identity was reshaped in Chinese society. The reshaped identity of the priest can be seen in three ways: Western Confucianist, religious professional, and conspirator. Since an indigenous clergy had not been initiated for more than one hundred years in Chinese society, the majority of Catholic priests in late Ming and early Qing were missionaries. Among them, the Jesuits had established contact with Chinese society for a longer time and had a wider network.

At first, early Jesuits such as Ruggieri and Ricci presented themselves as Western monks (*xiseng* 西僧). After learning more about Chinese society, they adapted their strategy to distinguish themselves from Buddhist monks and reshaped their identity as Western Confucianists, in order to make connections among the literati. Early in the Jin 晉 dynasty (266–420), the combination of famous monk and famous literatus enabled the propagation of Buddhism in Chinese society. It seems that missionaries in late Ming and early Qing unintentionally followed this Buddhist strategy.[49] As religious professionals of a foreign religion, both Buddhist monks and Catholic missionaries adapted their identity in order to approach the literati, so as to influence the broader culture. The Jesuits tried to build connections with the literati to gain their support and protection. Western knowledge and technology attracted attention from many literati, whose openness toward different religions offered the opportunity to build connection.[50]

To shorten the distance from the literati, the Jesuits began to dress like them, to talk like them, and to act like them. For example, they limited the contact with women not only to observe the severe gender segregation in Chinese society but also to adapt to the lifestyle of the literati.[51] Moreover, some Jesuits

---

[49] Sun Shangyang 孫尚揚, "Li Madou dui fojiao de pipan jiqi dui Yesuhui zaihua chuanjiao huodong de yingxiang 利瑪竇對佛教的批判及其對耶穌會在華傳教活動的影響," *Shijie zongjiao yanjiu* 世界宗教研究 4 (1998): 86.

[50] Lin Jinshui organizes a table of the communication between Ricci and 140 literati. Lin, *Li Madou yu Zhongguo*, 286–316.

[51] Nadine Amsler, *Jesuits and Matriarchs: Domestic Worship in Early Modern China* (Seattle: University of Washington Press, 2018), 35–36, 59.

mastered Chinese well and studied the ancient Chinese classics, such as Ricci, Longobardo, Aleni, and Buglio. Qu Rukui 瞿汝夔 (courtesy name: Taisu 太素, 1549–1611) began introducing Ricci as a Western literatus in Nanchang 南昌.[52] As a result, a number of literati treated the missionaries respectfully. In the Preface to *The True Meaning of the Lord of Heaven* (1601), Feng Yingjing 馮應京 (1555–1606), who was close to the Catholic faith, respectfully called Ricci as *"Lizi* 利子*"* (Master Li).[53] Li Zhi 李贄 (1527–1602) praised how Ricci absorbed Chinese culture yet wondered why Ricci stayed in China: "Now he is able to speak our language in this place, to write our words in this place, and to follow our etiquette in this place. He is an extremely excellent person … Yet, I do not know why he comes here."[54] Li Zhi knew Ricci as a learned westerner in this place (*cijian* 此間), not as a Catholic priest. Similarly, Jiang Dejing at first did not know missionaries as priests but praised them as intellectuals. In 1638 (Chongzhen 11.7), in the "Preface of *Anthology of Destroying the Pernicious*" (*Poxie ji xu* 破邪集序), Jiang Dejing said that he used to communicate with missionaries and learned their knowledge and technology but he had not heard of the Teaching of the Lord of Heaven. Later on, he renounced the Teaching yet still respected missionaries.[55] In the preface of the anti-Catholic book, Jiang Dejing kept calling missionaries "Western intellectuals" (*xishi* 西士).

Among various ways used to address missionaries, the most common one was to call them "Western Confucianists" (*xiru* 西儒). Catholic literati propagated this title as a prominent identity, such as in *Expounding How to Fear Heaven and to Love Human Beings* by Wang Zheng.[56] The early version of *Compilation of Doubts [on Behalf of Literatus]* called missionaries "Western intellectuals" (*xishi* 西士), whereas the later version changed it into Western Confucianists.[57] The *Sketch of Landscape in Capital Beijing* mentioned this identity:

---

52   Bernard, *Le père Matthieu Ricci*, deuxième partie, 249. For an introduction of Qu Rukui, see Fang, *Zhongguo tianzhujiaoshi shang*, 274–276.
53   Feng Yingjing 馮應京, "*Tianzhu shiyi* xu 天主實義序," fol. 1a2, in DCFY, vol. 2, 26. Feng Yingjing, courtesy name Keda 可大, born in the county Xuyi 盱眙, Anhui 安徽, won the *Jinshi* degree in 1592 (Wanli 20). Zhang Tingyu 張廷玉 et al., *Mingshi* 明史, *juan* 237, Eruson, 2423.
54   "今盡能言我此間之言，作此間之文字，行此間之儀禮，是一極標緻人也。…… 但不知此何為，" Li Zhi 李贄, *Yu youren shu* 與友人書, in *Xu Fenshu* 續焚書, *juan* 1, Eruson, 24.
55   "其教可斥，遠人則可矜，" Jiang, "*Poxie ji* xu," fol. 2a2, 254.
56   Wang, *Weitian airen*, fol. 48a3–5.
57   For an early version, see Yang, *Daiyi pian*, 1–170. For a later version, see Yang Tingyun 楊廷筠, *Daiyi bian* 代疑編, in CCT BAV (1), vol. 23, 171–310.

"According to the study of the Western visitors, they take distance from Buddhism and Taoism yet approach Confucianism, so they are called the Western Confucianists in China."[58]

Moreover, certain officials strengthened the missionaries' identity as Western Confucianists in the official proclamation. In 1635 (Chongzhen 8.6), Lei Chong 雷翀, the prefect in Jiangzhou 绛州, Shanxi, criticized Buddhism and Taoism for inciting people not to honor heaven (*bu zuntian* 不尊天) in one official proclamation; worse were the Non-Action Teaching (*wuwei jiao* 無為教) and the Golden Cicada Teaching (*jinchan jiao* 金蟬教), which deceived heaven (*qitian* 欺天).[59] Nevertheless, he highly praised Vagnone, who went back in China in 1624 under the new Chinese name Gao Yizhi 高一志.[60]

> Fortunately, there is the Western Confucianist Master Gao, who cultivates his moral character to serve heaven, loves others as himself, and considers the teachings of loyalty and filial piety the primary issue. Even the holy Son of Heaven and the wise prime minister respect him, consequently, the officials and the gentlemen [who teach] at schools honor him as master and love him as brother; common people who follow his Teaching all change into law-abiding people. Great are his merits contributed to the court and his benefits to public morality![61]

In the end of the official proclamation, Lei Chong exhorted local people to abandon the pernicious and to convert to the orthodox (*qixie guizheng* 棄邪

---

58 "按西賓之學也，遠二氏，近儒，中國稱之曰西儒。" Liu and Yu, *Dijing jingwu lüe*, juan 5, 207.

59 Lei Chong 雷翀, "*Jiangzhou Leicishi gaoshi* 绛州雷刺史告示," in Huang, ed., *Zhengjiao fengzhuan*, fol. 1a7–9. For the prefect Lei's name, see Erik Zürcher, "Un 'contrat communal' chrétien de la fin des Ming: le Livre d'Admonition de Han Lin (1641)," in Catherine Jami and Hubert Delahaye, ed., *l'Europe en Chine: Interactions scientifiques, religieuses et culturelles aux XVIIe et XVIIIe siecles* (Paris: Collège de France. Mémoires de l'Institut des hautes études chinoises 34, 1993), 4. For a translation of the whole official proclamation in French, see Zürcher, "Un 'contrat communal' chrétien," 3–4.

60 During the Nanjing persecution, Vagnone and Álvaro de Semedo suffered in prison and were exiled to Macao. Louis Pfister, *Notices biographiques et bibliographiques sur les Jésuites de l'ancienne mission de Chine. 1552–1773: XVIe & XVIIe siècles* (Chang-hai [Shanghai]: La Mission Catholique, 1934), 89.

61 "幸有西儒高先生，修身事天，愛人如己，以教忠教孝為第一事。上自聖天子、賢宰相，莫不敬禮之，以致縉紳、學校諸君子，尊之如師傅，愛之如兄弟；百姓從其教者，皆化為良民。其有功朝廷，裨益世道大矣！" Lei, "Jiangzhou Leicishi," fol. 1b2–7.

歸正).⁶² The prefect Lei officially acknowledged Vagnone as a Western Confucianist who reinforced orthodox Confucianism.⁶³ Similarly in 1641 (Chongzhen 14.6), Zuo Guangxian as the local official in Jianning addressed missionaries as Western Confucianists in the official proclamation.⁶⁴ Zuo Guangxian thought that their knowledge and technology could improve the imperial sovereignty and gave several references, such as *The Owl and the Phoenix Do Not Sing Together* (*Xiao luan bubingming shuo* 鴞鸞不並鳴說, ca. 1622), *Compilation of Doubts* [*on Behalf of Literatus*] (*Daiyi pian* 代疑篇, 1621), and *Sequel to Compilation of Doubts* (*Daiyi xupian* 代疑續篇, 1635), all written by Yang Tingyun, and *Explanation on Using Chinese Culture* (*Yongxia jie* 用夏解, ca. 1630) by Zhang Geng.⁶⁵ Catholic literati, such as Yang Tingyun, Zhang Geng, and Zuo Guangxian, justified and propagated the missionary's identity as Western Confucianist.

1.3 Religious Professional

From the second perspective, missionaries found themselves in fierce competition with many religious professionals in Chinese society. They competed with local religious professionals in chasing away demons, curing diseases, and dispelling natural disasters, thus reshaping their identity as Chinese religious professionals. It is necessary to notice that the distinction between clergy and lay people in Chinese society is complex. Joël Thoraval points out the fundamental difference in how religious communities are structured between the Western context and the Chinese one. His emphasis lies in the distinction between the status of lay people and that of religious professionals. There are different religious communities in the West, each with their own priests, own place of cult, own creed, and own rituals, however, the religious communities in China perform their rituals without the intervention of religious specialists.⁶⁶ As a result, it is difficult to draw a line between the performer and the attendee of worship. Similarly, Philip Kuhn points out that the distinction between clergy and lay people in the Qing dynasty was much hazier than in the West.⁶⁷ The

---

62 Lei, "Jiangzhou Leicishi," fol. 2a1–2.
63 Zürcher, "Un 'contrat communal' chrétien," 5–6.
64 "自是西儒接踵來都，⋯⋯ 而艾思及先生，在西儒中尤稱拔萃，⋯⋯ 泰西諸儒，" Zuo, "Jianning xian Zuomingfu," fol. 3a7–b9.
65 "深知西儒之學，足輔王化，⋯⋯ 則有《鴞鸞說》、《用夏解》、及《代疑》正續二編在，" Zuo, "Jianning xian Zuomingfu," fol. 4a4–8.
66 Joël Thoraval, "Pourquoi les 'religions chinoises' ne peuvent-elles apparaître dans les statistiques occidentales?" *Perspectives chinoises* numéro 1 (1992): 38–40.
67 Kuhn, *Soulstealers*, 241.

majority of religious professionals were not ordained or did not even belong to a religious organization.[68] They did not live in a temple or a monastery and only served specific rituals in local communities.

Because of the complex distinction, the word "lay" in this book only refers to people with a specific affiliation, mostly the faithful in the Christian communities, whereas "the performer of worship" refers to religious professionals in a broad sense. The performer of worship in popular religion is usually a religious professional without any specific affiliations. The distinction between a performer of worship and an attendee only appears occasionally during the worship. By contrast, clergy refers to full-time religious professionals who are affiliated with a specific religion. To become a member of the clergy requires specific preparations, such as learning to read and write, studying prayers, and training to perform rituals.[69] The clergy's identity is confirmed by a solemn ordination and the distinction between clergy and lay people remains in daily life. In the category of clergy, the Catholic priest is entitled to certain exclusivity because certain rituals can only be performed by them. As the intermediary between the Lord of Heaven and human beings, the Catholic priest has the power to perform efficacious rituals for various intentions. The power to ask the Lord of Heaven to answer the prayer can be seen as efficacy (*lingyan* 靈驗), which has been a distinctive factor in the religious life in Chinese society as well as in the whole world.

Especially in rural areas, missionaries, as religious professionals who performed efficacious rituals, attracted a number of Chinese converts.[70] Catholic rituals, such as reciting prayers, baptism, and Mass, took place frequently as examples to prove their efficacy. In order to dispel natural disasters in Changshu, Brancati and his successor Rougemont advised local Catholics to pray to the Lord of Heaven and to attend Mass. As Rougemont recorded, their practice was successful.[71] Étienne Faber (Fang Dewang 方德望, SJ, 1597–1657) wore the sacrificial vestment and sprinkled the holy water to dispel locusts in Shaanxi 陝西. As a result, some local people believed him to be a deity capable of dispelling locusts and taming tigers. After Faber's death, local people built a temple for him and named him "Fang, the local guardian god" (*Fang tudi* 方土地).[72]

---

68 Kuhn, *Soulstealers*, 107.
69 These preparations are not necessary for religious professionals in popular religion. Valerie Hansen, *Changing Gods in Medieval China, 1127–1276* (Princeton: Princeton University Press, 1990), Introduction, 10–11.
70 Brockey, *Journey to the East*, 95–96.
71 Golvers, *François de Rougemont*, 403.
72 Lecomte, *Un jésuite à Pékin*, 402–403. See also Zhang Xianqing 張先清, *Guanfu, zongzu yu*

This example shows the pervasive power of popular religion to elevate a great figure to become a deity. The emperor was as interested as common people in the power of the missionaries to petition the Lord of Heaven to answer the prayer. For example, the Shunzhi emperor asked Schall how a Catholic priest prays for rain in a drought, noticing the missionary's identity as a religious professional.[73] As Louis Pfister points out, some horologers in Shanghai honored Ricci, who pleased the Wanli emperor with Western horologes, as their patron and called him Ricci Bodhisattva (*Li Madou pusa* 利瑪竇菩薩).[74]

In the letter written on 26 November 1702 to Duke de la Force, Jean-François Fouquet (Fu Shengze 傅聖澤, SJ, 1665–1741) recounted several examples where Buddhist monks and Taoist priests failed to save local people yet Emeric Langlois de Chavagnac (Sha Shouxin 沙守信, SJ, 1670–1717) succeeded. One example took place in a non-Christian area in Fuzhou 撫州, Jiangxi 江西, where three families suffered from dysentery. Seeing that the child in the first family died despite the prayers and sacrifices made by Buddhist monks, the parents in the second family ran to the church, asking for baptism for their dying son. The baptism soothed the child and the Mass celebrated by de Chavagnac for him cured the disease, then the whole family received baptism. As for the third family, let them learn from their neighbors.[75]

In competition with various other religious professionals, the Jesuits reinforced their identity as religious professionals who perform efficacious rituals in order to gain conversions. Moreover, they required their Chinese converts to accept Catholic rituals as the only efficacious ones and to abandon the rituals performed by other religious professionals. Although many Chinese acknowledged the Catholic rituals' efficacy, they did not want to abandon other rituals.[76] Instead of being exclusively affiliated with the Catholic priest, common people were accustomed to inviting different religious professionals when needed. In this regard, to convert to the Catholic Church was a resolute move in

---

      tianzhujiao: 17–19 shiji Fu'an xiangcun jiaohui de lishi xushi 官府、宗族與天主教：17–19世紀福安鄉村教會的歷史敘事 (Beijing: Zhonghua shuju 中華書局, 2009), 266.

73   Schall, *Relation historique*, 287.
74   Pfister, *Notices biographiques*, 29–30.
75   Jean-François Fouquet, "Lettre du Père Fouquet, missionnaire de la Compagnie de Jésus, à monseigneur le duc de la Force, pair de France," Charles Le Gobien, ed., *Lettres édifiantes et curieuses, écrites des Missions étrangères, par quelques missionnaires de la Compagnie de Jésus*, vol. 5 (Paris: Nicolas Le Clerc, 1708), 193–194. For the identification of Fuzhou, see Jean-Baptiste Du Halde 杜赫德, ed., *Yesuhuishi Zhongguo shujianji* 耶穌會士中國書簡集 vol. 1, trans. Zheng Dedi 鄭德弟 and Zhu Jing 朱靜 (Zhengzhou: 大象出版社 Elephant Press, 2001), 210.
76   Brockey, *Journey to the East*, 301.

Chinese society. For example, Fouquet administered baptism for the first time to an ill woman in Fuzhou, Jiangxi. When asked if she still believed the idols, the woman answered that to believe the morsels made of stone and wood have virtue or power is blind. After receiving baptism, she recovered and became a fervent Catholic laywoman.[77]

The well-known poet Chen Weisong 陳維崧 (1626–1682) vividly described Rougemont as a strange foreigner from a strange country in a lyric poem (*ci* 詞). The poem praised Rougemont's skill to play Chinese chess and wondered at his ability to recite a particular incantation on people (*zhouren jing* 咒人經).[78] Since Chen Weisong talked about Rougemont in a friendly way, he probably did not mean that the incantation was putting a curse on people. Perhaps he heard Rougemont reciting a Catholic prayer and considered the missionary a foreign religious professional as in popular religion.

1.4   *Conspirator*

The performance of Catholic rituals incited suspicion toward missionaries as the conspirators. Both the early Jesuits and the Dominicans who arrived decades later noticed how rarely the pagans visited their temples and almost never out of obligation.[79] Yet, missionaries exhorted Chinese Catholics to assemble in the church on designated dates to attend Mass or other rituals. Moreover, in Catholic rituals such as Mass, Chinese Catholics from different social classes assembled together, as if there was no difference between the rich and the poor. According to Xu Dashou, missionaries claimed to common people: "Once you follow the Teaching, even those who are noble and who are rich will call you 'brother of the Teaching' and treat you as an honored guest; even the poorest can become rich quickly, obtain fame, and definitely receive assistance when needed."[80] This new type of relation which acknowledges brother of the Teaching (*jiaoxiong* 教兄) incited Xu Dashou's weariness. Although missionaries may not have said seductive words such as the poorest can become rich quickly, their performance of rituals already incited suspicion of violating the five cardinal relationships in Chinese tradition. Chinese Catholics were a unity in the Teaching of the Lord of Heaven, regardless of consanguinity and gender, which threatened kinship in local communities.[81]

---

77   Fouquet, "Lettre du Père Fouquet," 163–164.
78   Liu, *Yitian liyi*, 58–59.
79   Bürkler, *Die Sonn-und Festtagsfeier*, 3–4.
80   "汝但從教，即某某大老、某某中貴，亦稱曰 '教兄'，禮為上客；雖酷貧者可驟富，功名可掇，患難必援。" Xu, "Wupi fanlun 五闢反倫," *Shengchao zuopi*, 116.
81   Xiao, *Tianhui yu wudang*, 184.

Anti-Catholics thought that missionaries deluded Chinese Catholics. The literatus-official Wei Jun 魏濬 (1553–1625) thought that the missionaries after Ricci founded the Teaching of the Lord of Heaven with Ricci's words.

> Not long ago Li Madou deluded people with his pernicious words, and the literati all believed these words. After Madou's death, his disciples propagated these words as the Teaching of the Lord of Heaven, assembled groups of people, and deluded them.[82]

Unsanctioned religious leaders were seen as a threat to the state's authority. Such misunderstanding reflected Ricci's achievement in Chinese society in a distorted way. In fact, João Rodrigues described in a similar way that Ricci was like the founder of the Jesuit mission in China.[83] In the official proclamation, Xu Shiyin 徐世蔭 called Dias and Aleni "the leaders of the Teaching of the Lord of Heaven such as Yang Manuo and Ai Rulüe."[84] Missionaries in the seventeenth century were aware of their reshaped identity as conspirators. They tried to avoid being regarded as the founder of a new sect.[85] Moreover, the rumor of the Catholic priest spending money to win people over had been repeated frequently as a firm proof of their conspiracy. Both Yu Chunxi 虞淳熙 (1553–1621) and Xu Dashou recorded how missionaries bought people with money.[86] In addition, both the superiors of the mission, Ricci and Longobardo, informed Rome how some Chinese regarded missionaries as spies of the Portuguese in Macao.[87]

During the calendar case (liyu 曆獄) roused by Yang Guangxian in 1664, anti-Catholics considered Schall the head of a conspiracy against the state and other

---

82 "近利瑪竇以其邪說惑眾，士大夫翕然信之。竇既死，其徒倡為天主之教，呼群聚黨，所至譸張。" Wei Jun 魏濬, Lishuo huangtang huoshi 利說荒唐惑世, fol. 37a3–4, in Poxie ji, vol. 3, 272.
83 Cooper, Rodrigues the Interpreter, 276.
84 "天主教首楊瑪諾艾儒畧等，" Xu Shiyin 徐世蔭, "Tixing anchasi gaoshi 提刑按察司告示," fol. 36b7–8, in Poxie ji, vol. 2, 253. The character "yang 楊" should be "yang 陽."
85 Bontinck, La Lutte, 10.
86 "抑且潛通利貨，以誘貪愚，誘一庶人入其教者賞，誘一庠士賞十倍，誘一縉紳賞百倍。" Yu Chunxi 虞淳熙, Tianzhu shiyi shasheng bian 《天主實義》殺生辨, fol. 15b1–3, in Poxie ji, vol. 5, 302. "夷又爲令曰：'能勸百人從者，賞自鳴鐘、自鳴琴各一，金帛稱是。若得一青衿准十人，得一縉紳准百人。'⋯⋯ 且其以金買民，" Xu, "Wupi," 116–117.
87 Edmond Lamalle, "La propagande du P. Nicolas Trigault en faveur des missions de Chine (1616)," Archivum historicum Societatis Iesu 9 (Rome: Institutum historicum Societatis Iesu, 1940): 67.

Catholic officials co-conspirators.[88] They claimed that the churches and settlements were hiding places; consecrated objects were symbols of identity; Chinese Catholics' assemblies were meetings of the conspirators, whereby money was collected for their enterprise; baptism signified the acceptance into the conspiratorial union (*den Verschwörerbund*); confession served as treacherous communications; and the Catholic liturgical calendar showed days of the control meetings (*der Kontrollversammlungen*).[89]

It was rare for a Chinese Catholic to attack the Jesuits with harsh words in late Ming and early Qing. One exceptional example was Johan Su (Xu Ruohan 徐若翰), who depicted the Jesuits as disloyal officials and hypocrites within a Christian community. Johan Su was an assistant of Jean Basset (Bai Risheng 白日昇, MEP, 1662–1707) in Sichuan 四川. Around 1707, he listed crimes committed by the Jesuits in an undelivered letter, including an allegation that the Jesuits had embarrassed the papal legate Charles-Thomas Maillard de Tournon (Duo Luo 多羅, 1668–1710) during his trip in China. Johan Su claimed offenses not only against the hierarchy of the Catholic Church but also the Chinese bureaucratic hierarchy, accusing the Jesuits of a double betrayal: "deluding our Emperor, embarrassing your cardinal, and betraying the pope."[90]

Chinese society reshaped the identity of Catholic priests as Western Confucianists, religious professionals, and conspirators, which incited fierce attacks on priests, the majority of whom were Western missionaries. The missionaries such as the Jesuits tried to be priests and scholars at the same time, which were two incompatible identities in Chinese society.[91] Certain Jesuits thought that the double identity weakened or contradicted the identity of Catholic priests. Longobardo thought that the best preaching tools in China were Western teachings (*xijiao* 西教), such as the Cross, the holy statue, and the Gospels, instead of Western learning (*xixue* 西學).[92] Gabriel de Magalhães (An Wensi 安

---

88   Commonly used in the research field, "the calendar case" is in fact a modern term introduced by Huang Yi-long. Christopher Cullen and Catherine Jami, "Christmas 1668 and After: How Jesuit Astronomy Was Restored to Power in Beijing," *Journal for the History of Astronomy* 51: 1 (2020): 6.
89   Bürkler, *Die Sonn-und Festtagsfeier*, 5.
90   "欺罔于我皇上，困陁于爾大主教，背叛于教化皇，" Song Gang 宋剛, "Xiao renwu de da lishi: Qingchu Sichuan tianzhujiaotu Xu Ruohan ge'an yanjiu de qishi 小人物的大歷史：清初四川天主教徒徐若翰個案研究的啟示," in *Guoji hanxue* 國際漢學 1 (2017): 49–55.
91   Erik Zürcher, "The Spread of Buddhism and Christianity in Imperial China: Spontaneous Diffusion Versus Guided Propagation," in *Buddhism in China: Collected Papers of Erik Zürcher*, ed. Jonathan A. Silk, trans. Thomas Cruijsen (Leiden: Brill, 2013), 390.
92   It is noteworthy that although the Jesuits were known for their approach to the social elite, they did not oppose the approach to the lower social class. In fact, they wanted to convert

文思, SJ, 1609–1677) protested to Rome against Schall's service at the Imperial Astronomical Bureau, which involved superstitious predictions.[93] The double identity as Western Confucianist and religious professional incited the suspicion toward missionaries and deepened the worry that they were conspirators. The next section explores anti-Catholic movements from an anticlerical angle.

2 Anticlericalism against Catholic Priest

2.1 *Anticlericalism in Chinese Society*

Coined during the French Revolution in the nineteenth century, the term *anticléricalisme* implies the state's hostility toward a well-organized church that depends on the exterior authority in Rome.[94] In *Dictionnaire Français-Chinois*, the Chinese translation for anticlericalism is "to oppose the church's manipulation of politics, to oppose clericalism."[95] *Le Grand Ricci* only records the word "*jiaoquan* 教權," which means "religious power; religious authority; ecclesiastical power; clerical power," followed by the term "*jiaoquan zhuyi* 教權主義."[96] Therefore, this section suggests "*fan jiaoquan zhuyi* 反教權主義" as the translation in Chinese.

In 2002, the journal *Extrême-Orient Extrême-Occident* published an issue on the study of anticlericalism in Imperial China. The introduction brings forth the hypothesis of Chinese anticlericalism; several articles in the issue study the anticlerical movement toward Christianity in the eighteenth century and the nineteenth century Chinese society.[97] Chinese anticlericalism aimed at the clergy, that is, male and female religious professionals affiliated with a specific religion. Vincent Goossaert poses three major themes in the Chinese anticlericalism: sexuality, violence, and sorcery,[98] all relate to the physical contact between the clergy and the people.

---

as many from the lower social class as possible. Li Tiangang 李天綱, "Long Huamin dui Zhongguo zongjiao benzhi de lunshu jiqi yingxiang 龍華民對中國宗教本質的論述及其影響," *Xueshu yuekan* 學術月刊 5 (2017): 167–168.

93 Cullen and Jami, "Christmas 1668 and After," 8.
94 Sylvie Hureau, "L'apparition de thèmes anticléricaux dans la polémique anti-bouddhique médiévale," *Extrême-Orient Extrême-Occident* 24 (2002): 17.
95 "反對教會干預政治，反教權主義，" *Dictionnaire Français-Chinois* 法漢詞典 (Shanghai: Shanghai yiwen chubanshe 上海譯文出版社, 1978), 55.
96 *Le Grand Ricci* I, 687.
97 Vincent Goossaert and Valentine Zuber, "Introduction: La Chine a-t-elle connu l'anticléricalisme?" *Extrême-Orient Extrême-Occident* 24, 8.
98 Goossaert, "Anatomie d'un discours," 113.

Moreover, Erik Zürcher studied fourth and fifth century anticlericalism in a Buddhist context. Buddhism competed against other religions in India whereas in China it confronted the powerful bureaucratic system. Since the beginning of the fourth century, the upper class used strong anticlerical rhetoric both on *sangha* (*seng* 僧) as an organization and monks as individuals. The anticlerical rhetoric against Buddhism can be categorized in four types: political and economic arguments; utilitarian arguments; feelings of cultural superiority; and moral arguments.[99] As a response, Buddhist apologetic arguments insisted that *sangha* as an organization should not be blamed because of some clerics' evil deeds.[100] In late Ming and early Qing, similar anticlerical rhetoric reappeared in Buddhist attacks against Catholic priests. This section examines anti-Catholic movements from the three major themes in anticlericalism.

In late Ming and early Qing anti-Catholic movements were more anticlerical than antireligious.[101] The attacks were often not against the religion itself but against part or all of its clergy. It is plausible that the intolerance toward priests was a primary cause of the attacks toward the Teaching of the Lord of Heaven. Since there had not been indigenous clergy in the Catholic Church in China until 1688, the Catholic priest under attack were mainly missionaries. Anticlericalism in late Ming and early Qing took place at two levels which are closely related: at the state level, the bureaucratic system and those who followed it worked against the clergy and their growing influence; at the local level, people in local communities treated the clergy with suspicion and hostility.

2.2 *Sexuality*

Seen from the first theme sexuality, Catholic rituals violate the taboo of sexuality in Chinese society. The administration of the sacraments involve physical contact between missionaries and Chinese Catholics regardless of the gender. Yet, daily physical contact and bodily practices were considered taboo to the Confucian values concerning the individual and the family, consequently, all religious professionals faced pressure to keep gender segregation in reli-

---

99   Erik Zürcher, *The Buddhist Conquest of China: The Spread and Adaptation of Buddhism in Early Medieval China* (Leiden: Brill, 2007), 255–256.
100 Zürcher, *Buddhist Conquest of China*, 262.
101 As Laamann points out, the anti-Christian action during the eighteenth century was against the activity of preachers and leaders in the Christian communities, not against the religion. Laamann, "Anti-Christian Agitation," 47. See also Goossaert, "Anatomie d'un discours," 126.

gious practices and to limit contact with women.[102] Tang Bin 湯斌 (1627–1687), one governor of Jiangsu Province under the reign of the Kangxi emperor, issued the *Edict to Control Area Wu* (*Fuwu gaoyu* 撫吳告諭) accusing Buddhist monks in various temples of seducing women, causing men and women to mingle together to the detriment of custom. His successors one after another forbade women from going to the temple and attending religious services in public.[103] During the Qing dynasty, supervisory institutions were set up across China to control Buddhist monks, Taoist priests, and both Buddhist and Taoist nuns. Ordination certificates (*dudie* 度牒) were issued to prevent imposters from disguising themselves as monks; and it was forbidden for temples and monasteries in the capital to establish sects and to hold assemblies where men and women mingled together.[104] With an indication of moral degeneracy, the phrase "men and women mingle together" (*nannü hunza* 男女混雜) became a typical rhetoric of anticlericalism and repeatedly appeared in the anti-Catholic texts.

At the state level, in 1617 (Wanli 45.5), Shen Que criticized that missionaries such as Ricci "smear oil and sprinkle water even on women, greatly harming customs."[105] In the same month, Xu Congzhi 徐從治 (1574–1634) denigrated the Chinese Catholics such as Zhong Mingren for helping missionaries to "publicly pour water to women, without avoiding suspicion."[106] On 20 December 1637 (Chongzhen 10.11.5), Xu Shiyin declared in the official announcement that "men and women mingle together without segregation" in the Teaching of the Lord of Heaven.[107] At local levels, probably in 1623 (Tianqi 3),[108] Xu Dashou depicted how missionaries "mingle with all the women."[109] Probably in 1634 (Chongzhen 7), Huang Zhen reiterated that missionaries made "men and women mingle together."[110]

---

102 Goossaert, "Anatomie d'un discours," 128.
103 "男女混雜，傷風敗俗，" Zhao Shiyu 趙世瑜, *Kuanghuan yu richang—Mingqing yilai de miaohui yu minjian shehui* 狂歡與日常——明清以來的廟會與民間社會 (Beijing: Sanlian shudian 三聯書店, 2002), 261–263.
104 Kuhn, *Soulstealers*, 109.
105 "至於擦油灑水，婦女皆然，而風俗之壞極矣！" Shen Que 沈㴶, *Faqian yuanyi huizou shu* 發遣遠夷回奏疏, fol. 3b2–3, in *Poxie ji*, vol. 2, 236.
106 "至於公然淋婦女之水，而瓜嫌不避，" Xu Congzhi 徐從治, *Huishen Zhong Mingren dengfan yi'an* 會審鐘鳴仁等犯一案, fol. 17a1–2, in *Poxie ji*, vol. 2, 243.
107 "男女混雜無分，" Xu, *Tixing anchasi*, fol. 36b4, 253.
108 Ad Dudink, "*Shengchao Zuopi* (1623) by Xu Dashou: the Date and Background of the Longest Anti-Christian Essay of Late Ming Times," in *Christianity in Late Ming China: Five Studies*, (PhD diss., University of Leiden, 1995), 250–257.
109 "混諸婦女，" Xu, "Liupi," 121.
110 "男女混雜，" Huang, *Zunru jijing*, fol. 19a7, 263.

Among anti-Catholics, Xu Dashou was the most concerned about the mingling of men and women. As a Buddhist, he first talked about how strict the segregation between men and women (*nannü zhi bie* 男女之別) in Buddhism is. Then, he pointed a finger at other religious groups, such as the Non-Action Teaching founded by Luo Zu 羅祖, the White Lotus Teachings (*bailian jiao* 白蓮教), and the Smelling Fragrance Teaching. Xu Dashou claimed that "men and women mingle for the sake of mixing" in these religious groups. He procedes with a stronger criticism that according to "the pernicious talk of the Lord of Heaven … men and women do not mingle only nominally but in actuality mingle the most."[111] Furthermore, Xu Dashou denigrated missionaries for being hypocritical in exhorting others to observe gender segregation.

> They themselves allure foolish women behind the red veil at night, close the door then dab the holy oil and confer the holy water to these women, and put their hands intimately on the women's heads. Can the segregation between men and women be more disordered than that?[112]

Xu Dashou's vivid depiction mixed his imagination with actual Catholic rituals such as baptism. In fact, missionaries tried to avoid physical contact with female Chinese Catholics. They established indirect communication with women through male relatives, children, servants in the households, and eunuchs, moreover, female Catholics were the most important catechists.[113] Since Buddhism was under great criticism pertaining to gender segregation in late Ming and early Qing, Xu Dashou probably wanted to remove the attack toward Buddhist monks and nuns and turn it toward the Catholic priests.

2.3 Violence

In the second theme violence, missionaries were considered conspirators who might disturb the social stability. C.K. Yang categorizes the religions in Chinese society in two forms: institutional religion with its theological system, rituals, and organizations, which is a social institution itself, independent from other secular social institutions; and diffused religion, whose theology, rituals, and organizations are closely combined within other secular institu-

---

[111] "男女之別⋯⋯慨自羅祖、白蓮、聞香等妖輩出，而男女以混而混。今天主之邪說，⋯⋯而男女名不混而實最混；" Xu, "Qipi," 138.
[112] "然其自處，又延無智女流夜入猩紅帳中，闔戶而點以聖油，授以聖水，及手按五處之秘媟狀；男女之亂，曷以加諸？" Xu, "Bapi yi suowei shan zhi shi feishan 八闢夷所謂善之實非善," *Shengchao zuopi*, 147.
[113] Amsler, *Jesuits and matriarchs*, 50–51.

tions and social orders.[114] He points out that institutional religion in Chinese society lacked organizational strength. For example, the structural position of Buddhist and Taoist priesthood has been weak in history and since the Song dynasty, the functions and structure of Buddhism and Taoism have been noticeably reduced.[115] In addition, Buddhism and Taoism never developed the sophisticated structure and pervasive influence as the Catholic Church did in medieval Europe.[116]

At the state level, Taoism, as an indigenous religion, and Buddhism, as foreign in origin but inherently decentralized, differed from the Catholic Church in China which maintained a close connection with Macao and Rome. The close relationship with an authority outside mainland China brought great concern to some literati-officials. At the local level, religious professionals in Imperial China usually exerted very limited power in people's daily life, and the relation between the clergy and people was loose and distant, however, the Jesuits introduced a typical Western conception.[117] Missionaries built a close relationship with Chinese Catholics, who should obey the Spiritual Father's decision even in their private life.[118] Such a close relationship between priests and the faithful broke the boundary of the familial sphere and brought the familial sphere into the ecclesiastical sphere. Nevertheless, some people considered this close relationship a threat to Confucianism.

Anticlericalism against Catholic priests belongs to the enduring campaign between the state and the clergy of various religions in Imperial China. The state did not care about theological arguments of Catholicism or Buddhism, such as heaven and hell, karma, or fasting; it aimed to restrict the clergy's political role in Chinese society.[119] In 1381 (Hongwu 14), the Ming court made a regulation and began issuing ordination certificates to the clergy. In 1674 (Kangxi 13), the Qing court issued its first general instructions for the state's control of the clergy.[120] Buddhism, Taoism, and popular religion all tried to thrive despite the state's control, while they competed with each other but with mutual tolerance. Catholicism joined the multilateral competition yet tossed away tolerance toward Buddhism, Taoism, or popular religion. As to Confu-

---

114   Yang, *Religion in Chinese society*, 20.
115   Yang, *Religion in Chinese society*, 307.
116   Jochim, *Chinese Religions*, 77.
117   Zürcher, "The Spread of Buddhism," 389.
118   "聽神父定奪，" de Mailla, *Shengti ren'aijing guitiao*, fol. 26b6–7, 346. See also "⋯⋯ 再三不改，即應到堂通知神父。" Anon., *Sheng Fangjigehui gui* 聖方濟各會規, in CCT ARSI, vol. 12, 486.
119   Goossaert and Zuber, "Introduction," 8.
120   Kuhn, *Soulstealers*, 108.

cianism, missionaries dealt with it delicately and made adaptations to avoid conflicts with the state. Nevertheless, Catholic priests still became a target of anticlericalism in Chinese society.

From the state's stance, the primary target of anticlericalism was not creed nor doctrine but the suspicious clerical lifestyle and their strange practices. The state considered all heretical beliefs a threat to social stability and state security. The suspicion and the following persecution of one religion can and often affected another religion that seemed to be similar in the state's view. For example, Nestorian Christianity entered China in the Tang dynasty (618–907) and was similar to a Buddhist branch. When the Wuzong emperor (814–846) launched an anti-Buddhist movement, Nestorian Christianity lost its support and all but disappeared in Chinese society.[121] By the middle of the sixteenth century, some officials realized the increased tensions at all social classes and began to link various heterodox religious groups together. The officials applied the label "White Lotus Teachings" to various religious groups and considered these unrelated groups a unity from the perspective of persecution.[122] In the late sixteenth century, more and more religious groups were attacked under the label "White Lotus Teachings."

In late Ming and early Qing, the Teaching of the Lord of Heaven began to be associated with popular religions which were especially popular among lower social classes. To contemporary Chinese, Catholicism and popular religion have four similar characteristics: first, the Teaching of the Lord of Heaven requires regular assembly of worship, just as popular religions usually require burning incense and assembly (*shaoxiang juhui* 燒香聚會); second, the Teaching of the Lord of Heaven propagates beliefs such as one true God and eschatology, while popular religions have similar beliefs, for instance, the Non-Action Teaching propagates that one should only worship the Lord of Non-Action Teaching and sacrifice to ancestors was forbidden; third, it is common for popular religious sects to use titles such as "Heaven" and "Lord," which resembles the usage in the Teaching of the Lord of Heaven; and lastly, some specific rituals were so similar that they easily caused misunderstanding.[123] In some officials' descriptions, forbidding sacrifice to ancestors was a major characteristic of the White Lotus movement.[124] Furthermore, followers of various religious groups labeled as the "White Lotus Teachings" mainly came from lower social classes, such

---

121 Fang Hao 方豪, *Zhongxi jiaotongshi* 中西交通史 (Changsha: Yuelu shushe 嶽麓書社, 1987), 425.
122 ter Haar, *The White Lotus Teachings*, 209–212.
123 Zhang, "Bailian," 74.
124 ter Haar, *The White Lotus Teachings*, 202.

as household servants, peddlers, soldiers, and eunuchs; the majority of the Catholic population was also poor people from lower social classes. Although literati such as Xu Guangqi, Yang Tingyun, and Li Zhizao attract much attention in the research field, the social elite was but a small portion of Chinese Catholics in late Ming and early Qing.[125] Missionaries were aware of the danger of being considered a heterodox religious group. In 1638, a local medium in Nanjing suddenly admonished people to adore the true God and a secret cult soon developed. Sambiasi went to persuade the people to cease the cult.[126]

The role of the Ministry of Rites (*Libu* 禮部) in anticlericalism is noteworthy. Since to preserve ideological orthodoxy was its principal charge, the Ministry of Rites had already participated in the combat against heterodox religious groups by applying the label "White Lotus Teachings" in the 1590's.[127] In 1616 (Wanli 44), the state commenced the first large-scale persecution of the Teaching of the Lord of Heaven.[128] The initiator was Shen Que, the official in the Ministry of Rites in Nanjing. Shen Que wrote three memorials to beg the Wanli emperor to expel the Western missionaries from China and to extinguish the Teaching of the Lord of Heaven.[129] His memories were compiled in the anthology *Documents of the South Palace* (*Nangong shudu* 南宮署牘, 1620) and later were compiled into *Anthology of Destroying the Pernicious* (*Poxie ji* 破邪集, 1640).

In the first preface of the *Documents of the South Palace* in 1620 (Wanli 48), Chen Yidian 陳懿典 (1554–1638), Shen Que's colleague in the Ministry of Rites, gave high praise to Shen Que.[130] More than half of Chen Yidian's preface explains how insightful Shen Que was to attack the "Western barbarians" (*xiyang yiren* 西洋夷人) and the attack toward Western missionaries was an essential part in Shen Que's career. In the third preface written by Wen

---

125 In the beginning of the seventeenth century, the social elite, those who passed the imperial examinations, was about one percent in Chinese Catholics. In the eighteenth century, their number diminished. Even take the Confucianists who did not passe the examinations into account, the rate was no more than ten percent. See Standaert, *L'«autre»*, 80.
126 Zürcher, "Strange Stories," 372.
127 Given the social background and the similar discipline, it was justifiable for the officials to associate the Teaching of the Lord of Heaven with the White Lotus Teachings. ter Haar, *The White Lotus Teachings*, 219–221.
128 Compared to the severe persecutions in Japan, those in China were little persecutions and local incidents. Claudia von Collani, "Parishes, Priests and Lay People: Christian Communities as Described in the Neue Welt-Bott," in *A Life Long Dedication*, 701.
129 The three memorials are: *Can yuanyi shu*, 1616 (Wanli 44.5); *Zaican yuanyi shu* 再參遠夷疏, 1616 (Wanli 44.8); *Can yuanyi sanshu* 參遠夷三疏, 1616 (Wanli 44.12). For six explanations of Shen's intention, see Sun and Standaert, *1840 nian qian*, 256–258.
130 "惟蚤見遠慮者能預察其端而力防其漸，" Chen Yidian 陳懿典, "Nangong shudu xu 南宮署牘序," fol. 5a2–3, in *Nangong shudu* 南宮署牘, *juan* 1.

Xiangfeng 文翔鳳 (1577–1642) in the same year (1620), to repel the barbarian (*rangyi* 攘夷) is traced back to the reign of the Hanwu emperor (156 BC–87 BC). Wen Xiangfeng pointed out that the catastrophe of barbarian intrusion (*yiyi huaxia zhi huo* 夷裔猾夏之禍) stepped into China along with Buddhism.[131] He made a comparison by claiming that Shen Que's attack toward the Teaching of the Lord of Heaven resembles the refutation of Han Yu 韓愈 (768–824) against Buddhism.[132] For officials such as Wen Xiangfeng, Buddhism is a breach against Confucianism,[133] thus as heterodox as the Teaching of the Lord of Heaven.

In 1618 (Wanli 46), Shen Que also wrote a memorial on the Non-Action Teaching.[134] Although he did not explicitly link the Teaching of the Lord of Heaven to the White Lotus Teachings or the Non-Action Teaching, Shen Que strongly attacked them all as heterodox religious groups. It is remarkable that Shen Que objected to the Jesuits first as a heterodox religious group, then as suspicious foreigners. Yu Maoci 余懋慈, a Censor of the Office of Scrutiny for Rites (*like jishizhong* 禮科給事中), explicitly linked the Teaching of the Lord of Heaven to the White Lotus Teachings in one memorial.[135] There was a growing tendency of the officials to link the Teaching of the Lord of Heaven with the Non-Action Teaching and the White Lotus Teachings,[136] and Xu Changzhi 徐昌治 (1582–1672) compiled many of the accusations in the the *Anthology of Destroying the Pernicious*. His elder brother Xu Congzhi was an official in the Ministry of Rites in Nanjing. The official backgrounds of Shen Que, Yu Maoci, and Xu Congzhi were essential factors in their participation in anticlericalism.

During the Song and Yuan dynasties, there were many isolated critiques of various religious groups,[137] while in late Ming, the literati's suspicion toward religious groups outside the traditional framework of monasteries increased. On 20 December 1637 (Chongzhen 10.11.5), an official in Fujian, Xu Shiyin issued a decree, declaring: "Teachings such as the Non-Action Teaching and the Teaching of the Lord of Heaven all belong to the heterodox sects."[138] Xu Shiyin called

---

131　Wen Xiangfeng 文翔鳳, "*Nangong shudu* xu 南宮署牘序," fol. 2a5, in *Nangong shudu*, *juan* 1. Since the first preface and the third one share the same title, it is necessary to notice the author in order to distinguish which preface it is.
132　Wen, *Nangong shudu xu*, fol. 11a2–b2.
133　"自是夷狄之一法與周公孔子之道統必不可以並驅而治。" Wen, *Nangong shudu xu*, fol. 7a3–5.
134　ter Haar, *The White Lotus Teachings*, 223.
135　ter Haar, *The White Lotus Teachings*, 224.
136　"不得妄習無為、天主邪教。" Xu, *Tixing anchasi*, fol. 36b10, 253.
137　ter Haar, *The White Lotus Teachings*, 242.
138　"若無為、天主等教，悉屬左道，" Xu, *Tixing anchasi*, fol. 36a4–5, 252.

these heterodox sects "the pernicious teachings" (*xiejiao* 邪教), which "do not offer sacrifice to ancestors, mingle men and women without any segregation, ... and assemble groups of people to meet at night and disperse at dawn."[139] In the early seventeenth century, the state ordered all local officials to search for similar religious groups in an edict specifically using the label "White Lotus Teachings."[140] The edict embodied the concerns for social stability and state security. In 1647 (Shunzhi 4), the prominent lineage of Chen 陳 in Fu'an 福安, which had been anti-Catholic since the 1630s, persuaded the local magistrate to denounce the Teaching of the Lord of Heaven as a heterodox sect, consequently, missionaries had to escape from official arrest.[141]

At non-official level, attacks against Catholic priests mainly came from Buddhism. The compilation of the *Anthology of Destroying the Pernicious* embodied the Buddhists' rather active role in anticlericalism against Catholic priests. As Jacques Gernet points out, the Buddhists could not stand fierce attacks from the Christian communities any more so they fought back.[142] Nevertheless, being scorned by the Teaching of the Lord of Heaven, which was marginal in Chinese society, did not mean much in Imperial China. It was being judged as heterodox by the state that indicated potential danger. In the Ming dynasty, Buddhism was confronted with religious groups in popular religion citing Buddhist teaching such as the White Lotus Teachings. Moreover, with the secularization of its own clergy, Buddhism was exposed to anticlericalism from the state. In 1595 (Wanli 23), the well-known monk Hanshan Deqing 憨山德清 (1546–1623) was sent to jail for secretly establishing a Buddhist temple and later was banished to Guangdong 廣東.[143] In 1603 (Wanli 31), the monk Zibo Daguan 紫柏達觀 (1543–1603) got involved into the case of evil book (*yaoshu an* 妖書案) and was sentenced to death in jail.[144]

It was high time for the Buddhists to draw a clear line from the heterodox religious groups. By attacking the heterodox religious groups they not only defended their teachings but also proved their orthodoxy to the state. When Hanshan Deqing arrived at Jimo 即墨 county in Shandong, he introduced orthodox Buddhist doctrines to fight against the Luo Teaching (*Luo jiao* 羅教)

---

139 "祖宗神主不祀，男女混雜無分，⋯⋯且呼群引類，夜聚曉散，" Xu, *Tixing anchasi*, fol. 36b3–5, 253.
140 ter Haar, *The White Lotus Teachings*, 234.
141 Menegon, *Ancestors, Virgins, and Friars*, 97.
142 Jacques Gernet, *Chine et christianisme Action et réaction* (Paris: Gallimard, 1982), 104, 232.
143 "憨系獄良久，後始謫發粵中充戍，" Shen Defu 沈德符, *Wanli yehuo bian* 萬曆野獲編, *juan* 27, Eruson, 515.
144 "後妖書事起，紫柏逮入獄，尋卒，上亦不問。" Shen, *Wanli yehuo bian*, *juan* 27, 506.

in the birthplace of its founder Luo Qing 羅清 (1443–1527). Under the Wanli emperor's reign, another well-known monk Zhuhong also expressed deep concern about the Luo Teaching. Citations of the Buddhist canon by the Luo Teaching may mislead the people to link Buddhism with heterodoxy, thus provoking persecutions by the state.[145] In the same period Zhuhong wrote *On Heaven* to criticize the Teaching of the Lord of Heaven, a text which echoed his concern of heterodox religious groups. The White Lotus Teachings were even more confusing. The monk Huiyuan 慧遠 (334–416) established "*bailianhua she* 白蓮華社" (the White Lotus movement), abbreviated as "*bailian she* 白蓮社" or "*lian she* 蓮社*.*" Because of the resemblance of name, Buddhist monks considered the White Lotus Teachings "the pernicious teaching which is pseudo-Buddhism."[146]

Confronted with Catholic priests, the Buddhists went from being attacked by anticlericalism to perpetrating the attacks themselves. Missionaries and Chinese Catholics focused mainly on theological points in anti-Buddhist texts. While in anti-Catholic texts, the Buddhists focused mainly on the Western missionary, although critiques of theological points and doctrines were also present. For example, Huang Zhen had talked with Aleni personally and considered missionaries barbarian and pernicious (*yixie* 夷邪).[147] In the anti-Catholic texts, Huang Zhen called missionaries various discriminatory words, such as barbarian sorcerers (*yiyao* 夷妖),[148] sorcerous barbarians (*yaoyi* 妖夷),[149] and cunning barbarians (*jiaoyi* 狡夷).[150]

Moreover, the Buddhists attached the label "the White Lotus Teaching" to the Teaching of the Lord of Heaven. In the beginning of Xu Dashou's refutation, he implied that the Teaching of the Lord of Heaven is as big a threat as the White Lotus Teaching.[151] As the refutation continues, Xu Dashou claimed straightforwardly that the Teaching of the Lord of Heaven was the same as the White Lotus Teaching, maybe even more seductive.[152] The literatus Li Can 李

---

145 Timothy Brook, *Praying for Power: Buddhism and the Formation of Gentry Society in Late-Ming China* (Cambridge, MA: Harvard University Press, 1993), 204.

146 "偽託佛教之邪教也," Ding, *Foxue*, 457.

147 Huang Zhen 黃貞, *Qing Yan Zhuangqi xiansheng pi tianzhujiao shu* 請顏壯其先生闢天主教書, fol. 8a7, in *Poxie ji* vol. 3, 257. See also Huang, *Qing Yan Zhuangqi*, fol. 10b4, 259.

148 Huang, *Zunru jijing xu*, fol. 15b2–3, 260. See also Huang, *Zunru jijing xu*, fol. 20b9–10, fol. 21a2–3, 264.

149 Huang, *Zunru jijing xu*, fol. 12b3–5, b10, 260. See also Huang, *Zunru jijing xu*, fol. 19a8, 263; fol. 21a5, 264.

150 Huang, *Zunru jijing xu*, fol. 13b3, fol. 14a1, 260.

151 "目擊乎東省白蓮之禍，" Xu, "*Shengchao zuopi* zixu 聖朝佐闢自敘," *Shengchao zuopi*, 82.

152 "與白蓮等何異？……則較白蓮之攫金錄用者，其眾又易集，而其心又叵測矣。" Xu, "Wupi," 117.

璨 expressed a similar view that missionaries caused "the fierce disaster which is ten times worse than the White Lotus Teaching."[153] The monk Miyun Yuanwu 密雲圓悟 (1566–1642) pointed out the similarity between the Teaching of the Lord of Heaven and the heterodox religious groups: they both keep their pernicious teachings as secrets from the outside.[154] In late Ming and early Qing, Buddhist monks were under the attack of anticlericalism as well as Catholic priests. Following the state's action, the Buddhists linked the Teaching of the Lord of Heaven with heterodox religious groups, in order to distinguish Buddhism from the heterodox religious groups and to prove Buddhism's orthodoxy.

2.4 Sorcery

Around a third theme, namely sorcery, attacks against missionaries were spread by rumors. Written information usually circulated among social elite while oral information circulated among common people. Although written information's impact had been increased with the development of printing technology, local communities widely maintained communication through oral information. The rapid spread of oral information shows local social network's strength and local people's ability to preserve a cultural memory that can shape perception and action,[155] whereas written information did not have as profound an influence on the spread of rumors and people's subsequent reactions.[156] Moreover, a well-established tradition of orally transmitted rumors has been passed by in Imperial China, which incited fear and provoked anticlericalism among the people. A stranger was often considered suspicious and dangerous in local communities. A man from another province can easily cause fear, let alone a Western missionary.

In the early stage of the mission in China, the majority of the Jesuits evangelized and did pastoral work outside Beijing.[157] The Jesuits could only visit some local communities one or two times annually, asking local Chinese Catholics about catechism, rewarding them with holy objects as encouragement, and

---

153 "揣其烈禍，十倍白蓮，" Li Can 李璨, *Pixie shuo* 劈邪說, fol. 23b2, in *Poxie ji*, vol. 5, 306.
154 "唯聞香白蓮等教，其說妖妄，非入其教者不得預聞。今余又不知汝書果何書，汝教果何教，而謂外人縱欲求之不可得也耶。" Shi Yuanwu 釋圓悟, *Biantian ershuo* 辨天二說, fol. 17a7–9, in *Poxie ji*, vol. 7, 330.
155 Most contemporaries probably tended to treat the orally transmitted information as a historical fact. B.J. ter Haar, *Telling Stories: Witchcraft and Scapegoating in Chinese History* (Leiden: Brill, 2006), 324–325.
156 ter Haar, *Telling Stories*, 330. No clear causal link has been found between the written propagation and the riots, see ter Haar, *Telling Stories*, 186.
157 Standaert, *L'«autre»*, 80.

exhorting those who did not know much to learn catechism.[158] As itinerant missionaries, the Jesuits competed with the Buddhist monks, Taoist priests, and shamans in local communities. Because of the suspicious role as intermediary between the supernatural world and human beings, people considered priests from various religions fearful figures. Consequently, anticlericalism was connected with the anti-sorcery movement and the latter aggravated the former.[159] The constant fear of itinerant sorcerer was common in Imperial China as in preindustrial Europe.[160] In Ming and Qing dynasties, people's fear was frequently directed to those relatively marginal people, such as beggars, itinerant priests, and merchants.[161] Various new religious groups got involved into the rumors caused by fear, including the Teachings of the Lord of Heaven. In a letter written in 1702, Franchi recorded that missionaries only visited the villages twice a year to administer the sacraments, that they had to be prudent since Chinese people were very sensitive.[162] Leaders of Catholic families and itinerant catechists were also targeted by local officials as heretical and suspected by some unsympathetic neighbors for their strange behavior.[163]

Yet, missionaries were the main target because anti-Catholics thought that they allured Chinese Catholics by money and sorcery; that those who were greedy or foolish can be easily deluded.[164] With the fear of cannibalism, Xu Dashou repeated one rumor that circulated in Macao: "According to *Admonition of the Wild Grass* (*Lihuo jiyan* 藜藿卮言), they barbarians are so cruel that they often kidnap the children under ten years old to cook and eat."[165] In *Solid Evidence of Pernicious Poison* (*Xiedu shiju* 邪毒實據, 1638), Su Jiyu 蘇及寓 claimed that missionaries made medicine to numb the children and to

---

158 "神父到鄉報聞，候其面問，賞以聖物，勉勵其心，使未能曉者亦上緊習學。" Augery, *Shengmuhui gui*, 492.
159 In 1768, Catholic missionaries and Chinese converts were involved into the fear of sorcery. To certain extant, the popular anti-sorcery movement became anti-missionary, see Kuhn, *Soulstealers*, 224.
160 Laamann, "Anti-Christian Agitation," 51.
161 ter Haar, *Telling Stories*, 116–122.
162 Collani, "Neue Welt-Bott," 677.
163 So they are counted by Laamann as clerics in the wider sense. Laamann, "Anti-Christian Agitation," 56.
164 "且其以金買民，動輒蠱人曰，彼徒錢糧不可計量。" Xu, "Wupi," 117. See also "布金錢而賈眾，" Shi Chengyong 釋成勇, *Pi tianzhujiao xi* 闢天主教檄, fol. 24a8, in *Poxie ji*, vol. 8, 353.
165 "且按《藜藿卮言》中，言彼夷殘甚，數掠十歲以下小兒，烹食之，" Xu, "Qipi," fol. 26b6–7, 286. The book *Admonition of the Wild Grass* is only mentioned by Xu Dashou.

draw women into sexual promiscuity.[166] Once Fouquet was about to baptize a dying woman, however, her husband changed his mind and forbid Fouquet to enter their home, saying that the missionary will take his wife's eyes to make telescope.[167] A similar rumor said that the missionaries took children's eyes to make glasses.[168] These claims creatively combined the missionary's Western science activity with the fear of organ-snatching. Before the missionaries' arrival, the fear of organ-snatching, kidnapping, and fetus-theft had already formed a consistent tradition in Chinese society for centuries.[169] Marginal people such as travelling beggars and itinerant clergy were taken habitually as the preferable suspects.[170] In this regard, the aforementioned rumors were not specifically against missionaries, and the fear toward them belongs to a long tradition in Chinese society.

In 781 (Jianzhong 2), the rumor of an evil spirit called chengcheng 棖棖 eating human hearts and children began to circulate. Sent directly by the emperor or his official, chengcheng collected human organs as a sacrifice to the Dog of Heaven (*tiangou* 天狗).[171] Respectively in 835 (Taihe 9) and in 845 (Huichang 5), the rumor described the emperor as a bogeyman.[172] The rumor of chengcheng betrays the popular fear of the emperor, which resulted from two main reasons: the distance between the emperor and local people, which made him a marginal person to local communities; the emperor's identity as the intermediary between humanity and heaven, which made him a marginal person with enormous power in terms of ritual.[173] The rumor of the emperor

---

166 "教中默置淫藥以婦女入教為取信，" Su Jiyu 蘇及寓, *Xiedu shiju* 邪毒實據, fol. 34a8, in *Poxie ji*, vol. 3, 270. "至於擦孩童之口藥皆能製，" Su, *Xiedu shiju*, fol. 34b1, 271.
167 Fouquet, "Lettre du Père Fouquet," 147.
168 Collani, "Neue Welt-Bott," 702.
169 ter Haar, *Telling Stories*, 152. These rumors were circulated nationally and the larger context within which they initially arose is still unknown. ter Haar, *Telling Stories*, 107.
170 The marginality is determined by cultural, social or geographical distance. It changes according to the perspective of those who marginalize it. Someone's marginal status is always relative. ter Haar, *Telling Stories*, 123.
171 "夏六月，都下訛言有棖棖，取人肝肺及血，以飴天狗。" Li Yanshou 李延壽, "Wudi 武帝," *Nanshi* 南史, Eruson, 82. "秋七月庚辰，京城訛言雲：'上遣棖棖取人心肝，以祠天狗。' 遞相驚悚。" Liu Xu 劉煦, "Taizong ji xia 太宗紀下," *Jiu Tangshu* 舊唐書, Eruson, 26. "貞觀十七年七月，民訛言官遣棖棖殺人，以祭天狗。" Ouyang Xiu 歐陽修 et al., "Wuxing zhi er 五行志二," *Xin Tangshu* 新唐書, Eruson, 366.
172 ter Haar, *Telling Stories*, 111.
173 ter Haar, *Telling Stories*, 320. Local Cantonese myths reflect the public fear toward the emperor and his representatives, see James Watson, "Waking the Dragon: Visions of the Chinese Imperial State in Local Myth," in *An Old State in New Settings: studies in the Social Anthropology of China in Memory of Maurice Freedman*, ed. Hugh D.R. Baker and Stephan Feuchtwang (Oxford, 1991), 162–177.

forcibly recruiting women had also been circulated in Chinese society over the centuries.[174] In 1687 (Kangxi 26), the rumor circulated again in Zhangzhou and Quanzhou 泉州, betraying the popular fear of the Qing emperor, a new ruler from a different ethnic group. This time the rumor had a new element that the Western barbarians offered a tribute and demanded a thousand girls in return.[175] The popular fear linked the emperor and missionaries together because they both had no direct relationship with the local communities, thus being considered suspicious and dangerous.

In addition, the rumor of alchemy may link the emperor and missionaries in local people's eyes. On the one hand, the emperor and his advisors were suspected of evil alchemy which required children and organs;[176] on the other, missionaries were misunderstood as alchemists ever since their entry in China. In the late sixteenth century, local people in Zhaoqing assumed that missionaries had mysterious sources of richness. Missionaries tried to deny the rumor but failed, however, their Chinese friends said that it is better than assuming that they are paid by the Portuguese in Macao.[177] The rumor lingered despite the clarification made by Chinese Catholics over and over again.[178] Philip Kuhn reveals the deep intention behind the popular fear in Qing dynasty. In Imperial China, political power was inaccessible to most people, however, in an anti-sorcery movement the powerless can seize a chance to improve their own life or to beat their enemy. To accuse itinerant clergy of evil sorcery became an accessible power to people, whose accusations are projections of powerlessness.[179] Nevertheless, it happened that some Chinese Catholics used the misunderstanding to evangelize. In the early eighteenth century, a Chinese Catholic convinced a nobleman that the missionary would tell him the secret of making elixir (*liandan* 煉丹), which referred to alchemy or a means to achieve immor-

---

174　The recruitment fear probably derived from the ancient practice to ritually marry or sacrifice female virgins to a local deity. Since the basic fear was that the virgins might be given away without any reciprocal benefits, the rumours betray how local people doubted the emperor's willingness or ability to bestow favours on them. ter Haar, *Telling Stories*, 317.
175　ter Haar, *Telling Stories*, 307.
176　ter Haar, *Telling Stories*, 135.
177　Bernard, *Le père Matthieu Ricci*, première partie, 132.
178　The rumor had already circulated in Ricci's time. For instance, Qu Rukui spent a lot of inheritance on alchemy and he visited Ricci in order to learn alchemy. Sun and Standaert, *1840 nian qian*, 115–116. Yang Tingyun made clarification. "世意其習爐火點化之術所自來亦，而實不然也。" Yang, *Daiyi pian, juan shang*, fol. 17b8–9, 245. Around 1630 to 1640, Lin Guangyuan 林光元 wrote a text to clarify the rumor, see Lin Guangyuan 林光元, *Dianjin shuo* 點金說, in CCT BnF, vol. 7, 49–52.
179　Kuhn, *Soulstealers*, 229–230.

tality. The nobleman began reading Christian books and converted with his family, although the Chinese Catholic told him that the secret of making elixir was a lie.[180]

One may wonder if the celebration of Mass caused the rumor of cannibalism related to missionaries, since it was a particular source of misunderstanding in late Imperial China. To consume the consecrated wine and bread may have been seen as a way to obtain the life-force in order to attain health and a long life.[181] The doctrine of transubstantiation might be misunderstood. The consuming of the body and blood might have incited the Confucian horror of bodily mutilation and the culturally deeper horror of cannibalism.[182] In late Ming and early Qing, similar misunderstandings already existed but did not circulate widely enough to cause any upheavals. Only a limited number of non-Catholics obtained certain knowledge about the celebration of Mass, so the carnivorous accusation pertaining to transubstantiation from the Protestant movement in Europe did not occurred in late Ming and early Qing.

The fear at the local level is individual, referring to lifeforce-loss (as ter Haar puts it) or soul-loss (as Kuhn puts it), while the fear at the national level is collective, referring to the bureaucratic hierarchy. The fear of the state was not sorcery *per se* but that people may be easily deluded and rebel. The real concerns were social stability and state security, and the state considered unauthorized communication with the supernatural world a threat. The role sorcery played in the political system was political crime, including religious heterodoxy, literary innuendo, and outright revolt.[183] The state ritual confirmed the emperor and his officials as legitimate agents of Heaven's Mandate. Communications with the supernatural world outside the state's supervision may threaten the bureaucratic hierarchy.[184]

Yet, it seemed that missionaries tried to break down the state's supervision. Nicolas Standaert draws a comparison of the Chinese Great Sacrifice and the European Catholic Mass in late Ming. The comparison is based on *Collective Rites of the Great Ming* (*Da Ming jili* 大明集禮, 1530) and *The Classics of the Mass* (translation of the Roman Missal in 1570).[185] Common people were not allowed

---

180 Collani, "Neue Welt-Bott," 682.
181 ter Haar, *Telling Stories*, 168.
182 Kuhn, *Soulstealers*, 102.
183 Kuhn, *Soulstealers*, 187.
184 Kuhn, *Soulstealers*, 118. Here Kuhn posed a marvelous contrast: for the people, the evil sorcery threatens the vulnerable connection between body and soul while for the state, it threatens the vulnerable connection with supernatural powers.
185 Nicolas Standaert, "The 'Theory' of Rituals Related to Heaven," in *A Life Long Dedication*, 521. This article describes in detail Catholic rituals in China and compares Mass, the

to attend or watch the imperial sacrificial ritual, for the power of the Grand Sacrifice derived from the emperor's passivity and the taboo around the ritual.[186] In this sense, the Mass celebrated by the Catholic priest can be seen as a violation of the taboo of communication with heaven. The exclusive priest of Mass confronted the exclusive priest of the worship of Heaven. In addition, the state ritual was celebrated in the sanctuary with the liturgy entirely enclosed.[187] The celebration of Mass was an enclosed liturgy as well, yet the congregants came from various social classes, the majority being common people. In addition to the exclusive celebrant, another similarity is that the emperor is a human intermediary through whom the ruling power passed.[188] In the two grand rituals, the emperor and the Catholic priest are respectively the powerful intermediary between heaven (be it Heaven or the Lord of Heaven) and human beings.

Some literati-officials considered the similarities between the emperor and the Catholic priest a great transgression. Jiang Dejing told the missionary (probably Aleni): "In our China only the Son of Heaven is allowed to worship the High Lord. No one else dares to offend."[189] In the conversation cited in section 1 of the Introduction, Chen Zhongdan asked: "Now every family in your Teaching reverence the Lord of Heaven. Is this not a usurpation?" Aleni drew the comparison between the Son of Heaven and the Catholic priest but explained that the former values the esteem (*shi* 事) of being intermediary more while the latter focuses on the responsibility (*zhi* 職) entrusted by the Lord of Heaven.[190] The emperor is exclusive celebrant in the bureaucratic hierarchy while the Catholic priest is exclusive celebrant in the hierarchy of the Catholic Church, therefore the latter commits no transgression against the Son of Heaven. The conversation between Aleni and Chen Zhongdan is also recorded in *Analects of Master Aleni from the Western Sea* (*Xihai Ai xiansheng yulu* 西海艾先生語錄, ca. 1650).

> Someone asked: "The Son of Heaven sacrifices to Heaven and Earth; the feudal lords sacrifice to mountains and rivers; the senior officials sacrifice to the five gods; the common people sacrifice to their ancestors. Now you say that it is good for everyone to reverence the Lord of Heaven. Is this not

---

Catholic worship to Heaven, with the traditional Chinese worship to Heaven. For the comparison of the procedure in the *Family Rituals* and that in *The Classics of the Mass*, see Wang, "Misa shifou jisi," 113–115.

186 Standaert, "The 'Theory' of Rituals," 539–540.
187 Goossaert, *Dans les temples*, 203.
188 Jochim, *Chinese Religions*, 148.
189 "吾中國惟天子得祀上帝，餘無敢干者。" Jiang, "*Poxie ji* xu," fol. b3–5, 254.
190 "夫郊社之禮，在中邦，非天子不舉，重其事也；彌撒之禮，在聖教，非鐸德不行，重其職也。" Li, *Kouduo richao, juan* 3, fol. 21b6–8, 220.

a usurpation? Moreover, the homes of common people, small and shabby, also reverence the Lord of Heaven's image. Is that not a grave blasphemy?"

The master said: "Sacrifice and reverence are different. The ritual to Heaven and Earth in China can only be conducted by the Son of Heaven. Yet, to reverence the Lord of Heaven's image is because the Lord of Heaven creates heaven to cover us, creates earth to hold us, creates angels to guard us, and creates all things to nourish us. All these great graces, who does not receive them daily? Who does not want to repay? Nevertheless, even to reverence day and night can only express one ten-thousandth of gratitude. How can this be called a sacrifice? How can that be called a blasphemy?"[191]

The author of *Analects of Master Aleni from the Western Sea* Stephan Li Sixuan 李嗣玄 (?–1661) and the editor Li Jiugong participated in the compilation of *Diary of Oral Admonitions*. Several questions & answers in the analects resemble those in *Diary of Oral Admonitions*, yet usually without mentioning when, where, and who asked the question. The two questions are the same as in *Diary of Oral Admonitions*, yet the conversation omits Chen Zhongdan's name and shortens Aleni's answer.

The answer in the analects only explains that sacrifice and reverence are different, without mentioning the ritual of Mass and the Catholic priest. It is uncertain whether Li Sixuan intentionally omitted the comparison of the two exclusive celebrants. Decades later, Yan Mo repeated the comparison and insisted that the sacrifice to Heaven and the celebration of Mass are different rituals.[192] From cosmological perspective, the Son of Heaven is the legitimate representative of the power that rules the cosmos.[193] Being the exclusive celebrant in the sacrifice to Heaven signifies the emperor's double identity as the highest priest and the highest ruler in the state, whereas being the exclusive celebrant in the celebration of Mass signifies the Catholic priest's power

---

191 "或問：'天子祭天地，諸侯祭山川，大夫祭五祀，庶人祭其先。今日人人宜事天主，不亦僭乎？況士庶鶉螭居蓬戶，亦奉主像，毋乃太褻耶？' 先生曰：'祭祀與奉事異。夫郊社之禮，非天子不行。若奉事主像，則為天主生天、生地以覆載我，生神、生萬物以守護我，贍養我。何人不受恩？何人不當報？然則朝夕瞻依，亦聊盡感謝萬一耳，豈曰祭之云乎？亦何僭褻之有？'" Li, *Yulu, xia*, 298–299.

192 "祭天主自是事天主之禮，如聖教彌撒，惟鐸德可行，或古郊天，惟天子行之。" Yan Mo 嚴謨, *Bianji zaoqi chaoben* 辨祭（早期抄本）, fol. 19a, in CCT ARSI, vol. 11, 42–43. The later version replaced "*wei* 惟" with "*wei* 唯." Yan Mo 嚴謨, *Bianji jinqi chaoben* 辨祭（近期抄本）, fol. 4a, in CCT ARSI, vol. 11, 55.

193 Standaert, "The 'Theory' of Rituals," 537–538.

within the ecclesiastical sphere. In addition, the Catholic priest is not the only one under suspicion because of being the intermediary between heaven and human beings. Some officials in the Qing court also opposed the Taoist sacrificial ceremony (*jiaohui* 醮會), in which a Taoist priest acts as the intermediary between heaven and human beings, thus easily threatening the state's authority.[194]

In light of these three themes in anticlericalism, the Teaching of the Lord of Heaven was not only attacked for its own sake but was also involved in contemporary social changes. Moreover, forces at the national level and at the local level sometimes collaborated in anticlerical movements. For example, the state, the local force, and the gentries collaborated in the Nanjing persecution from 1616 to 1617.[195] The fierce attack on Catholic priests put the Christian communities in crisis. Under the circumstances some missionaries found establishing indigenous clergy and indigenous liturgy to be effective methods of defending the young mission in China.

3 Indigenous Clergy and Indigenous Liturgy

3.1 *Establishment of Indigenous Clergy*

Since the beginning of the mission in China, the Jesuit visitor to the East Indies Alessandro Valignano (Fan Li'an 范禮安, SJ, 1539–1606) thought that indigenous clergy was the *sine qua non* for the Catholic Church to take root in China as well as in Japan.[196] Ricci began to recruit Chinese Jesuits who were destined to be indigenous priests.[197] On 1 January 1591 (Wanli 18.12.6), Zhong Mingren and Franciscus Huang Mingsha 黃明沙 (SJ, 1568–1606) started their novitiate at Chaozhou 潮州 under his direction.[198] On 15 August 1605 (Wanli 33.7.2), three Chinese began their novitiate at Beijing, and in 1608 (Wanli 36), four began their novitiate at Nanchang. Eight out of the nine Chinese Jesuit brothers studied Latin, however, the Jesuit Superior General Claudio Aquaviva (SJ, 1543–1615,

---

194　Faure, *Mingqing shehui*, 56.
195　Zou Zhenhuan 鄒振環, "Mingmo Nanjing jiaoan zai Zhongguo jiaoanshi yanjiu zhong de fanshi yiyi—yi Nanjing jiaoan de fanjiao yu poxie moshi wei zhongxin 明末南京教案在中國教案史研究中的范式意義——以南京教案的反教與破邪模式為中心," *Xueshu yuekan* 學術月刊 5 (2008): 126.
196　Bontinck, *La Lutte*, 11–13.
197　A. Brou, "Notes pour servir à l'histoire des origines du clergé indigène en Chine," *Revue d'histoire des missions* 3 (Paris: Amis des missions, 1926): 519.
198　For Zhong Mingren, see Fang, *Zhongguo tianzhujiaoshi shang*, 90–91. For Huang Mingsha, see Fang, *Zhongguo tianzhujiaoshi shang*, 92.

term as General: 1581–1615) thought that Chinese Catholics were still young in faith, therefore unqualified to be ordained.[199] By the time of Ricci's death in 1610, there were five Jesuit residences in Nanjing, Nanchang, Hangzhou 杭州, Chaozhou, and Beijing, with eight European priests and eight Chinese brothers in total. Jesuit missionaries, especially their superior Longobardo, desired a sufficient administrative and financial autonomy for the mission in China, which depended on the province of Japan at that time.[200]

In the end of 1612 (Wanli 40), Longobardo decided to send Trigault back to Europe to be the procurator of the mission in China.[201] On 9 February 1613, Trigault set off from Macao and arrived at Rome on 11 October 1614. His task was to report to Paul V (1550–1621, papacy: 1605–1621) the situation of the Catholic Church in China and to ask for more support, an indigenous clergy being one crucial request. Trigault first brought the requests to the Jesuit Superior General Aquaviva, who asked a commission of Jesuit theologians for advice. After receiving a positive response from the commission, Aquaviva submitted two requests from the Catholic Church in China to Paul V: the privilege to celebrate Mass with the priest's head being covered; the privilege of Chinese liturgy, i.e., to celebrate Mass and the Divine Office in the language of Chinese doctors (*de Missa et Officio divino in lingua Sinensi doctorum celebrandis*).[202] Moreover, in the end of 1614, Aquaviva detached the mission in China from the province of Japan to be an independent mission (*sui iuris*) and the superior of the mission received the authority of a provincial.[203]

With the support of Cardinal Robert Bellarmine (SJ, 1542–1621),[204] the Holy Office granted three privileges to the Catholic Church in China after a careful consideration: the Jesuits can cover their heads during Mass; the Jesuits can translate the Bible into literary Chinese; Chinese priests can celebrate Mass and the Liturgy of the Hours in literary Chinese. On 15 January 1615, the Holy Office issued the decree to grant the privileges and an edited decree with critiques on 26 March. On 27 June the same year, Paul V issued the pontifical letter *High Priest of the Roman See* (*Romanae Sedis Antistes*), which confirmed and extended the privileges of indigenous liturgy: all the priests in China can cover

---

199 Bontinck, *La Lutte*, 18. See also Joseph Jennes, "A propos de la liturgie chinoise: Le Bref *Romanae Sedis Antistes* de Paul V (1615)," *Neue Zeitschrift für Missionswissenschaft* 2 (1946): 242.
200 Lamalle, "La propagande," 53–54.
201 Longobardo appreciated Trigault's talent and capability. Lamalle, "La propagande," 53.
202 Bontinck, *La Lutte*, 37.
203 Lamalle, "La propagande," 58.
204 Cardinal Robert Bellarmine was a constant supporter of Chinese liturgy. Jennes, "La liturgie chinoise," 244.

their heads during Mass; Chinese priests can administer sacraments and other ecclesiastical functions in literary Chinese.[205] On 16 April 1618, Trigault took off from Lisbon, with 21 new recruits from various provinces, including Schall and Johannes Schreck Terrentius (Deng Yuhan 鄧玉函, SJ, 1576–1630).[206] Yet, the superiors of Macao opposed using literary Chinese as liturgical language. Seeing that the missionaries disagreed with each other, the Jesuit Superior General Mutio Vitelleschi (SJ, 1563–1645, term as General: 1615–1645) decided not to employ the privilege of Chinese liturgy.[207]

Despite privileges pertaining to indigenous liturgy—or at least the presupposition of indigenous clergy—being approved, the Catholic Church in China needed a bishop to ordain Chinese priests. Early in the Yuan dynasty, Franciscan missionaries had one bishop in Beijing in 1307 and one in Quanzhou in 1313, however, missionaries in late Ming and early Qing had to start all over again.[208] During his stay in Rome, Trigault mentioned the plan to nominate a bishop for mainland China. Contrary to his support for the privileges of indigenous liturgy, Vitelleschi showed a rather dilatory attitude toward the nomination of a bishop.[209] On the one hand, the young mission needed a bishop to realize an indigenous clergy which can strengthen its root in China; on the other hand, a foreign superior's entry in China might incite suspicion, therefore, the nomination of a bishop for mainland China became an unsolved problem.[210] While discussions over indigenous liturgy and indigenous clergy was held in Rome, the persecution issued by Shen Que took place in Nanjing in 1616, thus making an indigenous clergy for the mission in China even more urgent.

Other young missions in Asia shared the desire for indigenous clergy and bishops. On 20 December 1645, Alexandre de Rhodes (Luo De 羅德, SJ, 1591–1660) set off from Macao to Europe, with three tasks: to ask the pope to appoint bishops for the mission in Annam; to obtain financial support from the kings and princes; to recruit new missionaries for Indochina.[211] Arrived in Rome on 27 June 1649, de Rhodes explained to Propaganda Fide the necessity of appoint-

---

205 Bontinck, *La Lutte*, 40–42. Brou, "Clergé indigène en Chine," 520–521.
206 There were four Jesuits from the Gallo-Belgic province, three from Germany, one from Austria, three from Italy, and ten from Portugal. Lamalle, "La propagande," 86–87. To select the recruits required careful consideration to the Padroado. Lamalle, "La propagande," 78–81.
207 Jennes, "La liturgie chinoise," 254. Chinese liturgy specifically refers to using literary Chinese as liturgical language. Jennes, "La liturgie chinoise," 248.
208 A. Brou, "Le développement des églises de Chine," *Revue d'histoire des missions* 13 (Paris: Amis des missions, 1936): 283.
209 Lamalle, "La propagande," 87–88.
210 Brou, "Clergé indigène en Chine," 522.
211 Bontinck, *La Lutte*, 68.

ing bishops and the urgency of establishing an indigenous clergy in Annam. Rome had to gradually shake off the Portuguese Padroado with prudence and patience. With an indigenous clergy in the East as its specific goal, the Society of Foreign Missions of Paris was founded.[212] Finally, in a pontifical letter issued on 29 July 1658, Alexander VII (1599–1667, papacy: 1655–1667) appointed three members of the Society of Foreign Missions of Paris as bishops. François Pallu (Lu Fangji 陸方濟, MEP, 1626–1684) was the Vicar Apostolic of Tonkin and the apostolic administrator of Yunnan 雲南, Guizhou 貴州, Sichuan, Guangxi 廣西, and the Huguang 湖廣 area; Pierre Lambert de la Motte (MEP, 1624–1679) was the Vicar Apostolic of Cochin and the apostolic administrator of Zhejiang, Fujian, Guangdong, Jiangxi, and Hainan 海南; Ignace Cotolendi (MEP, 1630–1662) was the Vicar Apostolic of Nanjing and in charge of Beijing, Shanxi, Shandong, Henan, Shaanxi, Korea and Tartary. Yet, Mgr. Cotolendi died in India in 1662 and the other two bishops did not enter China. In 1684, Mgr. Pallu finally arrived China but lived less than one year.[213]

A Catholic priest was obliged to use Latin to administer the sacraments, however, Trigault talked about an enormous difficulty of Chinese people mastering Latin during his trip in Europe. He told Cardinal Bellarmine that Chinese priests who celebrated in Latin were impossible to find. Trigault suggested that it is necessary to take Chinese as a replacement, not the plain language spoken by people but the literary one mastered by literati only.[214] Since the privileges granted by Paul V pertaining to liturgical language had not been acted upon, Trigault's suggestion became an insistent request from the Catholic Church in China. In 1658, Alexander VII formed a particular commission to discuss indigenous liturgy, however, no one during the discussion mentioned the privileges granted by Paul V and the cardinals thought the question was premature.[215] In 1659, Alexander VII granted the privilege that Chinese candidates need only master the prayers in Latin before being ordained. In 1660, the privileges granted by Paul V were discovered in the archives of the Holy Office. Propaganda Fide did not promulgate these privileges immediately but did permit Chinese priests to use the Roman Missal and the Roman Breviary (*Breviarium Romanum*) written in literary Chinese.[216] The privilege granted by Alexander VII preserved the study of Latin as a basic training before priest ordination.

---

212 Brou, "Clergé indigène en Chine," 525–526.
213 Brou, "Des églises de Chine," 283–284.
214 Bontinck, *La Lutte*, 30.
215 Brou, "Clergé indigène en Chine," 526.
216 Bontinck, *La Lutte*, 92.

From 18 December 1667 to 26 January 1668, the Canton Conference was held, during which indigenous clergy had been a heated issue. The majority of missionaries were in favor of the establishment of indigenous clergy, such as Couplet, Rougemont, Prospero Intorcetta (Yin Duoze 殷鐸澤, SJ, 1625–1696), Jean-Dominique Gabiani (Bi Jia 畢嘉, SJ, 1623–1696), Jacques Le Faure (Liu Diwo 劉迪我, SJ, 1613–1675), Buglio, and Magalhães. Meanwhile, some missionaries opposed the ordination of Chinese priests, such as Feliciano, Antoine de Gouvea (He Dahua 何大化, SJ, 1592–1677), Jacques Motel (Mu Diwo 穆迪我, SJ, 1619–1692), Michel Trigault, Pietro Canevari (Nie Boduo 聶伯多, SJ, 1596–1675), and Brancati.[217] In 1661, Jacques Motel saw how a literatus baptized by Rodrigo de Figueiredo acted as a priest in Wuchang 武昌. This literatus said Mass, consecrated holy water, and told fortunes. As mentioned in the beginning of this chapter, the distinction between the performer of worship and the attendee in traditional Chinese society is hazy. Motel worried that Chinese Catholics could not understand that Catholic priests were the exclusive celebrants of Mass and that they might ruin the ritual purity of the Catholic Church.[218] Finally, the majority of the Jesuits in Canton 廣州 decided to solve the problem of indigenous clergy by the privilege of indigenous liturgy.[219]

On 21 January 1669, the Procurator Intorcetta set off to Europe and on 10 December 1671 he submitted a petition to Clement X (1590–1676, papacy: 1670–1676), which contained a request for indigenous clergy. Intorcetta requested the permission to ordain aged literati and eunuchs, because the former mastered well literary Chinese and the latter had great advantage to evangelize in the court. On 11 January 1672, Propaganda Fide examined Intorcetta's petition then rejected to exert the privileges granted by Paul V and maintained the privilege by Alexandre VII.[220] Since aged literati who were qualified for the ordination were rare to find, and even with the privilege granted by Alexandre VII, their clerical formation was still difficult. Therefore, the Vice Provincial Verbiest and his successor Gabiani suggested a clerical formation of young Chinese to the Jesuit Superior General Giovanni Paolo Oliva (SJ, 1600–1681, term of General: 1664–1681). On 16 June 1672, Oliva allowed the mission in China to open a new novitiate and gave the superior Verbiest the authority to recruit Chinese Jesuits who were destined to be indigenous priests.[221]

---

217   Bontinck, *La Lutte*, 109.
218   Brockey, *Journey to the East*, 147.
219   Bontinck, *La Lutte*, 110.
220   Bontinck, *La Lutte*, 130–134.
221   Brou, "Clergé indigène en Chine," 532.

In December 1681, the Procurator Couplet set off to Europe and arrived in Holland on 8 October 1683. In February 1684, he met the hagiographer Daniel Papebroch (SJ, 1628–1714) in Antwerp. Papebroch showed great interest to the liturgical books in Chinese brought by Couplet, including the Roman Missal, the Roman Breviary, and the Roman Ritual.[222] When Couplet talked about the privileges granted by Paul V, Papebroch pointed to an excellent example that similar privilege had been granted to the Slavs.[223] In December 1684, Couplet requested Innocent XI (1611–1689, papacy: 1676–1689) to exert the privileges granted by Paul V since the Roman Missal and the Roman Ritual had been translated in Chinese. On 6 June 1685, Couplet and the Chinese Catholic Michel Shen Fuzong 沈福宗 (1657–1692) met Innocent XI. The pope highly praised the Catholic Church in China and was supportive of indigenous liturgy. Couplet asked why the privileges granted by Paul V have not been exerted after all these years. Innocent XI replied that these privileges will be exerted.[224] Yet, Propaganda Fide gave no positive reply and the privileges granted by Paul V could not be exerted. Couplet insisted on privileges pertaining to Chinese liturgy, arguing in one report that without Chinese liturgy there would be no Chinese clergy, however, the cardinals at the particular commission insisted on following the Church's tradition.[225]

Meanwhile, the Catholic Church in China achieved a breakthrough on the nomination of a Chinese bishop. In 1654, the Chinese Dominican Luo Wenzhao was ordained to the priesthood in Manila.[226] Because of the calendar case launched in 1664, most of the European missionaries were exiled to Guangdong. Luo Wenzhao was the only one who traveled across different provinces to provide pastoral care, embodying the indigenous priest's advantage. In the

---

222 Golvers, *François de Rougemont*, 73.
223 Bontinck, *La Lutte*, 203.
224 "Quae causa fuit quod a me quaereret Innocentius XI, Pontifex Sanctus cur tot annis non fuisset executioni mandatum. Omnio id fieri oporteret." Lettre de Couplet au Général, Madrid, 6 juillet 1690. See Bontinck, *La Lutte*, 210, note 52.
225 Albert Chan, SJ, "Towards a Chinese Church: The Contribution of Philippe Couplet S.J. (1622–1693)," in *Philippe Couplet, S.J. (1623–1693): The Man Who Brought China to Europe*, ed. Jeroom Heyndrickx (Monumenta Serica Monograph Series XXII, Nettetal: Steyler Verlag, 1990), 80–83.
226 Instead of the common usage (name: Luo Wenzao 羅文藻, courtesy name: Wocun 我存), Song Liming promotes another one (name: Luo Wenzhao 羅文炤, courtesy name Zonghua 宗華) with sufficient evidence, such as two epitaphs in ARSI. Song Liming 宋黎明, "Luo Wenzhao haishi Luo Wenzao?—wei Zhongguo shouwei guoji zhujiao Luo zhujiao zhengming 羅文炤還是羅文藻?——為中國首位國籍主教羅主教正名," *Haijiaoshi yanjiu* 海交史研究 3 (2019): 40–51. For an introduction of Luo Wenzhao, see Fang, *Zhongguo tianzhujiaoshi zhong*, 145–152.

1670s, the Holy See appointed and confirmed this Chinese priest as the Vicar Apostolic of Nanjing and Titular Bishop of Basilinopolis. After overcoming various obstacles, on 8 April 1685 (Kangxi 22.3.5), Luo Wenzhao was ordained as the first Chinese bishop by Mgr. della Chiesa in a Franciscan church in Canton. He was appointed as the Bishop of Nanjing in 1690.[227] As regards Chinese liturgy, Luo Wenzhao was on the Jesuits' side. On 2 October 1685 (Kangxi 22.9.5), Mgr. Luo requested Rome to permit using Chinese in the celebration of Mass and the Divine Office.[228] On 1 August 1688 (Kangxi 27.7.6), Mgr. Luo ordained three Chinese Jesuits as priests, thus finally realizing the establishment of indigenous clergy in mainland China.[229]

Yet, the difficulty of celebrating Mass in Latin haunted indigenous priests. Pronunciation as a particular obstacle made some missionaries think that Chinese priests were unable to celebrate Mass properly. Some missionaries feared that an incorrect pronunciation of Latin ruined the ritual purity and rendered the ritual invalid. As Verbiest recorded in a letter to Europe, Chinese people pronounced *est corpus* in the consecration prayer as *es-e-te colepuse*.[230] Le Comte also pointed out that the different pronunciation between Chinese and Western languages caused "a particular difficulty for the consecration of the Host among the Chinese priests."[231] In the "Opinion on the Mission of China" written in 1702, Basset reiterated that Chinese people cannot pronounce *hoc est corpus meum*. Basset wrote that one Chinese priest spent all his time to learn the Mass in Latin which he would celebrate the next day and he may not dare to celebrate Mass in Latin in front of a European.[232]

In the seventeenth century, a number of missionaries, mostly the Jesuits, spared no effort to request the privilege in favor of indigenous clergy from Rome. It is noteworthy that indigenous liturgy in their requests was not a final goal but an expedient for indigenous clergy. Nevertheless, developments of

---

227 Brou, "Clergé indigène en Chine," 536.
228 "usus linguae sinicae in Missa et Officio permittatur," Bontinck, *La Lutte*, 235.
229 Around 1700, there were 122 foreign missionaries yet only four or five Chinese priests in China, while in 1810, the former shrank to thirty-one and the later increased to eighty. Joseph Jennes, *Four Centuries of Catechetics in China: Historical Evolution of Apologetics and Catechetics in the Catholic Mission of China from the 16th Centry until 1940*, trans. Fr. Albert Van Lierde and Fr. Paul T'ien Yung-cheng (Taipei: Huaming shuju 華明書局, 1975), 96.
230 Bontinck, *La Lutte*, 32.
231 Lecomte, *Un jésuite à Pékin*, 231.
232 Jean Basset, *Jean Basset (1662–1707), pionnier de l'église au Sichuan, précurseur d'une église d'expression chinoise: correspondance (oct. 1701–oct. 1707), avis sur la Mission de Chine (1702)* (Éditions You Feng Librairie & Éditeur, 2012), 125.

indigenous liturgy fostered the establishment of indigenous clergy, which in turn developed indigenous liturgy, especially those pertaining to Mass.

3.2 Ritual Manuals for Mass

In the aforementioned requests made by Trigault to Paul V, two relate to indigenous liturgy. The first is to celebrate Mass in Chinese, pertaining to liturgical language and liturgical books used in Mass; the second is to cover the priest's head during Mass, pertaining to the liturgical vestment dressed in Mass. The sacrificial hat as an innovative vestment is discussed in section 3.3, and this section examines developments of the ritual manuals for Mass in Chinese. From the seventeenth century to the early eighteenth century, the Christian communities in China published a number of ritual manuals for Mass, first as a chapter or a section in a book then as a monograph as well.

In 1619, Longobardo published the prayer booklet *Daily Services of the Holy Teaching* (*Shengjiao rike* 聖教日課) using a press built in Yang Tingyun's residence in Hangzhou.[233] Based on contemporary prayer books in Europe, this primitive Chinese prayer book contained the prayers for Mass.[234] In 1628, the Jesuits published *General Collection of Prayer Recitation in the Holy Teaching of the Lord of Heaven* using the same press.[235] Ferreira, Dias, de Figueiredo, Lazzaro Cattaneo (Guo Jujing 郭居靜, SJ, 1560–1640), and Francisco Furtado (Fu Fanji 傅汎際, SJ, 1589–1653) edited (*ding* 訂) two volumes (*juan* 卷) in total. The first volume includes an enriched version of Longobardo's *Daily Services of the Holy Teaching*.[236] The second volume, collected (*ju* 聚) by de Figueiredo, provides [Prayer] Recited before Receiving the Holy Body and [Prayer] Recited after Receiving the Holy Body (*yiling shengti nian* 已領聖體念).[237]

With eleven related prayers and seven notes in *Daily Services of the Holy Teaching*, Longobardo in fact provided an untitled ritual manual for the congregants of Mass.[238] The prayers in Longobardo's ritual manual, six of which were titled, comply with the celebration of Mass: before Mass, Dip in the Holy Water (*dian shengshui* 點聖水), Sprinkle the Holy Water (*sa shengshui* 灑聖

---

233 The prayer booklet contained Longobardo's translation and his own works in Chinese in 16 or 22 folios. Yang Tingyun probably polished the language. Brunner, *L'euchologe*, 27.
234 Brunner, *L'euchologe*, 28–29.
235 Brunner, *L'euchologe*, 15–16.
236 Niccolò Longobardo 龍華民, *Shengjiao rike* 聖教日課, *Nianjing zongdu, juan* 1, fol. 7–fol. 22, 21–52.
237 *Nianjing zongdu, juan* 2, fol. 84b4–fol. 87a7, 438–443.
238 Longobardo, *Shengjiao rike*, fol. 10b7–fol. 14b7, 28–36. For an English translation, see Dudink, "Manual for Attending Mass," 229–231.

水, *Asperges me*), the Our Father one time, the Hail Mary one time, one short prayer to praise the Lord, one long thanks-giving prayer, and one long prayer to praise the Great Father (*dafu* 大父); at Mass, The Elevation of the Holy Body (*juyang shengti* 舉揚聖體), The Elevation of the Holy Chalice (*juyang shengjue* 舉揚聖爵), and one prayer of the spiritual reception to the Lord Jesus; after Mass, one short thanks-giving prayer to the Lord Jesus. The seven notes in smaller size provide brief instructions on how to properly attend Mass: before Mass, the exhortation to "see Mass" (*kan misa* 看彌撒), actions at the entrance of the church; before the priest enters, three identical short notes on reciting the prayers; actions when the priest enters, explanation of the meaning of Mass; actions and thoughts when the priest receives the holy body; actions and thoughts after seeing Mass.

In 1629, Aleni published the first monograph on the Mass in Chinese *The Meaning of the Sacrifice of Mass* in Fuzhou. The word "*jiyi* 祭義" (meaning of sacrifice) in the title may remind people of *Jiyi* 祭義 in the *Book of the Rites*. The first volume (*juan* 卷) gives a comprehensive explanation in ten chapters: the Name (*mingyi* 名義), the Origin (*yuanshi* 原始), the Solemnity (*chongyan* 崇嚴), the Hall and Altar (*tangtai* 堂臺), the Order (*pinji* 品級), the Liturgical Vestment (*zhangfu* 章服), the Rite of Attending Mass (*yu misa liyi* 與彌撒禮儀), the Grace Repaid by Attending Mass (*yu misa enbao* 與彌撒恩報), the Rite for the Acolyte (*fu misa liyi* 輔彌撒禮儀), and the Prayers for the Acolyte (*fu misa jingwen* 輔彌撒經文).[239] The second volume expounds the procedure of Mass in three parts with thirty-three sections (*jie* 節) in total: the approach of the sacrifice (*jiangji* 將祭), with eighteen sections; the solemn sacrifice (*zhengji* 正祭), with nine sections; the withdrawal of the sacrifice (*cheji* 撤祭), with six sections.[240] As an allegorical commentary on the texts and actions of Mass, the second volume is probably the first exposition of Mass (*expositio missae*) in Chinese.[241] *The Prayers of Sufferings* (*Tongku jingji* 痛苦經蹟, ca. 1640s) included an anonymous text called *The Exposition of Mass* (*Misa lijie* 彌撒禮節).[242] In the end of the text is a note written in smaller size, giving *The Meaning of the Sacrifice of Mass* as a reference.[243] Composed by the same

---

239 Aleni, *Misa jiyi*, *mulu*, fol. 1a–b, 483–484.
240 Dudink translates the three parts as "the preparation of the sacrifice, the sacrifice proper, and the conclusion of the sacrifice." Dudink, "Manual for Attending Mass," 237. The translation in the current section conforms to the Chinese context of the original text.
241 For the exposition of Mass, see Dudink, "Manual for Attending Mass," 211–212.
242 Anon., *Misa lijie* 彌撒禮節, in Anon., *Tongku jingji*, fol. 19a–fol. 34b, 1147–1180. No content in the last folio.
243 "詳見《彌撒祭義》," Anon., *Misa lijie*, fol. 34a5, 1179.

three parts with thirty-three sections,[244] *The Exposition of Mass* is an abridged second volume of Aleni's monograph.[245] The following text in *The Prayers of Sufferings* is *Abridged Meaning of the Sacrifice of Mass* (*Misa jiyi lüe* 彌撒祭義畧) by Aleni.[246] It is an abridged version of four chapters in the first volume of his monograph (i.e., the Name, the Hall and Altar, the Liturgical Vestment, and the Rite for the Acolyte). These two abridged texts have been included in many books, yet there are other texts taking same titles which can be confusing.[247]

Around 1665, the Jesuits enriched *General Collection of Prayer Recitation in the Holy Teaching of the Lord of Heaven* into three volumes and renamed it *Daily Services of the Holy Teaching*.[248] Without mentioning date and place, this edition kept the five aforementioned editors and marked Buglio and Verbiest as two new revisers (*chongding* 重訂). The first volume included the Rite of Attending Mass (*yu misa li* 與彌撒禮),[249] giving *The Meaning of the Sacrifice of Mass* as a reference in the end with a note in smaller size;[250] Prayer before Mass (*misaqian zhuwen* 彌撒前祝文),[251] The Elevation of the Holy Body (*juyang shengti* 舉揚聖體),[252] The Elevation of the Holy Chalice (*juyang shengjue* 舉揚聖爵),[253] [Prayer] Recited before Receiving the Holy Body (*ling shengti qian song* 領聖體前誦),[254] and [Prayer] Recited after Receiving the Holy Body (*yiling shengti song* 已領聖體誦).[255] The second volume included the Litany of Jesus' Holy Body by Aleni.[256] This mature prayer book became the definitive (*ne varietur*) edition, *Daily Services of the Holy Teaching* in later generations always included this edition and only made slight changes.[257]

---

244   Anon., *Misa lijie*, fol. 19a2–4,1147.
245   Dudink, "Manual for Attending Mass," 208.
246   Giulio Aleni 艾儒畧, *Misa jiyi lüe* 彌撒祭義畧, in Anon., *Tongku jingji*, fol. 23a–fol. 28a3, 1181–1191.
247   Brunner attributed folios 18–34 in *The Prayers of Sufferings* to Longobardo. Brunner, *L'euchologe*, 90. For detailed information of the two abridged texts from Aleni's monograph, see Dudink, "Manual for Attending Mass," 322–323.
248   Brunner, *L'euchologe*, 27.
249   Anon., *Shengjiao rike* 聖教日課, *shang juan*, BnF Chinois 7353, fol. 16a1–b1.
250   "見《彌撒祭義》," Anon., *Shengjiao rike, shang juan*, fol. 16b1.
251   Anon., *Shengjiao rike, shang juan*, fol. 16b2–fol. 17a2.
252   Anon., *Shengjiao rike, shang juan*, fol. 17a3–6.
253   Anon., *Shengjiao rike, shang juan*, fol. 17a7–b2.
254   Anon., *Shengjiao rike, shang juan*, fol. 48a4–b7.
255   Anon., *Shengjiao rike, shang juan*, fol. 49a1–b7.
256   Anon., *Shengjiao rike, zhong juan*, BnF Chinois 7353–7354, fol. 2a1–fol. 9b6.
257   Brunner, *L'euchologe*, 84, 98.

In 1670, the translation of the Roman Missal published in Beijing.[258] The front cover reads the Chinese title *"Misa jingdian* 彌撒經典*"* (The Classics of the Mass). The next page introduces the translator Buglio; the five editors Herdtricht, Couplet, Magalhães, Rougemont, and Grelon; the authorizer Verbiest. The following page is a cover in Latin decorated with the Jesuit symbol and images of the four Evangelists. The cover in Latin reads: "MISSALE ROMANUM auctoritate PAULI V. PONT. M Sinice redditum A P LUDOVICO BUGLIO SOC. IESU PEKIM[NI] In Collegio eiusd. Soc. AN. M. DC. LXX" (Roman Missal with the Sanction of Pope Paul V reedited in Chinese by Father Ludovico Buglio of the Society of Jesus at Beijing in the College of the Same Society in the year 1670). The following page provides a detailed table of content in Chinese.[259] The translation is incomplete because the missionaries decided to translate essential parts first.[260] In a letter written to the Visitor and the revisers in Canton, Buglio talked about the difficulty of translating the Roman Missal into literary Chinese. His translation was an expedient which conformed to

---

258 Audrey Seah, "The 1670 Chinese Missal: A Struggle for Indigenization Amidst the Chinese Rites Controversy," in *China's Christianity: From Missionary to Indigenous Church*, ed. Anthony E. Clark (Leiden: Brill, 2017), 86–120.

259 According to the appendix to *The Classics of the Mass* edited by Couplet, Bontinck makes a list of sixteen sections, yet the list is more like a summary than a table of content and the section sequence does not conform with the original text. Bontinck, *La Lutte*, 156. In the *Sequel to Chinese Christian Texts from the Zikawei Library*, the editors provide a brief table of contents before the original text, which offers sections with precise page numbers and corresponding Latin titles. Yet, the brief table is incomplete; its three parts and fourteen sections do not conform with the original text. Based on the brief table, the current section provides the content of the original text. *The Classics of the Mass* contains nine parts with seventy-five sections in total: part 1, *Xili nianyue* 西曆年月 (year and month in Western calendar, *Calendarium*), nine sections; part 2, *Misa gongli* 彌撒公例 (*Rubricae generales Missalis*), twenty-one sections; part 3, *Misa lijie* 彌撒禮節 (*Ritus servandus in celebratione Missarum*), thirteen sections; part 4, *Zuo misa huo que zhe* 做彌撒或缺者 (*De defectibus Missae*), eight sections; part 5, *Duode zuo misa yubei nian* 鐸德做彌撒預備念 (what said by the priest at the preparation of Mass), seven sections; part 6, *Duode yubei misa qian zhuwen* 鐸德預備彌撒前祝文 (prayers by the priest before the preparation of Mass), one section; part 7, *Misa hou zhuwen* 彌撒後祝文 (prayers by the priest after Mass), two sections; part 8, *Misa jingdian* 彌撒經典 (classics of the Mass), seven sections; part 9, *Zhushengshui guiyi* 祝聖水規儀 [etc.] (*Benedictio aquae*), seven sections, this part is in fact *Benedictiones diversae*. See *Missale Romanum* (1570), 660, 719–720.

260 Bontinck, *La Lutte*, 155. Pfister claims that the translation is complete. Pfister, *Notices biographiques*, 240. Luo Guohui also claimed that the whole Roman Missal was translated into Chinese. Luo Guohui 羅國輝, "Li Leisi *Misa jingdian* fanyi shimo 利類思《彌撒經典》翻譯始末," in *Colletanea Theologica* [*Universitatis Fujen*] 輔仁大學神學論集 vol. 120, trans. Qu Fengling 瞿鳳玲 (1999), 260.

Chinese structure and needed the missionary's explanation.[261] In the following years, Buglio continued translating and publishing ritual books, such as the translation of the Roman Breviary *Prayer Book for the Priest* (*Siduo kedian* 司鐸課典, 1674);[262] *Ritual Manual for Sacraments* (*Shengshi lidian* 聖事禮典, 1675);[263] and *Instructions of the Priest* which was published in 1676.[264] Buglio's fruitful translations contained the explanation and manual of Mass, yet these ritual books did not obtain the approval from Rome and could not be used in liturgy.[265] As Le Comte recorded, after some consideration missionaries continued to celebrate Mass in Latin.[266]

On 30 July 1673, the cardinals in the particular commission to discuss indigenous liturgy approved the first privilege granted by Paul V, i.e., priest's head being covered in the celebration of Mass, but they refused to exert the other two privileges pertaining to the Roman Missal and the Roman Ritual in Chinese. On 23 December 1673, their decision was confirmed by the brief *The Roman Pontiff* (*Romanus Pontifex*).[267] In December 1684, Couplet presented *The Classics of the Mass* to Innocent XI but received no comment.[268] During his trip in Europe, Couplet planned to make a refined version of the Roman Missal in Chinese. In a letter written to Papebroch on 26 May 1686, he asked for twenty or more copies of images in the Roman Missal published by Plantin-Moretus in Antwerp. These images preceded the Canon and the Mass on feasts such as the Advent, Christmas, Epiphany, Easter, and Ascension.[269] Couplet received the images but it was impossible to make a great number of movable characters. The plan to publish a refined version of *The Classics of the Mass* in Europe had to stop. Around 1694, the Visitors of the Vice-Province requested that copies of

---

261 The Roman Missal includes four elements: the Gospels, the Epistles, prayers, and Psalms. Buglio could translate the first three elements in one or another way but the Psalms were extremely difficult to translate. St. Jerome had translated them literally instead of according to the meaning, yet it would be unreasonable for the literati to comprehend the Psalms translated literally. Bontinck, *La Lutte*, 157.
262 Bernard, *Les Adaptations chinoises*, 374.
263 Bernard, *Les Adaptations chinoises*, 375. It was adapted from the *Manuals for Administering the Sacraments of the Church* (*Manuale ad sacramenta Ecclesiae ministranda*, 1605) by Luís Cerqueira (SJ, 1552–1614). Dudink, "Manual for Attending Mass," 315, note 345.
264 It was adapted from the *On the Education of Priests and Mortal Sins* (*De instructione sacerdotum et peccatis mortalibus*, 1604) by Francisco Toledo (SJ, 1532–1596). Bernard, *Les Adaptations chinoises*, 376.
265 Standaert, *The Interweaving of Rituals*, 107.
266 Lecomte, *Un jésuite à Pékin*, 427.
267 Bontinck, *La Lutte*, 146–147.
268 Bontinck, *La Lutte*, 208.
269 Bontinck, *La Lutte*, 226.

The Classics of the Mass should not circulate among Chinese Catholics or even among coadjutors, for fear that the Roman Missal in Chinese might tempt Chinese people to impersonate priests.[270] Nevertheless, requests to use *The Classics of the Mass* continued. In a letter written to Mgr. de Lionne on 5 September 1702, Basset talked about the Roman Missal and the Roman Ritual printed in Chinese. He argued that if Rome confirms Paul V's permission, the Catholic Church in China only have to review, correct, and refine the translation.[271] In the eighteenth century, various missionaries reiterated the request to use *The Classics of the Mass* but Rome refused.

In contrast, prayer books in Chinese had been developed and continued to be circulated in the Christian communities. In the late seventeenth century, the Franciscans published *General Collection of Prayers in the Holy Teaching* (*Shengjiao zongdu jingwen* 聖教總牘經文, ca. 1698) in Ji'nan.[272] This first non-Jesuit prayer book was also called *Daily Services of the Holy Teaching* and kept the majority content of the definitive edition.[273] In addition, the Franciscan *General Collection* included new prayers pertaining to Mass. Included into the book for the first time, the Rite of Five Thanks (*Wuxie li* 五謝禮) has been a popular prayer recited after Mass to this day.[274] In the first volume, the Franciscans attached Spritual Practice to Communicate Merits (*Tonggong shenke* 通功神課) to *The Exposition of Mass*.[275] It was a prayer that Chinese Catholics preferred to chant after the consecration.[276] In the fifth volume, de la Piñuela selected (*xuanding* 選定) Holy Body's Mysterious Meaning (*Shengti aoyi* 聖體奧義) and Questions & Answers of Receiving the Holy Body (*Ling shengti wenda* 領聖體問答).[277] Around the same time, de la Piñuela published *Directions for Hearing Mass* (*Ting misa fanli* 聽彌撒凡例, ca. 1698), yet this ritual manual was not included in the Franciscan prayer book and has not been reprinted.[278]

---

270 The request had been reiterated in a letter by the Vice-Provincial Antoine Thomas (An Duo 安多, SJ, 1644–1709) in 1704. Brockey, *Journey to the East*, 174.
271 Bontinck, *La Lutte*, 291.
272 Dudink, "Manual for Attending Mass," 223.
273 Brunner, *L'euchologe*, 99.
274 Anon., OFM, *Wuxie yi* 五謝禮, *Shengjiao zongdu* 聖教總牘, *juan* 1, fol. 1b1–6, in CCT BAV (1), vol. 44, 22. For a French translation, see Brunner, *L'euchologe*, 100.
275 Anon., OFM, *Tonggong shenke* 通功神課, *Shengjiao zongdu*, *juan* 1, fol. 33a1–fol. 34a4, 91–93. See Dudink, "Manual for Attending Mass," 224.
276 Brunner, *L'euchologe*, 106.
277 Pedro de la Piñuela 石鐸琭, *Shengti aoyi* 聖體奧義, *Shengjiao zongdu*, *juan* 5, fol. 39a3–fol. 41b5, 641–646. Pedro de la Piñuela 石鐸琭, *Ling shengti wenda* 領聖體問答, *Shengjiao zongdu*, *juan* 5, fol. 41b7–fol. 45a4, 646–653. See Brunner, *L'euchologe*, 108.
278 Dudink, "Manual for Attending Mass," 223. *Directions for hearing Mass* was published around 1698, see Dudink, "Manual for Attending Mass," 221, note 42.

PERFORMER OF WORSHIP   173

In 1715, Ignacio Noruega (Yi-na-jue 依納爵, OSA,?–1731) published *Daily Services of the Holy Teaching of the Lord of Heaven* in Canton.[279] Composed by two volumes, the Augustinian prayer book kept much of the definitive edition and a few prayers from the Franciscan prayer book.[280] For the first time, the prayer book included "Praise to the Holy Body and the Holy Mother" and liturgical hymns by Aquinas. Saint Master Thomas' Four Character Poem to the Holy Body (*Duo-ma-si shengshi xiang shengti sizi shi* 多瑪斯聖師向聖體四字詩) translated Devoutly I Adore Thee (*Adoro te devote*, 1264) from poetic Latin into literary and poetic Chinese.[281] Similarly, Four Character Classic to Praise the Holy Body (*Zan shengti sizi jingwen* 讚聖體四字經文) translated Sion Lift Thy Voice and Sing (*Lauda Sion*, 1264).[282] Furthermore, Noruega included new texts pertaining to Mass, such as Merits Suitable to Make before and after Receiving the Holy Body (*Ling shengti qianhou kexing zhi gong* 領聖體前後可行之功),[283] Seven Points to Meditate before and after Receiving the Holy Body (*Ling shengti qianhou moxiang qiduan* 領聖體前後默想七端),[284] Summary of Miraculous Events at Mass (*Misa qimiao shiqing lüeshuo* 彌撒奇妙事情畧說),[285] and Method of Listening to the Mass Every Day (*Meiri ting misa zhi fa* 每日聽彌撒之法).[286] These anonymous texts taught Chinese Catholics how to pray and meditate during the celebration of Mass, especially when receiving the Host.

In the early eighteenth century, the Jesuits published *Manual for Attending Mass* (*Yu misa gongcheng* 與彌撒功程, ca. 1721), which was attributed to one of its censors Romain Hinderer (De Manuo 德瑪諾, SJ, 1668–1744). This Order of the Mass (*Ordinarium Missae*) in Chinese became a huge success and shaped Chinese Catholics' eucharistic piety.[287] Since the beginning of the

---

279   Brunner, *L'euchologe*, 109.
280   Ignacio Noruega 依納爵, *Tianzhu shengjiao rike* 天主聖教日課, BnF Chinois 7433, fol. 1a1–fol. 5a4.
281   Noruega, *Shengjiao rike*, juan 1, fol. 53b5–fol. 54b4. Buglio had translated Saint Master Thomas' Four Character Poem to the Holy Body under the same title decades before. See Lodovico Buglio 利類思, *Misa jingdian* 彌撒經典, fol. 61a13–b10, SCCT ZKW, vol. 15, 127–128.
282   Noruega, *Shengjiao rike*, juan 2, fol. 144a1–fol. 145a5. The Chinese version omitted the last word "Alleluia."
283   Noruega, *Shengjiao rike*, juan 1, fol. 54b5–fol. 56a8.
284   Noruega, *Shengjiao rike*, juan 1, fol. 56b1–fol. 59a8.
285   Noruega, *Shengjiao rike*, juan 2, fol. 172b1–fol. 174b8.
286   Noruega, *Shengjiao rike*, juan 2, fol. 175a1–fol. 179b8.
287   Paul Brunner, "La Messe chinoise du Père Hinderer," *Neue Zeitschrift für Missionswissenschaft* 15 (1959): 271. A variant title of this ritual manual is *Manual for Mass* (*Misa guicheng* 彌撒規程). For a translation in English, see Dudink, "Manual for Attending Mass," 245–294.

Catholic Church in China, receiving the Host has been an essential part in catechism books. As the Catholic Church developed, manual books to guide Chinese Catholics to attend Mass were published. In Europe manual books on Mass were published for priests, whereas in China ritual manuals were written for all the Chinese Catholics, providing detailed procedure for the acolyte and the congregants as well as for priests.[288] From history to meaning, from procedure to suggestion, missionaries made every effort to propagate Mass in the Christian communities.

3.3   Sacrificial Hat

Contrary to the rejection of using *The Classics of the Mass*, Rome approved the request that priests in China be allowed to cover their heads during the celebration of Mass. Ever since their arrival, the Jesuits paid special attention to their clothing and its meaning in Chinese society. At first, the early Jesuits in China such as Ruggieri and Ricci dressed like common people. In 1583, the official in Zhaoqing suggested them to dress like Buddhist monks. In 1592, Qu Rukui told Ricci that those who were respected in Chinese society were not Buddhist monks but literati, so Ricci wrote to Valignano the visitor of the Jesuit missions in East Asia, suggesting that missionaries should dress like literati, the well-educated Chinese.[289] Valignano agreed that the Jesuits in China should dress according to Chinese tradition and reported this decision to the Jesuit Superior General and the pope.[290] In May 1595, Ricci began to wear a Confucian outfit in Zhangshu 樟樹, Jiangxi.[291] When visiting the officials in Nanchang, Ricci wore a whole Confucian outfit, including a beautiful silk garment, a matching belt, a pair of embroidered shoes, and a tall hat covered with black veil, which was called "Dongpo hat" (*Dongpo jin* 東坡巾).[292] Before long, the Jesuits in China intended to wear hats not only in formal meetings with literati but also in Mass.

---

288   Dudink, "Manual for Attending Mass," 313.
289   Bernard, *Le père Matthieu Ricci*, première partie, 194.
290   Qi Yinping 戚印平 and He Xianyue 何先月, "Zailun Li Madou de yifu yu Fan Li'an de wenhua shiying zhengce 再論利瑪竇的易服與范禮安的文化適應政策," *Zhejiang daxue xuebao renwen shehui kexueban* 浙江大學學報人文社會科學版 3 (2013): 121.
291   There are various opinions about the specific time and place, see Qi and He, "Zailun," 117, note 1.
292   Bernard, *Le père Matthieu Ricci*, première partie, 199–200; deuxième partie, 249. Dongpo hat is a kind of ancient Chinese hat. Tradition has it that the literatus Su Shi 蘇軾 (1037–1101, art name: hermit Dongpo 東坡居士) invented this hat. Shen Congwen 沈從文, *Zhongguo gudai fushi yanjiu* 中國古代服飾研究 (Shanghai: Shanghai shudian chubanshe 上海書店出版社, 2011), 443.

In 1603, Valignano had already permitted the Jesuits to cover their heads when celebrating Mass. The theologians in Rome disagreed, however, they suggested that the Jesuits can ask the pope for a pontifical privilege.[293] During his trip in Europe, Trigault emphasized to Paul V that it is the entire Catholic Church in China—both missionaries and Chinese Catholics—that demand wearing a special hat to cover head at Mass.[294] Paul V granted the privilege and Propaganda Fide approved it. The anonymous article "A Liturgical Practice Specific to China: The *jijin* 祭巾 or Bonnet of Mass" (Un pratique liturgique propre à la Chine: Le *Tsikin* 祭巾 ou bonnet de messe) lists two major reasons given by Rome to grant the privilege, both were based on the report brought by Trigault. The first reason pertaining to material order and practical commodity. To evangelize in China, missionaries had to conform to Chinese customs. Contrary to Europeans who began to wear wigs as a fashion, missionaries shaved their heads and had a long braid. Since some regions in China were very cold in winter, Rome approved the head covering as a sacred ornament of adaptation for the health of missionaries.[295] Nevertheless, this description complies more with the situation in the Qing dynasty than the Ming dynasty. The second reason was pertaining to moral order, because to uncover one's head was a sign of humiliation and contempt in the Chinese tradition. A subordinate always covered his head in front of a superior, let alone in front of the emperor. Therefore, Chinese neophytes were astonished to watch a priest uncovering his head in the presence of Jesus Christ on the altar. Rome granted the approval with the faculty of assimilation which is a mark of its catholicity.[296]

Having heard about the privilege granted by Rome, the Catholic Church in China began to design a special hat for priests to wear when celebrating Mass.[297] With the assistance of Xu Guangqi, Li Zhizao, and other Catholic literati, the missionaries finally chose one design out of several models and named it "the sacrificial hat" (*jijin* 祭巾). The word "*jinji* 祭巾" is not recorded in *Le Grand Ricci* dictionary, yet there is the similar word "*jiguan* 祭冠," which means the bonnet of sacrifice used in traditional Chinese sacrificial rituals.[298]

---

293 Bontinck, *La Lutte*, 36. The Jesuits probably wore different hats for different occasions. More research is needed to find out if priests wore a specific hat when celebrating Mass before inventing the sacrificial hat.
294 Bontinck, *La Lutte*, 36–37. Jennes, "La liturgie chinoise," 247.
295 Anon., "Un pratique liturgique propre à la Chine: Le *Tsikin* 祭巾 ou bonnet de messe," *Bulletin catholique de Pékin* 11 (1924): 377. This anonymous article gives a brief introduction on the history of the sacrificial hat exclusively for priests in China.
296 Anon., "Un pratique liturgique," 404.
297 Fang, *Zhongguo tianzhujiao shang*, 180.
298 *Le Grand Ricci* I, 855, 476.

The similarity of naming is not accidental because the sacrificial hat is a kind of bonnet wore by priests in the Catholic sacrificial ritual. The aforementioned article on the sacrificial hat calls it *tsikin* and "bonnet of Mass" (*bonnet de messe*). Bontinck translated it as *tsi-kin*, "bonnet of sacrifice" (*bonnet de sacrifice*), and "Chinese barrette" (*barrette chinoise*).[299] In the chapter of liturgical vestment, *The Meaning of the Sacrifice of Mass*, Aleni gave a vivid description.

> Now in China, the pope permits use of the black bonnet. The style is square on the top and round on the bottom; all four sides are hung with the flowing piece, all have three folded lines, with one angle toward the front and two long ribbons falling on the back. This is the sacrificial hat.[300]

The sacrificial hat housed in the Scheuts China Museum corresponds to Aleni's description (figure 10).

Following the description is the corresponding allegorical explanation. This section attaches the allegorical explanation to each specific detail of the sacrificial hat. For the square top and the round bottom, "The highest level of the celestial body created by the Lord of Heaven is unmoved and constantly unchangeable, while its lowest level is infinitely circling."[301] For the quadrilateral formed by the square top, "The east, the west, the south, and the north has its position respectively and each position demonstrates the meaning of our Lord's Trinity."[302] The aforementioned three folded lines form one triangle on each side of the quadrilateral, signifying the Trinity. The flowing piece near the stable triangle signifies human beings' situation, posing a contrast: "Yet, human beings doubt themselves that since their faith is incomplete, they cannot enter heaven directly, thus having the floating and unstable look."[303]

The black covering is decorated with colorful embroidery, which presents Christian images with traditional Chinese pattern. The Cross embroidered on the covering is a remarkable image.

---

299   Bontinck, *La Lutte*, 58.
300   "今在中華，教皇許用玄色為冠。其制上方下圓，四圍俱有飄版，俱有三折線路，以一角向前，後有二長垂帶，即祭巾也。" Aleni, *Misa jiyi, juan* 1, fol. 15a6–9, 513.
301   "取義指天主所造天體，最上一層，不動而常定。其下則圓轉不窮，" Aleni, *Misa jiyi, juan* 1, fol. 15a9–b1, 513–514.
302   "東西南北各有方位。每方各顯吾主三位一體之義。" Aleni, *Misa jiyi, juan* 1, fol. 15b1–2, 514.
303   "但人自疑信不齊，不能直入天堂，故猶有飄搖不定之象。" Aleni, *Misa jiyi, juan* 1, fol. 15b2–3, 514.

FIGURE 10 Sacrificial hat
COURTESY OF THE SCHEUTS CHINA MUSEUM.

Nevertheless the Holy Cross rules over the flowing piece. The world shares one ancestor and in the beginning there was no distinction between one and the other. One shall always keep the virtue of humility and reveal the heart that loves the Lord of Heaven and human beings. That is the reason our Lord deigned to come to the Cross and instructed that the Cross is the wooden boat ascending to the Heaven. [The Cross] also signifies the crown of thorns worn by our Lord during the Crucifixion. These are the examples originally established by our Lord Jesus and these are the examples for those who are in charge of the Teaching and those who follow the Teaching.[304]

---

304 "然十字聖架，則常統攝于上，四海共宗，初無彼此，惟常存謙下之德，發其

Those who are in charge signify priests and those who follow the Teaching signify the Catholic faithful. Both shall take the Cross as an example. The embroidery on the sacrificial hats varied in details. In figure 10, the Cross is embroidered on each long ribbon, while "RM" (for *Regina Maria* "Mary, Queen") and "IHS" (*Iesus Hominum Salvator* "Jesus, Savior of Men" or the first three letters of Jesus' name in Greek) are embroidered on the covering.

The only Chinese text on the sacrificial hat in late Ming and early Qing that has been found so far is *The Regulation of the Cap of Mass* (*Misa guan yi* 彌撒冠儀). In a matter of fact, there are three undated texts under the title: *Regulation of the Cap of Mass*, page 625 to page 629, and page 630 is blank; *The Hat of Mass is the Implicit Sign of the Fall of Ming Dynasty* (*Misa jin shi Mingwang zhi anxin* 彌撒巾是明亡之暗信, hereafter *The Hat of Mass is the Implicit Sign*), page 631 to page 632; *Matteo Ricci Entering China is the Implicit Sign of Ming Dynasty Losing the Reign* (*Li Madou jin Zhongguo wei Ming shi tianxia zhi anxin* 利瑪竇進中國為明失天下之暗信), page 633. The first text is complete and probably indicates the author, while the last two are anonymous and probably incomplete. Since the third text only contains two paragraphs which do not mention the sacrificial hat, the current section examines *The Regulation of the Cap of Mass* and *The Hat of Mass is the Implicit Sign*.

The Regulation of the Cap of Mass contains the introduction, description, and allegorical explanation of the sacrificial hat, occasionally giving the author's opinion. At the beginning, the author notified the different connotations of uncovering the head: "The subordinate commits a crime when he meets the superior but does not wear a cap (*mianguan* 免冠). Such is the rule in China. Yet, in the West people do not wear a cap during the worship."[305] What is considered disrespect in the Chinese custom is an expression of respect in the West. The indigenous priest Wu Li notified the difference in his poem as well. In the spring in Macao, people go to the bistro for a drink, "Every one who comes to drink talks about their homeland, their etiquette is the same except for not wearing a cap (*mianguan* 免冠)."[306] As the missionaries told Rome about the

---

愛天主愛人二者之心。則吾主所以降諭升天堂之筏也。又指吾主受難曾戴茨冠之義。此以上皆吾主耶穌原立之表，而主教者與奉教者，其表亦卽在于此焉。" Aleni, *Misa jiyi, juan* 1, fol. 15b3-8, 514.

305 "夫以卑見尊，免冠稱罪，中國之制也。西洋則以行於瞻禮。" Anon., *Misa guanyi* 彌撒冠儀, fol. 1a2, in SCCT ZKW, vol. 5, 625.

306 "禮數還同只免冠。（原注：髮有金絲拳被者，矜重戴黑絨帽；帽式如笠，見人則免之為禮敬。）" Wu Li 吳歷, "Aozhong zayong 9 嶴中雜詠九," *Sanba ji* 三巴集, Fang Hao 方豪, "Wu Yushan xiansheng *Sanba ji* jiaoshi 吳漁山先生《三巴集》校釋," in *Wu Yushan (Li) yanjiu lunji* 吳漁山（歷）研究論集, ed. Zhou Kangxie 周康

connotation of uncovering the head in the Chinese custom, the author of *The Regulation of the Cap of Mass* and Wu Li told Chinese people about the Western custom. Through the whole text of *The Regulation of the Cap of Mass*, the author took the West Sea (*xiyang* 西洋) into consideration to propagate Catholic rituals in China. The author emphasized that it took a long time to make covering the head during the celebration of Mass an actual practice because one should be obedient to the superior.

> Therefore, it took several years to carry the discussion of having the cap to the West and it took several years to carry the order of having the cap back to the East. The day on which the order from the West arrived was the day on which having the cap started, and the arrival is in the year of Wuwu.[307]

In late Ming and early Qing, the year of Wuwu 戊午 took place twice: 1618 (Wanli 46) and 1678 (Kangxi 17).[308] Since the text did not mention that the year is in the reign of the Ming dynasty, the author probably lived in Ming dynasty. Furthermore, the year 1618 is close to the actual year when the message of the privilege granted by Rome arrived China. In 1615, Paul V granted the privilege of covering the head during the celebration of Mass to all the missionaries in China. In April 1619, Trigault came back to Macao with the news of the privilege. Then, Aleni and some Chinese Catholics spent some time to design the sacrificial hat. In this regard, the year given in *The Regulation of the Cap of Mass* is 1618.

The description and allegorical explanation of the sacrificial hat in *The Regulation of the Cap of Mass* do not totally conform with Aleni's. To begin with, the author called the sacrificial hat "the cap of Mass" (*misa guan* 彌撒冠) with a strong Catholic connotation. In addition, the author always attached the allegorical explanation right behind the corresponding description. Similarities and dissimilarities between the description and allegorical explanation

---

燮 (Hongkong: Chongwen shudian 崇文書店, 1971), 110. For an English translation of the whole poem, see Jonathan Chaves, *Singing of the Source: Nature and God in the Poetry of the Chinese Painter Wu Li* (Honolulu: University of Hawaii press, 1993), 56.

307 "故有冠之議，約數載而西歸；有冠之命，又數載而東至。其至之日，則冠之日矣，其至則戊午也。" Anon., *Misa guanyi*, fol. 1a7–9, 625. The character "*gui* 歸" has been corrected into "*chen* 陳."

308 The lunisolar calendar calculates years by the Heavenly Stems and Earthly Branches. This calculative system has a sixty-year calendrical cycle. The year of Wuwu 戊午 is the fifty-fifth year in the calendrical cycle.

in *The Regulation of the Cap of Mass* and those in *The Meaning of the Sacrifice of Mass* can be divided in four categories. First, the description conforms with Aleni's but the allegorical explanation does not. For example, "Its shape is square, which signifies that the Teaching circulates in the four directions."[309] The word "the four directions" (*sifang* 四方) refers to the world in this context, producing a paronomasia together with the character "square" (*fang* 方). The shape of the cap of Mass signifies the wide spread of the Teaching of the Lord of Heaven.

Second, both the description and allegorical explanation differ from Aleni's. On the top of the cap, instead of the round bottom, "In the middle is the round hole, which signifies that the Trinity is without beginning and without end. Since the top of the priest's head reveals, wearing a cap looks like not wearing a cap."[310] In addition, what Aleni called the flowing piece (*piaoban* 飄版) is now called the surplus cloth (*yufu* 餘幅). Only one side of the surplus cloth hangs on one side of the top, leaving three other sides of the surplus cloth open, therefore "each of the four [surplus] cloth forms the three doors respectively to signify the mouth of the apostles."[311]

Third, the description conforms with Aleni's yet the allegorical explanation is not what Aleni mentioned. The author of *The Regulation of the Cap of Mass* attached the allegorical explanation to the two long ribbons on the back: "Behind are the two ribbons, which signify the rules of the Teaching."[312]

Fourth, both the description and allegorical explanation conform with Aleni's, yet more detailed, simplified or deepened. For example, the allegorical explanation of the three folded lines became more detailed.

> On the top of the cap is the equilateral triangle with the angles *jia*, *yi*, and *bing*. The triangle signifies the three Persons; the equal literals signify the unity. The two angles *jia* and *yi* are side by side in the front while the angle *bing* is at the middle in the back, because the third Person is proceeds from the first and the second.[313]

---

309 "其形方，象教之周以四方也。" Anon., *Misa guanyi*, fol. 1b1, 626.
310 "中為圓孔，象三位之無始無終也。而撒責之頂露矣，冠猶弗冠矣。" Anon., *Misa guanyi*, fol. 2a7–8, 627.
311 "其四幅各為三門，以象宗徒氏之口。" Anon., *Misa guanyi*, fol. 1b4–5, 626.
312 "後為二条，以象教規。" Anon., *Misa guanyi*, fol. 1b5, 626.
313 "冠之頂，為甲乙丙平邊三角形，三角者，象三位；平邊者，象一體也。甲乙兩角而前而並列，丙角在後而居中，第三位，從第一第二而生也。" Anon., *Misa guanyi*, fol. 2a5–7, 627.

The author pointed out the equilateral triangle (*pingbian sanjiaoxing* 平邊三角形) with the three angles *jia*, *yi*, and *bing*.[314] The author presented the relationship among the three Persons by quoting a verse from the Nicene Creed (*Qui ex Patre Filioque procedit*). The author also pointed out the location of the Cross, which is an appropriate image on the sacrificial vestment.

> Look at the front. There is the holy symbol of the Cross, which shows respect to the Crucifixion of Jesus. During the Mass, the priest faces up toward the Lord of Heaven, faces down toward the people and toward the one whom the people surround and worship. On the front of the cap is the most honorable holy symbol of the Cross, the most illustrious and deeply [illegible], therefore it is appropriate to face toward the Lord of Heaven and the people.[315]

Unlike Aleni who talked about humility, love, the wooden boat, and the crown of thorns, the author presented the scene where the priest celebrates the Mass with the cap of Mass on the head, thus simplifying yet deepening the allegorical explanation of the Cross. In the end of the allegorical explanation, the author summarized: "Thus the meaning of Mass is briefly enumerated."[316] The allegorical explanation of the cap of Mass directly relates to its function as a sacrificial vestment worn by priests in the celebration of Mass.

In addition to the description and allegorical explanation, the author gave his opinion on the cap of Mass. The regulation of the design for the cap of Mass shall be as followed: "Having the cap complies with the Chinese custom, but the cap itself does not have to; the color of the cap complies with the Chinese custom, but its shape does not have to."[317] Although priests should follow the Chinese custom of covering the head to show respect, the cap of Mass shall have some characteristics in its design to differentiate with traditional Chinese hats. The author raised three traditional Chinese hats as the comparison with the cap of Mass: the square hat (*fangjin* 方巾), Dongpo hat, and Letian hat

---

314 The equilateral triangle is called "*dengbian* 等邊" in Modern Chinese. *Jia*, *yi*, and *bing* are the first three in the cycle of the Heavenly Stems (*tiangan*天干).
315 "視其前，有十字聖號焉，尊耶穌受難也。彌撒時撒賚上對天主，下向眾人，及眾人所拱而禮者。冠之前也，十字聖號至尊者，至顯且切□，宜以對天主又眾人也。" Anon., *Misa guanyi*, fol. 2a8–b2, 627–628.
316 "於是乎彌撒之義，畧舉矣。" Anon., *Misa guanyi*, fol. 3a3, 629.
317 "有冠從中國，其冠不必從中國也；冠之色從中國，其形不必從中國也。" Anon., *Misa guanyi*, fol. 1b7–8, 626.

(*Letian jin* 樂天巾).[318] Missionaries often wore a Dongpo hat in daily life.[319] The cap of Mass resembles the three hats in respective details yet differentiates from them in other respective details, thus "making Chinese people think that [the cap of Mass] looks like the other hat and not look like the other hat, that [the cap of Mass] can be imitated and impossible to imitate."[320] What the author aimed at was the effect of "*you* 猶" (to look like). In the aforementioned description, the round hole on the top of the cap produces the effect that "wearing a cap looks like not wearing a cap" (*guan you fuguan* 冠猶弗冠). Because of such ambiguous effect, Chinese people cannot identify this cap with any traditional hats, "then they have no choice but to name it the cap of Mass."[321]

In the Ming dynasty, the official regulation on hats soon ceased to take effect and various designs of hats were developed for the literati and the people. The intellectuals, the feudal lords, and the retired officials usually wore the square hat, while the merchants, the official servers, and the urban citizens wore the hat of six directions (*liuhe mao* 六合帽).[322] Under such a loose control of the official regulation, the Christian communities were able to propagate the hat exclusive for the Catholic priest in Chinese society. The author underlined: "This is not only a creation in the Chinese Mass but a creation since the origin of Mass."[323] The cap of Mass is a remarkable example of adaptation. Behind the creation is the collaboration between missionaries and Chinese Catholics, along with the interaction between Rome and the Catholic Church in China. The new sacrificial vestment not only strengthened the root of the Catholic Church in China but also added more diversity to the universal Church. Moreover, the author thought that the Catholic Church in China had developed "the Chinese Mass" (*Zhongguo misa* 中國彌撒), the Mass with Chinese characteristics.

318　The square hat was popular in the Ming dynasty. Shen, *Zhongguo gudai*, 549–550. Letian hat is one kind of Taoist hat, named after the poet in the Tang dynasty Bai Juyi 白居易 (772–846, courtesy name: Letian 樂天), also called Chunyang hat (*Chunyang jin* 純陽巾), named after the Taoist god Lü Dongbin 呂洞賓 (798–?, art name: Chunyang zi 純陽子). Shen, *Zhongguo gudai*, 505.
319　For example, Ricci was wearing a Dongpo hat in his portrait painted by You Wenhui 游文輝 (Manuel Pereira, SJ, 1575–1633) around 1610. The portrait is housed in the Church of the Gesù in Rome.
320　"使中國之人，以為猶夫冠而不猶夫冠，若可倣而必不可倣，" Anon., *Misa guanyi*, fol. 1b8–9, 626.
321　"而後乃不得不名之彌撒巾矣。" Anon., *Misa guanyi*, fol. 3a7–8, 629.
322　Shen, *Zhongguo gudai*, 545.
323　"此不獨中國彌撒創見，自有彌撒而創見矣。" Anon., *Misa guanyi*, fol. 1a9, 625.

The Regulation of the Cap of Mass was written in the tone of a Chinese Catholic in literary Chinese, and the allegorical explanation exemplified the author's knowledge of Catholic theology and mathematics. Furthermore, the author highlighted priests as the exclusive celebrants of Mass, that their virtue is extraordinary and he usurped (*jian* 僭) their position to talk about the cap of Mass.[324] In addition, if the text was written in the Qing dynasty, the author would have specified that it is the year Wuwu in the last dynasty. Therefore, *The Regulation of the Cap of Mass* was probably written by a Catholic literatus in the Ming dynasty around 1620–1644. The most plausible evidence is the only name mentioned in the main body of the text: "On the twenty-eighth day in the ninth month, Mass was celebrated in Lianchuan. Ignatius Sun saw it."[325] Lianchuan 練川 is a variant name for Jiading, and the last word "it" refers to the cap of Mass. The description of the cap of Mass begins right after this sentence. Another name appears in the end of the text where usually the author's name is presented: "Preserved text by Mr. Xu Wending" (*Xu Wending gong cungao* 徐文定公存稿). "Wending 文定" is the posthumous title of Paulus Xu Guangqi. Yet, as one of the designers, Xu Guangqi did not need to describe the cap of Mass through Ignatius Sun's eyes. Moreover, two characters "*juefei* 決非" (certainly not) were added right before "preserved text by Mr. Xu Wending" and four characters "*Sun Yi-nuo-jue* 孫意諾爵" (Ignatius Sun) were added in the next vertical line. The six characters added by an unknown editor support that the author is a Chinese literatus whose surname is Sun and baptismal name is Ignatius.

Given the analysis above, the author is probably Ignatius Sun Yuanhua 孫元化 (1581–1632). As a disciple of Xu Guangqi, Sun Yuanhua converted to the Catholic Church under Xu Guangqi's guidance before 1621.[326] Sun Yuanhua invited Álvaro de Semedo (Zeng Dezhao 曾德昭, SJ, 1586–1658) and Cattaneo to initiate the Christian community in his hometown Jiading, and he paid to build the church and the residence for missionaries.[327] In fact, Huang Yi-long identifies a certain Ignatius Sun with Sun Yuanhua: "Xu Guangqi once wrote a text which mentioned that Ignatius Sun attended one Mass in Lianchuan on the twenty-eighth day in the ninth month the forty-sixth year of the reign of the Wanli emperor. The 'Ignatius Sun' here should also be Sun Yuanhua."[328] The

---

324 Anon., *Misa guanyi*, fol. 2a4–5, 627.
325 "九月二十有八日，行彌撒於練川。孫意諾爵見之。" Anon., *Misa guanyi*, fol. 1a9–b1, 625–626.
326 Liu, *Yitian liyi*, 5.
327 Fang, *Zhongguo tianzhujiaoshi shang*, 234–236.
328 "徐光啟曾撰文提及孫意諾爵嘗於萬曆四十六年九月二十八日參加在練川(嘉定之別名)所舉行的一場彌撒, 此一孫意諾爵應亦為孫元化，" Huang Yi-long 黃

text Huang Yi-long uses is called *A Discussion of the Cap of Mass* (*Misa guan yi* 彌撒冠議) by Xu Guangqi.[329] The text is probably another version of *The Regulation of the Cap of Mass*, the one without the six added characters. It is justifiable to identify Ignatius Sun with Sun Yuanhua under the premise that the author is Xu Guangqi, however, it was unlikely for Ignatius Sun to see the cap of Mass in Lianchuan in the year of Wuwu (1618, Wanli 46).

The following text is *The Hat of Mass is the Implicit Sign*, which calls the sacrificial hat "the hat of Mass" (*misa jin* 彌撒巾). Since the text only contains three short paragraphs, it is difficult to determine the author and date. The text may be incomplete as both the beginning and the end are abrupt. The first paragraph begins with "*Jia, yi,* and *bing* are *jiashen, yiyou,* and *bingxu* these three years."[330] The abrupt mention of *jia, yi,* and *bing* probably refers to certain parts of the hat of Mass. The three characters might mean the angles *jia, yi,* and *bing* of the equilateral triangle described in *The Regulation of the Cap of Mass*. The author of *The Hat of Mass is the Implicit Sign* interpreted the three characters as three continuous years in the Heavenly Stems and Earthly Branches (*tiangan dizhi* 天干地支): the twenty-first year *jiashen*, the twenty-second year *yiyou*, and the twenty-third year *bingxu*. Then, the author enumerated the events took place in the three years: "For the fall of Ming, Beijing [was conquered] in the year *jiashen*; Nanjing was lost in the year *yiyou*; by the year *bingxu*, various provinces and counties in the southern part all surrendered to Great Qing, thus the Ming territory has been entirely lost."[331] The Qing court indeed conquered Beijing in the year *jiashen* (1644), Nanjing in the year *yiyou* (1645), and many places in southern China in the year *bingxu* (1646).

The second paragraph continues the same interpretation: "[*Yi, geng,* and *xin*] are *yiwei, gengshen,* and *xinyou* these three years, which certainly are the eighteenth year, the nineteenth year, and the twentieth year of the reign of the Kangxi emperor."[332] Given the context, the three missing characters should be "*yi* 乙, *geng* 庚, *xin* 辛," which probably refer to certain parts of the hat of Mass. Again, the author interpreted them as three continuous years in the Heavenly Stems and Earthly Branches: the fifty-sixth year *yiwei*, the fifty-seventh year

---

一農, "Tianzhujiaotu Sun Yuanhua yu Mingmo chuanhua de xiyang huopao 天主教徒孫元化與明末傳華的西洋火炮," *Zhongyang yanjiuyuan lishi yuyan yanjiusuo jikan* 中央研究院歷史語言研究所集刊 67, 4 (1996): 918.

329 See Huang, "Tianzhujiaotu," 918, note 31.

330 "甲乙丙，即甲申、乙酉、丙戌三年也。" Anon., *Misa guanyi*, fol. 4a1, 631.

331 "明之亡，北京□在甲申；南京失於乙酉；至丙戌年，南路各省郡縣，俱歸降大清，是明地盡失□也。" Anon., *Misa guanyi*, fol. 4a2–4, 631.

332 "□□□即已未庚申辛酉三年，實康熙之十八、十九、二十年也。" Anon., *Misa guanyi*, fol. 4a5, 631.

gengshen, and the fifty-eighth year *xinyou*. The author identified the three years with 1679 (Kangxi 18), 1680 (Kangxi 19), and 1681 (Kangxi 20). Then, the author pointed out that these are "the years when the old subjects of Ming died."[333] By raising the imprecise example of Wu Sangui 吳三桂 (1612–1678), the author said that the old subjects of Ming were either conquered or killed in the three years.

The third paragraph gives the allegorical meaning to specific parts of the hat of Mass.

> The top of the hat echoes the emperor who is superior and honorable. Therefore *jia*, *yi*, and *bing* are the years when the Ming court lost its territory. The hat being tied up from the back echoes the subject, who is obedient to the king and is humble. Therefore *yi*, *geng*, and *xin* are the years when all the old subjects of Ming were killed. The scattered tassels falling down echoes the people who suffered the war.[334]

The author is probably a non-Catholic Chinese in the Qing dynasty, who learned about the sacrificial hat from somewhere. Unlike the theological interpretation in the Catholic Church, the author interpreted certain details of the sacrificial hat as signs of certain social events in a traditional Chinese way. To consider the sacrificial hat an ominous sign for the fall of Ming betrays certain anti-Catholic connotations. *The Hat of Mass is the Implicit Sign* presents a distorted yet intriguing Sinicization of the sacrificial hat. Its special interpretation shows that the Catholic Church in China was not isolated from Chinese society but was affected by it as a part of it.

In the nineteenth century, as European norms were introduced into Chinese society, the sacrificial hat became a "victim" of the Chinese social evolution.[335] In 1883, Propaganda Fide ordered priests in China to cease wearing the sacrificial hat yet allowed them to adapt to local customs when necessary.[336] Since the order was not strict, the practice of wearing the sacrificial hat continued for decades. In 1922, at the funeral ceremony of the martyr Julianus Adons

---

333 "是明舊臣致命之年也。" Anon., *Misa guanyi*, fol. 4a7–8, 631.
334 "冠之頂，應國王，上也，尊也。故甲乙丙，為明失天下之年也。冠後繫，應臣。臣從君者也，微也。故乙庚辛，為明舊臣盡殺之年也。垂以散絲，應被兵遭难之民也。" Anon., *Misa guanyi*, fol. 4a9–b2, 631–632. The character "*wang* 王" was later corrected as "*huang* 皇."
335 Anon., "Un pratique liturgique," 405.
336 Carine Dujardin, *Missionering en moderniteit. De Belgische minderbroeders in China 1872–1940*, KADOC-Studies 19 (Leuven: Leuven University Press, 1996), 393. Gratitude to Dr. Dujardin for explaining the content in her book pertaining to the sacrificial hat to me.

(OFM, 1879–1922) in the south-west of Hubei, two European missionaries and a Chinese priest were wearing the sacrificial hat as a sign of honor and respect. Carine Dujardin presents a black and white photo of this grand ceremony celebrated in the open air, as a remarkable example of combining Chinese and Western culture.[337] Today, the sacrificial hat is a rather unfamiliar object to Chinese Catholics.

3.4   Wu Li and "The Musical Sound of Mass"

Almost one hundred years after the introduction of Catholic clergy, the Catholic Church in China finally had her first indigenous priests. On 1 August 1688 (Kangxi 27.7.6), Mgr. Luo ordained three Chinese Jesuits Wu Li, Liu Yunde 劉蘊德 (Blaise Verbiest, SJ, 1628–1703), and Wan Qiyuan 萬其淵 (Paul Banhes, SJ, 1635–1700) in the cathedral of Nanjing.[338] Among the three indigenous priests, Wu Li had "the most outstanding fame, the highest life expectancy, and the longest propagation of Teaching."[339] The information of the other two indigenous priests is comparatively sparse.[340]

Wu Li (courtesy name: Yushan 漁山, art names: hermit Taoxi 桃溪居士 and the Taoist Mojing 墨井道人) was a versatile artist in the Qing dynasty.[341] Born in a family near the church in Changshu, Wu Li was probably baptized in his childhood.[342] Yet, he did not come close to the Catholic Church until in his middle age, which explains the Buddhist and Taoist connotation of his art names. Around the beginning of 1681 (Kangxi 19.11), Wu Li arrived Macao and spared no effort to prepare for the ordination during his stay.[343] He entered the Society of

---

337   Dujardin, *Missionering en moderniteit*, 421. Since this funeral ceremony did not necessarily include a Mass, the photo indicates that Catholic priests in China perhaps wore the sacrificial hat in other occasions as well.

338   Fang Hao 方豪, "Wu Yushan shenfu lingxi niandai, jinduo didian ji ladingwen zaoyi kao 吳漁山神父領洗年代、晉鐸地點及拉丁文造詣考," in *Wu Yushan*, 133, 137. According to Pfister, Wu Li was born in 1631. Pfister, *Notices biographiques*, 395–396, no. 156.

339   "漁山名最顯，壽最高，宣教最久，" Chen Yuan 陳垣, "Wu Yushan jinduo 250 nian jinian 吳漁山晉鐸二百五十年紀念," in *Wu Yushan*, 36.

340   For Liu Yunde, see Pfister, *Notices biographiques*, 402–403, no. 162. For Wan Qiyuan, see Pfister, *Notices biographiques*, 388–389, no. 146.

341   Contemporary literati gave Wu Li high praise. "漁山不獨善畫，其於詩尤工，" Qian Qianyi 錢謙益, "*Taoxi shigao* xu 桃溪詩稿序," in Zhang, *Wu Yushan ji*, 1. "鼓琴作書，潔清自好，尤善畫山水，" Chen Hu 陳瑚, "*Congyou ji* xu 從遊集序," in Zhang, *Wu Yushan ji*, 13. "吳子雅工詩，擅書畫，" You Tong 尤侗, "*Sanba ji* xu 三巴集序," in Zhang, *Wu Yushan ji*, 21.

342   Fang, "Zaoyi kao," 136.

343   Wang Zongyan 汪宗衍, "Wu Yushan wang Aomen nianfen zhi yanjiu ziliao ji qita 吳漁山往澳門年份之研究資料及其它," in *Wu Yushan*, 148.

Jesus in 1682 and after the novitiate studied theology and Latin. After the ordination, Wu Li was first assigned to Shanghai and then served in Jiading since 1691, where he mainly evangelized in rural areas.[344]

Fruitful research on Wu Li has been done, such as a broad chronicle biography, specific details of his life, his paintings, and his poems.[345] The current section focuses on how the indigenous priest Wu Li understood Mass, concerning the ritual performance and descriptions. The research material comes from his poetry anthologies and the record by the Chinese Catholic Zhao Lun. After his conversion to the Catholic Church, Wu Li began writing the poetry of Heavenly Learning (*tianxue shi* 天學詩).[346] The poetry of Heavenly Learning belonged to the Chinese Christian poetry, which was new in Chinese literature.[347] Jonathan Chaves categorizes Wu Li's poems into four types: traditional Chinese poems on standard themes; transitional poems on life in Macao, where Christian themes appeared; poems fully devoted to Christian themes; and the *Compendium of Orthodox Sounds of Heavenly Music* (*Tianyue zhengyin pu* 天樂正音譜), which represents Wu Li's attempt at the Chinese Christian poetry.[348] The current section examines poems in the last three types.

In the second type, the poems written in Macao vividly described the ritual life in the Catholic Church, such as the procession with St. Francis Xavier's statue,[349] the decoration of the nativity scene during the Christmas season,[350]

344　Xiao, *Tianhui yu wudang*, 206–207.
345　For the artistic aspect of his life, see Chaves, *Singing of the source*; Xiaoping Lin, *Wu Li (1632–1718): His Life, His Paintings* (Lanham: University Press of America, 2001); Jonathan Chaves, "Wu Li and the first Chinese Poetry," *Journal of the American Oriental Society* vol. 122, No. 3 (2002): 506–519. For the chronological biography, see Chen Yuan 陳垣, "Wu Yushan nianpu 吳漁山年譜," in *Wu Yushan*, 1–28. For a summary of study on Wu Li, see Jiang Xiangyan 蔣向艷, "Wu Li yanjiu zongshu 吳歷研究綜述," *Guoji hanxue* 國際漢學 2 (Beijing: Waiyu jiaoxue yu yanjiu chubanshe 外語教學與研究出版社, 2016): 165–170.
346　The term first appeared in "The poetry of Heavenly Learning is the most difficult to write, which is incomparable with other poems. (作天學詩最難，比不得他詩。)" Zhao, *Xu Kouduo*, 616.
347　Chaves, *Singing of the Source*, 47.
348　Chaves, *Singing of the Source*, 48–49.
349　"捧臘高燒迎聖來，旗幢風滿砲成雷。四街鋪草青如錦，未許遊人踏作埃。" Wu, "Aozhong zayong 4," *Sanba ji*, Fang, "Jiaoshi," 108–109. According to Wang Zongyan, the character for Macao should be "*ao* 隩." Wang Zongyan 汪宗衍, "Wu Yushan Aozhong zayong bushi 吳漁山隩中雜詠補釋," in *Wu Yushan*, 141. For an English translation and explanation, see Chaves, *Singing of the Source*, 54–55. As Chaves points out, this poem is the first detailed and firsthand account of Catholic procession in Chinese literature.
350　"百千燈耀小林崖，錦作云巒蠟作花。粧點冬山齊慶賞，黑人舞足應琵琶。（原注：冬山以木為石骨，以錦為山巒，染蠟紅藍為花樹，狀似鼇山。黑人歌

and the worship before the icon.[351] The ninth and the tenth poems in "Praising Origin and Development of the Holy Church" (*Song Shenghui yuanliu* 誦聖會源流) depicted the celebration of Mass:[352]

> Gloriously being bestowed the jade crown and golden fine clothes,
> these are merits gained in bloody battles by the pure heart.
> Ten thousand colors, ten thousand fragrances, ten thousand valleys,
> one root, one vine, one vineyard.
> The souls full of grace drink abundantly from Jesus' chalice,
> their bodies leap like a fish while listening to David's harp.
> *Sanctus Sanctus Sanctus* sounds of cheering without end,
> these are antiphonal singings under the throne of the Lamb.[353]

The ninth poem presents the celebration of Mass more by figure of speech than by the description of actual practice.[354] The first sentence depicts Catholics' spiritual battles and merits. In the second sentence, "*wan* 萬" (ten thousand)

唱，舞足與琵琶聲相應，在耶穌聖誕前後。）" Wu, "Aozhong zayong 27," *Sanba ji*, Fang, "jiaoshi," 114. For an English translation and explanation, see Chaves, *Singing of the Source*, 55.

351 "畫壁年年瞻配像，" Wu Li 吳歷, "Song shenghui yuanliu 8 誦聖會源流第八首," *Sanba ji* 三巴集, in Zhang, *Wu Yushan ji*, 242. For an English translation and explanation, see Chaves, *Singing of the Source*, 70–71. According to Zhang Wenqin, the character "*xiang* 像" refers to paintings of saints in the Society of Jesus. Zhang, *Wu Yushan ji*, 242, note 6. Yet, given this poem's context and its historical background, "*xiang*像" probably refers to the icon of Jesus or of Virgin Mary. Also, Zhang attributes the twelfth poem to the activity on the feast of the Assumption of Mary. The phrase "*chaoyuan* 朝元" refers to the meeting of God in heaven, and the sentence "*hedang shoufu chaoyuan ri* 何當受福朝元日" refers to the feast day on 15, August. Zhang, *Wu Yushan ji*, 247–248. Yet, previous sentences in the poem are praise to Mary and the following (also the last) sentence means to worship the beauty of Mary in person. Moreover, the desire to meet Mary in heaven is often expressed at the end of a prayer to her. Given the context and the Catholic tradition, this sentence means when shall the poet be blessed and meet Mary in heaven. Therefore, the twelfth poem is not a record of ritual activity.

352 Chaves translates the title as "Singing of the Source and Course of Holy Church," Chaves, *Singing of the Source*, 43.

353 "榮加玉冕錫衣金，血戰功勞赤子心。萬色萬香萬花谷，一根一幹一萄林。靭靈飫飲耶穌爵，躍體傾聽達味琴。聖聖聖聲呼不斷，羔羊座下唱酬音。" Wu, "Song shenghui yuanliu 9," *Sanba ji*, in Zhang, *Wu yushan ji*, 243.

354 Zhang Wenqin thinks this poem is a record of the ceremony of a priest's ordination yet is unaware of the elements of Mass. Instead of a bishop, he explains that the celebrant of the ordination ceremony is a priest and that the newly ordained priest has a jewelry crown. Wu, "Song shenghui yuanliu 9," *Sanba ji*, in Zhang, *Wu Yushan ji*, 243.

and "*yi* 一" (one) form a comparison, where both characters appear three times to strengthen the effect—to extol the diversity and unity of the Catholic Church. As one of the first indigenous priests, Wu Li experienced deeply the necessity and urgency to cultivate indigenous clergy in Chinese society. He probably indicated that an indigenous clergy can exemplify the diversity and solidify the unity of the Catholic Church. The last two sentences describe the scene in the Book of Isaiah (Isaiah 6:2–3, 11:1). Chaves points out the references, such as the harp of King David, the Tree of Jesse, and the Mass.[355] In addition, these sentences refer to the Gospel of John, where Jesus emphasized the necessity of unity by a parable of the vine and branch (John 15:1–17).[356] The poem not only intertwines the image in the Old Testament with that in the New Testament but also combines the image in the Bible with that in the Mass. To drink from Jesus' chalice (*Yesu jue* 耶穌爵) signifies receiving communion as well as the Last Supper.

As a powerful singing of the Lord of Heaven's holiness, the repetition of *sanctus* (holy) originated from the scene in the Book of Isaiah (Isaiah 6:2–3) and became an important prayer in the Mass since the early church. Wu Li attached the character "*sheng* 聲" (sounds) to the character "*sheng* 聖" (holy), thus forming "*Sanctus Sanctus Sanctus* sounds" (*sheng sheng sheng sheng* 聖聖聖聲), a phrase with the same pronunciation in different tones. The rhyme articulates the solemnity of Mass smoothly and powerfully. The phrase "*hu buduan* 呼不斷" (cheering without end) derives from *sine fine dicentes* (as without end we acclaim) in the Preface (*songxie ci* 頌謝詞, *Praefatio*) in the Mass. Today, the corresponding Chinese verse is "*butingde huanhu* 不停地歡呼" (to cheer without end). Right after the Preface is *Sanctus*, which is now called "*huanhu ge* 歡呼歌" (cheering song) in Chinese. More than a citation from the Book of Isaiah, the prayer *Sanctus* has its independent importance—the seraphim's singing reminds the Church on the earth to participate in the singing in heaven.[357]

Derived from "the Lamb who is in the center of the throne" (Revelation 7:17), the phrase "*gaoyang zuoxia* 羔羊座下" (under the throne of the Lamb) confirms the dimension of future. Furthermore, the banquet which satiates Catholics' bodies and souls signifies the Mass and the banquet in heaven. To

---

355 For an English translation and explanation, see Chaves, *Singing of the Source*, 71–72. For a painting of The Tree of Jesse, see Standaert, *An Illustrated Life*, 131–134.
356 Charles Pan Jiajun 潘家駿, *Gan'en shengshi—liyi yu shenxue* 感恩聖事——禮儀與神學 (Taipei: Wenhua shiye 文化事業, 2005), 81.
357 Jungmann, *La liturgie*, 128.

receive the Host at Mass is to partake the foretaste of everlasting life. The celebration of Mass combines the three dimensions of time—the past, the present, and the future. In addition to biblical images and the celebration of Mass, Wu Li cited from the ancient Chinese classics, such as "*chizi xin* 赤子心" (the pure heart) from *Mencius* (*Mengzi* 孟子),[358] "*renling* 牣靈" (the souls full of grace) and "*yueti* 躍體" (their bodies leap like a fish) from the *Book of Songs* (*Shijing* 詩經).[359] The ninth poem interwove the language, image, and classics in the Catholic tradition with those in the Chinese tradition.

Wu Li fully developed the theme of Mass in the tenth poem.[360] Similar to the ninth poem, the tenth poem presents the celebration of Mass more by figure of speech than by the description of actual practice.

> The supernatural mysterious body originally is not limited in any sorts,
> to save the lives of all people, he is present then hides.
> Vividly as one round new bread,
> still the almighty king in the universe he is.
> Now there is the holocaust in the world,
> and in Heaven the daily bread is permanently stored.
> Through so many faults yet we are allowed to approach,
> as our body and soul are satiated, our teardrops touch the robe.[361]

The first sentence tells that the supernatural mysterious body (*chaochao miaoti* 超超妙體) first came to the world then hides in the bread to save human beings. The second sentence depicts the contrast of the supernatural mysterious body as the round new bread (*yigui xin bing'er* 一規新餅餌) and the almighty king in the universe (*liuhe dajunwang* 六合大君王) at the same time. The third sentence draws a comparison between the holocaust (*quanfan zuo* 全燔胙) which is now in the world and the daily bread (*riyong liang* 日用糧) which is perma-

---

358 "大人者，不失其赤子之心者也。" "*Lilou xia* 離婁下," fol. 7b1–2, Zhao Qi 趙岐, annot., Sun Shi 孫奭, comm., *Mengzi* 孟子, vol. 8, *Shisanjing zhushu*, vol. 8, 144.
359 "王在靈沼，於牣魚躍。" "*Lingtai* 靈台," *Daya* 大雅, fol. 6a1, Zheng Xuan 鄭玄, annot., Kong Yingda 孔穎達, comm., *Shijing* 詩經, vol. 16, *Shisanjing zhushu*, vol. 2, 580. For another usage of "*renling* 牣靈," see "領時惟祈聖輝，主卽牣靈。" Dias, *Qingshi jinshu*, *juan* 4, fol. 14b1–2.
360 Chaves, *Singing of the Source*, 72.
361 "超超妙體本無方，為活蒸民顯復藏。宛爾一規新餅餌，依然六合大君王。人間今有全燔胙，天上恒存日用糧。曾是多愆容接近，形神飫處淚霑裳。" Wu, "Song shenghui yuanliu 10," *Sanbaji*, in Zhang, *Wu Yushan ji*, 244. For an English translation of the poem and the explanation, see Chaves, *Singing of the Source*, 72.

nently in heaven. The holocaust means the celebration of Mass in the world, and it is by attending Mass that human beings receive the daily bread as the spiritual food. The first three sentences show five diverse images of Jesus in the Mass: the supernatural mysterious body, the round new bread, the almighty king, the holocaust, and the daily bread. The fourth sentence changes the focus from Jesus to the Catholics who attend Mass and receive the Host. Although Catholics commit many faults, they are allowed to approach Jesus in Mass. Their bodies and souls are satiated by the Host and they are moved to tears.

"Praising Origin and Development of the Holy Church" shows Wu Li's efforts to create the Chinese Christian poetry, which adheres to the Chinese tradition of poetic techniques and to orthodox Catholic theology and liturgy.[362] As Chen Yuan praised, "Beautiful sentences often appear in the poems of Holy Learning in the *Anthology of St. Paul* compiled by Li Wenyu, such as in 'Praising Origin and Development of the Holy Church,' ... 'The souls full of grace drink abundantly from Jesus' cup,' 'their bodies leap like a fish while listening to David's harp,' 'Now there is the holocaust in the world,' 'and in Heaven the daily bread is permanently stored,' ... the coinage is very new, totally in a league of its own."[363] Chen Yuan addressed the poetry of Heavenly Learning as the poem of Holy Learning (*shengxue shi* 聖學詩).

In the third type, the poems fully devoted to Christian themes highlight Wu Li's identity as the Catholic priest. For example, he wrote a poem to congratulate a certain Guo for being newly baptized. In the poem "Sent to Guo" (*Zeng Guo* 贈郭), the crucial sentence pertaining to the Mass is "*xuanxiang zhenliang jie shengtai* 旋享真糧結聖胎."[364] Chaves translates the sentence as "Now you will enjoy the real bread, formed in the Holy womb."[365] In fact, the character "*tai* 胎" means fetus more often than womb.[366] The *Regulation of Reciting the Beads* uses "*shengtai* 聖胎" (the holy fetus) in the first joyful mystery,[367] which Wu Li must have learned. Therefore, the sentence can be translated as "Soon you will

---

362   Chaves, *Singing of the Source*, 73.
363   "今李本三巴集聖學詩，時有佳句，如誦聖會源流云， …… 牣靈飫飲耶穌爵，躍體傾聽達味琴，人間今有全燔胙，天上恆存日用糧， …… 造語甚新，獨闢境界，" Chen, "Jinian," 56.
364   "刪除舊染摧魔陣，旋享真糧結聖胎。" Wu Li 吳歷, "Zeng guo 贈郭," *Sanba ji*, in Zhang, *Wu Yushan ji*, 198.
365   For an English translation of the whole poem and the explanation, see Chaves, *Singing of the Source*, 62–63.
366   See *Le Grand Ricci* v, 762.
367   "天主費略，選爾爲母，將降孕於爾最淨最純的聖胎，爲人救世。" da Rocha, *Nianzhu guicheng*, fol. 4b2–3, 522.

enjoy the true food and conceive the holy fetus." The true food (*zhenliang* 真糧) is a quotation from *caro enim mea vere est cibus et sanguis meus vere est potus* (John 6:56). Since Guo had been baptized, he would soon receive the Host at Mass, thus receiving Jesus in himself as the Virgin Mary did. Similar content appears in *Golden Book with Contempt of the World*: "You can think that when you receive [the holy body], the Lord enters into your soul, like descending into the Holy Mother as a fetus conceived without intercourse."[368]

For another example, Wu Li urged the Chinese Catholic Wang Hui 王翬 (courtesy name: Shigu 石谷, 1632–1717) to revive his fervor for the Host. According to Chen Yuan, the poem was written in 1712 (Kangxi 51), when Wu Li and Wang Hui both were eighty-one years old. Wu Li pointed out the necessary task for Catholics: "To receive piously Jesus' holy body and to receive the holy grace, in order to increase the spiritual power, thus having the qualification to ascend into Heaven. This is the first necessary task."[369] In the third type of poems, Wu Li showed his pastoral care toward Chinese Catholics and underlined the importance of receiving the Host.

In the fourth type the *Compendium of Orthodox Sounds of Heavenly Music*, Wu Li wrote a series on the Mass in the form of *qu* 曲 called "The Musical Sound of Mass" (*Misa yueyin* 彌撒樂音). In 1946, Fang Hao discovered the *Compendium of Orthodox Sounds of Heavenly Music* in the Zikawei Library in Shanghai. It is an undated manuscript of *qu* written by Wu Li, including "The Musical Sound of Mass." Fang Hao asked the expert of *qu* Lu Qian 盧前 for help. In 1950, Fang Hao and Zheng Qian 鄭騫 edited and printed the manuscript in Taiwan.[370] In 1968, Fang Hao re-edited "The Musical Sound of Mass" in reference with *Rite of Attending Mass* (*Yu misa li* 與彌撒禮), the variant of *Manual for Attending Mass*.[371] Yet, *Manual for Attending Mass* was published around 1721 after Wu Li's death and the references made by Fang Hao are incomplete. Based on this prior research, the current section analyzes "The Musical Sound of Mass" in detail from a ritual perspective.

Since Wu Li was probably acquainted with the second volume of *The Meaning of the Sacrifice of Mass* or its abridged version,[372] the current section takes

---

368 "可念領時，主入汝靈，如降聖母淨胎，" Dias, *Qingshi jinshu*, juan 4, fol. 4b1.
369 "虔領耶穌聖體，兼領聖寵，以增神力，卽有升天之劑。此乃第一要務也，" Wu Li, "Zhi Wang Shigu chidu," 致王石谷尺牘, Chen, "Nianpu," 24.
370 Fang Hao 方豪, "Wu Yushan xiansheng *Sanyu ji* jiaoshi 吳漁山先生《三餘集》校釋," in *Wu Yushan*, 86.
371 Fang, "Jiaoshi," 84.
372 Since *The Meaning of the Sacrifice of Mass* is not a manual exclusively for priests, Dudink assumes that Wu Li wrote "The Musical Sound of Mass" before his ordination in August 1688. Dudink, "Manual for Attending Mass," 227.

the second volume as the reference in Chinese. "The Musical Sound of Mass" is a series of eight *qu* written in beautiful style with rhyme, yet the content is both concise and intense, thus difficult to understand. Both Fang Hao and Chaves noticed the emphasis on the priest. Chaves thinks that "The Musical Sound of Mass" has a particular emphasis on the priest's movements and utterances.[373] In fact, "The Musical Sound of Mass" contains two emphases but the second one is less apparent and can only be revealed after the examination in reference with the second volume of *The Meaning of the Sacrifice of Mass*. In addition, Wu Li may have consulted the Roman Missal in Latin,[374] meanwhile the second volume of *The Meaning of the Sacrifice of Mass* was based on *Ritus servandus in celebratione Missarum* (shortened as *Ritus servandus*) in the Roman Missal in 1570. Therefore, the current section takes *Ritus servandus* as the reference in Latin. In table 2, the content of "The Musical Sound of Mass" is categorized into two parts: the act of priest; the allegorical explanation. The sentence in each *qu* is numbered according to the version edited by Fang Hao and the smaller and auxiliary characters are omitted.[375] The corresponding act of priest in *The Meaning of the Sacrifice of Mass* (shortened as *The Meaning*) and that in *Ritus servandus* are given ("section, part" shortened as "s, p"). The table is followed by a further examination mainly on the allegorical explanation.

TABLE 2   Act of priest and allegorical explanation

Qu	Act	Explanation	*The Meaning*	*Ritus servandus*
1st 南南呂 一枝花	1 來親 彌撒經	2 莫不相冲凜	s 1, p 1 默道斂心	s 1, p 1 orationi aliquantulum vacet; et Orationes inferius positas pro temporis opportunitate dicat
	3 詣臺 將祭也	4 禮尤兢 6 謙躬謹行 7 萃我一堂忻信	s 1, p 1 陳聖經聖爵 于臺	s 1, p 2 accedit ad Altare
	5 儀注西秦		—	

---

373   Chaves, *Singing of the Source*, 75.
374   Chaves, *Singing of the Source*, 196, note 181.
375   Wu Li 吳歷, "Misa yueyin 彌撒樂音," in Fang Hao 方豪, "Wu Yushan xiansheng *Tianyue zhengyinpu* jiaoshi 吳漁山先生《天樂正音譜》校釋," *Fang Hao liushi zidinggao* 方豪六十自定稿 (Taipei: Taiwan xuesheng shuju 臺灣學生書局, 1969), *xia*, 1627–1629.

TABLE 2 Act of priest and allegorical explanation (*cont.*)

Qu	Act	Explanation	*The Meaning*	*Ritus servandus*
2nd 紅衲襖	1 拜臺前	–	–	s 1, p 3 convertit se ad ipsum Altare … facta genuflexione
	2 三位稱	3 內包含 4 無別性 5 造成物我功難罄 6 享用生存何現成	s 2, p 1 畫聖號，誦天主一體三位云云	s 4, p 3 producens manu dextera a fronte ad pectus signum crucis, dicit intelligibili voce: In nomine Patris, et Filii, et Spiritus Sancti. Amen.
	7 各虔祈、悔罪經	8 除免我罪因其敬	s 3, p 1 悔罪誦解罪經	s 7, p 3 dicit: Confiteor Deo
	9 聽誦古經一段於臺左	10 古聖當年求降生	s 4, p 1 就臺左誦古經一段	s 2, p 4 accedit ad cornu ejus sinistrum … incipit intelligibili voce Introitum Missae
3rd 繡太平	3 臺中正讀西音			–
	4 基利厄陀勒依算 5 三聲 6 連祈九遍為分形	1 開天路、垂慈汲引 2 救我人、墮孽靈魂	s 5, p 1 誦基利厄陀勒依算九遍	s 2, p 4 dicit eadem voce ter Kyrie, eleison, ter Christe, eleison, et iterum ter Kyrie, eleison … novies dicit
	7 把兩手、分開赦允	8 從教自省	s 6, p 1 將手兩開	s 3, p 4 Sacerdos stans in medio Altaris et manus extendens, elevansque usque ad humeros
	–	9 天神歌獎	s 6, p 1 復合掌，誦厄樂利亞云云	s 3, p 4 Gloria in excelsis. Cum dicit Deo, jungens manus
	–	10 世人稱慶	s 7, p 1 轉身對衆云："鐸彌奴斯，阿比斯公。"	s 1, p 5 vertit se a sinistro latere ad dexterum versus populum … dicit voce praedicta: Dominus vobiscum

PERFORMER OF WORSHIP   195

TABLE 2   Act of priest and allegorical explanation (*cont.*)

Qu	Act	Explanation	*The Meaning*	*Ritus servandus*
4th 宜春樂	1 瞻臺左	–	s 8, p 1 就臺左，開手誦經	s 1, p 5 respicit cornu Epistolae … extensis manibus, dicit Orationem
	2 手按經	3 指經中、若翰聖人 4 預為開徑	s 9, p 1 按手經上誦古經	s 1, p 6 Celebrans positis super librum, vel super Altare manibus, ita ut palmae librum tangant … legit Epistolam intelligibili voce
	5 移經臺右 申誠謹	–	s 10, p 1 移經臺右……誦萬熱略經一段	s 1, p 6 portat librum Missalis ad alteram partem Altaris in cornu Evangelii s 2, p 6 primo librum super principio Evangelii, quod est lecturus
	6 示堂中、敬服當同	–	s 11, p 1 就臺中誦信經	s 3, p 6 stans in medio Altaris … incipit … Credo
	–	7 主降我、靈臺方寸 8 邪魔畏遁 9 那時見我 10 聖蹟昭明	s 12, p 1 轉身又念："鐸彌奴斯，阿比斯公"	s 1, p 7 vertit se ad populum … dicit: Dominus vobiscum
5th 太師引	1 看開樽 2 元分品	3 獻耶穌、經言訓人 4 十字架、血流垂盡 5 與今朝、彌撒洪恩 6 從前負罪常逆命 7 我本待、報答慈恩 8 無終定 9 規程永遵 10 使我就捐軀 11 纔為致命	s 13, p 1 開聖爵，奉窩斯帝亞	s 2, p 7 discooperit Calicem … accipit Patenam cum Hostia … dicit: Suscipe, sancte Pater, etc.

TABLE 2   Act of priest and allegorical explanation (*cont.*)

Qu	Act	Explanation	*The Meaning*	*Ritus servandus*
6th 東甌令	1 重盥手	4 乾乾洗滌無須剩 5 纔不負、耶穌憫	s 14, p 1 盥手指	s 6, p 7 lavat manus
	2 復轉身 3 請禱佇同衆罪人		s 14, p 1 轉身向衆說："阿辣得，法德勒斯"	s 7, p 7 vertit se ad populum … dicit voce aliquantulum elata: Orate, fratres
		–	s 15, p 1 微聲念經	s 7, p 7 et secreto prosequens: ut meum ac vestrum sacrificium, etc.
		–	s 16, p 1 高聲念三都斯云云	s 8, p 7 dicit: Sanctus
		–	s 17, p 1 合掌默存，祈求 天主為保祐當今教化主，帝王，及諸司教者，與父母親友普天下之奉教者。	s 1, p 8 ac manibus junctis … secreto dicens: Te igitur etc.
	6 元何十字劃頻頻	7 聖死因他釘	s 18, p 1 聖爵上先後畫多許十字	s 1, p 8 Cum dicit: Haec + dona, haec + munera, haec sancta + sacrificia, dextera manu signat ter communiter super Hostiam et Calicem
7th 劉潑帽	1 舉揚聖體明飡飲	–	s 1, p 2 舉揚聖體聖爵	s 5, p 8 quantum commode potest, elevat in altum Hostiam s 7, p 8 et accipiens Calicem discoopertum cum Sanguine ambabus manibus, ut prius, elevat eum, et erectum quantum commode potest

TABLE 2   Act of priest and allegorical explanation (*cont.*)

Qu	Act	Explanation	*The Meaning*	*Ritus servandus*
–	–	–	s 2, p 2 聖體上畫十字聖號五次	s 1, p 9 et cum dicit: Hostiam + puram, Hostiam + sanctam, Hostiam + immaculatam, manu sinistra posita super Altare intra Corporale, dextera signat ter communiter super Hostiam et Calicem … et semel super Hostiam tantum, et semel super Calicem tantum, dicens: Panem + sanctum vitae aeternae, et Calicem + salutis perpetuae
	–	2 並求為、煉處靈魂	s 3, p 2 又合掌默然存主經	s 2, p 9 Cum dicit: Memento, Domine, famulorum famularumque tuarum, etc., extensis et junctis manibus ante pectus
	3 撫心響誦求慈允	–	s 4, p 2 拊心高聲念諾比斯郭國云云	s 3, p 9 Cum dicit: Nobis quoque peccatoribus, vocem aliquantulum elevat et dextera manu pectus sibi percutit
	–		s 5, p 2 高聲頌主經在天我等云云	s 1, p 10 incipit: Pater noster
	–		s 6, p 1 分開窩斯帝亞	s 2, p 10 accipit Hostiam inter pollicem et indicem dexterae manus … reverenter frangit per medium
	–	4 天上人間 5 地獄三般幸	s 7, p 2 又三分窩斯帝亞	s 2, p 10 de alia media … frangit cum pollice et indice dexterae manus particulam
		–	s 8, p 2 又念罷斯，鐸彌尼，云云	s 2, p 10 dicit: Pax Domini sit semper vobiscum

TABLE 2 Act of priest and allegorical explanation (cont.)

Qu	Act	Explanation	*The Meaning*	*Ritus servandus*
	–		s 9, p 2 叩心悔罪，隨領聖體	s 4, p 10 dextera tribus vicibus percutit pectus suum, interim etiam tribus vicibus dicens voce aliquantulum elevata: Domine, non sum dignus ... reverenter easdem ambas partes sumit
8th 尾聲	–		s 1, p 3 既斂聖爵等物，又請經復過臺左，誦經一段，卽轉身仍念鐸彌奴斯阿比斯公	s 1, p 11 dum Calicem collocat in Altari, liber Missalis defertur per ministrum ad cornu Epistolae ... vertit se ad populum ... et dicit: Dominus vobiscum
	–		s 2, p 3 又誦經謝恩	s 1, p 11 dicit Orationes post Communionem
	–		s 3, p 3 又轉身念： "鐸彌奴斯，阿比斯公"	s 1, p 11 vertit se ad populum, et dicit, ut supra: Dominus vobiscum
	1 依彌撒	2 歸思省	s 4, p 3 又向眾人念依得彌撒云云	s 1, p 11 versus populum, dicit ... Ite, Missa est
	–	3 殘疾疲癃 同是心	s 6, p 3 在臺右立，誦經一段，捧聖爵歸	s 2, p 12 accedit ad cornu Evangelii, et dicit Evangelium S. Joannis s 6, p 12 interim Sacerdos accipit sinistra Calicem ... redit ad Sacristiam
	–	4 陽奉陰違 自失真	s 5, p 3 畫十字，祝福于眾	s 1, p 12 semel benedicit populo dicens: Pater, et Filius, + et Spiritus Sanctus

In the entire series of the eight *qu*, the act of priest and the allegorical explanation unfold the procedure of Mass. The first part provides the act of priest in the celebration of Mass; the second provides the corresponding allegorical explanation of the act. Seen from table 2, sections of the procedure of Mass are shown sometimes by both parts and sometimes by one. In the first *qu*, to approach the altar is described by the act of priest and the allegorical explanation. In the third *qu*, the prayer of *Gloria in excelsis* is hidden in the allegorical explanation, so is the following saying of *Dominus vobiscum*. In the fourth *qu*, the act of looking at the left side of the altar has no corresponding allegorical explanation.

The procedure in "The Musical Sound of Mass" conforms to the formula of Mass (*formula missae*), only the last two sentences in the eighth *qu* are reversed in sequence. Nevertheless, some sections of the procedure are not mentioned, including to receive the Host. The act of priest corresponds to the three parts of *The Meaning of the Sacrifice of Mass* and the first twelve parts of *Ritus servandus* (thirteen parts in total).[376] For the part of the act of priest, all sentences in "The Musical Sound of Mass" have corresponding acts in *Ritus servandus*, however, two differences are found in *The Meaning of the Sacrifice of Mass*. First, to kowtow before the altar (*bai taiqian* 拜臺前), the act of priest in the first sentence of the second *qu*, corresponds to *convertit se ad ipsum Altare ... facta genuflexione* in section 1, Part 3, *Ritus servandus*, yet the act has no corresponding section in *The Meaning of the Sacrifice of Mass*. Second, to look at the left side of the altar (*zhan taizuo* 瞻臺左), the first sentence of the fourth *qu*, corresponds to *respicit cornu Epistolae* in section 1, Part 5, *Ritus servandus*, yet in *The Meaning of the Sacrifice of Mass*, the act is to come close to the left side of the altar (*jiu taizuo* 就臺左). The two differences suggest that Wu Li took the Roman Missal as reference. In contrast wiht *Ritus servandus*, the act of priest in "The Musical Sound of Mass" is very concise. Still take the first sentence of the fourth *qu* "to look at the left side of the altar" (*zhan taizuo* 瞻臺左) for example. The following act is omitted, which is *extensis manibus, dicit Orationem* in the Roman

---

376 The first twelve parts of *Ritus servandus* are: Part 1, *De Praeparatione Sacerdotis celebraturi*; Part 2, *De Ingressu Sacerdotis ad Altare*; Part 3, *De Principio Missae, et Confessione facienda*; Part 4, *De Introitu, Kyrie, eleison, et Gloria in excelsis*; Part 5, *De Oratione*; Part 6, *De Epistola, Graduali, et aliis usque ad Offertorium*; Part 7, *De Offertorio, et aliis usque ad Canonem*; Part 8, *De Canone Missae usque ad Consecrationem*; Part 9, *De Canone post Consecrationem usque ad Orationem Dominicam*; Part 10, *De Oratione Dominica, et aliis usque ad factam Communionem*; Part 11, *De Communione et Orationibus post Communionem dicendis*; Part 12, *De Benedictione in fine Missae et Evangelio sancti Joannis*. "Ritus servandus in celebratione Missarum," *Missale Romanum* (1570), 9–19, no. 20*–31*.

Missal or to extend the hands and to recite the prayer (*kaishou songjing* 開手誦經) in *The Meaning of the Sacrifice of Mass*. "For what reason to draw the cross so many times" (*yuanhe shizi hua pinpin* 元何十字劃頻頻), the sixth sentence of the sixth *qu*, does not mention the place to draw the cross, which is over the Host and the chalice (*super Hostiam et Calicem*) in the Roman Missal, and *The Meaning of the Sacrifice of Mass* only mentions the holy *jue* (chalice). The first sentence of the seventh *qu* only mentions to raise up the Host, omitting the chalice.

For the part of the allegorical explanation, the sentences in "The Musical Sound of Mass" have corresponding sections in both of the two references. *Ritus servandus* does not provide the allegorical explanation *per se*, while all the corresponding sentences to the part of the allegorical explanation can be found in the second volume of *The Meaning of the Sacrifice of Mass*. Each of the thirty-three sections in the second volume first describes the act of priest and occasionally the act of acolyte, then provides the allegorical explanation.[377] The allegorical explanation not only attaches the specific meaning to the act of priest but also gives suggestions to the congregants. The formula "Now those who attend Mass shall …" (*yu misa zhe zhici dang* 與彌撒者至此，當) appears in almost all the thirty-three sections.[378] Only section 15 in part 1 omits the phrase "those who attend Mass" (*yu misa zhe* 與彌撒者) yet keeps "one shall" (*dang* 當).[379] Sentences in the part of the allegorical explanation can be considered the condensed version of the allegorical explanation in *The Meaning of the Sacrifice of Mass*, especially the content following the formula "Now those who attend Mass shall …" Table 3 lists the corresponding sentences in *The Meaning of the Sacrifice of Mass* and underlines the same characters.[380]

Seen from table 3, the allegorical explanation in "The Musical Sound of Mass" partly resembles that in *The Meaning of the Sacrifice of Mass*. The same characters suggest that Wu Li directly used *The Meaning of the Sacrifice of Mass*. Similar to *The Meaning of the Sacrifice of Mass*, "The Musical Sound of Mass"

---

377   For an English translation, see Dudink, "Manual for Attending Mass," 237–241.
378   The character in the formula occasionally varies, see section 1, part one, "與彌撒者此時，當……" Aleni, *Misa jiyi*, juan 2, fol. 4a9–b1, 559–560. See also section 7, part two, "與彌撒者至此，想……" Aleni, *Misa jiyi*, juan 2, fol. 29a6–7, 609.
379   Aleni, *Misa jiyi*, juan 2, fol. 20a2, 591.
380   Aleni, *Misa jiyi*, juan 2, fol. 4a8–9, 559; fol. 4b1–3, 560; fol. 4b6–7, 560; fol. 4b8–fol. 5a2, 560–561; fol. 5b8, 562; fol. 6b1–3, 564; fol. 7a2–4, 565; fol. 8a8–9, 567; fol. 8 b4–6, 568; fol. 12b1–4, 576; fol. 12b1–4, 576; fol. 18a8–9, 587; fol. 18b2–4, 588; fol. 18b6–fol. 19a3, 588–589; fol. 19b1–4, 590; fol. 22a8–b3, 595–596; fol. 26a3–6, 603; fol. 28b5–8, 608; fol. 36b4–7, 624; fol. 40b3–5, 632; fol. 38b9–fol. 39a1, 628–629.

TABLE 3   Comparison of allegorical explanation

Qu	Allegorical explanation	Corresponding sentence
1st 南南呂 一枝花	7 萃我一堂忻信 2 莫不相冲凛	s 1, p 1 又萃一堂之精神，無不謙冲自抑，悚凛反觀也。
	4 禮尤兢 6 謙躬謹行	s 1, p 1 當致心兢業，既幸躬逢在堂，……一畨提醒，一畨虔恭，
2nd 紅衲襖	3 內包含 4 無別性	s 2, p 1 一主之內，卽含三位。其體非分，其位不雜，純一靈明之性。
	5 造成物我功難罄 6 享用生存何現成	s 2, p 1 造成萬類，……俾得各享焉。……感謝大主為我等預備如此大世界，令其享用。
	8 除免我罪因其敬	s 3, p 1 求天主赦宥，
	10 古聖當年求降生	s 4, p 1 正是古聖人所錄，……承天主之旨，而切望吾主之降生救世者也。
3rd 繡太平	1 開天路、垂慈汲引 2 救我人、墮孽靈魂	s 5, p 1 古聖人……哀痛號求真主，速發無窮之慈，降臨于世，以救萬民也。
	8 從教自省 9 天神歌獎	s 6, p 1 吾主應其苦求，……當陪天神讚誦上主，務求自新，
	10 世人稱慶	s 7, p 1 吾主既降生後，有傳播于世為人類稱慶者，欲人盡知，不至錯認恩主，致加罪戾也。
4th 宜春樂	3 指經中、若翰聖人 4 預為開徑	s 9, p 1 若望保第斯達大聖，署在吾主降生前為之先驅，……凡有阻礙于天主者，為之清闢其路，以俟主來。
	7 主降我、靈臺方寸 8 邪魔畏遁 9 那時見我 10 聖蹟昭明	s 12, p 1 吾主降生，宗徒傳教，萬民信從，得天主所授寵愛，既逐邪魔，則其本心如成一天主國然。……故鐸德轉而慶慰眾人言"主在爾輩中"矣。

TABLE 3 Comparison of allegorical explanation (*cont.*)

Qu	Allegorical explanation	Corresponding sentence
5th 太師引	3 獻耶穌、經言訓人	s 13, p 1 吾主耶穌降生之時，……故不惟以正言訓人，以聖蹟立表，且願以己之肉體為祭品，奉獻于天主罷德肋，
	4 十字架、血流垂盡	s 13, p 1 爵中酌酒者，指吾主常願以己體中聖血，流散于十字架上，成洗萬民之罪之寶藥。
	5 與今朝、彌撒洪恩 6 從前負罪常逆命 7 我本待、報答慈恩 8 無終定 9 規程永遵 10 使我就捐軀 11 纔為致命	s 13, p 1 與彌撒者至此，當想自己如負萬金重債，……幸有大富長者，肯為我盡發己貲，破格償還，特令我略出絲毫，聊表自贖之意。……俱要遵守主命。即使我可為天主致命，流血亦所不辭，稍補我向來無數之罪，以盡我奉主萬分之一也。
6th 東甌令	4 乾乾洗滌無須剩 5 纔不負、耶穌憫	s 14, p 1 與彌撒者至此，當想洗心滌慮，固是我等本分，而一念虔誠，必使洗之又洗，滌之又滌，至于無復可洗可滌，乃為敬謹之至云。
	7 聖死因他釘	s 18, p 1 此節之意，指吾主受難之日，諸般苦痛，如在石柱上受笞，首戴茨冠，負十字架登山，種種諸苦，與彌撒者至此，當存想此義，
7th 劉潑帽	2 並求為、煉處靈魂	s 3, p 2 鐸德到此，亦為奉教已歿之人，在煉罪處者，默求天主速救之。與彌撒者亦當于此致情，為煉罪之人祈求天主。此為聖神相通功也。
	4 天上人間 5 地獄三般幸	s 7, p 2 此節之意，指吾主受難之功既成，復生升天，而加全福于天上人間地獄。蓋聖教之體雖一，而教會之處有三。
8th 尾聲	2 歸思省	s 4, p 3 與彌撒者至此，當轉思彌撒雖畢，而或有忽畧觀面錯過，雖有，與彌撒之事，未必有與彌撒之功，即當肅然退省，日加精進，方以得，與此勝會為喜矣。
	3 殘疾疲癃同是心	s 6, p 3 凡我同類，隨其賢愚貴賤，老幼男女及殘疾疲癃者，一體隨時勸誘，必以吾主為父，在天為歸，欽崇為事，

TABLE 3   Comparison of allegorical explanation (cont.)

Qu	Allegorical explanation	Corresponding sentence
4	陽奉陰違自失眞	s 5, p 3 斷當勉勵相警，無使空為善迹，而自失眞福也。

can be considered a Mass manual in musical form, which is for the faithful as well as for priests. As shown in table 2, the fifth sentence in the first *qu* "[conform to] the ritual regulation of the West" (*yi zhu xiqin* 儀注西秦) and the third sentence in the third *qu* "in the middle of the altar [the priest] is reading in the Western language" (*taizhong zhengdu xiyin* 臺中正讀西音) have no corresponding sections in the two references. Because the two sentences neither belong to the act of priest nor to the allegorical explanation. They are two additional comments on the procedure of Mass, indicating that in the late seventeenth century the Christian communities in China probably celebrated Mass in Latin as in Europe.

"The Musical Sound of Mass" might be the most remarkable work on Mass written by Chinese people in late Ming and early Qing. Claiming that the genre is completely original in Chinese literature,[381] Chaves may be exaggerating its originality in order to highlight the poetry of Heavenly Learning as a new type in Chinese poetry. In fact, *qu* is a traditional and rather popular type of poetry in Chinese literature. Written in literary Chinese, the diction and rhyme in each *qu* share the same tradition with earlier Chinese poetry. It is in the subject matter that the originality of "The Musical Sound of Mass" lies. The celebration of Mass was an unfamiliar ritual in a marginal religion in Chinese society. The combination of literary Chinese and the transliteration of Latin produces an aesthetic strangeness. The allegorical explanation may be restricted to literate Chinese Catholics,[382] yet the series of *qu* is different from the normal ritual manuals. The singing of *qu*, which Chinese Catholics were familiar with, can assist them to memorize the procedure of Mass and what they shall do during Mass. Nevertheless, since the content of "The Musical Sound of Mass" is concise and condense, it is necessary to learn the catechism beforehand.

To apply *qu* to religious music is a tradition originating in the Yuan dynasty (1271–1368). "Prayer of Golden Character" (*Jinzi jing* 金字經) and "Five Supplies" (*Wu gongyang* 五供養) were composed in the Buddhist tradition; "Song

---

381   Chaves, *Singing of the Source*, 75.
382   Dudink, "Manual for Attending Mass," 227.

of Blue Sky" (*Qingtian ge* 青天歌) and "Song of Taiqing Fairyland" (*Taiqing ge* 太清歌) in the Taoist one.[383] "The Musical Sound of Mass" was an innovative move in the Christian music in China.[384] Fang Hao gave a proper comment: "Following musical scores and vocal lines, Yushan explained prayers and the ritual of Mass, which truly opened a new type in the literature of our country."[385] In addition, "The Musical Sound of Mass" opened a new type in the propagation of Catholic rituals in China. Wu Li's efforts to describe and to explain the Mass in an indigenous way exemplify that the establishment of indigenous clergy fostered the development of indigenous liturgy.

4 Conclusion

This chapter reveals the close relationship between indigenous clergy and indigenous liturgy in Chinese society. Reshaped in Chinese society, the Catholic priest's multiple identities incited anti-Catholic movements. Confronted with a cultural imperative, the Christian communities considered the establishment of indigenous clergy an urgent measure not only to defend but also to strengthen the Catholic Church in China, and the establishment of indigenous liturgy was the effective method for training indigenous clergy. Indigenous liturgy, especially the celebration of Mass in an indigenous way, was one major step toward the establishment of indigenous clergy, and the latter in turn fostered the development of the former.

Some missionaries and Chinese Catholics insistently asked Rome for the privileges to establish indigenous clergy and indigenous liturgy. Regardless of their success, the efforts illustrate cooperation between missionaries and Chinese Catholics, opposition at the state and the local level, struggle between the

---

383 Shi Junjing 時俊靜, "Yuanqu qupai yu zongjiao yinyue 元曲曲牌與宗教音樂," *Huangzhong (Wuhan yinyue xueyuan xuebao)* 黃鐘武漢音樂學院學報 1 (2012): 82–87.

384 In order to reconstruct Christian music in the seventeenth and eighteenth centuries in China, Jean-Christophe Frisch and François Picard made a series of recordings: "Teodorico Pedrini: Concert Baroque à la cité interdite" (Auvidis Astree E8609, rec 1996); "Messe des Jésuites de Pékin" (Auvidis Astree E8642, rec 1998); "Chine: Jésuites & courtisanes" (Buda Records 1984872, rec 1999); "Vêpres à la Vierge en Chine" (K617 K617155, rec 2003). The fourth recording includes examples of sung Mass and hymns from the *Compendium of Orthodox Sounds of Heavenly Music* (*Tianyue zhengyin pu* 天樂正音譜). Joyce Lindorff, "The Sweet Sound of Cultures Clashing," *Early Music* 33, no. 3 (Aug. 2005): 538–539.

385 "漁山尋聲按譜, 以解彌撒經文與儀禮, 實為我國文學別開生面。" Fang, "Zhuri misa jingdian zixu 主日彌撒經典自序," in *Fang Hao liushi*, 2243.

Catholic Church in China and Rome, and a contrast of diversity in local communities and unity in the universal Church. The various embodiments unfold the glocalization of rituals in the Christian communities in China. The next chapter examines the ritual space and ritual time of Mass.

CHAPTER 4

Place of Worship: Ritual Space and Ritual Time of Mass

In late Ming and early Qing the Christian communities celebrated Mass in a closed environment and at a low frequency in general. Nevertheless, the celebration of Mass is essential for the place of worship in the Teaching of the Lord of Heaven, which is constituted by ritual space and ritual time. This chapter argues that with Mass as the essential ritual, ritual space and ritual time of the Catholic Church were effectively rooted in Chinese society, thus realizing the foundation of Christendom. The first section focuses on the "hall" of the Lord of Heaven, the most important ritual space in the Teaching of the Lord of Heaven. The following section focuses on the Catholic liturgical calendar and related worship practices. The third section explores the foundation of Christendom in Chinese society.

1   Ritual Space of Mass

1.1   *Hall of the Lord of Heaven*

With their peculiar names, architecture, sacrificial objects, and decorations, churches built in late Ming and early Qing were remarkable symbols of the Teaching of the Lord of Heaven. In 1583, local official Wang Pan approved Ruggieri and Ricci to settle in Zhaoqing, Guangdong, and to build the first church in mainland China.[1] At that time Ruggieri and Ricci called themselves "*Tianzhu seng* 天竺僧" (the Indian monks), therefore Wang Pan gave the church a rather Buddhist name "*Xianhua si* 仙花寺" (the Temple of Immortal Flower). In the end of 1584, the construction of the Temple of Immortal Flower was finished. The two-stage European architecture seemed an odd Buddhist temple in local people's eyes.[2] For Ricci the temple's name carried the connotation of the Virgin Mary, while for local people it indicated the Bodhisattva of Compassion (*guanyin* 觀音).[3]

---

1 Ricci, *Yesuhui yu tianzhujiao*, 96.
2 Zhang Xianqing 張先清, "Zhishi yishou shi: wenhua xiangyu zhongde Xianhua si gushi 只是一首詩：文化相遇中的仙花寺故事," in *Xiao lishi*, 15–17.
3 Bernard, *Le père Matthieu Ricci*, première partie, 133.

The early mission in China used various words to refer to the church, such as the temple (*si* 寺), the palace (*dian* 殿), and the Holy Palace of the Lord of Heaven (*tianzhu shengdian* 天主聖殿).[4] In 1611, the official of the Ministry of Rites named the Jesuit's residence at Zhalan er "*tianzhu tang* 天主堂" (the hall of the Lord of Heaven).[5] This name became the fixed term for Catholic churches, in accordance with the term for Catholicism "*tianzhu jiao* 天主教" (the Teaching of the Lord of Heaven). Missionaries and Chinese Catholics frequently used the hall (*tang* 堂) as an abbreviation. Thus, going to church was going to the hall (*fu tang* 赴堂).[6] Another abbreviation was the hall of the Lord (*zhutang* 主堂).[7] Names such as the holy place (*shengsuo* 聖所) and the holy hall (*shengtang* 聖堂) were also in use.[8] The holy hall had already been used in Buddhism and Taoism but with a lower frequency. The character "*sheng* 聖" (holy) underlines the church's holiness. The primary reason for the church structure to be holy is that it is the ritual space to celebrate Mass. Moreover, some churches have a tabernacle to keep the Host—the real presence of God. The hall of the Lord of Heaven signifies that it is the place to worship the Lord and that the Lord is present under the appearance of the Host.

It is necessary to notice the complexity of the terminology for religious architecture in Chinese. For architectures in Confucianism, Buddhism, Taoism, and popular religion, characters are used with no strict distinction of religions, such as "*si* 寺," "*miao* 廟," "*tang* 堂," "*gong* 宮," and "*ci* 祠." The outstanding example is the temple of the Heavenly Empress (*tianhou* 天后), a goddess in popular religion. Several names are used to address her temple, such as "*tianhou gong* 天后宮," "*tianhou si* 天后寺," "*tianhou ci* 天后祠," and "*tianhou miao* 天后廟." Such a variety of usage exemplifies how complex the terminology of religious architecture in Chinese can be. Some missionaries were aware of the complex terminology and tried to take advantage of it. In order to prove that the wor-

---

4 "謁寺，" Ruggieri, *Tianzhu shilu*, fol. 35a6, 71. "入殿，" Vagnone, *Jiaoyao jielüe, shang juan*, fol. 17a3, 157. "天主聖殿，" João Soeiro 蘇如望, *Shengjiao yueyan* 聖教約言, fol. 9a5, in CCT ARSI, vol. 2, 271.

5 Jozef Jennes, *Four Centuries of Catechetics*, 26.

6 "一、每月以第三主日之六日，蚤赴堂作會，" Humbert Augery 洪度貞, *Tianzhu Yesu kuhui gui* 天主耶穌苦會規, fol. a5–6, in CCT ARSI, vol. 12, 465. "但無大緣故而自寬自慢，不赴堂瞻禮者，" Brancati, *Tianshen huike*, fol. 63a3, 129.

7 "擴建主堂，" Ding, *Yang Qiyuan*, fol. 4b3, 224. "至杭州主堂，" Anon., *Taixi Yin Juesi xiansheng xinglüe* 泰西殷覺斯先生行畧, in CCT BnF, vol. 12, 600.

8 For "*shengsuo* 聖所," see de Mailla, *Shengti ren'aijing*, fol. 6a4, 305. For "*shengtang* 聖堂," see Manuel Dias 陽瑪諾, *Tang jingjiao beisong zhengquan* 唐景教碑頌正詮, fol. 9b, in CCT BnF, vol. 23, 18, 19.

ship of Confucius was never a religious cult, Le Comte argued: "The palaces which bear his name are not temples, but houses destined to the assemblies of the scholars."[9] Simao Rodrigues emphasized that the meaning of the Chinese character can vary in different context. He explained that although both are called a temple, the temple for Confucius (*Kongzi miao* 孔子廟) and the temple for ancestors (*zumiao* 祖廟) have two different functions: the former serves as a place for lecture, the latter as a place to worship the ancestors. One shall not avoid using a name just because one character in it was used by other religions, since "in China there is no character that cannot have an orthodox usage and there is no character that cannot have a pernicious usage. And what choice shall the preacher make?"[10]

In the texts written in Western languages by missionaries, "temple" (*templum*) refers to the church as well as to religious architecture of other religions. Similarly, this chapter uses the word "temple" in an encompassing sense. Every religious edifice can be called a temple, regardless of its religious affiliation. "Church" is used exclusively for the Catholic temple. According to Ad Dudink, the usage of "hall" dissociated the Catholic church from the Buddhist or Taoist monasteries (*si* 寺, *guan* 觀, *gong* 宮), because the character "*tang* 堂" was also used for local administrative buildings, juridical buildings, and gathering places of learned discussions.[11] Yet, the usage did not dissociate the church from the temples of popular religion, where there were various halls, such as the Hall of Buddha (*fotang* 佛堂), the Hall of Bodhisattva of Compassion (*Guanyin tang* 觀音堂), and the Hall of General [Liu] Meng (*Mengjiang tang* 猛將堂). In this regard, the resemblance of names made the hall of the Lord of Heaven indigenous, by sociating the church with local religious buildings in Chinese society.

Under the general name of the hall of the Lord of Heaven, each church has its specific name, usually named after its patron. For instance, the church under the patronage of Holy Mary is called the hall of the Holy Mother (*shengmu tang* 聖母堂), which was the common name for the church exclusively for female Catholics.[12] The name resembles the temple of the Holy Mother (*shengmu miao* 聖母廟) and the altar of the Holy Mother (*shengmu tan* 聖母壇), two other

---

9   Lecomte, *Un jésuite à Pékin*, 382.
10   "中國無一字不可正用亦無一字不可邪用。傳教者又何擇焉？" Rodrigues, *Bianji canping*, 424.
11   Ad Dudink, "Church buildings," *Handbook of Christianity*, 580. Terms such as "*si* 寺" and "*gong* 宮" are not only used in Buddhism and Taoism. For instance, a mosque is called "*qingzhen si* 清真寺."
12   Dudink, "Church buildings," 580–581.

names for the temple of the Heavenly Empress. There were halls under the patronage of various saints: in 1684, the Hall of St. Thomas Aquinas was built in Zhangzhou;[13] in 1697, the Hall of St. Francis Xavier was built in the county Xinhui 新會 in the south of Canton.[14] There were also churches named after events in the church history: in 1685, the Hall of Our Lady of Annunciation was built in Shaozhou 韶州;[15] in 1717–1718, the Hall of the Sacred Heart was built at the north of Hangzhou, as the first church under this title in the Far East.[16] In addition, names that barely with religious connotation in Chinese were used: in 1696, the Hall of Rose (*Meigui tang* 玫瑰堂) was built in Fuzhou;[17] in 1703, the Hall of the Supreme Good (*Shoushan tang* 首善堂) was built on the land which the Kangxi emperor bestowed to the Jesuits in 1694;[18] from 1659–1663, the Hall of the Supernatural (*Chaoxing tang* 超性堂) was built in Hangzhou. Chinese Catholics could recognize these halls as the ritual space for the Lord of Heaven. Yet, the Catholic connotation was too implicit for non-Catholics to catch. They might have seen these halls only as places for Catholic publication,[19] and they often considered the hall of the Lord of Heaven a school, because the catechist taught children in the hall.[20]

Moreover, a church's name in Chinese sometimes differed from that in Western languages written by missionaries to the European readers. The Hall of Rose was called the Church of Our Lady of the Rosary;[21] the Hall of the Supernatural was called the Church of the Savior (*Templum Salvatoris*) and the Church of the Holy Name of Jesus by the Europeans.[22] Consequently, European readers missed the connotation of original names in Chinese. Noël Golvers gives a summary of words in Western languages referring to places of worship built in China. The Latin words *templum* and *ecclesia* refer to a church which was part of the house; *templum* can also mean a church and a mostly adjoining house; the Latin word *oratoria* refers to smaller places of worship; the Spanish words *casa*

---

13   Dehergne, *La Chine centrale*, 331.
14   Joseph Dehergne, *La Chine du Sud-Est: Guangxi (Kwangsi) et Guangdong (Kwuangtung). Étude de géographie missionnaire* (Rome: Archivum Historicum Societatis Iesu, 1976): 32.
15   Dehergne, *La Chine du Sud-Est*, 42.
16   Dehergne, *La Chine centrale*, 314.
17   Dehergne, *La Chine centrale*, 336.
18   For a detailed clarification, see Dudink, "Church buildings," 581, note 3.
19   Dudink, "Church buildings," 581.
20   Collani, "Neue Welt-Bott," 685.
21   Dehergne, *La Chine centrale*, 336.
22   In the mid-nineteenth century the church was re-named as Hall of Holy Mother without Original Sin (*Shengmu wuyuanzui tang* 聖母無原罪堂, the Church of Immaculate Conception). D.E. Mungello, *The Forgotten Christians of Hangzhou* (Honolulu: University of Hawaii Press, 1994), 30.

iglesia and *sala* refer to a room in a Chinese Catholic's house for Mass, prayers, and catechism. Among these places of worship, large ones usually located in a city while small ones in a country.[23] Early in 1579, Ruggieri built the Oratorio of Saint Martin in a mountain in Canton.[24] In the end of the sixteenth century, Wang Pan's father received baptism and built a domestic oratory in Zhaoqing, where he knelt down and recited the Rosary everyday.[25] Oratories were not necessarily smaller than churches. In the end of the seventeenth century, some oratories were even larger.[26]

Generally, a church was built in a growing Christian community with enough financial and material support. When the condition was not sound, smaller constructions such as chapels and oratories were built. Since the Christian community often did not have a fixed residence for the missionary, when an itinerant missionary visited there, he administered sacraments, such as baptism, confession, and the Eucharist, in a room in the house of a Catholic family. In this case, the room being used was a temporary ritual space. Once the ritual was finished, the ritual space returned to an ordinary room.[27] In the second half of the seventeenth century, missionaries encouraged poor families to set a niche in the main room of their house and wealthy families to establish a chapel.[28] An exceptional case was found in Ningde, where the Hall of the Conception of Our Lady was started on 20 August 1675 with only one Chinese Catholic.[29] As for churches exclusively for female Catholics, there is also an exceptional case. In 1696 the church exclusively for female Catholics in Nanxiong 南雄 was called the Hall of St. Monica instead of the hall of the Holy Mother.[30] In addition, churches for the lepers were built in various Christian communities. In Fujian, there was a church and hospital for the lepers in the East of Fu'an and a church and hospital for the lepers in the North of Fu'an around the 1700s.[31] In Guangdong, there was a church for the lepers in Nan-

---

23 Rougemont distinguished *templum* and *ecclesia* from *aedes* and *domus*. Golvers, *François de Rougemont*, 377–378.
24 Lin, *Li Madou yu Zhongguo*, 11.
25 Bernard, *Le père Matthieu Ricci*, première partie, 112.
26 Brockey, *Journey to the East*, 363.
27 Ad Dudink gives a brief introduction of churches in China, with an emphasis on those in Beijing. The chapel and the room in a Catholic family are mentioned. Dudink, "Church buildings," 580–586.
28 "本家各宜設一小堂。力或不能，作一木龕，內供主像。" Verhaeren, "Ordonnances," 469.
29 Dehergne, *La Chine central*, 351.
30 Dehergne, *La Chine du Sud-Est*, 41.
31 Dehergne, *La Chine central*, 328.

hai 南海 before 1723 and a chapel for the lepers in Chao'an 潮安 after 1703;[32] a church for the lepers in Xinxing 新興 around the 1700s and a leprosarium with a chapel in Huizhou 惠州 in 1695.[33]

Together with missionaries, Chinese Catholics offered financial and material support to build churches.[34] Wealthy Chinese Catholics were generous to assist the construction of churches. In 1627 (Tianqi 7), the family of Han Lin bought two houses in East South of Jiangzhou and transformed them into churches.[35] This is a very early example of local Chinese Catholics supporting to build churches.[36] In 1639 (Chongzhen 12), Han Lin supported Vagnone to build a church in Pingyang 平陽, Shanxi. In 1641 (Chongzhen 15), he supported Trigault to build a church in Taiyuan 太原.[37] Candida Xu showed great fervor in building churches and chapels, not only in Shanghai but also in provinces such as Jiangxi, Hubei, and Hunan 湖南.[38] Her father Jacques Xu Ji 徐驥 (1582–1645) assisted Brancati to build a number of churches, chapels, and domestic oratories.[39] Her son Basil Xu Zuanzeng 許纘曾 (1627–1696?) built churches in Sichuan and Henan.[40] From 1627 to 1633, Yang Tingyun supported Dias to build the first church in Hangzhou. Later in 1645, Tong Guoqi 佟國器 (1648–1684) urged Martino Martini (Wei Kuangguo 衛匡國, SJ, 1614–1661) to build a large church in Hangzhou. The construction began in 1659 with financial support from Madame Agathe who was Tong Guoqi's wife and from Madame Judith who was a certain Mr. Zhao's concubine. In 1663, Augery completed the construction of the Hall of the Supernatural.[41]

In addition to these eminent figures, common Catholics and some non-Catholic literati also offered great support.[42] In 1702, the Chinese Catholics in Ji'nan, the majority being poor, made huge sacrifice to build the new East Hall. The non-Catholic literatus Zhu, a circuit intendant (*daotai* 道臺), contributed

---

32 Dehergne, *La Chine du Sud-Est*, 28, 35.
33 Dehergne, *La Chine du Sud-Est*, 46.
34 Dudink, "Church buildings," 581.
35 Xu Guangqi 徐光啟, *Jingjiao tang beiji* 景教堂碑記, in *Sanzhushi*, 72.
36 Sun Shangyang 孫尚揚, "Shangdi yu Zhongguo huangdi de xiangyu—*Duoshu* zhongde ruye hudong yu lunli jiangou 上帝與中國皇帝的相遇——《鐸書》中的儒耶互動與倫理建構," in *Duoshu jiaozhu*, 5.
37 Sun, "Shangdi," 5.
38 Couplet, *Histoire d'une dame*, 24, 46.
39 Couplet, *Histoire d'une dame*, 31–32.
40 Couplet, *Histoire d'une dame*, 47, 49.
41 Mungello, *The Forgotten Christians*, 28–30.
42 Chinese Catholics' support for the construction of churches embodied their religious commitment. Sun, "Zongjiao weishen," 19.

to decorate the new church.[43] Non-Catholic literati assisted the construction perhaps in order to improve their personal reputation and influence at local levels. In 1693, female Catholics in Beijing donated their rings, earrings, and other ornaments to build a new church dedicated to the Annunciation.[44] In the seventeenth century, decorations made from precious textiles were popular gifts from female Catholics to churches.[45] It also happened that local Christian communities built churches without the missionary's guidance. In 1654, the Chinese Catholics in Shangtang 上塘, Funing 福寧 began to build a church by themselves.[46] In 1699 (Kangxi 38) during his third Southern Inspection Tour, the Kangxi emperor saw the large golden characters "*tianzhu tang* 天主堂" at the Jesuit residence's portal in Hangzhou and asked about the church's situation. Then, the emperor bestowed a large amount of silver to support Emmanuel Laurifice (Pan Guoliang 潘國良, SJ, 1646–1703) to complete its reconstruction.[47] In addition, local Christian community may receive support from Europe as well. In his letter written on 17 July 1707, François-Xavier Dentrecolles (Yin Hongxu 殷弘緒, SJ, 1664–1741) recorded that M. le Marquis de Brossia supported the construction and maintenance of the church in Jingdezhen 景德鎮, Jiangxi.[48]

As the Catholic Church in China grew, churches were gradually built in various places. This section examines the hall of the Lord of Heaven from three perspectives: architectural, liturgical, and spiritual. From the architectural perspective, the construction of a church introduced the architecture of European style into Chinese society. In the 1670s, only four churches were built in Baroque style, and the rest were in Chinese style.[49] The West Hall in Ji'nan was in typical Chinese style, with an altar at the north end and an entrance at the south end.[50] On the contrary, the church rebuilt at Xuanwu men was in typical Baroque style.

---

43   The new church was thirty paces long and fifteen paces wide, including a baptistry and a sacristy. Mungello, *Spirit and the Flesh*, 87–88.
44   Brockey, *Journey to the East*, 364.
45   Amsler, *Jesuits and matriarchs*, 139.
46   Dehergne, *La Chine central*, 350.
47   François Froger, *Relation du premier voyage des François à la Chine fait en 1698, 1699 et 1700 sur le vaisseau „L'Amphitrite"*, ed. E.A. Voretzsch (Leipzig: Verlag der Asia major, 1926), 118.
48   François-Xavier Dentrecolles, "Lettre du Père d'Entrecolles, missionnaire de la Compagnie de Jésus, au Père procureur-général des missions des Indes et de la Chine," Charles Le Gobien, ed., *Lettres édifiantes et curieuses, écrites des Missions étrangères, par quelques missionnaires de la Compagnie de Jésus*, vol. 10 (Paris: Jean Barbou, 1713), 154–155.
49   Golvers, *François de Rougemont*, 378.
50   Mungello, *Spirit and the Flesh*, 98.

Schall praised: "That Temple truly surpasses the remaining shrines of Idols by artistic rarity and beauty."[51] The Hall of the Supernatural in Hangzhou was also remarkable for its Baroque style. Missionaries often described this church with three naves (*ecclesia trium navium*) to European readers.[52] The Hall of the Supernatural's Baroque design probably came from the Church of the Gesù in Rome, the prototype of many Jesuit churches,[53] yet its style also had Chinese elements. According to Le Comte, a number of churches in China were as beautiful as those in Europe, and the church in Hangzhou which was enriched by Chinese people with varnish, golden flowers, and other figures achieved the most beautiful effect in the world.[54] A construction of the temple of the true God, as Le Comte called,[55] became a new mark on the Chinese religious landscape.

From the liturgical perspective, the hall of the Lord of Heaven was constructed for the assembly of Chinese Catholics. The early Catholic Church considered a church the house where Christians assembled (*domus in qua Christiani conveniebant*),[56] the place where Christians assembled to worship God as a unity. Le Comte proposed that this ritual space already existed in ancient China: "Huangdi, the third Emperor, built a temple for the sovereign the Lord of Heaven; ... it is not a small glory that China has sacrificed to the Creator in the most ancient temple of the universe."[57] It is this proposition that was condemned by the theologians of the University of Paris. According to David Mungello, Le Comte probably referred to early sacrifices to God in a temple in ancient China without a specific temple in mind.[58] Despite Le Comte's creative proposition for evangelization, a church was a new type of religious architecture in Chinese society. As the place to celebrate Mass the grand sacrifice to the Lord of Heaven, the church signified the visible church, where the members visibly assemble to have a common meal and to honor God together.[59]

---

51 "Templum equidem istud et artis raritate et formae nitore reliqua Idolorum fana exsuperat." Schall, *Relation historique*, 327.
52 Dehergne, *La Chine centrale*, 313.
53 Mungello compares this church with the Church of the Gesù, the mother church of the Society of Jesus in Rome, Mungello, *The Forgotten Christians*, 31–33.
54 Lecomte, *Un jésuite à Pékin*, 464–465.
55 Lecomte, *Un jésuite à Pékin*, 376.
56 Jungmann, *La liturgie*, 30.
57 "Hoamti, troisième empereur, bâtit un temple au souverain Seigneur du Ciel; ... ce n'est pas une petite gloire à la Chine d'avoir sacrifié au Créateur dans le plus ancien temple de l'univers." Lecomte, *Un jésuite à Pékin*, 359.
58 Mungello, *Curious Land*, 338.
59 Jungmann, *La liturgie*, 25.

From the spiritual perspective, Aleni interpreted the visible church and the invisible one to the Chinese Catholics in Longjiang 龍江. On 24 September 1636 (Chongzhen 9.8.26), Aleni first acknowledged the local Catholics' many merits (*gongduo* 功多) to (re)build the holy hall,[60] then he exhorted them that the exterior hall (*waitang* 外堂) has been built, now it is high time to build the interior hall (*neitang* 內堂).[61] Aleni made an indirect reference to the First Letter of St. Paul to the Corinthians: "In your heart, you should build a hall of *Spiritus Sanctus* (*si-bi-li-duo-san-duo zhi tang* 斯彼利多三多之堂)."[62] Following the exhortation is a detailed analogy between the exterior hall and the interior hall. It takes three steps to build the exterior hall: the first step is to pull away weeds and to clean the ground (*bachu* 拔除); the second is to construct the wooden and stone parts of the hall in right order (*jianshu* 建豎); the third is to assemble the parts into the hall (*hecheng* 合成).[63] It takes the same steps to build the interior hall: first, to receive baptism is to pull away the wrong words and clean the pernicious deeds; second, to establish merits (*ligong* 立功) in various ways is to construct the parts; third, to attach to the Lord's heart in thoughts, words, and deeds is to assemble the parts into the hall.[64] When the interior hall is built, it shall receive the presence of the Supreme Lord (*shangzhu zhi lin'ge* 上主之臨格). The term "*lin'ge* 臨格" (presence) had already been used in Buddhism and Taoism.[65] In late Ming and early Qing, the Teaching of the Lord of Heaven connected it with the real presence (*praesentia realis*).[66]

---

60 Longjiang 龍江 is a variant name for Haikou 海口. The original text says "newly built" (*xinjian* 新建). According to Zürcher, a new church had been built in Haikou in 1631 and was probably rebuilt in 1636. Zürcher, *Kou duo ri chao*, vol. 1, VI. 47, 519, note 1.
61 For the whole conversation, see Li, *Kouduo richao*, juan 6, fol. 18a7–fol. 19a4, 441–443. Zürcher, *Kou duo ri chao*, vol. 1, VI. 47 (Haikou, Wednesday, 24 September 1636), 518–519.
62 The original sentence is "nescitis quia templum Dei estis et Spiritus Dei habitat in vobis" (1 Corinthians 3:16). According to Song Gang, St. Paul referred to the Holy Spirit which dwells in human body, while Aleni changed the words into "in your heart" to combine Mencius' theory of four branches of the mind (*sixin shuo* 四心說) and Wang Yangming's theory of mind (*xinxue* 心學). Song, *Giulio Aleni*, 238–239.
63 These three steps were taken from the construction of a traditional Chinese wooden architecture. Zürcher, *Kou duo ri chao*, vol. 1, VI. 47, 519–520, note 2.
64 Song Gang suggests that the three steps to build the interior hall referred to works written by St. Bonaventure and by Thomas Aquinas, and *The Spiritual Exercises* of St. Ignatius. Song, *Giulio Aleni*, 239.
65 "至真臨格," Shi Zhiqing 釋志磬, *Fozu tongji* 佛祖統紀, *juan* 43, Eruson, 482. "臨格," Xiaoshan laoren 曉山老人, *Taiyi tongzong baojian* 太乙統宗寶鑒, *juan* 6, Eruson, 51.
66 Exceptionally in *Life of the Holy Mother*, Vagnone used "*lin'ge* 臨格" to describe Mary's apparition. "以何功可致聖母臨格," Vagnone, *Shengmu xingshi*, *juan* 3, fol. 8a8–9, 1435.

Early in the *Brief Record of Holy Prayers*, Ricci introduced the profound meaning of the Eucharist.[67] After the celebrant reciting the holy prayer (*shengjing* 聖經), the real presence of the Lord manifests at Mass in the exterior hall. Aleni exhorted the Chinese Catholics to prepare the interior hall in order to embrace the real presence within themselves. In *The Meaning of the Sacrifice of Mass*, Aleni had used a similar indirect citation: "All the hearts of the faithful can be one living hall (*huotang* 活堂) together for the Holy Spirit to dwell."[68] The term "*si-bi-li-duo-san-duo* 斯彼利多三多" (the Holy Spirit) is a transliteration of the Portuguese word *Spirito Santo*.[69] In this sense, human body becomes a ritual space.[70] The most ancient appellation of the house of God is *ecclesia*, the Greek word for reunion and assembly. The Christians consider the visible church the shadow of the interior edifice, which is constructed from the living stones.[71] In The Second Letter to the Corinthians, Paul described that the Christians themselves are the living stones which construct the invisible church (II Cor. 6:16, *Vos enim estis templum Dei vivi*).

The church as the ritual space is constructed for the function of the community.[72] To stress the notion of community, Aleni distinguished the private sphere and public sphere to worship the Lord of Heaven: "The home, a place where one cultivates oneself alone, is private. The hall, a place where the crowd worship together, is public. The private cannot compare with the public."[73] He acknowledged the religious practices in the familial sphere while urged those in the ecclesiastical sphere. "All gathering in the hall, the faithful worship the Great Father together."[74] The assembly of the Christians was emphasized by "*xian* 咸" (all) and "*gong* 共" (together). To attend Mass is the principal purpose of the assembly.[75] In the interior of the church, the altar as the ritual center reveals the close relationship between the celebration of Mass and the church.

---

67 "念經後，麵色、餅味存，而其體變易為耶穌之體。其體既為活體，併有寬靈，併有聖血。…… 故有天主性在其中焉。惟酒亦然。" Vagnone, *Jiaoyao jielüe*, shang juan, fol. 53a7–b2, 229–230.

68 "凡我等奉教人心，皆可共成一活堂，為斯彼利多三多所居。" Aleni, *Misa jiyi*, juan 1, fol. 6b9–fol. 7a2, 496–497.

69 Dudink, "Sacramental Initiation," 190.

70 Human body could also be a space, in some cases a sacred space, see Mircea Eliade, ed., *The Encyclopedia of Religion* (New York: Macmillan Publishing Company, 1987), volume 12, 532.

71 Jungmann, *La liturgie*, 32.

72 Jungmann, *La liturgie*, 32.

73 "家者獨脩之處，私也。堂者眾仰之地，公也。私不如公。" Aleni, *Misa jiyi*, xu, fol. 3b2–3, 476.

74 "奉教者咸集堂中，共仰一大父。" Aleni, *Misa jiyi*, juan 1, fol. 16b8–9, 516.

75 Jungmann, *La liturgie*, 27.

1.2 *The Altar and Objects around It*

The interior of the church is constructed to fulfill its function as the ritual space for the Christians to worship God as a unity. From the liturgical perspective, the altar is the ritual center of the church. Because Mass is celebrated in front of the altar and the Host is consecrated on it, the altar is called the Lord's table.[76] Rodrigues highlighted: "The most noble and the most important ritual must be Mass which must be offered to the Lord of Heaven and must be performed on the altar by the priest everyday without any changes."[77] Appearing three times, the character "*bi* 必" (must) underlines the close relationship between the celebration of Mass and the altar.

Ad Dudink summarizes the thirty-three sections in *The Exposition of Mass*. Seven sections mention the altar, one time in each section.[78] Below are the corresponding sections in the second volume of *The Meaning of the Sacrifice of Mass*.

> Put the holy classic and the holy chalice on the altar (section 1, part one);[79]
>
> Ascend the altar, approach the altar's left side, and read a part of the ancient scriptures (section 4, part one);[80]
>
> Approach the altar's center to read *Kyrie eleison* nine times (section 5, part one);[81]
>
> Approach the altar's left side to extend the hands and recite a prayer (section 8, part one);[82]
>
> Move the [holy] classic to the altar's right side, offer incense, and recite the *Evangelium* classic (section 10, part one);[83]

---

76 Jungmann, *The Mass*, 315.
77 "則極尊之礼方為至重必屬彌撒必献天主必鐸德每日行之於聖臺不可更易者也。" Rodrigues, *Bianji canping*, 437.
78 Each section has its allegorical explanation. Dudink, "Manual for Attending Mass," 237–241.
79 "陳聖經聖爵于臺，" Aleni, *Misa jiyi, juan* 2, fol. 4a5, 559. The word "*shengjing* 聖經" (holy classic) here refers to the Roman Missal. In the Chinese Christian texts in late Ming and early Qing, the meaning of the character "*jing* 經" varies in different context.
80 "上臺，就臺左，誦古經一段，" Aleni, *Misa jiyi, juan* 2, fol. 6a2, 563.
81 "就臺中誦基利厄陀勒依算九遍，" Aleni, *Misa jiyi, juan* 2, fol. 6b9, 564.
82 "就臺左開手念經，" Aleni, *Misa jiyi, juan* 2, fol. 9a2, 569.
83 "移經臺右，奉香，誦萬熱略經，" Aleni, *Misa jiyi, juan* 2, fol. 12b7, 576. According to the allegorical explanation, the book is moved from the left to the right side of the altar. For the clarification of the altar's left and right sides, see Appendix 11, Dudink, "Manual for Attending Mass," 313–316.

Approach the altar's center to recite the prayer *Credo* (section 11, part one);[84]

Then carry the [holy] classic to the altar's left side again, and recite a prayer (section 1, part three);[85]

Stand at the altar's right side, and recite a prayer (section 6, part three).[86]

Directions for Hearing Mass mentions the altar nine times.[87] The two additional times are "After washing hands, the priest approaches the altar's center and puts the hands together to recite a prayer in a low voice" (*duode xishou hou xiang taizhong hezhang weisheng songjing* 鐸德洗手後向臺中合掌微聲誦經), which fits section 15, part one in the second volume of *The Meaning of the Sacrifice of Mass*; "The priest extends the hands to recite a prayer" (*duode taizhong kaishou langsheng songjing* 鐸德臺中開手朗聲誦經), which fits section 16, part one in the second volume.

The altar and the objects around it are necessary materials to celebrate Mass and visible symbols of theological thoughts on Mass. In the first volume of *The Meaning of the Sacrifice of Mass*, the fourth chapter on the hall and altar provides a detailed explanation of the altar and various sacrificial objects around it, with twenty items in total.[88] Table 4 is based on Aleni's explanation on the name, location, description, and allegorical meaning. It offers the corresponding Latin words in the Roman Missal in 1570 and an English translation of Aleni's explanation.

TABLE 4   Altar and objects around it

Latin	Chinese	English	Location	Description	Meaning
altare	*tai* 臺	altar	in the deepest place of the hall	—	Mount Calvary

84 "就臺中誦信經，" Aleni, *Misa jiyi, juan* 2, fol. 15b4, 582.
85 "又請經復過臺左，誦經一段，" Aleni, *Misa jiyi, juan* 2, fol. 32b7–8, 616.
86 "在臺右立，誦經一段，" Aleni, *Misa jiyi, juan* 2, fol. 39a2, 629.
87 Appendix 13, Dudink, "Manual for Attending Mass," 318–319.
88 "堂之最深處必有一臺，設一聖像于上，帷帳蔽之，以時開閉；臺中置聖石一座，冪以潔白細布，凡三層；⋯⋯ 左右各置燭臺，其燭必以黃蠟為之；臺前護以繒帛，旁飾以綵綉；⋯⋯ 臺下有升降階級；臺邊兩旁設祭器；案左列葡萄酒注、淨水罐、淨手帨、阿斯地亞之奩，各種供具；⋯⋯ 聖爵為第一品祭器，⋯⋯ 聖爵上用拭爵帨；帨上金銀蓋爵之盤；盤上四角方綿蓋；蓋上有紗羅之冪；冪上有少許方綉函以含藏里諾布袱，" Aleni, *Misa jiyi, juan* 1, fol. 7b1–fol. 9a4, 498–501.

TABLE 4   Altar and objects around it (cont.)

Latin	Chinese	English	Location	Description	Meaning
crux	shengxiang 聖像	holy statue	on the altar	with a cross	salvation of the world
velum	weizhang 帷帳	curtain	hang over the holy statue	—	movable barrier
sepulchrum	shengshi 聖石	holy stone	in the centre of the altar	—	our Lord's body
palla altaris	xibu 細布	fine cloth	covered on the holy stone	Three-layered, white, clean	the most clean holy body of our Lord
candelabra	zhutai 燭臺	candle-stick	on the altar's left and right sides	candle made of yellow wax	our Lord's holy light
pallium altaris	taiwei 臺幃	altar frontal	hang in front of the altar	made of silk, decorated with colorful embroidery	our Lord's perfect vertues
gradus altaris	shengjiang jieji 升降階級	up-and-down steps	below the altar	—	—
parva mensa	xiang'an 香案	incense table	beside the altar	—	—
ampulla vini	putaojiu zhu 葡萄酒注	grape wine flagon	on the incense table's left side	—	—
ampulla acquae	jingshui guan 淨水罐	jar for clean water	—	—	—
manutergium	jingshou shui 淨手帨	towel for hand cleaning	—	—	—
ciborium	a-si-di-ya zhi lian 阿斯地亞之奩	casket of *Hostia*	—	—	—
calix	shengjue 聖爵	holy chalice	held by the celebrant to the altar	First-class sacrificial object, must be made of gold, silver or tin	our Lord's tomb
purificatorium	shijue shui 拭爵帨	towel for wiping chalice	on holy chalice	—	shroud
patena	pan 盤	plate	covered on the towel	made of gold or silver	stone over the tomb
palla	gai 蓋	lid	on the plate	Four-corner, square, made of silk	
velum calicis	mi 羃	cloth covering	on the lid	made of fine woven fabric	—
bursa	han 函	casket	on the cloth cover	square, decorated with colorful embroidery	—

TABLE 4 Altar and objects around it (cont.)

Latin	Chinese	English	Location	Description	Meaning
corporalis	linuobu fu 里諾布袱	linen covering	kept in the casket, spreaded under the holy body during Mass	made of linen	shroud

Aleni first mentioned the altar: "At the deepest part of the hall, there must be an altar … In the middle of the altar one holy stone is placed."[89] In accordance with table 4, when visiting the newly-(re)built holy hall in Longjiang, Aleni explained to local Catholics the analogy of the living hall. Pointing to the altar, Aleni deepened the analogy by saying that in the ancient ritual the altar must be made of stone, but today it was made of wood yet must be solidified by a holy stone. Then, he pointed out the connection and distinction between Jewish ritual and Catholic ritual: "If you want to establish the interior hall, you must put a stone to solidify it."[90] The ancient ritual (*guli* 古禮) refers to the ancient Jewish ritual which used the stone altar. The early Catholic Church used a wooden altar as a distinction from Judaism. Yet, in the fifth century, the stone altar gradually took over the wooden one, and one council in 517 decided that only the stone altar can be consecrated. The corresponding theological explanation said that the stone altar signifies Jesus who himself is the cornerstone.[91] In the sixth or seventh century, the devotion of the martyr went popular in Europe and so did the placement of the martyr's relic in the altar, eventually, to place the martyr's relic in the altar became a rule.[92]

Aleni's explanation in Longjiang was partly inherited from the history of the Catholic Church and partly adapted to Chinese society. To place the holy stone in the altar was aimed at not to forget the ancient (*bu wanggu* 不忘古), which highly conformed with the Chinese tradition to cherish the ancient.

---

89 "堂之最深處必有一臺，……臺中置聖石一座，" Aleni, *Misa jiyi, juan* 1, fol. 7b1–2, 498.
90 "徐觀堂臺，先生又曰：'古禮之為臺也，必砌以石。今雖以木為之，亦必鎮以聖石，示不忘古也。顧子等欲立內堂，亦必鎮之以石。何則？石方正堅確，不可動搖，非若木之游移而靡定者巳。'" Li, *Kouduo richao, juan* 6, fol. 19a5–8, 443. Zürcher, *Kou duo ri chao*, vol. 1, VI. 47 (Haikou, Wednesday, 24 September 1636), 519.
91 Jungmann, *The Mass*, 315. For the cornerstone, see Psalm 118:22, "The stone which the builders rejected has become the cornerstone" (*lapis quem reprobaverunt aedificantes factus est in caput anguli*). See also Matthew 21:42, Luke 20:17.
92 Jungmann, *The Mass*, 258, 315.

Moreover, the holy stone (*sepulchrum*) was the spot to place the relic, however, Aleni did not mention the relic itself to the Chinese Catholics in Longjiang. Perhaps he worried that the mention of relic might cause misunderstanding. As shown in table 4, Aleni did not mention the relic in *The Meaning of the Sacrifice of Mass* neither, where the holy stone was explained as the body of Jesus.

Similar to the sacrificial vestment, the table frontal is a vivid demonstration of the ritual time's rhythm. The sacrificial vestment's color changes among white, red, black, blue, and green according to the time (*suishi* 隨時), that is, according to the liturgical calendar in the Catholic Church.[93] The table frontal's color changes in accordance with the sacrificial vestment's.[94]

In *Reception of Suffering of the Lord of Heaven Jesus from the Beginning to the End*, de Pantoja transliterated *calix* as "*jia-li-zeng* 加理增" and explained in a note that it means "*jiujue* 酒爵" (wine container).[95] Later on, "*shengjue* 聖爵" (the holy chalice) became a fixed translation for the chalice. This translation conforms with the terminology of traditional Chinese rituals, for the wine container "*jue* 爵" is a bronze sacrificial object used in ancient China.[96] In the prayers during Mass translated by Buglio, the chalice is called the chalice of salvation of the soul (*jiuling zhi jue* 救靈之爵) and the chalice of life (*shengming zhi jue* 生命之爵), with the Catholic connotation.[97] In *The Classics of the Mass* and *Instructions of the Priest*, Buglio gave the prescriptions of some sacrificial objects and the allegorical meanings, which can serve as the complements of table 4.

The Chinese translation of the sacrificial objects are inconsistent even in the same book. Aleni called the purificator (拭爵帨 *shijue shui*) "the towel for holy chalice" (聖爵帨 *shengjue shui*) in the same section,[98] whereas Buglio simply called it "the wiping towel" (*shijin* 拭巾).[99] In addition to "the casket of *Hostia*" (*a-si-di-ya zhi lian* 阿斯地亞之奩), Buglio called the ciborium "the casket of

---

93 "若其祭服之色，隨時而用，或白，或紅，或玄，或天青，或綠。" Aleni, *Misa jiyi*, juan 1, fol. 16 a1–2, 515.

94 "臺前護以繒帛，旁餘以綵綉，其色隨時更易，與祭服同。" Aleni, *Misa jiyi*, juan 1, fol. 7b4–5, 498.

95 de Pantoja, *Shounan shimo*, fol. 3a4, 65.

96 "爵，禮器也。象爵之形，中有鬯酒，又持之也。" Xu Kai 徐鍇, "Tongshi juan 10 通釋卷十," *Shuowen jiezi xizhuan* 說文解字系傳, Eruson, 122.

97 "念主奉獻救靈之爵云云，" Buglio, *Misa jingdian*, fol. 43a13–14, 91. "念將取生命之爵云，" Buglio, *Misa jingdian*, fol. 48b7–8, 102.

98 Aleni, *Misa jiyi*, juan 1, fol. 9a6, 501.

99 Buglio, *Misa jingdian*, fol. 43a9, 91.

bread" (*bingxia* 餅匣), "the small casket of the holy body" (*xiao shengtixia* 小聖體匣), and "the holy casket" (*shengxia* 聖匣).¹⁰⁰ The character "*xia* 匣" (casket) means a small covered container and can refer to a coffin as well. The casket of bread echoes the holy bread (*shengbing* 聖餅), which is another translation by Buglio for *Hostia* (*a-si-di-ya* 阿斯底亞).¹⁰¹ Aleni did not mention the tabernacle on the altar in the fourth section, whereas Buglio translated it in several terms, such as the holy cabinet (*shenggui* 聖櫃), the cabinet of the holy body (*shengti gui* 聖體櫃), and the holy casket (*shengxia* 聖匣), which is also one translation of the ciborium.¹⁰² In the early stage of translating the objects pertaining to Mass, there was no strictly consistent terminology. In fact, certain objects still have various translations in the Catholic Church in China today. For instance, the tabernacle is called "the niche of the holy body" (*shengti kan* 聖體龕), "the cabinet of the holy body" (*shengti gui* 聖體櫃), and "the holy niche" (*shengkan* 聖龕).

Because of its essential ritual function in Mass, the altar attracted Chinese Catholics. As Le Comte described, "The lively faith they have for the adorable sacrament of the Eucharist attached them continuously to the altars."¹⁰³ Chinese Catholics expressed their adoration to the Lord of Heaven in front of the altar. Before and after celebrating Mass, they knelt before the altar and recited prayers. In the seventeenth century, Chinese Catholics in the East Hall in Ji'nan knelt before the altar and prayed before the Sunday Mass, and they recited "Praise to the Holy Body and the Holy Mother" in the conclusion. In some villages outside Ji'nan, Chinese Catholics knelt before the altar and prayed after the Sunday Mass.¹⁰⁴ Chinese Catholics' frequent and long kowtow caught Le Comte's attention. This posture was more common in Asia than in Europe, "the face glued to the ground, moaning and ordinarily shedding tears."¹⁰⁵ In tradi-

---

100 "餅匣，" Buglio, *Misa jingdian*, fol. 45a8, 95. "小聖體匣，" Buglio, *Misa jingdian*, fol. 49a2–3, 103. "聖匣，" Buglio, *Misa jingdian*, fol. 49a6, 103.
101 Buglio, *Misa jingdian*, fol. 43a7, 91.
102 "臺上聖櫃，" Buglio, *Siduo dianyao, juan shang*, fol. 14a10, 41. "臺上有聖體櫃，" Buglio, *Misa jingdian*, fol. 38b9, 82. "聖匣，" Buglio, *Misa jingdian*, fol. 48b5, 102. "盍聖體供在聖匣內，" Buglio, *Siduo dianyao, juan shang*, fol. 18a5, 49. For the description of a tabernacle in the church in Hangzhou in late Ming and early Qing, see Mungello, *The Forgotten Christians*, 49.
103 "La foi vive qu'ils avaient pour l'adorable sacrement de l'Eucharistie les attachait continuellement aux autels," Lecomte, *Un jésuite à Pékin*, 428.
104 Mungello, *Spirit and the Flesh*, 13–16. Mungello translates this prayer as "Praise be to the Most High Sacrament and the Immaculate Conception."
105 Lecomte, *Un jésuite à Pékin*, 428.

tional Chinese rituals, kowtow before an altar is a common act. Therefore it is not surprising that some non-Catholics also knelt and kowtowed before the altar in a church.

On 5 February 1689 (Kangxi 28.1.16), the Kangxi emperor arrived Ji'nan during the second Southern Inspection Tour and talked with Joseph de Osca (Ke Ruose 柯若瑟, OFM, 1659–1735). De Osca prepared some gifts from Europe for the Kangxi emperor: two bottles of wine,[106] one glass bottle or cup, a pair of linen handkerchiefs with point lace, two candles made of white wax, and some incense. The Kangxi emperor then sent two courtiers Zhao Chang 趙昌 and the Venerable Wu 哈鄔 to the church to meet de Osca. In the Chinese source *Documents in the Reign of the Kangxi Emperor* (*Xichao ding'an* 熙朝定案), the two courtiers "arrived the hall and kowtowed (*bai* 拜) toward the Lord of Heaven first," then they met de Osca and told him that "the Master of ten thousand years ordered us to come in order to kowtow and to worship (*baikou* 拜叩) the Lord of Heaven and to bestow silver."[107] Similarly, Le Comte mentioned how the emperor passed by and sent two officials to the hall to offer presents to the true God on his behalf. The emperor ordered the officials to kowtow in front of the altars of the true God.[108]

On 16 March 1689 (Kangxi 28.2.25), the Kangxi emperor arrived Jiangning 江寧. On 18 March (Kangxi 28.2.27), he sent the same two courtiers to meet Gabiani and Jean de Fontaney (Hong Ruo 洪若, SJ, 1643–1710). The courtiers "arrived the hall. They kowtowed (*bai* 拜) the Lord of Heaven first."[109] On 21 March (Kangxi 28.3.1), the Kangxi emperor sent the two courtiers to deliver three plates of food to the hall. Gabiani and de Fontaney followed the courtiers to the front of the Lord of Heaven's altar (*tianzhu tai* 天主臺) and placed the food. Zhao Chang delivered the emperor's order that it is fine for the two missionaries to "thank for the [emperor's] grace in front of the Lord of Heaven's

---

106 Bernard Rhodes (Luo Dexian 羅德先, SJ, 1646–1715) recommended the Kangxi emperor to develop a habit of drinking wine. Dentrecolles, "Lettre du Père d'Entrecolles," 133. Western wine, once only used during Mass, became a tribute which maintained the communication between the Kangxi emperor and missionaries. Li, *Zhongguo liyi*, 101–104.

107 "有侍衛趙、御前一等哈伍，捧欽賜賚銀二十兩，到堂先拜天主。趙、伍二位云：'萬歲爺命我們來拜叩天主，頒賜銀兩。'" Han Qi 韓琦 and Wu Min 吳旻, annot., *Xichao chongzheng ji, xichao ding'an* (*wai sanzhong*) 熙朝崇正集，熙朝定案（外三種） (Beijing: Zhonghua shuju 中華書局, 2006), 172.

108 Lecomte, *Un jésuite à Pékin*, 474. Zhao Chang and the Venerable Wu struck their heads nine times before the altar of the Lord of Heaven. Mungello, *Spirit and the Flesh*, 68.

109 "廿七日早，皇上差侍衛趙、御前一等哈鄔，賚捧黃袱，內包白金到堂。先叩拜天主，" Han and Wu, *Xichao chongzheng*, 175.

altar."[110] The altar in the hall was the place where Chinese Catholics kowtowed and worshiped the Lord of Heaven, yet it was but one among many altars for non-Catholics.

Nevertheless, the Shunzhi emperor's attitude toward the altar in the hall is remarkable. According to Schall, once when the emperor passed the front of the main altar in the hall at Xuanwu men, "in the presence of all who were there, bending his head and striking his chest, he honored the image of our Savior with great devotion" (*coram omnibus adstantibus inclinato capite percussoque pectore Imaginem Salvatoris nostri honoravit magna cum devotione*). In Schall's eyes, such a move showed respect if not faith toward the Lord of Heaven.[111] Later, the bibliophile Wang Qishu 汪啟淑 (1728–1799) recorded his visit to the church at Xuanwu men, "The image of Buddha in the hall is painted by oil. It looks lifelike from a distance. The objects there are rather peculiar and strange."[112] The image of Buddha probably refers to the image of Christ or Mary above the altar. The use of perspective in the oil painting gives a three-dimensional and lifelike effect, which is different from the traditional Chinese painting. The objects which Wang Qishu described as peculiar and strange probably include various sacrificial objects used in the celebration of Mass and other Catholic rituals.

The altar can also be examined from the spiritual perspective. In the end of the fourth chapter "the Hall and Altar," Aleni encouraged people to think about the allegorical meaning of each object used in Mass because such thinking constructed a spiritual altar in the heart (*yi xinzhong shentai* 一心中神臺).[113] Once again human body was considered ritual space. According to Aleni's analogy of the living hall in section 1.1, human body shall be a church. Now the analogy takes a step further to consider human heart an altar where the Lord descends and dwells. One sentence in Wu Li's poem "Sent to Guo" is in accordance with Aleni's analogy: "How glorious it is that your heart becomes the altar for the almighty King!"[114] One may wonder if Wu Li thought about Aleni's analogy while writing the poem. In the *Golden Book with Contempt of the World*, Dias

---

110 "三月初一日黎明，皇上臨行又差趙、鄔二大人，賫送食物三盤，木箱一擡到堂。畢、洪……次隨二大人到天主臺前，擺設御賜。……侍衛趙又云：'奉旨不必往行宮謝恩，就在天主臺謝恩罷了。'" Han and Wu, *Xichao chongzheng*, 176.
111 Schall, *Relation historique*, 289.
112 "堂中佛像，用油所繪，遠望如生，器皿頗光怪陸離。" Wang Qishu 汪啟淑, *Shuicao qingxia lu* 水曹清暇錄, *juan* 4, Eruson, 21.
113 "夫不以外之儀節為禮，而以中心參究為禮，豈不又成一心中神臺也哉？" Aleni, *Misa jiyi*, *juan* 1, fol. 9b1–3, 502.
114 "榮哉心作大君臺。" Wu, "Zeng Guo," in Zhang, *Wu Yushan ji*, 198. For a translation of the whole poem, see Chaves, *Singing of the Source*, 63.

used a similar expression in the discourse of the Lord: "You shall make your heart the altar, where you dust and illuminate with various virtues and where I will feast with the apostles."[115] The altar to the church is as the heart to the body. Yet, anti-Catholics did not mention the interior of the hall often. It is the exterior of the hall that caught their attention.

1.3 Beamless Palace

The construction of a church was an outstanding vista in China's religious landscape. Churches attracted much attention from Chinese Catholics, curious visitors, and anti-Catholics. Since late Ming and early Qing, churches had often been the primary target in persecutions.[116] Anti-Catholics attributed various names to this new type of religious architecture in Chinese society.

From 1615 to 1619, Shen Que was the Right Vice Minister of the South Palace (*Nangong* 南宮), the Ministry of Rites in Nanjing. In the beginning of 1620, Shen Que published *Documents of the South Palace*, a collection of memorials and other official documents issued by him and his Ministry.[117] Four memorials and twelve documents in the collection are related to the Nanjing persecution.[118] Xu Changzhi compiled most of them into the large-scaled work *Anthology of Destroying the Pernicious*, because She Que's memorials served powerfully for the anti-Catholic purpose.[119] One peculiar accusation in the memorials is that the Western missionaries built the beamless palace (*wuliang dian* 無梁殿). In the *Second Memorial to Accuse Distant Barbarians* (*Zaican yuanyi shu* 再參遠夷疏), written in 1616 (Wanli 44.8), Shen Que described how Wang Fengsu 王豐肅 (Alfonso Vagnone) "dared to sneak into the City Gate of Zenith Sun, to build the beamless palace to the west of the Hongwu Hill, to hang the barbarian statue in the air, and to delude foolish people."[120]

---

115 "子以心為臺，蕩污拂塼，耀以眾德，吾偕宗徒宴厥內。" Dias, *Qingshi jinshu*, juan 4, fol. 12a3–4.

116 Zou Zhenhuan 鄒振環, "Mingqing zhi ji Lingnan de 'jiaotang wenhua' jiqi yingxiang 明清之際嶺南的'教堂文化'及其影響," *Xueshu yanjiu* 學術研究 11 (2002): 82.

117 The publication aimed to promote Shen Que to Grand Secretary. After much effort, he became Grand Secretary in August 1620. Adrian Dudink, "*Nangong Shudu* (1620), *Poxie Ji* (1640), and Western Reports on the Nanjing Persecution (1616/1617)," *Monumenta Serica* 48, 1 (2000): 138.

118 For a table of content with marks on texts pertaining to Catholics, see Dudink, "*Nangong Shudu*," 138–140.

119 Only a few texts were omitted in *Anthology of Destroying the Pernicious*, because they did not serve for anti-Catholic purpose. Dudink, "*Nangong Shudu*," 140–141.

120 "而豐肅神姦，公然潛住正陽門裏，洪武岡之西，起蓋無樑殿，懸設胡像，誆誘愚民。" Shen Que 沈㴶, *Zaican yuanyi shu* 再參遠夷疏, fol. 11b6–9, in *Poxie ji*, vol. 1, 223. See also Shen, *Zaican yuanyi*, fol. 5b4–7. The character "*liang* 樑" in *Documents of the*

After a series of strong accusations, Shen Que emphasized the places chosen by the missionary: "What is most hateful is that they not only occupy the imperial place of Hongwu Hill as the residence inside the city but also have one garden outside the city right before the Filial Mausoleum Guard."[121] The Hongwu Hill (*Hongwu gang* 洪武岡) lies inside the City Gate of Zenith Sun (*Zhengyang men* 正陽門), and the Filial Mausoleum Guard (*Xiaoling wei* 孝陵衛) is the imperial mausoleum in Nanjing. Shen Que suggested that the missionaries' choice of place betrayed their rebellious intention. In the *Third Memorial to Accuse Distant Barbarians* (*Can yuanyi sanshu* 參遠夷三疏), written in the same year (Wanli 44.12), Shen Que reiterated the missionaries' choice of place and asked the Wanli emperor to send officials to examine that "the beamless palace built by the missionary is really a few five hundred meters (*li* 里) away from the City Gate of Zenith Sun, is it not suspicious for being so near to the city?"[122] As a summary of the memorial, the missionaries made an illicit entrance into the city and built illicit constructions near imperial places for illicit activities.

Seeing that the three memorials did not receive any response, Shen Que enlisted the help of Fang Congzhe 方從哲 (?–1628), a high-ranking official who grew up in Shen Que's hometown, to attack the church in Nanjing and to capture missionaries and Chinese Catholics. Thus, the first large-scaled persecution toward the Teaching of the Lord of Heaven broke out in China. In "Memorial to Expel Distant Barbarians" (*Faqian yuanyi huizou shu* 發遣遠夷回奏疏), written in 1617 (Wanli 45.5), Shen Que repeated the accusation of illicit construction.

> It is forbidden to construct monasteries privately, ... the form of the beamless palace threatens the Honorable; the Hall of Serving Heaven (*Shitian tang* 事天堂) transgresses greatly, how can we not sweep these away but allow them to change the perspective of people in the capital?[123]

South Palace is written as "*liang* 梁." For a description of how the Jesuits bought the place near Hongwu Hill, see Bernard, *Le père Matthieu Ricci*, deuxième partie, 347–348.

121 "尤可恨者，城內住房既據洪武岡王地，而城外又有花園壹所，正在孝陵衛之前。" Shen, *Zaican yuanyi*, fol. 12a9–b1, 223–224. See also Shen, *Zaican yuanyi*, fol. 6a9–b3. The place was called the Filial Mausoleum Guard because the guard of the Ming Filial Mausoleum garrisoned there.

122 "皇上試差官踏勘，其所蓋無樑殿，果於正陽門相去幾里，是否緣城近堞蹤跡可疑？" Shen Que 沈㴶, *Can yuanyi sanshu* 參遠夷三疏, fol. 15a7–8, in *Poxie ji*, vol. 1, 225.

123 "惟是私剏庵觀有禁，…… 而況乎無樑殿，其制逼尊；事天堂，其名大僭，豈容不掃除以易都人耳目之觀？" Shen, *Faqian yuanyi*, fol. 3b7–fol. 4a1, 236.

Although not the capital anymore, Nanjing was still a crucial city, with the Hongwu Hill and the Filial Mausoleum Guard as the symbols of imperial reign. Shen Que considered both the construction and name of the church in Nanjing rebellious.

It is noteworthy that Shen Que called the church the beamless palace. The beamless palace was a traditional Chinese architecture made of brick and stone, without wooden beams and pillars. It originated from the mausoleum made of brick and stone in the end of the West Han dynasty (202 BC–8) and first appeared in the Jin dynasty (1115–1234). Because of the low cost and fire-resistant quality, the beamless palace became popular in the Ming dynasty.[124] It had been constructed throughout China, mainly in Buddhist temples but also in Taoist ones. In 1381 (Hongwu 14) a large beamless palace was built in Nanjing to worship Buddha of Immeasurable Life (*wuliang shou fo* 无量寿佛, *amitayus*), thus also being called the Immeasurable Palace (*Wuliang dian* 無量殿). Because of its architecture, the homophonous name the Beamless Palace (*Wuliang dian* 無梁殿) was more known. Ad Dudink provides three possible reasons why Shen Que called the church the beamless palace: Shen Que simply referred to the architecture made of brick and stone; the church's European style; Shen Que accused the church as a sacrilegious imitation of the aforementioned Immeasurable Palace.[125] The current section suggests that Shen Que considered the church not a strange European building but an illicit religious one. As Vice Minister of Rites, Shen Que was concerned with the imperial places such as the Hongwu Hill and the Filial Mausoleum Guard. In 1618, he accused the improper location of a Taoist canon bestowed by the Wanli emperor to a Taoist temple of being close to the forbidden area (*jindi* 禁地).[126] Similarly, Shen Que treated the church as an indigenous religious construction in an improper location.

Other names attributed to churches appeared in *Anthology of Destroying the Pernicious*. As the propagation of the Teaching of the Lord of Heaven grew, Huang Zhen demanded people to be alert and to face the current situation: "Please look that which place does not have the hall of Jesus and the Teaching of rebellion today?"[127] The two phrases—the hall of Jesus (*Yesu zhi tang* 耶穌

124　Guo Jinfeng 郭晉峰, "Woguo xiancun zuigulao de yuanluoshi wuliang dian jianzhuqun: Taiyuan Cangshan shenmiao 我國現存最古老的院落式無梁殿建築群：太原藏山神廟," *Gujian yuanlin jishu* 古建園林技術 4 (2012): 70.
125　Dudink, "*Nangong Shudu*," 239, note 312.
126　Dudink, "*Nangong Shudu*," 240.
127　"試觀今日何處非耶穌之堂，叛逆之教也乎？" Huang Zhen 黃貞, "*Poxie ji* zixu 破邪集自敘," fol. 24a4–5, in *Poxie ji*, vol. 3, 265.

之堂) and the Teaching of rebellion (*panni zhi jiao* 叛逆之教)—correspond to each other. Since anti-Catholics considered Jesus the leader of a rebellious Teaching, the hall of Jesus indicated a place where people assemble for conspiracy. Wang Chaoshi 王朝式 (1603–1640) compared the situation in the past with the current one: "It was only in the Hongwu Hill in the old capital that the missionary built the Hall of Serving Heaven to assemble and to delude people; today, the establishment of Great Bright Teaching (*jingjiao* 景教) spreads to several provinces."[128] The construction of a church was a remarkable symbol of local Christian community and the material evidence of the Teaching of the Lord of Heaven's development.

Xu Dashou repeated Shen Que's accusation: "The hall of the Lord of Heaven was established privately," and "it is clearly forbidden by the law to construct monasteries privately."[129] Then his accusation went further: "I do not know according to which imperial edict they order people that everyone shall establish one hall of the Lord of Heaven and that every house shall worship one cross. Is it a convention or a creation? Secret or public?"[130] Xu Dashou emphasized that churches were secretly built. The character "*si* 私" (secret) refers to a church that was constructed without official approval, which is different than the usage of "*si* 私" by Aleni in section 1.1. In fact, Xu Dashou's accusation was true. As Schall acknowledged, the Society of Jesus had been in China for almost eighty years, "but has not opened publicly any temple" (*nec tamen ullum templum palam aperuit*). In general, missionaries administrated the sacraments in private chapels inside houses. Schall listed three reasons for not opening temples publicly: the lack of proper places for the construction; Catholicism had not been widely promulgated; the fear that some non-Catholics may invade churches. When talking about the construction of the church at Xuanwu men, Schall gave the fourth reason that it was very difficult to obtain permission from the Ministry of Rites, "so we did not ask for any permission" (*nulla quidem tum petita licentia*).[131]

Some local officials decided to tear down the secretly built churches. On 20 December 1637 (Chongzhen 10.11.5), the official Xu Shiyin issued an official notice: "Where there are the halls of Teaching and the pernicious books, they

---

128 "建事天堂，聚眾惑民，止留都洪武岡一處耳。今則景教之設延及數省矣。" Wang Chaoshi 王朝式, *Zuiyan* 罪言, fol. 26b4–6, in *Poxie ji*, vol. 3, 267. Great Bright Teaching (*jingjiao* 景教) is the Chinese name of Nestorian Christianity. In late Ming and early Qing, it also referred to the Teaching of the Lord of Heaven.
129 "所私設天主堂，" "且私剏庵院，律有明禁。" Xu, "Liupi," 120–121.
130 "不知彼所令民間人設一天主堂，戶供一十字枷，奉何勅旨，因耶穌耶？私耶公耶？" Xu, "Liupi," 120–121.
131 Schall, *Relation historique*, 319.

should all be destroyed and burnt out."[132] Since a church was a place where the followers of the Teaching of the Lord of Heaven assembled, Xu Shiyin called it the hall of Teaching (*jiaotang* 教堂), which is now a common usage to call a church. The two words—the hall of Teaching and the pernicious books (*yaoshu* 妖書)—correspond to each other, both carrying negative connotation. All the aforementioned anti-Catholics underlined that the hall is the place where people assemble, and the majority of them imagined that missionaries assembled Chinese people and deceived them into rebellion. Only a few people such as Xu Dashou knew about Catholic rituals performed in a church. In the seventeenth century, the celebration of Mass in churches was not widely known. Yet, the assembly in a church was suspicious enough to incite anti-Catholic sentiments, so churches in various Christian communities suffered from local accusations and attacks.

During the Nanjing persecution, the Hall of Serving Heaven accused by Shen Que was tore down in 1617 (Wanli 45), and objects in the church were inventoried by local governments in Shangyuan 上元 county and Jiangning 江寧 county. In the Case of Inventorying Barbarian Objects (*Qingcha yiwu yi'an* 清查夷物一案), "one niche of the Lord of Heaven inside the Hall of Serving Heaven" (*Shitian tang nei tianzhu kan yizuo* 事天堂內天主龕一座) referred to a tabernacle;[133] "one small golden painted niche" (*jinqi xiaokan yige* 金漆小龕一個) and "gilded and black painted niche" (*miaojin heiqi kan* 描金黑漆龕) probably also referred to tabernacles;[134] one package of frankincense (*ruxiang yibao* 乳香一包) was probably to be burned in Mass.[135] In addition, a number of objects in the inventory, such as various boxes, caskets, plates, cups, censers, candlesticks, curtains, and table coverings, were probably objects used in Mass.

In 1617 (Wanli 45.8), Xu Changzhi's brother, the official of the Ministry of Rites Xu Congzhi wrote the Case of Demolishing House and Garden Which Violate the System (*Chaihui weizhi louyuan yi'an* 拆毀違制樓園一案). According to this official document, the materials of the Jesuit residence were transported for the reconstruction of the Temple of Master Huang (*Huanggong ci*

---

132 "其地方若有教堂妖書，盡行拆毀焚除，" Xu, *Tixing anchasi*, fol. 37a6–7, 253.
133 Yingtian fu Shangyuan, Jiangning erxian chaobao 應天府上元、江寧二縣抄報, *Qingcha yiwu yi'an* 清查夷物一案, fol. 35b1, in *Nangong shudu*, juan 3. In 1637 (Chongzhen 11), the official in Fujian Shi Bangyao 施邦曜 recorded the inventory of "one large niche of the Lord of Heaven and one small niche of the Lord of Heaven" (*daxiao tianzhu kan ge yizuo* 大小天主龕各一座). Shi, *Fujian xunhaidao*, fol. 31a10, 250.
134 Shangyuan and Jiangning, *Qingcha yiwu*, fol. 33a2, b2.
135 Shangyuan and Jiangning, *Qingcha yiwu*, fol. 30b9.

黃公祠).¹³⁶ Dudink suggests that Shen Que used these materials for a traditional Chinese temple in order to emphasize that missionaries and Chinese Catholics should show proper loyalty to the state and its orthodox teaching.¹³⁷ Later on, local geomancers in Jianchang 建昌, Jiangxi criticized the hall built by Intorcetta, arguing that this tall hall destroyed the official court's harmony of geomancy (*fengshui* 風水).¹³⁸ Also, the hall in Pinghu 平湖 county, Jiaxing, Zhejiang was destroyed in the 1664–1671 persecution.¹³⁹

2 Ritual Time of Mass

As mentioned in the beginning of this chapter, the place of worship is constituted by ritual space and ritual time together. The assembly of Christians in the church was not random, because a fixed order of coming and going is an expression for a closed society to reveal itself.¹⁴⁰ The early church already noticed the necessity to assemble at determined hours for the common ritual.¹⁴¹ Therefore a rhythm of ritual time had been composed in the form of the liturgical calendar. The first part of this section focuses on the rhythm of the Catholic liturgical calendar in Chinese context. The following part analyzes the liturgical calendar in the form of the list of worship. The third part examines how missionaries urged Chinese Catholics to live according to the liturgical calendar. This section argues that the promotion of the Catholic liturgical calendar achieved a synthesis of time.

2.1 *Day of Worship*

In the early church, the Catholic ritual's new spirit manifested not only by ritual place but also by ritual time.¹⁴² The notion of time in the Roman empire had been gradually Christianized. In the Catholic Church, the rhythm of ritual time is composed with seven days. The Christians shall gather in the church on the Lord's day to celebrate Mass, and the emphasis on the Lord's day attaches to the

---

136   Xu Congzhi 徐從治, *Chaihui weizhi louyuan yi'an* 拆毀違制樓園一案, fol. 2a5, in *Nangong shudu, juan 4.*
137   Dudink, "*Nangong Shudu,*" 151.
138   "未幾建昌郡伯高君聽形家者言，以主堂高聳礙伊衙署風水，捏詞控於上臺。" Anon., *Taixi Yin Juesi*, 601.
139   Dehergne, *La Chine centrale*, 318.
140   Jungmann, *The Mass*, 235.
141   Jungmann, *La liturgie*, 26.
142   Jungmann, *La liturgie*, 37.

whole week a religious consecration.[143] In late Ming and early Qing, missionaries introduced the rhythm of ritual time in the Catholic Church to Chinese society. The implantation of this rhythm of ritual time in Chinese context began with the translation of terms.

The word "*zhanli* 瞻禮" in Chinese is originally used as a verb, meaning to adore and to worship.[144] The reference of the word in *Dictionary of Etymology* (*Ciyuan* 辭源) is from *Record of the Transmission of the Lamp* (*Chuandeng lu* 傳燈錄, 1004), a Buddhist text written in the North Song dynasty. Earlier references are found in *Complete Collection of All Surviving Prose Literature in the Tang Dynasty* (*Quan Tangwen* 全唐文, compiled in 1808–1814).[145] A number of references confirm the clear Buddhist origin of the word. The Catholic Church in China chose the Buddhist term to present its own rhythm of ritual time in Chinese. The current chapter translates "*zhanli* 瞻禮" as "day of worship" when used as a noun and as "to worship" when used as a verb.[146] It is necessary to notice that "*zhanli* 瞻禮" used in the Catholic Church often means "Mass" as a noun and "go to Mass" as a verb.[147] Moreover, its usage as a noun extends to all the seven days.

In the explanation of "*zhanli* 瞻禮," Buglio called a week "seven" (*qi* 七), "Every seven is called a day of worship. A year has in total fifty-two sevens and one day."[148] Then, Buglio described the whole seven days one by one.

> The first day is called the Lord's day; the second day is called the second day of worship; the third day is called the third day of worship; the fourth day is called the fourth day of worship; the fifth day is called the fifth day

---

143 Jungmann, *La liturgie*, 44.
144 "瞻禮：瞻仰禮拜，" *Ciyuan* 辭源 (Beijing: The Commercial Press 商務印書館, 1979), 2223.
145 "每梵音瞻禮，" Li Baiyao 李百藥, "Huadu si guseng yong chanshi sheli ta ming 化度寺故僧邕禪師舍利塔銘," in *Quan Tangwen* 全唐文, *juan* 143, comp. Dong Gao 董誥, Eruson, 1428. "獲瞻禮於千輻輪足畢，" Wang Bo 王勃, "Shijia rulai chengdao ji 釋迦如來成道記," in *Quan Tangwen*, *juan* 182, Eruson, 1837. "瞻禮雲集，" Li Yong 李邕, "Donglin si bei bingxu 東林寺碑並序," in *Quan Tangwen*, *juan* 264, Eruson, 2665.
146 Dudink notices the Buddhist origin and translates "*zhanli* 瞻禮" as "performing ritual," see Dudink, "Manual for Attending Mass," 301.
147 Zürcher used to translate the noun as "ritual of veneration," see Erik Zürcher, "Confucian and Christian Religiosity in Late Ming China," *The Catholic Historical Review* vol. 83, no. 4 (Washington D.C.: Catholic University of America Press, 1997): 631. Later he changed the translation into "rite of worship." Zürcher, *Kou duo ri chao*, vol. 1, I. 39 (Fuzhou, Saturday, 22 March 1631), 244.
148 "每個七謂之一瞻禮。一年共具五十二個七，零一日。" Buglio, *Misa jingdian*, fol. 4a4–5, 13.

PLACE OF WORSHIP   231

TABLE 5   Names of days of worship

Catholic terms	Latin	Modern Chinese	English
zhuri 主日	*Dominica*	*zhou ri* 周日	Sunday
zhanli er 瞻禮二	*Feria Secunda*	*zhou yi* 周一	Monday
zhanli san 瞻禮三	*Feria Tertia*	*zhou er* 周二	Tuesday
zhanli si 瞻禮四	*Feria Quarta*	*zhou san* 周三	Wednesday
zhanli wu 瞻禮五	*Feria Quinta*	*zhou si* 周四	Thursday
zhanli liu 瞻禮六	*Feria Sexta*	*zhou wu* 周五	Friday
zhanli qi 瞻禮七	*Feria Septima*	*zhou liu* 周六	Saturday

of worship; the sixth day is called the sixth day of worship; the seventh day is called the seventh day of worship.[149]

Le Grand Ricci marks "*zhanli* 瞻禮" as a Catholic term with two meanings: liturgical feast; liturgical feria.[150] According to the explanation in *Le Grand Ricci*, table 5 lists the Catholic terms of days of worship, the corresponding Latin words, the common usage in Modern Chinese, and its translation in English.

Both ferial days and feast days are translated as "*zhanli* 瞻禮," and the method for distinguishing them is that every ferial day is always marked by a number while every feast day has its specific name. The feast day is attached with the name of certain saint(s) or of certain event(s), such as the Feast of St. Joseph, the feast day of St. Francis Xavier, and the feast day of the Institution of the Holy Body.

As the feast day celebrated every week, Sunday (*Dominica*) has special names in Chinese. Usually it is not called "the first day of worship" (*zhanli yi* 瞻禮一) but simply "the day of worship" (*zhanli* 瞻禮) or literally "the Lord's day." The Lord's day (*zhuri* 主日) was a new Chinese term specifically coined to describe Catholic ritual time. Back in the early church, to name the first day of worship as the Lord's day was a typical Christianization of time, with a new meaning, a new character, and a new name.[151] In late Ming and early Qing, the

---

149   "每七日謂之一瞻禮。第一日，謂之主日；第二日，謂瞻禮二；第三日，謂瞻禮三；……第七日，謂瞻禮七。" Buglio, *Misa jingdian*, fol. 4b4, 14.
150   *Le Grand Ricci* I, 275, 138.
151   Jungmann, *La liturgie*, 38. In the end of the first century, a new Greek term was coined,

Catholic Church in China began Christianization of time in Chinese society. To use the Lord's day had always been a profession of faith.[152] Among the seven days, some missionaries and Chinese Catholics especially explained the seventh day, which shall not be confused with the seventh day of worship. Traced back to Genesis and the Jewish tradition, the Lord's day is called the seventh day. Yet, the Catholic liturgical calendar acknowledges it as the first [worship] day. There were various explanations of the seventh day in late Ming and early Qing. According to de Pantoja, "The work of opening the sky and the earth is accomplished on the seventh day. Therefore the Lord of Heaven designates this day as the holy day. Ever since the ancient Teaching, the seventh day is the day of worship (*zhanli* 瞻禮)."[153] The creation of the world is addressed in an indigenous way as the work of opening the sky and the earth.[154] Tracing back to Genesis and addressing ancient Judaism as the ancient Teaching (*gujiao* 古教), de Pantoja underlined the role of the Lord of Heaven who sanctifies the seventh day.

The second explanation connects the calculation of the Lord's day with traditional Chinese calendar. When explaining the days of fasting and abstinence in the Catholic Church, Rho made a peculiar note of the Lord's day.

> The days of Room (*fang* 房), Emptiness (*xu* 虛), Hair (*mao* 昴), and Star (*xing* 星) are the four days of the Sun among the Twenty-Eight Mansions recorded in the calendar. In the Holy Teaching they are called the Lord's day, the Sun's day, and the first day of worship. The following day is the second day of worship, which successively increases to the seventh day of worship.[155]

Then Rho made concise description of the name of all the seven days. He connected the Four Symbols (*sixiang* 四象) in the Twenty-Eight Mansions

---

        which equals to "the day of the Christ" and "the supper of the Lord," Jungmann, *La liturgie*, 39.

152 Jungmann, *La liturgie*, 40.

153 "開天地之功，第七日盡。故天主定此日，為聖日，從古教中，以第七日為瞻禮也。" de Pantoja, "Renlei yuanshi 人類原始," *Pangzi yiquan*, fol. 20b1–2, 230.

154 In ancient Chinese myth of genesis, a man named Pan Gu 盤古 broke the egg-shaped chaos, thus separating the sky and earth. "Pan Gu opened the sky and the earth" (*Pan Gu kai tiandi* 盤古開天地) is one popular understanding of the genesis in Imperial China.

155 "主日者，曆載二十八宿內房虛昴星四太陽日，聖教謂之主日，亦名曜日，又名瞻禮一。次日為瞻禮二，挨次遞至瞻禮七云。" Rho, *Zhaike, juan* 3, fol. 2b8–9, 580.

(*ershiba xingxiu* 二十八星宿) with the Sun's day (*yaori* 曜日, *dies Solis*) in Western astronomy.[156] Seen from this note, "the Sun's day" is the name used from the perspective of astronomy, while "the Lord's day" and "the first day of worship" are names used from the perspective of religion. The note is peculiar because the first day of worship (*zhanli yi* 瞻禮一) is rarely used in the Chinese Christian texts in late Ming and early Qing. In *Direct Explanation of Sacred Scripture* (*Shengjing zhijie* 聖經直解, ca. 1636–1642), Dias explained the Lord's day in a similar way and cited Augustine's praise that "The first day when the Lord of Heaven created the world is the first Lord's day in the world."[157]

Decades later, Buglio also mentioned the calculation which is connected with traditional Chinese calendar: "When it is the day of Room (*fang* 房), Emptiness (*xu* 虛), Hair (*mao* 昴), and Star (*xing* 星) on the calendar, it is the Lord's day."[158] Zhou Zhi continued using the connection: "According to the Chinese calendar, whenever it is [the day of] Room (*fang* 房), Emptiness (*xu* 虛), Hair (*mao* 昴), and Star (*xing* 星), it is the Lord's day."[159] Furthermore, he pointed out human beings' intention to celebrate the seventh day: "The seventh day is the day when human beings thank for the Lord's grace. Therefore there is a worship every seven days ever since the opening of the world and it shall never change."[160] Again, the creation of the world is called "the opening of the world," despite its mythical origin. Different than de Pantoja's explanation, Zhou Zhi underlined the role of human beings who express their gratitude toward God on the seventh day. Then, Zhou Zhi even tried to argue that the seventh day had already been celebrated in ancient Chinese tradition: "Because of the Lord's day, the ancient calendar in China still spreads that whenever there is birth, marriage, funeral, illness, and brewing, there is the saying of coming and reviving each seven days (*qiri laifu* 七日來復)."[161] Zhou Zhi made a rather bold

---

156 Among the Twenty-Eight Mansions, in Four Symbols (*sixiang* 四象), Room belongs to Azure Dragon 青龍 (East 東), Emptiness belongs to Murky Warrior 玄武 (North 北), Hair head belongs to white Tiger 白虎 (West 西), Star belongs to Vermillion Bird 朱雀 (South 南). Jean-Claude Martzloff, étoile et constellations, *Le Grand Ricci*, "Dossiers et Index," 351–352.
157 "天主開世之首日，是世之第一主日也。" Manuel Dias 陽瑪諾, *Shengjing zhijie* 聖經直解, *juan* 1, fol. 2a3, in CCT BAV (1), vol. 17, 457.
158 "又凡遇曆上房虛星昴之日，即是主日。" Buglio, *Misa jingdian*, fol. 4b4, 14.
159 "按今中曆，凡遇房虛昴星即是主日。" Zhou, "Mengyin lüeshuo 蒙引畧說," *Tianxue mengyin*, fol. 1b, 360.
160 "第七日，係人感謝主恩之日。故于每七日為一瞻禮，自開闢至今，永無能改。" Zhou, "Mengyin lüeshuo," fol. 1b, 360.
161 Zhou, "Mengyin lüeshuo," fol. 1b–fol. 2a, 360–361. "反復其道，七日來複。" Wang Bi 王弼, annot., *Zhouyi* 周易, *juan* 3, Eruson, 23.

argument that the ancient Chinese calendar had been the result of Catholic ritual time. The connection of Catholic ritual time with the traditional "Room (*fang* 房), Emptiness (*xu* 虛), Hair (*mao* 昴), and Star (*xing* 星)" became a major target in the anti-Catholic discourse.

Wang Zheng developed another explanation for the seventh day.

> Everyone worships daily, and every seventh day is designated as the public worship. On this day all people stop working and go to the hall of the Lord of Heaven to worship and to listen to the Master of the Teaching explaining scriptures and classics, exhorting good and quitting evil.[162]

The word "public" (*gonggong* 公共) is noteworthy because the public day of worship (*gonggong zhanli* 公共瞻禮) echoes to Aleni's distinction between the private sphere and the public sphere discussed in section 1.1. Moreover, according to the Catholic teaching in Europe, to celebrate the sacraments is a public cult (*cultus publicus*) and to pray on one's own is a private cult (*cultus privatus*).[163] Wang Zheng depicted the typical Catholic practice in the place of worship: Catholics go to church on the Lord's day to attend Mass and other activities as an assembly. As people enter the ritual space, they feel living in the ritual time more intensively and are confronted with specific acts and symbols.[164] In order to introduce Catholic ritual time into Chinese society, missionaries gave new usages to old words and coined new terms. They and Chinese Catholics introduced the rhythm of seven days with a strong liturgical connotation. Nevertheless, probably in every new mission, it is difficult to teach the converts the concept of the Lord's day and to persuade them to celebrate it.[165] The Jesuits made the Catholic liturgical calendar to help Chinese Catholics to adapt to the new type of ritual time.

2.2　　*List of Worship*

Missionaries propagated the Catholic liturgical calendar in the form of the list of worship (*zhanlidan* 瞻禮單), which was convenient to distribute and to keep. *Le Grand Ricci* marks this word as a Catholic term, meaning "liturgical calendar; ordo."[166] Since the early mission in China, the Jesuits began

---

162　"人々日瞻禮，每七日，定為公共瞻禮。此日四民悉罷業，上下俱歸天主殿堂瞻禮，聽掌教士講鮮經典，勸善戒惡。" Wang, *Renhui yue*, fol. 40b7–9, 608.
163　*Christian Theological Lexicon*, 241.
164　Jochim, *Chinese Religions*, 3.
165　Bürkler, *Die Sonn-und Festtagsfeier*, 61.
166　*Le Grand Ricci* I, 275, 138.

producing and distributing the list of worship. Ricci made a liturgical calendar in accordance with traditional Chinese calendar to inform the Chinese Catholics in Zhaoqing to assemble on Sundays and feast days.[167] Ricci told the noblemen the European Catholics' assembly as an example of the good customs in his homeland. He explained how all Catholics, regardless of their profession, dedicate many festive days of a year solely to God and to the salvation of the soul, by chanting psalms, attending Mass, and listening to a homily.[168] Reprinted year after year, the Catholic liturgical calendar in Chinese lists the Sundays and feast days on which Chinese Catholics should assemble.

Trigault published *Calculating Method of Day of Worship in Calendar Year* (*Tuiding linian zhanlirifa* 推定曆年瞻禮日法, 1636). Rougemont recorded the production of a new list of worship in December 1675 and in January 1676.[169] Couplet published *Eternal List of Worship of the Holy Teaching of the Lord of Heaven* (*Tianzhu shengjiao yongzhanlidan* 天主聖教永瞻禮單, ca. 1680) and its later edition was published in 1712. *The Classics of the Mass* contains four tables: the table of unmovable days of worship in the whole year (*zhounian buyidong zhanlibiao* 周年不移動瞻禮表); the table of movable days of worship in the whole year (*zhounian yidong zhanlibiao* 周年移動瞻禮表); the table of calculating the day of worship in the calendar year (*linian tuizhanlifa* 歷年推瞻禮法); the table of all ranks of days of worship in the same year (*tongnian gedeng zhanliri* 同年各等瞻禮日).[170] The Table of Dates for Worship and Fasting of the Holy Teaching of the Lord of Heaven (*tianzhu shengjiao zhanli zhaiqibiao* 天主聖教瞻禮齋期表) was published in three consecutive years: 1695 (Kangxi 34),[171] 1696 (Kangxi 35),[172] and 1697 (Kangxi 36).[173] In these lists of worship, the Jesuits tried to intertwine the Catholic liturgical calendar with the traditional Chinese

---

167   Bernard, *Le père Matthieu Ricci*, première partie, 142.
168   Bürkler, *Die Sonn-und Festtagsfeier*, 9.
169   Golvers, *François de Rougemont*, 383.
170   Buglio, "*zhounian buyidong zhanlibiao* 周年不移動瞻禮表," *Misa jingdian*, fol. 4b–fol. 6b, 14–18. Buglio, "*zhounian yidong zhanlibiao* 周年移動瞻禮表," *Misa jingdian*, fol. 7a–fol. 11a, 19–27. Buglio, "*linian tuizhanlifa* 歷年推瞻禮法," *Misa jingdian*, fol. 11b, 28. Buglio, "*tongnian gedeng zhanliri* 同年各等瞻禮日," *Misa jingdian*, fol. 12a–fol. 21b, 29–48.
171   *Kangxi sanshisi nian tianzhu shengjiao zhanli zhaiqibiao* 康熙三十四年天主聖教瞻禮齋期表, in CCT BAV (1), vol. 37, 621–626.
172   *Kangxi sanshiwu nian tianzhu shengjiao zhanli zhaiqibiao* 康熙三十五年天主聖教瞻禮齋期表, in CCT BAV (1), vol. 37, 629–634.
173   *Kangxi sanshiliu nian tianzhu shengjiao zhanli zhaiqibiao* 康熙三十六年天主聖教瞻禮齋期表, in CCT BAV (1), vol. 37, 637–642.

one. Whereas in *Direct Explanation of Sacred Scripture*, Dias listed Sundays in A Year (*zhousui zhuri* 周歲主日) and Days of Worship in A Year (*zhousui zhanli* 周歲瞻禮) not as a calendar but as a book rich in detailed index and annotations.[174]

The rhythm of traditional Chinese ritual time had been composed in ancient China. The royal ritual and consequently all the official rituals followed a double rhythm: the rhythm of the peasant life; and the regular rhythm of the year with its four astronomic seasons.[175] The liturgical year began in the spring, with the sacrifice to the High Lord as the first ceremony in the Round Mound (*Yuanqiu* 圜丘) at the southern suburb (*nanjiao* 南郊). It was the first religious act in a new year, and only the king had enough virtue to accomplish such a solemn and dangerous act.[176] The rhythm of traditional Chinese ritual time was so overwhelming that the foreign rituals had to make adaptations. For instance, the Ghost Festival was celebrated on various days in India yet its date was unified when introduced in China.[177] Similarly, Catholic ritual time gradually shaped the rhythm of European ritual time, however, when confronted with the rhythm of traditional Chinese ritual time, it had to go through adaptations. Missionaries tried to intertwine the two liturgical time in the form of the list of worship, thus making a synthesis of time.

Some Chinese Catholics not only learned to read the list of worship but also tried to produce it. On 26 August 1696 (Kangxi 35.7.29), Zhao Lun brought a draft of the list of worship for next year which had been newly made by himself to Wu Li's residence. Wu Li told Zhao Lun: "It is not proper to print the list of worship for next year now, because the liturgical calendar produced by the Ministry of Rites has not been published yet." As Zhao Lun later pointed out, Wu Li did not want some foolish people to misuse the list of worship.[178] Since human life finds rhythm in liturgical time and the time of the agricultural work,[179] the time of the agricultural work depended intimately on the natural rhythm both in Europe and in China. Yet, liturgical time was controlled by the Catholic Church in Europe and by the state in China. The Catholic liturgical calendar had to refer to traditional Chinese liturgical calendar. Otherwise, it would be difficult for Chinese Catholics to follow the European liturgical calendar.

---

174 Dias, *Shengjing zhijie*, *mulu*, fol. 1a1, 307; fol. 5a1, 315.
175 Maspero, *La Chine antique*, 186.
176 Maspero, *La Chine antique*, 187.
177 Teiser, *The Ghost Festival*, 34.
178 "'明年《瞻禮單》未便付梓，緣時憲歷未頒也。'先生之意，蓋戒愚賤之流，不可自用自專耳。" Zhao, *Xu Kouduo*, 585.
179 Le Goff, *La naissance du Purgatoire*, 389.

Moreover, anti-Catholics considered the calendar made by missionaries illicit. In the ninth refutation of *Help to the Refutation of the Heresy* (*Zuopi* 佐闢, ca. 1623), Xu Dashou harshly said: "The astronomy discussed by them is the most absurd!"[180] In the tenth refutation, he accused missionaries and Chinese Catholics of following the secret calendar (*cong sili* 從私曆).[181] Yet, the missionaries' mastery of astronomy not only served for the making of the list of worship but also earned them high positions at the Imperial Astronomical Bureau. Ricci used the introduction of science as a strategy for evangelization, which was inherited mostly by the Jesuits. The missionaries' efforts on astronomy and calendar-making were outstanding. Issued in the name of the emperor, the calendar in Imperial China symbolized great political importance.[182] In order to gain the emperor's protection, the Jesuits planned to reform the traditional Chinese calendar.[183] In 1629 (Chongzhen 2), the Chongzhen emperor could not put up with the mistakes made by the Imperial Astronomical Bureau anymore. The Catholic literatus in the Ministry of Rites Xu Guangqi introduced the German Jesuit Terrentius to the emperor. With the Chongzhen emperor's approval, the Jesuits began their service in the Imperial Astronomical Bureau. After Terrentius' death, Schall and Rho became his successors.[184] A new Calendar Office (*Liju* 曆局) was established and supervised by Xu Guangqi. Edited by Xu Guangqi and Schall, the *Chongzhen Calendar Compendium* (*Chongzhen lishu* 崇禎曆書, 1631–1635) contributed to the restoration of social order.[185] By means of astronomy, the Jesuits entered the court yet faced cultural and political tensions.[186]

The missionaries serving at the Imperial Astronomical Bureau aroused fierce opposition. In the calendar case from 1664 to 1669, the Jesuits suffered in prison and their eight Chinese colleagues were killed. In 1669, the Jesuits were restored to their management of the imperial calendar replacing Muslim astronomers.[187] Despite the Manchu official's support recorded by Mag-

---

180 "況彼所言之天文，又最荒唐悠謬乎！" Xu, "Jiupi yiji buzu shang, yihuo buzu tan, yizhan buzu xin 九闢夷技不足尚、夷貨不足貪、夷占不足信," *Shengchao zuopi*, 154.
181 Xu, "Shipi xing sili, rang ruiying, mou bugui, wei qiangu weiwen zhi dani 十闢行私曆、攘瑞應、謀不軌、為千古未聞之大逆," *Shengchao zuopi*, 158.
182 Catherine Jami, "General reception," *Handbook of Christianity*, 695.
183 Schall, *Relation historique*, 7.
184 Schall, *Relation historique*, 9–15.
185 Jami, "General reception," 696.
186 Nicole Halsberghe and Keizô Hashimoto, "astronomy," *Handbook of Christianity*, 711.
187 Cullen and Jami, "Christmas 1668 and After," 5–6.

alhães,[188] some Confucianists kept a hostile attitude toward the European astronomers. The famous scholar Gu Yanwu 顧炎武 (1613–1682) disapproved the missionaries' service at the Imperial Astronomical Bureau, although he acknowledged their mastery of astronomy.[189] In 1686, Gu Yanwu's disciple Pan Lei 潘耒 (1646–1708) denounced the westerner's meddling in the Chinese calendar.[190] Fully aware of the ritual perspective of traditional Chinese calendar, anti-Catholics seemed to hardly notice the ritual perspective of the Catholic liturgical calendar.

The liturgical calendar was so crucial for Catholic ritual life that an indigenous priest encouraged Chinese Catholics to make the list of worship. On 9 June 1697 (Kangxi 36.4.21), Zhu Yuanrong 朱園榮 criticized Zhao Lun in Wu Li's residence: "That you made the list of worship without order is close to being arrogant." Yet, Wu Li replied right away: "What kind of sin is it to make the list of worship? To edit and to publish [the list of worship] so it is convenient for people to worship and to fast. This is merit, not sin."[191] On the following day (10 June 1697), Wu Li encouraged Zhao Lun again.

> It is necessary for you to make the list of worship. Why did the emperor of the Teaching (*jiaohuang* 教皇, the pope) order me to be a priest? It is for fear that people from the Great West in China might sacrifice their life one day, then no one would propagate the Teaching in China and the list of worship would be nowhere to be seen. This is why. Be courageous.[192]

As the first indigenous priest, Wu Li was well aware that the evangelization shall not depend on Western missionaries alone, furthermore, it shall not depend on the clergy alone. Therefore, he wanted to preserve Zhao Lun's fervor to make the list of worship. Wu Li was insightful to realize the necessity of cultivating Chinese Catholics' ritual knowledge.

The list of worship was not only the most remarkable demonstration of the synthesis of time but also a symbol of faith, an object that contained the

---

188 Cullen and Jami, "Christmas 1668 and After," 28.
189 Liu, *Yitian liyi*, 63–64.
190 Liu, *Yitian liyi*, 65–66.
191 "園榮曰：'子擅作《瞻禮單》，近於驕傲。'先生曰：'作《瞻禮單》何罪？校正刊佈，以便人瞻禮守齋，功也，非罪也。'" Zhao, *Xu Kouduo*, 612.
192 "子所著《瞻禮單》在所必需。教皇命我為司鐸為何意乎？恐大西人在中國，或有致命之日，則中國行教無人，而《瞻禮單》亦無由而見。正此意也，子其勉之。" Zhao, *Xu Kouduo*, 613.

essence of Mass—to worship the Lord of Heaven as an assembly. Having read the list of worship, Shen Que considered the assembly on designated dates in churches suspicious.

> Every month besides the first day and the fifth day, the four days of Room, Emptiness, Hair, and Star are also the assembly dates. Every reunion has fifty persons at least and two hundred at most. One can look up the assembly dates which are engraved in *Tianzhu jiaojie yaolüe* 天主教解要略.[193]

"*Tianzhu jiaojie yaolüe* 天主教解要略" might be a mis-spelling of *Brief Explanation of Catechism* (*Jiaoyao jielüe* 教要解畧). In *Brief Introduction to the Holy Teaching of the Lord of Heaven* (*Tianzhu shengjiao xiaoyin* 天主聖教小引, ca. 1630), the Chinese Catholic in Hangzhou Timothy Fan Zhong 范中 depicted how Chinese Catholics used the list: "[They] ask for the list of the day of worship every year and go to the hall to attend Mass according to the date. If there is no hall, one can also do some work to pay respect by oneself."[194] One characteristic custom of the Christian community at Mopan Mountain is that the majority of the Catholic families keep the list of worship.[195] Kept at home, the list of worship is the symbol of faith, a constant reminder of the worship as an assembly, and a material extension of the ecclesiastical sphere into the familial sphere.

In the seventeenth century, the list of worship had a rather wide circulation in Jiangsu and Zhejiang. Moreover, some non-Catholics used the list of worship as well, with two major intentions: to gain commercial profit by ferrying Chinese Catholics on the date for the assembly; to use it as a talisman. Some non-Catholic Chinese used the list of worship as one kind of door gods (*menshen* 門神), which they attached to the front door of their houses in order to avoid evil spirits. For them the list of worship was but one among various religious objects kept at home. In this regard, this Catholic ritual object was absorbed into traditional Chinese polytheist practices.[196] In the letter of 1718 to the Jesuit Visitor Kilian Stumpf (Ji Li'an 紀理安, SJ, 1655–1720), Fernandez-Oliver told that some members of secret societies wanted to gain protection

---

193 "每月自朔望外，又有房虛星昴四日為會期。每會少則五十人，多則二百人。此其自刻《天主教解要略》中，明開會期，可查也。" Shen, *Zaican yuanyi*, fol. 12a1–4, 223.
194 "每年求得瞻禮日單，依日期詣堂與彌撒，若或無堂，亦依日期自己行工致敬可也。" Fan Zhong 范中, *Tianzhu shengjiao xiaoyin* 天主聖教小引, fol. 9a9–b1, in CCT BnF, vol. 7, 21–22.
195 Kang, *Shangzhu*, 259.
196 Golvers, *François de Rougemont*, 384.

from Christianity. They put the list of worship, rosary beads, and crosses on the doors of their houses to show the Catholic identity, but they often hung the symbols incorrectly.[197] These members of secret societies noticed that the list of worship was a symbol of Christian faith yet they did not know its ritual usage. Chinese Catholics usually kept the list of worship inside the house. In 1747 when the Qing court prohibited the Teaching of the Lord of Heaven, the Christian communities in Beijing secretly made and propagated the list of worship to remote areas.[198] For centuries, the list of worship has been popular among Chinese Catholics. According to its clear instruction about feast days, Chinese Catholics can go to church to attend Mass on designated dates.[199] Since the early mission, missionaries required Chinese Catholics to observe the day of worship.

2.3   To Observe the Day of Worship

The Jesuits taught Chinese Catholics that to observe the day of worship (*shou zhanli* 守瞻禮) was a basic obligation. In the early catechism book *Veritable Record of the Lord of Heaven* (*Tianzhu shilu* 天主實錄, 1584), a primitive Chinese version of the Ten Commandments articulated: "Thirdly, on the day of worship (*libai zhi ri* 禮拜之日), it is forbidden to work; you shall visit the temple and recite prayers to worship the Lord of Heaven."[200] In *Brief Introduction of the Holy Teaching* (*Shengjiao yueyan* 聖教約言, ca. 1606), João Soeiro (Su Ruwang 蘇如望, SJ, 1566–1607) kept the same version of the third commandment. Then, he explained the reason to assemble on the Lord's day in the hall to attend Mass.

> Thirdly, observe the day of worship. In the beginning, the Lord of Heaven began the merits of opening the sky and the earth, of growing all things to nurture us human beings, and of creating all kinds of things in six days. Therefore, people who follow the Holy Teaching of the Lord of Heaven in various countries all assemble in the holy palace of the Lord of Heaven

---

197   Mungello, *Spirit and the Flesh*, 115.
198   Kang Zhijie 康志傑, "Zhanlidan shulun: jianshuo xili de dongchuan 瞻禮單述論：兼說西曆的東傳," *Beijing xingzheng xueyuan xuebao* 北京行政學院學報 3 (2014): 123.
199   For a study of the list of worship in the twenty-first century China, see Wu Fei 吳飛, *Maimang shangde shengyan: yige xiangcun tianzhujiao qunti de xinyang he shenghuo* 麥芒上的聖言：一個鄉村天主教群體的信仰和生活 (Beijing: Zongjiao wenhua chubanshe 宗教文化出版社, 2013), 66–77. In the field research of Wu Fei, local Catholics in Duanzhuang 段莊 consider the list of worship a regular calendar.
200   "三，當禮拜之日，禁止工夫，謁寺誦經，禮拜天主。" Ruggieri, *Tianzhu shilu*, 82. See also "第三誡者，當禮拜之日，禁止工夫，謁寺誦經，禮拜天主。" Ruggieri, *Tianzhu shilu*, fol. 35a6–7, 71.

every seven days each year, to worship and to thank for the grace, to watch the sacrificial ritual (*guan jisi liyi* 觀祭祀禮儀), and to listen to the discussion about doctrines and the explanation of scriptures.[201]

The discussion about doctrines and the explanation of scriptures refer to the homily which usually includes exegesis. The description which traced back to Genesis, the intention to worship and to express gratitude, and the practices of attending Mass resemble the explanations of the seventh day in section 2.1. Soeiro underlined the first three commandments as the most necessary (*zhiyao* 至要).[202]

The later versions of the Ten Commandments in late Ming and early Qing used "*zhanli* 瞻禮" more frequently than "*libai* 禮拜," such as *Brief Explanation of Catechism*, *Four Rules of the Holy Teaching*, *Statutes of the Confraternity of the Angels*, and *One Hundred Questions and Answers of the Lord of Heaven's Holy Teaching*.[203] In *Brief Explanation of Catechism*, Vagnone inherited Soeiro's explanation, saying that the third commandment "teaches human beings to worship the Lord of Heaven by the exterior ritual (*waili* 外禮)." After the creation of the world, the Lord of Heaven made the covenant with the ancient saint that "every seventh day is the date of worship, his people are obliged to observe it."[204] The following note in smaller characters explains that the seventh day is Room (*fang* 房), Emptiness (*xu* 虛), Hair (*mao* 昴), and Star (*xing* 星) in the *Official Calendar in the Ming Dynasty* (*Datong li* 大統曆) used since 1384 (Hongwu 17). On the seventh day, people shall enter the palace to watch the sacrificial ritual (*guan jisi* 觀祭祀), to worship, and to thank the Lord's grace.[205]

---

201 "三、守禮拜之日。天主始開闢天地，化生萬物以養吾人，六日之內，造化萬品之功。故從天主聖教列國之人，一年每七之一日，皆聚於天主聖殿，禮拜謝恩，觀祭祀禮儀，并聞談道觧經。" Soeiro, *Shengjiao yueyan*, fol. 9a2–6, 271.

202 "此三誡者俱為至要者矣。" Soeiro, *Shengjiao yueyan*, fol. 9a6, 271. For the first two commandments, see "一、欽崇一天主萬物之上。 …… 二、毋呼天主名而設發虛誓。" Soeiro, *Shengjiao yueyan*, fol. 6a6–fol. 8b2, 265–270.

203 "問：何謂天主十誡？答： …… 三、守瞻禮之日。" Couplet, *Baiwenda*, fol. 3a, 225. "三、守瞻禮之日，" Brancati, *Tianshen huike*, fol. 46a4, 95. "問：'請講第三誡、守瞻禮之日。'答：'第三誡，命人以肉身之禮恭敬天主，凡遇瞻禮日，當與彌撒。'" Brancati, *Tianshen huike*, fol. 49a3–5, 101. "三、守瞻禮之日。" Raux, *Shengshi wenda*, fol. 3b1, 396.

204 "第三誡、守瞻禮之日。此誡，教人以外禮奉事天主也。天主制作天地人物凡六日。迨七日則諸事輟矣。故天主與古聖人約令以每七日為瞻禮之期，命其民守焉。" Vagnone, *Jiaoyao jieliie, shang juan*, fol. 16b5–fol. 17a2, 156–157.

205 "第七日，大統曆遇房星昴虛使得入殿觀祭祀，瞻望羅拜，稱謝主恩焉。" Vagnone, *Jiaoyao jieliie, shang juan*, fol. 17a3–4, 157.

In addition to the Ten Commandments, missionaries taught the four rules of the Holy Teaching to Chinese Catholics as a step into the Teaching (*jinjiao zhi jie* 進教之堦) and a road ascending to Heaven (*dengtian zhi lu* 登天之路).[206] *Four Rules of the Holy Teaching* especially underlines observing the day of worship as the very first rule, which originates from the third commandment. Brancati's explanation of the first rule also originates from that of the third commandment. Brancati pointed out that the intention of Mass is to repay (*baoben* 報本) the great grace of the Lord of Heaven who creates the world for human beings. In addition, it is the observation of the day of worship which distinguishes people of the Holy Teaching (*shengjiao zhi ren* 聖教之人) from those who are not.[207] Observing the day of worship expresses one's virtue of loving the Lord of Heaven by the material rituals (*youxing zhi liyi* 有形之禮儀). On the day of worship, Catholics cease their work and offer the Lord of Heaven the material holy merit (*youxing zhi shenggong* 有形之聖功), such as kowtow, prayer, and sacrificial rite. Brancati emphasized the importance of the material (*youxing* 有形) religious practice to Chinese Catholics.

> Today, because there are too many rules of the material rituals, the holy emperor of the Teaching (*sheng jiaohuang* 聖教皇, the pope) only issues one rule, that is, on the day of worship, people of the Teaching must go to the hall and attend Mass respectfully.[208]

To attend Mass on designated days of worship is Chinese Catholics' obligation and a remarkable symbol of their identity. The celebration of Mass is a two-

---

206 "故聖教皇于天主十誡之外，爰定四規：一、守瞻禮；一、守齋期；一、解罪過；一、領聖體。此四規者，與教中人作進教之堦，開登天之路。" Brancati, *Shengjiao sigui*, 262–263. "聖教定規，其要有四。一、凡主日暨諸瞻禮日，宜與彌撒。二、遵守聖教所定齋期。三、解罪至少者，每年一次。四、領聖體至少者，每年一次，宜于復活瞻禮前後、瞻禮日與彌撒。" Brancati, *Shengjiao sigui*, 267. See also "聖教會規有四：一、凡主日暨諸瞻禮之日宜與彌撒；二、遵守聖教所定齋期；三、解罪至少每年一次；四、領聖體至少每年一次。" Brancati, *Tianshen huike*, fol. 61a2–6, 125. See also "聖教定規有四，一、凡主日，暨諸瞻禮日，宜與彌撒；二、遵守聖教，所定齋期；三、解罪至少，每年一次；四、領聖體至少，每年一次，即於復活，瞻禮前後。" Anon., *Tianzhu jiaoyao*, fol. 13a1–b4, 333–334.
207 "此天主十誡中第三誡，命守瞻禮之日，要世人常記始初，天主專為吾人，生天地萬物，感其大恩，因瞻禮而報本也。亦以此分別聖教之人，與不在聖教之人焉。" Brancati, *Shengjiao sigui*, 267–268.
208 "今因有形之禮，其規甚多，聖教皇止定一規，惟于瞻禮之日，教中人必宜赴堂，敬與彌撒。" Brancati, *Shengjiao sigui*, 267–269.

PLACE OF WORSHIP 243

way street: it is the visible way for the Lord of Heaven to convey grace to human beings; and it is also the material way for human beings to repay holy merits to the Lord of Heaven.

Meanwhile, to not observe the day of worship is a major sin. Nevertheless, the sin of not attending Mass can be exempted for good reasons.[209] Brancati summarized five categories of exemptions and listed various specific situations in each category. The first four categories aim to protect the soul, the body, the reputation, and the materials. The fifth is for those who cannot go to church due to legitimate reasons, such as illness, captivity, and long distance.[210] Then, Brancati urged Chinese Catholics to observe the day of worship as far as possible: "Although there are many exemptions for those who cannot attend Mass, people in the Holy Teaching must spare no effort to go to worship respectfully and to attend Mass solemnly, thus being bestowed countless graces by the Lord of Heaven."[211] In the mission to Japan, the Jesuits only asked Japanese Catholics to attend Mass on Sundays and certain principle feasts. Because they were aware that Japanese Catholics, by following the Catholic liturgical calendar strictly, might be cut out of local communities.[212] Similarly, the early Jesuits encouraged Chinese Catholics to observe the day of worship but did not force them. On the one hand, to attend Mass costs the poor most, if not all, of their daily wages. On the other hand, the Catholic Church in China had always faced the lack of priests, therefore a lack of adequate pastoral care. The Jesuits left to the individual Chinese Catholics' discretion to decide whether to attend Mass at Christmas or Easter, to abstain from meat on Good Friday, and to confess on Easter.[213]

On September 8, 1609 (Wanli 37.8.11), Ricci established the first confraternity in China, that is, the Confraternity of the Lord of Heaven's Mother (*tianzhu zhi mu shanhui* 天主之母善會).[214] It was the feast of the Nativity of the

---

209 "若居恒無故，而不與彌撒，則是日雖行別大聖功，必不作為守瞻禮之規，而大得罪于天主。倘有眞實緣絲，而不與彌撒，庶可無罪也。" Brancati, *Shengjiao sigui*, 269. See also "問：瞻禮之日，不與彌撒，有大罪否？答：若懈怠于善，無故而不與彌撒，有大罪。非懈怠而有故，雖于瞻禮之日不與彌撒，可無罪也。" Brancati, *Tianshen huike*, fol. 49a7–9, 101.
210 Brancati, *Shengjiao sigui*, 269–273. See also Brancati, *Tianshen huike*, fol. 49b6–8, 102.
211 "夫不與彌撒而無罪，雖有多端，然聖教之人，必當殫力竭心，敬赴瞻禮，恭與彌撒，而蒙天主賜無數之恩惠。" Brancati, *Shengjiao sigui*, 273.
212 Hélène Vu Thanh, *Devenir japonais: La mission jésuite au Japon (1549–1614)* (Paris: Presses de l'université Paris-Sorbonne, 2016), 238.
213 Bürkler, *Die Sonn-und Festtagsfeier*, 10–12.
214 D. de Gassart, "Esquisse historique sur les congrégations de la Sainte Vierge dans l'ancienne mission de Chine (1609–1664)," *Collectanea commissionis synodalis in Sinis* 8 (Peking: Commissio synodalis in Sinis, 1935): 35.

Blessed Virgin Mary. The chosen date shows the Catholic penchant to begin an important event on certain feast days according to the Catholic ritual calendar. The first member was a mandarin called Lucas Li whose full name is still unknown. Lucas Li wrote down statutes for the Confraternity of the Lord of Heaven's Mother, then Ricci revised the statutes and added some chosen from the statutes of *Prima Primaria*.[215] The principal European element added by Ricci is the insistence that the members shall receive the sacraments regularly. The obligation to receive communion frequently aims at the member's spiritual improvement.[216] Statutes of confraternities express an ideal ritual life of the Christian communities in late Ming and early Qing, however, the actual frequency of the celebration of Mass varied from community to community. In some Christian communities where the itinerant missionary visited only a few times annually, the frequency of the celebration of Mass was very low. On the other hand, for Christian communities in larger cities where the missionary lived, pious Catholics fulfilled the obligation to attend Mass on the Lord's day and other designated dates.

The Mass in late Ming and early Qing is like an obscured light. Although the non-Catholic Chinese could not see the light directly, they saw objects lit by it, such as the hall of the Lord of Heaven, the list of worship, and the assembly in the hall on designated dates. Christianization of space and time was embodied concretely by materials such as the hall of the Lord of Heaven and the list of worship. On the one hand, these materials helped Chinese Catholics to establish and to strengthen their new identity as followers of the Teaching of the Lord of Heaven. On the other hand, the remarkable materials incited suspicion from anti-Catholics, so the early Jesuits were very cautious. The annual letter in 1610 reported how the festivals in Nanjing were abolished. Yet, the Provincial for Japan Valentino Carvalho (SJ, 1559–1630) was against too much caution. With the apostolic frankness ordered by Carvalho, the Christian community in Nanjing began assembling freely and celebrating Mass, however, the persecution broke out in 1616 and spread throughout the country the following year.[217] The official documents in the Nanjing persecution recorded the regular assembly of Chinese Catholics on the Lord's day.

---

215 Paul Bornet, SJ, "L'apostolat laïque en Chine aux XVIIe et XVIIIe siècles," *Bulletin catholique de Pékin* 35 (Pékin: Imprimerie des Lazaristes du Pei-t'ang, 1948): 50. In 25 March 1563, the first Sodality of Our Lady *Prima Primaria* was begun in the Roman College by the Belgian Jesuit John Leunis. Before his entrance into the Society of Jesus, Ricci joined *Prima Primaria*. Gassart, "Esquisse historique," 34; Bornet, "L'apostolat laïque," 50.
216 Brockey, *Journey to the East*, 372.
217 Bürkler, *Die Sonn-und Festtagsfeier*, 13.

In October 1616 (Wanli 44.10), eight Chinese Catholics were arrested and interrogated in Nanjing.[218] In the Case of Joint Hearing of Zhong Mingli and Other Prisoners (*Huishen Zhong Mingli dengfan yi'an* 會審鍾明禮等犯一案), written by the official of the Ministry of Rites Wu Ercheng 吳爾成, three of the eight arrested Chinese Catholics confessed that they worshiped as an assembly every seven days. Zhang Cai 張寀 (twenty-six-year-old, Shanxi) said: "Since then, we worship every seven days, recite the Lord of Heaven's Prayer 'Our Father in Heaven …' as a group, and dismiss when the sun is about to rise. We are accustomed to such practice."[219] Similarly, Yu Chengyuan 余成元 (twenty-nine-year-old, Nanjing) described: "Since then, we worship every seven days. We arrive before the daybreak and dismiss before the sunrise. Sometimes there are thirty or forty people, sometimes fifty or sixty."[220] Fang Zheng 方政 (thirty-two-year-old, Huizhou 徽州) confessed: "The group assembles together every seven days, non-stop in all seasons."[221] The phrase "since then" (*zihou* 自後) means since they received baptism. Their confession recorded in the official documents testified that Chinese Catholics in Nanjing observed the rhythm of seven days.

Because of the Nanjing persecution, the Christian communities became doubly cautious. In Nanjing local Catholics assembled in small groups on fixed days; in Shanghai only five Chinese Catholics met missionaries on certain days for confession, Mass, and spiritual discussion; in Beijing local Catholics assembled in different houses every month and five or six times a year with more solemnity in the hall.[222] Although the Chinese Catholics' assembly became low-profile in the following decades, the Buddhist anti-Catholic campaign still noticed the rhythm of seven days. On 8 August 1634 (Chongzhen 7.8.15), the monk Shi Purun criticized a number of the Chinese Catholics' activities, including the ritual of seven days (*qiri zhi li* 七日之禮).

> Therefore, whoever follow their Teaching cut out sacrifice to ancestors and only offer flattering sacrifice to the Lord of Heaven; they burn the holy

---

218 "南京禮部主客清吏司為緝獲人犯事,據東城兵馬司呈解犯人鍾明禮、張寀、余成元、方政、湯洪、夏玉、周用、吳南等八名,到部。" Wu, *Huishen Zhong Mingli*, fol. 5a2–4, 237.
219 "自後七日一瞻拜,群誦天主經,'在天我等父者' 云云。日將出,乃散,習以為嘗。" Wu, *Huishen Zhong Mingli*, fol. 7a8–9, 238.
220 "自後七日一聚會,天未明而至,日未出而散,每次或三四十人,或五六十人不等。" Wu, *Huishen Zhong Mingli*, fol. 8a5–7, 238.
221 "其眾俱同七日一會,歲時不絕。" Wu, *Huishen Zhong Mingli*, fol. 8b6–7, 239.
222 Bürkler, *Die Sonn-und Festtagsfeier*, 13–14.

statues and only worship the torture instrument the cross; they abolish the three-year mourning for parents and practice the rebel leader's ritual of seven days.[223]

In *Sketch of Landscape in Capital Beijing*, Liu Tong and Yu Yizheng gave a short yet specific description of the Catholic ritual life: "To offer sacrifice to *Deus* (*Tusi* 徒斯) every seventh day and it is called Mass (*misa* 米撒). The sacrifice on days such as the day of the Nativity of Jesus and the day of the Ascension of Jesus is called High Mass (*damisa* 大米撒)."[224] Tan Qian gave a highly similar description in *Record of Visiting Beijing*: "To offer sacrifice to *Deus* (*Tusi* 徒斯) every seventh day and it is called Mass (*misa* 米撒). On days such as the day of his nativity and the day of his ascension [the sacrifice] is called High Mass (*damisa* 大米撒)."[225] "*Tusi* 陡斯" (*Deus*) and "*misa* 米撒" (*missa*) are transliterations from the Latin or Portuguese in the early stage of the mission. Rarely used in late Ming and early Qing, "*misa* 米撒" is an exceptional variant of "*misa* 彌撒." Vagnone used this term when talking about a Catholic priest's power: "[A priest] performs the ritual of the grand sacrifice, which is called Mass (*misa* 米撒)."[226] The three Chinese historians not only noticed the rhythm of seven days but also knew that Chinese Catholics assembled for the celebration of Mass. Moreover, they knew that the Mass celebrated on certain important feast days were called High Mass.

Seeking the conversion of the whole country, the Jesuits respected Chinese customs and traditions as far as possible and treated the new mission mildly.[227] The mendicants, however, sought more individual conversions and strengthened their new converts by strict training. Early in 1636, Caballero explained to Chinese Catholics when they were obliged to attend Mass and when they should abstain from meat. Nevertheless, the mendicants did not require Chinese Catholics to celebrate as many feasts as in Europe.[228] Morales asked Propaganda Fide whether Chinese Catholics were obliged to observe the positive

---

223 "故凡入其教者斬祖宗之祀，唯謟祭一天主；火神聖之像，但供十字刑枷；廢父母三年之喪，行渠魁七日之禮，" Purun, *Zhuzuo ji*, fol. 21b3–6, 352.
224 "祭徒斯以七日，曰米撒，於耶穌降生升天等日，曰大米撒。" Liu and Yu, *Dijing jingwu lüe*, juan 4, 153.
225 "祭陡斯以七日，曰米撒。其降生升天等日，曰大米撒。" Tan, *Beiyou lu*, 46. For an English translation, see Chan, "Johann Adam Schall," 276.
226 "行大祭之禮，所謂米撒是也。" Vagnone, *Jiaoyao jielüe, shang juan*, fol. 58a3, 239.
227 In order to spread Catholicism over China, the Jesuits aimed at a great number of conversions rather than the conversion of individuals. Jennes, *Four centuries of catechetics*, 43.
228 Bürkler, *Die Sonn-und Festtagsfeier*, 21–22.

law regarding fasting, annual confession and communion, and observing the festivals. He received an affirmative response from the decree on 12 September, 1645.[229]

On behalf of the Jesuits in China, Martini explained in Rome that it is impossible for most Chinese Catholics to attend Mass on Sundays and feast days, to confess and to receive communion once a year. Firstly, the majority of Chinese Catholics were poor people who had to continue working to earn their living; secondly, Christian mandarins had to fulfil their official responsibility even on Sundays and feast days; thirdly, there were not enough priests to administer sacraments in this large empire. On 23 March, 1656, Propaganda Fide reaffirmed that Chinese Catholics should observe the church's precepts, at the same time, the faithful can be excused in certain cases.[230] With the missionaries' instructions and exhortation, Chinese Catholics attended Mass in churches according to the list of worship, indicating the foundation of Christendom in Chinese society.

3 Christendom in Chinese Society

3.1 Ritual of the Assembly

The ritual space and ritual time explored in the previous sections are constituted firstly as the place of worship to celebrate Mass, whose essence is to worship the Lord of Heaven as an assembly. The early catechism books written in late Ming had already underlined the notion of assembly. Ricci explained the seven sacraments in *Brief Record of Holy Prayers*,[231] and he transliterated the terms from Portuguese to Chinese, such as from *sacramentos* to "*sa-ge-la-meng-duo* 撒格辣孟多."[232] Table 6 presents the transliteration of the seven sacraments in *Brief Record of Holy Prayers* and the corresponding version in Portuguese, English, and Modern Chinese.

Ricci's transliteration is totally different from the version in Modern Chinese.[233] Six of the seven terms coined by Ricci do not make any sense in Chi-

---

229 Bürkler, *Die Sonn-und Festtagsfeier*, 24.
230 Bürkler, *Die Sonn-und Festtagsfeier*, 27–28.
231 Ricci, *Shengjing yuelu*, fol. 12a3–fol. 14a4, 111–115. See also Vagnone, *Jiaoyao jieliie, shang juan*, fol. 49a1–7, 221.
232 Dudink, "Sacramental Initiation," 191–193.
233 Todays, the Eucharist (*gan'en shengshi* 感恩聖事), penance and reconciliation (*chanhui yu hehao shengshi* 懺悔與和好聖事), and anointing of the sick (*bingren fuyou shengshi* 病人傅油聖事) are more commonly used than their variants in table 6.

TABLE 6   Transliteration of seven sacraments

Ricci's transliteration	Portuguese	English	Modern Chinese
ba-di-si-mo 拔弟斯摩	*baptismo*	baptism	*shengxi shengshi* 聖洗聖事
gong-fei-er-ma-cang 共斐兒瑪藏	*confirmaçam*	confirmation	*jianzhen shengshi* 堅振聖事
gong-meng-yang 共蒙仰	*comunhão*	communion	*shengti shengshi* 聖體聖事
bai-ni-deng-ji-ya 白尼登濟亞	*penitentia*	penitence	*gaojie shengshi* 告解聖事
e-si-de-le-ma-weng-cang 阨斯得肋麻翁藏	*extrema unçam*	extreme unction	*zhongfu* 終傅
a-er-deng 阿兒等	*ordem*	holy orders	*shengzhi shengshi* 聖秩聖事
ma-di-li-mo-niu 瑪地利摩紐	*matrimonio*	matrimony	*hunyin shengshi* 婚姻聖事

nese, whereas the one referring to communion is a combination of transliteration and literal translation. Firstly, the pronunciation of *"gong mengyang* 共蒙仰*"* resembles that of *comunhão*; secondly, the first character *"gong* 共*"* means together and the last two characters *"mengyang* 蒙仰*"* resemble the word *"yangmeng* 仰蒙*"* which means to respectfully receive the benefits; therefore, the whole term means co-receiving which conforms to the meaning of *communio*. *Brief Record of Holy Prayers* gives a brief explanation to each sacrament, and the explanation of *"gong mengyang* 共蒙仰*"* is below.

> The translation means to assemble with each other. When people in the Holy Teaching grow up, they shall often absolve sins to pacify the heart, then receive Jesus' holy body by the appearance of bread and wine, in order to benefit from the Lord of Heaven's enormous grace.[234]

---

234 "譯言相取也。聖教中人年既壯，則當時常解罪，使心志安定，乃因麵餅及酒像，領受耶穌聖體，以沾天主洪恩。" Ricci, *Shengjing yuelu*, fol. 12b7–fol. 13a2, 112–113. See also "三、聖體。原文曰：共蒙仰。聖教中人，年既壯，則當時常解罪，清潔靈冕，安定心志，于是領受以沾天主洪恩。" Anon., *Tianzhu jiaoyao*, fol. 17a6–b2, 341–342.

Ad Dudink translates *"xiangqu* 相取" as "to communicate mutually,"[235] yet the current section considers the character *"qu* 取" the variant of *"ju* 聚" (to assemble).

Based on *Brief Record of Holy Prayers*, the explanation in *Brief Explanation of Catechism* gives a note in three smaller characters behind the sub-title *"gong mengyang* 共蒙仰"—to receive the holy body (*ling shengti* 領聖體).[236] Then, Vagnone deepened the explanation by describing how Jesus instituted the Eucharist.

> This is the third sacrament, which takes care of our spirit and let it have communion with (*xiang tonghe* 相通和) Jesus and those who also enter the Teaching. Co-receiving (*gong mengyang* 共蒙仰) is the translation which means to assemble with each other (*xiangqu* 相取). On the day before the Crucifixion, the Lord of Heaven Jesus assembled (*ju* 聚) the holy apostles, wanting to abolish the ancient sacrificial ritual and to replace it with the new sacrificial ritual which is true. Therefore he took the bread and gave it to the holy apostles, saying: "Eat it, for this is my body." Then he poured the wine in the chalice and gave it to them, saying: "Drink it, for this is my blood. From now on, it is proper for you to use the two objects to perform the ritual in memory of me."[237]

Vagnone cited Jesus' words both from the Gospel accounts,[238] and from the words of the consecration in the Roman Missal.[239] Because before the description Vagnone mentioned the replacement of the ancient sacrificial ritual (*gu jili* 古祭禮, ancient Jewish sacrifice) by the new one (*xin jili* 新祭禮, Mass).

---

235   Dudink, "Sacramental Initiation," 192.
236   "三、共蒙仰領聖體，" Vagnone, *Jiaoyao jielüe, shang juan*, fol. 52b7, 228. See also "共蒙仰，領受耶穌聖體，" da Rocha, *Shengjiao qimeng*, fol. 13a8, 401.
237   "此第三撒格辣孟多，用以育存吾神，而於耶穌及同進教者，相通和也。共蒙仰，譯言相取也。天主耶穌，未受難前一日，聚聖宗徒，欲令革去古祭禮，而易真切之新祭禮，因以麵餅授聖徒曰：'爾等食此，吾體也。'又以爵注葡萄酒授之曰：'爾等飲此，吾血也。從此後，爾等宜當用此二物為禮，以記憶吾也。'" Vagnone, *Jiaoyao jielüe, shang juan*, fol. 53a1–5, 229.
238   Luke 22:19–20, "Then he took bread, and when he had given thanks, he broke it and gave it to them, saying, 'This is my body given for you; do this in remembrance of me.' He did the same with the cup after supper, and said, 'This cup is the new covenant in my blood poured out for you.'" See also Matthew 26:26–28, Mark 14:22–24.
239   "Hoc est enim corpus meum ... Hic est enim calix sanguinis mei: novi et aeterni testamenti: mysterium fidei: qui pro vobis et pro multis effundetur in remissionem peccatorum." "Ordinarium Missae," *Missale Romanum* (*1570*), 343–344, no. 1515–1519.

Afterward, he described the consecration and transubstantiation as the brief meaning of the new sacrificial ritual.

> The celebrant who wants to offer sacrifice to the Lord of Heaven firstly takes the bread, which contains the appearance, the taste, and the substance (*ti* 體) of bread before the celebrant recites the holy prayer. After the celebrant recites the prayer, the appearance and taste of bread remain but the substance transforms into the body (*ti* 體) of Jesus ... This is the same with the wine.[240]

The holy prayer (*shengjing* 聖經) here refers to the words of the consecration recited by a priest.

In *Rudiments of the Holy Teaching of the Lord of Heaven* (*Tianzhu shengjiao qimeng* 天主聖教啓蒙, ca. 1619), da Rocha gave a similar explanation of the Eucharist when discussing the *Pater Noster*: "Co-receiving (*gong mengyang* 共蒙仰), to receive Jesus' holy body."[241] Yet, he made a slight change when discussing the seven sacraments (*qi sa-ge-la-meng-duo* 七撒格辣孟多): "Master: What does '*gong mengyang* 恭蒙仰' mean? Student: It is the translation of 'to receive Jesus Christ's holy body'."[242] In this conversation, the character "*gong* 共" was changed into "*gong* 恭," producing the variant of co-receiving—to receive solemnly (*gong mengyang* 恭蒙仰). The early missionaries were searching for the translation of terms, and they used variants even in the same text. With an approach to daily life, Aleni interpreted the bread and wine consecrated at Mass as the proof that Catholics shall love each other and communicate with each other.

> Unlike the rice formed by each separated grain, the bread is one body mingled by many grains. And the wine is fermented from the juice taken from grapes. Our Lord used the bread and wine because he wanted us who receive the holy body to love each other as one body without division.[243]

---

240 "主祭者，欲祭天主，先取麵餅，未念聖經，此時但有餅色、餅味、餅體。念經後，麵色、餅味存，而其體變易為耶穌之體。……惟酒亦然。" Vagnone, *Jiaoyao jieliie, shang juan*, fol. 53a6–b2, 229–230.

241 "共蒙仰，領受耶穌聖體，" da Rocha, *Shengjiao qimeng*, fol. 13a8, 401. This catechism book takes the form of questions and answers.

242 "師：恭蒙仰，有什麼意思？學：譯言'領耶穌基利斯多聖體'。" da Rocha, *Shengjiao qimeng*, fol. 56a3–4, 487.

243 "麵以多粒相渾而成一體，比米飯各自一粒不侔。葡萄酒則取葡萄實，以其本汁，醞釀而成。吾主用此，意欲吾輩領其聖體，必相親愛猶如一體，

The consecration at Mass transforms the bread which is made from wheat grains ("unless a wheat grain falls into the earth and dies ..." John 12:24) into living body which signifies human body in general.[244] The comparison between the bread and rice reveals indigenous characteristics and evangelical creativity during the introduction and propagation of Mass. Although there is no evidence that rice was proposed as a substitute for bread in the ritual of the Mass, the missionaries recognized the cultural significance of rice as a staple food more than bread.

Furthermore, there was a concern about procuring wine suitable for use in the sacrament. The missionaries were unable to find a suitable type of grape grown locally and so had to import wine for the celebration of Mass. Dentrecolles mentioned that they imported wine of the Canary Islands from Manila.[245] Some did try to make wine by themselves, leading to a discussion of the proper way to ferment grape juice. On 6 August 1706, Tournon doubted the validity of the wine made in the Portuguese Jesuit residence in Beijing, because he thought the wine did not taste good enough.[246]

The anti-Catholic Chinese in 1616 were acquainted with the Catholic catechism and doctrines and those in the 1630's knew about Aleni's works and preaching, yet they barely knew Catholic rituals, such as the celebration of Mass.[247] Specific description of the Mass was rare to see in contemporary anti-Catholic texts. One exceptional example was found in the text "On the Calendar" (*Lifa lun* 曆法論, ca. 1630s) written by Xie Gonghua 謝宮花, who accused missionaries of illicitly making a calendar. Surprisingly, Xie Gonghua described Mass with a few details: "To drink the wine is to drink the blood of the Lord of Heaven, and to eat the bread is to eat the flesh of the Lord of Heaven. There is a stone placed on the table, which is called the bone of the Lord of Heaven."[248] The stone probably refers to the holy stone kept in the altar, as shown in table 4, and the bone probably refers to a relic of certain saint. Xie Gonghua gained rather clear information about transubstantiation, a theological notion which was unknown to most Chinese people.

Around the 1630s, the Buddhist monk Shi Ruchun 釋如純 derided the missionaries' discussion about transubstantiation: "All their absurd and vulgar

---

不分彼此爾我。" Aleni, *Shengti yaoli, shang juan*, fol. 2b8–fol. 3a3, 238–239. For Gianni's translation, see Criveller, *Preaching Christ*, 186–187.
244 Macherel, "Le corps du pain," 123.
245 Dentrecolles, "Lettre du Père d'Entrecolles," 133.
246 Stumpf, *The Acta Pekinensia*, volume I, 569–570.
247 Criveller, *Preaching Christ*, 402.
248 "食酒為食天主之血，食麵為食天主之肉。有一石置于案頭，謂是天主之骨。" Xie Gonghua 謝宮花, *Lifa lun* 曆法論, fol. 22b9–fol. 23a1, in *Poxie ji*, vol. 6, 321.

discourse is not worthy of accusation, for instance, they take the red juices in vegetables as blood."[249] The "red juices" are probably a distortion of red wine which is consecrated at Mass. In general, the contemporary anti-Catholic authors noticed the hall, the list of worship, and the assembly but missed the ritual itself. In the seventeenth century, the notion of transubstantiation did not incite any cannibalistic rumors. In the nineteenth century, Catholic rituals became more accessible to the non-Catholic Chinese and Mass became a particular source of misunderstanding. To consume the consecrated bread and wine was seen as a way to obtain the life-force in order to attain health and long life.[250]

A remarkable exception in the late Ming would be Xu Dashou, possibly a former catechumen,[251] who might have participated in the celebration of Mass.[252] Xu Dashou described Catholic rituals in detail, as if he was present.

> As to the wives and daughters of those who follow the barbarians, the barbarians order them to live in groups and to receive the secret Teaching of the barbarians. The barbarians sprinkle the holy water on them, drip the holy oil, confer the holy locket, and make them swallow the holy salt, light the holy candle, distribute the holy bread, and wave the holy fan. Dressed in bizarre vestments, the barbarians murmur the instructions to them behind the red veil. What are these nocturnal meetings with mixed genders for?[253]

The vivid depiction mixes several Catholic rituals with the imagination of missionaries deluding female Chinese Catholics. The holy water, the holy oil, the holy salt, and the holy candle refer to baptism; the distribution of the holy bread refers to the communion; and the nocturnal meetings, as Ad Dudink suggests, refers to confession.[254] The "holy locket" (*shengdu* 聖櫝, *Agnus Dei*), a type of portable reliquary, was widely distributed to Chinese Catholics in late Ming and early Qing.[255] The bizarre vestments perhaps refer to liturgical vestments

---

249 "至以菜中紅液為血，種種謬妄、鄙俚之談不足斥。" Shi Ruchun 釋如純, *Tianxue chupi* 天學初闢, fol. 30a5–6, in *Poxie ji*, vol. 8, 356.
250 ter Haar, *Telling Stories*, 168.
251 Dudink, "Longest Anti-Christian Essay," 266.
252 Criveller, *Preaching Christ*, 382.
253 "至若從夷者之妻女，悉令其群居而受夷之密教，為之灌聖水，滴聖油，授聖櫝，嚥聖鹽，燃聖燭，分聖麵，揮聖扇，蔽絳帳，披異服，而昏夜混雜又何歟？" Xu, "Wupi," 115–116.
254 Dudink, "Longest Anti-Christian Essay," 264.
255 It refers to round or oval discs of wax impressed with a figure of the lamb of God (*Agnus*

wore by a priest. The holy fan and the red veil probably belong to the imagination. The character "*sheng* 聖" (holy) appears often in the ritual description in the Chinese Christian texts. The frequent repetition of this character shows Xu Dashou's derision at Catholic rituals. Nevertheless, to distribute the holy bread (*fen shengmian* 分聖麵) is a vivid description of the communion. Xu Dashou criticized female Chinese Catholics' participation in Catholic rituals, and his rhetorical question indicates that missionaries deluded female Chinese Catholics to violate the severe gender segregation in Chinese society. The following section examines whether Xu Dashou's accusation of gender integration was accurate among the Christian communities.

3.2   *Female Catholics' Participation*

In late Ming and early Qing, female Chinese Catholics attended Mass with great fervor. Because of the severe gender segregation in Imperial China, missionaries prepared separate ritual place and ritual time for them. Gender segregation in the Christian communities in late Ming and early Qing took several phases. In the early stage of the mission, missionaries encouraged male Catholics to go to church while asked female Catholics to adore the Lord of Heaven at home. In the beginning of the seventeenth century, female Catholics had house oratories as their ritual space, and the wealthy family even built a chapel in their house. For example, Yang Tingyun had a beautiful chapel built in his residency exclusively for his female family members to attend Mass and to listen to the homily delivered by the Jesuit priests.[256] Moreover, spacious ritual space in the wealthy family was not only for family members but also for local female Catholics to assemble.[257]

With a growth of Chinese Catholics in the 1630s, the Christian communities built "the female hall" (*nütang* 女堂) exclusively for female Catholics. The name might have been an abbreviation of "the hall of the Lord of Heaven for females" (*nü tianzhu tang* 女天主堂).[258] The first female hall was built in Jianchang in 1633; the second was in Jiangzhou in 1634; the third in Nanjing in 1635; and another in Xi'an 西安 in 1639. From the 1630s onward, the female hall became a major ritual space for female Chinese Catholics to receive the sacra-

---

Dei). This holy object can be worn round the neck or be preserved in a locket. Dudink, "Longest Anti-Christian Essay," 251, note 74. Dudink translates "*shengdu* 聖櫝" as "the holy casket," which might reminds people of a burial casket or a relic casket.

256   Manuel Dias, Wenceslaus Pantaleon Kirwitzer, Nicolas Trigault, *Histoire de ce qui s'est passé*, 45.
257   Amsler, *Jesuits and matriarchs*, 56.
258   Dudink, "Church buildings," 585, note 20.

ments while the house oratory was predominantly used for the devotions.[259] As Le Comte recorded, "All of their churches are dedicated under the title of Sheng-Mu-Tang; that is to say the temple of the Holy Mother. It is there that they assemble, because never do they enter the men's church, just as men dare never to be found in the women's."[260] When building the church at Xuanwu men in 1650, the Jesuits reserved one place for a chapel where women assembled separately from men (*sacello in quo mulieres convocarentur seorsim a viris*).[261] In separate ritual spaces, men and women assembled separately on the fixed day (*die constituta conveniunt seorsim viri et feminae*).[262] The twice appearance of *seorsim* (separately) underlines the Jesuits' adherence to gender segregation. The contemporary book *Sketch of Landscape in Capital Beijing* mentioned the chapel as "the hall of the Holy Mother on the right side [of the hall at Xuanwu men]."[263]

Where a local Christian community did not have a female hall, the missionary generally invited female and male Catholics to the same church at different hours. Caballero said Mass for female Catholics on Saturday and for male Catholics on Sunday.[264] In some villages outside Ji'nan, male and female Catholics gathered in a church at the same time. After the Sunday Mass, they lined up in the church, men on one side and women on the other, chanting prayers.[265] At first, the Dominicans also tried to have male and female Catholics attend Mass at the same time. Later on, they built female halls or separated female and male Catholics in one church. They started building churches where two aisles met toward the altar in a right angle.[266] It happened in some Christian communities that during Mass a screen was set between the altar and female Catholics to create a partially separated ritual space.[267]

---

259 Amsler, *Jesuits and matriarchs*, 56–58.
260 "Toutes leurs églises lui sont dédiées sous le titre de Chin-Mou-Tam; c'est-à-dire temple de la Sainte Mère. C'est là qu'elles s'assemblent, car jamais elles n'entrent dans l'église des hommes, comme aussi les hommes n'oseraient jamais se trouver dans la leur." Lecomte, *Un jésuite à Pékin*, 428.
261 Schall, *Relation historique*, 321. In Bornet's translation, the chapel is called the chapel of Our Lady (la chapelle de Notre-Dame). Schall, *Relation historique*, 320.
262 Schall, *Relation historique*, 331.
263 "右聖母堂，" Liu and Yu, *Dijing jingwu lüe*, juan 4, 153.
264 Mungello, *Spirit and the Flesh*, 18.
265 Mungello, *Spirit and the Flesh*, 13.
266 Jennes, *Four centuries of catechetics*, 45.
267 Kang Zhijie 康志傑, *Jidu de xinniang—Zhongguo tianzhujiao zhennü yanjiu* 基督的新娘——中國天主教貞女研究 (Beijing: Zhongguo shehui kexue chubanshe 中國社會科學出版社, 2013), 28.

Missionaries in Beijing tried to celebrate Mass with men and women in the same church but separated by a high wall, yet they were unable to spread this method.[268]

Female Chinese Catholics also participated actively in the confraternity activities, however, in Imperial China female or mixed-gender confraternities were considered a deviant from the state-supported model of religious groups, such as territorial cults, guilds, and lineages.[269] Therefore, it was necessary for the Christian communities to write statutes of confraternities that underlined gender segregation. Female Catholics must (*xu* 須) have their own confraternity and their own prefect;[270] and a female confraternity shall assemble to attend Mass in another place instead of in the same room with male Catholics.[271] The Christian communities underlined the adherence to gender segregation even more when under persecutions. During the Canton Conference in 1667, the Jesuits and the Dominicans discussed the female Catholic's participation in Mass. The thirty-third rule in *Ordinances of the Holy Teaching* shows the missionaries' prudence.

> In the villages, when women hear Mass in the chapel, it is absolutely interdict for men to enter the interior or even to examine from the outside. Women on their side should not hold the meetings of penitence to give themselves the discipline, nor convoke their confraternities on the same days with men; may all the people in the Teaching strictly observe this rule.[272]

The assembly space for a female confraternity can be a female hall or someone's house.[273] The second rule in *Ordinances of the Holy Teaching* exhorted Chinese Catholics to attend Mass in a church yet made adjustments for the female Catholics who were unable to go out of the familial sphere.

---

268 Bürkler, *Die Sonn-und Festtagsfeier*, 36.
269 Vincent Goossaert, "Irrepressible Female Piety: Late Imperial Bans on Women Visiting Temples," *Nan Nü* 10 (2008): 236.
270 de Mailla, *Shengti ren'aijing*, fol. 12a3–4, 317.
271 Wang, *Renhui yue*, fol. 41a1, 609.
272 "三十三、鄉間小堂中，如女人聽彌撒，男人決不許入堂，亦不許在外窺探。若女人亦不得同聚做苦會行苦功，併與男人同日做會。教中人必宜嚴守。" Verhaeren, "Ordonnances," 475. For a French translation, see Verhaeren, "Ordonnances," 463.
273 "Elles ont leurs réunions de Congrégation, surtout des Congrégations de la Ste Vierge, soit dans des églises dédiées à Marie, soit dans des maisons privées, où elles peuvent commodément réciter leurs prières, assister à la messe et recevoir les sacrements." Bornet, "L'apostolat laïque," 46.

The followers of the Teaching adore the Lord's image at home, yet whenever it is the grand day of worship, they must still come to the main hall to attend the worship solemnly. Because people often make sacrifices to the Lord of Heaven in the main hall and the Lord is constantly present there. Those who are unable to come to the main hall can come to the chapel in their own village. If they are still unable or if women are unable to go out, one must (*xu* 須) yearn for the Lord with the whole heart and look at [the direction of] the main hall or the chapel, as the official looks at the imperial palace and kowtows.[274]

Traditional Chinese culture specifically prohibits the presence of women in public spaces.[275] Confucianism restricts female activities to within the familial sphere. Couplet described how difficult it was to convert and to instruct Chinese women because they always stayed at home.[276] Missionaries did not visit female Catholics unless someone was ill and the latter almost never visited the former. Female Catholics assembled in a female hall on designated dates to attend Mass and to participate in other sacraments, and missionaries administered the sacraments to them with much precaution.[277]

Female Catholics often dared not go out of the familial sphere for fear of scandal, so it was much more embarrassing for the missionary to instruct them.[278] Le Comte explained that their fear resulted from the state law that women should not go to the temple. Then, he blamed Buddhist monks: "The disorders which occur whenever the pagan women visit the temples of the monks make our assemblies suspicious and always give the Gentiles a specious pretext to describe the religion."[279] Chinese women enjoyed going to the temple because it was their only occasion to appear outdoors, however, their husbands did not like this occasion and men of the high class obliged their wives

---

274 "二、奉教人家雖然供奉主像，然每遇大瞻禮日，必當赴大堂中瞻拜恭敬，因大堂中常祭天主，主恆降臨也。倘有不便不能到大堂，或在本鄉小堂中亦可。若更有不能或女人不便出入，亦須一心向主，或望大堂或望小堂，如官府望闕而拜可也。" Verhaeren, "Ordonnances," 469. For a French translation, see Verhaeren, "Ordonnances," 454. For a German translation, see Bürkler, *Die Sonn-und Festtagsfeier*, 32.
275 Goossaert, "Irrepressible Female Piety," 232.
276 Couplet, *Histoire d'une dame*, 7.
277 Couplet, *Histoire d'une dame*, 8.
278 Lecomte, *Un jésuite à Pékin*, 428.
279 "Les désordres qui arrivent toutes les fois que les femmes païnnes visitent les temples des bonzes rendent nos assemblées suspectes et donnent toujours aux gentils un prétexte spécieux de décrire la religion." Lecomte, *Un jésuite à Pékin*, 429–430.

to restrict their fervor to their houses.[280] Furthermore, the state restricted the female participation in the temple. Goossaert's article on female piety in late Imperial China sheds light on the study of gender segregation in religious rituals. Prohibitions against women entering temples cannot be isolated from the regulations aiming at controlling religious life and public morality. These prohibitions consider five specific problems: temples' ritual purity, women's active ritual role, the control over young women, nighttime activities, and anticlericalism.[281] Such comprehensive consideration reminds scholars to examine gender segregation as a pervasive aspect of the whole society.

In late Ming and early Qing, it was common to keep gender segregation during religious activities. The Catholic Church was not the only religion being challenged, yet her measures were rather particular. The statutes for the Confraternity of Guardian Angels (*hushou tianshenhui* 護守天神會) require that little girls in the Catholic Church especially should (*youyao* 尤要) master the classical prayers well and understand basic disciplines clearly for fear that once they get married their souls might be led astray. If a girl has lost her parents or her parents are unable to teach her, the prefect must (*dingyao* 定要) try to find a way to teach her.[282] In addition, the fourteenth rule in *Ordinances of the Holy Teaching* requires that if a female Catholic marries a non-Catholic man, the man should convert to the Catholic Church.[283]

Despite the severe gender segregation, the female Catholics' participation in Catholic rituals increased. The Christian community in Fu'an in late Ming and early Qing contained a high percentage of women.[284] In the Christian community at Mopan Mountain, female Catholics were the basic force of the faith, running their own charity confraternity—the Confraternity of the Holy Mother.[285] In the seventeenth century, a large number of female Catholics assembled in churches on major feast days. In order to avoid crowds of women in the hall, the missionaries designated different dates around the feast to the confraternities. Although the Catholic rituals which based in the church were performed at a low frequency in general, Chinese women defined their identity as Catholic

---

280 Lecomte, *Un jésuite à Pékin*, 140.
281 Goossaert, "Irrepressible Female Piety," 217–219.
282 "教中女孩，尤要習熟經典，講明要理六端。" Anon., *Shengtihui gui*, fol. 4a5–7, 263.
283 "十四、教中女子或與教外聯姻，先當講明聖教之禮，願信願從方可為婚。否則恐有自悞也。" Verhaeren, "Ordonnances," 470. For a French translation, see Verhaeren, "Ordonnances," 456.
284 Zhang, *Guanfu*, 171.
285 Kang, *Shangzhu*, 25.

through their participation in these rituals.[286] Chinese Catholics' participation in Catholic rituals helped to build the foundation of Christendom in Chinese society.

3.3 Foundation of Christendom

Medieval writers coined the term *Christianitas* (Christendom) with two basic understandings: a self-conscious defense against Islam, and a universal society of believers subject to the pope.[287] John Van Engen offers a third understanding: the term medieval folk used to identify their religious culture. An early Dutch-Latin lexicon (ca. 1480) explained that Christendom is the rite and/or property (*ritus vel proprietas*) by which people are called Christian.[288] In medieval Europe, the parish was the center of village life where the local community found its identity and at the heart of the parish life were the rituals.[289] Nevertheless, in the seventeenth and eighteenth centuries, Chinese Catholics were not organized by parish which is a geographical unity around the church but by the confraternity (*hui* 會).[290] The confraternity was the center of local Christian community where local Chinese Catholics found their identity as Catholic and at the heart of the confraternity life were the rituals. Therefore, it is justifiable to apply the term "Christendom" to the Christian communities in China.[291] Similarly, Richard Madsen points out that missionaries in the nineteenth century tried to make the Christian communities "like little Christendoms" where the social, economical, and political life was closely intertwined with the Catholic Church.[292] In fact, missionaries in late Ming and early Qing had already established the foundation of Christendom in Chinese society. Missionaries at that time naturally applied this word to the Catholic Church in China.[293] As Henri Bernard suggests, the Zhalan er cemetery, the very first Christian cemetery in China, signified the definitive foundation of Christendom.[294]

Christianization in Chinese society consisted rituals as well as faith. Catholic rituals were essential in the faithful's daily life, be it in Europe from the Middle

---

286 Amsler, *Jesuits and matriarchs*, 107.
287 Van Engen, "The Christian Middle Ages," 539–540.
288 Van Engen, "The Christian Middle Ages," 541.
289 Van Engen, "The Christian Middle Ages," 542–543.
290 Standaert, *L'«autre»*, 81.
291 Standaert, *L'«autre»*, 87.
292 Richard Madsen, *China's Catholics: Tragedy and Hope in an Emerging Civil Society* (Berkeley: University of California Press, 1998), 32.
293 Fouquet, "Lettre du Père Fouquet," 162.
294 Bernard, *Le père Matthieu Ricci*, quatrième partie, 374.

Ages to the Renaissance or in China from late Ming to early Qing. The foundation of Christendom can be measured by the extent to which time, space, and ritual observances are defined according to the Christian liturgical year.[295] In the 1580's, the Chinese Catholics in Zhaoqing had already begun a Christian life by regularly attending Mass and listening to homilies on Sundays and feast days.[296] As the Catholic Church in China grew, more and more Christian communities began and continued living the Christian life.

> On fixed day they assemble, men and women each on their side; and each one, as much as one could, put on the table of incense the almsgiving for the expense of the confraternity. Then they devoutly attend the sacrifice of Mass. Up to the end of Mass, they listen to a small homily, and finally at the same time they recite the litanies or other prayers in common.[297]

As Schall recorded, following the designated dates on the list of worship, Chinese Catholics assembled in the hall to attend Mass and to perform other religious practices.

Missionaries delivered the homily after Mass, in order to preach to Chinese Catholics in Chinese. *Li Jiubiao's Diary of Oral Admonitions* used a formula to express the homily following the celebration of Mass: first notify the date in the traditional lunisolar calendar, then right after the worship (*zhanli fubi* 瞻禮甫畢), a priest preaches according to the Gospel of the day. For example, "On the fifth day, right after the worship, Master Lu instructs the crowd, saying: 'In today's Gospel …'"[298] *Sequel to Li Jiubiao's Diary of Oral Admonitions* (*Xu Kouduo richao* 續口鐸日抄, ca. 1698) used a similar formula: notify the date in the lunisolar calendar and the name of the worship of the day, then after Mass a priest preaches according to the worship of the day, wearing sacrificial vestments.

295　Van Engen, "The Christian Middle Ages," 543.
296　Bernard, *Le père Matthieu Ricci*, première partie, 128.
297　"Die constituta conveniunt seorsim viri et foeminae; et quisque, quantum vocat, nummorum pro congregationum expensis in mensa incensi deponit. Tum Missae sacrificio devote intersunt. Sub hujus finem conciunculam pro re proposita auscultant, et tandem simul vel litanias vel alias preces in communi recitant." Schall, *Relation historique*, 331.
298　"初五日，瞻礼甫畢。盧先生詔于眾曰：'今日经中有云……'" Li, *Kouduo richao*, juan 1, fol. 19b6, 74. See also "二十日，瞻禮甫畢。盧先生語余輩曰：'子等知天主之尊嚴，亦知天主之慈悲乎？今日《萬日略經》，載吾主設譬有云……'" Li, *Kouduo richao*, juan 1, fol. 23a9–b1, 81–82. See also "初六日，瞻禮甫畢。盧先生謂眾曰：'今日經中……'" Li, *Kouduo richao*, juan 2, fol. 3a4, 103.

On the thirteenth day of the eighth month, the worship of the Holy Mother's Nativity. After Mass, wearing the sacrificial vestment, Master [Wu Li] stands on the altar's left and faces south. He orders the crowd to line up from the senior to the young and speaks to them, saying: "Today is the Holy Mother's nativity …"[299]

Moreover, Wu Li sometimes organized Chinese Catholics to deliver the homily after Mass. Zhao Lun, the author of *Sequel to Li Jiubiao's Diary of Oral Admonitions*, gave a homily on 9 September 1696 (Kangxi 35.8.14): "On the fourteenth day, the worship of the Lord's day. I talked about the chapter of Jesus ordering the leper to be clean."[300] On 21 September 1697 (Kangxi 36.8.7, the worship day of St. Matthew), Wu Li who was nearly sixty years old got tired after Mass and asked the members of the Confraternity of St. Francis to deliver the homily. Again Zhao Lun delivered the homily in replacement of a priest.[301]

A Day of Worship for St. Andrew [etc.] (*Sheng An-de-le zongtu zhanli* 聖安德肋宗徒瞻礼, ca. 1658) recorded homilies given by Brancati and Girolamo de Gravina (Jia Yimu 賈宜睦, SJ, 1603–1662) from 1646 (*xinmao nian* 辛卯年) to 1656 (*yichou nian* 乙丑年). Its title came from the first homily given on the feast day of St. Andrew. Homilies for the initiation of the holy body take more pages than those for other days of worship.[302] The two Jesuits are called Mr. Pan (*Pan xiansheng* 潘先生) and Mr. Jia (*Jia xiansheng* 賈先生). One record reads, "When the Mass is ended, Mr. Jia says: 'Today is the eighth day after Christmas, the day when Jesus was circumcised …'"[303]

The Franciscans trained the Chinese Catholics in Shandong to live a fervent Christian life according to the Catholic liturgical calendar. Arriving in Ji'nan in November 1650, Caballero taught Chinese Catholics to kneel in front of the altar in two choirs before Mass and to recite prayers such as the Rosary and

---

299 "八月十三日，聖母聖誕瞻禮。先生彌撒畢，服祭衣，從台左南向立，命眾昭穆分序立，謂之曰：'今日聖母聖誕……'" Zhao, *Xu Kouduo*, 586–587. Pfister, *Notices biographiques*, 396, no. 156. See also "十一月九日，聖方濟各瞻禮。先生彌撒甫畢，祭衣未解，命眾東西序立，詔眾於堂曰：'凡聖人瞻禮，須學聖人行實……'" Zhao, *Xu Kouduo*, 600.

300 "十四日，主日瞻禮。余講耶穌令癩者潔篇。" Zhao, *Xu Kouduo*, 591.

301 "余年遲暮，彌撒後津涎每竭，不能日日宣講聖道，惟賴方濟各會中人代講為荷。" Zhao, *Xu Kouduo*, 625.

302 Francesco Brancati 潘國光 and Girolamo de Gravina 賈宜睦, *Sheng An-de-le zongtu zhanli* 聖安德肋宗徒瞻礼, fol. 53a7–fol. 70a1, CCT BnF, vol. 17, 205–239.

303 "彌撒畢，賈先生云：'今日乃聖誕後第八日耶穌行割損礼……'" Brancati and de Gravina, *Sheng An-de-le*, fol. 23a9, 145.

"Praise to the Holy Body and the Holy Mother" with him in a loud voice. Then, everyone stood up and Caballero asked and explained basic catechism questions. Next they celebrated Mass, following by Caballero's short homily.[304] His co-worker Ibáñez reported to Propaganda Fide that in 1665 more than three thousand Chinese Catholics in Shandong attended Mass and listened to the homily on Sundays and feast days all year round.[305]

Christendom in late Ming and early Qing China was composed of local Christian communities rather than by parishes. Furthermore, the lack of diocesan structures made every mission station a *de facto* cathedral and every subordinate Christian community a *de facto* parish.[306] By assembling in churches to attend Mass on designated dates, Chinese Catholics professed their faith and shaped their identity as members of the local Christian community as well as in the universal Church. The study of ritual unfolds how people set up spatial and temporal boundaries to represent and to identify.[307] The introduction and propagation of Mass reveal the missionaries' evangelical method. How Chinese Catholics understood Mass mentally and attended Mass physically reveal their embrace of faith.

In late Ming and early Qing, the celebration of Mass was a rather rare event for many Christian communities, where missionaries could not visit often. Those who lived in urban areas received continual pastoral care, while those in rural areas said confession and attended Mass at a low frequency.[308] Take the Christian communities in Guangdong for example. There were seven or eight churches in Canton since 1693. During the 1690s, some urban female confraternities in Canton received the sacraments every other week, while the confraternities in small towns or cities without a resident missionary met a priest every few months or less frequently.[309] As François Froger (1676–1715?) recorded in January 1700, there were several chapels for female Catholics in Canton, and there were seven churches where people celebrated Mass "with as much freedom as in all the cities in France" every day.[310] As for the rural areas, the low frequency did not necessarily decrease the importance of Mass in the Christian communities. Although the rituals performed by a priest in a church

---

304 Bürkler, *Die Sonn-und Festtagsfeier*, 28–29.
305 Bürkler, *Die Sonn-und Festtagsfeier*, 30.
306 Brockey, *Journey to the East*, 329.
307 Stephan Feuchtwang, *The Imperial Metaphor: Popular Religion in China* (New York: Routledge, 1992), 14.
308 Brockey, *Journey to the East*, 367.
309 Amsler, *Jesuits and matriarchs*, 107.
310 Froger, *Relation du premier voyage*, 138.

were comparably rare, they were "highly meaningful moments" when Chinese Catholics gained intense religious experience.[311]

For the purpose of apologetics, Chinese Catholics in late Ming and early Qing generally focused on discussing various questions more than describing their actual Christian life. Nevertheless, two exceptional books below described how the Christian communities piously observed the day of worship. *Li Jiubiao's Diary of Oral Admonitions* recorded the celebration of Mass on various feast days in eight volumes.[312] Similarly, the majority of *Sequel to Li Jiubiao's Diary of Oral Admonitions* recorded accounts of the celebration of Mass.[313] In order to exemplify their fruits in the mission in China, missionaries often described the Chinese Catholics' fervor of Mass in the letters and books written to European readers. For example, some Chinese Catholics in Beijing lived far away from the church, but they came to attend Mass all year round, and "nothing has driven them away, either snow, or cold, or mud, or rain" (*nequidquam absterrentibus, seu nive, seu frigore, seu luto, seu pluvia*).[314] Magalhães was impressed by the members in Beijing. They knelt during Mass for the whole time and only stood during the gospel reading; they did not talk or look or act indecently.[315]

Caballero's letter records the Christmas celebration in 1695 in Ji'nan. The local Christian community prepared this major event for three weeks. First females then males, the Chinese Catholics arranged their offerings and came to the church to confess in order to receive communion. On Christmas Eve, they gathered in the East Hall from small villages outside Ji'nan to celebrate Mass at night. Ibáñez said three Masses in the morning and two more Masses at dawn the following day for those who arrived late and those who stayed the entire night. Jean Valat (Wang Ruwang 汪儒望, SJ, 1599/1614–1696) traveled twenty leagues to celebrate Christmas with small Christian communities, where flutes and other musical instruments were played.[316]

In 1701, François Noël (Wei Fangji 衛方濟, SJ, 1651–1729) prepared the "holy tomb" and the veneration of the Cross for Holy Week. From Holy Thursday night to Good Friday, some Chinese Catholics adored the Host by praying or singing. On Easter Sunday, they confessed then received communion and the

---

311 Amsler, *Jesuits and matriarchs*, 108.
312 For the mention of the celebration of Mass in each volume, see Xiao, *Tianhui yu wudang*, 174.
313 For a detailed record of the celebration of Mass, see Xiao, *Tianhui yu wudang*, 208–210.
314 "Letterae Annae, Collegium Pekinense, Anno 1677," ARSI Jap. Sin. 116, fol. 216.
315 Brockey, *Journey to the East*, 382.
316 Mungello, *Spirit and the Flesh*, 21–22.

communion always deeply touched them.³¹⁷ In 1702 Fouquet described how the Chinese Catholics in Nanchang piously celebrated Holy Week. On Palm Sunday, the congregation of people made the large church look small. Fouquet blessed tree branches, as well as perfumes and candles which Chinese Catholics burnt before holy images all year round. On Holy Thursday, Chinese Catholics adored the Host in turn. From the afternoon to the night, there were always many reciting the Rosary and the litanies to the Most Blessed Sacrament in a loud voice. On Good Friday the crowd made the church look small again to adore the Cross in the same way as in Europe. Afterward, the fervent neophytes took a discipline to practice the mortification of the flesh. On Holy Saturday, they held the ordinary ceremonies. On Easter Sunday, more than one hundred people received communion and the church was full all day.³¹⁸

In 1702, Joseph de Prémare (Ma Ruose 馬若瑟, SJ, 1666–1736), Pierre de Goville (Ge Weili 戈維里, SJ, 1668–1758), and João Duarte (Nie Ruowang 聶若望, SJ, 1671–1752) planned to make church ceremonies more splendorous to attract the Chinese Catholics in Nanfeng 南豐. On Holy Thursday, they said High Mass with the deacon and subdeacon. Before the communion, de Prémare loudly pronounced how to approach the Host in his imperfect Chinese, and about forty Chinese Catholics piously received communion. Then, they placed the Host in the chapel decorated with the images of the Passion which were delivered from France that year. That evening, de Prémare tried to persuade some neophytes to participate in the foot-washing ritual, yet the Chinese Catholics did not want to see the missionaries humiliating themselves. After praying to the Lord, they selected twelve names by lot. The three Jesuits administered the foot-washing ritual according to the Roman Ritual. With lit candles, they recited prayers in Chinese as well as in Latin, which vividly impressed the Chinese Catholics. On Good Friday after the adoration of the Cross, the three Jesuits and the Chinese Catholics took a discipline while praying and crying before the Crucifixion. That evening, they celebrated *Tenebrae* and the Chinese Catholics were satisfied to learn the signification of the fifteen candles extinguished one by one and the loud noise made in the end.³¹⁹ On Good Friday 1707, three hundred of boats arrived near Wuxi 無錫. Catholic fishermen first landed their wives in a church built by themselves; then they waited there together to celebrate Easter.³²⁰

---

317 Collani, "Neue Welt-Bott," 687–689.
318 Fouquet, "Lettre du Père Fouquet," 209–211.
319 Fouquet, "Lettre du Père Fouquet," 221–225.
320 Dentrecolles, "Lettre du Père d'Entrecolles," 136–137.

In medieval Europe, the growing worship of the Host resulted from the decreased frequency of communion during Mass. Since the tenth century, European Catholics had to confess before receiving the Host. Yet, several elements restricted people from confession and preparation for communion became more strict, thus causing limited reception of communion and even lower Mass attendance. In the end of the twelfth century, the notion of spiritual communion (*spiritualis communio*) had been developed. It was believed that gazing on the Host allows for the reception of the Host in some way.[321] As a result, people longed to look at the Host raised by a priest during Mass, then the adoration of the Host and the Feast of *Corpus Christi* became popular. Promoted by the local Norbertine canoness Julienne de Cornillon (1193–1258), the Feast of *Corpus Christi* was first celebrated in 1246 in Liège, Belgium, and it was adopted for the universal Church in 1264.

When the Society of Jesus was established, the adoration of the Host became one basic spiritual activity for the Jesuits.[322] Earlier in Japan, the Jesuits already attached much importance to the Host. Missionaries and Japanese Catholics celebrated the Feast of *Corpus Christi* with many processions.[323] Since late Ming and early Qing, this feast was celebrated in China as well. In *Eternal List of Worship of the Holy Teaching of the Lord of Heaven*, the Belgian Jesuit Couplet marked the date of the Feast of *Corpus Christi*: "The fourth day after [the Feast of] the Holy Trinity (*shengsan* 聖三) is [the Feast of] Jesus' Holy Body (*Yesu shengti* 耶穌聖體)."[324] The Feast of the Holy Trinity means Trinity Sunday, which is the first Sunday after Pentecost, and the fourth day is the Thursday after Trinity Sunday.

The Jesuits in China translated the notion of spiritual communion as spiritual reception (*shenling* 神領), which became the fixed translation. Brancati explained: "There are two kinds of reception of the holy body: the first one is called actual reception; the second spiritual reception."[325] Brancati asked Augustine Qiu Aoding 丘奧定, a Chinese Catholic from Shangyang 上洋 (Shanghai), to write the preface for *Ritual Rules of the Holy Body*. In his preface, Qiu Aoding exclaimed: "Few are the people who read this book yet do not

---

321 Jungmann, *The Mass*, 363–364.
322 Criveller, *Preaching Christ*, 428.
323 Vu Thanh, *Devenir japonais*, 227.
324 "聖三後四日，是耶穌聖體。" Philippe Couplet 柏應理, *Tianzhu shengjiao yongzhanlidan* 天主聖教永瞻禮單, in CCT BnF, vol. 20, 575. See also Nicolas Trigault 金尼閣, *Tuiding linian zhanlirifa* 推定曆年瞻禮日法, CCT ARSI, vol. 5, 331.
325 "領聖體有二樣：一曰實領，二曰神領。" Brancati, *Shengti guiyi*, fol. 27b3, 364. See also Brancati, *Tianshen huike*, fol. 68b3, 140.

spiritually receive (*shenling* 神領) the holy grace!"³²⁶ Buglio translated the second kind of reception of the holy body as the reception by heart (*xinling* 心領).³²⁷ Aleni categorized three kinds of the reception: "One is false reception; one actual reception; and one spiritual reception."³²⁸ The false reception (*maoling* 冒領) happens when a receiver does not prepare well for the reception, such as no confession before the Mass or a receiver commits major sin and is not supposed to receive communion. In late Ming and early Qing, either priests alone took the actual reception and the faithful took the spiritual reception, or the latter prepared well and took the actual reception as well.³²⁹ In order to avoid the false reception, the *Ritual Rules of the Holy Body* included four stories where people who committed the false reception died a horrific death.³³⁰ Franchi noticed a Chinese Catholic always receiving communion yet living an unchaste life. Sometimes the man even received communion without confession first. Since mild talk was ineffective, Franchi harshly warned him and the man finally repented.³³¹

The Jesuits introduced the adoration of the Host in Chinese society. Schall recorded how the Chinese Catholics in Beijing held the Eucharistic procession on Holy Thursday.

> The regular feasts of the Christian devotion are celebrated in the European manner. In the processions of the Holy Sacrament, people carry triumphantly God hidden beneath the veil of the Eucharistic appearances; to commemorate the death of Christ, people light the funeral candles, and in the middle of the angels who are represented in tears, the assistants express their sentiments. When people carry the Eucharist in the accustomed ceremony, they shelter it under the cloth of great price, interwoven with gold and silk, which was dedicated to this service by one of the princes.³³²

---

326 "讀是書而不神領聖寵者，幾希矣！" Qiu Aoding, "*xu* 敘," in Brancati, *Shengti guiyi*, fol. 1b6–7, 310.
327 "領聖體有實領，有心領。" Buglio, *Siduo dianyao, juan shang*, fol. 45b5, 104.
328 "一冒領，一實領，一神領。" Aleni, *Shengti yaoli, shang juan*, fol. 17a2, 267.
329 Song, *Giulio Aleni*, 312.
330 Brancati, *Shengti guiyi*, fol. 16a8–fol. 18a6, 341–345.
331 Collani, "Neue Welt-Bott," 694.
332 "Festa pietatis christianae vulgaria, ut Theophoriae ac Christi morientis, ibi triumphali apparatu deferendo velatum sub speciebus Eucharisticis DEUM, hic lugubri per funalia luce pie accendendis ad sepulchrum inter Angelorum repraesentata studia affectibus accurrentium, more Europaeo celebrantur. Deferendae ritu consueto Eucharistiae, qui

The Eucharistic procession was an excellent occasion for Chinese Catholics to profess their faith in public. On 8 June 1651, the Dominican priests and the Chinese Catholics in Fu'an assembled in a newly-built hall at Dingtou 頂頭 to celebrate the Feast of *Corpus Christi*. Local Catholics, including the future bishop Luo Wenzhao, decorated the altar and prepared the path for the procession at evening. The priests sang the Mass and almost everyone confessed and received communion. The adoration of the Host continued for a whole day.[333] *Statutes of Confraternity of the Holy Mother* prescribes the Eucharistic adoration: "If the day before the Lord's day is the date of the Holy Mother's feast, all the members shall hold the candle and adore the holy body solemnly (*gongchao shengti* 恭朝聖體)."[334] These religious rituals celebrated according to the list of worship either encouraged or urged Chinese Catholics to live in the rhythm of Catholic ritual time.

In late Ming and early Qing, missionaries, together with Chinese Catholics, introduced and propagated Catholic rituals with Mass at the core. It is these effective rituals that shaped and strengthened the identity of Chinese Catholics, individually as well as collectively. Among the effective rituals, the celebration of Mass and confession are most important.[335] Chinese Catholics fasted and confessed beforehand as preparation, then attended Mass on Sundays and other designated days of worship. Thus, they began to live according to the Catholic liturgical calendar, which was a brand new ritual time in Chinese society.[336] With great cohesive power in the Christian communities, Mass and confession attracted Chinese Catholics to assemble from various villages usually to a church or to someone's house. As an assembly, Chinese Catholics attended the two sacraments which were exclusively administered by a priest.

The Franciscans instructed new converts especially about Mass and confession.[337] The Catholic Church requires annual confession and communion. In late Ming and early Qing, one must confess before Mass as a well preparation for receiving communion. Moreover, when confessing, one shall reflect on whether one has attended Mass and urged one's children to attend Mass.[338] In this regard, Mass and confession were closely connected and the latter under-

---

illam inumbret magni pretii pannum, auro et serico intertextum, huic officio dedicatum unus e Regulis donavit." Schall, *Relation historique*, 333.

333   Menegon, *Ancestors, Virgins, and Friars*, 206–207.
334   "若主日前一日，為聖母瞻禮日期，俱要執蠟燭，恭朝聖體。" Augery, *Shengmuhui gui*, fol. 4a7–b2, 453–454.
335   Standaert, *L'«autre»*, 81. Menegon, "Deliver Us from Evil," 49.
336   Standaert, *The Interweaving of Rituals*, 162.
337   Jennes, *Four centuries of catechetics*, 46.
338   Liam Matthew Brockey and Ad Dudink, "A Missionary Confessional Manual: José Mon-

lined the former as the Sacrament of sacraments. The two rituals also had a strong individual dimension, for the bodily presence in the two sacraments constructed and affirmed each individual's identity as a member of the communion of merits of saints.[339] Chinese women married to pagans tried to participate in confession and Mass as a way to strengthen their identity as Catholics.[340] Members of the Christian communities gained meaning and a sense of salvation by attending Mass and participating in other Catholic rituals. In this regard, the Catholic Church in China had already constructed communities of effective rituals.[341]

Where the celebration of Mass was rarely held because of the lack of priests, the local Christian community took other religious practices as substitutes, such as praying together, preaching to each other, and doing charitable work. What might have been the closest substitute for Mass was reciting prayers in a church on designated dates as an assembly. The church and the list of worship signify the material perspective of the rite, and the Christian assembly as the living hall signifies the spiritual perspective. Despite difficulties such as the lack of priests and persecutions, Chinese Catholics tried to preserve the place of worship and the essence of Mass, which is to worship the Lord of Heaven as an assembly. When unable to go to church, they worshiped the Lord of Heaven according to the list of worship kept in their houses. The rhythm of Catholic ritual time continued in the familial sphere. Furthermore, it connected Chinese Catholics in one family with local Christian community and the universal Church, bringing the familial sphere into the ecclesiastical sphere. Since a church can be considered the house where Christians assemble, the cel-

---

teiro's *Vera et Unica Praxis breviter ediscendi, ac expeditissime loquendi Sinicum idioma*," *Forgive Us Our Sins*, 212.

339 About the relationship between bodily presence and the identity of a group member, see Randall Collins, *Interaction Ritual Chains* (New Jersey: Princeton University Press, 2004), 52–61.

340 Menegon, "Deliver Us from Evil," 54. When discussing the relationship between the participation in rituals and the testification of individual identity, Standaert suggests that to participate in Chinese New Year celebrations testifies to a Chinese identity, and to attend Mass testifies to a Catholic identity. Standaert, *The Interweaving of Rituals*, 230.

341 Communities of effective rituals are the groups of Christians whose lives are organized around certain rituals, such as mass and confession. Organized by a liturgical calendar, these rituals are related to the faith and doctrine. They are effective in the sense that they build a group and that the group members consider these rituals methods to bring meaning and salvation. Nicolas Standaert, "Christianity Shaped by the Chinese," in *The Cambridge History of Christianity: Reform and Expansion 1500–1660*, ed. R. Po-Chia Hsia (Cambridge: Cambridge University Press, 2007), 573.

ebration of Mass held in the house is the celebration of God's family.[342] When this family celebration could not be held, Chinese Catholics took replacements such as reciting prayers in their own families.

Forming the familial sphere was an effective method for evangelization because religions in Chinese society functioned in the first place within the institutions such as the family, the community, and the state.[343] The familial sphere is an important ritual space in Chinese society, where all major rites of passage are celebrated, such as rituals pertaining to birth, marriage, and death. The early development of one religion in Fu'an, be it Buddhism, Taoism or popular religion, is often closely related to the local kinship group.[344] One remarkable characteristic of divinities in the local temple is their "attachment of the kinship" (*zongzu yifuxing* 宗族依附性), which the Teaching of the Lord of Heaven also adapted to in Fu'an in late Ming.[345] In the seventeenth century the Teaching of the Lord of Heaven became more predominantly a family religion.[346] The Christian communities inherited the effective rituals in the familial sphere, thus preserving Christendom in Chinese society.

In addition to acknowledging Catholic rituals as effective, the local Catholics' attitude toward the traditional rituals was one crucial factor to the foundation of Christendom. According to Hélène Vu Thanh, the Christian communities in Japan were fragile because although Japanese Catholics accepted Catholic rituals such as Mass and confession, they kept performing certain Buddhist practices and other traditional rituals, which were considered superstitious by the Jesuits.[347] It was necessary for local Catholics to abandon the traditional rituals which were considered heterodox or superstitious by the Catholic Church. In order to strengthen young Christian communities in China, missionaries urged Chinese Catholics to abandon certain traditional rituals. Although different opinions were held about which traditional rituals were heterodox or superstitious, there was a consensus that only Catholic rituals are effective. Some missionaries and Chinese Catholics supported keeping sacrifice to ancestors as an important custom in Chinese society, but they did not acknowledge it as an effective ritual which produces merits. To acknowledge Catholic rituals as the only effective ones helped Chinese Catholics to

---

342   Jungmann, *The Mass*, 275. As regards the sacrament, the word "communion" denotes "sublime Good that holds together the society of the faithful," rather than the union of the individual with Christ. Jungmann, *The Mass*, 275, note 1.
343   Teiser, *The Ghost Festival*, 15.
344   Zhang, *Guanfu*, 39.
345   Zhang, *Guanfu*, 264.
346   Brockey, *Journey to the East*, 346.
347   Vu Thanh, *Devenir japonais*, 257.

strengthen their Catholic identity, maintained a ritual unity in the Christian communities, and ensured the foundation of Christendom.

Another crucial factor to the foundation of Christendom is the establishment of indigenous clergy. Jesuit missionaries in Paraguay and the Chiquitos region rejected establishing an indigenous clergy, so did the church officials in Europe. In this regard, Robert H. Jackson suggests that indigenous peoples who converted were not full members of the Christian community.[348] The establishment of indigenous clergy is an acknowledgement from both Rome and the missionaries that local Catholics are qualified to be trained as priests. Furthermore, an ephemeral flourishing of local Christian communities can hardly be counted as Christendom. Indigenous clergy is a *sine qua non* for maintaining local Christian communities, which are the components of Christendom in Chinese society. When foreign missionaries were expelled from mainland China, indigenous priests, such as Luo Wenzhao, Wu Li, and those in later generations, maintained Christendom in Chinese society, which was fragile but persistent.

4 Conclusion

Through the introduction and propagation of Mass, Chinese Catholics accepted the idea to worship the Lord of Heaven as an assembly and put it into practice. Catholic rituals with Mass at the core attracted Chinese Catholics, both male and female, from the familial sphere into the ecclesiastical sphere, meanwhile the list of worship brought the ecclesiastical sphere into the family one. Although the celebration of Mass was at a low frequency in general, its essence as worship of the Lord of Heaven as an assembly was inherited in the familial sphere and connected Chinese Catholics into the ecclesiastical sphere. With Mass as the essential ritual, the ritual space and ritual time in the Christian communities were effectively rooted in late Ming and early Qing. The pious Chinese Catholics kept performing Catholic rituals as the only effective ones, thus realizing the foundation of Christendom in Chinese society. The next chapter shows how the series of ritual interactions around Mass in late Ming and early Qing were fruitful.

---

348 Jackson, *Demographic Change*, 41.

CHAPTER 5

On-going Interactions

After exploring the object of worship, intention of worship, performer of worship, and place of worship, this book now reflects on the three major questions posed in the Introduction: How was Mass introduced and propagated in China? At what levels, between whom, and on what questions did ritual interactions around Mass take place in late Ming and early Qing Chinese society? In comparison with the ritual in Europe, what was the inheritance and adaptation of the Mass in China? The first three sections in this chapter respond respectively to each of the three major questions, and the fourth one concludes, offering a prospect of further research in Catholic rituals in Chinese society.

1   Glocalization of Catholic Rituals in Chinese Society

As mentioned in the Introduction, after the historiographical shift in the twentieth century European medieval study began to focus on rituals' social dimension rather than theological one. In addition, Durkheim and some scholars in later generations considered a ritual a social act that concerns social cohesion. Among the group activities in medieval Europe, a ritual was an act of sociability.[1] As shown in the previous chapters, this book focuses on a social dimension of Mass, in order to explore Christianization in Chinese society and Sinicization of Catholic rituals. In addition, a theological dimension smoothly pervades this book as the scent of incense spreads in the celebration of Mass.

This book applies contextual studies to unfold a glimpse of the intriguing visage of ritual interactions between China and Europe. As regards this methodology, the introduction and propagation of Mass in Chinese society went through the transition of time, space, thinking modes, and languages, indicating a shift from an old context to a new one.[2] This dynamic process was like a wrestling between local Christian communities and the universal Church.[3] At present, only a few works have applied contextual studies to the history of Christian-

---

1   Palazzo, *Liturgie et société*, 14–15.
2   Hans Waldenfels, "Introduction," *Contextual Fundamental Theology*, trans. Susan Johnson (Paderborn: Ferdinand Schöningh, 2018), 27–30.
3   The metaphor of wrestling reminds people of Jacob's wrestling (Genesis 32:25). It is borrowed from Hans Waldenfels, see Waldenfels, "Introduction," 24.

ity in China.[4] In *The Nestorian Stele in Xi'an—Encounter between Christianity and Chinese Culture*, Xu Longfei raises inspiring questions about a notion translated into another language, a thought understood in another language, Christian salvation theory and theological notions introduced in Chinese culture, and the influence from contemporary mainstream religions.[5] Erik Zürcher suggests that the Catholic Church in China under the cultural imperative formed a recontextualized faith—a Confucian monotheism.[6] Yet, ritual interactions around Mass prove the foundation of Christendom in Chinese society rather than the formation of a Confucian monotheism.

Since their arrival in China, missionaries began to introduce Mass as the essential Catholic ritual. At the early stage, the Teaching of the Lord of Heaven required a strong ritual unity. All Christian communities across China celebrated Mass according to the same procedure. At the level of text, the early mission in China introduced basic knowledge pertaining to the Mass in paragraphs, sections, or chapters of books, such as *Brief Record of Holy Prayers* and *Brief Explanation of Catechism*. Since the seventeenth century, the Christian communities printed several monographs on the Mass, such as *The Meaning of the Sacrifice of Mass, Treatise on the Holy Body, The Classics of the Mass*, and *Answers to Questions about the Holy Body*. These monographs explained in detail the meaning, intention, procedure, and merits of Mass, providing instructions not only for priests but also for acolytes and congregants. The Mass was not propagated separately but related closely to Catholic dogmas and doctrines. The relation between Mass and Jesus' reception of suffering is most remarkable. From the late sixteenth century to the early seventeenth century, mainly missionaries discussed Mass. Later on, more and more Chinese Catholics joined the discussions, among whom Yang Tingyun, Zhou Zhi, and Xia Dachang made notable contributions. In the second half of the seventeenth century, the indigenous priest Wu Li wrote "The Musical Sound of Mass," a manual book on the Mass in the form of traditional Chinese music.

Ritual unity was required both in thoughts and in actions. At the level of practice, at first Mass was only celebrated among missionaries in China. As the

---

4 Xu Longfei, *Die nestorianische Stele in Xi'an. Begegnung von Christentum und chinesischer Kultur* (Bonn: Borengässer, 2004). Zhao Shilin 趙士林 and Duan Qi 段琦, ed., *Jidujiao zai Zhongguo: chujinghua de zhihui* 基督教在中國：處境化的智慧 (Beijing: Zongjiao wenhua chubanshe 宗教文化出版社, 2009). Li Wei 李韋, *Wu Leichuan de jidujiao chujinghua sixiang yanjiu* 吳雷川的基督教處境化思想研究 (Beijing: Zongjiao wenhua chubanshe 宗教文化出版社, 2010).
5 Xu Longfei, *Die nestorianische Stele in Xi'an. Begegnung von Christentum und chinesischer Kultur* (Bonn: Borengässer, 2004), 94.
6 Zürcher, "Jesuit Accommodation," 63–64.

conversion of Chinese people grew, the number of people who attended Mass increased. Gradually, the ritual space of Mass extended from a simple altar in a room to churches and chapels across the country. The Christian communities based in large cities were able to celebrate Mass according to the Catholic liturgical calendar. While for those based in small towns and villages, the celebration of Mass became infrequent because of the lack of priests, but remained highly meaningful to local Chinese Catholics. Missionaries exhorted Chinese Catholics to attend Mass by on the one hand explaining the rules of observing the day of worship, and on the other hand emphasizing various merits of attending Mass, especially the salvation of souls. Furthermore, with the propagation of Catholic funeral rituals, Chinese Catholics increasingly valued Mass said for deceased souls. By inviting a priest to celebrate Mass for a deceased, the family member brought the care of the souls of the deceased from the familial sphere into the ecclesiastical sphere.

As the ritual of an assembly, the celebration of Mass shaped and strengthened the Chinese convert's new identity as Catholic. In turn, the Chinese Catholics' practices, such as building churches and attending Masses, strengthened the Catholic Church's development in China. To study the Teaching of the Lord of Heaven as a Chinese marginal religion is an insightful perception,[7] which extends the exploration in this book not only from European missionaries to Chinese Catholics, but also from the Christian communities to Chinese society, including sympathizers of the Catholic Church, questioners, and anti-Catholics. Moreover, the comparison with Confucianism, Buddhism, Taoism, and popular religions helps to better elucidate the Teaching of the Lord of Heaven as a Chinese marginal religion.

Following the missionaries' correspondence and travels, this book's exploration extends to Europe, especially to Rome. Missionaries in China submitted various reports about rituals in the Catholic Church in China, including requests for privileges to adapt to the cultural imperative. Rome made decisions on these reports and missionaries brought the decisions to China. Through communications between China and Europe, the local Christian communities had ritual interactions with Rome not only about Catholic rituals but also about traditional Chinese rituals. Furthermore, the Catholic Church in Europe provides background and comparison for the study of the Catholic Church in China. As Peng Xiaoyu points out, in order to study the missionaries who came to China and Christianity in China, it is necessary to learn about the thoughts and cultures of evangelical orders such as the Society of Jesus in

---

7 Zürcher, "Jesuit Accommodation," 63.

a global context.[8] Since the Catholic Church in China was closely connected to Rome, ritual interactions around Mass had two dimensions: one within Chinese society, the other between China and Europe. The Christian communities in Chinese society tried to obtain ritual diversity, whereas Rome tried to maintain ritual unity in the universal Church. Ritual interactions around Mass unfolded the glocalization of Catholic rituals in Chinese society.[9]

With its cultural prosperity and religious diversity, Chinese society provided an environment conducive to ritual interactions. Being conducive does not mean that the environment was favorable to the introduction and propagation of Catholic rituals, but it did encourage and even compel the Catholic Church in China to produce a series of diverse and complex ritual interactions. Moreover, concrete traces of ritual interactions have been preserved to date. There are not only tangible materials, such as architectures and objects, but also abundant written materials, especially those written by Chinese people. Ritual interactions in this conducive environment are easier to explore in contrast to contemporary missions in other regions, such as the Christian communities in Paraguay and the Chiquitos in the seventeenth century. On the frontiers of Spanish territory in South America, the Jesuits attracted a number of indigenous peoples and achieved certain autonomy in local Christian communities built within the Spanish colonial empire. They built churches in combination of indigenous and European architectures; they recorded numbers of those who received baptism, communion, and confession. Yet, it is difficult to explore how local Catholics in Paraguay and the Chiquitos accepted and understood their Catholic faith, how they incorporated their new faith with their old world view and traditional beliefs.[10]

On the contrary, Chinese Catholics in local Christian communities wrote a number of texts in various forms and most are preserved. These precious sources reveal their daily discussions, thoughts, and practices of Catholic rituals. It is accessible to explore their understanding of Catholic rituals, their acceptance of their new faith, and their struggles to be Catholic and Chinese at the same time.

---

8   Peng Xiaoyu 彭小瑜, "Ai tianzhu zhi xiao mochenghu airen—quanqiushi yujing zhongde jindai zaoqi Yesuhui 愛天主之效, 莫誠乎愛人——全球史語境中的近代早期耶穌會," *Huazhong Normal University xuebao renwen shehui kexueban* 華中師範大學學報人文社會科學版 5 (2011): 47.
9   Pan Feng-chuan suggests reflecting on relationships between various cultures and those between various religions from a perspective of glocalization. Pan, *Xilai Kongzi*, 332.
10 Jackson, *Demographic Change*, 40–44.

2 Applications of the Metaphor of Weaving

This book has explored ritual interactions around Mass in diverse categories, from persons to objects, from the material to the spiritual, and from historical events to theological arguments. In all these categories, ritual interactions took place between the Mass and various cultural expressions of Chinese society, including traditional religion, architecture, art, literature, government, and theology. The exploration in these categories relates to three levels of religious expression in the inculturation of Catholicism in late Ming and early Qing China: the expression at the level of thought and theology; the expression at the level of action; the expression at the level of structure, organization, and personnel.[11] In this regard, the introduction and propagation of Mass was a vital part in the inculturation of the Catholic Church in Chinese society.

At the level of language, missionaries and Chinese Catholics borrowed words from Confucianism, Buddhism, and Taoism, such as benevolence (*ren'ai* 仁愛), worship day (*zhanli* 瞻禮), presence (*lin'ge* 臨格), merit (*gong* 功), and everlasting life (*changsheng* 常生). They also coined new Chinese terms, such as Mass (*misa* 彌撒), the Lord's day (*zhuri* 主日, Sunday), and the cabinet of the holy body (*shengti gui* 聖體櫃, tabernacle). They developed expressions with indigenous characteristics as well, such as the Great Father and Mother (*dafumu* 大父母), the Lord of Heaven Jesus (*tianzhu Yesu* 天主耶穌), and the hall of the Lord of Heaven (*tianzhu tang* 天主堂).

At the level of thought, missionaries introduced profound theological notions to Chinese Catholics, such as transubstantiation, the real presence of the Lord of Heaven, and the communion of merits. With paintings that illustrate the life of Christ, they vividly explained essential events, such as the reception of suffering and the institution of the Eucharist. The missionaries' method for introducing and propagating Mass related to their daily life in Chinese society. Aleni referred rice to explain why use bread at Mass; Verbiest referred the knowledge of astronomy and cannon which he used daily at the Qing court to explain the Host; and Wu Li used traditional Chinese music to explain a priest's act and allegorical explanation during Mass. After absorbing discussions with missionaries, Chinese Catholics, such as Yang Tingyun, Han Lin, Wang Zheng, and Li Jiugong, made new interpretation of the Lord of Heaven and of the relationship between the Lord of Heaven and human beings.

At the level of practice, the homily was delivered in Chinese right after Mass, occasionally by Chinese Catholics. The Christian communities cautiously kept

---

11   See Standaert, *L'«autre»*, 74.

gender segregation, with male and female Catholics attending Mass at separate ritual space and time. They actively sought indigenous liturgy and obtained the privilege of wearing sacrificial hat at Mass. The Jesuits invented the list of worship (*zhanlidan* 瞻禮單) by intertwining the Catholic liturgical calendar with the traditional Chinese one. They also introduced trilogy of aids for the dead—Mass, prayer, and almsgiving—into Chinese society as the most effective practices to express filial piety to deceased ancestors.

In the past, the voices from Chinese people were ignored in the study of the Catholic Church in late Ming and early Qing China.[12] Today, the field has gradually shifted its attention to their voices. Based on the abundant sources written in late Ming and early Qing, this book presents discussions on the four elements of worship from different groups and individuals in China and Europe, such as missionaries, Chinese Catholics, anti-Catholics, emperors, popes, and European theologians. Ritual interactions around Mass took place in various groups, such as between missionaries and Chinese Catholics, between missionaries from different religious orders, between local Christian communities in China and Rome, between missionaries and anti-Catholics. During interactions in these groups, discussions on the Mass transcended knowledge about Mass itself and expanded to various questions. The main actors in ritual interactions around Mass were missionaries and Chinese Catholics. They interacted with each other to achieve cooperation, and their cooperation faced opposition from two forces: a national force both from state and local anti-Catholics; and an international force from Rome, European theologians, and missionaries who opposed indigenous clergy and indigenous liturgy in China. The missionaries and the Chinese Catholics had to answer different questions from different groups. To Chinese society, they answered "Is Mass a usurpation of the worship of Heaven?" and "Is Heaven identical to the Lord of Heaven?" To Rome, "Why is it urgent to initiate indigenous clergy and indigenous liturgy?" To both Chinese society and Rome, "How to deal with traditional Chinese rituals such as sacrifice to ancestors?"

It is suitable to apply the metaphor of weaving a tapestry to stress the complexity and variety of ritual interactions. Different threads and fibers are connected in complex ways during the weaving process. This metaphor allows an examination of specific threads and fibers, as well as the whole piece of fabric.[13] I make ten applications of the metaphor of weaving with examples in ritual interactions around Mass below.[14]

---

12 Zürcher, "Jesuit Accommodation," 32.
13 Standaert, *The Interweaving of Rituals*, 220.
14 For the ten applications of the metaphor of weaving, see Standaert, *L'«autre»*, 122–123. For other metaphors of cultural interaction, see Standaert, *L'«autre»*, 120–121.

1. A fiber is detached from among others in one fabric and added to a part of another. This represents a concept being taken from existing contexts, and developed with a new interpretation in a new context. For example, heaven (*tian* 天) and the High Lord (*shangdi* 上帝) were detached from Neo-Confucianism and were interpreted as the object of Mass—the Lord of Heaven (*tianzhu* 天主), whose notion was based on heaven.
2. One fiber is removed and another fiber from the same thread is highlighted in its place. For example, the Christian communities forbade Chinese Catholics from asking ancestors for blessings while propagated the trilogy of aids for the dead.
3. An existent fiber is reenforced. For example, the Christian communities underlined filial piety, not only toward parents but even more toward the Great Father and Mother.
4. A new thread is introduced, but only after certain existing part has been pulled out: the Christian communities forbade Chinese Catholics from inviting Buddhist monks or Taoist priests to funerals while propagated Catholic funeral rituals with Mass at the core.
5. A new thread is introduced and is restored in its original status: the transliteration of Mass as "*misa* 彌撒" and of communion as "*gong mengyang* 共蒙仰."
6. A new thread is inserted into the existent fabric: a new idea, for instance that the celebrant of Mass is the intermediary between the Lord of Heaven and human beings; or a new interpretative element, for instance to consider Mass as the sacrificial ritual to the Great Father and Mother of all human beings.
7. A new thread replaces an old one with the same signification or function: a church replaced a Buddhist temple.
8. An existent thread receives a new color: Wu Li wrote "The Musical Sound of Mass" in the form of "*qu* 曲."
9. A new thread, woven into the existent fabric, receives a new context: the missionary's identity had been reshaped in Chinese society as the Western Confucianist, religious professional, and conspirator.
10. An existent thread is juxtaposed with a new one: the Jesuits invented the list of worship according to Catholic liturgical calendar and traditional Chinese one.

Finally, in addition to these ten applications, there is one more, that is, an existent fiber intertwines with a new one to form a new thread. The invention of the sacrificial hat is an outstanding example. On the one hand, the sacrificial hat was made to reconcile with the Chinese custom; on the other hand, only after obtaining the privilege from Rome could it be put into practice and only

Catholic priests in China could wear it; furthermore, the non-Catholic Chinese interpreted the sacrificial hat with social changes in late Ming, which strengthened the new thread. Another example is the communion of merits, the key notion to propagate Catholic rituals, formed by the intertwining of traditional Chinese notion of merit with Catholic teaching of the communion of saints.

As shown from these applications of the metaphor of weaving, ritual interactions around Mass took place in a diverse and dynamic process. Nevertheless, it is necessary to notice that these interactions were not woven into a perfect tapestry, which is always colorful and seamless. Certain interactions were threads and fibers which faded over time, such as the temporary usage of the Great Father and Mother and the wearing of the sacrificial hat. Certain interactions took place under strong forces which caused wrinkles and even tears in the fabric, such as conflicts within the Christian communities, local attacks from different religions, and persecutions from the state. Moreover, the weaving process did not follow a well-designed pattern. Certain interactions were unpredictable, such as the incidents between Mgr. Maigrot and local Catholics in Fuzhou; and certain results were uncontrollable, such as the Kangxi emperor's expulsion of missionaries.[15] In this diverse and dynamic process, ritual interactions around Mass enriched the fabric of religions in Chinese society.

In summary, the introduction and propagation of the Mass in Chinese society was a dynamic process that varied in times and regions. With complexity and variety, ritual interactions around Mass have begun the inculturation process of Catholic rituals in late Ming and early Qing, laying the foundation for inculturation in later generations. During ritual interactions, it was difficult to measure to what extent the Mass in China should inherit from the Catholic tradition and adapt to Chinese society.

3   Tension between Inheritance and Adaptation

With her organization, dogmatic formation, and liturgical ceremony closely connected to Greco-Roman culture, how can Catholicism enter Chinese culture without thrusting a foreign culture to Chinese people? Meanwhile, how can she adapt to this new culture without losing her doctrinal content? The two questions raised by Joseph Jennes summarize the tension in the Catholic

---

15   This notice is developed from the limits of the metaphor of weaving, see Standaert, *The Interweaving of Rituals*, 220–222.

Church in late Ming and early Qing.[16] Between the Catholic tradition and that of Chinese society, missionaries and Chinese Catholics made every effort to find a balance. During the introduction and propagation of Mass, they tried to interweave the inheritance of the Catholic Church with the adaptation to Chinese society. Confronted with the cultural imperative, the Catholic Church in China tried to measure the extent of inheritance and adaptation of Mass. The missionaries and Chinese Catholics reflected on their interactions with sympathizers of the Catholic Church, questioners, and anti-Catholics.

When introducing and propagating Mass in Chinese society, it is necessary to distinguish the orthodox and the pernicious. In consideration of cultural integration, James Watson suggests that the state in late Imperial China imposed a structure but not the content and promoted symbols not beliefs.[17] In this sense, orthopraxy became more important than orthodoxy to Chinese people: "Practice—correct performance—was infinitely more significant than adherence to a creed or a codified set of beliefs."[18] As regards Catholic rituals in late Imperial China, Watson's study and other scholars' further studies are inspiring. Certain cases show that in China proper procedure was more important than proper belief, while in Europe correct articulation of faith was more important than correct ritual practice.[19] Nevertheless, the distinction between orthopraxy and orthodoxy does not mean a total separation, because the actual process of rituals is very complex.[20]

In order to keep being orthodox in the context of the Catholic Church,[21] some missionaries opposed traditional Chinese rituals as well as adaptations of Catholic rituals. The mandate that forbade sacrifice to ancestors and sacrifice to Confucius, with the new lifestyle and strange practices, provoked conflicts at

---

16   Jennes, *Four centuries of catechetics*, 8. Erik Zürcher raises a similar question: to what extent can Christianity remove its European post-Renaissance shell and adapt to other cultures' thought-patterns, norms, and ritual lore without losing its identity? Zürcher, "Jesuit Accommodation," 63.

17   James Watson, "Standardizing the Gods: The Promotion of T'ien-hou ('Empress of Heaven') along the South China Coast, 960–1960," in *Popular Culture in Late Imperial China*, ed. David Johnson, Andrew J. Nathan, Evelyn S. Rawski (Berkeley: University of California Press, 1985), 323.

18   James Watson, "Orthopraxy Revisited," *Modern China* 33, 2007, 155.

19   Standaert, *The Interweaving of Rituals*, 36.

20   For a cultural paradox where Verbiest stressed on correct belief yet made correct praxis more important and that the Kangxi emperor insisted on correct expression of feeling yet disregarded correct practice, see Standaert, *The Interweaving of Rituals*, 182.

21   In the Catholic Church's context, orthodoxy means standard, correct doctrine and belief, while orthopraxy means to act and work according to correct doctrine; these two complement each other. *Christian Theological Lexicon*, 763.

local and state levels. Attacks on Catholic rituals in Chinese society focused not on Catholic rituals being barbarian (*yi* 夷) and foreign (*wai* 外) but on them being pernicious (*xie* 邪) and evil (*yin* 淫). According to Sun Shangyang, the Christian communities in Fujian in late Ming weighed orthopraxy more than orthodoxy, and the government cared about whether the practice and behavior of one religious group were orthodox more than the belief. Therefore, the Teaching of the Lord of Heaven and the government achieved conformity at least in the form, however, forbidding sacrifice to ancestors and sacrifice to Confucius contradicted the orthopraxy in the government's view, thus making the Teaching of the Lord of Heaven unorthodox and pernicious (*yiduan xiejiao* 異端邪教).[22]

Missionaries took two approaches to protect the young mission in crisis. One approach is to allow Chinese Catholics to perform certain traditional Chinese rituals; the other is to establish indigenous clergy and indigenous liturgy. Paul R. Katz points out that local elites and religious specialists used rituals to assert the legitimacy of their own interests. These two groups sometimes overlapped, for instance, some prominent Taoist priests were also local elites. Moreover, the belief and practice to worship gods need religious specialists to promote. For instance, the wide-spread cult of Bodhisattva Guanyin mainly relied on Buddhist monks and nuns.[23] In the Christian communities, Chinese Catholics who were local elites acted as the missionaries' strong supporters. In close collaboration, these two groups sought Rome's approval of the two approaches.

For the first approach, missionaries, mainly the Jesuits, interpreted that certain traditional Chinese rituals were political and moral obligations rather than religious ones, such as sacrifice to ancestors and sacrifice to Confucius. Chinese Catholics in various regions provided arguments to support this approach. For instance, Xia Dachang took most advantage of filial piety to build a connection between Mass and sacrifice to ancestors, that is, to take the sacrifice to honor parents as the introduction of the sacrifice to worship the Lord of Heaven. Benoît Vermander suggests that religions in China tend to become religion of interpretation (*quanshi de zongjiao* 詮釋的宗教), aimed at defining orthopraxy rather than orthodoxy.[24] To make interpretations, missionaries

---

22   Sun, "Zongjiao weishen," 24.
23   Paul R. Katz, "Orthopraxy and Heteropraxy beyond the State: Standardizing Ritual in Chinese Society," in *Modern China*, vol. 33 (2007): 75–76.
24   Benoît Vermander 魏明德, "Gaoxie de 'zongjiao tuichu' shuo yu Zhongguo zongjiao geju chonggou de zhexue sikao 高歇的 '宗教退出' 說與中國宗教格局重構的哲學思考," *Zhexue yu wenhua* 哲學與文化 (Taipei: Zhexue yu wenhua yuekan zazhishe 哲學與文化月刊雜誌社, Oct., 2011): 175.

and Chinese Catholics had to consider both the context of Chinese society and that of the Catholic Church. Nevertheless, some interpretations, such as Xia Dachang's, were considered dangerous in the Catholic Church in late Ming and early Qing.

As for the second approach, the establishment of indigenous clergy and indigenous liturgy in Japan around the sixteenth century served as a precedent for the mission in China. With the Counter-Reformation underway in Europe, the Jesuits made every effort to preserve orthodoxy of Catholic doctrines and rituals. According to Hélène Vu Thanh, despite certain necessary adaptations, the Jesuits intended to maintain the liturgy in Japan as practiced in Europe.[25] They were cautious about training Japanese Jesuits as the preparation for indigenous clergy, consequently, some Japanese Jesuits' maladaptation of the strict European training caused tension between them and their European brothers.[26] Yet, the precedent in Japan did not make adaptations in China any easier. Missionaries in China had different attitudes toward adaptations to Chinese society. In fact, the mission in China had a wider choice between the inheritance from the Catholic Church and the adaptation to Chinese society. The Christian communities in China did not endure persecutions as severe and violent as in Japan. Moreover, Confucianism, Buddhism, and Taoism shared "an open, flexible, and inclusive character" in Chinese society.[27] Nevertheless, the mission in China was unable to take full advantage of its wider choice.

Institutional religions in Chinese society can be divided into three categories: classical religions; universal salvific religions, such as Buddhism and Taoism; and comprehensive religions.[28] The Teaching of the Lord of Heaven had organizational strength, yet this strength hindered its spread in Chinese society. Although both Buddhism and the Teaching of the Lord of Heaven belonged to the second category of the institutional religion with a foreign origin, the former was much more widely spread than the latter. There are three explanations to the marginal status of the Teaching of the Lord of Heaven in Chinese society: xenophobia and conservative elements; cultural isolation; different modes of thought and the almost insurmountable incompatibility between ideas.[29] These three explanations are not sufficient though because Buddhism faced similar situation in Chinese society. As an institutional reli-

---

25 Vu Thanh, *Devenir japonais*, 230.
26 Cooper, *Rodrigues the Interpreter*, 176–177.
27 Yu Ying-shih, "Confucianism and China's Encounter with the West in Historical Perspective," *Dao: A Journal of Comparative Philosophy*, vol. 4, No. 2 (2005): 206.
28 Yang, *Religion in Chinese society*, 301.
29 Zürcher, "The Spread of Buddhism," 381–382.

gion of foreign origin, Buddhism went through much more severe persecutions than the Teaching of the Lord of Heaven yet continued to grow. Thus, Zürcher suggests a fourth explanation: the contrast of spontaneous diffusion versus guided propagation. Buddhism was developed by the spontaneous diffusion. The monastic system extended naturally and continuously as the surplus monks built new communities in new places, so Buddhism grew by many separate centers across China. The spread of Buddhism was "great institutional force, coupled with organizational weakness."[30] On the contrary, the spread of the Teaching of the Lord of Heaven was a guided propagation. Local Christian communities were in unity with each other and all were obedient to Rome. Yet, powerful instructions from Rome created obstacles to the Catholic Church in China, causing its weak growth in Chinese society.[31]

Missionaries and Chinese Catholics tried to vindicate the Teaching of the Lord of Heaven in Chinese society, yet their competence was limited by orders from Rome. Missionaries from different religious orders and Chinese Catholics from different regions kept asking Rome to approve indigenous liturgy, which was a long process full of ups and downs. Take the example of liturgical language used in the Catholic Church in China. Under the cultural imperative in Chinese society, missionaries witnessed how necessary it was for them to learn Chinese in order to communicate with Chinese people.[32] Yet, Rome and some missionaries in China were reluctant to the adaptation of liturgical language. The cautious and sometimes reluctant attitude toward adaptations was common in overseas missions around the seventeenth century. Rome and some missionaries worried that diverse adaptations in local Christian communities may threaten the unity in the universal Church, and that Catholic rituals may be syncretized with traditional rituals, thus losing Catholic characteristics. In the conclusion of his book on the Jesuit mission in Ethiopia, Andreu Martínez d'Alòs-Moner points out that the Jesuit missions in India, Japan, and Ethiopia were fragile in the seventeenth century. The foreign missionaries incited antipathy from traditional religious professionals and local officials in these powerful states. Meanwhile, mismanagement and quarrels arose inside the Society of Jesus. In addition, the Portuguese empire which was the primary supporter of the overseas missions was shrinking. Because of these internal and

---

30   Zürcher, "The Spread of Buddhism," 384–386.
31   Zürcher, "The Spread of Buddhism," 391.
32   Nicolas Standaert, "Christianity in Late Ming and Early Qing China as a Case of Cultural Transmission," in *China and Christianity: Burdened Past, Hopeful Future*, ed. Stephen Uhalley Jr. and Wu Xiaoxin (Armonk, New York: M.E. Sharpe, 2001), 84.

external causes, the Jesuits were expelled from India, Japan, and Ethiopia.[33] Then, d'Alòs-Moner suggests that the Jesuits had to accept significant compromises to continue the mission in China.[34] This suggestion seems to indicate that the Jesuits' adaptations in China were passive reactions to the tension they faced in Chinese society.

In fact, action and reaction were intertwined in ritual interactions, where the Jesuits, other missionaries, and their supporters in China and Europe made positive efforts. Since compromises are not the most desirable settlements, the missionaries considered some adaptations expedient, such as to use literary Chinese as liturgical language and to cover the priest's head during Mass. Nevertheless, even these expedient adaptations resulted in fruits of interactions, such as various ritual manuals in Chinese and the sacrificial hat. For the missionaries and Rome in the seventeenth century, the privileges pertaining to Catholic rituals and the tolerance of certain traditional Chinese rituals were temporarily given to local Christian communities, yet they did not know how long this situation would last. Through the interweaving of inheritance and adaptation, the Christian communities with effective rituals remained even after the expulsion of foreign missionaries.

Among these effective rituals, Mass was at the core in the Christian communities. Missionaries affirmed Mass as the most important and the ultimately noble ritual (*jizhong zhizun zhi li* 極重至尊之礼). Despite adaptations made under the cultural imperative, the introduction and propagation of the Mass in China complied with contemporary norms in Europe. Occasionally, certain points were controversial in Europe as well as in Chinese society, such as identifying the Lord of Heaven with heaven in the ancient Chinese classics. In general, no fundamental changes were made during the introduction and propagation. Chinese Catholics acknowledged Mass as the grand ritual of sacrifice to the Lord of Heaven (*ji tianzhu zhi dali* 祭天主之大禮). It is noteworthy that the importance of other Catholic rituals, such as baptism and confession, did not overshadow Mass at the core. Receiving baptism is the necessary condition for communion and confession is the proper preparation. Catholic rituals which were less open to public did not undergo any significant changes in China, such as Mass, baptism, and confession.[35] Fervent Catholics in China and those in Europe shared a number of similarities, such as their zeal for Mass, their adoration of the Host, and their reverence for the priest as exclusive cele-

---

33   Andreu Martínez d'Alòs-Moner, *Envoys of a Human God: The Jesuit Mission to Christian Ethiopia, 1557–1632* (Leiden: Brill, 2015), 343.
34   d'Alòs-Moner, *Envoys*, 344.
35   Standaert, *The Interweaving of Rituals*, 228.

brant of Mass. Moreover, some Chinese Catholics defended orthodox teachings and developed innovative interpretation of Mass. Confronted by various difficulties caused by differences between China and Europe, they managed to embrace and to preserve their faith in the tension. In this regard, Mass could be considered as having adapted to Chinese culture without losing its Catholic identity.

4   The Intermediary

The identity of missionaries and of Chinese Catholics were caught up between the Catholic tradition and the Chinese one, in which sense they were all intermediaries. Missionaries fell in the dilemma of multiple identities, while Chinese Catholics fell in the dilemma of being deprived of their old identity. The latter accepted their new identity as followers of the Teaching of the Lord of Heaven, which was professed and reinforced by participating in effective rituals, such as Mass. Some of them not only accepted the catechism and doctrines taught by the missionaries, but also made their own interpretation and innovative theological points which enriched the Catholic tradition. Yet, anti-Catholics claimed that the poor and uneducated Chinese were misled into the Teaching of the Lord of Heaven by lies and money. They denigrated Catholic literati more fiercely, because the literati were supposed to be the main force to support Confucianism, and their conversion to the Teaching of the Lord of Heaven was considered a thorough betrayal. Anti-Catholics thought that whenever a Chinese converted to the Catholic Church, he or she was not Chinese anymore.[36]

At state level, anti-Catholic movements in Chinese society did not result from xenophobia but from the concern that the Teaching of the Lord of Heaven was a threat to social stability and state security. In fact, Chinese Catholics were considered particularly dangerous, because their conversion to the Catholic Church was the betrayal of the Chinese tradition.[37] At local levels, on the one hand, Chinese Catholics participated in new rituals such as Mass and kept strange objects at home such as the list of worship; on the other hand, they were forbidden from attending certain important traditional Chinese rituals, including sacrifice to ancestors and sacrifice to Confucius. Performing sacrifice to ancestors was one principal obligation to the family and lineage and

---

36   Sun, *Mingmo tianzhujiao*, 244.
37   Standaert, "Case of cultural transmission," 114.

performing sacrifice to Confucius was one principal obligation to the officials of the state. A Chinese would face tremendous pressure to abandon either of these two rituals.[38] In this case, the Chinese Catholics' new identity threatened their old identity as a member of the family, of the local community, and even of the state.

Nevertheless, the new identity could reinforce the old one when the family or the local community converted to the Teaching of the Lord of Heaven, because local Chinese Catholics became more united when facing the outside pressure. Richard Madsen suggests that villages where the Teaching of the Lord of Heaven has been passed on for generations form a "quasi-ethnic" identity.[39] Chinese Catholics tried to be both true Chinese and true Catholic. Their double identity was shaped during interactions with non-Catholics as well as with missionaries. In interactions at the level of thought, as You Bin points out, the Confucian-Catholics selected and reinterpreted the ancient Chinese classics in order to weave them into the Catholic belief system. The Confucian-Catholics in late Ming and early Qing did not have to choose only one identity in the struggle of being Christian or Chinese Confucian.[40] Nevertheless, in interactions at the level of religious practice, as Henrietta Harrison shows, Chinese Catholics have faced the constant tension between following Chinese culture and the universal Church.[41] Catholic families and villages have passed on their faith as a heritage from their ancestors for generations. Yet, the Teaching of the Lord of Heaven is still a foreign or Western religion to many Chinese people. After taking root for hundreds of years, the Catholic Church is still marginal in Chinese society and being confronted with various difficulties.

Devoted to the research of Catholic rituals in late Ming and early Qing, researchers enter their subject's context through diverse sources. They listen to dialogues between different groups at different levels, thus discovering their own voices in the research. In this sense, researchers can be considered intermediaries as well. From collecting sources to discussing questions, these modern intermediaries face much tension. For example, I intend to translate the Chinese texts more literally yet sometimes end up sacrificing accuracy for fluency or clarity. Translating words and phrases which express Catholic teaching yet also have strong connotations of traditional Chinese thoughts is most challenging. When I am struggling through these challenges, my appreciation and sympathies for the missionaries and Chinese Catholics increase. As challenging

---

38   Zürcher, "Jesuit Accommodation," 31.
39   Madsen, *China's Catholics*, 57.
40   You, "Hetian," 33.
41   Harrison, *The Missionary's Curse*, 33.

as it is, the research of Catholic rituals in Chinese society is very promising, with diverse themes and objects from the sacraments to daily prayers, with a large perspective from local to global history, with a wide time frame from late Ming to today. The harvest is abundant but the laborers are few (Mt 9:37); continuations, interruptions, and renewals during hundreds of years await research in depth. Considering the church history, four hundred years is not long enough to draw a final conclusion from the history of Christianity in China, with her on-going interactions. Meanwhile, these four hundred years provide the Catholic Church in China today lessons, courage, and hope.

Bibliography

Aleni, Giulio 艾儒略. *Tianzhu shengjiao sizi jingwen* 天主聖教四字經文 [*Four Character Classic of the Lord of Heaven's Holy Teaching*]. in CCT ARSI, vol. 2, 297–384.

Aleni, Giulio 艾儒略. *Tianzhu jiangsheng chuxiang jingjie* 天主降生出像經解 [*Explanation of the Incarnation and Life of the Lord of Heaven*]. in CCT ARSI, vol. 3, 527–582, 2002.

Aleni, Giulio 艾儒略. *Misa jiyi* 彌撒祭義 [*The Meaning of the Sacrifice of Mass*]. in CCT BnF, vol. 16, 467–632.

Aleni, Giulio 艾儒略. *Shengti yaoli* 聖體要理 [*Treatise on the Holy Body*]. in CCT BnF, vol. 18, 229–288.

Aleni, Giulio 艾儒略. *Misa jiyi lüe* 彌撒祭義畧 [*Abridged Meaning of the Sacrifice of Mass*]. *Tongku jingji* 痛苦經蹟 [*The Prayers of Sufferings*], in TZJDCWXSB, vol. 3, fol. 23a–fol. 28a3, 1181–1191.

Aquinas, Thomas. *Summa Theologiae*. Steubenville, Ohio: St. Paul Center, accessed January 28, 2021. https://aquinas.cc/la/en/~ST.I.

Amsler, Nadine. *Jesuits and Matriarchs: Domestic Worship in Early Modern China*. Seattle: University of Washington Press, 2018.

Anon. *Huigui zongyao* 會規總要 [*Summary of Confraternity Statutes*]. in CCT ARSI, vol. 12, 471–494.

Anon. *Misa lijie* 彌撒禮節 [*The Exposition of Mass*]. in *The Prayers of Sufferings* [*Tongku jingji* 痛苦經蹟], 1147–1180.

Anon. *Misa guanyi* 彌撒冠儀 [*The Regulation of the Cap of Mass*]. in SCCT ZKW, vol. 5, 623–634.

Anon. *Sheng Fangjigehui gui* 聖方濟各會規 [*Statutes of Confraternity of St. Francis Xavier*]. in CCT ARSI, vol. 12, 479–488.

Anon. *Shengjiao rike* 聖教日課 [*Daily Services of the Holy Teaching*]. BnF Chinois 7353–7354.

Anon. *Shengtihui gui* 聖體會規 [*Statutes of Confraternity of the Holy Body*]. in CCT BnF, vol. 20, 253–281.

Anon. *Taixi Yin Juesi xiansheng xinglüe* 泰西殷覺斯先生行畧 [*Life of Master Prosper Intorcetta from the Great West*]. in CCT BnF, vol. 12, 595–611.

Anon. *Tianzhu jiaoyao* 天主教要 [*Catechism of the Lord of Heaven*]. in CCT ARSI, vol. 1, 307–374.

Anon., and Rui de Figueiredo 費樂德, SJ. *Tianzhu shengjiao nianjing zongdu* 天主聖教念經總牘 [*General Collection of Prayer Recitation in the Holy Teaching of the Lord of Heaven*]. CCT BAV (1), vol. 16, 1–478.

Anon. *Tonggong dan* 通功單 [*Cards of the Communion of Merits*]. CCT BnF, vol. 18, 631–635.

Anon., OFM. *Tonggong shenke* 通功神課 [*Spritual Practice to Communicate Merits*].

Shengjiao zongdu 聖教總牘 [*General Collection of Prayers in the Holy Teaching*], juan 1, fol. 33a1–fol. 34a4, in CCT BAV (1), vol. 44, 91–93.

Anon., OFM. *Wuxie yi* 五謝禮 [Rite of Five Thanks]. *Shengjiao zongdu* 聖教總牘 [*General Collection of Prayers in the Holy Teaching*], juan 1, fol. 1b1–6, in CCT BAV (1), vol. 44, 22.

Anon. "Un pratique liturgique propre à la Chine: Le *ji jin* 祭巾 ou bonnet de messe." *Bulletin catholique de Pékin* 11 (1924): 376–377, 404–406.

Atsutoshi Hamashima 濱島敦俊. *Mingqing Jiangnan nongcun shehui yu minjian xinyang* 明清江南農村社會與民間信仰 [*Folk Religion in Rural Society in Jiangnan during the Ming and Qing Periods*]. Translated by Zhu Haibin 朱海濱. Xiamen: Xiamen University Press 廈門大學出版社, 2008.

Augery, Humbert 洪度貞. *Shengmuhui gui* 聖母會規 [*Statutes of Confraternity of the Holy Mother*]. in CCT ARSI, vol. 12, 439–462.

Augery, Humbert 洪度貞. *Tianzhu Yesu kuhui gui* 天主耶穌苦會規 [*Statutes of Confraternity of the Lord of Heaven Jesus' Suffering*]. in CCT ARSI, vol. 12, 463–470.

Augustinus. *De civitate Dei*, tomus II, libri XIV. Caroli Tauchnitii, 1825.

Bailey, Gauvin Alexander. "The Image of Jesus in Chinese Art during the Time of the Jesuit Missions (16th–18th Centuries)." in *The Chinese face of Jesus Christ*, vol. 2, edited by Roman Malek. 395–415. Netteltal: Steyler Verlag, 2003.

Basset, Jean. *Jean Basset (1662–1707), pionnier de l'église au Sichuan, précurseur d'une église d'expression chinoise: correspondance (oct. 1701–oct. 1707), avis sur la Mission de Chine (1702)*. Éditions You Feng Librairie & Éditeur, 2012.

Bell, Catherine. *Ritual: Perspectives and Dimensions*. New York: Oxford University Press, 1997.

Bernard, SJ, Henri. *Le père Matthieu Ricci et la société chinoise de son temps (1552–1610)*. Tientsin [Tianjin]: Hautes études, 1937.

Bernard, SJ, Henri. *Les Adaptations chinoises d'ouvrages européens: Bibliographie chronologique depuis la venue des Portugais à Canton jusqu'à la mission française de Pékin 1514–1688*. Monumenta serica, vol. 10, 1945.

Bontinck, François. *La Lutte autour de la liturgie chinoise aux XVIIe et XVIIIe siècles*. Louvain et Paris Nauwelaerts et Béatrice-Nauwelaerts, 1962.

Books of the Bible. United States Conference of Catholic Bishops, accessed January 28, 2021. https://bible.usccb.org/bible.

Bornet, SJ, Paul. "L'apostolat laïque en Chine aux XVIIe et XVIIIe siècles." *Bulletin catholique de Pékin* 35 (Pékin: Imprimerie des Lazaristes du Pei-t'ang, 1948): 41–67.

Brancati, Francesco 潘國光. *Shengjiao sigui* 聖教四規 [*Four Rules of the Holy Teaching*]. in CCT ARSI, vol. 5, 257–300.

Brancati, Francesco 潘國光. *Shengti guiyi* 聖體規儀 [*Ritual Rules of the Holy Body*]. in CCT BnF, vol. 18, 303–373.

Brancati, Francesco 潘國光. *Tianshen huike* 天神會課 [*Statutes of the Confraternity of the Angels*]. in CCT BnF, vol. 20, 1–162.

Brancati, Francesco 潘國光, and Girolamo de Gravina 賈宜睦. *Sheng An-de-le zongtu zhanli* 聖安德肋宗徒瞻礼 [*A Day of Worship for St. Andrew etc.*]. CCT BnF, vol. 17, 99–378.

Brockey, Liam Matthew. "Illuminating the Shades of Sin: The Society of Jesus and Confession in Seventeenth-Century China." in *Forgive Us Our Sins: Confession in Late Ming and Early Qing China*. Edited by Nicolas Standaert and Ad Dudink. 129–181, Monumenta Serica Monograph Series LV, Sankt Augustin: Institut Monumenta Serica, 2006.

Brockey, Liam Matthew. *Journey to the East: The Jesuit Mission to China, 1579–1724*. Cambridge: Harvard University Press, 2008.

Brockey, Liam Matthew, and Ad Dudink. "A Missionary Confessional Manual: José Monteiro's *Vera et Unica Praxis breviter ediscendi, ac expeditissime loquendi Sinicum idioma*." in *Forgive Us Our Sins: Confession in Late Ming and Early Qing China*. Edited by Nicolas Standaert and Ad Dudink. 183–239, Monumenta Serica Monograph Series LV, Sankt Augustin: Institut Monumenta Serica, 2006.

Brook, Timothy. *Praying for Power: Buddhism and the Formation of Gentry Society in Late-Ming China*. Cambridge, MA: Harvard University Press, 1993.

Brou, A. "Notes pour servir à l'histoire des origines du clergé indigène en Chine." *Revue d'histoire des missions* 3 (Paris: Amis des missions, 1926): 519–540; (1927): 391–406.

Brou, A. "Le développement des églises de Chine." *Revue d'histoire des missions* 13 (Paris: Amis des missions, 1936): 283–294.

Brunner, Paul. "La Messe chinoise du Père Hinderer." *Neue Zeitschrift für Missionswissenschaft* 15 (1959): 271–284.

Brunner, Paul. *L'euchologe de la mission de Chine: Editio princeps 1628 et développements jusqu'à nos jours (Contribution à l'histoire des livres de prières)*. Münster: Aschendorffsche, 1964.

Buglio, Lodovico 利類思. *Shengshi lidian* 聖事禮典 [*Ritual Manual for Sacraments*]. in CCT ARSI, vol. 11, 305–598.

Buglio, Lodovico 利類思. *Siduo dianyao* 司鐸典要 [*Instructions of the Priest*]. in CCT BnF, vol. 19, 1–144.

Buglio, Lodovico 利類思. *Misa jingdian* 彌撒經典 [*The Classics of the Mass*]. SCCT ZKW, vol. 15, 1–718,

Bürkler, Xaver. *Die Sonn-und Festtagsfeier in der katholischen Chinamission: Eine geschichtlich pastorale Untersuchung*. Roma: Herder, 1942.

Chan, SJ, Albert. "Towards a Chinese Church: The Contribution of Philippe Couplet S.J. (1622–1693)." in *Philippe Couplet, S.J. (1623–1693): The Man Who Brought China to Europe*, edited by Jeroom Heyndrickx. 55–86, Monumenta Serica Monograph Series XXII, Nettetal: Steyler Verlag, 1990.

Chan, SJ, Albert. "Johann Adam Schall in the Pei-Yu Lu of T'an Ch'ien and in the Eyes of His Contemporaries." in *Western Learning and Christianity in China: The Contribution and Impact of Johann Adam Schall von Bell, S.J. (1592–1666)*, vol. 1, edited by Roman Malek, SVD. 273–301, Monumenta Serica monograph series XXXV, Nettetal: Steyler Verlag, 1998.

Chan, SJ, Albert. *Chinese Books and Documents in the Jesuit Archives in Rome: A Descriptive Catalogue: Japonica-Sinica I–IV*. Armonk&London: M.E. Sharpe, 2002.

Chen Zhanshan 陳占山, annot. *Budeyi fu erzhong 不得已附二種 [I Cannot Do Otherwise]*. Hefei: Huangshan shushe 黃山書社, 2000.

Chaves, Jonathan. *Singing of the Source: Nature and God in the Poetry of the Chinese Painter Wu Li*. Honolulu: University of Hawaii press, 1993.

Chen Hu 陳瑚. "*Congyouji* xu 從遊集序 [Preface to *Anthology of Visiting and Studying*]." in *Wu Yushan ji, juanshou*, 13–14.

Chen Yuan 陳垣. "Wu Yushan jinduo 250 nian jinian 吳漁山晉鐸二百五十年紀念 [In Commemoration of Wu Yushan's 250th Anniversary of his Ordination to Priesthood]." in *Wu Yushan (Li) yanjiu lunji* 吳漁山（歷）研究論集 [*Collection of Research Essays on Wu Yushan (Li)*], edited by Zhou Kangxie 周康燮. 35–58, Hongkong: Chongwen shudian 崇文書店, 1971.

Chen Yuan 陳垣. "Wu Yushan nianpu 吳漁山年譜 [Chronological Biography of Wu Yushan]." in *Wu Yushan (Li) yanjiu lunji* 吳漁山（歷）研究論集 [*Collection of Research Essays on Wu Yushan (Li)*], edited by Zhou Kangxie 周康燮. 1–28, Hongkong: Chongwen shudian 崇文書店, 1971.

Chen Yuan 陳垣, ed. *Kangxi yu Luoma shijie guanxi wenji* 康熙與羅馬使節關係文集 [*Collection of Documents about Relationship between the Kangxi Emperor and Ambassador from Rome*]. Taipei: Wenhai chubanshe 文海出版社, 1974.

Chen Yidian 陳懿典. "*Nangong shudu* xu 南宮署牘序 [Preface to *Documents of the South Palace*]." fol. 1–fol. 11, in *Nangong shudu* 南宮署牘 [*Documents of the South Palace*], juan 1.

Ciyuan 辭源 [*Dictionary of Etymology*]. Beijing: The Commercial Press 商務印書館, 1979.

Collani, Claudia von. "Jing Tian—The Kangxi Emperor's Gift to Ferdinand Verbiest in the Rites Controversy." in *Ferdinand Verbiest (1623–1688): Jesuit Missionary, Scientist, Engineer and Diplomat*, edited by John W. Witek. 453–470, Monumenta Serica Monograph Series XXX, Nettetal: Steyler Verlag, 1994.

Collani, Claudia von. "Charles Maigrot's Role in the Chinese Rites Controversy." in *The Chinese Rites Controversy: Its History and Meaning*, edited by D.E. Mungello. 149–183, Monumenta Serica Monograph Series XXXIII, Nettetal: Steyler Verlag, 1994.

Collani, Claudia von. "Parishes, Priests and Lay People: Christian Communities as Described in the Neue Welt-Bott." in *A Life Long Dedication to the China Mission: Essays Presented in Honor of Father Jeroom Heyndrickx CICM, on the Occasion of His*

75th Birthday and the 25th Anniversary of the F. Verbiest Institute, K.U.Leuven, edited by Noël Golvers and Sara Lievens. 669–704, Leuven Chinese studies XVII, Leuven: Ferdinand Verbiest Institute, K.U.Leuven, 2007.

Collins, Randall. *Interaction Ritual Chains*. New Jersey: Princeton University Press, 2004.

Cooper, SJ, Michael. *Rodrigues the Interpreter: An Early Jesuit in Japan and China*. New York and Tokyo: Weatherhill, 1974.

Couplet, Philippe 柏應理. *Tianzhu shengjiao yongzhanlidan* 天主聖教永瞻禮單 [*Eternal List of Worship of the Holy Teaching of the Lord of Heaven*]. in CCT BnF, vol. 20, 575–580.

Couplet, Philippe 柏應理. *Tianzhu shengjiao baiwenda* 天主聖教百問答 [*One Hundred Questions and Answers of the Lord of Heaven's Holy Teaching*]. in CCT BnF, vol. 24, 213–250.

Couplet, Philippe 柏應理. *Histoire d'une dame chrétienne de la Chine où par occasion les usages de ces peuples, l'établissement de la religion, les manieres des missionaires, & les exercices de pieté des nouveaux chrétiens sont expliquez*. Paris: Estienne Michallet, 1688.

Criveller, Gianni. *Preaching Christ in Late Ming China*. Taipei: Taipei Ricci Institute, 1997.

Criveller, Gianni. "Christ Introduced to Late Ming China by Giulio Aleni S.J. (1582–1649)." in *The Chinese face of Jesus Christ*, vol. 2, edited by Roman Malek. 437–460, Netteltal: Steyler Verlag, 2003.

Cullen, Christopher, and Catherine Jami. "Christmas 1668 and After: How Jesuit Astronomy Was Restored to Power in Beijing." *Journal for the History of Astronomy* 51:1 (2020): 3–50.

da Rocha, João 羅儒望. *Song nianzhu guicheng* 誦念珠規程 [*Regulation of Reciting the Beads*]. in CCT ARSI, vol. 1, 515–574.

da Rocha, João 羅儒望. *Tianzhu shengjiao qimeng* 天主聖教啓蒙 [*Rudiments of the Holy Teaching of the Lord of Heaven*]. in CCT ARSI, vol. 1, 375–514.

Darrobers, Roger. *Zhu Xi et la synthèse confucéenne*. Paris: Éditions Points, 2016.

de la Piñuela, Pedro 石鐸琭. *Sheng Fanjige disanhui gui* 聖方濟各第三會規 [*Statutes of Confraternity of the Third Order of St. Francis*]. in CCT BnF, vol. 20, 163–212.

de la Piñuela, Pedro 石鐸琭. *Aijin lianling shuo* 哀矜煉靈說 [*Description of Mercy on Souls in Purgatory*]. in CCT BnF, vol. 24, 251–272.

de la Piñuela, Pedro 石鐸琭. *Shengti aoyi* 聖體奧義 [Holy Body's Mysterious Meaning]. *Shengjiao zongdu* 聖教總牘 [*General Collection of Prayers in the Holy Teaching*], juan 5, fol. 39a3–fol. 41b5, in CCT BAV (1), vol. 44, 641–646.

de la Piñuela, Pedro 石鐸琭. *Ling shengti wenda* 領聖體問答 [Questions & Answers of Receiving the Holy Body]. *Shengjiao zongdu* 聖教總牘 [*General Collection of Prayers in the Holy Teaching*], juan 5, fol. 41b7–fol. 45a4, in CCT BAV (1), vol. 44, 646–653.

de Gassart, D. "Esquisse historique sur les congrégations de la Sainte Vierge dans l'ancienne mission de Chine (1609–1664)." *Collectanea commissionis synodalis in Sinis* 8 (Peking: Commissio synodalis in Sinis, 1935): 34–441.

de Mailla, Joseph 馮秉正. *Shengti ren'aijing guitiao* 聖體仁愛經規條 [*Rules of Prayer to the Holy Body's Benevolence*]. in CCT BnF, vol. 20, 283–386.

de Pantoja, Diego 龐迪我. *Pangzi yiquan* 龐子遺詮 [*Explanations left by Master de Pantoja*]. in CCT ARSI, vol. 2, 1–252.

Dehergne, Joseph. *Les Missions du Nord de la Chine vers 1700. Étude de géographie missionnaire* (Rome: Archivum Historicum Societatis Iesu, 1955): 291–294.

Dehergne, Joseph. *La Chine centrale vers 1700. II. Les vicariats apostoliques de la côte. Étude de géographie missionnaire* (Rome: Archivum Historicum Societatis Iesu, 1961): 307–366.

Dehergne, Joseph. *La Chine du Sud-Est: Guangxi (Kwangsi) et Guangdong (Kwuangtung). Étude de géographie missionnaire* (Rome: Archivum Historicum Societatis Iesu, 1976): 3–55.

Dentrecolles, François-Xavier. "Lettre du Père d'Entrecolles, missionnaire de la Compagnie de Jésus, au Père procureur-général des missions des Indes et de la Chine." *Lettres édifiantes et curieuses, écrites des Missions étrangères, par quelques missionnaires de la Compagnie de Jésus*, edited by Charles Le Gobien, vol. 10, 119–155, Paris: Jean Barbou, 1713.

Dias, Manuel 陽瑪諾. *Tang jingjiao beisong zhengquan* 唐景教碑頌正詮 [*True Commentary on the Tang Nestorian Monument*]. in CCT BnF, vol. 23, 1–22.

Dias, Manuel 陽瑪諾. *Shengjing zhijie* 聖經直解 [*Direct Explanation of Sacred Scripture*] (*mulu, juan* 1–2). in CCT BAV (1), vol. 17, 287–624.

Dias, Manuel 陽瑪諾. *Qingshi jinshu* 輕世金書 [*Golden Book with Contempt of the World*]. S.L.: S.N., 1848.

Dias, Manuel 陽瑪諾, Wenceslaus Pantaleon Kirwitzer, and Nicolas Trigault. *Histoire de ce qui s'est passé à la Chine, tirée des lettres escrites és années 1619. 1620. & 1621, adressées au R.P. Mutio Vitelleschi, general de la Compagnie de Iesus: Traduicte de l'Italien en François par le P. Pierre Morin de la mesme Compagnie*. Paris: Sébastien Cramoisy, 1625.

Dictionnaire de théologie catholique, tome troixième. Paris: 1908.

Dictionnaire de théologie catholique, tome septième (deuxième partie). Paris: 1923.

Dictionnaire de théologie catholique, tome dixième (première partie). Paris: 1928.

Dictionnaire Français-Chinois 法漢詞典. Shanghai: Shanghai yiwen chubanshe 上海譯文出版社, 1978.

Ding Fubao 丁福保, ed. *Foxue dacidian* 佛學大辭典 [*The Great Dictionary of Buddhism*]. Beijing: Wenwu chubanshe 文物出版社, 1984.

Ding Zhilin 丁志麟. *Yang Qiyuan xiansheng chaoxing shiji* 楊淇園先生超性事蹟 [*Supernatural Events of Mr. Yang Qiyuan*]. in CCT ZKW, vol. 1, 217–238.

Dong Gao 董誥, comp. *Quan Tangwen* 全唐文 [*Complete Collection of All Surviving Prose Literature in the Tang Dynasty*]. Qing Jiaqing neifu keben 清嘉慶內府刻本, Eruson.

Dong Shaoxin 董少新, and Liu Geng 劉耿, trans., annot. "1618 nian Yesuhui Zhongguo nianxin yizhu bing xu shang 1618年耶穌會中國年信譯注並序（上）[Translation, Annotation and Introduction of the Annual Letter of 1618 of the Society of Jesus in China]." *Guoji hanxue* 國際漢學 [*International Sinology*] 4 (2017): 133–204.

Du Halde, Jean-Baptiste 杜赫德, ed. *Yesuhuishi Zhongguo shujianji* 耶穌會士中國書簡集 [*Collection of Letters from China Written by the Jesuits*]. Vol. 1, translated by Zheng Dedi 鄭德弟 and Zhu Jing 朱靜. Zhengzhou: 大象出版社 Elephant Press, 2001.

Dudink, Ad, and Nicolas Standaert. Chinese Christian Texts Database (CCT-Database) https://www.arts.kuleuven.be/sinologie/english/cct.

Dudink, Ad. "*Shengchao Zuopi* (1623) by Xu Dashou: the Date and Background of the Longest Anti-Christian Essay of Late Ming Times." in *Christianity in Late Ming China: Five Studies*, 227–271, PhD thesis: University of Leiden, 1995.

Dudink, Ad. "*Nangong Shudu* (1620), *Poxie Ji* (1640), and Western Reports on the Nanjing Persecution (1616/1617)." *Monumenta Serica* 48: 1 (2000): 133–265.

Dudink, Ad. "The Image of Xu Guangqi as Author of Christian Texts: A Bibliographical Appraisal." in *Statecraft and Intellectual Renewal in Late Ming China: The Cross-Cultural Synthesis of Xu Guangqi (1562–1633)*, edited by Catherine Jami, Peter Engelfriet, and Gregory Blue. 99–152, Leiden: Brill, 2001.

Dudink, Ad. "The Holy Mass in Seventeenth-and Eighteenth-Century China: Introduction to and Annotated Translation of 與彌撒功程 (1721), Manual for Attending Mass." in *A Life Long Dedication to the China Mission: Essays Presented in Honor of Father Jeroom Heyndrickx, CICM, on the Occasion of His 75th Birthday and the 25th Anniversary of the F. Verbiest Institute, K.U.Leuven*, edited by Noël Golvers and Sara Lievens. Leuven Chinese studies XVII, 207–326, Leuven: Ferdinand Verbiest Institute, K.U.Leuven, 2007.

Dudink, Ad. "Sacramental Initiation in Matteo Ricci's Mission." in *Scienza, Ragione, Fede: Il genio di Padre Matteo Ricci*, edited by Claudio Giuliodori. 189–197, Macerata: Edizioni universita di Macerata, 2012.

Dujardin, Carine. *Missionering en moderniteit. De Belgische minderbroeders in China 1872–1940*. KADOC-Studies 19, Leuven: Leuven University Press, 1996.

Dunyn-Szpot, Thomas-Ignatius, ms. *Hist. Sin. 1610–1625*, ARSI, Jap. Sin. 107.

Eliade, Mircea, ed. *The Encyclopedia of Religion*. Volume 12, New York: Macmillan Publishing Company, 1987.

Fan Zhong 范中. *Tianzhu shengjiao xiaoyin* 天主聖教小引 [*Brief Introduction to the Holy Teaching of the Lord of Heaven*]. in CCT BnF, vol. 7, 1–24.

Fang Hao 方豪. "Wu Yushan xiansheng *Tianyue zhengyinpu* jiaoshi 吳漁山先生《天樂正音譜》校釋 [Revision and Annotation of the *Compendium of Orthodox Sounds of Heavenly Music* by Master Wu Yushan]." *Fang Hao liushi zidinggao* 方豪六十自定稿

[*Collected Works of Fang Hao Revised and Edited by the Author on His 60th Birthday*], 1627–1642, Taipei: Taiwan xuesheng shuju 臺灣學生書局, 1969.

Fang Hao 方豪. "Zhuri misa jingdian zixu 主日彌撒經典自序 [The Author's Preface to *The Classics of the Mass on Sundays*]." *Fang Hao liushi zidinggao* 方豪六十自定稿 [*Collected Works of Fang Hao Revised and Edited by Himself on His 60th Birthday*], 2243–2244, Taipei: Taiwan xuesheng shuju 臺灣學生書局, 1969.

Fang Hao 方豪. "Wu Yushan shenfu lingxi niandai, jinduo didian ji ladingwen zaoyi kao 吳漁山神父領洗年代、晉鐸地點及拉丁文造詣考 [Research on the Year of Fr. Wu Yushan's Baptism, Place of His Ordination to Priesthood, and His Level of Latin]." in *Wu Yushan (Li) yanjiu lunji* 吳漁山（歷）研究論集 [*Collection of Research Essays on Wu Yushan (Li)*], edited by Zhou Kangxie 周康燮. 131–140, Hongkong: Chongwen shudian 崇文書店, 1971.

Fang Hao 方豪. "Wu Yushan xiansheng *Sanba ji* jiaoshi 吳漁山先生《三巴集》校釋 [Revision and Annotation of *Anthology of the Church St. Paul* by Master Wu Yushan]." in *Wu Yushan (Li) yanjiu lunji* 吳漁山（歷）研究論集 [*Collection of Research Essays on Wu Yushan (Li)*], edited by Zhou Kangxie 周康燮. 103–116, Hongkong: Chongwen shudian 崇文書店, 1971.

Fang Hao 方豪. "Wu Yushan xiansheng *Sanyu ji* jiaoshi 吳漁山先生《三餘集》校釋 [Revision and Annotation of *Anthology of Leisure Times* by Master Wu Yushan]." in *Wu Yushan (Li) yanjiu lunji* 吳漁山（歷）研究論集 [*Collection of Research Essays on Wu Yushan (Li)*], edited by Zhou Kangxie 周康燮. 85–102, Hongkong: Chongwen shudian 崇文書店, 1971.

Fang Hao 方豪. *Zhongxi jiaotongshi* 中西交通史 [*History of Communications between China and the West*]. Changsha: Yuelu shushe 嶽麓書社, 1987.

Fang Hao 方豪. *Zhongguo tianzhujiaoshi renwu zhuan* 中國天主教史人物傳 [*Biographies of Historical Persons in Chinese Catholic History*]. Beijing: Zhonghua shuju 中華書局, 1988.

Faure, David 科大衛. *Mingqing shehui yu liyi* 明清社會與禮儀 [*Society and Rituals in Ming and Qing*]. Translated by Zeng Xianguan 曾憲冠. Beijing: Beijing Normal University Press 北京師範大學出版社, 2016.

Feliciano, Pacheco 成際理. *Shengjiao guicheng* 聖教規程 [*Ordinances of the Holy Teaching*]. Hubert Germain Verhaeren, "Ordonnances de la Sainte Église," *Monumenta serica* 4 (1939–1940): 469–477.

Feng Yingjing 馮應京. "*Tianzhu shiyi* xu 天主實義序 [Preface to *The True Meaning of the Lord of Heaven*]." in DCFY, vol. 2, 26–28.

Feuchtwang, Stephan. *The Imperial Metaphor: Popular Religion in China*. New York: Routledge, 1992.

Fouquet, Jean-François. "Lettre du Père Fouquet, missionnaire de la Compagnie de Jésus, à monseigneur le duc de la Force, pair de France." in *Lettres édifiantes et curieuses, écrites des Missions étrangères, par quelques missionnaires de la Compagnie de Jésus*, vol. 5, edited by Charles Le Gobien. 129–238, Paris: Nicolas Le Clerc, 1708.

Froger, François. *Relation du premier voyage des François à la Chine fait en 1698, 1699 et 1700 sur le vaisseau „L'Amphitrite"*. Edited by E.A. Voretzsch. Leipzig: Verlag der Asia major, 1926.

Fu Jen Theological Publications Association 輔仁神學著作編譯會. *Jiduzongjiao waiyu Hanyu shenxue ciyu huibian* 基督宗教外語漢語神學詞語彙編 [*A Foreign Languages-Chinese Christian Theological Lexicon of Terms and Persons*]. Shanghai: Guangqi Press 天主教上海教區光啟社, 2007.

Gernet, Jacques. *Chine et christianisme Action et réaction*. Paris: Gallimard, 1982.

Golvers, Noël. *François de Rougemont, S.J., Missionary in Ch'ang-Shu (Chiang-Nan): A Study of the Account Book (1674–1676) and the Elogium*. Leuven: Leuven University Press, 1999.

Goossaert, Vincent, and Valentine Zuber. "Introduction: La Chine a-t-elle connu l'anticléricalisme?" *Extrême-Orient Extrême-Occident* 24 (2002): 5–16.

Goossaert, Vincent. *Dans les temples de la Chine. Histoire des cultes Vie des communautés*. Paris: Albin Michel, 2000.

Goossaert, Vincent. "Anatomie d'un discours anticlérical: le *Shenbao*, 1872–1878." *Extrême-Orient Extrême-Occident* 24 (2002): 113–131.

Goossaert, Vincent. "Irrepressible Female Piety: Late Imperial Bans on Women Visiting Temples." *Nan Nü* 10 (2008): 212–241.

Gu Gangzi 孤剛子. *Huangdi jiuding shendan jingjue* 黃帝九鼎神丹經訣 [*Instructions on the Scripture of Divine Elixirs of Nine Tripods of the Huangdi Emperor*]. Ming zhengtong daozang ben 明《正統道藏》本, Eruson.

Guo Jinfeng 郭晉峰. "Woguo xiancun zuigulao de yuanluoshi wuliang dian jianzhuqun: Taiyuan Cangshan shenmiao 我國現存最古老的院落式無梁殿建築群：太原藏山神廟 [The Most Ancient Extant Architectural Complex of Beamless Palace in Our Country: the Temple in Cangshan, Taiyuan]." *Gujian yuanlin jishu* 古建園林技術 [*Traditional Chinese Architecture and Gardens*] 4 (2012): 70–74.

Haar, B.J. ter, *The White Lotus Teachings in Chinese Religious History*. Leiden: E.J. Brill, 1992.

Haar, B.J. ter. *Telling Stories: Witchcraft and Scapegoating in Chinese History*. Leiden: Brill, 2006.

Hai Rui 海瑞. *Hai Zhongjie gong wenji* 海忠介公文集 [*Collected Works of Mr. Hai Zhongjie*]. *Ming jingshi wenbian* 明經世文編 [*Collected Essays about Statecraft in the Ming Dynasty*], *juan* 390, Ming Chongzhen Pinglutang keben 明崇禎平露堂刻本, Eruson.

Han Lin 韓霖. *Duoshu* 鐸書 [*The Book of the Warning Bell*]. in *Duoshu jiaozhu* 鐸書校注 [*Critical and Annotated Edition of The Book of the Warning Bell*], annotated by Sun Shangyang 孫尚揚, Xiao Qinghe 肖清和, et al. Beijing: Huaxia chubanshe 華夏出版社, 2007.

Han Qi 韓琦, and Wu Min 吳旻, annot. *Xichao chongzheng ji, xichao ding'an (wai sanzhong*) 熙朝崇正集，熙朝定案（外三種）[*The Veneration of Glorious Ming Dynasty. Judgments of Glorious Qing Dynasty*]. Beijing: Zhonghua shuju 中華書局, 2006.

Hansen, Valerie. *Changing Gods in Medieval China, 1127–1276*. Princeton: Princeton University Press, 1990.

Harrison, Henrietta. *The Missionary's Curse and Other Tales from a Chinese Catholic Village*. Berkeley: University of California Press, 2013.

He Yan 何晏, annot., Xing Bing 邢昺, comm. *Lunyu* 論語 [the *Analects*]. Ruan Yuan 阮元, ed., *Shisanjing zhushu* 十三經注疏 [*Commentaries on the Thirteen Confucian Classics*], vol. 8, Taipei: Yiwen yinshuguan 藝文印書館, 1981.

Hong, Ignatius 洪依納爵. *Jisi wenda* 祭祀問答 [*Questions & Answers of Sacrificial Rituals*]. in CCT ARSI, vol. 11, 235–256.

Huang Bolu 黃伯祿, ed. *Zhengjiao fengbao* 正教奉褒 [*In Praise of the Orthodox Teaching*]. Shanghai: Cimu tang 慈母堂, 1894, vol. 1.

Huang Wendao 黃問道. *Pixie jie* 闢邪解 [*Explanation of Refutation against Heterodoxy*]. in *Shengchao poxie ji* 聖朝破邪集 [*Anthology of Destroying the Pernicious*], edited by Xu Changzhi 徐昌治. Lan Jifu 藍吉富, ed., *Dazangjing bubian* 大藏经补编, vol. 28, 322–324, Taipei: Huayu chubanshe 華宇出版社, 1986, vol. 5, 303–305.

Huang Yi-long 黃一農. "Tianzhujiaotu Sun Yuanhua yu Mingmo chuanhua de xiyang huopao 天主教徒孫元化與明末傳華的西洋火炮 [Christian Convert Sun Yüan-Hua (1581–1632) and the Import of Western Cannons]." *Zhongyang yanjiuyuan lishi yuyan yanjiusuo jikan* 中央研究院歷史語言研究所集刊 [Bulletin of the Institute of History and Philology Academia Sinica] 67, 4 (1996): 911–966.

Huang Yi-long 黃一農. *Liangtoushe: Mingmo Qingchu diyidai tianzhujiaotu* 兩頭蛇：明末清初第一代天主教徒 [*Two-Head Snakes: The First Generation of Chinese Catholics in Late Ming and Early Qing*]. Shanghai: Shanghai guji chubanshe 上海古籍出版社, 2006.

Huang Zhen 黃貞. *Qing Yan Zhuangqi xiansheng pi tianzhujiao shu* 請顏壯其先生闢天主教書 [*Letter to Invite Mr. Yan Zhuangqi to Refute the Teaching of the Lord of Heaven*]. in *Shengchao poxie ji* 聖朝破邪集 [*Anthology of Destroying the Pernicious*], vol. 3, 257–259.

Huang Zhen 黃貞. *Zunru jijing* 尊儒亟鏡 [*Mirror for Honoring Confucianism*]. in *Shengchao poxie ji* 聖朝破邪集 [*Anthology of Destroying the Pernicious*], vol. 3, 259–264.

Huang Zhen 黃貞. "*Poxie ji* zixu 破邪集自敘 [The Author's Preface of *Anthology of Destroying the Pernicious*]." in *Shengchao poxie ji* 聖朝破邪集 [*Anthology of Destroying the Pernicious*], vol. 3, 264–266.

Hureau, Sylvie. "L'apparition de thèmes anticléricaux dans la polémique anti-bouddhique médiévale." *Extrême-Orient Extrême-Occident* 24 (2002): 17–29.

Jackson, Robert H. *Demographic Change and Ethnic Survival among the Sedentary Pop-*

ulations on the Jesuit Mission Frontiers of Spanish South America, 1609–1803. Leiden: Brill, 2015.

Jennes, Joseph. "A propos de la liturgie chinoise: Le Bref *Romanae Sedis Antistes* de Paul V (1615)." Neue Zeitschrift für Missionswissenschaft 2 (1946): 241–254.

Jennes, Joseph. *Four Centuries of Catechetics in China: Historical Evolution of Apologetics and Catechetics in the Catholic Mission of China from the 16th Centry until 1940*. Translated by Van Lierde, Fr. Albert, and Fr. Paul T'ien Yung-cheng. Taipei: Huaming shuju 華明書局, 1975.

Jiang Dejing 蔣德璟. "*Poxie ji* xu 破邪集序 [Preface of *Anthology of Destroying the Pernicious*]." in *Shengchao poxie ji* 聖朝破邪集 [*Anthology of Destroying the Pernicious*], vol. 3, 254–255.

Jochim, Christian. *Chinese Religions: A Cultural Perspective*. Englewood Cliffs (N.J.): Prentice Hall, 1986.

Jungmann, Joseph. *The Mass of the Roman Rite: Its Origins and Development* (*Missarum Sollemnia*). Translated by F. Brunner. London: Burns & Oates, 1961.

Jungmann, Joseph. *La liturgie des premiers siècles jusqu'à l'époque de Grégoire le Grand*. Paris: Cerf, 1962.

Kangxi sanshisi nian tianzhu shengjiao zhanli zhaiqibiao 康熙三十四年天主聖教瞻禮齋期表 [Table of Dates for Worship and Fasting of the Holy Teaching of the Lord of Heaven in 1695]. in CCT BAV (1), vol. 37, 621–626.

Kangxi sanshiwu nian tianzhu shengjiao zhanli zhaiqibiao 康熙三十五年天主聖教瞻禮齋期表 [Table of Dates for Worship and Fasting of the Holy Teaching of the Lord of Heaven in 1696]. in CCT BAV (1), vol. 37, 629–634.

Kangxi sanshiliu nian tianzhu shengjiao zhanli zhaiqibiao 康熙三十六年天主聖教瞻禮齋期表 [Table of Dates for Worship and Fasting of the Holy Teaching of the Lord of Heaven in 1697]. in CCT BAV (1), vol. 37, 637–642.

Kang Zhijie 康志傑. *Shangzhu de putaoyuan: E xibei Mopan shan tianzhujiao shequ yanjiu, 1634–2005* 上主的葡萄園：鄂西北磨盤山天主教社區研究，1634–2005 [*The Lord's Vineyard: A Study of the Catholic Community in Mopan Mountain, Northwest Hubei*]. Xinbei: Fu Jen Catholic University Press 輔仁大學出版社, 2006.

Kang Zhijie 康志傑. *Jidu de xinniang—Zhongguo tianzhujiao zhennü yanjiu* 基督的新娘——中國天主教貞女研究 [*Bride of the Christ: Research on Chinese Catholic Virgins*]. Beijing: Zhongguo shehui kexue chubanshe 中國社會科學出版社, 2013.

Kang Zhijie 康志傑. "Zhanlidan shulun: jianshuo xili de dongchuan 瞻禮單述論：兼說西曆的東傳 [On the List of Worship: also On the Introduction of Western Calendar to the East]." *Beijing xingzheng xueyuan xuebao* 北京行政學院學報 [*Journal of Beijing Administrative College*] 3 (2014): 122–128.

Katz, Paul R. "Orthopraxy and Heteropraxy beyond the State: Standardizing Ritual in Chinese Society." *Modern China* vol. 33 (2007): 72–90.

Kuhn, Philip A. *Soulstealers: The Chinese Sorcery Scare of 1768*. Cambridge, MA: Harvard University Press, 1990.

Laamann, Lars. "Anti-Christian Agitation as an Example of Late Imperial Anticlericalism." *Extrême-Orient Extrême-Occident* 24 (2002): 47–64.

Lamalle, Edmond. "La propagande du P. Nicolas Trigault en faveur des missions de Chine (1616)." *Archivum historicum Societatis Iesu* 9 (Rome: Institutum historicum Societatis Iesu, 1940): 49–120.

Lecomte, Louis. *Un jésuite à Pékin: Nouveaux mémoires sur l'état présent de la Chine, 1687–1692*. Texte établi, annoté et présenté par Frédérique Touboul-Bouyeure. Paris: Phébus, 1990.

Le Goff, Jacques. *La naissance du Purgatoire*. Paris: Gallimard, 1981.

Le Grand Dictionnaire Ricci de la langue chinoise. Paris: Desclée de Brouwer, 2001.

Lei Chong 雷翀. "Jiangzhou Leicishi gaoshi 绛州雷刺史告示 [Official Proclamation by Prefect Lei of Jiangzhou]." in *Zhengjiao fengzhuan* 正教奉傳 [*In Heritage of the Orthodox Teaching*], edited by Huang Bolu 黃伯祿. 1–2, Shanghai: Cimu tang 慈母堂, 1877.

"Letterae Annae, Collegium Pekinense, Anno 1677," ARSI, Jap. Sin. 116.

Lewis, SJ, Mark A. "Annotations and Meditations on the Gospels by Jerome Nadal." *Renaissance Quarterly*, vol. 59, no. 3 (2006): 877–879.

Li Andang 李安當. "*Linsang chubin yishi* 臨喪出殯儀式 [Ritual Sequence for Attending Funerals and Organizing the Procession]." in CCT ARSI, vol. 5, 447–466.

Li Andang 李安當. "*Sangzang yishi* 喪葬儀式 [Ritual Sequence for Funerals and Burials]." in CCT ARSI, vol. 5, 467–480.

Li Can 李璨. *Pixie shuo* 劈邪說 [*On Refutation against the Pernicious*]. in *Shengchao poxie ji* 聖朝破邪集 [*Anthology of Destroying the Pernicious*], vol. 5, 305–307.

Li Jiubiao 李九標. *Kouduo richao* 口鐸日抄 [*Li Jiubiao's Diary of Oral Admonitions*]. in CCT ARSI, vol. 7, 1–594.

Li Jiugong 李九功. *Lisu mingbian* 禮俗明辯 [*Clear Discussion on Ritual and Custom*]. in CCT ARSI, vol. 9, 21–50.

Li Jiugong 李九功. *Zhengli chuyi* 證禮芻議 [*A Rustic Opinion about Rites*]. in CCT ARSI, vol. 9, 63–90.

Li Jiugong 李九功. "*Zhengli chuyi yin* 證禮芻議引 [Introduction of *A Rustic Opinion about Rites*]." in CCT ARSI, vol. 9, 91–118.

Li Jiugong 李九功. *Shensi lu* 慎思錄 [*Meditations*]. in CCT ARSI, vol. 9, 119–238.

Li Jiugong 李九功. *Lixiu yijian* 勵修一鑑 [*A Mirror for Self-Cultivation*]. in CCT BnF, vol. 7, 67–326.

Li Mei 李梅. *Haishuidi* 海水滴 [*Drop of Seawater*]. in CCT BnF, vol. 7, 427–520.

Li Mei 李梅. *Juehuo ji* 爝火集 [*Collection of Fire Torch*]. in CCT BnF, vol. 7, 521–627.

Li Sancai 李三才. *Jichen guojia zhiluan daguanshu* 極陳國家治亂大關疏 [*Report of Essential Points in Statecrafts*]. *Wanli shuchao* 萬曆疏鈔 [*Official Reports during the*

Reign of the Wanli Emperor], *juan* 1, compiled by Wu Liang 吳亮, Ming Wanli sanshiqinian keben 明萬曆三十七年刻本, Eruson.

Li Sixuan 李嗣玄. *Xihai Ai xiansheng xinglüe* 西海艾先生行略 [*Biography of Master Aleni from the Western Sea*]. in CCT ARSI, vol. 12, 243–263.

Li Sixuan 李嗣玄. *Xihai Ai xiansheng yulu* 西海艾先生語錄 [*Analects of Master Aleni from the Western Sea*]. in CCT ARSI, vol. 12, 265–322.

Li Tiangang 李天綱. *Zhongguo liyi zhi zheng: lishi, wenxian he yiyi* 中國禮儀之爭：歷史、文獻和意義 [*The Chinese Rites Controversy: Its History, Texts, and Meaning*]. Shanghai: Shanghai guji chubanshe 上海古籍出版社, 1998.

Li Tiangang 李天綱, comp. and annot. *Mingmo tianzhujiao sanzhushi wenjianzhu—Xu Guangqi, Li Zhizao, Yang Tingyun lunjiao wenji* 明末天主教三柱石文箋注——徐光啟、李之藻、楊廷筠論教文集 [*Catholic Documents of Xu Guangqi, Li Zhizao, Yang Tingyun: an Exposition of Three Great Late Ming Thinkers in China*]. Hongkong: Logos and Pneuma Press 道風書社, 2007.

Li Tiangang 李天綱, "Sanjiao tongti: shidafu de zongjiao taidu 三教通體：士大夫的宗教態度 [Three Teachings Rooted to One Believing: On Literati's Religious Attitude]." *Xueshu yuekan* 學術月刊 [*Academic Monthly*] 5 (2015): 108–126.

Li Tiangang 李天綱, "Long Huamin dui Zhongguo zongjiao benzhi de lunshu jiqi yingxiang 龍華民對中國宗教本質的論述及其影響 [Niccolo Longobardi's Discourse on Essence of Chinese Religion and Its Influence]." *Xueshu yuekan* 學術月刊 [*Academic Monthly*] 5 (2017): 165–184.

Li Xiyue 李西月. *Zhang Sanfeng xiansheng quanji* 張三丰先生全集 [*The Complete Collection of Mr Zhang Sanfeng*]. Qing Daoguang keben 清道光刻本, Eruson.

Li Yanshou 李延壽. *Nanshi* 南史 [*The History of the Southern Dynasties*]. Qing Qianlong Wuyingdian keben 清乾隆武英殿刻本, Eruson.

Li Zhi 李贄. *Yu youren shu* 與友人書 [*Letter to a Friend*]. *Xu Fenshu* 續焚書 [*Another Book to Burn*], *juan* 1, Ming keben 明刻本, Eruson.

Li Zhizao 李之藻. "Ke *Shengshui jiyan* xu 刻《聖水紀言》序 [Preface of *Records of the Holy Water*]." in *Shengshui jiyan* 聖水紀言 [*Records of the Holy Water*], CCT ARSI, vol. 8, 3–11.

Lin Jinshui 林金水. "Shilun Ai Rulüe chuanbo jidujiao de celue yu fangfa 試論艾儒略傳播基督教的策略與方法 [On Julio Aleni's Strategy and Method for Disseminating Christianity]." *Shijie zongjiao yanjiu* 世界宗教研究 [*Studies In World Religions*] 1 (1995): 36–45, 156.

Lin Jinshui 林金水. *Li Madou yu Zhongguo* 利瑪竇與中國 [*Matteo Ricci and China*]. Beijing: Zhongguo shehuikexue chubanshe 中國社會科學出版社, 1996.

Lin Jinshui 林金水. "Ai Rulüe yu Ye Xianggao Sanshan lunxue jiqi shidi kao 艾儒略與葉向高三山論學及其時地考 [Research on Conversation in Sanshan between Julio Aleni and Ye Xianggao, the Place, and the Date]." *Zongjiaoxue yanjiu* 宗教學研究 [*Religious Studies*] 1 (2015): 193–198, 223.

Lindorff, Joyce. "The Sweet Sound of Cultures Clashing." *Early Music* 33, no. 3 (Aug. 2005): 538–539.

Liu Tong 劉侗, and Yu Yizheng 于奕正. *Dijing jingwu lüe* 帝京景物略 [*Sketch of Landscape in Capital Beijing*]. Beijing: Beijing guji chubanshe 北京古籍出版社, 1983.

Liu Xu 劉昫. *Jiu Tangshu* 舊唐書 [*Old Book of the Tang Dynasty*]. Qing Qianlong Wuyingdian keben 清乾隆武英殿刻本, Eruson.

Liu Yunhua 劉耘華. *Yitian liyi: Qingdai qianzhongqi Jiangnan wenren yingdui tianzhujiao wenhua yanjiu* 依天立義；清代前中期江南文人應對天主教文化研究 [*Defending Righteousness with the Heaven: Study of the Literati's Responses to the Catholic Culture in Jiangnan Region during the Early to Mid Qing Dynasty*]. Shanghai: Shanghai guji chubanshe 上海古籍出版社, 2014.

Longobardi, Nicolò. *Traité sur quelques points de la religion des Chinois*. Paris: Louis Guerin, 1701.

Longobardo, Niccolò 龍華民. *Shengjiao rike* 聖教日課 [*Daily Services of the Holy Teaching*]. *Nianjing zongdu*, juan 1, fol. 7–fol. 22, in CCT BAV (1), vol. 16, 21–52.

Luo Guohui 羅國輝. "Li Leisi *Misa jingdian* fanyi shimo 利類思《彌撒經典》翻譯始末 [The Whole Process of How Lodovico Buglio Translated *The Classics of the Mass*]." in *Colletanea Theologica* [*Universitatis Fujen*] 輔仁大學神學論集, vol. 120, Translated by Qu Fengling 瞿鳳玲 (1999), 255–264.

Macherel, Claude. "Le corps du pain et la maison du père." *L'Uomo*, volume 3, n.s.–n. 1 (1990): 123–137.

Madsen, Richard. *China's Catholics: Tragedy and Hope in an Emerging Civil Society*. Berkeley: University of California Press, 1998.

Maspero, Henri. *La Chine antique*. Paris: Presses Universitaires de France, 1965.

Masson, J., "L'Église ouverte sur le monde," *Nouvelle Revue Théologique* 84 (1962): 1032–1043.

Mayr, Georg. *Fasciculus sacrarum litaniarum ex sanctis scripturis et patribus*. Mayer, 1614.

Menegon, Eugenio. "Deliver Us from Evil: Confession and Salvation in Seventeenth- and Eighteenth-Century Chinese Catholicism." in *Forgive Us Our Sins: Confession in Late Ming and Early Qing China*, edited by Nicolas Standaert and Ad Dudink. 1–101, Monumenta Serica Monograph Series LV, Sankt Augustin: Institut Monumenta Serica, 2006.

Menegon, Eugenio. *Ancestors, Virgins, and Friars: Christianity as a Local Religion in Late Imperial China*. Harvard-Yenching Institute Monograph Series 69, Cambridge (Massachusetts) and London: Harvard University Press, 2009.

Meynard, Thierry 梅謙立. "Fojiao zhaijie nengfou rongru tianzhujiao—yi 1668 nian Guangzhou huiyi yu Nie Zhongqian de baogao weili 佛教齋戒能否融入天主教——以1668年廣州會議與聶仲遷的報告為例 [Could Catholics Adopt Buddhist Vegetarianism? The Canton Conference and Adrien Grelon's Report of 1688]." *Foguang xuebao* 佛光學報 [*Fo Guang Journal of Buddhist Studies*] *xinsi juan*, 2 (2018): 475–500.

Meynard, Thierry, and Yang Hongfan 楊虹帆, annot. *Shengchao zuopi jiaozhu* 聖朝佐闢校注 [*Critical and Annotated Edition of Help to the Refutation of the Heresy*]. Gaoxiong: Foguang wenhua shiye youxian gongsi 佛光文化事業有限公司, 2018.

Monteiro, João 孟儒望. *Yesu shenghao daowen* 耶穌聖號禱文 [the Litany of Jesus' Holy Name]. Anon., *Tongku jingji* 痛苦經蹟 [*The Prayers of Sufferings*], TZJDCWXSB, vol. 3, 1065–1084.

Mungello, David. *Curious Land: Jesuit Accommodation and the Origins of Sinology*. Stuttgart: F. Steiner, 1985.

Mungello, David. *The Forgotten Christians of Hangzhou*. Honolulu: University of Hawaii Press, 1994.

Mungello, David. *The Spirit and the Flesh in Shandong, 1650–1785*. Lanham, New York, Boulder, and Oxford: Rowman and Littlefield, 2001.

Nanjing libu zhuke qinglisi 南京礼部主客清吏司. *Qingcha yiwu you yi'an* 清查夷物又一案 [Another Case of Inventorying Barbarian Objects]. in *Nangong shudu* 南宮署牘 [*Documents of the South Palace*], juan 3, fol. 35b–45a.

Ouyang Xiu 歐陽修, Song Qi 宋祁, et al. *Xin Tangshu* 新唐書 [*New Book of the Tang Dynasty*]. Qing Qianlong Wuyingdian keben 清乾隆武英殿刻本, Eruson.

Palazzo, Éric. *Liturgie et société au Moyen Âge*. Paris: Aubier, 2000.

Pan Feng-chuan 潘鳳娟. *Xilai Kongzi Ai Rulüe: Gengxin bianhua de zongjiao huiyu* 西來孔子艾儒略——更新變化的宗教會遇 [*Confucius from the West: Giulio Aleni (1582–1649) and the Religious Encounter between the Jesuits and the Chinese*]. Taipei: Shengjing ziyuan zhongxin 聖經資源中心, 2002.

Pan Jiajun 潘家駿, Charles. *Gan'en shengshi—liyi yu shenxue* 感恩聖事———禮儀與神學 [*Eucharist—Liturgy and Theology*]. Taipei: Wenhua shiye 文化事業, 2005.

Peng Xiaoyu 彭小瑜. "Ai tianzhu zhi xiao mochenghu airen—quanqiushi yujing zhongde jindai zaoqi Yesuhui 愛天主之效, 莫誠乎愛人——全球史語境中的近代早期耶穌會 [The Society of Jesus in Early Modern Period in the Context of Global History]." *Huazhong Normal University xuebao renwen shehui kexueban* 華中師範大學學報人文社會科學版 [*Journal of Huazhong Normal University (Humanities and Social Sciences)*] 5 (2011): 47–56.

Pfister, Louis. *Notices biographiques et bibliographiques sur les Jésuites de l'ancienne mission de Chine. 1552–1773: XVIe & XVIIe siècles*. Chang-hai: La Mission Catholique, 1934.

Qian Qianyi 錢謙益. "*Taoxi shigao* xu 桃溪詩稿序 [Preface to Manuscript of Poetry in Taoxi]." in *Wu Yushan ji jianzhu* 吳漁山集箋注 [*Annotated Collection of Wu Yushan's Works*]. Annotated by Zhang Wenqin 章文欽. *juanshou*, 1–2, Beijing: Zhonghua shuju, 2007.

Qilu Zhuren 杞廬主人, comp. "Huaxue 1 化學一 [Chemistry]." *Shiwu tongkao* 時務通考 [*Comprehensive Examination of Current Affairs*], juan 24, Qing Guangxu ershisannian Dianshizhai shiyinben 清光緒二十三年點石齋石印本, Eruson.

Qi Yinping 戚印平, and He Xianyue 何先月. "Zailun Li Madou de yifu yu Fan Li'an de wenhua shiying zhengce 再論利瑪竇的易服與范禮安的文化適應政策 [Matteo Ricci's Change of Clothing and Alexandro Valignano's Cultural Accommodation Policy Revisited]." *Zhejiang daxue xuebao renwen shehui kexueban* 浙江大學學報人文社會科學版 [*Journal of Zhejiang University (Humanities and Social Sciences)*] 3 (2013): 116–124.

Qu Yi 曲藝. "Mingmo jidujiao chatu zhong de rujia yuansu: yi *Tianzhu jiangsheng chuxiang jingjie* weili 明末基督教插圖中的儒家元素：以《天主降生出像經解》為例 [Confucian elements in Christian Illustrations in Late Ming: Take the Example of *Explanation of the Incarnation and Life of the Lord of Heaven*]." *Shijie zongjiao yanjiu* 世界宗教研究 [*Studies In World Religions*] 2 (2015): 140–148.

Qu Jiusi 瞿九思, comp. *Wanli wugong lu* 萬曆武功錄 [*Report of Military Campaigns in the Reign of the Wanli Emperor*]. Ming Wanli keben 明萬曆刻本, Eruson.

Raux, Nicolas-Joseph 羅廣祥. *Shengshi wenda* 聖事問答 [*Questions & Answers of the Holy Sacrament*]. in CCT BnF, vol. 20, 387–475.

Ricci, Matteo 利瑪竇. *Shengjing yuelu* 聖經約錄 [*Brief Record of Holy Prayers*]. in CCT ARSI, vol. 1, 87–116.

Ricci, Matteo 利瑪竇. *Tianzhu shiyi* 天主實義 [*The True Meaning of the Lord of Heaven*]. in DCFY, vol. 2, 23–96.

Ricci, Matteo 利瑪竇. *Yesuhui yu tianzhujiao jinru Zhongguo shi* 耶穌會與天主教進入中國史 [*Della entrata della Compagnia di Giesù e Christianità nella Cina*]. Translated by Wen Zheng 文錚, edited by Eugenio Menegon 梅歐金. Beijing: The Commercial Press 商務印書館, 2014.

Rho, Giacomo 羅雅谷. *Aijin xingquan* 哀矜行詮 [*Explanation on Works of Mercy*]. in CCT ARSI, vol. 5, 1–256.

Rho, Giacomo 羅雅谷. *Zhaike* 齋克 [*Victory over Fasting*]. in CCT BnF, vol. 19, 479–648.

Rodrigues, Simao 李西滿. *Bianji canping* 辯祭參評 [*Commentary on Dialogue on Sacrifice*]. in CCT ARSI, vol. 10, 363–438.

Ruggieri, Michele 羅明堅. *Tianzhu shilu* 天主實錄 [*Veritable Record of the Lord of Heaven*]. in CCT ARSI, vol. 1, 1–85.

Sambiasi, Francesco 畢方濟, and Xu Guangqi 徐光啟. *Lingyan lishao* 靈言蠡勺 [*Humble Attempt at Discussing Matters Pertaining to the Soul*]. in DCFY, vol. 2, 497–532.

Schall, SJ, Joannes Adamus. *Relation historique, texte latin avec traduction française de Paul Bornet*. Tientsin [Tianjin]: Hautes études, 1942.

Seah, Audrey. "The 1670 Chinese Missal: A Struggle for Indigenization Amidst the Chinese Rites Controversy." in *China's Christianity: From Missionary to Indigenous Church*, edited by Anthony E. Clark. 86–120, Leiden: Brill, 2017.

Shen Congwen 沈從文. *Zhongguo gudai fushi yanjiu* 中國古代服飾研究 [*The Study of Ancient Chinese Clothing and Ornaments*]. Shanghai: Shanghai shudian chubanshe 上海書店出版社, 2011.

Shen Defu 沈德符. *Wanli yehuo bian* 萬曆野獲編 [*An Unofficial History of the Wan Li*

BIBLIOGRAPHY

Period]. Qing Daoguang qinian Yaoshi ke tongzhi banian buxiuben 清道光七年姚氏刻同治八年補修本, Eruson.

Shen Que 沈㴶. *Can yuanyi shu* 參遠夷疏 [*Memorial to Impeach Barbarians from Far Away*]. in *Shengchao poxie ji* 聖朝破邪集 [*Anthology of Destroying the Pernicious*], vol. 1, 220–222.

Shen Que 沈㴶. *Zaican yuanyi shu* 再參遠夷疏 [*Second Memorial to Accuse Distant Barbarians*]. in *Shengchao poxie ji* 聖朝破邪集 [*Anthology of Destroying the Pernicious*], vol. 1, 223–224.

Shen Que 沈㴶. *Can yuanyi sanshu* 參遠夷三疏 [*Third Memorial to Accuse Distant Barbarians*]. in *Shengchao poxie ji* 聖朝破邪集 [*Anthology of Destroying the Pernicious*], vol. 1, 224–226.

Shen Que 沈㴶. *Faqian yuanyi huizou shu* 發遣遠夷回奏疏 [*Memorial to Repatriate Barbarians from Far Away*]. in *Shengchao poxie ji* 聖朝破邪集 [*Anthology of Destroying the Pernicious*], vol. 2, 235–236.

Śikṣānanda 實叉難陀, trans. *Dafang guang fo huayan jing* 大方廣佛華嚴經 [*Flower Adornment Sutra*]. Dazheng xinxiu Dazangjing ben 大正新修大藏經本, Eruson.

Shi Bangyao 施邦曜. "*Fujian xunhaidao gaoshi* 福建巡海道告示 [Official Proclamation by the Marine Inspector of Fujian]." in *Shengchao poxie ji* 聖朝破邪集 [*Anthology of Destroying the Pernicious*], vol. 2, 249–252.

Shi Chengyong 釋成勇. *Pi tianzhujiao xi* 闢天主教檄 [*Announcement to Refute the Teaching of the Lord of Heaven*]. in *Shengchao poxie ji* 聖朝破邪集 [*Anthology of Destroying the Pernicious*], vol. 8, 353–354.

Shi Hao 史浩. *Shangshu jiangyi* 尚書講義 [*Explanation of The Book of Documents*]. Vol. 8, Qing Wenyuange Siku quanshu ben 清文淵閣四庫全書本, Eruson.

Shi Junjing 時俊靜. "*Yuanqu qupai yu zongjiao yinyue* 元曲曲牌與宗教音樂 [On Yuanqu Qupai and Religious Music]." *Huangzhong (Wuhan yinyue xueyuan xuebao)* 黃鐘武漢音樂學院學報 [*Journal of Wuhan Conservatory of Music*] 1 (2012): 82–87.

Shi Purun 釋普潤. *Zhuzuo ji yuanqi* 誅左集緣起 [*Origin of Anthology to Eliminate the Heterodoxy*]. in *Shengchao poxie ji* 聖朝破邪集 [*Anthology of Destroying the Pernicious*], vol. 8, 352–353.

Shi Ruchun 釋如純. *Tianxue chupi* 天學初闢 [*First Refutation against the Study of Heaven*]. in *Shengchao poxie ji* 聖朝破邪集 [*Anthology of Destroying the Pernicious*], vol. 8, 354–362.

Shi Yuanwu 釋圓悟. *Biantian ershuo* 辨天二說 [*Dialogue on Heaven*]. in *Shengchao poxie ji* 聖朝破邪集 [*Anthology of Destroying the Pernicious*], vol. 7, 328–330.

Shi Zhiqing 釋志磐. *Fozu tongji* 佛祖統紀 [*Comprehensive History of the Buddhist Patriarchs*]. Vol. 43, Dazheng xinxiu Dazangjing ben 大正新修大藏經本, Eruson.

Shi Zhuhong 釋袾宏. *Tian shuo* 天說 [*On Heaven*]. in *Shengchao poxie ji* 聖朝破邪集 [*Anthology of Destroying the Pernicious*], vol. 28, 322–324.

Soares, José 蘇霖. *Shengmu lingbaohui gui* 聖母領報會規 [*Statutes of the Confraternity of the Annunciation to the Holy Mother*]. in CCT BnF, vol. 20, 213–251.

Sodi, Manlio and Achille Maria Triacca, eds. *Missale Romanum: editio princeps (1570)*. Città del Vaticano: Libreria editrice Vaticana, 2012.

Soeiro, João 蘇如望. *Shengjiao yueyan* 聖教約言 [*Brief Introduction of the Holy Teaching*]. in CCT ARSI, vol. 2, 253–280.

Song Gang 宋剛. "Xiao renwu de da lishi: Qingchu Sichuan tianzhujiaotu Xu Ruohan ge'an yanjiu de qishi 小人物的大歷史：清初四川天主教徒徐若翰個案研究的啟示 [A Minor Figure, a Large History: A Study of Johan Su, a Sichuan Catholic Convert in the Early Qing Dynasty]." in *Guoji hanxue* 國際漢學 [*International Sinology*] 1 (2017): 30–57, 202.

Song Gang 宋剛. *Giulio Aleni, Kouduo richao, and Christian-Confucian Dialogism in Late Ming Fujian*. Abingdon, Oxon New York: Routledge, 2018.

Song Liming 宋黎明. "Luo Wenzhao haishi Luo Wenzao?—wei Zhongguo shouwei guoji zhujiao Luo zhujiao zhengming 羅文炤還是羅文藻?——為中國首位國籍主教羅主教正名 [Luo Wenzhao (羅文炤) or Luo Wenzao (羅文藻)? A Study on the Chinese Name of the First Chinese Bishop Gregorio Lopez (1617–1691)]." *Haijiaoshi yanjiu* 海交史研究 [*Journal of Maritime History Studies*] (2019:3): 40–51.

Soothill, William Edward, and Lewis Hodous, eds. *A Dictionary of Chinese Buddhist Terms: with Sanskrit and English Equivalents and a Sanskrit-Pali Index*. Taipei: Ch'eng Wen Publishing Company (reprinted), 1975.

Standaert, Nicolas. *Yang Tingyun, Confucian and Christian in Late Ming China: His Life and Thought*. Leiden: Brill, 1988.

Standaert, Nicolas. "Chinese Christian Visits to the Underworld." in *Conflict and Accommodation in Early Modern East Asia*, edited by Leonard Blussé and Harriet T. Zurndorfer. 54–70, Leiden: Brill, 1993.

Standaert, Nicolas. *The Fascinating God: A Challenge to Modern Chinese Theology Presented by a text on the name of God written by a 17th century Chinese student of theology*. Rome: Pontificia Università Gregoriana, 1995.

Standaert, Nicolas. "The Bible in Early Seventeenth-century China." in *Bible in Modern China: The Literary and Intellectual Impact*, edited by Irene Eber, Knut Walf, and Wan Sze-kar, 31–54, Sankt Augustin: Institut Monumenta Serica, 1999.

Standaert, Nicolas. "The Jesuits Did NOT Manufacture 'Confucianism'." *East Asian Science, Technology and Medicine* 16 (1999): 115–132.

Standaert, Nicolas, ed. *Handbook of Christianity in China. Volume One: 635–1800*. Leiden: Brill, 2001.

Standaert, Nicolas, "Christianity in Late Ming and Early Qing China as a Case of Cultural Transmission." in *China and Christianity: Burdened Past, Hopeful Future*, edited by Stephen Jr. Uhalley and Wu Xiaoxin. 81–116, Armonk, New York: M.E. Sharpe, 2001.

Standaert, Nicolas, *L'«autre» dans la mission: leçon à partir de la Chine*. Bruxelles: Lessius, 2003.

Standaert, Nicolas, "The Composition of Place: Creating Space for an Encounter." *The Way* 46, no. 1 (2007): 7–20.

Standaert, Nicolas, "The 'Theory' of Rituals Related to Heaven." in *A Life Long Dedication to the China Mission: Essays Presented in Honor of Father Jeroom Heyndrickx CICM, on the Occasion of His 75th Birthday and the 25th Anniversary of the F. Verbiest Institute, K.U.Leuven,* edited by Noël Golvers and Sara Lievens, Leuven Chinese studies XVII. 521–543, Leuven: Ferdinand Verbiest Institute, K.U.Leuven, 2007.

Standaert, Nicolas, "Christianity Shaped by the Chinese." in *The Cambridge History of Christianity: Reform and Expansion 1500–1660,* edited by R. Po-Chia Hsia, 558–576, 707–709, Cambridge: Cambridge University Press, 2007.

Standaert, Nicolas, *An Illustrated Life of Christ Presented to the Chinese Emperor. The History of the Jincheng shuxiang (1640)*. Monumenta serica monograph series LIX, Sankt Augustin: Institut Monumenta Serica, 2007.

Standaert, Nicolas, *The Interweaving of Rituals: Funerals in the Cultural Exchange between China and Europe*. Seattle: University of Washington Press, 2008.

Standaert, Nicolas, *Chinese Voices in the Rites Controversy: Travelling Books, Community Networks Intercutural Arguments*. Rome: Institutum Historicum Societatis Iesu, 2012.

Stumpf, SJ, Kilian. *The Acta Pekinensia or Historical Records of the Maillard de Tournon Legation*. volume I, December 1705–August 1706, edited by Paul Rule and Claudia von Collani, Rome: Institutum Historicum Societatis Iesu, 2015.

Su Jiyu 蘇及寓. *Xiedu shiju* 邪毒實據 [*Solid Evidence of Pernicious Poison*]. in *Shengchao poxie ji* 聖朝破邪集 [*Anthology of Destroying the Pernicious*], vol. 3, 269–271.

Sun Shangyang 孫尚揚, and Nicolas Standaert. *1840 nian qian de Zhongguo jidujiao* 一八四零年前的中國基督教 [*Christianity in China before 1840*]. Beijing: Xueyuan chubanshe 學苑出版社, 2004.

Sun Shangyang 孫尚揚. "Li Madou dui fojiao de pipan jiqi dui Yesuhui zaihua chuanjiao huodong de yingxiang 利瑪竇對佛教的批判及其對耶穌會在華傳教活動的影響 [Criticism on Buddhism by Matteo Ricci and Its Influence on the Missionary Activities of Jesuits in China]." *Shijie zongjiao yanjiu* 世界宗教研究 [*Studies In World Religions*] 4 (1998): 85–94, 149.

Sun Shangyang 孫尚揚. *Zongjiao shehuixue* 宗教社會學 [*Sociology of Religion*]. Beijing: Peking University Press, 2001.

Sun Shangyang 孫尚揚. "Lüelun Mingmo shidafu tianzhujiaotu dui qixinyang de bentuhua quanshi 略論明末士大夫天主教徒對其信仰的本土化詮釋 [Brief Discussion on Catholic Literati's Indigenous Interpretation of Their Faith in Late Ming]." *Beijing xingzheng xueyuan xuebao* 北京行政學院學報 [*Journal of Beijing Administrative College*] 4 (2006): 77–81.

Sun Shangyang 孫尚揚. "Shangdi yu Zhongguo huangdi de xiangyu—*Duoshu* zhongde ruye hudong yu lunli jiangou 上帝與中國皇帝的相遇——《鐸書》中的儒耶互動與倫理建構 [The Encounter between God and Chinese Emperor: Interaction between Confucianism and Christianity and Ethics Construction in *The Book of the Warning Bell*]." in *Duoshu jiaozhu* 鐸書校注 [*Critical and Annotated Edition of The Book of the Warning Bell*], annotated by Sun Shangyang 孫尚揚, Xiao Qinghe 肖清和, et al., 1–37, Beijing: Huaxia chubanshe 華夏出版社, 2007.

Sun Shangyang 孫尚揚. "Fengbi de jidutu yu danfang shouyi de ruye duihua—yi Huang Baoluo de yanjiu weili 封閉的基督徒與單方受益的儒耶對話——以黃保羅的研究為例 [Narrow-minded Christian and Unilateral-beneficial Dialogue between Confucianism and Christianity: Taking Dr. Paulos Huang's Studies for Example]." *Zhexue yanjiu* 哲學研究 [*Philosophical Researches*] 5 (2009): 51–57.

Sun Shangyang 孫尚揚. *Mingmo tianzhujiao yu ruxue de hudong: yizhong sixiangshi de shijiao* 明末天主教與儒學的互動：一種思想史的視角 [*A Study of the Interaction Between Catholicism and Confucianism in Late-Ming Dynasty: from a Perspective of History of Thoughts*]. Beijing: Zongjiao wenhua chubanshe 宗教文化出版社, 2013.

Sun Shangyang 孫尚揚. "Cong *Kouduo richao* kan Mingmo Fujian tianzhujiaotu de zongjiao weishen 從《口鐸日抄》看明末福建天主教徒的宗教委身 [On Catholics' Commitment in Fujian in the Late Ming Dynasty: from the Perspective of *Diary of Oral Admonitions*]." *Hangzhou shifan daxue xuebao: shehui kexue ban* 杭州師範大學學報：社會科學版 [*Journal of Hangzhou Teachers College (Social Sciences Edition)*], vol. 35, 6 (2013): 17–24, 45.

Sun Xueshi 孫學詩. *Shengshui jiyan* 聖水紀言 [*Records of the Holy Water*]. in CCT ARSI, vol. 8, 1–30.

Sun Yuming. "Cultural Translatability and the Presentation of Christ as Portrayed in Visual Images from Ricci to Aleni." in *The Chinese face of Jesus Christ*, vol. 2, edited by Roman Malek. 461–498, Nettetal: Steyler Verlag, 2003.

Tan Qian 談遷. *Beiyou lu* 北游錄 [*Record of Trip in Beijing*]. in *Qingdai shiliao biji congkan* 清代史料筆記叢刊 [*Compendia of Qing Dynasty Historical Miscellanies*], revised by Wang Beiping 汪北平. Beijing: Zhonghua shuju 中華書局, 1997.

Teiser, Stephen F. *The Ghost Festival in Medieval China*. Princeton, N.J.: Princeton University Press, 1996.

"The Sacrament of the Eucharist." *Catechism of the Catholic Church*, last accessed September 29, 2021. https://www.vatican.va/archive/ENG0015/__P3X.HTM.

Thoraval, Joël. "Pourquoi les 'religions chinoises' ne peuvent-elles apparaître dans les statistiques occidentales?" *Perspectives chinoises*, numéro 1 (1992): 37–44.

Trigault, Nicolas 金尼閣. *Tuiding linian zhanlirifa* 推定曆年瞻禮日法 [*Method to Count Days of Worship in Each Year*]. in CCT ARSI, vol. 5, 301–332.

Vagnone, Alfonso 王豐肅. *Jiaoyao jielüe* 教要解畧 [*Brief Explanation of Catechism*]. in CCT ARSI, vol. 1, 117–306.

Vagnone, Alfonso 高一志. *Shengmu xingshi* 聖母行實 [*Life of the Holy Mother*]. in TZJD-CWXSB, vol. 3, 1273–1552.

Van Engen, John. "The Christian Middle Ages as an Historiographical Problem." *American Historical Review* 91, 3 (1986): 519–552.

Verbiest, Ferdinand 南懷仁. *Tianzhujiao sangli wenda* 天主教喪禮問答 [*Questions and Answers of Catholic Funeral Rituals*]. in CCT ARSI, vol. 5, 493–508.

Verbiest, Ferdinand 南懷仁. *Jiaoyao xulun* 教要序論 [*Methodical Exposition of the Essence of the Faith*]. in CCT BnF, vol. 24, 1–152.

Verbiest, Ferdinand 南懷仁. *Shengti dayi* 聖體答疑 [*Answers to Questions about the Holy Body*]. in CCT BnF, vol. 18, 375–404.

Verhaeren, Hubert Germain. "Ordonnances de la Sainte Église." *Monumenta serica* 4 (1939–1940): 451–477.

Vermander, Benoît 魏明德. "Gaoxie de 'zongjiao tuichu' shuo yu Zhongguo zongjiao geju chonggou de zhexue sikao 高歌的 '宗教退出' 說與中國宗教格局重構的哲學思考 [Marcel Gauchet, "Exit from Religion" and the Reconfiguration of the Chinese Religious Landscape—A Philosophical Excursus]." *Zhexue yu wenhua* 哲學與文化 [Universitas: Monthly Review of Philosophy and Culture] (Taipei: Zhexue yu wenhua yuekan zazhishe 哲學與文化月刊雜誌社, Oct., 2011): 165–181.

Vu Thanh, Hélène. *Devenir japonais: La mission jésuite au Japon (1549–1614)*. Paris: Presses de l'université Paris-Sorbonne, 2016.

Waldenfels, Hans. "Introduction." *Contextual Fundamental Theology*, translated by Susan Johnson. 23–37, Paderborn: Ferdinand Schöningh, 2018.

Wang Bi 王弼, annot. *Zhouyi* 周易 [the *Book of Changes*]. Sibu congkan jing Song ben 四部叢刊景宋本, Eruson.

Wang Chaoshi 王朝式. *Zuiyan* 罪言 [*Discourse from a Sinner*]. in *Shengchao poxie ji* 聖朝破邪集 [*Anthology of Destroying the Pernicious*], vol. 3, 266–267.

Wang Ding'an 王定安. "Zhongguo liyi zhi zheng zhong de rujia zongjiaoxing wenti 中國禮儀之爭中的儒家宗教性問題 [Confucian Religiosity in "Chinese Rites Controversy"]." *Xueshu yuekan* 學術月刊 [Academic Monthly] 7 (Shanghai: Shanghai shi shehui kexue lianhehui 上海市社會科學聯合會, 2016): 174–184.

Wang Ding'an 王定安. "Misa shifou jisi: Mingqing zhi ji bei yizhi huati zhi chongxin zhankai 彌撒是否祭祀：明清之際被抑制話題之重新展開 [Whether Missa is Sacrifice or Not: Research on a Restrained Topic in Late Ming and Early Qing Dynasty]." *Zhexue yu wenhua* 哲學與文化 [Universitas: Monthly Review of Philosophy and Culture] 46 (Taipei: Zhexue yu wenhua yuekanshe 哲學與文化月刊社, 2019): 103–120.

Wang, Petrus 王伯多祿 et al. *Jingdu zonghuizhang Wang Bo-duo-lu deng shiba ren zhi waisheng getang huizhang shu, gao Kangxi wushiwu nian jiuyue zhuren yu Shandong Linqing daizhujiao Kang shenfu tan liyi wenti* 京都總會長王伯多祿等十八人致外省各堂會長書，告康熙五十五年九月諸人與山東臨清堂代主教康神父談禮儀問題 [Discussion of Rituals between Catholics and Fr. da Castorano in Linqing, Shandong in 1716, Recorded by Eighteen Persons, including the Confraternity Prefect in Beijing Petrus Wang, to the Prefects of Churches in Provinces]. in CCT ARSI, vol. 10, 479–534.

Wang Qishu 汪啟淑. *Shuicao qingxia lu* 水曹清暇錄 [*Record from the Leisurely Office of the Board of Works*]. Qing Qianlong wushiqinian Wangshi Feihongtang keben 清乾隆五十七年汪氏飛鴻堂刻本, Eruson.

Wang Zheng 王徵. *Renhui yue* 仁會約 [*Rules of Confraternity of Charity*]. in CCT BnF, vol. 6, 521–616.

Wang Zheng 王徵. *Weitian airen jilun* 畏天愛人極論 [*Expounding How to Fear Heaven and to Love Human Beings*]. BnF Chinois 6868.

Wang Zongyan 汪宗衍. "Wu Yushan wang Aomen nianfen zhi yanjiu ziliao ji qita 吳漁山往澳門年份之研究資料及其它 [Research Materials of the Year When Wu Yushan Went to Macao etc.]." in *Wu Yushan (Li) yanjiu lunji* 吳漁山（歷）研究論集 [*Collection of Research Essays on Wu Yushan (Li)*], edited by Zhou Kangxie 周康燮. 147–150, Hongkong: Chongwen shudian 崇文書店, 1971.

Wang Zongyan 汪宗衍. "Wu Yushan Aozhong zayong bushi 吳漁山墺中雜詠補釋 [Additional Annotation of Wu Yushan's *Various Poems in Macao*]." in *Wu Yushan (Li) yanjiu lunji* 吳漁山（歷）研究論集 [*Collection of Research Essays on Wu Yushan (Li)*], edited by Zhou Kangxie 周康燮. 141–146, Hongkong: Chongwen shudian 崇文書店, 1971.

Waterworth, J., ed. and trans. *The Canons and Decrees of the Sacred and Oecumenical Council of Trent*. London: Dolman, 1848.

Watson, James. "Standardizing the Gods: The Promotion of T'ien-hou ('Empress of Heaven') along the South China Coast, 960–1960." in *Popular Culture in Late Imperial China*, edited by David Johnson, Andrew J. Nathan, and Evelyn S. Rawski. 292–324, Berkeley: University of California Press, 1985.

Watson, James. "Waking the Dragon: Visions of the Chinese Imperial State in Local Myth." in *An Old State in New Settings: studies in the Social Anthropology of China in Memory of Maurice Freedman*, edited by Hugh D.R. Baker and Stephan Feuchtwang. 162–177, Oxford, 1991.

Watson, James. "Orthopraxy Revisited." *Modern China* 33 (2007): 154–158.

Wei Jun 魏濬. *Lishuo huangtang huoshi* 利說荒唐惑世 [Ricci's Talks are Absurd and Deluding People]. in *Shengchao poxie ji* 聖朝破邪集 [*Anthology of Destroying the Pernicious*], vol. 3, 272–273.

Wen Xiangfeng 文翔鳳. "*Nangong shudu xu* 南宮署牘序 [Preface to *Documents of the South Palace*]." fol. 1–14, in *Nangong shudu* 南宮署牘 [*Documents of the South Palace*], juan 1.

Wu Ercheng 吳爾成. *Huishen Zhong Mingli dengfan yi'an* 會審鐘明禮等犯一案 [the Case of Joint Hearing of Zhong Mingli and Other Prisoners]. in *Shengchao poxie ji* 聖朝破邪集 [*Anthology of Destroying the Pernicious*], vol. 2, 237–241.

Wu Fei 吳飛. *Maimang shangde shengyan: yige xiangcun tianzhujiao qunti de xinyang he shenghuo* 麥芒上的聖言：一個鄉村天主教群體的信仰和生活 [Sacred Word above the Awn of the Wheat: Faith and Life in a Rural Catholic Community]. Beijing: Zongjiao wenhua chubanshe 宗教文化出版社, 2013.

Wu Li 吳歷. *Wu Yushan ji jianzhu* 吳漁山集箋注 [*Annotated Collection of Wu Yushan's Works*]. Annotated by Zhang Wenqin 章文欽. Beijing: Zhonghua shuju, 2007.

Wu Li 吳歷. "Misa yueyin 彌撒樂音 [The Musical Sound of Mass]." in "Wu Yushan xiansheng *Tianyue zhengyinpu* jiaoshi 吳漁山先生《天樂正音譜》校釋, [Revision and Annotation of the *Compendium of Orthodox Sounds of Heavenly Music* by Master Wu Yushan]." *Fang Hao liushi zidinggao* 方豪六十自定稿 [*Collected Works of Fang Hao Revised and Edited by the Author on His 60th Birthday*], xia, 1627–1629, Taipei: Taiwan xuesheng shuju 臺灣學生書局, 1969.

Wu Min 吳旻, and Han Qi 韓琦. "Liyi zhi zheng yu Zhongguo tianzhujiaotu—yi Fujian jiaotu he Yan Dang de chongtu weili 禮儀之爭與中國天主教徒——以福建教徒和顏璫的衝突為例 [The Chinese Rites Controversy and Chinese Catholics: A Case Study of Conflict between the Christians in Fujian Province and Bishop Charles Maigrot (1652–1730)]." *Lishi yanjiu* 歷史研究 [*Historical Research*] 6 (2004): 83–91, 191.

Xia, Mathias 夏瑪第亞. *Jili paozhi* 祭禮泡製 [*Imitation of Sacrificial Rituals*]. in CCT ARSI, vol. 10, 79–104.

Xiao Qinghe 肖清和. "Quanshi yu qibian: Yesu xingxiang zai Mingqing shehuili de chuanbo jiqi fanying 詮釋與歧變：耶穌形象在明清社會裡的傳播及其反應 [Interpretation and Distortion: Spread of Jesus' Image and Its Reaction in Ming and Qing Society]." *Guangdong shehui kexue* 廣東社會科學 [*Social Sciences In Guangdong*] 4 (2011): 137–147.

Xiao Qinghe 肖清和. *Tianhui yu wudang: mingmo qingchu tianzhujiaotu qunti yanjiu* 天會與吾黨：明末清初天主教徒群體研究 [*"Tianhui" and "Wudang": Study on Catholics in the Late Ming Dynasty and Early Qing Dynasty*]. Beijing: Zhonghua shuju 中華書局, 2015.

Xiaoshan laoren 曉山老人. *Taiyi tongzong baojian* 太乙統宗寶鑒 [*Precious Mirror of Unified Origins of the Taiyi*]. Ming chaoben 明鈔本, Eruson.

Xie Gonghua 謝宮花. "*Lifa lun* 曆法論 [On the Calendar]." in *Shengchao poxie ji* 聖朝破邪集 [*Anthology of Destroying the Pernicious*], vol. 6, 319–322.

Xu Congzhi 徐從治. *Chaihui weizhi louyuan yi'an* 拆毀違制樓園一案 [the Case of Demolishing House and Garden Which Violate the System]. in *Nangong shudu* 南宮署牘 [*Documents of the South Palace*], juan 4, Shen Que 沈㴶, 1a–3b.

Xu Congzhi 徐從治. *Huishen Zhong Mingren dengfan yi'an* 會審鐘鳴仁等犯一案 [the Case of Joint Hearing of Zhong Mingren and Other Prisoners]. in *Shengchao poxie ji* 聖朝破邪集 [*Anthology of Destroying the Pernicious*], vol. 2, 241–245.

Xu Dashou 許大受. *Shengchao zuopi* 聖朝佐闢 [*Help to the Refutation of the Heresy*].

in *Shengchao zuopi jiaozhu* 聖朝佐闢校注 [*Critical and Annotated Edition of Help to the Refutation of the Heresy*], annotated by Thierry Meynard and Yang Hongfan 楊虹帆. Gaoxiong: Foguang wenhua shiye youxian gongsi 佛光文化事業有限公司, 2018.

Xu Guangqi 徐光啟. *Pi shishi zhuwang* 闢釋氏諸妄 [*Refutation of the Buddhist's Absurdities*]. in CCT ZKW, vol. 1, 37–70.

Xu Guangqi 徐光啟. *Jingjiao tang beiji* 景教堂碑記 [*Stone Inscription for the Hall of Great Bright Teaching*]. in *Sanzhushi*, 70–73.

Xu Kai 徐鍇. "Tongshi juan 10 通釋卷十 [Volume 10, Explanation]." *Shuowen jiezi xizhuan* 說文解字系傳 [*Commentary of Explaining Graphs and Analyzing Characters*], Sibu congkan jing Shugutang jing Song chaoben 四部叢刊景述古堂景宋鈔本, Eruson.

Xu Longfei. *Die nestorianische Stele in Xi'an. Begegnung von Christentum und chinesischer Kultur*. Bonn: Borengässer, 2004.

Xu Shiyin 徐世蔭. "Tixing anchasi gaoshi 提刑按察司告示 [*Official Proclamation by Provincial Surveillance Commission*]." in *Shengchao poxie ji* 聖朝破邪集 [*Anthology of Destroying the Pernicious*], vol. 2, 252–253.

Yan Mo 嚴謨. *Jizu kao* 祭祖考 [*Study on Sacrifice to Ancestors*]. in CCT ARSI, vol. 11, 1–28.

Yan Mo 嚴謨. *Bianji zaoqi chaoben* 辨祭（早期抄本）[*Discerning Sacrifices* (early version)]. in CCT ARSI, vol. 11, 37–46.

Yan Mo 嚴謨. *Bianji jinqi chaoben* 辨祭（近期抄本）[*Discerning Sacrifices* (recent version)]. in CCT ARSI, vol. 11, 47–60.

Yan Weisheng 顏維聖. *Tianzhu shenpan mingzheng* 天主審判明證 [*Clear Evidence of Judgement of the Lord of Heaven*]. *Jingjiao yiban* 景教一斑 [*A Part of Great Bright Teaching*], in CCT BnF, vol. 23, 201–212.

Yang Guangxian 楊光先. *Lin Tang Ruowang jincheng tuxiang shuo* 臨湯若望進呈圖像說 [*On Copies of Pictures Presented by Adam Schall*]. *Budeyi* 不得已 [*I Cannot Do Otherwise*], in SCCT ZKW, vol. 5, 509–622.

Yang, C.K., *Religion in Chinese Society: A study of Contemporary Social Function of Religion and Some of Their Historical Factors*. California: University of California Press, 1967.

Yang Tingyun 楊廷筠. *Daiyi pian* 代疑篇 [*Compilation of Doubts on Behalf of Literatus*]. in CCT BAV (1), vol. 23, 1–170.

Yingtian fu Shangyuan, Jiangning erxian chaobao 應天府上元、江寧二縣抄報. *Qingcha yiwu yi'an* 清查夷物一案 [the Case of Inventorying Barbarian Objects]. fol. 25b–35b, in *Nangong shudu* 南宮署牘 [*Documents of the South Palace*], juan 3.

You Bin 游斌. "Hetian, heren yu heji: Wanming tianzhujiao rushi Li Jiugong de bijiaojingxue shijian 和天、和人與和己：晚明天主教儒士李九功的比較經學實踐 [To Be Harmonious with Heaven, Others, and Self: A Case Study of Late Ming Catholic

Literatus, Li Jiugong, and His Method of Comparative Scripture]." in *Bijiao jingxue* 比較經學 [*Journal of Comparative Scripture*], vol. 1, 11–37, Beijing: Zongjiao wenhua chubanshe 宗教文化出版社, 2013.

You Tong 尤侗. "*Sanba ji* xu 三巴集序 [Preface to *Anthology of the Church St. Paul*]." in *Wu Yushan ji, juanshou*, 21.

Yu Chunxi 虞淳熙. *Tianzhu shiyi shasheng bian* 《天主實義》殺生辨 [*Discerning Killing Life in The True Meaning of the Lord of Heaven*]. in *Shengchao poxie ji* 聖朝破邪集 [*Anthology of Destroying the Pernicious*], vol. 5, 300–302.

Yu Ying-shih. "Confucianism and China's Encounter with the West in Historical Perspective." *Dao: A Journal of Comparative Philosophy*, vol. 4, no. 2 (2005): 203–216.

Zhang Geng 張賡. *Tianxue jiehuo* 天學解惑 [*Answering Questions in the Study of Heaven*]. in CCT BnF, vol. 7, 25–48.

Zhang Guangtian 張廣湉. *Pixie zhaiyao lüeyi* 闢邪摘要畧議 [*Brief Discussion of Extracts of Refutation against the Pernicious*]. in *Shengchao poxie ji* 聖朝破邪集 [*Anthology of Destroying the Pernicious*], vol. 5, 308–309.

Zhang Tingyu 張廷玉, et al. *Mingshi* 明史 [*History of the Ming Dynasty*]. Vol. 237, Qing Qianlong Wuyingdian keben 清乾隆武英殿刻本, Eruson.

Zhang Xiangcan 張象燦. *Jiali hejiao lu* 家禮合教錄 [*Family Rituals Comply with the Teaching*]. in CCT ARSI, vol. 11, 279–296.

Zhang Xianqing 張先清. *Guanfu, zongzu yu tianzhujiao: 17–19 shiji Fu'an xiangcun jiaohui de lishi xushi* 官府、宗族與天主教：17–19世紀福安鄉村教會的歷史敘事 [*The Official, the Lineage, and Catholicism: Historical Narratives of the Village Church in Fu'an during 17–19 Centuries*]. Beijing: Zhonghua shuju 中華書局, 2009.

Zhang Xianqing 張先清. *Xiao lishi: mingqing zhiji de zhongxi wenhua xiangyu* 小歷史：明清之際的中西文化相遇 [*Micro-history: Cultural Encounters of China and the West during the Ming-Qing Transition*]. Beijing: The Commercial Press 商務印書館, 2015.

Zhang Xianqing 張先清. "'Bailian,' 'wuwei' yu 'tianzhu': qingqianqi de tianzhujiao yu minjian zongjiao guanxi '白蓮'、'無為' 與 '天主'：清前朝的天主教與民間宗教關係 ["The White Lotus," "the Non-Action," and "the Lord of Heaven": The Relationship between Catholicism and Folk Religions in the Early Qing]." *Aomen ligong xuebao* 澳門理工學報 [*Journal of Macao Polytechnic Institute*] 1 (2017): 73–84.

Zhang Xingyao 張星曜. *Tianru tongyi kao* 天儒同異考 [*Examination on Similarity & Dissimilarity between the Study of Heaven and Confucianism*]. in CCT BnF, vol. 8, 429–558.

Zhao Lun 趙侖. *Xu Kouduo richao* 續口鐸日抄 [*Sequel to Li Jiubiao's Diary of Oral Admonitions*]. in *Wu Yushan ji jianzhu* 吳漁山集箋注 [*Annotated Collection of Wu Yushan's Works*], juan 8, annotated by Zhang Wenqin 章文欽. 583–628, Beijing: Zhonghua shuju, 2007.

Zhao Qi 趙岐, annot., Sun Shi 孫奭, comm. *Mengzi* 孟子 [*Mencius*], Ruan Yuan 阮元, ed., *Shisanjing zhushu* 十三經注疏 [*Commentaries on the Thirteen Confucian Classics*], vol. 8, Taipei: Yiwen yinshuguan 藝文印書館, 1981.

Zhao Shiyu 趙世瑜. *Kuanghuan yu richang—Mingqing yilai de miaohui yu minjian shehui* 狂歡與日常——明清以來的廟會與民間社會 [*Carnivals in Daily Life: The Temple Fairs and Local Society Since Ming and Qing Dynasties*]. Beijing: Sanlian shudian 三聯書店, 2002.

Zheng Xuan 鄭玄, annot., Kong Yingda 孔穎達, comm. *Shijing* 詩經 [the *Book of Songs*]. Ruan Yuan 阮元, ed., *Shisanjing zhushu* 十三經注疏 [*Commentaries on the Thirteen Confucian Classics*], vol. 2, Taipei: Yiwen yinshuguan 藝文印書館, 1981.

Zheng Xuan 鄭玄, *Liji* 禮記 [the *Book of the Rites*]. Ruan Yuan 阮元, ed., *Shisanjing zhushu* 十三經注疏 [*Commentaries on the Thirteen Confucian Classics*], vol. 5, Taipei: Yiwen yinshuguan 藝文印書館, 1981.

Zhou Zhi 周志. *Tianxue mengyin* 天學蒙引 [*Basic Knowledge of the Study of Heaven*]. in CCT BnF, vol. 7, 327–390.

Zhu Xi 朱熹. *Zhuzi yulei* 朱子語類 [*Classified Conversations of Master Zhu*]. Edited by Li jingde 黎靖德. Beijing: Zhonghua shuju 中華書局, 2004.

Zou Zhenhuan 鄒振環. "Mingqing zhi ji Lingnan de 'jiaotang wenhua' jiqi yingxiang 明清之際嶺南的 '教堂文化' 及其影響 ["Church Culture" in Lingnan and Its Influence during the Ming and Qing Transition]." *Xueshu yanjiu* 學術研究 [*Academic Research*] 11 (2002): 73–83.

Zou Zhenhuan 鄒振環. "Mingmo Nanjing jiaoan zai Zhongguo jiaoanshi yanjiu zhong de fanshi yiyi—yi Nanjing jiaoan de fanjiao yu poxie moshi wei zhongxin 明末南京教案在中國教案史研究中的范式意義—以南京教案的反教與破邪模式為中心 ["Paradigm" Significance of Nanjing Religion Case in Late Ming Dynasty in Chinese Religion Case History Studies: with Nanjing Religion Case's Anti-Religion and "De-Heretic" as Center]." *Xueshu yuekan* 學術月刊 [*Academic Monthly*] 5 (2008): 122–131.

Zuo Guangxian 左光先. "Jianning xian Zuomingfu gaoshi 建寧縣左明府告示 [Official Proclamation by Official Zuo of Jianning County]." in *Zhengjiao fengzhuan* 正教奉傳 [*In Heritage of the Orthodox Teaching*], edited by Huang Bolu 黃伯祿. 3–4, Shanghai: Cimu tang 慈母堂, 1877.

Zürcher, Erik. "The Lord of Heaven and the Demons—Strange Stories from a Late Ming Christian Manuscript." in *Religion und Philosophie in Ostasien: Festschrift für Hans Steininger zum 65. Geburtstag*, edited by Gert Naundorf, Karl-Heinz Pohl, and Hans-Hermann Schmidt. 359–375, Würzburg: Köningshausen & Neumann, 1985.

Zürcher, Erik. "Un 'contrat communal' chrétien de la fin des Ming: le Livre d'Admonition de Han Lin (1641)." in *l'Europe en Chine: Interactions scientifiques, religieuses et culturelles aux XVIIe et XVIIIe siecles*, edited by Jami Catherine and Hubert Delahaye. 3–22, Mémoires de l'Institut des hautes études chinoises 34, Paris: Collège de France, 1993.

Zürcher, Erik. "Jesuit Accommodation and the Chinese Cultural Imperative." in *The*

Chinese Rites Controversy: Its History and Meaning, edited by D.E. Mungello. 31–64, Monumenta Serica Monograph Series XXXIII, Nettetal: Steyler Verlag, 1994.

Zürcher, Erik. "Confucian and Christian Religiosity in Late Ming China." *The Catholic Historical Review*, vol. 83, no. 4 (Washington D.C.: Catholic University of America Press, 1997): 614–653.

Zürcher, Erik. "Buddhist Chanhui and Christian Confession in Seventeenth-Century China." in *Forgive Us Our Sins: Confession in Late Ming and Early Qing China*, edited by Nicolas Standaert and Ad Dudink. 103–127, Monumenta Serica Monograph Series LV, Sankt Augustin: Institut Monumenta Serica, 2006.

Zürcher, Erik. *The Buddhist Conquest of China: The Spread and Adaptation of Buddhism in Early Medieval China*. Leiden: Brill, 2007.

Zürcher, Erik. *Kou duo ri chao: Li Jiubiao's Diary of Oral Admonitions: A Late Ming Christian Journal*. Sankt Augustin: Institut Monumenta Serica, 2007.

Zürcher, Erik. "The Spread of Buddhism and Christianity in Imperial China: Spontaneous Diffusion Versus Guided Propagation." in *Buddhism in China: Collected Papers of Erik Zürcher*, translated by Thomas Silk Cruijsen, edited by Jonathan A. 377–391, Leiden: Brill, 2013.

Index

Abridged Meaning of the Sacrifice of Mass (*Misa jiyi lüe* 彌撒祭義畧)   169
abstinence   103–105, 232
acolyte   129, 131, 174, 200, 271
Acts of St. John   79
adaptation   5, 9, 48, 148, 175, 182, 236, 270, 277–282
Adons, Julianus, OFM   185
adoration   221, 263–266, 282
affiliation   109, 138, 208
Agathe, Madame   211
alchemy   156
Aleni, Giulio, SJ (Ai Rulüe 艾儒略)   1–2, 6–9, 14–17, 23–34, 39, 44, 47–52, 58–62, 67–79, 89–92, 102, 105, 109–114, 126–135, 141, 152, 158–159, 168–169, 176–181, 214–223, 227, 234, 250–251, 265, 274
Alexander VII (pope)   163
All Saint's Day   81
almsgiving   86–87, 110–114, 121, 259, 275
Ambrose   5
Analects of Master Aleni from the Western Sea (*Xihai Ai xiansheng yulu* 西海艾先生語錄)   158–159
Analects, the (*Lunyu* 論語)   92–94
analogy   40, 71–72, 75–76, 80, 99–100, 107–108, 214, 219, 223
Andrzej, Rudomina, SJ (Lu Ande 盧安德)   33, 53, 113–114, 259
Anhui 安徽
   Huizhou 徽州   245
Answers to Questions about the Holy Body (*Shengti dayi* 聖體答疑)   112, 129–130, 271
Anthology of Destroying the Pernicious (*Poxie ji* 破邪集)   39–40, 135, 149–151, 224–226
anti-Catholics   9, 16, 56, 141, 146, 154, 224–228, 237–238, 244, 272, 275, 278, 283
anticlericalism   143–145, 147–154, 160, 257
Apostles' Creed, the   71, 107
apparition   113–115
Aquaviva, Claudio, SJ   160–161
Aquinas, Thomas, OP   97, 112–115, 173
Aristotle   80
assembly   52, 62, 70, 133, 148, 213–215, 228–229, 234–235, 239, 244–247, 252, 255, 266–269, 272

astronomy   130, 233, 237–238, s274
Augery, Humbert, SJ (Hong Duzhen 洪度貞)   118, 211
Augustine   32, 112–113, 233

baptism   8–9, 35, 80, 87, 105, 132, 138–142, 146, 210, 214, 245, 248, 252, 273, 282
Baroque style   212–213
Basic Knowledge of the Study of Heaven (*Tianxue mengyin* 天學蒙引)   54
Basset, Jean, MEP (Bai Risheng 白日昇)   142, 166, 172
beads   62, 240
beamless palace, the (*wuliang dian* 無梁殿)   224–226
Beijing 北京   10, 19, 81, 153, 160–163, 170, 184, 212, 240, 245, 251, 255, 262, 265
Bellarmine, Robert, SJ   161, 163
bitter image (*kuxiang* 苦像)   54, 56
Bodhisattva   206, 279
Book of Songs, the (*Shijing* 詩經)   190
Book of the Rites, the (*Liji* 禮記)   89, 92–94, 100, 168
Book of the Warning Bell, The (*Duoshu* 鐸書)   26, 35
Brancati, Francesco, SJ (Pan Guoguang 潘國光)   11, 32, 37–38, 114, 129, 138, 164, 211, 242–243, 260, 264
bread   30–32, 36–38, 42–45, 49–55, 69–72, 89, 111, 126–129, 157, 190–191, 221, 248–253, 274
Brief Account of the Lord of Heaven's Incarnation, Sayings, and Acts (*Tianzhu jiangsheng yanxing jilüe* 天主降生言行紀畧)   47
Brief Explanation of Catechism (*Jiaoyao jielüe* 教要解畧)   31, 36, 41, 55, 107, 239, 241, 249, 271
Brief Introduction of the Holy Teaching (*Shengjiao yueyan* 聖教約言)   240
Brief Introduction to the Holy Teaching of the Lord of Heaven (*Tianzhu shengjiao xiaoyin* 天主聖教小引)   239
Brief Record of Holy Prayers (*Shengjing yuelu* 聖經約錄)   125, 215, 247–249, 271

INDEX

Buddhist monk   12, 57, 80–83, 95, 109–110, 121, 134, 139, 145–146, 152–154, 174, 251, 256, 276, 279
Buddhist nun   81, 145–146, 279
Buglio, Lodovico, SJ (Li Leisi 利類思)   102–103, 126–128, 135, 164, 169–171, 220–221, 230, 233, 265

Caballero, Antonio de Santa Maria, OFM (Li Andang 利安當)   41, 89, 246, 254, 260–262
Calculating Method of Day of Worship in Calendar Year (*Tuiding linian zhanlirifa* 推定曆年瞻禮日法)   235
calendar case, the   141, 165, 237
Calendar Office (*Liju* 曆局)   237
Candida Xu 許甘第大   18, 122, 211
candle   218, 222, 252, 263–266
Canevari, Pietro, SJ (Nie Boduo 聶伯多)   164
cannibalism   154, 157
Canton Conference, the   105, 164, 255
Cao Xuequan 曹學佺   28
cap of Mass, the (*misa guan* 彌撒冠)   179–184
card of the communion of merits (*tonggong dan* 通功單)   123
Carvalho, Valentino, SJ   244
Case of Demolishing House and Garden Which Violate the System, the (*Chaihui weizhi louyuan yi'an* 拆毀違制樓園一案)   228
Case of Inventorying Barbarian Objects, the (*Qingcha yiwu yi'an* 清查夷物一案)   228
Case of Joint Hearing of Zhong Mingli and Other Prisoners, the (*Huishen Zhong mingli dengfan yi'an* 會審鍾明禮等犯一案)   245
Catechism of the Lord of Heaven (*Tianzhu jiaoyao* 天主教要)   39
catechist   82, 90, 133, 146, 154, 209
catechumen   2, 5, 31, 41, 252
Cattaneo, Lazzaro, SJ (Guo Jujing 郭居靜)   167, 183
celebrant   2, 134, 158–159, 164, 183, 215, 250, 276, 283
chalice   37, 72, 101–102, 188–189, 200, 216–220, 249

changsheng 長生→ See also everlasting life   70–71, 76
chapel   210–211, 227, 253–256, 261–263, 272
Chen Hao 陳澔   100
Chen Rutiao 陳汝調   53
Chen Weisong 陳維崧   140
Chen Yidian 陳懿典   149
Chen Zhongdan 陳衷丹   1–2, 9, 14, 17, 23, 158–159
Cheng Yi 程頤   94
chengcheng 根根   155
Chinese liturgy   161–162, 165–166
Chinese Mass, the (*Zhongguo misa* 中國彌撒)   182
Chinese Rites Controversy   3, 7, 77–78, 88, 106
Chongzhen Calendar Compendium, the (*Chongzhen lishu* 崇禎曆書)   237
Chongzhen emperor, the   49, 56, 237
Christendom   206, 247, 258–259, 261, 268–269, 271
Christianization   4–5, 231–232, 244, 258, 270
Christmas   8, 34, 171, 187, 243, 260, 262
Church of the Gesù, the   213
ciborium   218–221
Classics of the Mass, The (*Misa jingdian* 彌撒經典)   10, 157, 171–174, 220, 235, 271
classics
    from ancient China   13, 21, 106, 135, 190, 282, 284
    of Buddhism   12–13
    of Catholicism   125, 190, 234
    of Confucianism   12, 14, 40, 98
Clear Discussion on Ritual and Custom (*Lisu mingbian* 禮俗明辯)   99
Clear Evidence of Judgement of the Lord of Heaven (*Tianzhu shenpan mingzheng* 天主審判明證)   116
Clement X (pope)   164
Clement XI (pope)   21
Collective Rites of the Great Ming (*Da Ming jili* 大明集禮)   157
Communion   9, 70, 103, 111, 189, 244, 247–249, 252–253, 262–267, 273, 276, 282
    of merits   79, 107–111, 114, 123, 267, 277
    of saints   85, 106–111, 116–118, 121–123, 277
Compendium of Orthodox Sounds of Heavenly Music, the (*Tianyue zhengyin pu* 天樂正音譜)   187, 192

Compilation of Doubts [*on Behalf of Literatus*] (*Daiyi pian* 代疑篇)   23, 135, 137
composition of place (*compositio loci*)   48
confession   8–9, 129, 133, 142, 210, 245–247, 252, 261, 264–268, 273, 282
confirmation   9, 248
confraternity   53, 117–122, 131, 243–244, 255–260
Confucius   93, 96, 208
congregant   6, 47, 85, 131, 158, 167, 174, 200, 271
congregation   5, 263
Cotolendi, Ignace, MEP   163
Council of Trent, the   31
Counter-Reformation, the   280
Couplet, Philippe, SJ (Bo Yingli 柏應理)   17, 35, 164–165, 170–171, 235, 256, 264
Credo   195, 217
cross   27, 33, 43–44, 49, 52–58, 111–112, 142, 176–178, 181, 200, 218, 227, 240, 246, 262–263
Crucifixion, the   33, 41–43, 56–58, 111, 177, 181, 249, 263
cultural imperative, the   5, 204, 271–272, 278, 281–282

da Castorano, Carlo di Orazio, OFM (Kang Hezi 康和子)   86
da Rocha, João, SJ (Luo Ruwang 羅儒望)   27, 108, 250
Daily Services of the Holy Teaching (*Shengjiao rike* 聖教日課)
  of Longobardo   167
  of the Augustinians   173
  of the Franciscans   172
  of the Jesuits   169
day of worship (*zhanli* 瞻禮)   75, 230–235, 239–243, 256, 262, 272
Day of Worship for St. Andrew [*etc.*], *A* (*Sheng An-de-le zongtu zhanli* 聖安德肋宗徒瞻礼)   260
de Chavagnac, Emeric Langlois, SJ (Sha Shouxin 沙守信)   139
de Cornillon, Julienne   264
de Figueiredo, Rodrigo, SJ (Fei Lede 費樂德)   53, 164, 167
de Fontaney, Jean, SJ (Hong Ruo 洪若)   222
de Gouvea, Antoine, SJ (He Dahua 何大化)   164

de Goville, Pierre, SJ (Ge Weili 戈維里)   263
de Gravina, Girolamo, SJ (Jia Yimu 賈宜睦)   260
de la Motte, Pierre Lambert, MEP   163
de la Piñuela, Pedro, OFM (Shi Duolu 石鐸琭)   113, 118, 120, 172
de Loyola, Ignacio, SJ   47
de Mailla, Joseph, SJ (Feng Bingzheng 馮秉正)   80–81, 117
de Matos, Bento, SJ (Lin Bendu 林本篤)   33, 70
de Nobili, Roberto, SJ   22
de Osca, Joseph, OFM (Ke Ruose 柯若瑟)   222
de Pantoja, Diego, SJ (Pang Diwo 龐迪我)   12, 42–43, 108, 220, 232–233
de Prémare, Joseph, SJ (Ma Ruose 馬若瑟)   263
de Rhodes, Alexandre, SJ (Luo De 羅德)   162
de Saa, João, SJ (Yang Ruowang 楊若望/Yang Ruohan 楊若翰)   19–20
deacon   5, 263
della Chiesa, Bernardino, OFM (Yi Daren 伊大仁)   19, 94, 166
Dentrecolles, François-Xavier, SJ (Yin Hongxu 殷弘緒)   212, 251
Description of Mercy on Souls in Purgatory (*Aijin lianling shuo* 哀矜煉靈說)   113
Dialogue on Miracles (*Dialogus miraculorum*)   114
Dialogue on Sacrifice (*Bianji* 辯祭)   97
Dias, Manuel, SJ (Yang Manuo 陽瑪諾)   70, 76, 129, 141, 167, 211, 223, 233, 236
Ding Zhilin 丁志麟   31
Dip in the Holy Water   167
Direct Explanation of Sacred Scripture (*Shengjing zhijie* 聖經直解)   233, 236
Directions for Hearing Mass (*Ting misa fanli* 聽彌撒凡例)   172, 217
discipline   263
Divine Office, the   161, 166
Documents of the South Palace (*Nangong shudu* 南宮署牘)   149, 224
Dongpo hat (*Dongpo jin* 東坡巾)   174, 181–182
door gods (*menshen* 門神)   239
Duarte, João, SJ (Nie Ruowang 聶若望)   263

INDEX

East Hall, the (*dongtang* 東堂)   18, 211, 221, 262
Easter   20, 171, 243, 262–263
Easter Sunday   262–263
Edict to Control Area Wu (*Fuwu gaoyu* 撫吳告諭)   145
effect
    as an impression   182, 189, 213, 223
    in rituals   8, 37, 55
effective ritual   266–268, 282–283
efficacy   109, 112, 138–139
Elevation of the Holy Body, The   168, 169
Elevation of the Holy Chalice, The   168, 169
elixir (*dan* 丹)   70–71, 76, 156–157
Eternal List of Worship of the Holy Teaching of the Lord of Heaven (*Tianzhu shengjiao yongzhanlidan* 天主聖教永瞻禮單)   235, 264
Eucharist, the   5–9, 31, 36, 58–61, 89, 129–130, 133, 210, 215, 221, 249–250, 265, 274
everlasting life (*changsheng* 常生)   54–55, 70–72, 76, 190, 274
Examination on Similarity & Dissimilarity between the Study of Heaven and Confucianism (*Tian ru tongyi kao* 天儒同異考)   14, 27, 76
Explanation of Baptism and Confession Two Important Rules Set by the Lord of Heaven Himself (*Tianzhu qinli lingxi gaojie er yaogui zhi li* 天主親立領洗告解二要規之理)   8
Explanation of Mass (*Misa jie* 彌撒解)   24
Explanation of the Incarnation and Life of the Lord of Heaven (*Tianzhu jiangsheng chuxiang jingjie* 天主降生出像經解)   44, 47–48
Explanation on Using Chinese Culture (*Yongxia jie* 用夏解)   137
Explanation on Works of Mercy (*Aijin xingquan* 哀矜行詮)   115
Exposition of Mass, The (*Misa lijie* 彌撒禮節)   168–169, 172, 216
Expounding How to Fear Heaven and to Love Human Beings (*Weitian airen jilun* 畏天愛人極論)   26, 35, 135
extreme unction   9, 133, 248

Faber, Étienne, SJ (Fang Dewang 方德望)   138

Family Rituals (*Jiali* 家禮)   94–95
Fan Zhong 范中   239
Fang Congzhe 方從哲   225
Fang Zheng 方政   245
fasting   9, 102–106, 112, 121, 147, 232, 235, 247
Feast of *Corpus Christi*   264, 266
Feast of St. Joseph, the   231
Feliciano, Pacheco, SJ (Cheng Jili 成際理)   117, 164
female Catholics   146, 208–212, 253–257, 261, 275
female hall (*nütang* 女堂)   253–256
Feng Yingjing 馮應京   135
Fernandez-Oliver, Michael, OFM (Nan Huaide 南懷德)   18, 89, 93–94, 239
Festival of Water and Land, the (*shuilu hui* 水陸會)   121
filial piety   25–28, 43, 77, 81, 85–86, 89–97, 101, 110, 136, 275–276, 279
five cardinal relationships, the (*wulun* 五倫)   110, 140
Flower Adornment Sutra (Avataṃsaka Sūtra)   55
foot-washing ritual, the   263
Fouquet, Jean-François, SJ (Fu Shengze 傅聖澤)   139–140, 155, 263
Four Books, the (*sishu* 四書)   13, 21
Four Character Classic of the Lord of Heaven's Holy Teaching (*Tianzhu shengjiao sizi jingwen* 天主聖教四字經文)   25
Four Character Classic to Praise the Holy Body (*Zan shengti sizi jingwen* 讚聖體四字經文)   173
Four Rules of the Holy Teaching (*Shengjiao sigui* 聖教四規)   32, 37, 42, 241–242
Franchi, Girolamo, SJ (Fang Quanji 方全紀)   93–94, 154, 265
Froger, François   261
Fróis, João, SJ (Fu Ruowang 伏若望)   44
Fujian 福建   1, 10, 19, 21, 58, 89, 132, 150, 163, 279
    Fu'an 福安   151, 210, 257, 266, 268
    Funing 福寧   212
    Fuzhou 福州   19–21, 28, 33, 52–54, 70, 113–114, 168, 209, 277
    Haikou 海口   32, 39, 68–71
    Jianning 建甯   29, 137
    Jinjiang 晉江   31

318　INDEX

Longjiang 龍江→ *See also* Haikou 海口
　　214, 219–220
Ningde 寧德　96, 210
Quanzhou 泉州　116, 156, 162
Shaowu 邵武　28
Wuyi Mountain (*Wuyi shan* 武夷山)
　　105
Xianyou 仙遊　2
Yongchun 詠春　33, 75
Zhangzhou 漳州　56, 156, 209
funeral　9, 79, 81–87, 93–95, 109, 185, 233, 276
Furtado, Francisco, SJ (Fu Fanji 傅汎際)
　　167

Gabiani, Jean-Dominique, SJ (Bi Jia 畢嘉)
　　164, 222
gender segregation　134, 144–146, 253–257, 275
General Collection of Prayer Recitation in the Holy Teaching of the Lord of Heaven (*Tianzhu shengjiao nianjing zongdu* 天主聖教念經總牘)　26, 167, 169
General Collection of Prayers in the Holy Teaching (*Shengjiao zongdu jingwen* 聖教總牘經文)　172
Genesis　232, 241
geomancy (*fengshui* 風水)　229
Ghost Festival, the　95, 122, 236
glocalization　205, 270–273
Golden Book with Contempt of the World (*Qingshi jinshu* 輕世金書)　70, 76, 129, 192, 223
Golden Cicada Teaching (*jinchan jiao* 金蟬教)　136
Goltzius, Hendrick　49
Good Friday　33, 243, 262–263
Gozani, Giampaolo, SJ (Lu Baolu 魯保祿/Luo Baolu 駱保祿)　19–21
grace
　　e-la-ji-ya 額辣濟亞, *gratia*　108
　　for souls of the deceased　75
　　of parents　101
　　of the bishop　20
　　of the emperor　222
　　of the holy body　38, 47, 70, 112, 114–116, 188–192, 265
　　of the Lord of Heaven　1–2, 24, 38, 42, 67–68, 74–75, 101, 103, 106, 108, 131, 159, 168, 233, 241–243, 248

　　of the Lord's nativity　33
　　of the reception of suffering　35, 42
　　Thomistic understanding　100
gratitude　1–2, 9, 24, 79, 98, 159, 233, 241
Great Father (*dafu* 大父)　25–27, 29–30, 168, 215
Great Father and Mother (*dafumu* 大父母)　25–30, 77, 99–100, 274, 276–277
Gregory the Great (pope)　112
Grelon, Adrien, SJ (Nie Zhongqian 聶仲遷)　105, 170
Gu Yanwu 顧炎武　238
Guangdong 廣東　151, 163, 165
　　Canton 廣州　164, 166, 170, 173, 210, 261
　　Chao'an 潮安　211
　　Chaozhou 潮州　160–161
　　Huizhou 惠州　211
　　Nanhai 南海　211
　　Shaozhou 韶州　209
　　Xinhui 新會　209
　　Xinxing 新興　211
　　Zhaoqing 肇慶　6–7, 156, 174, 206, 210, 235, 259
Guangxi 廣西　163
Guizhou 貴州　163
Guo Bangyong 郭邦雍　96, 98

Hail Mary, the　120, 168
Hainan 海南　163
Hall of Bodhisattva of Compassion, the (*Guanyin tang* 觀音堂)　208
Hall of Buddha, the (*fotang* 佛堂)　208
Hall of General [Liu] Meng, the (*Mengjiang tang* 猛將堂)　208
hall of Jesus, the　226–227
Hall of Our Lady of Annunciation, the　209
Hall of Rose, the　209
Hall of Serving Heaven, the　225, 227, 228
Hall of St. Francis Xavier, the　209
Hall of St. Monica, the　210
Hall of St. Thomas Aquinas, the　209
hall of Teaching, the (*jiaotang* 教堂)　228
Hall of the Conception of Our Lady, the　210
hall of the Holy Mother, the (*shengmu tang* 聖母堂)　208, 210, 254
Hall of the Honorable and Intimate, the (*Zunqin tang* 尊親堂)　29
Hall of the Sacred Heart, the　209
Hall of the Supernatural, the　209, 211–213

INDEX

Hall of the Supreme Good, the   209
Han Lin 韓霖   22, 26, 35, 71, 73, 211, 274
Han Yu 韓愈   150
Han Yun 韓雲   71
Hanshan Deqing 憨山德清   151
Hat of Mass is the Implicit Sign of the Fall of Ming Dynasty, The (*Misa jin shi Mingwang zhi anxin* 彌撒巾是明亡之暗信)   178, 184–185
hat of Mass, the (*misa jin* 彌撒巾)   184–185
hat of six directions, the (*liuhe mao* 六合帽)   182
heaven's order (*tianming* 天命)   16
Heavenly Stems and Earthly Branches, the (*tiangan dizhi* 天干地支)   184
Hebei 河北
    Chengde 承德   21
Heisterbach, Caesarius of, OCist   114
Help to the Refutation of the Heresy (*Zuopi* 佐闢)   237
Henan 河南   163, 211
    Kaifeng 開封   53
Herdtricht, Christian, SJ (En Lige 恩理格)   85, 170
heterodoxy   15, 98, 152, 157
hierarchy
    bureaucratic   2, 13–15, 142, 157–158
    of the Church   125–128, 142, 158
High Lord, the (*shangdi* 上帝)→ *See also tianzhu* 天主   12–14, 16, 19, 28–29, 31, 39–40, 92, 102, 110, 158, 236, 276
High Mass   246, 263
Hinderer, Romain, SJ (De Manuo 德瑪諾)   173
Holy Body's Mysterious Meaning (*Shengti aoyi* 聖體奧義)   172
holy locket (*shengdu* 聖櫝)   252
holy oil   57, 146, 252
holy salt   252
Holy Saturday   263
Holy Thursday   75, 262–263, 265
holy water   57, 138, 146, 164, 252
homily   33–34, 235, 241, 253, 259–261, 274
Hong, Ignatius 洪依納爵   101–102
Host, the   37–39, 69–72, 111–118, 121, 131, 166, 173–174, 190–192, 199–200, 207, 216, 262–266, 274, 282
Huang Dacheng 黃大成   96, 98
Huang Mingsha 黃明沙, SJ   160

Huang Wendao 黃問道   16
Huang Zhen 黃貞   16, 40, 57, 145, 152, 226
Hubei 湖北   186, 211
    Mopan Mountain (Mopan shan 磨盤山)   83–84, 239, 257
    Wuchang 武昌   164
Huguang 湖廣 area, the   163
Huiyuan 慧遠   152
Humble Attempt at Discussing Matters Pertaining to the Soul (*Lingyan lishao* 靈言蠡勺)   73, 80
Hunan 湖南   211

Ibáñez, Buenaventura, OFM (Wen Dula 文都辣)   133, 261–262
Idea of the Holy, The   23
Imitation of Sacrificial Rituals (*Jili paozhi* 祭禮泡製)   90, 96, 100
Immeasurable Palace, the   226
Imperial Astronomical Bureau, the (*Qintian jian* 欽天監)   130, 143, 237–238
Incarnation   22, 28, 73
inculturation   30, 77, 274, 277
indigenous liturgy   124–125, 160–167, 171, 204, 275, 279–281
indulgence   118, 120–121
Innocent X (pope)   14, 18
Innocent XI (pope)   165, 171
Innocent XII (pope)   19
institutional religion   79, 146–147, 280–281
Instructions of the Priest (*Siduo dianyao* 司鐸典要)   102, 126, 128, 171, 220
intermediary   128, 131, 138, 154–155, 158, 160, 276, 283
Intorcetta, Prospero, SJ (Yin Duoze 殷鐸澤)   164, 229

Japan   12–13, 22, 160–161, 243–244, 264, 268, 280–282
Jiajing emperor, the   89
Jiang Dejing 蔣德璟   40, 135, 158
Jiangsu 江蘇   10, 145, 239
    Changshu 常熟   18, 130, 138, 186
    Jiangning 江寧   222, 228
    Nanjing 南京   15, 56–57, 149–150, 161–163, 166, 184–186, 224–226, 244–245, 253
    Shangyuan 上元   228
    Wuxi 無錫   263

Jiangxi 江西　163, 211
　　Fuzhou 撫州　139–140
　　Ganzhou 贛州　90
　　Jianchang 建昌　229, 253
　　Jingdezhen 景德鎮　212
　　Nanchang 南昌　135, 160–161, 174, 263
　　Nanfeng 南豐　263
　　Zhangshu 樟樹　174
Judith, Madame　211

Kangxi emperor, the　6–7, 16–18, 21, 130, 145, 184, 209, 212, 222, 277
kinship (*zongzu* 宗族)　89, 140, 268
kowtow　102, 199, 221–223, 242, 256
Kyrie eleison　62, 194, 216

Last Supper, the　37, 43, 45, 48–49, 128, 189
Laurifice, Emmanuel, SJ (Pan Guoliang 潘國良)　212
Le Comte, Louis, SJ (Li Ming 李明)　18–19, 80, 166, 171, 208, 213, 221–222, 254, 256
Le Faure, Jacques, SJ (Liu Diwo 劉迪我)　164
Le Gobien, Charles, SJ (Guo Bi'en 郭弼恩)　19
Lei Chong 雷翀　136
Letian hat (*Letian jin* 樂天巾)　181–182
Li Andang 李安當　82
Li Anrui 李安瑞　82
Li Can 李璨　152–153
Li Jiubiao 李九標　52, 113–114, 132
Li Jiubiao's Diary of Oral Admonitions (*Kouduo richao* 口鐸日抄)　1, 132, 159, 259, 262
Li Jiugong 李九功　8, 26, 36, 85, 89, 92, 95, 99, 111, 159, 274
Li Sixuan 李嗣玄　159
Li Zhi 李贄　135
Li Zhizao 李之藻　26, 149, 175
Life of Christ (*Vita Christi*)　47–49
Life of the Holy Mother (*Shengmu xingshi* 聖母行實)　39
list of worship (*zhanlidan* 瞻禮單)　229, 234–240, 244, 247, 252, 259, 266–267, 269, 275–276, 283
Litany of Jesus' Holy Body (*Yesu shengti daowen* 耶穌聖體禱文)　10–11, 58–62, 70–71, 74, 77, 169

Litany of Jesus' Holy Name (*Yesu shenghao daowen* 耶穌聖號禱文)　29, 71
Litany of Jesus' Reception of Suffering (*Yesu shounan daowen* 耶穌受難禱文)　44, 53
literati　12–15, 48, 56, 80, 89, 106, 134–137, 141, 147, 149–150, 158, 163–164, 174–175, 182, 211–212, 283
　　literatus　18, 23, 28, 134, 141, 152, 164, 211
　　Catholic literatus　23–26, 29, 80, 183, 237
　　Western literatus　135
liturgical calendar　52, 142, 206, 220, 229, 232, 234–238, 243, 260, 266, 272, 275–276
Liturgy of the Hours, the→ See also Divine Office, the　161
Liu Tong 劉侗　126–127, 246
Liu Yunde 劉蘊德, SJ (Blaise Verbiest)　186
Longobardo, Niccolò, SJ (Long Huamin 龍華民)　13, 81, 135, 141–142, 161, 167
Lord of Heaven Jesus, the (*tianzhu Yesu* 天主耶穌)　11, 36–42, 48–49, 57–58, 98, 249, 274
Lord's day, the (*zhuri* 主日)　229–234, 240, 244, 260, 266, 274
Lucas, Li　244
Ludolf of Saxony　47
Luo Qing 羅清　152
Luo Teaching, the (*Luo jiao* 羅教)　151–152
Luo Wenzhao 羅文炤, OP (Gregorio López)　17, 165–166, 186, 266, 269

Ma Tang 馬堂　56
Macao 澳門　30, 56, 141, 147, 154, 156, 161–162, 178–179, 186–187
Magalhães, Gabriel de, SJ (An Wensi 安文思)　142, 164, 170, 262
Maigrot, Charles, MEP (Yan Dang 顏璫)　19–22, 54, 277
Maillard de Tournon, Charles-Thomas (Duo Luo 多羅)　142, 251
manna　68–70, 72–73
Manual for Acolytes, A (*Fu misa jing* 輔彌撒經)　131
Manual for Attending Mass (*Yu misa gongcheng* 與彌撒功程)　173, 192
marriage　9, 102, 233, 268
Martini, Martino, SJ (Wei Kuangguo 衛匡國)　211, 247

INDEX

Matteo Ricci Entering China is the Implicit Sign of Ming Dynasty Losing the Reign (*Li Madou jin Zhongguo wei Ming shi tianxia zhi anxin* 利瑪竇進中國為明失天下之暗信) 178
Mayr, Georg, SJ 61, 67
Meaning of the Sacrifice of Mass, The (*Misa jiyi* 彌撒祭義) 6, 10, 25, 69, 79, 102, 106, 111, 126, 168–169, 176, 180, 192–193, 199–200, 215–217, 220, 271
Meditations (*Shensi lu* 慎思錄) 36
Memorial to Expel Distant Barbarians (*Faqian yuanyi huizou shu* 發遣遠夷回奏疏) 225
Memorial to Impeach Barbarians from Far Away (*Can yuanyi shu* 參遠夷疏) 15
Mencius (*Mengzi* 孟子) 190
merit 38, 52, 67, 75, 86, 104, 107–118, 123, 136, 188, 214, 238, 240, 242–243, 268, 271–272, 274, 277
Merits Suitable to Make before and after Receiving the Holy Body (*Ling shengti qianhou kexing zhi gong* 領聖體前後可行之功) 173
Method of Listening to the Mass Every Day (*Meiri ting misa zhi fa* 每日聽彌撒之法) 173
Methodical Exposition of the Essence of the Faith (*Jiaoyao xulun* 教要序論) 73
Mezzabarba, Carlo Ambrogio (Jia Le 嘉樂) 7
Ministry of Rites (*Libu* 禮部) 15, 149–150, 207, 224, 227–228, 236–237, 245
Mirror for Self-Cultivation, A (*Lixiu yijian* 勵修一鑑) 95
Miyun Yuanwu 密雲圓悟 153
monotheism, Confucian 22–23, 271
Monteiro, João, SJ (Meng Ruwang 孟儒望) 29–30, 71
Morales, Juan Bautista de, OP (Li Yufan 黎玉範) 41, 246
Motel, Jacques, SJ (Mu Diwo 穆迪我) 164
Musical Sound of Mass, The (*Misa yueyin* 彌撒樂音) 10, 192–204, 271, 276

Nadal, Jerónimo, SJ 43–44
Nanjing persecution, the 132, 160, 224, 228, 244–245
Neo-Confucianism 32, 94, 276

neophyte 175, 263
New Testament, the 189
Nicene Creed, the 181
Noël, François, SJ (Wei Fangji 衛方濟) 262
Non-Action Teaching, the (*wuwei jiao* 無為教) 136, 146, 148, 150
Noruega, Ignacio, OSA (Yi-na-jue 依納爵) 173

Official Calendar in the Ming Dynasty, the (*Datong li* 大統曆) 241
Old Testament, the 68–70, 72, 189
Oliva, Giovanni Paolo, SJ 164
On Copies of Pictures Presented by Adam Schall (*Lin Tang Ruowang jincheng tuxiang shuo* 臨湯若望進呈圖像說) 58
On Heaven (*Tian shuo* 天說) 12, 152
On the Calendar (*Lifa lun* 曆法論) 251
One Hundred Questions and Answers of the Lord of Heaven's Holy Teaching (*Tianzhu shengjiao baiwenda* 天主聖教百問答) 35, 241
oratory 210, 254
Order of the Mass (*Ordinarium Missae*) 173
Ordinances of the Holy Teaching (*Shengjiao guicheng* 聖教規程) 117, 255, 257
ordination 9, 19, 42, 125, 138, 163–164, 186–187
ordination certificate (*dudie* 度牒) 145, 147
orthodoxy 15, 94, 122, 149, 151, 153, 278–280
orthopraxy 278–279
Our Father, the→ *See also* Pater Noster 26, 120, 168, 245
Owl and the Phoenix Do Not Sing Together, The (*Xiao luan bubingming shuo* 鴞鸞不並鳴說) 137

Padroado 163
Pallu, François, MEP (Lu Fangji 陸方濟) 163
Palm Sunday 263
Palmeiro, André, SJ 14
Pan Lei 潘耒 238
Papebroch, Daniel, SJ 165, 171
parish 258, 261
Pater Noster 26, 62, 69, 120, 250
Paul V (pope) 161, 163–165, 167, 170–172, 175, 179

pernicious teaching (*xiejiao* 邪教)   75, 151–153

Person(s) of the Trinity   29–30, 36–41, 62, 73, 180–181

Pictures in a Booklet Presented to His Majesty (*Jincheng shuxiang* 進呈書像)   49, 56–57

Plantin-Moretus   171

poetry of Heavenly Learning, the (*tianxue shi* 天學詩)   187, 191, 203

Praise to the Holy Body and the Holy Mother (*Shengti shengmu hezan* 聖體聖母合讚)   39, 173, 221, 261

Praising Origin and Development of the Holy Church (*Song Shenghui yuanliu* 誦聖會源流)   188, 191

Prayer before Mass   169

Prayer Book for the Priest (*Siduo kedian* 司鐸課典)   171

Prayer of the Confraternity of the Holy Body's Benevolence to Give Thanks to the Lord of Heaven (*Shengti ren'aihui xianxie tianzhu zhuwen* 聖體仁愛會獻謝天主祝文)   38

Prayer Recited after Receiving the Holy Body   167, 169

Prayer Recited before Receiving the Holy Body   26, 167, 169

Prayers for the Acolyte, the   168

Prayers of Sufferings, The (*Tongku jingji* 痛苦經蹟)   168–169

prefiguration   68–69, 72

Prescription of Elixir that Revives Human Beings (*Huoren danfang* 活人丹方)   71

Prima Primaria   244

procession   187, 264–266

Propaganda Fide   162–165, 175, 185, 246–247, 261

purgatory   83, 85, 99, 106, 112–121, 123

purificator   220

qinchong tiandao 欽崇天道   16

Qiu Aoding 丘奧定   264

Qiu Lianghou 丘良厚, SJ   127

Qu Rukui 瞿汝夔   135, 174

Questions & Answers of Receiving the Holy Body (*Ling shengti wenda* 領聖體問答)   172

Questions & Answers of Sacrificial Rituals (*Jisi wenda* 祭祀問答)   101

Questions & Answers of the Holy Sacrament (*Shengshi wenda* 聖事問答)   38

real presence, the   31–33, 38, 55, 72, 207, 214–215, 274

reception of suffering (*shounan* 受難)   11, 34–36, 41–44, 47–49, 52–58, 77, 271, 274

Reception of Suffering of the Lord of Heaven Jesus from the Beginning to the End (*Tianzhu Yesu shounan shimo* 天主耶穌受難始末)   42, 220

Record of the Transmission of the Lamp (*Chuandeng lu* 傳燈錄)   230

Record of Trip in Beijing (*Beiyou lu* 北游錄)   128

Records of the Holy Water (*Shengshui jiyan* 聖水紀言)   25–26

Refutation of the Buddhist's Absurdities (*Pi shishi zhuwang* 闢釋氏諸妄)   90, 110

Regulation of Reciting the Beads (*Song nianzhu guicheng* 誦念珠規程)   27, 43, 191

Regulation of the Cap of Mass, The (*Misa guan yi* 彌撒冠儀)   10, 178–180, 183–184

reincarnation   80, 104, 110

Requiem Mass   6, 86–87, 118–121

Rho, Giacomo, SJ (Luo Yagu 羅雅谷)   103–104, 115, 232, 237

Ricci, Matteo, SJ (Li Madou 利瑪竇)   6–7, 12–14, 22–25, 41, 48, 56, 80–81, 91–94, 106, 116, 125–127, 134–135, 139–141, 145, 160–161, 174, 206, 215, 235–237, 243–244, 247

Ricci Bodhisattva (*Li Madou pusa* 利瑪竇菩薩)   139

Ricci's rule (*Li Madou de guiju* 利瑪竇的規矩)   22

Ripa, Matteo, SJ (Ma Guoxian 馬國賢)   93

Rite for the Acolyte, the   168–169

Rite of Attending Mass, the   192

Rite of Attending Mass, the   168–169

Rite of Five Thanks, the (*Wuxie li* 五謝禮)   172

ritual interaction   2, 7, 9–10, 269, 270–275, 277, 282

Ritual Manual for Sacraments (*Shengshi lidian* 聖事禮典)   171

INDEX 323

Ritual Rules of the Holy Body (*Shengti guiyi* 聖體規儀) 114, 264–265
Ritual Sequence for Attending Funerals and Organizing the Procession (*Linsang chubin yishi* 臨喪出殯儀式) 82, 84–85
ritual to Heaven and Earth, the 1, 2, 14–15, 159
Rodrigues, João, SJ (Lu Ruohan 陸若漢) 12, 13, 22, 141
Rodrigues, Simao, SJ (Li Ximan 李西滿) 97–99, 208, 216
Roman Breviary, the 163, 165, 171
Roman Missal, the 43, 69, 157, 163–165, 170–172, 193, 199–200, 217, 249
Roman Ritual, the 165, 171–172, 263
Romanae Sedis Antistes 161
Romanus Pontifex 171
Rome 6–9, 14, 22, 77, 141, 143, 147, 161–163, 166, 171–172, 174–175, 178–179, 182, 204–205, 213, 247, 269, 272–273, 275–276, 279, 281–282
Rosary, the 43, 210, 260, 263
Rougemont, François de, SJ (Lu Riman 魯日滿) 18, 130–131, 138–140, 164, 170, 235
Rudiments of the Holy Teaching of the Lord of Heaven (*Tianzhu shengjiao qimeng* 天主聖教啓蒙) 250
Ruggieri, Michele, SJ (Luo Mingjian 羅明堅) 6–7, 134, 174, 206, 210
Rules of Confraternity of Charity (*Renhui yue* 仁會約) 6
Rules of Prayer to the Holy Body's Benevolence (*Shengti ren'aijing guitiao* 聖體仁愛經規條) 39, 44, 80, 117–118
Rustic Opinion about Rites, A (*Zhengli chuyi* 證禮芻議) 85–86

sacrifice
    to ancestors 7, 15, 78, 79, 88–93, 96–102, 106, 124, 148, 151, 245, 268, 275, 278–279, 283
    to Confucius 7, 88, 97, 278–279, 283–284
    to the Lord of Heaven 11, 24, 86, 99–100, 111, 125, 129, 213, 245, 250, 282
sacrificial hat, the (*jijin* 祭巾) 167, 175–179, 184–186, 275–277, 282
Saint Master Thomas' Four Character Poem to the Holy Body (*Duo-ma-si shengshi xiang shengti sizi shi* 多瑪斯聖師向聖體四字詩) 173
Sambiasi, Francesco, SJ (Bi Fangji 畢方濟) 73, 80, 149
Sanctus 188–189
sangha (*seng* 僧) 144
sanshen 三身 (the three bodies) 41
Schall von Bell, Johann Adam, SJ (Tang Ruowang 湯若望) 48–49, 56, 58, 115, 132, 139, 141, 143, 162, 213, 223, 227, 237, 259, 265
Second Memorial to Accuse Distant Barbarians (*Zaican yuanyi shu* 再參遠夷疏) 224
Semedo, Álvaro de, SJ (Zeng Dezhao 曾德昭) 183
Sequel to Li Jiubiao's Diary of Oral Admonitions (*Xu Kouduo richao* 續口鐸日抄) 259–260, 262
Seven Points to Meditate before and after Receiving the Holy Body (*Ling shengti qianhou moxiang qiduan* 領聖體前後默想七端) 173
seven sevens, the (*qiqi* 七七) 83–84
Shaanxi 陝西 138, 163
    Xi'an 西安 253
Shandong 山東 163, 260–261
    Ji'nan 濟南 18, 93, 172, 211–212, 221–222, 254, 260, 262
    Jimo 即墨 151
    Linqing 臨清 56
Shanghai 上海 18, 123, 139, 187, 192, 211, 245, 264
Shanxi 山西 80, 133, 163, 245
    Donger gou 洞兒溝 117
    Jiangzhou 絳州 136, 211, 253
    Pingyang 平陽 211
    Taiyuan 太原 211
Shen Fuzong 沈福宗 165
Shen Que 沈㴶 15–16, 145, 149–150, 162, 224–229, 239
Shi Purun 釋普潤 57, 245
Shunzhi emperor, the 16, 139, 223
Sichuan 四川 142, 163, 211
Sinicization 5, 185, 270
Sketch of Landscape in Capital Beijing (*Dijing jingwu lüe* 帝京景物略) 126, 135, 246, 254
Soares, José, SJ (Su Lin 蘇霖) 121

Soeiro, João, SJ (Su Ruwang 蘇如望)   240–241
Solid Evidence of Pernicious Poison (*Xiedu shiju* 邪毒實據)   154
solidarity   106, 116–117, 121
Son of Heaven (*tianzi* 天子)   1–2, 13–17, 23–24, 136, 158–159
sphere
    ecclesiastical   83, 85, 87, 100, 107, 123, 147, 160, 215, 239, 267, 269, 272
    familial   2, 83, 87, 100, 117, 122–123, 147, 215, 239, 255–256, 267–269, 272
    private   215, 234
    public   215, 234
    state   122
Spiritual Exercises, the   47
Spiritual Father (*shenfu* 神父)   82–83, 86, 132, 147
spiritual reception   168, 264–265
Sprital Practice to Communicate Merits (*Tonggong shenke* 通功神課)   172
Sprinkle the Holy Water   167
square hat, the (*fangjin* 方巾)   181–182
Statutes of Confraternity of the Holy Body (*Shengtihui gui* 聖體會規)   118
Statutes of Confraternity of the Holy Mother (*Shengmuhui gui* 聖母會規)   118, 266
Statutes of Confraternity of the Third Order of St. Francis (*Sheng Fangjige disanhui gui* 聖方濟各第三會規)   118
Statutes of the Confraternity of the Angels (*Tianshen huike* 天神會課)   37, 42, 241
Statutes of the Confraternity of the Annunciation to the Holy Mother (*Shengmu lingbaohui gui* 聖母領報會規)   121
Study on Sacrifice to Ancestors (*Jizu kao* 祭祖考)   89, 93
Stumpf, Kilian, SJ (Ji Li'an 紀理安)   239
Su Jiyu 蘇及寓   154
Su, Johan (Xu Ruohan 徐若翰)   142
suffrage   112–113, 121
Summary of Confraternity Statutes (*Huigui zongyao* 會規總要)   117
Summary of Miraculous Events at Mass (*Misa qimiao shiqing lüeshuo* 彌撒奇妙事情畧說)   173
Sun Yuanhua 孫元化   183–184
Supernatural Events of Mr. Yang Qiyuan (*Yang Qiyuan xiansheng chaoxing shiji* 楊淇園先生超性事蹟)   30–31
superstition   4, 97

tabernacle   207, 221, 228, 274
Table of Dates for Worship and Fasting of the Holy Teaching of the Lord of Heaven, The (*tianzhu shengjiao zhanli zhaiqibiao* 天主聖教瞻禮齋期表)   235
tablet (*paibian* 牌匾)   16–21
Tan Qian 談遷   128, 246
Tang Bin 湯斌   145
Taoist nun   145
temple for ancestors (*zumiao* 祖廟)   208
temple for Confucius (*Kongzi miao* 孔子廟)   208
Temple of Immortal Flower, the (*Xianhua si* 仙花寺)   206
Temple of Master Huang, the (*Huanggong ci* 黃公祠)   228–229
temple of the Heavenly Empress   207–209
Ten Commandments, the   84, 91, 240–242
Ten Paradoxes (*Jiren shipian* 畸人十篇)   80
Tenebrae   263
Terrentius, Johannes Schreck, SJ (Deng Yuhan 鄧玉函)   162, 237
Third Memorial to Accuse Distant Barbarians (*Can yuanyi sanshu* 參遠夷三疏)   225
tianzhu 天主 (the Lord of Heaven)   7, 11–14, 17, 276
To Revere Heaven (*jingtian* 敬天)   16–19
Tong Guoqi 佟國器   211
transubstantiation   30–35, 37–38, 42, 111, 130, 157, 250–252, 274
Treatise on the Holy Body (*Shengti yaoli* 聖體要理)   61, 69, 76, 111–112, 271
Trigault, Michel, SJ (Jin Mige 金彌格)   115, 164
Trigault, Nicolas, SJ (Jin Nige 金尼閣)   12, 30, 33, 161–163, 167, 175, 179, 211, 235
trilogy of aids   112–114, 116, 275, 276
True Meaning of the Lord of Heaven, The (*Tianzhu shiyi* 天主實義)   25, 135
Twenty-Eight Mansions, the (*ershiba xingxiu* 二十八星宿)   232–233

Vagnone, Alfonso, SJ (Wang Fengsu 王豐肅/Gao Yizhi 高一志)   12, 27, 31, 36, 39,

INDEX

41–42, 55, 71, 107, 115, 136–137, 211, 224, 241, 246, 249
Valat, Jean, SJ (Wang Ruwang 汪儒望) 262
Valignano, Alessandro, SJ (Fan Li'an 范禮安) 160, 174–175
Varo, Francisco, OP (Wan Jiguo 萬濟國) 97
Verbiest, Ferdinand, SJ (Nan Huairen 南懷仁) 16, 73, 96, 106, 112, 129–130, 164, 166, 169–170, 274
Veritable Record of the Lord of Heaven (*Tianzhu shilu* 天主實錄) 240
Victory over Fasting (*Zhaike* 齋克) 103
Vitelleschi, Mutio, SJ 162

Wan Qiyuan 萬其淵, SJ (Paul Banhes) 186
Wang Chaoshi 王朝式 227
Wang Hui 王翬 192
Wang Pan 王泮 6, 206, 210
Wang Qishu 汪啟淑 223
Wang Zheng 王徵 6, 22, 26, 35–36, 71, 73, 135, 234, 274
Wanli emperor, the 56, 139, 149, 152, 183, 225–226
Wei Jun 魏濬 141
Wen Xiangfeng 文翔鳳 149–150
Western Confucianist (*xiru* 西儒) 24, 134–137, 142–143, 276
Western intellectual (*xishi* 西士) 135
Western monk (*xiseng* 西僧) 134
White Lotus movement, the (*bailianhua she* 白蓮華社) 148, 152
White Lotus Teachings, the (*bailian jiao* 白蓮教) 146, 148–152
wine 31, 37, 42, 45, 49, 52, 54–55, 72, 101–102, 112, 126, 128–129, 157, 222, 248–252
Wu Ercheng 吳爾成 245
Wu Li 吳歷, SJ (Simon-Xavier a Cunha) 34, 131, 178–179, 186–193, 199–200, 204, 223, 236–238, 260, 269, 271, 274, 276
Wu Sangui 吳三桂 185

Xavier, Francis, SJ (Sha Wulüe 沙勿略) 12, 131, 187, 231
Xia Dachang 夏大常 90, 92, 96, 99–102, 271, 279–280
Xie Gonghua 謝宮花 251
Xu Changzhi 徐昌治 150, 224, 228
Xu Congzhi 徐從治 145, 150, 228

Xu Dashou 許大受 40–41, 57, 104, 109, 140–141, 145–146, 152, 154, 227–228, 237, 252–253
Xu Guangqi 徐光啟 73, 80–81, 149, 175, 183–184, 237
Xu Ji 徐驥 211
Xu Shiyin 徐世蔭 141, 145, 150, 227–228
Xu Zuanzeng 許纘曾 211
Xuanwu men 宣武門 16, 212, 223, 227, 254

Yan Kuibin 顏魁賓 116
Yan Mo 嚴謨 89–90, 92–95, 159
Yan Weisheng 顏維聖 116
Yang Guangxian 楊光先 57–58, 141
Yang Tingyun 楊廷筠 23–25, 27–31, 33, 35, 87, 95, 137, 149, 167, 211, 253, 271, 274
Yang Zhaofang 楊兆坊 87
Ye Xianggao 葉向高 28
Yu Chengyuan 余成元 245
Yu Chunxi 虞淳熙 141
Yu Maoci 余懋慈 150
Yu Yizheng 于奕正 126, 127, 246
Yunnan 雲南 163
Yunqi Zhuhong 雲棲袾宏 12–13, 122, 152

Zhalan er 柵欄儿 81, 207, 258
Zhang Cai 張寀 245
Zhang Ergu 張爾谷 116
Zhang Geng 張賡 8, 30, 137
Zhang Xiangcan 張象燦 94
Zhang Xingyao 張星曜 14, 27, 76
Zhang Zai 張載 94
Zhao Chang 趙昌 222
Zhao Lun 趙侖 34, 131, 187, 236–238, 260
Zhejiang 浙江 10, 163, 239
    Hangzhou 杭州 161, 167, 209, 211–213, 239
    Jiading 嘉定 13, 34, 183, 187
    Jiaxing 嘉興 19, 229
    Songjiang 松江 18, 123
Zhong Mingren 鐘鳴仁, SJ (Sebastien Fernandes) 30, 33, 145, 160
Zhou Zhi 周志 54–55, 233, 271
Zhu Xi 朱熹 93–95
Zhu Yuanrong 朱圜榮 238
Zhu Zongyuan 朱宗元 73
Zibo Daguan 紫柏達觀 151
Zuo Guangxian 左光先 28–29, 137

Printed in the United States
by Baker & Taylor Publisher Services